A SELECTION OF
GREEK HISTORICAL
INSCRIPTIONS

A SELECTION OF GREEK HISTORICAL INSCRIPTIONS

TO THE END OF THE FIFTH CENTURY B.C.

REVISED EDITION

EDITED BY

RUSSELL MEIGGS

AND

DAVID LEWIS

CLARENDON PRESS · OXFORD

Oxford University Press, Walton Street, Oxford OX2 6DP

Oxford New York Toronto
Delhi Bombay Calcutta Madras Karachi
Petaling Jaya Singapore Hong Kong Tokyo
Nairobi Dar es Salaam Cape Town
Melbourne Auckland

and associated companies in
Berlin Ibadan

Oxford is a trade mark of Oxford University Press

Published in the United States
by Oxford University Press, New York

© Oxford University Press 1969

First published 1969
Reprinted 1971, 1975 (with corrections), 1980, 1984
Revised edition with Addenda and Concordance
First published 1988
First issued in Clarendon Paperbacks 1989
Reprinted 1992

British Library Cataloguing in Publication Data

A selection of Greek historical inscriptions:
to the end of the fifth century B.C.—Rev. ed.
1. Inscriptions in Greek, B.C.750–B.C.404
I. Title   II. Meiggs, Russell
III. Lewis, David
481.'7
ISBN 0–19–814487–3

Library of Congress Cataloging in Publication Data
Data available

Printed in Great Britain by
Biddles Ltd, Guildford & Kings Lynn

PREFACE TO REVISED EDITION

Reprints in 1971 and 1975 quietly tidied various misprints and some of our more blatant errors. At least a little more is now needed, and, besides continuing the tidying of the main text, we now add a few pages of Addenda to cover a crowded twenty years to which we cannot possibly do justice. The reader is asked to use the Concordance systematically; it contains references to *IG* I^3. 1 (1981), Hansen's *Carmina Epigraphica Graeca* I (1983), Fornara's *Translated Documents of Greece and Rome* I: *Archaic Times to the End of the Peloponnesian War* (1983), now an essential companion to the book, and, I hope, all references to *Supplementum Epigraphicum Graecum* since its welcome revival with Volume xxvi, which covered the years 1976–7. *SEG* covers the ground much more thoroughly than I could, and it is essential for those seeking complete coverage. The main text of the Addenda is intended to single out major treatments of whole inscriptions, major changes in the nature of the evidence, and more important references not yet included in *SEG*. The choice will sometimes seem capricious, but the fault for this and all error and omission lies with me, and not with my ever generous and trusting colleague.

D. M. L.

Oxford, February 1988

PREFACE

Marcus Niebuhr Tod's *Greek Historical Inscriptions*, first published in 1933 and reprinted, with a useful appendix to cover the interval, in 1947, has proved an indispensable companion to Greek historians and epigraphists. It is now out of print and the Delegates of the Oxford University Press have invited us, as they invited Tod when Hicks and Hill's *Manual of Greek Historical Inscriptions* went out of print, to write a fresh work on the same general lines.

How much we owe to Tod will be at once apparent to those who come to know both books. We have preserved Tod's title, and we are glad to follow the form of the *lemma* which he evolved. Like him we have in mind primarily the needs of university students but in selecting our bibliographies we have not ignored the interests of our colleagues at home and abroad. Though this book is in no sense a new edition of Tod's work we have not hesitated to take advantage of his generosity and have even repeated whole paragraphs from his commentaries. It was a very great pleasure to us as well as to him when in 1967 he was awarded by our university the Hon. D.Litt. that his great contribution to Greek epigraphy has so richly deserved.

While in most matters we have followed Tod's principles, in one important respect our practice has been different. Tod followed the precedent of Hicks and Hill and in transcribing epigraphic texts in a literary form wrote βουλή in place of βολέ and ʽόπως in place of hόπος. This method admittedly has the advantage of making the texts easier to read, but it can also lead to serious misuse; for in restoration the literary form obscures the number of letters that the space demands. We have therefore followed the general modern practice of maintaining epigraphic usage and preserving the layout of the original. We have also modified the form of Tod's indexes.

The main reason why a new book rather than a new edition is now needed is the impressive accumulation of new inscriptions,

from the Athenian Agora, the Acropolis, and many other scattered sources: no less than eleven of our inscriptions have been
discovered since 1933. To make way for this new material we
have reluctantly had to displace many inscriptions from Tod's
selection. This task, however, has been made easier by the comprehensive publication of *The Athenian Tribute Lists* by Meritt,
Wade-Gery, and McGregor; in view of the accessibility of
these texts (in Vol. II) we have reduced our own selection to
small samples from the lists. The new inscriptions mark the main
difference between the two books, but even in the inscriptions
that remain from Tod's selection there are many changes, some
due to the discovery of new fragments, others to the improvements reached by a further generation of study.

In the preparation of this book we have appreciated the help
of many good friends at home and abroad. In the Epigraphic
Museum the successive directors, M. Mitsos and Mme D. Peppa
Delmousou, gave us every facility that we could wish and more
than once adjudicated on doubtful readings. The generous
hospitality of the Institute for Advanced Study at Princeton in
the year 1964–5 gave Lewis unique opportunities to do work of
this kind. There and from there Professor Meritt, under whom
we both took our first steps in Greek epigraphy, kept us in continuous touch with his own work, and answered a number of our
queries from stones or squeezes. Professor Bean checked for us
the text of the Serpent Column in Istanbul. Eugene Vanderpool
sent us an up-to-date list of ostraka, though the most recent
discoveries of ostraka from the Kerameikos could not be included. He also considerably helped our work in the Agora
and was always ready to answer our questions. D. W. Bradeen,
J. K. Davies, K. J. Dover, W. G. Forrest, P. M. Fraser, P. J.
Rhodes, R. S. Stroud, W. E. Thompson, H. T. Wade-Gery,
and A. M. Woodward have also generously put their readings
and views at our disposal before publication. In Oxford Miss
Jeffery has modestly but firmly saved us from some serious mistakes
and, sharing the unlovable task of proof reading, has helped us to
reduce our misprints. Professor Andrewes has always been ready
with sensible advice or statesmanlike arbitration. To these scholars

and many others we are deeply grateful. We should also compliment one another, for we have found a surprising measure of agreement and our few differences of opinion have never escalated.

In the last two years we have gained an increasing respect for the patience and skill of the compositors and readers in the University Press. It is right that they should have a position of emphasis in this record of our debts.

R. M.

D. M. L.

Oxford, August 1968

CONTENTS

(Numbers in parentheses are those of Tod's edition)

NOTE ON TRANSCRIPTIONS

[   ]   enclose letters which we believe to have once stood in the text, but which are now lost.

(   )   enclose letters which complete words abbreviated by the stone-cutter.

⟨   ⟩   enclose letters accidentally omitted by the stone-cutter or letters which we think should stand in place of letters wrongly cut by him.

{   }   enclose superfluous letters added by the stone-cutter.

⟦   ⟧   enclose letters or spaces deliberately erased in antiquity.

ạ   A dot placed under a letter indicates that there are traces on the stone compatible with the letter which we print, which would not, in isolation, dictate the reading of that letter.

....   represent lost or illegible letters for which we suggest no restoration, equal in number to the number of dots. We number groups of more than four dots.

- - -   represent an uncertain number of lost or illegible letters.

v   represents a vacant letter-space.

vacat   indicates that the remainder of the line was left vacant.

| in texts not laid out in conformity with the layout of the stone indicates the beginning of a fresh line on the stone.

→ ←   indicate the direction in which lines of boustrophedon or retrograde texts were cut.

: ⁝ ⦙⦙ always represent punctuation-marks of the original text. All other forms of punctuation represent modern interpretation, and it should also be remembered that virtually all word-division is also modern. *h* represents an aspirate sign in the original text. Apart from it, all aspiration and accentuation in our transcriptions is interpretative, designed to direct the reader to the Attic form with which he will be familiar; it is not intended to express any view whatever about the correct aspiration and accentuation in individual dialects, and some of it is positively misleading in this respect.

References are given to assist the reader with the conventions of non-Attic alphabets, but a few notes on the Attic alphabet are given here. The Attic alphabet lacked the double consonants, ξ, ψ, which it represented by $\chi\sigma$, $\phi\sigma$. It also lacked eta and omega, employing H (eta in Ionic) as an aspirate sign, and therefore represented their sounds by epsilon and omikron. As a matter of spelling-convention rather than of alphabet, persisting after the Ionic alphabet came to be used in Athens, epsilon was also used to represent some sounds which we write epsilon-iota and omikron was also used to represent some sounds which we write omikron-upsilon. Strictly, the use of the single letter should have been confined to sounds resulting from the contraction or compensatory lengthening for the loss of a consonant of original short [e] or [o], e.g. νέεσθε → νεῖσθε → νἐσθε (Attic spelling), μισθόοντα → μισθοῦντα → μισθὀντα (Attic spelling), ἔσναι → εἶναι → ἔναι (Attic spelling), ἐλθόνσαν → ἐλθοῦσαν → ἐλθὀσαν (Attic spelling), and the spelling ει ου reserved for diphthongs, e.g. τεῖχος, Σπουδίας, but practice is not infrequently erratic. See W. S. Allen, *Vox Graeca*, 67–9, 72 f.

Numbers and coinage. The Attic system of numerals (Tod, *BSA* xviii (1911–12), 100 f., xxxvii (1936–7), 237 f.) was acrophonic, the symbol being taken from the first letter of the word represented, e.g. Γ (πέντε) = 5, Η (ἑκατόν) = 100. Some intermediate symbols were constructed by a combination of two others, e.g. ᚠ or ᚦ (50) is a combination of Γ and Δ. Complex numerals were produced by aggregation, the largest always appearing first. The basic system is therefore:

I	= 1	ΓI	= 6	H	= 100
II	= 2	Δ	= 10	HΔ	= 110
III	= 3	ΔΔ	= 20	Hᚠ	= 150
IIII	= 4	ᚠ	= 50	HH	= 200
Γ	= 5	ᚠΔ	= 60	ᚦ	= 500

ᚦH =	600
X =	1,000
XH =	1,100
ᚠ =	5,000
M =	10,000

ᚦ = 50,000

ᚦMMᚦXXXᚦHᚠΔΔΔΔΓI = 78,696

These numbers always represent cardinals, not ordinals.

When the system is applied to the Athenian system of coinage and weights:

> 6 obols = 1 drachma
> 100 drachmai = 1 mna
> 60 mnai or 6,000 drachmai = 1 talent,

certain modifications take place. The basic numerical system is understood to represent drachmai—in terms of coinage, silver drachmai—so that ᚠ can mean 50 dr. as well as 50, but the unit (1 drachma) is written ⊢, I being reserved for the obol. There are signs for subdivisions of the obol, $C = \frac{1}{2}$ ob., $\supset$ or T ($\tau\epsilon\tau\alpha\rho\tau\eta\mu\acute{o}\rho\iota o\nu$) $= \frac{1}{4}$ ob., and for the talent, T, and this last is also capable of combination: Ͱ = 5 T., 𐅄 = 10 T., Ͱ = 50 T., Ͱ = 100 T., Ͱ = 500 T., ✕ = 1,000 T. Hence ✕✕ͰͰͰͰͰ𐅄𐅄𐅄𐅄ͰΤͰͰΗΗͰΔΔΔΓͰͰͰͰΙΙΙC⊃ = 2,896 T. 5,789 dr. $3\frac{3}{4}$ ob.

The influence of the numerical system or possibly of working with the abacus can produce a way of writing out sums in full which seems strange at first sight (see no. 72, ll. 103–5).

Weights and non-Attic currency which need to be expressed in staters can also be expressed by combination, e.g. ΗΗΔΔΔΔͰΣΣΣ (p. 232) = 248 st.

ABBREVIATIONS

Abh. Berl.	*Abhandlungen der Preussischen Akademie der Wissenschaften:* philosophisch-historische Klasse.
AFD	B. D. Meritt, *Athenian Financial Documents of the Fifth Century*, Ann Arbor, 1932.
AJA	*American Journal of Archaeology.*
AJP	*American Journal of Philology.*
ALG³	*Anthologia Lyrica Graeca* (3rd edition), edited by E. Diehl, Leipzig, 1949–52.
Am. J. Sem. Lang.	*American Journal of Semitic Languages.*
Ant. Class.	*Antiquité Classique.*
Arch. Anz.	*Archäologischer Anzeiger: Beiblatt zum Jahrbuch der archäologischen Instituts.*
Ἀρχ. Δελτ.	Ἀρχαιολογικὸν Δελτίον.
Ἀρχ. Ἐφ.	Ἀρχαιολογικὴ Ἐφημερίς.
Arch. für Religionsw.	*Archiv für Religionswissenschaft.*
Ath. Mitt.	*Mitteilungen des deutschen archäologischen Instituts: Athenische Abteilung.*
ATL	The Athenian Tribute Lists by B. D. Meritt, H. T. Wade-Gery, M. F. McGregor. 4 vols. Cambridge, Mass., 1939–53.
Austin	R. P. Austin, *The Stoichedon Style in Greek Inscriptions*, Oxford, 1938.
BCH	*Bulletin de correspondance hellénique.*
Bechtel, *G. D.*	F. Bechtel, *Die griechischen Dialekte*, Berlin, 1921–4.
Berl. Phil. Woch.	*Berliner philologische Wochenschrift.*
Binnebössel	R. E. Binnebössel, *Studien zu den attischen Urkundenreliefs des 5. und 4. Jahrhunderts*, Kalderkirchen, 1932.
BMC	A Catalogue of the Greek Coins in the British Museum. London, 1873–1927.
BMI	The Collection of Ancient Greek Inscriptions in the British Museum, 1874–1916.
BSA	*Annual of the British School at Athens.*
Buck	C. D. Buck, *The Greek Dialects*, Chicago, 1955.
Busolt, *Gr. St.*	G. Busolt, *Griechische Staatskunde*, in I. von Müller's *Handbuch der Altertumswissenschaft*, (3rd edition), Munich, 1920–6.
CAH	*The Cambridge Ancient History*, Cambridge, 1923–
Cal. Publ. Class. Arch.	*California Publications in Classical Archaeology.*
Cavaignac, *Études*	E. Cavaignac, *Études sur l'histoire financière d'Athènes au Ve siècle*, Paris, 1908.
CIG	*Corpus Inscriptionum Graecarum*, 4 vols. 1828–77.
Class. Jour.	*Classical Journal.*
CP	*Classical Philology.*

CQ	*Classical Quarterly.*
CR	*Classical Review.*
CRAI	*Comptes rendus de l'Académie des Inscriptions et Belles-Lettres.*
DAA	A. E. Raubitschek, *Dedications from the Athenian Akropolis*, Cambridge, Mass., 1949.
DAT	B. D. Meritt, *Documents on Athenian Tribute*, Cambridge, Mass., 1937.
Deutsche Lit.-zeit.	*Deutsche Literaturzeitung.*
DGE	E. Schwyzer, *Dialectorum Graecarum exempla epigraphica potiora* (the 3rd edition of P. Cauer's *Delectus Inscriptionum Graecarum propter dialectum memorabilium*), Leipzig, 1923.
DM	*Mitteilungen des deutschen archäologischen Instituts*, 1948–53.
Dokl. Ak. Nauk, Ser. B.	*Dokladi Akademii Nauk*, Series B.
Ehrenberg Studies	*Ancient Society and Institutions*: Studies presented to Victor Ehrenberg on his 75th birthday, Oxford, 1966.
EM	Epigraphic Museum, Athens.
Eng. Hist. Rev.	*English Historical Review.*
FD	*Fouilles de Delphes*, Paris, 1909–
Ferguson, *Treasurers*	W. S. Ferguson, *The Treasurers of Athena*, Harvard, 1932.
FGH	F. Jacoby, *Die Fragmente der griechischen Historiker*, Berlin and Leyden, 1923–
Friedländer	*Greek Inscriptions in Verse, from the Beginnings to the Persian Wars* by Paul Friedländer with the collaboration of Herbert B. Hoffleit, Berkeley, 1948.
GD	F. Bechtel, *Die griechischen Dialekte*, Berlin, 1921–4.
GDI	*Sammlung der griechischen Dialekt-Inschriften*, ed. H. Collitz, F. Bechtel, O. Hoffmann, Göttingen, 1884–1915.
Geffcken	J. Geffcken, *Griechische Epigramme*, Heidelberg, 1916.
GG	*Griechische Geschichte.*
GGA	*Göttingische gelehrte Anzeigen.*
Gk. Rom. Byz. Stud.	*Greek, Roman and Byzantine Studies.*
Gomme, *HCT*	A. W. Gomme, *A Historical Commentary on Thucydides*, Oxford, 1945–56.
Gött. Nachr.	*Nachrichten von der Gesellschaft der Wissenschaften zu Göttingen*: philologisch-historische Klasse.
GVI	W. Peek, *Griechische Vers-Inschriften* (Vol. I), Berlin, 1955.
Harv. Stud.	*Harvard Studies in Classical Philology.*
Head, *H. N.*	B. V. Head, *Historia Numorum* (2nd edition), Oxford, 1911.
Hesp.	*Hesperia.*
H. Gr. Ep.	F. Hiller von Gaertringen, *Historische griechische Epigramme*, Bonn, 1926.

Hicks–Hill	E. L. Hicks and G. F. Hill, *A Manual of Greek Historical Inscriptions*, Oxford, 1901.
Hill, *Sources*[2]	G. F. Hill, *Sources for Greek History* (revised edition), 1951.
Hist.	*Historia, Zeitschrift für Alte Geschichte* 1950–
Historia	*Historia, Studi storici per l'antichità classica* (1927–35).
IC	*Inscriptiones Creticae*, 4 vols. 1935–50, edited by Margherita Guarducci.
IG	*Inscriptiones Graecae*, Berlin, 1873–
IGA	H. Roehl, *Inscriptiones Graecae antiquissimae praeter Atticas in Attica repertas*, Berlin, 1882.
IIA	J. Kirchner, *Imagines Inscriptionum Atticarum* (2nd edition, edited by G. Klaffenbach, 1948).
IJG	R. Dareste, B. Haussoullier, T. Reinach, *Recueil des inscriptions juridiques grecques*, Paris, 1891–1904.
Imag.	H. Roehl, *Imagines inscriptionum Graecarum antiquissimarum* (3rd edition), Berlin, 1907.
Jahresh.	*Jahreshefte des österreichischen archäologischen Institutes in Wien.*
JHS	*Journal of Hellenic Studies.*
JRIBA	*Journal of the Royal Institute of British Architects.*
Judeich, *Topographie*[2]	W. Judeich, *Topographie von Athen* (2nd edition), Munich, 1931.
Kahrstedt, *Staatsgebiet*	U. Kahrstedt, *Staatsgebiet und Staatsangehörige in Athen*, Stuttgart, 1934.
Kahrstedt, *Untersuchungen*	U. Kahrstedt, *Untersuchungen zur Magistratur in Athen*, Stuttgart, 1936.
Kern	O. Kern, *Inscriptiones Graecae*, Bonn, 1913.
Le Bas–Wadd.	P. Le Bas and W. H. Waddington, *Voyage archéologique en Grèce et en Asie Mineure, 1843–1844* ... (6 vols., Paris, 1853–70).
LGS	I. von Prott and L. Ziehen, *Leges Graecorum sacrae e titulis collectae*, Leipzig, 1896–1906.
LSAG	L. H. Jeffery, *The Local Scripts of Archaic Greece* Oxford, 1961.
Marcadé, *Signatures*	J. Marcadé, *Recueil des signatures des sculpteurs grecs*, Paris, 1953– .
Meritt, *AFD*	B. D. Meritt, *Athenian Financial Documents of the Fifth Century*, Ann Arbor, 1932.
Meritt, *Calendar*	B. D. Meritt, *The Athenian Calendar in the Fifth Century*, Cambridge, Mass., 1928.
Meritt, *Year*	B. D. Meritt, *The Athenian Year* (Sather Classical Lectures, 32), Berkeley, 1961.
Meyer, *Forsch.*	E. Meyer, *Forschungen zur alten Geschichte*, Halle, 1892–9.
Michel	C. Michel, *Recueil d'inscriptions grecques*, Paris–Brussels, 1900–27.
Moretti	L. Moretti, *Iscrizioni agonistiche greche*, Rome, 1953.

Neue Jahrb.	*Neue Jahrbücher für das klassische Altertum.*
Num. Chron.	*Numismatic Chronicle.*
PA	J. Kirchner, *Prosopographia Attica*, Berlin, 1901–3.
Pal. Soc. Facs.	*The Palaeographical Society: Facsimiles of Manuscripts and Inscriptions.*
Phil.	*Philologus.*
Phil. Woch.	*Philologische Wochenschrift.*
Pouilloux	Jean Pouilloux, *Choix d'inscriptions grecques*, Paris, 1960.
Proc. Afr. Class. Ass.	*Proceedings of the African Classical Associations.*
Proc. Mass. Hist. Soc.	*Proceedings of the Massachusetts History Society.*
RA	*Revue archéologique.*
RE	Paully–Wissowa–Kroll, *Real-Encyclopädie der classischen Altertumswissenschaft*, Stuttgart, 1894–
REA	*Revue des études anciennes.*
REG	*Revue des études grecques.*
Rend. Linc.	*Rendiconti della Classe di Scienze morali, storiche, e filologiche dell'Accademia dei Lincei.*
Rend. Pont. Acc.	*Rendiconti della Pontificia accademia romana di archeologia.*
Rev. Num.	*Revue numismatique.*
Rev. Phil.	*Revue de philologie, de littérature et d'histoire anciennes.*
RF	*Rivista di filologia e di istruzione classica.*
Rh. Mus.	*Rheinisches Museum für Philologie.*
RIDA	*Revue internationale des droits de l'antiquité.*
SEG	*Supplementum Epigraphicum Graecum.*
SIG	Dittenberger, *Sylloge Inscriptionum Graecarum* (3rd edition), Leipzig, 1915–24.
Sitz. Berl.	*Sitzungsberichte der Preussischen Akademie der Wissenschaften:* philosophisch-historische Klasse.
Sitz. Wien	*Sitzungsberichte der Akademie der Wissenschaften in Wien:* philosophisch-historische Klasse.
Solmsen	F. Solmsen, *Inscriptiones Graecae ad inlustrandas dialectos selectae* (4th edition by E. Fraenkel), Leipzig, 1930.
Staatsverträge	H. Bengtson, *Die Verträge der griechisch-römischen Welt*, vol. II, Munich and Berlin, 1962.
Stud. It. Fil.	*Studi italiani di filologia classica.*
TAM	*Tituli Asiae Minoris*, Vienna, 1901–
TAPA	*Transactions of the American Philological Association.*
Verh. d. Kon. Ned. Ak. v. Wet.	*Verhandelingen der Koninklijke Nederlandsche Academie van Wetenschapen.*
Wade-Gery, *Essays*	H. T. Wade-Gery, *Essays in Greek History*, Oxford, 1958.
Wien Anz.	*Anzeiger der philosophisch-historischen Klasse der Akademie der Wissenschaften in Wien.*
Wilhelm, *Beitr.*	A. Wilhelm, *Beiträge zur griechischen Inschriftenkunde*, Vienna, 1909.

1

'Nestor's Cup': 750–700 B.C.

Graffito on a Geometric skyphos (East Greek) from a grave in Ischia (Pithekoussai).

Euboean writing, retrograde, with punctuation. Phot.: *Rend. Linc.* 1955, 215–34, Pl. i–iv (whence *LSAG*, Pl. 47); *REA* lxvii (1965) Pl. xvi–xvii.

Buchner and Russo, *Rend. Linc.*, loc. cit.; Woodhead, *SEG* xiv. 604; Page, *CR* vi (1956) 95–7; Hampe, *Gymnasium*, lxiii (1956) 36–8; Picard, *RA* xlix (1957) 82 f.; Manganaro, *Siculorum Gymnasium*, xii (1959) 71–3; Webster, *Glotta*, xxxviii (1959) 253 f.; Guarducci, *Rend. Linc.* 1961, 3–7; *LSAG* 43–5, 235 f.; Carpenter, *AJP* lxxxiv (1963) 83–5; Metzger, *REA* lxvii (1965) 301–5.

> Νέστορος: ϵ[2–3]ι̣: ϵὔποτ[ον]: ποτέριο[ν:]   ←
> hὸς δ' ἂ⟨ν⟩ τόδε π[ίε]σι: ποτερί[ο]: αὐτίκα κῆνον ←
> hίμερ[ος: hαιρ]έσει: καλλιστϵ[φά]ο̣ο Ἀφροδίτης. ←

l. 1: ϵ̣[ρρο]ι̣, ϵ[ἰκο]ι̣, ϵ[ἴκε]ι̣ Buchner–Russo; ϵ̣[οτα]ι̣, ἀ̣[θλο]ν̣ Woodhead; ϵ̣[ν τ]ι̣ Page; ϵ̣[ν το]ι̣ Manganaro; μ[ὲ]ν̣ Guarducci; ϵ[ἰμ]ι̣ Webster, Jeffery, which seems most reasonable. In l. 2, Page believes the space to require ποτέρι[ον]. To the left of l. 2 are traces of two letters, interpreted rightly by Guarducci and Jeffery as a false start on Νέστορος.

The earliest of Greek colonies in the west (Str. v. 4. 9, p. 247) has produced this, the longest eighth-century Greek inscription (Carpenter's view that the inscription is sixth century is not compatible with the archaeological context in which it was found, and is clearly refuted by Metzger). As was to be expected, the letters are closely related to Euboean, and help to confirm the origin of the Etruscan alphabet and, eventually, our own from Euboean Kyme (cf. *LSAG* 236 f.; Guarducci, *Rend. Linc.* 1964, 3–10). The continuous retrograde is virtually unique in a Greek text (*LSAG* 43–5), though we would allow more weight in explaining it to closeness to Phoenician origins than does Jeffery, who attributes it to a desire to separate the verses clearly. That ll. 2–3 are hexameters is clear; l. 1 has been variously interpreted as a rough iambic trimeter, prose, or a trochaic trimeter catalectic (Guarducci).

Interpretations are divided between (a) the belief that a distinction is being drawn between the famous cup of Nestor (*Iliad* xi. 632–7) and this one, and (b) the belief that this cup is posing as Nestor's cup (so Webster). Unless, by a remarkable coincidence, the owner of this cup was really named Nestor, we have here evidence for knowledge in the eighth century of this item in the epic repertoire. In any case,

Picard is right to comment on the contrast between the literary sophistication and the artistic poverty exhibited by the verses and the cup. For the light thrown on the development of epic technique, see Notopoulos, *Hesp.* xxix (1960) 195 f.

2

Law on the Constitution: Dreros, 650–600 B.C.

Block of grey schist from the wall of the temple of Apollo Delphinios at Dreros; now in the Dreros Museum.

Archaic Cretan letters. Ll. 1–3 boustrophedon, l. 4 retrograde. Vertical strokes are used as punctuation, and Χ at the beginning of l. 4 marks a new clause (*LSAG* 311, no. 1a, with drawing and partial photograph, Pl. 59. 1a).

Demargne and van Effenterre, *BCH* lxi (1937) 333–48, lxii (1938) 194–5; Guarducci, *RF* lxvii (1939) 20–2; Ehrenberg, *CQ* xxxvii (1943) 14–18; Willetts, *Aristocratic Society in Ancient Crete*, 106, 167–9; Buck 116.

θιός ολοιον (sic). ἆδ' ἔϝαδε | πόλι· | ἐπεί κα κοσμήσει, | δέκα ϝετίον
τὸν ἀ- ←
ϝτὸν | μὴ κόσμεν· | αἰ δὲ κοσμησίε, | ὁ[π]ε δικακσίε, | ἀϝτὸν ὀπῆλεν |
διπλεῖ κἀϝτὸν →
ἄκρηστον | ἦμεν, | ἆς δόοι, | κότι κοσμησίε | μηδὲν ἤμην. vacat ←
Χ ὀμόται δὲ | κόσμος | κοὶ δάμιοι | κοὶ | ἴκατι | οἰ τᾶς πόλ[ιο]ς vacat ←

The crux of the inscription lies in the first two words. The first editors, thinking them intended as an insertion in l. 2, read κἀϝτὸν θιοσόλοιον ἄκρηστον ἦμεν, assuming an asyndeton and that θιοσόλοιον might mean 'cursed'. Buck followed them in their placing, but read θιὸς ὄλοι ὄν, 'may God destroy him' as an interjection. Guarducci rightly showed that the words were inscribed before l. 2 and belong to the beginning of l. 1 as an invocation, but felt difficulty about the comparative ὁ λοίον against the more normal θεὸς ἀγαθός. Her suggestion ὁ λόϊος, however, is not borne out by the photograph, and she seems to have abandoned it (*Epigrafia Greca*, i. 187 f.).

'May God be kind (?). The city has thus decided; when a man has been *kosmos*, the same man shall not be *kosmos* again for ten years. If he does act as *kosmos*, whatever judgements he gives, he shall owe double, and he shall lose his rights to office, as long as he lives, and whatever he does as *kosmos* shall be nothing. The swearers shall be the *kosmos* (i.e. the body of *kosmoi*) and the *damioi* and the twenty of the city.'

This may be the earliest surviving Greek law on stone, and is certainly the earliest which has survived complete. It is one of a group of eight, one in Eteocretan, from the same temple.

The ratification formula with its use of πόλις against the normal Cretan ethnic may reasonably be claimed as an early piece of evidence for the concept of the *polis*. The word does not appear elsewhere epigraphically until the late sixth century (Kyzikos, Thasos, Arkesine, Poseidonia (see no. 10)). We have no means of telling whether the word implies the participation of the assembly, as Willetts claims, or merely the authority of the city's officials (Ehrenberg).

The law forbids the repeated tenure of the office of *kosmos*, presumably, as elsewhere in Crete, the chief magistracy, before ten years have elapsed. The provision is paralleled at Gortyn (*IC* iv. 14, *g–p*, 2, τρι[ό]ν Ϝετίον τὸν ἀϝτὸν μὴ ϙοσμεν, δέκα μὲν γνόμονας, πέντε [δὲ κο]ενίος, sixth century), and it had generally been explained there by the need to make a break in the financial and legal immunity of a magistrate. The length of time which has to elapse in Dreros, however, suggests strongly that the motive was rather to limit the possibilities of using the office as a stepping-stone to tyranny (the first editors) or to bolster the power of an individual family (Ehrenberg, Willetts). How severe the penalty involved was depends on whether ἄκρηστος implies total deprivation of civic rights or deprivation merely of the right to hold certain magistracies. Dispute over the implications of the word involves the interpretation of the phrase χρηστοὺς ποιεῖν in the archaic treaty between Sparta and Tegea (Plutarch, *Greek Questions*, 5, Ehrenberg, op. cit., Jacoby *CQ* xxxviii (1944) 15–16).

The list of those who swear the oath, presumably every year, includes two unknown offices. The δάμιοι have been generally identified with the Gortynian τίται as financial supervisors. 'The twenty of the city' have been identified as a committee of the assembly (Willetts), a committee of the council (the first editors), the council itself (Ehrenberg). The last seems the most probable.

3

Glaukos Friend of Archilochos: 625–600 B.C.

A marble block set in a stepped poros base, perhaps an altar rather than a cenotaph, found in the Agora in Thasos; now in Thasos Museum.

Parian letters (C = β; Ω = o, ου; O = ω; Ⴂ = η), boustrophedon (see *LSAG* 300–1, no. 61). Phot.: *BCH* lxxix (1955) 76, Fig. 1 and Pl. iii; *LSAG*, Pl. 58. 61; Pouilloux and Dunant, *Recherches sur l'histoire et les cultes de Thasos*, ii, Pl. liv.

BCH lxxix 75–86, 348–51 (*GVI* 51a; *SEG* xiv. 565+); *LSAG*, loc. cit.

Γλαύρο εἰμὶ μνῆ-   →
μα τὸ Λεπτίνεω· ἔ-   ←
θεσαν δέ με οἱ Βρέντ-   →
εω παῖδες.   ←

Thasos, colonized from Paros at the end of the eighth or beginning
of the seventh century (Pouilloux, *Recherches sur l'histoire et les cultes de
Thasos*, i. 22 ff.), retained the alphabet of the mother city and close
links with her; Archilochos was active there in the middle of the seventh
century (Jacoby, *CQ* xxxv (1941) 97–109). Among the addressees of
his poems was Glaukos, son of Leptines (*ALG*³, frs. 13, 56, 59, 68; 51,
IV A), whose prominence in Thasos is attested by the dedication of
this μνῆμα in the Agora, hardly long before 600 B.C. and perhaps some
time after his death, an action which recalls the honours paid to
founders of colonies (cf., e.g., Thuc. v. 11. 1). We do not think the
text metrical (cf. *Entretiens Hardt*, x. 216, 218).

4

Cenotaph of a Corcyraean Proxenos:
(?) 625–600 B.C.

On a cylindrical limestone cenotaph at Καστράδες, a suburb of Corcyra town
(Crome, *Mnemosynon Theodor Wiegand*, 52, with Pl. 17–18).

Corinthian alphabet, in one continuous retrograde line round the monument. A lozenge marked the place where the reader had to start. Punctuation marks the ends of lines. Facs.: *IGA* 342; *IG* ix. 1. 867; *Imag.* 47. 26.

IG ix. 1. 867+; *DGE* 133 (1); Frisk, *Eranos*, xxix (1931) 31 f.; Friedländer 26; Buck 93; *GVI.* 42; *LSAG* 232, no. 9.

◊ hυιοῦ ΤλασίαϝΟ Μενεκράτεος τόδε σᾶμα:
Οἰανθέος γενεάν, τόδε δ' αὐτὸι δᾶμος ἐποίει:
ἐς γὰρ πρόξενϝος δάμου φίλος· ἀλλ' ἐνὶ πόντοι [:]
ὄλετο, δαμόσιον δὲ καρὸν [.]ọ[- - - - -]:
5 Πραξιμένες δ' αὐτὸι γ[αία]ς ἀπὸ πατρίδος ἐνθὸν:
σὺν δάμ[ο]ι τόδε σᾶμα κασιγνέτοιο πονέθε:

The missing letter in l. 4 seems to have been pi or rho: πρ[τὶ πάντας
ἀφῖκε] Hoffman; πρ[τὶ πάντας hίκανε] Peek; πό[λις ἄδε κέκαδε] Edmonds;
πρ[λλοῖσι φύτευσε] Friedländer; ϸό[θιον πόρε κῦμα] Frisk.

Corcyra used the Corinthian alphabet, though Syracuse, founded
in the same year, did not (*contra*, Guarducci, *Κώκαλος* x–xi (1964–5)

465 ff.). The date is approximate, from the pottery found in the tomb. The epigram has a fascinating tension between its Homeric echoes and the political circumstances of a new age, δᾶμος or a form of it four times repeated, and above all the πρόξενος, the earliest known to us. Menekrates was presumably normally resident at Oianthea in Ozolian Lokris, and he may owe this monument to dying near Corcyra.

For δημόσιον κακόν (l. 4) cf. Solon 3. 26. ἐνθόν (l. 5) = ἐλθών; πονέθε (l. 6) is transitive.

5

The Foundation of Cyrene: late seventh century B.C.

Marble stele from Cyrene; now in the museum there. Cutting in the top for a relief (?), now lost.

Fourth-century lettering, not stoichedon; ll. 1, 23 are larger. Phot.: *Abh. Berlin*, 1925, no. 5, Pl. ii. 2; *RF* lvi (1928) Pl. x–xii.

SEG ix. 3+; Chamoux, *Cyrène sous la monarchie des Battiades*, 105–11; Wilhelm, *Griech. Inschr. Rechtlichen Inhalts*, 5–7; Graham, *JHS* lxxx (1960) 94–111; Jeffery, *Hist.* x (1961) 139–47; Seibert, *Metropolis und Apoikie*, 9–67; Graham, *Colony and Mother City in Ancient Greece*, 27, 40, 224–6; Oliver, *Gk. Rom. Byz. Stud.* vii (1966) 25–9.

θεός.   τύχα ἀγαθά.

Δᾶμις Βαθυκλεῦς ἦιπε· περὶ ὧν λέγοντι τοι Θηραῖο[ι]
Κλευδάμας Εὐθυκλεῦς, ὅπως ἁ πόλις ὀρθῶται καὶ ὁ δ[ᾶ]-
μος εὐτυχῆι ὁ Κυραναίων, ἀποδόμεν τοῖς Θηραίοις τ-
5 ὰμ πολιτήιαν κατὰ τὰ πάτρια, τὰ οἱ πρόγονοι ἐποιήσαντο, οἵ τε Κυράναγ κα[τώ]ικιξαν Θήραθε καὶ οἱ ἐν Θήραι [μέ]-
νοντες, καθὼς Ἀπόλλων ἔδωκε Βάττωι καὶ τοῖς Θηρ[αί]-
οις τοῖς κατοικίξασι Κυράναν εὐτυχὲν ἐμμένοντας το[ῖς]
ὁρκίοις, τὰ οἱ πρόγονοι ἐποιήσαντο αὐτοὶ ποτ’ αὐτός, ὅκα
10 τὰν ἀποικίαν ἀπέστελλον κατὰ τὰν ἐπίταξιν τῶ Ἀπό[λ]-
λωνος τῶ Ἀρχαγέτα· ἀγαθᾶι τύχᾱι, δεδόχθαι τῶι δάμω[ι],
καταμεῖναι Θηραίοις ἴσαμ πολιτήιαν καὶ ἐγ Κυράναι κ[α]-
τὰ τὰ αὐτά· ποιεῖσθαι δὲ πάντας Θηραίους τὸς ἐπιδημέ[ον]-
τας ἐγ Κυράναι τὸν αὐτὸν ὅρκον ὅμπερ τοὶ ἄλλοι ποτ-
15 ὲ διώρκωσαν· καὶ καταστᾶμεν ἐς φυλὰν καὶ πάτραν ἔς θε
ἐννῆα ἑταιρήας. καταγράφεν δὲ τόδε τὸ ψάφισμα ἐν στάλ[αν]
λυγδίναν, θέμεν τὰν στάλαν ἐς τὸ ἱαρὸν πατρῶιον τῶ

Ἀπόλλωνος τῶ Πυθίω, καταγράφεν καὶ τὸ ὅρκιον ἐς τὰν στάλ[αν],
τὸ οἱ οἰκιστῆρες ἐποιήσαντο καταπλεύσαντες Λιβύανδε [σὺ]-
20 μ Βάττωι Θήραθεν Κυράνανδε. τό κα ἀνάλωμα τὸ δέηι ἐς τ[ὸν λ]-
ᾶον ἢ ἐς τὰγ καταγραφάν, οἱ ἐπιστάντες ἐπὶ τὸς ἀπολόγος [κο]-
μισάσθων ἀπὸ τῶν Ἀπόλλωνος προσόδων. vacat
    Ὅρκιον   τῶν   οἰκιστήρων.
[ἔ]δοξε τᾶι ἐκκλησίαι· ἐπεὶ Ἀπόλλων αὐτομάτιξεν Β[άτ]-
25 τωι καὶ Θηραίοις ἀποι[κίξαι] Κυράναν, ὁριστὸν δοκεῖ Θη[ραί]-
[ο]ις ἀποπέμπεν ἐς τὰν [Λιβ]ύαν Βάττομ μὲν ἀρχαγέτα[ν]
[τ]ε καὶ βασιλῆα, ἑταίρους δὲ τοὺς Θηραίους πλέν· ἐπὶ τᾶι ἴσα[ι κ]-
αὶ τᾶι ὁμοίαι πλὲν κατὰ τὸν οἶκον, υἱὸν δὲ ἕνα καταλ[έ]-
γεσθαί   ΤΟΣΔΕΕΛΟ.....c. 10.....καὶ τοὺς ἡβῶντας καὶ τῶν [ἄλ]-
30 [λ]ων Θηραίων ἐλεύθερος...6...πλέν. αἰ μὲν δέ κα κατέχ[ων]-
τι τὰν οἰκισίαν οἱ ἄποικοι, τῶν οἰκείων τὸγ καταπλέον[τα]
ὕστερον εἰς Λιβύαν καὶ πολιτήιας καὶ τιμᾶμ πεδέχ[εν]
καὶ γᾶς τᾶς ἀδεσπότω ἀπολαγχάνεν. αἰ δέ κα μὴ κατ[έχ]-
ωντι τὰν οἰκισίαν μηδὲ οἱ Θηραῖοί μιν δυνῶνται ἐπικου[ρέ]-
35 ν, ἀλλὰ ἀνάγκαι ἀχθῶντι ἔτη ἐπὶ πέντε, ἐκ τᾶς γᾶς ἀπίμ[εν]
ἀδιέως Θήρανδε ἐπὶ τὰ αὐτῶγ χρήματα καὶ ἦμεμ πολιάτ-
ας. ὁ δέ κα μὴ λῆι πλὲν ἀποστελλοίσας τᾶς πόλιος, θανά[σι]-
μος τένται καὶ τὰ χρήματα ἔστω αὐτοῦ δαμόσια. ὁ δὲ ἀπ-
οδεκόμενος ἢ ἀδήιζων ἢ πατὴρ υἱὸν ἢ ἀδελφεὸς ἀδελ-
40 φεὸν παισεῖται ἅπερ ὁ μὴ λέων πλέν. ἐπὶ τούτοις ὅρκια ἐποιήσαντο οἵ τε αὐτεῖ μένοντες καὶ οἱ πλέοντες οἰκίξοντε-
ς καὶ ἀρὰς ἐποιήσαντο τὸς ταῦτα παρβεῶντας καὶ μὴ ἐμμένοντας ἢ τῶν ἐλ Λιβύαι οἰκεόντων ἢ τῶν αὐτεῖ μεν-
όντων. κηρίνος πλάσσαντες κολοσὸς κατέκαιον ἐπα-
45 ρεώμενοι πάντες συνενθόντες καὶ ἄνδρες καὶ γυναῖκ-
ες καὶ παῖδες καὶ παιδίσκαι· τὸμ μὴ ἐμμένοντα τούτοις
τοῖς ὁρκίοις ἀλλὰ παρβεῶντα καταλείβεσθαί νιν καὶ κα-
ταρρὲν ὥσπερ τὸς κολοσός, καὶ αὐτὸν καὶ γόνον καὶ χρήματα, τοῖς δὲ ἐμμένοισιν τούτοις τοῖς ὁρκίοις καὶ τοῖς
50 πλέοισι ἐλ Λιβύαν κ[αὶ] τ[οῖς μέ]νοισι ἐν Θήραι ἦμεν πολλ-
ὰ καὶ ἀγαθὰ καὶ αὐ[τοῖς καὶ γό]νοις.

Our text, like other recent texts, depends heavily on Oliverio, *RF* lvi (1928)
224 f., but, since he read letters not seen by others before or since, some
caution is necessary. We have had the benefit of notes by P. M. Fraser

and have underlined readings of importance which depend solely on Oliverio; these should probably rank higher than mere restorations (cf. Fraser, *Berytus*, xii (1956–8) 120 ff.). L. 11 [τῷ ἐν Δελφοῖς] Ferri; l. 12, καταγεῖμαι Wilamowitz; l. 20, Θήραθεν is a new reading by Fraser. Various suggestions have been made for ll. 28–30: καταλ[έ]‖γεσθαί τ[ε ἀπὸ τῶν χώρων ἀπάντων] τοὺς ἡβῶντας, καὶ τῶν [ἀλ|λ]ων Θηραίων ἐλευθέρος, [ὅ κα λῆι,] πλέν Oliverio; καταλ[έ]‖γεσθαι τ[ῷ οἴκω ἑκάστω, πλὲν δὲ] τοὺς ἡβῶντας Wilhelm; καταλ[έ]‖γεσθαι· τῷ[ν δὲ ἀστῶν πλὲν (vel περιοίκων) ἑκατὸν] τοὺς ἡβῶντας καὶ τῶν [ἀλ|λ?]ων Θηραίων ἐλευθέρος [ἑκατὸν] πλέν Jeffery; see also Oliver's solution, with a new emendation of Herodotus; we print Fraser's readings, inconsistent with them all. L. 33, ἀδ[ά]στῳ Wilamowitz.

The inscription before us was divided by those responsible for its publication into two parts (see ll. 16–18 and the headings); at first sight we may be tempted further to subdivide the second part.

I (ll. 2–22): This is a fourth-century decree of Cyrene, replying to a request made by representatives of Thera (Κλευδάμας in l. 3 is apparently their leader), granting equal citizenship to Theraean residents in Cyrene in accordance with the arrangements made by their respective ancestors at the time of the founding of Cyrene, and ordering the publication of this decree and the original agreement (ὅρκιον is best translated thus, since the actual words of the oath are not reported). For phratries in Cyrene (l. 15) cf. Arist. *Pol.* 1319^b 22–4; *Hetaireiai* (l. 16) are a less widespread phenomenon in Greek political organization, being largely confined otherwise to Crete and Thera (Chamoux, op. cit. 214).

IIa (ll. 23–40): This is the original agreement, purporting to be a decree of the ἐκκλησία of Thera. The formulae in ll. 24–5 are surprising (Wilamowitz thought incredible) for seventh-century Thera, but compare the prescript of No. 2 (see Graham, *JHS* lxxx (1960) 104 f.). The decree, in response to a spontaneous declaration of Apollo (for αὐτομάτιξεν, see Parke, *JHS* lxxxii (1962) 145 f.), orders the dispatch to Libya of Battos as 'founder' (for ἀρχαγέταν see Jeffery, op. cit. 144) and king, and fixes the method by which the colonists are to be selected. The difficulties of the reading obscure this method, but it is agreed that it presents a strong similarity to the report of Herodotus (iv. 153): Θηραίοισι δὲ ἔαδε ἀδελφεόν τε ἀπ' ἀδελφεοῦ (ἀδελφεῶν Legrand) πέμπειν πάλῳ λαχόντα καὶ ἀπὸ τῶν χώρων ἀπάντων ἑπτὰ ἐόντων ἄνδρας (ἄνδρας ⟨σ'⟩ = διακοσίους Cobet), εἶναι δέ σφεων καὶ ἡγεμόνα καὶ βασιλέα Βάττον, at least in the demand for representation by families. For ἐπὶ τᾶι ἴσαι καὶ τᾶι ὁμοίαι (ll. 27–8) cf. Graham, *JHS* lxxx (1960) 108, who shows that this is a standard phrase for colonial foundations at least from the middle of the fifth century. Ll. 30–3, the only clause on which the fourth-century Theraeans were relying, guarantee rights in Libya for later arrivals from Thera.

Ll. 33–7 prescribe the terms on which the colonists may return to Thera (cf. No. 20, 6–10). Ll. 37–40 lay down the penalties against evasion (for θανάσιμος cf. *SEG* ix. 1. 53, Cyrene, late fourth century, the only parallel; τένται = τέλεται = ἔσεται (Buck, p. 65) and is also Cyrenaean).

II*b* (ll. 40–51); the ἀραί: This section, though also apparently part of the ὅρκιον, is couched in the form of a prose narrative, not dependent on ἔδοξε τᾶι ἐκκλησίαι in l. 24. The only parallel we know for such an abrupt transition (leaving aside such phenomena as lists of ambassadors and oath-takers) is Tod, vol. ii, no. 204, where a similar transition occurs at l. 46, again to describe an ἀρά, and again with no indication of a change of type of content within the one general heading. Leaving aside the general problems of authenticity and transmission for the moment, we would suppose that details of a noteworthy ἀρά were not infrequently transmitted along with the document it reinforced; cf. perhaps Aeschin. ii. 115, iii. 110 on the Amphictyonic oath, and Arist. *Ἀθ. Πολ.* 23. 5 on the covenant of the Delian League. The ἀρά is indeed noteworthy: the community here 'reinforces the magical potency of the curse with a magical act, identical with the practice of what we regard as anti-social black magic and directed at a prospective individual or individuals (including naturally their descendants). Such a proceeding is altogether different from the symbolic acts which often accompany an oath' (Nock, *Arch. für Religionsw.* xxiv (1926) 172 f.). (παρβεῶντας, l. 42, cf. l. 47 = παραβαίνοντας.)

Until 1960 the ὅρκιον was regarded as more or less apocryphal. There were difficulties in this view. The document, though it has close parallels to what Herodotus gives as the version of Thera, seems clearly independent of Herodotus and shows no signs of being constructed from his account. The alternative, to suppose the existence of a literary invention on which Herodotus and this document both drew, has seemed to run counter to the influential view of Jacoby (e.g. *Atthis*, 189, 199–202) that local history started later than Herodotus. Graham and Miss Jeffery, in simultaneously reopening the question, have argued for the possibility that we have here a genuine document which has had some later re-editing. If this is so, we are faced with a problem of distinguishing between authenticity of form and authenticity of content similar to that which we meet in the Decree of Themistocles (No. 23). That there is nothing which can be seriously objected to in the content has long been recognized. At the most, one might doubt that the original document can have actually named Cyrene as the destination of the colony (l. 25), and many scholars have doubted that Battos was named Battos (l. 26) before arriving at his destination. There are, however, many doubtful points about the form of the decree and the language (see Graham, *JHS* lxxx (1960)

103–9, for a detailed investigation); we incline to doubt whether it can be proved that they are all due to a single preparation for publication in the fourth century, and prefer to assume a long and complex moulding of a genuine original within the tradition of Thera. We would not care to make precise the elements of oral and written transmission in this tradition, but we are sure that we are dealing with a situation to which our standards of literal authenticity are inappropriate, and think it not unsafe to assume that we have before us genuine elements of what was said and done in seventh-century Thera.

For a translation of II see Graham, *Colony and Mother City*, 225 f.

6

The Athenian Archon-List

Four fragments of Pentelic marble found in the Agora at Athens; now in the Agora Museum.

Developed Attic writing, stoichedon. Phot.: (frag. *c* only) *Hesp.* viii (1939) 60; (all) *Hesp.* xxxii (1963) Pl. 58–9.

Meritt, *Hesp.* viii (1939) 59–65 (frag. *c*); Dinsmoor, *Studies in the History of Culture*, 197; Roussel, *RA* xviii (1941) 209–13; Guarducci, *Annuario*, N.S. iii–v (1941–3), 121–2; Cadoux, *JHS* lxviii (1948), 77–9, 109–12; Jacoby, *Atthis*, 171–6; Alexander, *Class. Jour.* liv (1958–9) 307–14; Thompson, *Class. Jour.* lv (1959–60) 217–20; Eliot and McGregor, *Phoenix*, xiv (1960) 27–35; Bradeen, *Hesp.* xxxii (1963) 187–208 (three new fragments).

a   *b*

	Col. i	Col. ii
[. . .]Ν[- -	[- - - - -] υ	Κ[- - - -]
[Κύ]φσελο[ς]	[- - - - -] υ υ	Φα[- - - -]
[Τε]λεκλε[- -	[- - - - -] υ υ	Τε[- - - -]
[Φιλ]όμβ[ροτος?] (595–	[- - - - -] υ	'Ερχ[σικλειδες] (548–
- - - - - - 4)	5[.......c.12......]ς	Θεσ[- - -] 7)
	- - - - - -	Φ[ο]ρ[- - -]
		- - - - -

c

['Ον]ετο[ρίδες]	(527–6)
[h]ιππία[ς]	(526–5)
[Κ]λεισθέν[ες]	(525–4)

			d	
[*M*]ιλτιάδες	(524–3)			
5 [*Κα*]λλιάδες	(523–2)	[Φαίν]ιπ[πος]?		(490–89)
[..5...]στρατ[ος]	(522–1)	[Ἀρ]ιστ[είδες]?		(489–8)
- - - - -		*vacat*		

a 1 the letter was alpha, gamma, or nu.

Meritt in publishing fragment *c* had little doubt that the appearance of names prominent in the sixth century on a stone carved *c.* 425 suggested that he was dealing with an inscribed archon-list. The doubts raised by Alexander were adequately dealt with by Thompson and Eliot and McGregor, and should now be laid to rest by the new fragments.

Since no traces of the back or sides are preserved, we can hardly do more than guess about the nature of the monument. Bradeen has argued that it was a stele, with the names arranged in four columns, sixty-five names to a column, beginning with Kreon in 683–2 and ending with Isarchos in 424–3. (Miller, *Klio* xxxvii (1959) 49–52, before the discovery of the new fragments, had argued for 426–5 as the date of the inscription, on rather shaky grounds.) This arrangement has the attraction of allowing the five letters at the bottom of a column on fragment *d* to fit into the names of known archons. Whatever the uncertainties of Bradeen's arrangement, the appearance on fragment *b* of a column to the left of names belonging to the 540s makes it impossible to arrive at a satisfactory arrangement if the list began with Solon, as might be assumed, e.g. from Plato, *Hipp. Maj.* 285 e, and leaves Kreon (683–2) as the only possible start.

Fragment *a* is placed by argument from the name of Kypselos (see below). The latest dates available for its four names before the likely date of his death happen to fit the restoration of]ομβ[as Φιλ]όμβ[ροτος, archon 595–4 (Cadoux, op. cit. 92). Earlier placings for the fragment would be possible. Fragment *b* is placed by the near-certainty that 'Ερχ[is Erxikleides, 548–7 (Paus. x. 5. 13), fragment *c* by the known archonship of Miltiades in 524–3 (Dion. Hal., *AR* vii. 3. 1). Fragment *d* is more uncertain, but the coincidence with the known archons of 490–89 and 489–8 is attractive.

We have no means of telling what material lay behind this late fifth-century publication of the archon-list, and how far it reflects an older document. Jacoby, laying stress on the apparent absence of patronymics, felt that the text on stone was in some sense an excerpt. The absence of any historical notes is also remarkable. We find it hard, however, to believe that the list contained nothing but names. There must have been some additional information about the archonship itself, at any rate, and we do not doubt that the two ἀναρχίαι and other difficulties of the 580s (Arist. Ἀθ. Πολ. 13. 1–2) were in some way recorded, a probability which weakens the tidiness of Bradeen's reconstruction.

Nor can we be confident about the occasion for the setting up of this list. It is possible, as Bradeen suggests, that it indicates an awakening of antiquarian interest. We are close in time to the activity of Hippias of Elis and of Hellanikos, but in default of all indication as to who was responsible we can only speculate.

For us these fragments give valuable new information about the names of archons in the sixth century, and some comment on individuals is necessary. The appearance of Κύ]ψσελο[ς (a 2) necessitates a reconsideration of the stemma of the Philaidai. (For earlier reconstructions see Hignett, *History of the Athenian Constitution*, 328–9, and the works cited there, Hammond, *CQ* vi (1956) 113–29. See now Bradeen, op. cit. 193–7, 206–8.) This Kypselos will be the father of the Miltiades who first went out to the Chersonese (Hdt. vi. 34 ff.). It no longer seems attractive to identify him with the Hippokleides who appears in Marcellinus, *Vit. Thuc.* 3, as Miltiades' father, for that Hippokleides must have appeared in the archon-list under 566–5 (Cadoux, op. cit. 104), and we doubt whether Marcellinus' confused and corrupt text can be used as evidence for anything. There has never been any doubt that this Kypselos was grandson of the Corinthian tyrant of that name, and we should think that his appearance as archon in 597 at the latest is decisive against attempts (most recently Will, *Korinthiaka*, 363–440) to lower the traditional dating of the tyranny at Corinth.

Fragment *c* has, since its discovery, been most fruitful for the study of the policy of the sons and successors of Pisistratus (see, e.g., Andrewes, *The Greek Tyrants*, 109–11). τὰ δὲ ἄλλα αὐτὴ ἡ πόλις τοῖς πρὶν κειμένοις νόμοις ἐχρῆτο, πλὴν καθ᾽ ὅσον ἀεί τινα ἐπεμέλοντο σφῶν αὐτῶν ἐν ταῖς ἀρχαῖς εἶναι (Thuc. vi. 54. 6). We can now see how the archonship was used for control and conciliation. Pisistratus died in the archonship of Philoneos, 528–7 (Arist. Ἀθ. Πολ. 17. 1). He may already have nominated Onetorides as archon for 527–6. (The alternative restoration Ὀν]έτο[ρ is ruled out by a study of the καλός-names on Athenian vases; Onetorides is associated with Exekias and other painters of the 540s, Onetor with the Edinburgh Painter and other painters of the last decade of the century. See Beazley, *ABV* 671 f.) Onetorides presumably comes from the rich but rarely conspicuous family of Melite, a city-deme (*PA* 11459–73). In 526–5 comes Hippias himself; in 525–4 Cleisthenes (Guarducci's Π]λεισθέν[ες is not probable), the head of the Alkmeonids and later lawgiver, the most spectacular gain from this inscription, since the literary evidence had suggested that the Alkmeonids were in continuous exile from

the Battle of Pallene to the fall of the tyranny. In 524–3 comes
Miltiades, heir to the position of the Philaids, and his archonship
gives body to Herodotus' assertion that the tyrants treated him well
(vi. 39. 1; see Wade-Gery, *Essays in Greek History*, 155–70). In 523–2
comes Kalliades, whose name is too common for his family to be
identified. The tempting restoration for 522–1 is Πεισί]στρατ[ος, the
son of Hippias. We do know he was archon under the tyranny (Thuc.
vi. 54. 6–7), and all the evidence for the Altar of the Twelve Gods,
built by him as archon, suggests 522–1 as a likely date (Crosby,
Hesp., Suppl. viii. 99–100). Were it not for the difficulties raised by
the lettering of No. 11, no one would doubt that the restoration
was correct.

7 (4)

Greek Mercenaries in Egyptian Service:
591 B.C.

Scratched on the left leg of a colossal statue of Rameses II before the great
temple of Abu Simbel in Nubia; *g* is below the knee of a second colossus.
   Bernand and Masson, *REG* lxx (1957) 1–20, with facs. + replaces all
earlier texts; *LSAG* 38, 48 (but the letters are not 'over a foot high', they
are never more than 9 cm.), 314, 340, 348, 355.

(*a*) Bernand–Masson 1. Doric Dialect, but mainly Ionic script, though
   o = o, ov, ω; koppa is present, the aspirate absent, Ⴃ = η, three-
   bar sigma.

   βασιλέος ἐλθόντος ἐς Ἐλεφαντίναν Ψαματίχο,
   ταῦτα ἔγραψαν τοὶ σὺν Ψαμματίχοι τὸι Θεοκλôς
   ἔπλεον, ἦλθον δὲ Κέρκιος κατύπερθε, υἷς ὁ πόταμος
   ἀνίη· ἀλογλόσος δ' ἦχε Ποτασιμτο, Αἰγυπτίος δὲ Ἄμασις·
 5 ἔγραφε δ' ἀμὲ Ἄρχον Ἀμοιβίχο καὶ Πέλεκος Οὐδάμο.

(*b*) Bernand–Masson 2. Ionic: Η = η, three-bar sigma.

   Ἐλεσίβιος ὁ Τήϊος.

(*c*) Bernand–Masson 4. Presumably Rhodian script: Ⴃ = η and the
aspirate.

   Τήλεφός μ' ἔγραφε ho Ἰαλύσιο[ς].

(*d*) Bernand–Masson 5.

   Πύθον Ἀμοιβίχου.

(e) Bernand–Masson 6; four-bar sigma.

    [- - - -] καὶ

    Κρῖθις ἔγρα⟨ψ⟩αν ἐμ[έ].

The psi was omitted.

(f) Bernand–Masson 6 bis (not seen by them). Ionic script, but
ο = ο, ω; three-bar sigma: koppa.

    Πάβις ὁ Ϙολοφόνιος

        σὺν Ψαμματᾶ.

(g) Bernand–Masson 2. Boustrophedon. ο = ο, ω; Ⴀ = the aspirate,
Ⴀε apparently = η; three-bar sigma; χσ = ξ; the shapes of psi
and chi in the last word are strange for Rhodian.

    Ἀναχσάνορ ε[. . . . .] ho ᾽Ιαλύσιος hόκα βασιλ-   →

    εὺς ἤλασε τὸν στράτον τὸ πρᾶτον [- - - -] Ψαμάτιχος.   ←

l. 1. ἐ[βάδισ᾽], doubtfully, B–M. In l. 2 they read, but do not draw,
Ἄμασις hάμα after τὸ πρᾶτον. Fraser (JEA xliv (1958) 108 f.) suggests that
Ποτασιμτο hάμα might be preferable.

(a) 'When King Psammetichos came to Elephantine, those who
sailed with Psammetichos son of Theokles wrote this; and they came
above Kerkis as far as the river allowed; and Potasimto had command
of those of foreign speech and Amasis of the Egyptians; and Archon
the son of Amoibichos wrote us and Peleqos the son of Eudamos.'

The king mentioned here is Psamtik II (the Ψάμμις of Herodotus).
His expedition to Ethiopia (Hdt. ii. 161) has fairly full documentation
from Egyptian sources, and is fully discussed by Sauneron and
Yoyotte, BIFAO l (1952) 157–207 (some further evidence on Potasimto in Yoyotte, Chr. d'Ég. xxviii (1953) 101–6). In their view the
expedition reached the Fourth and perhaps the Fifth Cataract,
though Préaux (Chr. d'Ég. xxxii (1957) 291) is inclined to maintain
the traditional view that it went no further than the Second Cataract.
Note that the king came only as far as Elephantine (a 1).

Jeffery suggests that the Greeks with no ethnics may be second- or
third-generation descendants of earlier settlers, and that this may
account for the mixed nature of their script; this must in any case be
true of Psammetichos, son of Theokles (a 2), presumably named
after Psamtik I. With ἀλογλόσος (a 4) cf. Hdt. ii. 154 πρῶτοι οὗτοι ἐν
Αἰγύπτῳ ἀλλόγλωσσοι κατοικίσθησαν and IG xii. 3. 328. 20. For the
singular form ἔγραφε cf., for example, Thuc. i. 51. 4 ἦρχε Γλαύκων τε
ὁ Λεάγρου καὶ Ἀνδοκίδης ὁ Λεωγόρου. Archon (a 5) and Python (d) are
presumably brothers. In (f) Πάβις may be shortened for Πάμβις or
Πάμβιος, and Ψαμματᾶ for Ψαμματίχωι.

8 (1)

Law from Chios: 575–550 B.C.

Upper part of a stele of reddish trachyte, with a cutting for a crowning member, found near Tholopotami in southern Chios; now in the Archaeological Museum at Istanbul.

Ionic alphabet (open eta, crossed theta, koppa), boustrophedon on all four sides, inscribed vertically on the front, right side and left side, horizontally on the back. Punctuation on front and right side only. Phot. and facs.: *Nordionische Steine* (*Abh. Berl.* 1909), 69 f., Pl. 2; *BSA* li (1956) 158 and Pl. 43 (whence *LSAG*, Pl. 65. 41). See *LSAG* 336 f.

Jeffery, *BSA* li 157–67+; Larsen, *CP* xliv (1949) 170–2; Wade-Gery, *Essays in Greek History*, 198 f.; Oliver, *AJP* lxxx (1959) 296–301.

Front (A)

[- - -]κατης: Ἱστίης δήμο   →
ῥήτρας : φυλάσσω[ν - - -]   ←
[- - -]ον : ηρει : ἦμ μὲν δημαρ-
χῶν : ἢ βασιλεύων: δεκασ[θῆι(?) - - -]
5 [- - -]s Ἱστίης ἀποδότω δημα-
ρχέων: ἐξπρῆξαι: τὸν ἐ[ξεταστὴν(?) - -]
[- - -]εν δήμο κεκλημένο
αλοιαι τιμὴ διπλησ[ίη - - -]
[- - -]ν ὄσην παραλοιω[.]

Right side (B)

[.c. 3..]ην δ' ἤκκλητος δί[κη - -]   →
[- - -,] ἦν δὲ ἀδικῆται: παρὰ   ←
δημάρχωι: στατῆρ[ας - - -]

Back (C)

ἐκκαλέσθω ἐς   →
βολὴν τὴν δημ-   ←
οσίην· τῆι τρίτηι
ἐξ Ἑβδομαίων
5 βολὴ ἀγερέσθ-
ω ἡ δημοσίη ἐ-
πιθώϊος λεκτ-

ἡ πεντήροντ' ἀπ-
ὸ φυλῆς· τά τ' ἄλ[λ]-
10   α πρησσέτω τὰ δή-
μο καὶ δίκα[ς ὁ]-
[ρό]σαι ἂν ἔκκλ-
ητοι γένων[τ]-
[αι] τô μηνὸς π-
15   άσας ἐπι[...]
[..c. 4..]σεερ[.c. 3..]
[- - - -]

Left side (D)

[- - - - Ἀ]ρτεμισιῶνος   →
[- - - -]ων ὅρκια ἐπι-   →
ταμνέτω ρὼ[μνύτω (?) - -]   ←
[- - - β]ασιλεῦσιν. vacat

Jeffery's re-examination of the text is now fundamental, and there can be little doubt that her arrangement of the order of the sides is the right one. It also seems reasonably certain that we have only one text, since any distinction based on the character of the script and the abandonment of punctuation would mean that a new text began with the beginning of C, which seems textually improbable. The main uncertainty that remains is the order of the lines in B, Jeffery and Oliver preferring to read them from left to right, whereas Wade-Gery slightly prefers the older arrangement from right to left. On any view, the principal difficulty is caused by the breaking of the stone, which entails that, after every second line on the three faces with vertical inscriptions, there is a lacuna of uncertain length. Oliver takes the view that relatively little is missing and suggests continuous restorations, but some of these are very compressed in language, and it is in our judgement unsafe to assume that much less than half the stele is missing.

A 1–3. [τῶν ἱερῶν ἔνε]κα: τῆς Ἱστίης δήμο | ῥήτρας: φυλάσσω[ν: - - - - - -]ον: ἢ (ἐ)ρεῖ, 'As for property sacred to Hestia, (the official) shall constantly observe rhetras of the demos and shall give an order that such and such be sacred by separately citing the rhetra which will so declare', Oliver, comparing ἡ (ἐ)κκλητος or ἢ (ἐ)κκλήτος in B 1. But Jeffery tells us that her facsimile is correct and not her transcript.

4. δεκασ[θῆι, 'accepts bribes', Jeffery; δεκάσ[ηι, 'levies a tithe' (an un-attested sense), Oliver.

4–5. τῶι ἱερεῖ τῆ]ς Ἱστίης Nachmannson; [x στατῆρας ἱερὸς τῆ]ς Ἱστίης Forrest; [τἀπιδέ|κατα τῆ]ς Ἱστίης Oliver.

6–8. τὸν ἐ[ξεταστὴν, or ἐ[πιστάτην Jeffery; τὸν ἐ[ξεταστὴ|ν ἔμπροσθ]εν δήμο κεκλημένο Oliver. Jeffery, followed by Oliver, ends a sentence after κεκλημένο, though there is no space or preserved punctuation, and takes ἀλοῖαι as a new heading, suggesting the meaning 'assaults' (Oliver prefers 'convictions'). Wade-Gery believes he can see traces of alpha under the eta of τιμή, and thinks that αἱ τιμαί was originally intended, that τιμαί was corrected to τιμή, but αἱ was left uncorrected; he would read [ὁ ἐκκαλεόμενος ἢμ μ]ὲν δῆμο κεκλημένο ἀλοῖ, ⟨ἡ⟩ τιμὴ διπλησ[ίη, 'if he appeal and lose his appeal before the assembled people, the fine is doubled'.

8–9. ἀλοῖαι, τιμὴ διπλησ[ίη· ἐξ ἐρήμο | δ' ἐξπρήσσε]ν ὅσην παρ' ἀλοίω[ν, 'Convictions: *poena dupli*. After a case lost by default, always exact a penalty as large as that which arises from convictions', Oliver. The choice in this complex situation is between an unattested word and the assumption of a partially corrected error.

B 1–2. [βολ]ὴν δ' ἡ (ἐ)κκλήτος δι̣[κάσει δημο|σίην εἶναι], 'The council which judges appeals shall be a people's council', Oliver; ἢν δ' ἡ (ἐ)κκλητος δι̣[κη Jeffery. Wade-Gery, reversing the order of B 1–3, suggests ἢν δὲ ἀδικῆται: παρα|[χωρ]ῆι δ' ἡ (ἐ)κκλητος δι̣[κη, 'if he be suffering wrong, and the judgement appealed against be (consequently) put aside'.

D. The *vacat* in l. 1 and the failure to continue the boustrophedon indicate that a new clause begins with l. 2. Ll. 3–4 ῥώ[μνυέτω ἐν τοῖς β]ασιλεῦσιν Oliver.

The stele has a small, normal taper, and Wilamowitz was mistaken in referring to it as a pyramid or κύρβις. Miss Jeffery has also, by bringing down the date from *c.* 600, reduced the part which this stone played for fifty years in discussions of Ionia's political advancement (cf. Mazzarino, *Fra Oriente e Occidente* 233–41). What we have is sufficiently remarkable, a view into a political organization where we have side by side βασιλεῖς (perhaps, as at Athens, the βασιλεύς plus the φυλοβασιλεῖς) and δήμαρχοι, whether they be high officials, like the archon at Athens, or officials specifically created to represent the δῆμος; and where we have a βουλὴ δημοσίη, which from the very formulation of its name must be a second council to supplement the aristocratic council, and which hears appeals, is elective, and meets regularly on the ninth day of each month to carry on the business of the δῆμος and to hear all cases which have come up on appeal in the last month. The power of the δῆμος, however widely or narrowly the term is to be interpreted, has become considerable by the time of this document, and there seems little reason to follow Oliver in believing that the popular council is now being appointed for the first time. The existence of this popular council has generally been thought to lend some support to the existence of Solon's Council of the Four Hundred at Athens (Arist. Ἀθ. Πολ. 8. 4; Plut. *Sol.* 19. 1), but its relevance has been denied by Hignett (*History of the Athenian Constitution*, 95). How great the power of the δῆμος in regard to appeals in fact is, we cannot determine because of the break in C 15. It has been generally thought that it is the council which determines the appeals, but Wade-Gery believes, somewhat improbably it seems to us, that the council only acts probouleutically in preparing the appeals for the δῆμος.

Faces A and B are likely to remain difficult to interpret. On Miss Jeffery's view of the text, the only point which would be at all clear would be the provision for the fining of officials who are bribed (A 3–6) ; a provision about assaults (?) would follow (A 8–9); Wade-Gery takes these clauses together. Oliver, on the other hand, taking A 1–7 together, regards them as a single edict about the administration of the property of Hestia. Miss Jeffery and Oliver, agreeing about the order of lines in B, differ as to whether παρὰ δημάρχωι should be taken with ἀδικῆται 'if he has been wronged in the demarch's court' (Jeffery) or with στατῆρ[ας '[he shall deposit so many] staters with the demarch' (Oliver). Wade-Gery, with his different arrangement of B, takes B 3 as the continuation of Face A, and lets B 1–2 lead into C. Face C is relatively straightforward, dealing with the procedure of appeal and the organization of the βουλὴ δημοσίη. A new section on oath-taking begins with D 2.

Some minor points call for notice. Ἱστίη (A 1, 5) seems rather more likely to be the goddess than the public hearth. Although the oldest occurrence of ῥήτρη (A 2) has the meaning 'covenant' (*Od.* xiv. 393, cf. No. 17), the prevalent later meaning is, as here, 'enactment' (Wade-Gery, *Essays in Greek History*, 62–4): the fact that nearly all uses of the word are in the Peloponnese or Peloponnesian colonies makes its appearance here more noteworthy (but see No. 83. 13). The Ἑβδομαῖα (C 4) was a festival held in honour of Apollo on the seventh day of each month (cf. *SIG* 57. 6, 21). ἐπιθώιος (C 6–7) should probably be taken actively, 'with power to inflict penalties', rather than passively, 'subject to a fine (for non-attendance)'. We do not know the number of tribes in archaic Chios (C 8–9).

One last doubt should be mentioned. Forrest tells us that he knows no other use of red trachyte for an inscription on Chios and suggests the possibility that the inscription originated in neighbouring Erythrae on the mainland.

9

Aristis, Son of Pheidon at Nemea: *c.* 560 B.C.

Shallow poros block with cuttings for a dedication, from the *gymnasion* by the Temple of Zeus at Nemea; now in the *apotheke* there.

Kleonaean script (see *LSAG* 144 f., 147 f.), boustrophedon. Phot.: *AJA* xxxi (1927) 432, Fig. 10; *Hesp.* xxxv (1966) Pl. 77; phot. and facs.: *LSAG*, Pl. 24.

Blegen, *AJA* xxxi. 432 f.; Peek, *Ἀρχ. Ἐφ.* 1931 103 f.; McGregor, *TAPA* lxxii (1941) 275; Friedländer 103; Buck 97; Moretti, 3; Bradeen, *Hesp.* xxxv (1966) 320.

> Ἀρίστις με ἀνέθ-   →
> ηκε Δὶ Ϙρονίονι Fά-   ←
> νακτι πανκράτιο-
> ν νιϙὸν τετράκις
> 5 ἐν Νεμέαι Φείδο-
> νος Fhιὸς τô Κλεο-
> ναίο.

This is one of the earliest surviving agonistic dedications. Jerome's version of Eusebius places the founding or refounding of the Nemean games in 573. If we allow Aristis the minimum time, he cannot have won his fourth victory in this trieteric festival earlier than 567, and the lettering does not suggest a much later date.

Kleonai was for long periods the patron of the Nemean games (cf. Pind. *Nem.* x. 42, iv. 17, *Hyp. Schol.* Pind. *Nem.*). Some interest attaches to the name Pheidon, appearing at a date where Herodotus (vi. 127), certainly wrongly, puts the great Pheidon. McGregor suggests that Leokedes, son of Pheidon in Herodotus, was son of Pheidon of Kleonai (cf. Huxley, *BCH* lxxxii (1958) 600 f.). Other combinations are perhaps possible, but there are clearly some attractions in seeing here a descendant of the Argive royal house in exile in Kleonai.

Down to Νεμέαι, the text is intended for an elegiac couplet; we do not share the view of Guarducci (*Epigrafia Greca*, i. 238–48) that the rest is an 'iambic pentapody'.

10

Treaty between Sybaris and the Serdaioi: (?) 550–525 B.C.

Bronze plate with nail-holes top and bottom, found at Olympia, probably from the Sybarite Treasury. Now in the Olympia Museum.

Achaean colonial script (for which see *LSAG* 248–51). Phot.: *VII Olympia-Bericht*, Pl. 86. 2; *Rend. Linc.* (see below) Pl. i.

Kunze, *VII Olympia-Bericht*, 207–10; *Staatsverträge* 120; Zancani Montuoro, *Rend. Linc.* Ser. viii, xvii (1962) 11–18; Guarducci, ibid. 199–210; Calderone, *Helikon*, iii (1963) 219–58 (see *REG* lxxix (1966) 380 f.).

> ἁρμόχθεν οἱ Συβαρῖ-
> ται κ' οἱ σύνμαχοι κ' οἱ

Σερδαῖοι ἐπὶ φιλότατ-
ι πιστᾶι κ' ἀδόλοι ἀε-
5 ίδιον· πρόξενοι ὁ Ζε-
ὺς κ' 'Οπόλον κ' ἄλλοι θ-
εοὶ καὶ πόλις Ποσειδα-
νία.

'The Sybarites and their allies and the Serdaioi made an agreement for friendship faithful and without guile for ever. Guarantors, Zeus, Apollo, and the other gods and the city Poseidonia.'

This is among the earliest, if it is not the earliest, of all preserved Greek treaties, and the only known epigraphical document of Sybaris, destroyed in 510. It shows Sybaris at the head of an alliance (cf. Strabo vi. 1. 13, p. 263). The other parties to the treaty, the Serdaioi, are unknown to literary sources. Kunze rightly associates them with a series of coins with the legend MEP sometimes wrongly attributed to Sergention in Sicily (*BM Italy*, 395; *HN²* 169; Panvini Rosati, *Rend Linc*. Ser. viii, xvii (1962) 278–85). The indications of the coins and this treaty are that they are an Achaean colony of south Italy. The hypothesis of Zancani Montuoro that the Sardinians are here referred to has been rebutted by Guarducci.

This treaty is by far the oldest surviving made 'for ever' (cf. Nos. 63, 64, and contrast No. 17). For this sense of πρόξενοι cf. Hesych. πρόξενος· προστάτης and *IG* xiv. 636. The guarantee offered by the gods was strengthened by the setting up of the treaty at Olympia. The function of Poseidonia is hard to determine; it is interesting that, though a colony of Sybaris, it appears to be outside her alliance.

11 (8)

Dedication of Pisistratus, Son of Hippias:

c. 521 B.C.

Two fragments of a sculptured marble cornice (Boardman, *Antiq. Journ.* xxxix. 206 f.), found in 1877 near the Ilissos; now in EM.

Late archaic Attic letters, *LSAG* 75, 78 (37). Phot.: *IIA* 12; Kern 12; facs.: *LSAG*, Pl. 4. 37.

IG i². 761; Meritt, *Hesp.* viii (1939) 62–5; Dinsmoor, *Studies in the History of Culture* (1942), 195–8; *DAA* pp. 449 f.; *SEG* x. 318; *LSAG* 75.

Μνῆμα τόδε hε̄ς ἀρχε̄ς Πεισίστ[ρατος hιππίο h]υιὸς
θε̄κεν Ἀπόλλονος Πυθ[ί]ο ἐν τεμένε̣ι.

Thucydides (vi. 54. 6) records that the grandson of the tyrant Pisistratus, to commemorate his archonship, dedicated the Altar of the Twelve Gods in the Agora and of Apollo in the Pythion. He quotes the inscription on the latter and adds: ἔτι καὶ νῦν δῆλόν ἐστιν ἀμυδροῖς γράμμασι λέγον τάδε. The epithet ἀμυδροῖς is surprising, since the letters are still clear; it almost certainly refers to the disappearance of the paint with which the letters had been filled. The elegance and comparative maturity of the letters have led some scholars to date the inscription to the early fifth century (Raubitschek, *DAA* p. 450; Meritt, *Hesp.* viii. 62). But Pisistratus cannot have been allowed to stay in Athens after the expulsion of his father Hippias in 510. He was archon before 510 and almost certainly in 522–1 (see No. 6); the altar must have been dedicated in or soon after his archonship. Dinsmoor's compromise (op. cit.), dating the inscription considerably later than the altar, is not needed. It is true that many later inscriptions (e.g. No. 18) have more archaic letters, and the straight bar of the alpha is surprising, but the early forms of theta and chi are used (⊕, +). We need only believe that Pisistratus chose a craftsman who was ahead of most of his contemporaries. The same hand can be seen in a dedication at the Ptoion sanctuary in Boeotia, by a Hipparchus, almost certainly the brother of Hippias (*BCH* xliv (1920) 237 ff., *Hesp.* viii. 65 n. 1).

12 (10)

Letter of Darius: 522–486 B.C.

On a marble corner-block from a wall found at Deirmendjik, on the road from Magnesia on the Maeander to Tralles; now in the Louvre. The side of the stone has traces of two other inscriptions.

'Letter-forms of the first half of the second century A.D.' (Kern).

Cousin and Deschamps, *BCH* xiii (1889) 529–42; *SIG* 22; Wilamowitz, *Griech. Lesebuch, Erläuterungen*, 252 f.; Olmstead, *Am. J. Sem. Lang.* xlix (1933) 156–9; van den Hout, *Mnemosyne*, ii (1949) 144–52; Schehl, *AJA* liv (1950) 265 (summary of an unpublished article).

> βασιλεὺς [βα]σιλέ-
> ων Δαρεῖος ὁ Ὑσ-
> τάσπεω Γαδάται
> δούλωι τάδε λέγε[ι]·
> 5 πυνθάνομαί σε τῶν
> ἐμῶν ἐπιταγμάτων

οὐ κατὰ πάντα πει-
θαρχεῖν· ὅτι μὲν γὰ[ρ]
[τ]ὴν ἐμὴν ἐκπονεῖς
10 [γ]ῆν, τοὺς πέραν Εὐ-
[φ]ράτου καρποὺς ἐπ[ὶ]
τὰ κάτω τῆς Ἀσίας μέ-
[ρ]η καταφυτεύων, ἐπαι-
[ν]ῶ σὴν πρόθεσιν καὶ
15 [δ]ιὰ ταῦτά σοι κείσεται
μεγάλη χάρις ἐμ βασι-
λέως οἴκωι· ὅτι δὲ τὴν
ὑπὲρ θεῶν μου διάθε-
σιν ἀφανίζεις, δώσω
20 σοι μὴ μεταβαλομένωι
πεῖραν ἠδικη[μέ]νου θυ-
μοῦ· φυτουργοὺς γὰρ
[ἱ]ερους Ἀπόλλ[ω]νος φό-
ρον ἔπρασσες καὶ χώραν
25 [σ]καπανεύειν βέβηλον ἐπ[έ]-
τασσες, ἀγνοῶν ἐμῶν
προγόνων εἰς τὸν θεὸν
[ν]οῦν, ὃς Πέρσαις εἶπε
[πᾶ]σαν ἀτρέκε[ι]αν καὶ τῃ.
- - -

The authenticity of this document has been denied by Beloch (*GG* ii². 2. 154 f.) for bad reasons, and is seriously doubted by van den Hout, but has generally been accepted. Though some of the points alleged in its support are invalid (πειθαρχεῖν with the genitive, l. 6, is not necessarily a trace of an original Ionic text, for it is a normal κοινή construction), it seems clear that the original was not in Greek and there is nothing incredible about the content.

Gadatas (the name recurs in Xen. *Cyrop.* v. 3. 10 ff.) seems to have been satrap of the Ionian province (Hdt. iii. 90; Meyer, *Entstehung des Judentums*, 19, prefers to see in him a more junior official, like Asaph in Nehemiah ii. 8) and may well have resided at Magnesia, as did Oroites (Hdt. iii. 122). Darius praises him for cultivating in western Asia Minor the fruit trees of Syria ('Beyond the River' is the normal Achaemenid phrase for this satrapy), but threatens him with punishment for levying a tax from the sacred gardeners of Apollo (for whom

perhaps see Paus. x. 32. 6 and the numismatic evidence collected by
Schehl) and ordering them to till profane soil, regardless of the
attitude shown to the god by the Achaemenid kings (for Persian religious toleration see *CAH* iv. 187 f.). The attention paid by the Persian
kings to the cultivation of trees and crops in their empire is emphasized in Xen. *Oec.* iv. 8; see also Poseidonios (*FGH* 87 F 68) in Ath.
i. 28d. The phrases βασιλεὺς βασιλέων (l. 1) and τάδε λέγει (l. 4; cf.
Rudberg, *Eranos*, xi (1913) 175 f. and van den Hout), as well as the
term δοῦλος applied to a satrap (l. 4), agree with the usage of Darius
as shown in the Behistun inscription: with the phrase used in ll. 15–17
compare Thuc. i. 129. 3 κείσεταί σοι εὐεργεσία ἐν τῷ ἡμετέρῳ οἴκῳ ἐς
αἰεὶ ἀνάγραπτος, Hdt. viii. 85. 3, and Esther vi. 1, 2.

13

A Lokrian Community settles New Territory: (?) 525–500 B.C.

A bronze plaque with nail-holes at the corners, said by different informants
to have come from Psoriani in Aetolia or the neighbourhood of Naupaktos;
now in the National Museum at Athens.

Script of the Ozolian Lokrians (see *LSAG* 104 f.), boustrophedon. Phot.:
Ἀρχ. Ἐφ 1924, Pl. 3; *LSAG*, Pl. 14.

Papadakis, Ἀρχ. Ἐφ. 1924, 119–41; Wilamowitz, *Sitzb. Berl.* (1927)
7–17; Luria, *Dokl. Ak. Nauk.*, Ser. B (1927) 216–18; Meillet, *Rev. Phil.* liv
(1928) 185–90; Pezopoulos, Πολέμων, i (1929) 97–105; Chatzes, Ἀρχ. Ἐφ.
1927–8, 181–5; Solmsen, 46; Lerat, *Les Locriens de l'Ouest*, i. 53 f.; ii. 9 f.;
Nilsson, *Hist.* iii (1954) 270–3; Buck 59; Georgacas, *CP* li (1956) 249–51;
LSAG 105 f. (Lokris 2); Graham, *Colony and Mother City in Ancient Greece*,
56 f., 65; Vatin, *BCH* lxxxvii (1963) 1–19; Asheri, *J. Jur. Pap.* xv (1965)
313–28; Larsen, *Greek Federal States*, 54.

(Obverse)

(A)   τεθμὸς ὅδε περὶ τᾶς γᾶς βέβαιος ἔστο κὰτ τὸν   →
      ἀνδαιθμὸν πλακὸς Ὑλίας καὶ Λισκαρίας καὶ τὸν ἀ-   ←
      ποτόμον καὶ τὸν δαμοσίον. ἐπινομία δ' ἔστο γο-
      νεῦσιν καὶ παιδί· αἰ δὲ μὲ παῖς εἴε, κόραι· αἰ δὲ μὲ κόρα εἴε,
 5   ἀδελφεοῖ· αἰ δὲ μὲ ἀδελφεό⟨ς⟩ εἴε, ἀγχιστέδαν ἐπινεμέσθο κὰ τὸ
      δίκαιον· αἰ δὲ μέ, τοῖ ἐπινόμοι OIION, hό τι δέ κα φυτεύσεται,
      ἄσυλος εἴστο. αἰ μὲ πόλεμοι ἀνανκαζομένοις δόξξαι ἀ-
      νδράσιν hενὶ κέκατον ἀριστίνδαν τοῖ πλέθει ἄνδρας δια-
      κατίος μεῖστον ἀξξιομάχος ἐπιϝοίκος ἐφάγεσθαι, hόστ-

10   ις δὲ δαιθμὸν ἐνφέροι ἒ ψᾶφον διαφέροι ἐν πρείγαι ἒ ᾽ν πόλι ἒ
᾽ν ἀποκλεσίαι ἒ στάσιν ποιέοι περὶ γαδαισίας, αὐτὸς μὲ-
ν Ϝερρέτο καὶ γενεὰ ἄματα πάντα, χρέματα δὲ δαμευόσθον
καὶ Ϝοικία κατασκαπτέσθο κὰτ τὸν ἀνδρεφονικὸν τετθμ-
όν. ὁ δὲ τετθμὸς ἱαρὸς ἔστο τô Ἀπόλλονος τô Πυθίο κ̣α̣ὶ τ̣ο̣ν̣ σ̣υ̣ν̣ν̣-
15   [άον· ἔμεν δὲ τôι τα]ῦτα παρβαίνοντι ἐξξόλειαν αὐτôι καὶ γενεᾶι
καὶ πα-
μ̣ά̣τ̣ε̣σ̣ι̣ν̣, τôι δ᾽ εὐσεβέοντι ℎίλαος ἔσστο. ἁ δὲ γ[ὰ τὸ μὲν ἔμισον]

(*Reverse*)

(C)   κομίζοιεν, ἀξιοδότας ἔστο τὰν αὐτô ℎιτινι χρέιζοι.   →
vacat

(**A** continued)
τὸν ℎυπαπροσθιδίον ἔστο, τὸ δ᾽ ἔμισον τὸν ἐπιϝοίκον ἔσ-   →
το.   vacat
vacat   ←

(**A** continued? Larger letters)
τὸς δὲ κοίλος μόρος διαδόντο: ἀλλαγὰ δὲ βέβαιο-   →
ς ἔστο, ἀλαζέσθο δὲ ἀντὶ τô ἀρχô.   ←
vacat

B (upside-down)
[αἰ δὲ τôι] δαμιοργοὶ κερδαίνοιεν ἄλλο   →
τὸν γεγραμένον, ℎιαρόντο Ἀπόλλο-   ←
νος: Ἐχέτο ἄγαλμα δι᾽ ἐννέα ϝετ-
έον καὶ μὲ ποτιγράψαι κέρδος.

Papadakis, followed by Jeffery, abandoned the enigmatic letters in l. 6
as an erasure, and regarded text C as an omitted line to be added at this
point. The text would then run αἰ δὲ μὲ τοι ἐπινόμοι κομίζοιεν, ἀξιοδότας
ἔστο τὰν αὐτô ℎιτινι χρέιζοι, 'If the heirs do not take the property, (the
owner) shall have the right to bestow his property on whomsoever he wishes.'
This view is not inherently probable, and Wilamowitz showed that there
were some orthographic reasons to detach text C from text A. Yet the alternative is to regard both text B and text C as parts of separate laws, of which
text C certainly and text B probably are continuations of texts on other
plaques, and this cannot be said to be an easy view either. Nor is it easy to
construct any hypothesis to explain at what stage in the plaque's history it
was firmly nailed to a wall so that only one side was visible. The enigmatic
letters remain a problem: ὀμ[όρ]ον (Wilamowitz), ὀμôν (= ὁμοίων) (Pezopoulos), rest on a false reading; ⟨ὀμ⟩οιίον (Buck) requires the assumption
of an error; δι ἰόν (sc. ἐστι = ᾧ καθήκει, Pezopoulos), οἷον (= οἵων, 'from
among whomsoever', Georgacas) are not convincing. In l. 2 πλακὸς Ὑλίας

(Pezopoulos), Πλακὸς ὑλίας (Wilamowitz). In ll. 10–11 ἐν πρείγαι, ἐν πόλι, ἐν ἀποκλησίαι is equally possible; ἐν Πόλι (cf. Thuc. iii. 101) Chatzes. In l. 15 [ἔμεν] Wilamowitz, [ἔμεν δέ] Jeffery. The version of B here followed is that of Wilamowitz; we do not understand the alternative ℎιαρὸν το Ἀπόλλο|νος ἐχέτο ἄγαλμα, 'If the demiourgoi gain anything other than the amounts prescribed, it shall be held sacred to Apollo as an offering for a period of nine years, and one shall not enter it in addition as profit.'

Text A: 'This law concerning the land shall be in force for the partition of the plain of Hyla and Liskara, both the separate lots and the public. The right of pasturage shall belong to parents and to the son; if there is no son, to the daughter; if there is no daughter, to the brother; if there is no brother, by relationship let a man pasture according to the law; if not, to the one who pastures . . .(?) [Vatin argues, by no means implausibly, that the words ἐπινομία, ἐπινεμέσθο, ἐπίνομος, simply refer to inheritance and not to pasturage at all.] Whatever a man plants, he shall be immune from its seizure. Unless under the pressure of war a majority of 101 men chosen from the best citizens decide to bring in at least 200 fighting-men as additional settlers, whoever [the δέ is apodotic] proposes a division or puts it to a vote in the council of elders or in the city or in the select-men or makes civil strife about the division of land, he himself and his family shall be accursed for all time, his property shall be confiscated and his house demolished just as under the law about murder. This law shall be sacred to Pythian Apollo and the gods who dwell with him; on the person who transgresses it may there be destruction, on him and his family and his possessions, but may (the god) be kindly to him who observes it. The land shall belong, half to the previous settlers, half to the additional settlers.' There follows an addition: 'Let them distribute the valley portions. Exchange shall be valid, but the exchange shall take place before the magistrate.'

Text C: '(If/when) they receive(?), one shall be entitled to give his share to whomever he wishes.'

Text B: 'If the demiourgoi gain more than the amount prescribed, let them dedicate a statue to Apollo Echetos at the end of nine years, and the money shall not be counted as a gain' (i.e. to the state treasury).

The topographic problems of this text are unlikely to be satisfactorily settled. The view of Chatzes which attributes the text to the town of Polis (cf. Keramopoullos, Ἀρχ. Ἐφ. (1927–8) 209 f.) is not easily reconcilable with either of the find-spots reported, and essentially rests on the mistaken belief that the Ὑαῖοι of Thuc. iii. 101 are attested only there and can be emended to Ὕλιοι (cf. l. 2). This is not so; see Lerat, op. cit. i. 31 f., 53 f. Lerat, on the other hand, wishes (ii. 9 f.) to regard the text as Aetolian, for dialect reasons, and to accept the find-spot of Psoriani. It is clear, however, that the alphabet is Ozolian Lokrian and not Aetolian. This does not rule out Psoriani, for the Lokrians may be contemplating a settlement across the Aetolian border, but Naupaktos is clearly much more likely, since the plaque was dedicated to Apollo (l. 14) and there was an Apollonion in Naupaktos (Thuc. ii. 91. 1). (So Papadakis; Jeffery's suggestion that the colony of No. 20 is the additional settlement contemplated in ll. 7–9 is attractive but not cogent.)

Whatever the community was, it has well-defined inheritance-laws (ll. 5–6); if the whole of ll. 11–13 applies to its homicide-law and not merely the confiscation of property and the destruction of the house, it has in theory progressed beyond the blood-feud; it has a council, a popular assembly, and something between the two in its ἀποκλησία (but see Schwahn, *Wien. Stud.* xlviii (1930) 141–9), though it may confide some business to a body selected aristocratically (l. 8); its magistrates include δαμιοργοί (see Murakawa, *Hist.* vi (1957) 390) and an ἀρχός. They are not new settlers; they are an old community extending their interests into a new area.

It has generally been assumed that the new area was being divided into κλῆροι, and Wilamowitz, for example, held that the particulars of the division had already been determined and perhaps inscribed on another plaque now lost. This has been challenged by Nilsson, who claims that it is primarily pasturage which is in question and that flocks and herds are no respecters of boundaries. He holds that the division contemplated is that of the pasture-land from the rest of the community's territory. He does not give an account of τὸν ἀποτόμον καὶ τὸν δαμοσίον, which are probably best interpreted as sacred precincts (cf. τέμενος, from the same root) and public property, and it is hard to see how he would explain the division of the territory with the new settlers, which certainly seems to be contemplated in ll. 16 ff. But his account needs serious consideration, particularly what he has to say about ll. 6–7, which he claims as the first known example of the rights gained by ἐμφύτευσις, very frequent in later Greek history.

The parallels with No. 49, extending to the formulae of l. 10, are of some interest.

14 (11)

Athenian Decree concerning Salamis: (?) late sixth century B.C.

Seven fragments of a marble stele from the Acropolis. The stele tapers upwards and the lines of the text read vertically downward; now in EM.

Archaic Attic letters, including ⊕ and ✛. Ll. 1–6 stoichedon 35; in
ll. 7–12 the letters are more widely spaced. Phot.: *IIA* 13; Austin, Pl. 4.
Facs. restored: *Hesp.* x (1941) 305. New frag.: *Hesp.* vii (1938) 265.

IG i². 1; *SEG* x. 1; Wilhelm, *Sitzb. Wien*, 217. 5 (1939) 5–11; Kahrstedt,
Staatsgebiet 359–62; Schweigert (new frag.), *Hesp.* vii (1938) 264; Meritt,
Hesp. x (1941) 301–7; Wade-Gery, *CQ* xl (1946) 101–4; Guarducci, *RF*
lxxvi (1948) 238–43; Bartsos, Ἀθηνᾶ, lxv (1961) 201–9; Luria, *Kadmos*, iii
(1964) 88–107.

> ἔδοχσεν τôι δέμοι· τ[ὸς ἐ Σ]αλαμ[ῖνι κλερόχος]
> οἰκên ἐâ Σαλαμῖνι [..5...]λεν [...7.... Ἀθένε]-
> σι τελên καὶ στρατ[εύεσθ]αι: τ[ὰ δ’ ἐ Σαλαμῖνι μ]-
> ἐ μι[σθ]ôν, ἐὰ μὲ οἰκ[...7....]ο[.μισθόμενο. : ἐὰ]-
> 5 ν δὲ μισθôι, ἀποτί[νεν τὸ μισθόμενον καὶ τὸ μ]-
> ισθôντα ηεκάτερο[ν........19..........]
> ἐς δεμόσιο[ν: ἐσπράτεν δὲ τὸν ἄ]-
> ρχο[ν]τα, ἐὰν [δὲ μέ, εὐθ]ύ[νεσθαι: τ]-
> ὰ δὲ [η]όπλα π[αρέχεσ]θα[ι αὐτὸς: τ]-
> 10 ριά[κ]οντα: δρ[αχμôν:] ηο[πλισμένο]-
> ν δὲ [τ]ὸν ἄρχοντ[α τὰ ηόπλα κρίν]-
> εν: [ἐπ]ὶ τês β[ο]λê[ς .....c. 11......]

l. 1: κλερόχος Luria; οἰκôντας Wilhelm; Ἀθεναῖος Meritt; τ[ὸν...
Ἀθεναῖον Wade-Gery. l. 2: αἰεὶ π]λὲν [ηότι δεῖ Ἀθένε]|σι Meritt; καὶ τε]λên
[ηά ἐστιν ἀστοῖ]σι τελên Wade-Gery; καὶ τε]λên [καθάπερ Ἀθένε]|σι τελên
Guarducci. l. 4: ἐὰ μὲ οἰκ[εῖος ἐι η]ο [μισθόμενος Wade-Gery; ἐὰ μὲ
οἰκ[ôσι καὶ η]ο[ι μισθόμενοι Meritt. l. 6: [τὸ τριπλάσιον τὸ μισθô]
Tod; [δεκάτεν τô μισθόματος] Wade-Gery. ll. 7–8: [χουλέγεν δὲ τὸν
ἄ]|ρχο[ν]τα, ἐάν [τι δέος η]υ[πάρχει] Wade-Gery. l. 12: [ταῦτ’ ἐγνόσθε]
Meritt; [ὁ δεῖνα εἶπε] Wade-Gery; ἐπ]ὶ τês Β[ο]λέ[κλεος ἀρχês] Luria,
Roussel.

This is the earliest Athenian decree to survive. It concerns the
status and obligations of men living on Salamis, but the keyword at
the end of the first line is lost: Ἀθεναῖος, κλερόχος, οἰκôντας equally
fit the space available, but the clauses that follow make better sense
if they refer to Athenians rather than natives (οἰκôντας). With Kahrstedt and others we believe that the decree concerns cleruchs recently
settled on the island. The direct evidence for a cleruchy on Salamis
is slight: a scholiast on Pindar, *Nem.* ii. 19, in honour of Timodemos
of Acharnai, says that there is no agreed explanation of the reference to
Ajax in the poem, but some think that Timodemos was one of the
Athenian cleruchs established on Salamis. It is likely that though
born in Athens he was brought up on Salamis. It is only a guess that

Timodemos was a cleruch, but the cleruchy itself is not questioned by the scholiast or his sources. There is also a reference to Salamis in a decree that dates from 386, just after the Peace of Antalkidas, when Athens was allowed to resume control over Lemnos through cleruchs: *IG* ii². 30, Frag. *b*, l. 4,]ναι μήτε μισθῶσαι πλήν - -. l. 6,] γῆν τὸς κλερόχος κα[- -. l. 7, καθάπ]ερ τοῖς ἐς Σαλαμ[ῖνα. This might be a reference back to regulations dating from Athens' first cleruchy. Hammond (following Macan, *Herodotus*, ad loc.) attractively identifies as cleruchs the force that Aristides landed on Psyttaleia at the battle of Salamis, described by Herodotus (viii. 95) as γένος ἐόντες Ἀθηναῖοι (*JHS* lxxvi (1956) 48).

The conditions laid down in the decree are: 1 (ll. 1–3): The cleruch must pay taxes and give military service to Athens. 2 (ll. 3–8): He must not lease his land on Salamis except to a ?kinsman (l. 4 οἰκ[εῖος], Wade-Gery). 3 (ll. 8–12): He must provide his own arms to the value of 30 dr. and the Athenian governor (cf. Arist. Ἀθ. Πολ. 54. 8, κληροῦσι δὲ καὶ ἐς Σαλαμῖνα ἄρχοντα) shall have some responsibility (either for approving his arms or of mobilizing cleruchs in an emergency).

The main evidence for the date of this important decree lies in the letter forms and the arrangement of the text. The stoichedon character of ll. 1–6 shows an early stage in the development of the style, which by 485–4 was mature in Athens (*IG* i². 3/4, Austin, 8). The letter forms might be found at any time between *c.* 520 and *c.* 480. They are probably cut by the same craftsman as a dedication on the Acropolis of a statue by Hegias (Raubitschek, *DAA* 94), who is presumably the teacher of Pheidias. This does not, however, compel a date after 490, and, if Salamis is the first Athenian cleruchy, the decree should be dated before the cleruchy sent to Chalkis after the Athenian victory of 506 (Hdt. v. 77. 2). The period immediately following the reforms of Cleisthenes offers a good context. Athens had broken with Sparta; it would have been a sound precaution to establish a permanent garrison on the island which Megara, with Spartan support, might attempt to recover.

The Boule is not mentioned in the opening formula, but was very probably referred to in the last line. No firm constitutional inferences, however, can be drawn, for the standard developed form of the preamble (ἔδοχσεν τὲι βολὲι καὶ τῶι δέμοι) was not reached for more than a generation after Cleisthenes (cf. *IG* i². 3/4; 5). Luria infers a pre-Cleisthenic date from prescript and postscript, Raubitschek a later date than ours from letter forms.

Wilhelm, *Beiträge* 240 n. 5, asserts that alternate lines of this text were coloured red and blue.

15 (12 and 43)

Athenian Victory over Boeotia and Chalkis:
c. 506 B.C.

A. Block of dark Eleusinian limestone, found north-east of the Propylaia
(? in the sanctuary of Artemis of Brauron, *IG* i². 394); now in EM.
Archaic Attic letters, not stoichedon. Phot.: *DAA* 168; *LSAG* Pl. 4. 43.
IG i². 394; *DAA* 168; *LSAG* 78 (43).

[Δεσμι ἐν ἀχνύεντι σιδερέοι ἔσβεσαν ηὑβ]ριν:
παῖδε[ς Ἀθεναίον ἔργμασιν ἐμ πολέμο]
[ἔθνεα Βοιοτν καὶ Χαλκιδέον δαμάσαντες]:
τν hίππος δ[εκάτεν Πάλλαδι τάσδ᾽ ἔθεσαν].

B. Four fragments from a base of Pentelic marble, found 'on the Acropolis';
now in EM.
Attic letters, Ϟ, Λ, P. Stoichedon. Phot.: *DAA* 173.
IG i². 394; *DAA* 173.

["Εθνεα Βοιοτν καὶ Χαλκιδέον δαμά]σαν[τες:]
[παῖδ]ες Ἀθεναίον ἔργμα[σιν ἐμ πολέμο]
[δεσμι ἐν ἀχνύεντι σιδερέοι ἔσβε]σαν [hύβριν:]
[τ]ν hίππος δεκά[τεν Πάλλαδι τάσδ᾽ ἔθεσαν]·

The manuscripts of Herodotus have ἀχλυόεντι, ἀχνυθέντι, ἀχνυνθέντι.
None of these words can be restored unless one of the iotas shared a stoichos
with another letter. The surviving lettering does not encourage this.

In *c.* 506 Cleomenes, expelled by the new democracy from Athens,
led a Peloponnesian army into Attica to coincide with an invasion
from the north by Boeotia and Chalkis. Opposition from Corinth and
his fellow king, Demaratos, led to the withdrawal of Cleomenes; the
Athenians defeated both Boeotians and Chalkidians on the same day.
Seven hundred Boeotians and an unknown number of Chalkidians
were taken prisoner and later ransomed for 2 minae each. The
Athenians commemorated the victories by setting up a chariot with
a tithe of the ransom money and hanging up the prisoners' chains.
Herodotus, who records these events, himself saw the monuments, and
copied the epigram (Hdt. v. 77).

Fragments of the base he saw have been found on the Acropolis (B),
but also part of another base (A) with the same lines. The letters of this
second base are markedly earlier and the two hexameters are trans-
posed. We can safely infer that the original monument was destroyed
or carried off by the Persians in 480, and that a replica was put
up later, presumably when the early victory seemed topical. The

association has commonly been thought to be with the crushing
of the Euboean revolt in 446, but we share Hauvette's preference
(*Hérodote*, 47 ff.), more fully argued by Raubitschek (*DAA* 173), for
the battle of Oenophyta (*c.* 457). The emphasis on Boeotia would
ring very hollow after the Athenian defeat at Koroneia, and the
letter forms (especially alpha with sloping bar) are more appropriate
to the earlier date.

The siting of the monument remains very controversial. Pausanias
(i. 28. 2) implies that when he visited the Acropolis the chariot was
near Pheidias' great bronze statue of Athena, and a rock-cutting that
would fit the monument can still be seen by the cutting for the base
of the Promachos (Stevens, *Hesp.* v (1936) 506). Herodotus' descrip-
tion is not easy to reconcile with Pausanias. In his day τὸ δὲ (the
chariot) ἀριστερῆς χειρὸς ἕστηκε πρῶτα ἐσιόντι ἐς τὰ προπύλαια τὰ ἐν
τῇ ἀκροπόλι, and this suggests that the chariot was then within or
immediately outside the entrance to the Acropolis, almost certainly
before Mnesikles began his great building in 437. The fetters, however, were some distance away, 'hanging on walls scorched by the
fire raised by the Mede, opposite the megaron that is turned towards
the west'. There is general agreement that the old temple (discovered
by Doerpfeld) is here referred to; the chains were near the Promachos.
It is tempting to see in this separation of chariot and chains the explanation for the transposition of the two hexameters, but an equally
simple explanation is equally valid. The chains signified the capture
and ransom of prisoners, from which the cost of the memorial was
met; this was irrelevant to the battle of Oenophyta, when it was
appropriate that the main emphasis should be on the victory over the
Boeotians. Attempts have been made to reconcile Herodotus with the
evidence of Pausanias, by understanding the Propylaia as the area
between the main entrance and the smaller entrance to the court in
front of the Parthenon's west face (L. Weber, *Phil. Woch.* liii (1933)
331–6) or this entrance itself (for the site see *Hesp.* v (1936) 445;
Holland, *AJA* xxviii (1924) 402; Raubitschek, *DAA* 173). This is not
the natural meaning of Herodotus. By τὰ προπύλαια τὰ ἐν τῇ ἀκροπόλι
he should mean the main entrance, and had the chariot stood next
to the Promachos, surely Herodotus would have described its site by
reference to the statue. We therefore prefer to accept the more complex
hypothesis of a double move. The chariot was originally sited where
Pausanias indicates (and the surviving block was found near this site).
It was destroyed or carried off in 480 and when it was restored after
Oenophyta it was set up outside the pre-Mnesiklean Propylaia. Later
it was returned to the original site, either when Mnesikles' Propylaia
were built or much later, in the Hellenistic or early Roman period
(Stevens, *Hesp.* v (1936) 505; Judeich, *Topographie²*, 236–9).

16 (7)

Dedication of Aiakes of Samos: *c.* 500 B.C.

Marble statue of a seated figure (possibly Hera, but there is no agreement about the sex) from the Samian Heraion. The inscription is engraved on the left side of the chair. Tigani Museum.

Ionic letters, with legless rho and upsilon, dotted theta and straight-barred alpha. Stoichedon, with slight irregularities at the end of the line (Austin, 13–15; note the tendency to stoichedon already manifest in the earlier Samian inscription, *DM* vi (1953) 15–20, with Pl. 3). Punctuation does not occupy a space. Phot.: *Ath. Mitt.* xxxi (1906) 152 f.; Kern 7; Buschor, *Altsamische Standbilder*, Abb. 141–3.

Curtius, *Ath. Mitt.* xxxi (1906) 151–85; *SIG* 10 (but cf. 20); *DGE* 714; Schede, *Abh. Berl.* 1929, no. 3, 22; Buschor, *Altsamische Standbilder*, 40–2; White, *JHS* lxxiv (1954) 38; *LSAG* 330 (Samos 13); Homann-Wedeking, Ἀρχ. Ἐφ., 1953–4, ii. 187 f.; Barron, *CQ* xiv (1964) 218 f., with 214 n. 4.

> Ἀεάκης ἀνέθηκεν
> ὁ Βρύχωνος: ὃς τῆι
> ῞Ηρηι: τὴν σύλην: ἔ-
> πρησεν: κατὰ τὴν
> 5   ἐπίστασιν.

l. 2: Βρύχωνος (cf. Βρυχωνίδας *IG* v. 387) is correct (Ἀρχ. Ἐφ. 1924, 64 n. 1), not Βρύσωνος.

Since Herodotus (ii. 182, iii. 39, etc.) gives the name of the father of the tyrant Polykrates as Aiakes, it is not surprising that there has always been a strong temptation to identify him with the dedicator of this inscription and date the dedication about 540, before Polykrates came to power. Epigraphists since Pomtow (*SIG* 20) have always found this date impossibly early for the forms of theta and alpha and for the stoichedon style; see, in particular, Klaffenbach, *DM* vi (1953) 16, n. 5. Although Jeffery, *LSAG* 330, dates 525–520, she herself sees the closest parallel to the lettering in a Milesian inscription of very shortly before 494, and is unduly influenced by an early dating for the statue. The early date for the statue has been maintained by Buschor, though there are strong indications that he was influenced by the identification of Aiakes, and by Homann-Wedeking, but the statue itself has been dated in the last third of the century by Richter (*Archaic Greek Art*, 168), and at the end of the century by Schede, Johnson (*CP* xli (1946) 189), Lippold (*Griechische Plastik*, 58), and Rumpf (Gercke–Norden, *Einleitung*, ii⁴. 3. 25), Rumpf at least confessedly influenced by the inscription.

The compromise view, first propounded by Pomtow, that the statue was early, but the inscription late, added by the later Aiakes, son of Syloson, tyrant of Samos in the early fifth century (Hdt. iv. 138, vi. 13, 14, 22, 25) has always won a certain amount of favour and was still held by White, but we agree with Barron that the weight of the probabilities is for dating the whole dedication about 500 and detaching this Aiakes from the direct tyrant line. The considerable body of evidence deployed by White, Homann-Wedeking, and Barron for believing in a powerful Samian tyranny before Polykrates, whether under Aiakes (White), Syloson the elder (Homann-Wedeking), or an elder Polykrates (believed by Barron to be the real name of the father of the Herodotean Polykrates), is not much affected.

σύλη (the root recurs in the name Συλοσῶν, which appears twice in the tyrant-house (Polyaen. vi. 45; Hdt. iii. 39, etc.)) occurs in the singular only here, though it is a plausible emendation in *FGH* 544 F 3, again in a Samian context. The connotation of the root is clearly 'officially recognized seizure', which might of course appear to the victims as simple piracy: for sixth-century Samian depredations compare Hdt. iii. 47. Aiakes as ἐπιστάτης (it is not clear whether this is a general word or a name for a particular office) exercises some state function in connection with the booty. Whether he exacted it (from πράττω) or sold it (from πέρνημι; Barron's view, but he has misunderstood Hdt. i. 70. 3) must remain uncertain. That 'he was committing piracy for Hera in the time of his presidency' (Bilabel, *Neue Heidelb. Jahrb.* 1934, 133) or burning the booty (from πίμπρημι, Bannier, *Berl. Phil. Woch.* xxxvi (1916) 646) seems less likely. For the use of κατά cf. *I. Priene* 60. 14.

For public recognition of piracy compare Livy's statement about the Liparaeans, *mos erat civitatis velut publico latrocinio partam praedam dividere* (v. 28), and for a covenant regulating the right of seizure see Tod, vol. i, no. 34.

17 (5)

Alliance between Eleans and Heraeans: *c.* 500 B.C.

A bronze tablet found at Olympia in 1813, with nail-holes at the top corners; now in the British Museum.

Archaic Elean alphabet (for which see *LSAG* 206 f., 216 f.). Phot.: *LSAG*, Pl. 42. 6; Guarducci, *Epigrafia Greca*, i. 202 fig. 69.

SIG 9+; *DGE* 413; Buck 62; *Staatsverträge* 110+; *LSAG* 219, no. 6.

       ἀ Ϝράτρα τοῖρ Ϝαλείοις: καὶ τοῖς Ἐρ-
       Ϝαοίοις: συνμαχία κ' ἔα ἑκατὸν Ϝέτεα:

ἄρχοι δέ κα τοῖ: αἰ δέ τι δέοι: αἴτε Ϝέπος αἴτε Ϝ-
άργον: συνέαν κ' ἀλάλοις: τά τ' ἄλ⟨α⟩ καὶ πὰ-
5 ρ πολέμο: αἰ δὲ μὰ συνέαν: τάλαντόν κ'
ἀργύρο: ἀποτίνοιαν: τῶι Δὶ 'Ολυνπίοι: τοὶ καδαλεμένοι: λατρειόμενον: αἰ δέ τιρ τὰ γ-
ράφεα: ταῖ καδαλέοιτο: αἴτε Ϝέτας αἴτε τ-
ελεστὰ: αἴτε δᾶμος: ἐν τἐπιάροι κ' ἐνεχ-
10 οιτο τῶι 'νταῦτ' ἐγραμένοι.

The alpha in l. 4 was omitted.

'This is the covenant between the Eleans and the Heraeans. There
shall be an alliance for a hundred years, and this (year) shall be the
first; and if anything is needed, either word or deed, they shall stand
by each other in all matters and especially in war; and if they stand
not by each other, those who do the wrong shall pay a talent of silver
to Olympian Zeus to be used in his service. And if anyone injures this
writing, whether private man or magistrate or community, he shall be
liable to the sacred fine herein written.'

For the Elean dialect, see Bechtel, *GD* ii. 827 ff., Buck, pp. 159 f. ἔα,
συνέαν (ll. 2, 4, 5) = Attic εἴη, συνεῖεν. τοῖ, ταῖ (ll. 3, 8) = τοδί, ταδί
(τόδε, τάδε). πὰρ (l. 4) = περὶ (Günther, *Indog. Forsch.* xx (1906–7)
139). καδαλεμένοι, καδαλέοιτο (ll. 6–7, 8) = καταδηλούμενοι, κατα-
δηλοῖτο. Ϝέτας survives in Arcadian prose until the first century B.C.
(*IG* v. 2. 20). ἐπιάροι (= ἐφιέρωι) (l. 9) seems to mean 'fine' rather
than 'curse' here. For Ϝράτρα cf. No. 8.

Jeffery, by confining her investigations to the allied alphabets of
Elis, Arcadia, and Laconia and avoiding the remoter parallels by
which this text has sometimes been dated, has lowered its date substantially. Arguments as to whether it should predate or postdate
572, the traditional date at which the Eleans finally wrested from the
Pisatans the control of Olympia and its festival (Paus. vi. 22. 2), now
seem beside the point. The circumstances in which Elis made this
alliance with Heraea of western Arcadia must remain unknown.
Heraea, to judge by its coins (Head, *HN²* 447), was not unimportant
at this date, and there is no trace of subordination in the terms of the
treaty.

The alliance was for a hundred years, beginning with 'this year'.
The indefiniteness may perhaps be due to the fact that a century's
alliance was regarded as practically unlimited (Keil, *Εἰρήνη*, 8) and
therefore its starting-point need not be precisely dated. It therefore differs in form rather than in practice from No. 10. The more
surprising feature, when we compare it with that text, is the absence
of oaths and divine sanctions. Olympian Zeus will gain from a breach

of the treaty, but he will not enforce it. Cf. Thuc. v. 31. 2, but by that time Olympian Zeus is practically functioning as the Elean sacred treasury, which does not seem to be the case here.

Neither Elis nor Heraea was a city at this date; they still dwelt κατὰ κώμας (Strabo, viii. 3. 2, p. 337).

18 (13)

Memorial of Kallimachos: 490 B.C.

Eight fragments of an Ionic marble column found on the Acropolis; now in EM.

Archaic Attic letters: ⊕, ⊖ (= phi), R, +. Phot.: *IIA* 18; *BSA* xlv (1950), Pl. 10, 11.

IG i². 609; Hampl, *Die Antike*, xv (1939) 168–74; Raubitschek, *AJA* xliv (1940) 53–9; *DAA* 13; Shefton, *BSA* xlv (1950) 140–64, xlvii (1952) 278; Fraenkel, *Eranos*, xlix (1951) 63 f.

> [Καλίμαχός μ' ἀν]έθεκεν Ἀφιδναῖο[ς] τἀθεναίαι·
> ἄγ[γελον ἀθ]ανάτον hοὶ 'Ο[λύμπια δόματ'] ἔχοσιν, |
> [....8.... πολέ]μαρχο[ς] Ἀθεναίον τὸν ἀγόνα·
> τὸν Μα[ραθον.... h]ελενονο[.....11......:]
> 5 παισὶν Ἀθεναίον μγ[..........21..........]

l. 3: [hοστέσας (= ὃς (σ)τέσας) πολέ]μαρχος Shefton.   l. 4: τὸν Μα[ραθονόθεν h]ἐλεν, ὃν ὄ[λεσε θόριος Ἄρες] Fraenkel; τὸν Μα[ραθόνι πρὸ h]ελ(λ)ένον ὄ[νομ' ἐστεφάνοσεν· Shefton.   l. 5: We regard ν after μ as probable rather than certain. μγ[έμεν δ' ἀρετές κατέλειπεν] Shefton; μγ[έμεν πένθος τε λιπόντα] Fraenkel.

Before 1940 all that was known of this monument was an Ionic column of which eight inscribed fragments were preserved, whose relative position was secure. The column was rough-picked all round but two flutings were cut to carry five hexameters (the first only quasi-metrical) in two lines. The first two verses seemed to record a dedication by Kallimachos of Aphidna. The three hexameters of the second line were more difficult to interpret; they seemed to refer to the services of the polemarch Kallimachos at Marathon, but Kallimachos died in the battle (Hdt. vi. 109, 114; cf. *PA* 8008) and dead men do not make dedications. One solution was that he had vowed the offering before the battle and that his vow was fulfilled on his behalf after his death; but in such cases two verbs are normally used for two people.

εὔξατο of the man who died and ἀνέθηκε of the man who carried out his vow. Hiller in *IG* i² therefore separated the two lines, the first recording a dedication by Kallimachos in his lifetime, the second added after his death in battle. Hiller assumed that the dedication was a figure of Hermes, but in 1940 Raubitschek (art. cit.) reported his discovery that the figure of a winged woman found on the Acropolis, and believed to be a Nike, fitted an Ionic capital which had the same diameter where it would have joined the shaft as the Ionic column bearing the Kallimachos inscription. The messenger of the gods is no longer Hermes, but Nike, or, perhaps more probably, Iris.

A further considerable advance was made when Shefton demonstrated that the two lines were contemporary and corrected two readings (in ll. 4 and 5). To explain away a dead man's dedication he inferred that the dedication was made by Kallimachos in his lifetime, and the inscription cut probably on the base of the column; after his death it was copied on the column in two flutings cut for the purpose and supplemented with a proud reference to Marathon. This, Shefton suggests, may have been intended to emphasize Kallimachos' role in the battle against the pretensions of Miltiades and his friends. To avoid the assumption of a secondary inscription Raubitschek suggests (*apud* Shefton, *BSA* xlv 164):

[τόνδε (surely a slip for τένδε) με δῆμος] ἔθεκεν Ἀφιδναῖο[ν] τἀθεναίαι :
ἄγ[γελον ἀθ]ανάτον, ϝοὶ ᾿Ο[λύμπια δόματα] ἔχοσιν.
[Καλίμαχος πολέ]μαρχος Ἀθεναίον τὸν ἀγόνα :
τὸν Μα[ραθόνι πρὸ h]ελένον ὀγ[ομαστὸν ἔθεκεν :]
παισὶν Ἀθεναίον μν[ῆμα λιπὸν ἀρετῆς].

This reconstruction solves one major problem, but it creates more. Epigraphically it satisfies the requirements of the stone, stylistically it is unacceptable. These are not the verses of an early fifth-century poet or craftsman, composed in honour of one of the most distinguished Athenians of his day, for a dedication on the Acropolis; nor (a less serious matter) do we know from literature or inscription of any similar honour paid by a deme to one of its members. Shefton's hypothesis of an original inscription before Marathon on the base and a second added after the battle is strengthened by the cutting of two flutes only, whereas all other inscribed columns known to us are either plain or fluted all round (*DAA*, pp. 3–60). Inscriptions, however, on bases of column dedications are very rare, and we may doubt whether the original inscription would have been repeated. It may be less difficult, in spite of the objection noted above, to believe that the dedication was vowed by Kallimachos before the battle and made on his behalf after his death.

19 (14)

Athenian Thank-offering for Marathon: 490 B.C.

On eight fragments of a long limestone base built against the front of the south wall of the Athenian Treasury at Delphi.

Attic alphabet, with Ϟ. The letters now seen are not earlier than the third century, but they copy the form of the original letters, some of which were deciphered by Keramopoullos (Ἀρχ. Ἐφ. 1911, 162 ff.). Phot.: *FD* iii. 2, Pl. 1.

SIG 23b.

> Ἀθεναῖοι τ[ô]ι Ἀπόλλον[ι ἀπὸ Μέδ]ον ἀκ[ροθ]ίνια
> τês Μαραθ[ô]νι μ[άχες].

Pausanias (x. 11. 5 with Frazer, *Pausanias*, v. 279 ff. and Hitzig and Blümner, *Pausanias*, iii. 697 ff.) says that the Athenian Treasury was built ἀπὸ τῶν ἐς Μαραθῶνα ἀποβάντων ὁμοῦ Δάτιδι, and the French excavators have agreed with him, referring the inscription to Treasury and base (G. Colin, *FD* iii. 2, no. 1). The bonding of the base with the Treasury, however, suggests that it was added later; the Treasury was more probably built between 506 and 490 (Pomtow, *RE*, Suppl. iv. 1280 ff.; Dinsmoor, *Studies in the History of Culture* (1942) 187–9). De La Coste-Messelière (*FD* iv. 4) thinks that the sculpture of the Treasury confirms Pausanias. E. B. Harrison (*The Athenian Agora*, vol. xi, *Archaic and Archaistic Sculpture*, 9–11), prefers a date in the 90s for the Treasury.

20 (24)

Law of the Eastern Lokrians relative to their Colony at Naupaktos: (?) 500–475 B.C.

Bronze plaque, engraved on both sides, found at Galaxidi (Chaleion, cf. l. 47; see Lerat, *Les Locriens de l'Ouest*, i. 198–209); now in the British Museum.

Script of the Ozolian Lokrians (*LSAG* 104 f.); unlike No. 13, it has koppa, but it is not engraved boustrophedon; the lines are separated by faint guide-lines. Phot.: *BMI* iv, p. 119. Facs.: *Imag.* 92. 1.

SIG 47, *BMI* 954+; *DGE* 362; Solmsen 44; Buck 57. (The best commentaries are still Meyer, *Forsch.* i. 291–305; Meister, *Ber. d. sächs. Gesell. d. Wiss. zu Leipzig, phil.-hist. Kl.*, 1895, 272–334.) Cf. Busolt, *GG* iii. 300; Bannier, *Berl. Phil. Woch.* xviii (1898) 862 f., xxxvi (1916) 956 f.; B. Keil, *Indog. Forsch.* xxxvi (1915–16) 236–42; Bechtel, *Gött. Nachr.* 1918, 397–400; Oldfather in *RE* xiii. 1240 ff.; Kent, *The Textual Criticism of Inscriptions*, 17 f.; Schulze, *Z. vergl. Spr.* lvii (1929–30) 297; O'Neill, *Ancient Corinth*, 250 f.; Lerat, op. cit. ii. 29–31; Schick, *RF* lxxxiii (1955) 377 f.; *LSAG* 106 (Lokris 3); Graham, *Colony and Mother City in Ancient Greece*, 40–60, 226–8; Larsen, *Greek Federal States*, 45–58.

Front

ἐν Ναύπακτον॰κα τόνδε॰ha 'πιϝοικία.॰ Λορρὸν τὸν॰hυποκναμιδίον॰ἐπ-
εί κα Ναυπάκτιος॰γένεται,॰Ναυπάκτιον ἐόντα,॰hόπο ξένον॰ὅσια
λανχάν-
ειν॰καὶ θύειν॰ἐξεῖμεν॰ἐπιτυχόντα,॰αἴ κα δείλεται·॰αἴ κα δείλεται,॰
θύειν καὶ λ-
ανχάνειν॰κὲ δάμο κὲ ροινάνον॰αὐτὸν καὶ τὸ γένος॰κατ' αἰϝεί·॰τέλος
το-
5 ὺς॰ἐπιϝοίκους Λορρὸν॰τὸν hυποκναμιδίον॰μὲ φάρειν॰ἐν Λορροῖς τοῖ-
ς hυποκναμιδίοις॰φρίν κ' αὖ τις Λορρὸς γένεται τὸν hυποκναμιδίον·॰αἰ
δείλετ' ἀνχορεῖν, καταλείπον॰τὰ ἐν τᾶι ἱστίαι παῖδα hεβατὰν ἒ 'δελφεόν,
॰ἐξ-
εῖμεν ἄνευ ἐνετερίον॰αἴ κα hυπ' ἀνάνκας ἀπελάονται॰ἒ Ναυπάκτο॰Λορ-
ροὶ τοὶ hυποκναμίδιοι,॰ἐξεῖμεν ἀνχορεῖν,॰hόπο ϝέκαστος ἐν, ἄνευ ἐ-
10 νετερίον.॰τέλος μὲ φάρειν μεδὲν॰hότι μὲ μετὰ Λορρὸν τὸν ϝεσπαρί-
ον.॰Α॰ἔνορρον τοῖς ἐπιϝοίροις ἐν Ναύπακτον॰μὲ 'ποστᾶμεν॰ἀπ'
'Ο⟨πο⟩ντίον
τέκναι καὶ μαχανᾶι॰μεδεμιᾶι॰ϝερόντας. τὸν hόρκον ἐξεῖμεν॰αἴ κα δεί-
λονται,॰ἐπάγεν μετὰ τριάροντα ϝέτεα॰ἀπὸ τô hόρρο hεκατὸν ἄνδρας 'Ο-
ποντίοις॰Ναυπακτίον καὶ Ναυπακτίοις 'Οποντίους॰Β॰hόσστις κα
λιποτελέε-
15 ι ἐγ Ναυπάκτο॰τὸν ἐπιϝοιρὸν,॰ἀπὸ Λορρὸν εἶμεν॰ἔντε κ' ἀποτείσει॰
τὰ νό-
μια Ναυπακτίοις॰Γ॰αἴ κα μὲ γένος ἐν τᾶι ἱστίαι॰ἒι ἒ 'χεπάμον॰τὸν ἐπι-
ϝοιρὸν॰ἒι ἐν Ναυπακτôι, Λορρὸν॰τὸν hυποκναμιδίον॰τὸν ἐπάνχισ-
τον॰κρατεῖν, Λορρὸν hόπο κ' ἒι,॰αὐτὸν ἰόντα, αἴ κ' ἀνὲρ ἒι ἒ παῖς,॰
τριôν
μενôν·॰αἰ δὲ μέ, τοῖς Ναυπακτίοις॰νομίοις χρêσται॰Δ॰ἒ Ναυπακτὸ
ἀνχορέ-
20 οντα॰ἐν Λορροὺς τοὺς hυποκναμιδίους॰ἐν Ναυπάκτοι॰καρῦξαι ἐν τἀ-
γορᾶι,॰κὲν Λορροῖς τοῖ⟨ς⟩ hυποκναμιδίοις॰ἐν τᾶι πόλι, hô κ' ἒι,॰
καρῦξαι ἐν
τἀγορᾶι॰Ε॰Περροθαριᾶν॰καὶ Μυσαχέον॰ἐπεί κα Ναυπάκτι⟨ός τι⟩ς॰
γένετα-
ι,॰αὐτὸς καὶ τὰ χρέματα॰τὲν Ναυπάκτοι॰τοῖς ἐν Ναυπάκτοι χρêσται,॰
τὰ δ' ἐν Λορροῖς τοῖς hυποκναμιδίοις॰χρέματα τοῖς hυποκναμιδί-
25 οις॰

Back

νομίοις χρέσται, ⋮ hόπος ἁ πόλις Ϝεκάστον νομίζει ⋮ Λορρὸν τὸν hυποκν-
αμιδίον· ⋮ αἴ τις hυπὸ τὸν νομίον τὸν ἐπιϜοίρον ⋮ ἀνχορέει Περροθαρια-
ν καὶ Μυσαχέον ⋮ τοῖς αὐτὸν νομίοις ⋮ χρέσται ⋮ κατὰ πόλιν Ϝεκάστους.
Ϝ ⋮ αἴ κ᾽ ἀδελφεοὶ ἔοντι ⋮ τὸ ᾽ν Ναύπακτον Ϝοικέοντος ⋮ hόπος καὶ Λορρὸ-
30 ν ⋮ τὸν hυποκναμιδίον ⋮ Ϝεκάστον νόμος ἐστί, ⋮ αἴ κ᾽ ἀποθάνει τὸν χ-
ρεμάτον κρατεῖν ⋮ τὸν ἐπίϜοικον, τὸ κατιρόμενον κρατεῖν ⋮ Ⅰ ⋮
τοὺς ἐπιϜοίρους ⋮ ἐν Ναύπακτον ⋮ τὰν δίκαν πρόδιρον ⋮ hαρέσται πὸ
τοὺς δ-
ικαστέρας, ⋮ hαρέσται ⋮ καὶ δόμεν ⋮ ἐν Ὀπόεντι κατὰ Ϝέος αὐταμαρόν. ⋮
Λορ-
ρὸν τὸν hυποκναμιδίον ⋮ προστάταν καταστᾶσαι ⋮ τὸν Λορρὸν τόπιϜ-
35 οίροι ⋮ καὶ τὸν ἐπιϜοίρον τôι Λορρôι, ⋮ hοίτινές κα ᾽πιατὲς ἔντιμοι ἐς ⋮ Η ⋮
hόσσ-
τις κ᾽ ἀπολίπει ⋮ πατάρα καὶ τὸ μέρος ⋮ τὸν χρεμάτον τôι πατρί, ⋮ ἐπεί κ᾽
ἀπογένεται, ⋮ ἐξεῖμεν ἀπολαχεῖν ⋮ τὸν ἐπίϜοιρον ⋮ ἐν Ναύπακτον.
⋮ ⊕ ⋮ hόσστις ⋮ κα τὰ ϜεϜαδερότα ⋮ διαφθείρει ⋮ τέχναι καὶ μαχανᾶι ⋮ κα-
ὶ μιᾶι, ⋮ hότι κα μὲ ἀνφοτάροις ⋮ δοκέει, ⋮ hοποντίον τε χιλίον ⋮ πλέθ-
40 αι καὶ Ναϝπακτίον ⋮ τὸν ἐπιϜοίρον πλέθαι, ⋮ ἄτιμον εἶμεν ⋮ καὶ χρέματα παματοφαγεῖσται· ⋮ τὸνκαλειμένοι ⋮ τὰν δίκαν ⋮ δόμεν τὸν ἀρ-
χόν, ⋮ ἐν τριάροντ᾽ ἀμάραις ⋮ δόμεν, ⋮ αἴ κα τριάροντ᾽ ἀμάραι ⋮ λείποντ-
αι τᾶς ἀρχᾶς· αἴ κα μὲ δίδοι ⋮ τôι ἐνκαλειμένοι ⋮ τὰν δίκαν, ⋮ ἄτιμον εἶμεν ⋮ καὶ χρέματα παματοφαγεῖσται, ⋮ τὸ μέρος μετὰ Ϝο-
45 ικιατᾶν· ⋮ διομόσαι hόρρον ⋮ τὸν νόμιον· ⋮ ἐν ὑδρίαν ⋮ τὰν ψάφιξ-
ξιν εἶμεν. ⋮ καὶ τὸ θέθμιον ⋮ τοῖς hυποκναμιδίοις Λορροῖς ⋮ ταὺ-
τὰ τέλεον εἶμεν ⋮ Χαλειείοις ⋮ τοῖς σὺν Ἀντιφάται ⋮ Ϝοικέταις.

This statute (θέθμιον, l. 46) defines the future relationship between those of the Eastern Lokrians who are going as colonists (ἐπίϜοιροι) to Naupaktos in Western (or Ozolian) Lokris and their mother people. The East Lokrians are here called Ὑποκνημίδιοι, from the mountain-range Κνῆμις which traverses their territory: elsewhere they are also named Ἐπικνημίδιοι, or Ὀπούντιοι, from the town of Opus, which formed their political (ll. 11, 13, 14, 39) and judicial (l. 33) centre (cf. Oldfather in *RE* xiii. 1157–62, Larsen, op. cit.).

The date of the law is certainly earlier than the seizure of Naupaktos by Athens Λοκρῶν τῶν Ὀζολῶν ἐχόντων c. 460 and its settlement by Messenians (Thuc. i. 103. 3); how much earlier, we cannot be sure. The law shows the normal desire to keep the colony up to strength (ll. 6–8) and a general provision against ἀπόστασις by the colonists from their mother city (ll. 11–12), but these are not sufficient grounds to impute imperialist motives to the East Lokrians. At least the West Lokrian community of Chaleion shared in the venture (l. 47); alphabet and find-spot show that we have a copy made for Chaleion.

The text, which has no preamble and bears no date, consists of an opening section followed by nine paragraphs bearing the letters A to ⊕ in succession. A fairly close translation will probably prove the most useful form of commentary; Graham's recent work will give further help.

For the dialect see Bechtel, *GD* ii. 3–44, and Buck, pp. 157–9, 250 f.

'The colony (shall go) to Naupaktos (ἐν = ἐς) on these terms (κα τόνδε = κὰτ τῶνδε = κατὰ τάδε). The Lokrian of the Hypoknemidians [cf. l. 6], after having become a Naupaktian, being a Naupaktian, may have civil rights and sacrifice as a ξένος, if he wishes [Meister and Graham prefer ὅπο ξένον ὁσία 'where it is right for foreigners' which has some advantages; against Graham, 49 ff., we prefer the view that these are rights in Lokris, not in Naupaktos; how could Lokris prescribe for Naupaktos?]; if he wishes, he shall sacrifice and participate both in a commune and in societies, he and his family for ever [but as a ξένος, presumably]. The colonists of the Hypoknemidian Lokrians shall pay no tax among the Hypoknemidian Lokrians until any one of them again becomes a Hypoknemidian Lokrian. If he desire to return [sc. to East Lokris] leaving in his home an adult son or brother, he may do so without (payment of) entry-fees. If the Hypoknemidian Lokrians are driven out perforce from Naupaktos, they may return, each to his own home, without (payment of) entry fees. They shall pay no tax save in common with the Western Lokrians.

I. The colonists to Naupaktos (are) under oath not to break away from the Opuntians of their own will on any pretext or by any device whatsoever. Thirty years after the (original) oath it shall be lawful, if they desire, for a hundred men of the Naupaktians to administer the oath to the Opuntians, and the Opuntians to the Naupaktians.

II. If any of the colonists leave Naupaktos without paying his taxes, he shall be (shut out) from the Lokrians until he has paid his lawful debts to the Naupaktians.

III. If there be no (member of the) family in the home or heir among the colonists of the Hypoknemidian Lokrians at Naupaktos, the next of kin among the Lokrians, whencesoever he be, shall take possession, going in person, whether he be man or boy, within three months; otherwise, the Naupaktian laws shall be observed.

IV. Anyone returning from Naupaktos to the Hypoknemidian Lokrians shall make proclamation in the market-place at Naupaktos, and among the Hypoknemidian Lokrians in the market-place in the city whence he comes.

V. When any of the Perkothariai and Mysacheis becomes a Naupaktian [the P. and M. are evidently two clans or castes, possibly sacerdotal (if the names are connected with περικαθαίρειν and μύσος ἀκεῖσθαι), standing in East Lokris on a different legal footing from the other citizens], he and his property at Naupaktos shall be subject to the laws at Naupaktos [we should have enough respect for the inscription's own punctuation not to punctuate after αὐτός, even though we might expect αὐτόν], but his property among the Hypoknemidian Lokrians shall be subject to the Hypoknemidian laws, as the law stands in the city of the Hypoknemidian Lokrians in each case. If any of the Perkothariai and Mysacheis return under the laws governing the colonists [i.e. under §§ II, IV, supra], each one shall be subject to his own laws in his several city [i.e. their special privileges, which disappeared while they were at Naupaktos, shall again become operative on their return to East Lokris].

VI. If there are brothers of the man who goes to live in Naupaktos, according to the laws of the Hypoknemidian Lokrians in each several case, if (a brother) dies, the colonist shall take possession of the property, take possession of his due share.

VII. The colonists to Naupaktos shall have precedence in legal suits before the judges, shall bring and submit to suits at Opus on the same day [the general sense cannot be affected whatever κατὰ Fέος, which we have suppressed, may mean; no suggested meaning is entirely convincing]. Whoever are in office for the year shall appoint a prostates from the Hypoknemidian Lokrians, one of the Lokrians for the colonist, one of the colonists for the Lokrian. [No interpretation of this sentence can be certain. That adopted here requires replacing ες, which cannot be right, by έοντι, and the assumption of an afterthought. The first thought will have been to provide for an official who would represent the colonist in court at Opus, just as a metic had to be represented at Athens; a later thought provides reciprocity at Naupaktos. Other less probable solutions need not be considered.]

VIII. Whoever leaves behind a father and his share of his property to his father, when (his father) passes away, the colonist to Naupaktos may recover his portion.

IX. Whoever subverts these decisions on any pretext or by any device whatsoever, save so far as is resolved by both parties, the assembly of the Opuntian Thousand and the assembly of the Naupaktian colonists, he shall be without rights and his property shall be confiscated. The magistrate shall grant the trial to the accuser, grant it within thirty days, if thirty days of his magistracy are left. If he does not grant the trial to the accuser, he shall be without rights and his property shall be confiscated, the estate together with the slaves. The judges shall swear the legal oath. The votes shall be cast into an urn.

And the statute for the Hypoknemidian Lokrians shall be valid in the same way for the Chaleian settlers under Antiphatas.'

21 (15 and 45)

Ostracism at Athens: 487–417 B.C.

Aristotle (Ἀθ. Πολ. 22) appears to date the first ostracism, that of Hipparchos, son of Charmos of Kollytos, to 487, and that of Megakles, son of Hippokrates of Alopeke, to 486. Since he goes on ἐπὶ μὲν οὖν ἔτη τρία τοὺς τῶν τυράννων φίλους ὠστράκιζον, ὧν χάριν ὁ νόμος ἐτέθη, μετὰ δὲ ταῦτα τῷ τετάρτῳ ἔτει καὶ τῶν ἄλλων εἴ τις δοκοίη μείζων μεθίσταντο· καὶ πρῶτος ὠστρακίσθη τῶν ἄπωθεν τῆς τυραννίδος Ξάνθιππος ὁ Ἀρίφρονος (Pericles' father), we must assume another ostracism of an unnamed tyrannophile in 485 before Xanthippos' ostracism in 484. He appears to place Aristides' ostracism in 482. Other ostracisms in the literary evidence which seem to have been important were those of Themistocles (475–470), Kimon (461?), Thucydides son of Melesias (443), and Hyperbolos (417; Woodhead, *Hesp.* xviii (1949) 78–83, and McGregor, *Phoenix* xix (1965) 43–6, prefer 416, Raubitschek, *Phoenix* ix (1955) 122–6, prefers 415).

The literary evidence is now supported by 1,658 ostraka, 1,238 from the Agora excavations, the rest mostly from the German excavations in the Kerameikos. Their contribution to our knowledge has been far-reaching, though it is not evenly spread throughout the period, since the Persian sack of Athens provided archaeologically more favourable conditions for the survival of votes cast before 480. Leaving aside for our purposes the evidence they provide for the development of the script and spelling of the private Athenian citizen (the institution in itself presupposes widespread literacy, and we have hardly enough evidence to refine that presupposition), we may group that contribution under the following, overlapping, heads:

1. The literary evidence had not led us to expect the size of the 'scatter vote' for persons either totally unknown to us or unexpected in this context. For the period 487–480 we appear to have votes for about twenty-five men besides those known to have been ostracized. Pre-eminent among these is Kallixenos, son of Aristonymos of Xypete, unknown from literary sources, but shown by his Sicyonian patronymic (Hdt. vi. 126) and one ostrakon reading, [Ἀλκ]μεον[ιδὸν | Καλ]λίχ-σεν[ος | Ἀρ]ιστο[νύμο, to be an Alkmeonid, descendant of the marriage

between Megakles and Agariste of Sicyon; the table below shows him second only to Themistocles in his total of preserved ostraka (for the evidence on him, see Stamires and Vanderpool, *Hesp.* xix (1950) 376-90). Another unknown Alkmeonid in the 480s is Ἱπποκράτες Ἀλκμεονίδο Ἀλοπεκέθεν; the guess that Ἱπποκράτες Ἀναχσιλέο is another Alkmeonid (see, e.g., Raubitschek, *DAA* pp. 339 f.) lacks cogency. None of the other unknowns can yet be given such importance, but among those known persons whose connection with ostracism had been unknown we may single out Melanthios, commander of the Athenian expedition to Ionia in 498 (Hdt. v. 97, if he is Μελάνθιος Φαλάνθο, *Hesp.* Suppl. viii. 400 f.), [Ἀνδο]κίδες [Λεογ]όρο (cf. No. 51) and [Τεί]σανδρος [᾽Ε]πιλύκο (cf. Andoc. i. 117), the two grandfathers of the orator Andocides (*Ath. Mitt.* xl (1915) 16 f.), Κλεινππίδες Δεινίο Ἀχαρνεύς, general in 428 (Thuc. iii. 3; *Ath. Mitt.* xl. 12-16) and Ἱπποκλ[ἐς] | Μενίππ[ο], general in 413 (Thuc. viii. 13; *Kerameikos*, iii. 86).

The range of voting thus illustrated weakens the doubts that some scholars have felt about some ostracisms which had seemed to be of improbable persons and inadequately attested. Three such ostracisms are those of Damon or Damonides (Arist. Ἀθ. Πολ. 27. 4; Plut. *Per.* 4, *Nik.* 6, *Arist.* 1; Raubitschek, *Class. et Med.* xvi (1955) 78-83), Menon (Hesych. s.v. Μενωνίδαι, fully discussed by Raubitschek, *Hesp.* xxiv (1955) 286-9), and of Kallias, son of Didymias ([Andoc.] iv. 32). All these have been doubted, all of them are now represented by ostraka, which proves at the minimum that some people thought ostracism appropriate for them.

2. New information about known persons consists firstly of new data about their patronymic or demotic. For example, Themistocles' associate Abronichos (Hdt. viii. 21; Thuc. i. 91. 3) is shown to come from Lamptrai (*CR* vi (1956) 199 f.), an out-of-town statesman like Themistocles himself. (The view has been held, e.g. by Koerte, *Ath. Mitt.* xlvii (1922) 6 f., that ostraka are more likely to give the demotic of *novi homines* and omit it for nobles. As the evidence increases, it seems better to say that, at any rate for a generation after Cleisthenes, country-demotics came more readily to mind as a means of identification than the names of the new, artificial town-demes; cf. Raubitschek, *Actes du deuxième congrès international d'épigraphie grecque et latine*, 67-9.) A previously unknown patronymic may reveal unsuspected relationships. The outstanding example here is that of the demagogue Kleophon, where the literary evidence is united on his low social status and foreign birth (*PA* 8638). His ostraka show, firstly, that he was prominent enough to be a 'candidate' at the last ostracism, five to seven years earlier than his first appearance in literature, and, secondly, that he was son of a Kleippides of Acharnai. This makes it highly probable

that he was son of the general of 428 (see above) and 'candidate' of 443 (see below), and forces modification of ideas about his social status (Vanderpool, *Hesp.* xxi (1952) 114 f., xxxvii (1968) 120; for a likely brother, Philinos, see Raubitschek, *Hesp.* xxiii (1954) 68–71).

Even more interesting are the rare instances where the voter felt the need to add something to the name of his 'candidate'. This might be purely descriptive; Εὐχαρίδην θεσμο(θέτην) | Εὐχάρος (*Ath. Mitt.* xl (1915) 17; note the accusative and the Ionic *eta*) serves no other purpose. The ostrakon quoted above, identifying Kallixenos as an Alkmeonid, may have both descriptive and pejorative motives. These last come out more strongly elsewhere. On one sherd (*Hesp.* xix (1950) 378 f., 389 f.) the restoration [Καλλ]ίχσενος | [ho πρ]οδότες seems inevitable, and this makes Μένον | ἐκκ προ[δοτ]ῶν tempting on *Kerameikos*, iii. 71–2 (*Hesp.* xix 379 n., xxiv 288 f.). [- - -]ς ἄτιμ[ος (*Hesp.* xix. 379, 390) may be more imprecatory than pejorative. More complex problems are raised by two pieces which on the face of them accuse Aristides of pro-Persian leanings and harshness to suppliants. As restored by Raubitschek (*Charites: Studien zur Altertumswissenschaft*, ed. K. Schauenburg, pp. 240–2) they run Ἀριστ[είδεν] | τὸν Δά[τιδος] | ἀδελφ[όν] and [Ἀριστείδες | ho Λυσιμ]άχο | [hὸς τὸ]ς hικέτας | [ἀπέοσ]εν.

Pride of place among these texts goes to a kylix-foot found on the western slope of the Areopagus, incised with an elegiac couplet in two concentric circles (Raubitschek, *AJA* li (1947) 257–61; Broneer, ibid. lii. 341–3; Schweigert, ibid. liii. 266–8; Wilhelm, *Wien. Anz.* 1949, 237).

> Χσάνθ[ιππον τόδε] φεσὶν ἀλειτερὸν πρυτάνειον
> τόστρακ[ον Ἀρρί]φρονος παῖδα μά[λ]ιστ' ἀδικε̃ν.

[κατά]φεσιν Raubitschek, Broneer, Schweigert; [τόδε] Wilhelm. ἀλειτερὸν Raubitschek, Broneer; ἀλειτέρον (= ἀλιτήριον) Schweigert; ἀλειτερὸν Wilhelm. πρυτανεῖον Raubitschek, Broneer; πρυτάνειον (= πρυτάνεων) Schweigert, Wilhelm.

Tempting though it was to suggest that ἀλειτερὸν was accusative and that Xanthippos had acquired the Alkmeonid curse through his marriage, neither 'the cursed Xanthippos wrongs the sacred hearth' (Raubitschek) nor 'wrongs the Prytaneion (by his excessive claims to public entertainment)' (Broneer) were really satisfactory. Schweigert's solution 'a curse to the leaders, doing most wrong' does not run easily, and we prefer Wilhelm's solution: 'This ostrakon says that Xanthippos son of Ariphron does most wrong of all the cursed leaders.'

3. So far we have been dealing with contributions of a type not essentially different from that of those made by inscriptions on stone or bronze. Many of the contributions made by ostraka, however, are

more peculiarly 'archaeological', making their point by their context rather than by their individual evidence.

The ostracism of the elder Alcibiades (Lys. xiv. 39, [Andoc.] iv. 34) used to be placed in the blank year 485 (see above; Carcopino, *L'ostracisme athénien*², 145–8; Hatzfeld, *Alcibiade*, 13–15). Against this we can now muster the negative fact that no ostrakon attributable to him has appeared in the large number of ostraka sealed in Persian debris, and the positive facts that, of the six ostraka which are attributable to him, two are from kylikes of the second quarter of the century and one of these is in a sealed deposit of that quarter-century (Vanderpool, *Hesp.* xxi (1952) 1–8). This and the patronymic, Kleinias, necessitate a rewriting of the stemma of the family and an abandonment of 485 as a date for the ostracism, whatever the ultimate fate of Vanderpool's suggestion of 460 as the exact date.

Light on the organization of an ostracism is thrown by a group of 191 ostraka, all designed for use against Themistocles, found in a well on the north slope of the Acropolis (Broneer, *Hesp.* vii (1938) 228–41). The types of pottery represented are so few that we are entitled to suggest that most of the pieces had formed part of a potter's stock. More striking still, it can be seen that the sherds were inscribed by only fourteen different hands. We have here the work of a *hetairia*, preparing votes for voters too illiterate or too lazy to do the job themselves, though the group presents such uniformity that it is highly improbable that it was ever used. Archaeologically, it seems slightly more likely that the sherds were prepared for an ostracism in the late 480s than for the final successful campaign against Themistocles.

The kind of evidence we should most like to have would be sealed deposits of ostraka, of which one could say with confidence that they all came from one ostrakophoria, with no intrusive evidence, earlier or later, and large enough in number to be statistically significant. We should then have some clear idea of who the principal candidates were in any particular year. Such evidence is still in very short supply. We list those deposits which may be helpful.

A (*Hesp.* xv (1946) 265 ff., esp. 271–5 = Hands, *JHS* lxxix (1959) 77 Group E). This deposit from a rock-cut shaft does not represent a single deposit, but is stratified and sealed. Lowest in the shaft, from 9 to 8.45 m. down, were three ostraka of Μεγακλῆς Ἱπποκράτος. Also at 8.45 m. was a sherd probably of [ℎίππαρχος Χά]ρμ[ο, and another of Βουτ[αλίον] | Ἐπ[- -] (Μαραθώνιος). At 8 m. there were two votes for ℎιπποκράτες Ἀναχσιλέο, at 7.40 m. two for Kallixenos. At 6 m. there were sherds of Hipparchos, Themistocles, Aristides, and [ℎιπ]ποκράτες Ἀλκμεονίδο. At 5 and 4.50 m. there were two more sherds of Aristides. All these were sealed by Persian debris. If we except the second Hipparchos sherd, which must have reached the shaft rather late, the stratification coheres with Aristotle's account and suggests that Boutalion and Hippokrates son of Anaxileos were candidates early in the decade, Themistocles, Aristides, and Hippokrates son of Alkmeonides rather later. The evidence for Kallixenos is inconclusive.

In the remaining pre-Persian deposits the names of Themistocles, Aristides, Kallixenos, and Hippokrates son of Alkmeonides are dominant. The excavators of the Agora have held (e.g. *Hesp.* Suppl. iv. 33 n.) that this is because the ostraka of 482 were still lying about when the Persians came. Hands (loc. cit.), rightly in our opinion, suggests that some of these deposits may belong to a vote in 483, unrecorded because the required number of votes was not cast and no one was ostracized. Statistically, our deposits B and C seem distinguishable from our D, E, F.

B (*Hesp.* ix (1940) 301–2, Suppl. viii. 395, Hands Group A (modified figures)). This apparently coherent deposit is distributed as follows: Themistocles 65, Kallixenos 43, Hippokrates son of Alkmeonides 43, Aristides 2, miscellaneous 5, uncertain 6.

C (*Hesp.* xvii (1948) 193 f., Hands Group B (modified figures)). This large group did not settle till *c.* 415 and there was ample time for both earlier and later pieces to have intruded. But the ostraka seem to be a coherent unit, and, with reservations, may be treated as such. The distribution is: Themistocles 172, Kallixenos 165, Hippokrates son of Alkmeonides 48, Aristides 5, miscellaneous (eight different names) 20, uncertain about 80.

D (*Hesp.* Suppl. iv. 33, Hands Group C). A closed deposit, distributed: Themistocles 18, Kallixenos 9, Hippokrates son of Alkmeonides 7, Aristides 5.

E (unpublished, Hands Group D). Distribution: Themistocles 23, Kallixenos 4, Hippokrates son of Alkmeonides 2, Aristides 18.

F (*Hesp.* xxiii (1954) 54, Hands Group F). Distribution: Themistocles 2, Kallixenos 9, Hippokrates son of Alkmeonides 3, Aristides 3.

Even in deposits D, E, F, Aristides is nowhere in a majority. This may be a by-product of the fact that they are smaller and less statistically significant than B, C, but if we take B and C on one hand and D, E, and F on the other, there does seem to be a noticeable shift of votes away from the Alkmeonids, Kallixenos and Hippokrates, against Aristides.

G Of the deposits after 480, the excavators of the Kerameikos seem reluctant to attribute any unity to a group found in 1932 which included 64 votes against Kimon and 80 against Menon (*Kerameikos,* iii. 51–83). It does include at least one obviously intrusive piece, against Phaiax, but we see no obvious reason to deny that the bulk of the Kimon and Menon ostraka belong to the same year, or, necessarily, to affirm that that year has to be the year of Kimon's ostracism.

H (*Ath. Mitt.* xl (1915) 7–20; Carcopino, op. cit. 80 f., 88). This deposit seems a unit. Distribution: Thucydides son of Melesias 11, Kleippides 24, miscellaneous (Andocides, Teisandros, Eucharides) 3, uncertain 5. The ostrakon of Damon son of Damonides (*Ath. Mitt.* xl. 20 f.) was not found in this deposit. Brueckner, in publishing this group, suggested a date between Kimon's death in 449 and the ostracism of Thucydides in 443, at which Pericles and not Kleippides must have been his principal opponent. The view was refined by Rosenberg (*Neue Jahrb.* xviii (1915) 205–12), who explained the absence of votes against Pericles by an agreement among the conservatives to concentrate against Kleippides, say in 445. This view has its attractions, but it is clearly vulnerable to suggestions that the absence of Pericles is due to the smallness of the sample or to the removal of votes against him for separate counting. Koerte (*Ath. Mitt.* xlvii (1922) 1–5) saw no reason to doubt that the deposit belonged to the ostracism of 443.

Vanderpool, *Hesp.* Suppl. viii. 408–11, gave a list of known ostraka with select bibliography to 1946, which had to be supplemented by *Hesp.* xvii (1948) 194 for the large finds of 1947. We owe to Vanderpool's generosity the revised summary list we print here. Through his bibliography and the articles cited above, most published photographs and drawings should be traceable; see also *IIA* Pl. 12, 16. For discussions of ostracism in the light of reasonably up-to-date knowledge of the ostraka, Raubitschek, *Actes du deuxième congrès international d'épigraphie grecque et latine*, 61–74 (= *Class. Journ.* xlviii (1952–3) 113–22), and Hands, *JHS* lxxix (1959) 69–79 stand more or less alone.

As we go to press, news reaches us of very large finds of ostraka in the Kerameikos, continuing those reported in *Archaeological Reports for 1965–66*, p. 5. We are told that they provide, for example, clear evidence that Themistocles was a candidate in 486.

KNOWN OSTRAKA

	Agora	Else-where	Total
Abronichos (Lysikleous) Lamptreus	4	0	4
Acharnion Xypetaion	3	0	3
Alkibiades Kleiniou Skambonides (the elder)	7	1	8
Alkibiades Kleiniou Skambonides (the younger)	3	0	3
[Ando]kides [Leog]orou	0	1	1
Archenos Philoxenou	1	0	1
Arist- Charop-	1	0	1
Arista- Timo-	1	0	1
Aristeides Lysimachou Alopekethen	61	0	61
Boutalion Ep- Marathonios	7	0	7
Charias Paianieus	1	0	1

	Agora	Else-where	Total
Charias Ph- -dou	I	o	I
Damon Damonidou	o	I	I
Dieitrephes Euthoinou (*Hesp.* xxxvii. 118 f.)	3	o	3
Dionysios -onou	3	o	3
Eratyllos Kattariou	3	o	3
Eret[rieus]	I	o	I
Eucharides Eucharous Thesmo(thetes)	o	I	I
Eukrates	I	o	I
Eupolis Thoraieus	I	o	I
Gnathon Echekleous	o	I	I
Habron Patrokleous Marathonios	11	o	11
Hierokl- Herma-	I	o	I
Hipparchos Charmou (Kollyteus)	11	o	11
Hippokles Menippou	2	I	3
Hippokrates Alkmeonidou Alopekethen	123	2	125
Hippokrates Anaxileo	8	2	10
Hippokrates (uncertain which)	21	o	21
Hyperbolos Antiphanous (Perithoides)	2	o	2
Kallias Didymiou	3	o	3
Kallias Kratiou	2	I	3
Kallixenos Aristonymou Xypetaion	262	I	263
Kimon Miltiadou (Lakiades)	4	67	71
Kleiboulos Nikodemou	2	o	2
Kleippides Deiniou Acharneus	o	25	25
Kleophon Kleippidou Acharneus	3	o	3
Kritias Leaidou	2	o	2
Kydrokles Timokratous Kriothen	17	2	19
Laispodias ek Koiles	?	o	I
Megakles Hippokratous Alopekethen	12	3	15
Melanthios Phalanthou	3	o	3
Menestratos	o	I	I
Menon Menekleidou Gargettios	4	80	84
Onomastos Konthyleus	I	o	I
Panaitios Agrylethen	I	o	I
Perikles Xanthippou (Cholargeus)	2	o	2
Phaiax Erasistratou Acharneus	3	I	4
Phalanthos Spintharou	I	o	I
Phileas Derketou	I	o	I
Phileriphos	o	I	I
Philinos Kleippidou (Acharneus)	I	o	I
Philippos	o	I	I
Polytimos Prasi(eus)	o	I	I
Sokrates Anagyrasios	I	o	I
[Sp]intharos Eu[boulou Probalinthios?]	I	o	I
[Tei]sandros [E]pilykou	o	I	I
Themistokles Neokleous Phrearrhios	373	195	568

	Agora	Else- where	Total
Theotimos Kleainou	0	1	1
Thrasykles	1	0	1
Thukydides Melesiou (Alopekethen)	1	13	14
Xanthippos Arriphronos (Cholargeus)	15	2	17
Fragments	240	14	254
	1,238	420	1,658

22

A Spartan Dedication: (?) 490–480 B.C.

A hollow cylindrical base of Laconian stone, found in the Altis at Olympia;
now in the Olympia Museum.

In one line, Laconian alphabet. Phot. and facs.: *JHS* lxix (1949) 27, 29.
SEG xi. 1203a+; Jeffery, *JHS* lxix. 26–30; Buck 68; *LSAG* 196, no. 49+.

[δέξ]ο Fάν[α]ξ Κρονίδα{ι} Δεῦ ’Ολύνπιε καλὸν ἄγαλμα
hιλέFο[ι θυ]μõι τοῖ(λ) Λακεδαιμονίοις.

τοῦ ναοῦ δέ ἐστιν ἐν δεξιᾷ τοῦ μεγάλου Ζεὺς πρὸς ἀνατολὰς ἡλίου,
μέγεθος μὲν δυόδεκα ποδῶν, ἀνάθημα δὲ λέγουσιν εἶναι Λακεδαιμονίων,
ἡνίκα ἀποστᾶσι Μεσσηνίοις δεύτερα τότε ἐς πόλεμον κατέστησαν. ἔπεστι
δὲ καὶ ἐλεγεῖον ἐπ’ αὐτῷ,
δέξο ἄναξ Κρονίδα Ζεῦ ’Ολύμπιε καλὸν ἄγαλμα
ἱλάῳ θυμῷ τοῖς Λακεδαιμονίοις. (Paus. v. 24. 3)

That this monument in fact refers to the Second Messenian War
of the seventh century is out of the question, and it has generally been
attributed to the Helot Revolt which started in 465. There is hardly
enough comparative material in the first half of the fifth century
to make a firm date for the lettering possible, though in some respects
it looks more archaic than one would expect *c.* 460. However, the
nature of the base suggests that the statue was not anthropomorphic,
but a human head and arms surmounting a circular core sheathed in
bronze, inserted directly into the base. This seems impossibly archaic
for *c.* 460, but just possible *c.* 488. Jeffery, therefore, followed by
Wallace (*JHS* lxxiv (1954) 32–5) and Huxley (*Early Sparta*, 88),
would add this base to the scattered evidence (Plato, *Laws* iii. 692 d,
698 d–e; Strabo, viii. 4. 10, p. 362; Paus. iv. 23. 5–10) for Spartan
trouble in Messenia around 490. Den Boer, on the other hand (*Hist.* v
(1956) 168–74), regards a Messenian revolt at this date as a historical
fiction. It must be noted that the epigram does not mention Messenia
and Pausanias’ information may be unreliable (cf. Pearson, *Hist.* xi
(1962) 421 n. 56).

23

The Decree of Themistocles: 480 B.C.

A marble stele, found near the church of Hagia Soteira at Damala (Troizen); now in EM.
Third-century lettering, ll. 4–47 stoichedon 42 (ll. 38–41, 43). Phot.: *Hesp.* xxix (1960) 200 (enlargement of part of ll. 30–5, ibid. xxxi. 413). All non-textual criteria for dating the stele are discussed by Dow, *AJA* lxvi (1962) 353–68.

Editio princeps: Jameson, *Hesp.* xxix (1960), 198–223; a new text incorporating suggestions by others, Jameson, ibid. xxxi (1962), 310–15. Critical bibliography: Dow, *Classical World*, lv. 105–8; Chambers, *Philologus* cxi (1967) 166–9. We confine ourselves to recommending as an introduction to the problems involved: Habicht, *Hermes*, lxxxix (1961) 1–35; Amandry, *Bull. de la Faculté des Lettres de Strasbourg*, xxxviii (1961) 413–35; Hignett, *Xerxes' Invasion of Greece*, 458–68; Burn, *Persia and the Greeks*, 364–77 (hostile to authenticity); the *editio princeps*; Berve, *Sitzb. Münch.* 1961, no. 3, 1–50; Jameson, *Hist.* xii (1963) 385–404; Meritt, *Lectures in Memory of L. T. Semple*, i. 119–32 (favourable).

[θεοί.]

ἔδοξ[εν] τῆι βουλῆι καὶ τῶι δήμωι·

Θεμισ[τοκλ]ῆς Νεοκλέους Φρεάρριος εἶπεν·

τὴ[μ] μὲγ πό[λιν παρ]ακατ[αθέ]σθαι τῆι Ἀθηνᾶι τῆι Ἀθηνῶ-

5 μ [μεδεο]ύ[σηι] κ[αὶ τοῖς ἄλλ]οις θεοῖς ἅπασιν φυλάττει-

ν κα[ὶ] ἀμ[ύνειν τὸμ βά]ρβαρ[ο]ν ὑπὲρ τῆς χώρας· Ἀθηναίου-

[ς δ' ἅπ]α[ντας καὶ τοὺς ξέν]ους τοὺς οἰκοῦντας Ἀθήνησι

[τὰ τέκ]ν[α καὶ τὰς γυναῖκ]ας ε[ἰς] Τροιζῆνα καταθέσθαι

τ[..........20..........] τοῦ ἀρχηγέτου τῆς χώρας· τ-

10 [οὺς δὲ πρεσβύτας καὶ τὰ] κτήματα εἰς Σαλαμῖνα καταθ-

έ[σ]θ[αι· τοὺς δὲ ταμίας καὶ τ]ὰς ἱερέας ἐν τῆι ἀκροπόλε-

[ι μένειν φυλάττοντας τὰ τῶ]ν θεῶν· τοὺς δὲ ἄλλους Ἀθη-

[ναίους ἅπαντας καὶ τοὺς ξέ]νους τοὺς ἡβῶντας εἰσβαί-

νειν ε[ἰς τὰς ἑτοιμασθ]ε[ί]σ[α]ς διακοσίας ναῦς καὶ ἀμύ-

15 νεσ[θαι] τ[ὸμ βάρβαρον ὑπὲρ τῆ]ς ἐλευθερίας τῆς τε ἑαυ-

τῶν [καὶ τῶν ἄλλων Ἑλλήνων] μετὰ Λακεδαιμονίων καὶ Κο-

ριν[θίων καὶ Αἰγινητῶν] καὶ τῶν ἄλλων τῶμ βουλομένω-

[ν] κοινω[νήσειν τοῦ κινδύνο]υ· καταστῆσαι δὲ καὶ τριη-

[ρ]ά[ρχους διακοσίους ἕνα ἐπὶ] τὴν ναῦν ἑκάστην τοὺς [σ]-

20 τρατη[γ]οὺ[ς ἀρχομένους τ]ῆι αὔριον ἡμέραι ἐκ τῶν κ[εκ]-

τημέν[ω]ν γ[ῆν] τ[ε κ]αὶ [οἰκί]αν Ἀθ[ή]νησι καὶ οἷς ἂμ παῖδ[ες]

ὦσι γνή[σιοι μὴ πρεσβυτέρο]υς πεντήκοντα ἐτῶν κα[ὶ ἐ]-
πικλ[ηρῶσαι αὐτ]οῖς [τ]ὰς ναῦς· υ υ καταλέξαι δὲ καὶ ἐπ[ι]-
βάτας [δ]έκα [ἐφ' ἑκάστη]ν ναῦν ἐκ τῶν ὑπὲρ εἴκοσιν ἔτη [γ]-
25 εγονότω[ν μέχρι τριά]κοντα ἐτῶν καὶ τοξότας τέτταρ-
ας· δια[κληρῶσαι δὲ κ]αὶ τὰς ὑπηρεσίας ἐπὶ τὰς ναῦς ὅτ-
αμπερ κ[αὶ τοὺς τριηράρ]χους ἐπικληρῶσιν· ἀναγράψα-
ι δὲ κα[ὶ τοὺς ἄλλους κατὰ] ναῦν τοὺς στρατηγοὺς εἰς λ-
ευκώ[ματα, τοὺς μὲν Ἀ]θηναίους ἐκ τῶν ληξιαρχικῶν γρ-
30 αμματεί[ων, τοὺς] δὲ ξ[έν]ους ἐκ τῶν ἀπογεγραμμένων πα-
[ρ]ὰ τῶι [πολε]μ[άρχ]ω[ι·] ἀναγράφειν δὲ νέμοντας κατὰ τάξεις [ε]ἰς διακοσίας ἀ[ν]ὰ ἑκατὸν ἀριθμὸν καὶ ἐπιγράψα-
ι τῆι [τάξ]ει ἑκάστηι τῆς τριήρους τοὔνομα καὶ τοῦ τρι-
ηράρχου καὶ τῆς ὑπηρε[σί]ας ὅπως ἂν εἰδῶσιν εἰς ὁποί-
35 αν τριήρη ἐ[μ]βήσεται ἡ [τ]άξις ἑ[κ]άστη· ἐπειδὰν δὲ νεμη-
θῶσιν ἅπα[σ]αι αἱ τάξεις καὶ ἐπικληρωθῶσι ταῖς τριήρεσι, πληροῦν ἁ[π]άσας τὰς διακοσίας ναῦς τὴμ βουλὴν
καὶ τ[ο]ὺστρατηγοὺ[ς θύ]σαντας ἀρεστήριον τῶι Διὶ τῶι
Παγκρατεῖ καὶ τῆι Ἀθηνᾶι καὶ τῆι Νίκηι καὶ τῶι Ποσει-
40 δῶνι τῶι Ἀσφα[λ]είωι· υ υ ἐπειδὰν δὲ πεπληρωμέναι ὦσιν
αἱ νῆες, τα[ῖ]ς μὲν ἑκατὸν αὐτῶν βοηθεῖν ἐπὶ τὸ Ἀρτεμίσ·
[ι]ον τὸ Εὐβοϊκόν, ταῖς δὲ ἑκατὸν αὐτῶν περὶ τὴν Σαλαμῖνα καὶ τὴν ἄλλην Ἀττικὴν ναυλοχεῖν καὶ φυλάττειν
τὴν χώραν· ὅπως δ' ἂν καὶ ὁμονοοῦντες ἅπαντες Ἀθηναῖοι
45 ἀμύνωνται τὸμ βάρβαρον, τοὺς μὲν μεθεστηκότας τὰ [δ]-
[έκα] ἔτη ἀπιέναι εἰς Σαλαμῖνα καὶ μένειν αὐτοὺς ἔ[κε]-
[ῖ ἕως ἄν τι τῶι δήμ]ωι δόξηι περὶ αὐτῶν· τοὺς δὲ [ἀτίμου]-
[ς - - - - - - - - -] traces [- - - - - - - - - -]

Jameson's second text is the basis of ours, but we have taken into account
Hardy and Pritchett, *BSA* lix (1964) 30–1, and further unpublished notes
by Jameson. The stone has suffered damage on the left, but some of the
restorations are assured by quotations in Plutarch and Aristides. In l. 7
δ' ἅπαντας was Habicht's restoration, which now seems to fit the traces better
than Jameson's [ς δὲ α]ὐτ[οὺς. For l. 9 Meritt suggests [προστάτου ὄντος
Πιτθέως], Habicht [εἰς παραθήκην τοῦ Θησέως or Πιθέως]. (Hardy and
Pritchett read the first letter as tau or zeta and Jameson accepts this.) In
l. 28 ναύτας (Woodhead, Stroud) is also possible. For l. 32 see Meritt,
Hesp. xxxi (1962) 413. In l. 34 τῆς seems more likely than τ[ὰ]ς. In ll. 38–9
Amandry suggests τῶι Διὶ ⟨καὶ⟩ τῶι Παγκρατεῖ καὶ τῆι Ἀθηνᾶι {καὶ}
τῆι Νίκηι, and Meritt concurs in excising the second καί.

In 348 Aeschines was reciting the decree of Themistocles (Dem. xix. 303), and, whatever the precise date at which the text before us was put on stone, it is not seriously maintained that it differed greatly from his recitation, though one might doubt whether he went much further than our l. 18. The question is to what extent the text current in 348 represents what Themistocles may have said in 480. Extreme positions seem to us untenable. At an absolute minimum, an adherent of the view that we have a documentary reproduction of a decree of Themistocles will concede that editing has added Themistocles' patronymic and demotic in l. 3, elements not found in Attic documents much before 350, and eliminated the Attic spelling Ἀθηναίαι in ll. 4, 39. Those who hold the view that the decree was composed shortly before 348 by Aeschines or another surely cannot be maintaining that it was fabricated without any regard to the source-material available, taking that phrase in its widest sense. Between these two positions, the possibilities seem to us to form a continuum without a sharp dividing-line; no very wide gap, for example, seems to separate the treatments of Burn and Meritt, cited above as representatives of divergent views. To disregard the historical kernel of the decree altogether on the ground that it is irreconcilable with the narrative of Herodotus seems to us to assume what needs to be proved, even if it were not clear that the most irreconcilable of the assumed divergences depend on the proposition that what was decreed was done, a proposition not self-evidently true. (Consider, for instance, the situation which would arise if the first decree of No. 78 were preserved complete, to be matched with a narrative slightly less explicit than that of Thucydides about the prehistory of the organization of the Sicilian Expedition.)

Ll. 4–12 order the evacuation of Attica except the Acropolis. The cult-title τῆι Ἀθηνῶν μεδεούσηι can be criticized as inappropriate and more normally used of Athena Polias looked at from outside Athens (cf. Preuner, *Ath. Mitt.* xlix (1924) 31–4), but Ar. *Knights* 763 perhaps defends it. βάρβαρον (ll. 6, 15, 45) is less dignified than the references to 'the Mede' usual in the period (cf. Nos. 24, 26), but, if Themistocles was being dignified, later paraphrases may have been less so, and cf. Thuc. i. 96. 1. ἐν τῆι ἀκροπόλει is an apparent anachronism for the Old Attic ἐν πόλει (cf. Thuc. ii. 15 and *CQ* xi (1961) 62); it can be accounted for by editing or a desire to avoid πόλις in a different sense from that in l. 4.

Ll. 12–18 order the mobilization of the fleet for the joint war of liberation. These lines have been accused of fourth-century rhetoric, but cf. Hdt. v. 64. 2, vii. 144. 3, 178. 2.

Ll. 18–35 contain the detailed provisions for mobilization (see Jameson, *Hist.* xii (1963) 385–404). They have been charged with being too detailed and redolent of fourth-century practice. We do not feel that these charges have been made out. We confess to surprise that the qualifications for the trierarchs in ll. 21–2 contain no reference to the Solonian property-classes, but Habicht's view that there were no bastards in Athens before Pericles' citizenship-law of 451–0 (Arist. *Ἀθ. Πολ.* 26. 4) seems to rest on a misunderstanding. The charge that ten ἐπιβάται is an impossibly small number for an Athenian fleet in 480, based on Hdt. vi. 15. 1, vii. 184. 2, Thuc. i. 49. 1, is substantially neutralized by Thuc. i. 14. 3, Plut. *Cimon* 12. 2. Some doubt attaches to the ὑπηρεσίαι (l. 26); in the classical period this word covers the specialist officers (cf. Richardson, *CQ* xxxvii (1943) 55–61, Lewis, *CQ* n.s. xi (1961) 64) and excludes the ἐπιβάται. Jameson rightly argues that, if this is the case here, provision is made for the selection of the ἐπιβάται, but not their assignment to ships, and for the assignment of the specialists, but not for their selection; he therefore concludes that here the ὑπηρεσίαι are the marines and archers, an unparalleled use, impossible for a fourth-century forger. It might, we suppose, be argued that the conclusion from the normal sense of the word is that the details of the mobilization are not logically worked out, thus betraying the hand of a forger; this seems less convincing. The ληξιαρχικὰ γραμματεῖα (ll. 29–30) are deme-registers; Habicht's belief that *thetes* were not listed on them in 480 is refuted by Meritt. Ll. 31–5 are very difficult, and have been read and interpreted variously. If the readings given here are right, which seems probable, we see no escape from the conclusion that the aim is to provide a minimum of 100 rowers for each trireme. The normal was 200 (cf. Hdt. viii. 17); is it really credible that a forger's desire for verisimilitude would be so strong as to reconstruct a procedure calculated to put as many ships to sea as possible rather than simply use the normal number?

Ll. 35–45 order the manning of the fleet after preliminary sacrifice, and outline a basic strategic plan by which 100 ships are to move to Artemision and 100 will remain near Salamis and Attica. Various doubts can be raised about the gods named in ll. 38–40, and there may be some misplacing of the καί's. Pankrates is certainly normally a hero distinct from Zeus, but cf. Aesch. *Eum.* 917–20. Nike is generally Athena Nike, but compare the oracle in Hdt. viii. 77. For Poseidon Asphaleios, cf. Ar. *Ach.* 682. Herodotus' account gives us the final disposition of forces at Artemision as 147 Athenian ships (20 manned by Chalkis; viii. 1. 2), reinforced later by another 53 (viii. 14. 1).

Ll. 44 ff. order those ostracized, perhaps already back in Athens, to Salamis and may have passed on to considering other exiles (cf. Andoc. i. 77).

Relatively few of the points of detail which have been raised against the decree have turned out to be decisive, but this is of course not the whole story. It can hardly be denied that the whole document runs more smoothly than other official documents of the period (cf. Amandry, op. cit. 416 f.) and that it is relatively free from hiatus (*CQ* xi (1961) 66). What importance is to be attached to this turns on the type of transmission which has to be assumed for the period 480–348, and on this our ignorance is nearly absolute. Against this superficial fluency it may be argued that ll. 41–3 are remarkably inelegant, and that it is surprising that a forger failed to call metics metics (ll. 7, 30) or the ostracized ostracized (ll. 45–6). (These seem to be the surviving points from an attempt to show that there was 'no reason to suspect forgery. There are too many traces of official and archaic language', Lewis, *CQ* xi. 61–6.)

This is not the place to discuss the allied strategy of the year 480, but a few points may be made. If our decree is a unit, it must be placed between the failure of the expedition to Tempe and the manning of the Artemision–Thermopylae position, which seems in any case to be the context of Hdt. vii. 144. 3: ἔδοξέ τέ σφι μετὰ τὸ χρηστήριον βουλευομένοισι ἐπιόντα ἐπὶ τὴν Ἑλλάδα τὸν βάρβαρον δέκεσθαι τῆσι νηυσὶ πανδημεί, τῷ θεῷ πειθομένους, ἅμα Ἑλλήνων τοῖσι βουλομένοισι. That the evacuation of civilians is ordered so early is not necessarily incompatible with the fact that, according to Herodotus, it happened later, nor is it entirely surprising that, at the time of the decree, Athens was not yet prepared to commit all her forces to Artemision. That our decree already has Salamis in view as a fleet-station (ll. 42–3) raises no problems other than those already caused by the appearance of Salamis in the closing lines of the second Delphic oracle to Athens (Hdt. vii. 141).

24 (16)

Epitaph of the Corinthians who died at Salamis: 480 B.C.

Marble block found at Ambelaki on the island of Salamis; now in EM. Archaic Corinthian alphabet. Phot.: Kern 9; *LSAG*, Pl. 21. 29.

IG i². 927; *LSAG* 129, 132 (29); Carpenter, *AJA* lxvii (1963) 209; Boegehold, *Gk. Rom. Byz. Stud.* vi (1965) 179–86.

['Ο ξένε, εὔhυδρ]όν ποκ' ἐναίομες ἄστυ Ϙορίνθο,

[νῦν δ' hαμὲ Αἴα]ϝτος [νᾶσος ἔχει Σαλαμίς].

[ἐνθάδε Φοινίσσας νᾶας καὶ Πέρσας hελόντες]

[καὶ Μέδους hιαρὰν hελλάδα ῥυσάμεθα].

Other letters have been added later. Four letters above letters 14–18 in l. 1 seem to be idle copying of the original letter-forms; there are also two letters, barely visible, just below letters 14 and 15 of l. 1.

In the Athenian version of the battle of Salamis, according to Herodotus (viii. 94), the Corinthian contingent fled as soon as battle was joined and returned only when the battle was won. Herodotus, however, knows that the Corinthian version was very different, and the rest of Greece, he says, agreed with them. Plutarch (*de Mal. Hdt.* 39), in attacking Herodotus, says that the Athenians allowed the Corinthians to bury their dead on Salamis and he quotes this epitaph. Together with [Dio Chrysostom], xxxvii. 18, he adds a second couplet:

> Ἐνθάδε Φοινίσσας νῆας καὶ Πέρσας ἑλόντες
> καὶ Μήδους, ἱερὰν Ἑλλάδα ῥυόμεθα.

l. 1. [Dio] has ῥεῖα δὲ. l. 2. ῥυσάμεθα Jacobs; Ἑλλάδ' ἱδρυσάμεθα [Dio.]

Rhys Carpenter, emphasizing the archaic character of the writing and the absence of the second couplet, attributed this epitaph to Corinthians who may have helped Megara in the fighting against Athens for Salamis in Solon's time, *c.* 600. He also thinks that the lettering is Megarian. These last lines do not survive on the stone and it was generally held that they derived from a literary tradition. Boegehold, however, in a thorough examination of the stone, points out that a hollow has been worn where two additional lines could have been inscribed. We follow his text, but in l. 4 we prefer ῥυσάμεθα to his ῥηνόμεθα. The epigram is attributed by [Dio] to Simonides; it is at least Simonidean. The triangular tailless rho, which led Rhys Carpenter to infer that the lettering was Megarian, is amply illustrated in Corinth (Boegehold, 181, n. 7).

25 (18)

Dedication of the Athenian Portico at Delphi:
(?) 479 B.C.

On the highest of the three steps of the stylobate of the Athenian Portico at Delphi, built on the north side of the Sacred Way against the polygonal wall that supports the terrace of the temple of Apollo.

Attic letters including ⊕, Ϛ. Phot.: *FD* ii (as below), Pl. 23. Facs.: *Imag.* 73 (23).

SIG 29; Pomtow, *Rh. Mus.* xlix (1894) 627–9; Amandry, *FD* ii, *La Colonne des Naxiens et le Portique des Athéniens*, 37–121.

Ἀθεναῖοι ἀνέθεσαν τὲν στοὰν καὶ τὰ hόπλ[α κ]αὶ τἀκροτέρια hελόντες τὸν πολε[μίο]ν.

Pausanias (x. 11. 6) associates the portico with Phormio's victories in the Corinthian Gulf in 429, and an inscription which he saw listed the allies who fought with Sparta, and also specified a sacrifice to Theseus and Poseidon at Rhion. In the portico he saw ships' prows and bronze shields. The inscription that survives, however, has letter forms that should not be later than 470, and might be as early as 510.

Until recently it was assumed that the hόπλα of the inscription were arms, and the Athenian victory commemorated was thought to be either over the Boeotians and Chalkidians (c. 506) or the Aeginetans (between 500 and 480), or over the Persians at Salamis. Amandry (op. cit.) has suggested that the hόπλα are cables from the Persian bridges over the Hellespont, and that the ἀκροτέρια are from the ships that formed the bridges; he emphasizes the suitability of the portico's design for this purpose. His attractive hypothesis is not quite compelling. Would ἑλόντες be the right word for the recovery of the cables which had been taken to Kardia when the bridges broke up, and were handed over to the Greeks at Sestos (Hdt. ix. 115)? Would the Mede not be called a Mede? If cables had been dedicated at Delphi, would they not have been a joint-dedication by the Greeks? The letter-forms have been used as evidence for both high and low dates. They are not decisive, but no other surviving Athenian public inscription, which can be dated, has ⊕ after 490.

26

Athenian Epigrams on the Persian Wars

Two fragments of a base; the right-hand one found in Hadrian Street to the north-east of the Acropolis, the left-hand one in the Agora, both in modern houses, so that no conclusion can be drawn about their original situation; both now in the Agora Museum. The dressing of the left edge, closely corresponding to that of the front, rules out Wilhelm's theory (*Anz. Wien.*, 1934, 105 f.) that the texts are to be read vertically downwards (Oliver, *Hesp.* v (1936) 228). The right-hand fragment has traces of a cutting in the top; if it is original, it must be at least one of a pair. These cuttings have been attributed to stelai (Raubitschek, *AJA* xliv (1940) 56–9) and to herms (Meritt in *The Aegean and the Near East, Studies Presented to Hetty Goldman*, 274 f.); the relevance of the cutting to the original form of the monument has been doubted (Oliver, *AJA* xliv. 483 f.; Amandry, in Θεωρία, *Festschrift für W.-H. Schuchhardt*, 8, n. 18).

There are two inscriptions. The first, on the original smooth band which ran round the face of the base, is stoichedon, with punctuation marks of three dotted circles, and is certainly by the same stone-cutter as *IG* i². 3–4 (485–4 B.C.). Later, a new panel was smoothed in the stippled area below the upper band to receive the second, non-stoichedon inscription. Our general impression of the letter-forms is that the two inscriptions might be as much as fifteen years apart, but they could be virtually contemporary. Phot.: *Hesp.* ii (1933) 481–2, *IIA* 19.

Work on the document falls into three phases. The first phase, before the publication of the left-hand fragment by Oliver (*Hesp.* ii (1933) 480–94), is now of little importance. Of the second phase, Jacoby, *Hesp.* xiv (1945) 161–85, gives a useful bibliography and *apparatus criticus*, to which add: *SEG* x. 404; Vollgraff, *Mélanges Grégoire*, i. 621–4; Gomme, *HCT* ii. 98–9; Peek, *Studies Presented to D. M. Robinson*, ii. 305–12. The third phase opened with Meritt, *The Aegean and the Near East* (*v. sup.*), 268–80, in which he published what is almost certainly a fourth-century copy of the first epigram. Thereafter add: Peek, *Hermes*, lxxxviii (1960) 494–8; Amandry, Θεωρία (*v. sup.*), 1–8; Pritchett, *Marathon* (*Cal. Publ. Class. Arch.* iv), 160–8 (these three simultaneous and independent of each other); Meritt, *AJP* lxxxiii (1962) 294–8.

I   ἀνδρῶν τōνδ' ἀρετε[....9.....ος ἄφθιτον] αἰεἱ[:]
     | ▩[....8....]ν[.]ρ[....9..... νέμοσι θεοί:] |
     ἔσχον γὰρ πεζοί τε [καὶ ὀκυπόρον ἐπὶ νεō]ν˙
     ἑλλά[δα μ]ὲ πᾶσαν δούλιο[ν ἔμαρ ἰδε͂ν:] |

II   ἐν ἄρα τοῖσζ' ἀδαμ[α - - - - - - - - - - - - - -] ℏότ' αἰχμὲν
     στέσαμ πρόσθε πυλōν ἀγ[- - - - - - - - - - -]|
     ἀνχίαλομ πρέσαι ρ[- - - - - - - - - - - - - - - - - -]
     ἄστυ βίαι Περσōν κλινάμενο[ι - - -]. |

I. The fourth-century copy (*v. sup.*) has:
     ]ος ἄφθι[- - -]
     ]νέμωσι θεοί˙
     ]ὠκυπόρων ἐπὶ νηῶν
     ]ον ἦμαρ ἰδεῖν.

By fixing the text of the second hexameter, it determines the length of the lacuna in the first hexameter, showing earlier suggestions to be two letters too long; of current suggestions, we would prefer ἀρετε͂[ς ἔσται κλέος (Peek) to ἀρετε͂ [δόχσει κλέος or λάμφσει φάος (Meritt), but it raises difficulties in the fourth-century text, maintained by Meritt to be substantially stoichedon. Readings in the first pentameter have been recently disputed (Pritchett, *AJP* lxxxv (1964) 50–5, Meritt, ibid. 417). Whether there is a vertical in the first space or not, and the balance of opinion is in its favour, we agree with Peek and Meritt that the punctuation mark before it does not take a letter-space and that there were nine, not eight, letters before the nu. The nu and the rho may be taken as certain; between them Meritt reads an epsilon, denied by Pritchett and which we cannot confirm. After the rho, Meritt, but not Pritchett, sees traces of the bottom of gamma or chi; we incline to agree. The only current restoration which fits the traces is ℏ[οῖς κᾶν εἰ]ν ἔργ[οις ἐσθλὰ νέμοσι θεοί] (Meritt), 'No matter to whom in deeds of war the gods may grant success'; we would prefer a clause with the sense 'as long as'; that exactly nine letters are missing after the rho depends on the fourth-century text's being stoichedon.

II. τοῖσζ' = τοῖσσδε. Nu is preferable to gamma at the end of the first pentameter, rho to beta at the end of the second hexameter, but neither reading is quite certain. To Jacoby's apparatus, and his preference for Wilhelm's text:

> ἐν ἄρα τοῖσζ' ἀδάμ[αντος ἐνὶ φρεσὶ θυμός], hότ' αἰχμὲν
> στέσαμ πρόσθε πυλôν ἀγ[τία τοχσοφόρον.]
> ἀγχίαλομ πρέσαι β[ολευσαμένον δ' ἐσάοσαν]
> ἄστυ, βίαι Περσôν κλινάμενο[ι στρατιάν.]

we add:

> ἐν ἄρα τοῖσζ' ἀδάμ[ας ἐν στέθεσι θυμός], hότ' αἰχμὲν
> στέσαμ πρόσθε πυλôν ἀγ[τία μυριάσιν,]
> ἀγχίαλομ πρέσαι β[ολευσαμένον ἐρικυδὲς]
> ἄστυ βίαι Περσôν κλινάμενο[ι στρατιάν.]   (Meritt),

and:

> ἐν ἄρα τοῖσζ' ἀδάμ[αντος ἐνὶ φρεσὶν ἔτορ], hότ' αἰχμὲν
> στέσαμ πρόσθε πυλôν ἀγ[τία δυσμενέσιν]
> ἀγχίαλομ πρέσαι β[ολευσαμένοις καὶ ἔσοσαν]
> ἄστυ, βίαι Περσôν κλινάμενο[ι δύναμιν.]   (Peek).

That the second epigram refers to a campaign in which the Athenians fought by land and saved the city from burning, i.e. Marathon, has been agreed by all save Gomme, and the connection of thought which he would have suggested to support his view that Salamis was referred to is not very clear to us. πρόσθε πυλôν is no serious obstacle to this view, if we take it to indicate the contrast between the Athenians' conduct and that of the Eretrians who stayed within their walls (Hdt. vi. 101) rather than a precise indication of place; the Maas–Raubitschek theory that the epigram refers to a skirmish at Phaleron or Kynosarges in 490, not mentioned by Herodotus, has not found support.

One would naturally expect two epigrams on the same stone to refer to the same thing, and the dominant view in the second phase of work was that the first epigram also referred to Marathon. Hiller and Gomme were virtually the only exceptions. Hiller's suggested restoration of ὀκυπόρον ἐπὶ νεôν after *Anth. Pal.* vii. 258, and his objection (not a very good one) that it could not have been asserted that Marathon saved all Greece from slavery (*Hermes*, lxix (1934) 204–6), were rejected with something very near contempt. The fourth-century copy shows that Hiller's restoration was right and strongly implies that his attribution was also right. Meritt still defends Marathon, but his interpretation of ὀκυπόρον ἐπὶ νεôν as referring to the fight by the ships (Hdt. vi. 113–15) is very difficult. Pritchett and Amandry come out firmly for Salamis (Pritchett's comparison with Aeschylus' *Persae* for the emphasis placed on the Athenian hoplite-engagement on Psyttaleia is particularly valuable), and, although Peek prefers to refer the text to all the operations of 480–79, this is largely because he wants to keep *SEG* xiii. 34 [- - - - - - πε]ζοί τε καὶ h[ιππῆς - - - - - - | - - - - -]ο νέσοι[- - -] as a text specifically about Salamis. It must then be held that to an epigram and a monument concerned with Salamis, an epigram about Marathon was later added, perhaps, as Amandry suggests, at the instigation of Cimon, son of the victor of Marathon and opponent of Themistokles.

The nature of the monument must remain uncertain. Oliver's view that τῶνδ' and τοῖσζ' referred specifically to the dead and his reconstruction of a cenotaph with a stele carrying lists of names now look very unattractive, since it is impossible to restore any reference to any deaths in the epigrams. It may well be that we have a monument parallel to the herm-monument set up for Eion (Aeschines iii. 183 ff., Plut. *Cimon* 7; Jacoby, *Hesp.* xiv. 185–211), but we still have very little to go on.

27 (19)

Greek Thank-offering for Victories in the Persian War: 479–8 B.C.

Engraved on the 'Serpent-Column', for which see commentary below. The bibliography of the monument as a whole is extensive, but unsatisfactory. For the surviving base at Delphi see Bourguet, *Les Ruines de Delphes*, 160–2, with Figs. 49–50; Pomtow, *RE*, Suppl. iv. 1406 f. For the monument as a whole see in particular Furtwängler, *Sitzb. München*, 1904, 413–17; Luckenbach, *Olympia und Delphi*, 54–7; Reisch, *RE* v. 1688 f.; Studniczka, *Zum platäischen Weihgeschenk in Delphi* (Leipzig 1928); S. Casson, *Preliminary Report upon the Excavations carried out in the Hippodrome of Constantinople in 1927*, 12–14, with Fig. 17. One of the snakes' heads survives in the Istanbul Museum (Devambez, *Grands Bronzes du musée de Stamboul*, pp. 9–12, with Pl. ii).

Phocian, i.e. Delphic, alphabet (*not* Laconian; see Carpenter, *AJA* xlix (1945) 455 f.). Facs.: *Imag.* 101. 16 (whence *LSAG* Pl. 13 (part)).

SIG 31 + ; *DGE* 11; Buck 69; von Domaszewski, *Sitzb. Heidelberg*, 1920, 5. 4–8; Tosti, *Historia*, vii (1933) 433–9; Giannelli, *Atene e Roma*, xxxvi (1934) 103 f.; Larsen, *CP* xxxix (1944) 151, 154; *ATL* iii. 95–100; Papantoniou, Πλάτων vi (1954) 322–30; Cozzoli, *Ann. Univ. Napoli*, iv (1954) 5–24; *Staatsverträge* 130 + .

Coil 1   το[ίδε τὸν]
πόλεμον [ἐ]-
πολ[έ]μεον·

2   Λακεδ[αιμόνιοι]
Ἀθαναῖο[ι]
Κορίνθιοι

3   Τεγεᾶ[ται]
Σικυόν[ιο]ι
Αἰγινᾶται

4   Μεγαρὲς
Ἐπιδαύριοι
Ἐρχομένιοι

5   Φλειάσιοι
Τροζάνιοι
Ἑρμιονὲς

6   Τιρύνθιοι
Πλαταιὲς
Θεσπιὲς

7   Μυκανὲς
Κεῖοι
Μάλιοι
Τένιοι

8   Νάξιοι
Ἐρετριὲς
Χαλκιδὲς

9   Στυρὲς
Ϝαλεῖοι
Ποτειδαιᾶται

10   Λευκάδιοι
Ϝανακτοριὲς
Κύθνιοι
Σίφνιοι

11   Ἀμπρακιδται
Λεπρεᾶται

We have numbered the inscribed coils only. For Coil 1 we follow the reading of Fabricius, supported by Jones, *Preliminary Report*, 43, and confirmed for us by Professor G. E. Bean in the essential point that $\dot{\epsilon}]|\pi o\lambda[\dot{\epsilon}]\mu\epsilon o\nu$ and not $A]|\pi o\lambda[\lambda o\nu\iota$ stands in l. 3; Meister, *Wien. Stud.* lxx (1957) 232 f., proposes $\tau o[\iota\delta\epsilon\ \tau o\nu\ |\ M\epsilon\delta o\nu]$. From squeezes made for us by Professor Bean, we are fairly confident that the intrusive name on coil 7 was $T\epsilon\nu\iota o\iota$, cut later, as has been generally thought, and not $M\upsilon\kappa\alpha\nu\epsilon\hat{s}$, the odd name geographically. More surprisingly, we find that the four names on coil 10 are not to be explained, with von Domaszewski, by the later intrusion of $K\upsilon\theta\nu\iota o\iota$ and $\Sigma\iota\phi\nu\iota o\iota$ into a list of Corinthian dependencies, but simply by the later addition of $\Sigma\iota\phi\nu\iota o\iota$, presumably placed here, rather than on coil 11, in order to group it with $K\upsilon\theta\nu\iota o\iota$.

After their victory at Plataea the allies dedicated thank-offerings to Apollo at Delphi, to Zeus at Olympia, and to Poseidon at the Isthmus (Hdt. ix. 81). The offering to Apollo took the form of a golden tripod resting upon a bronze column, about 6 m. high, representing three intertwined serpents (Herodotus thought it was one serpent with three heads). The tripod was melted down by the Phocians during their occupation of Delphi in the Third Sacred War (Paus. x. 13–19), but the column remained at Delphi until it was transported by Constantine to Constantinople, where it still stands in the ancient Hippodrome (*Atmaidan*), though the heads of the serpents dropped off, apparently by metal-fatigue, on 20 October 1700. The history of the monument is traced in *IGA* 70, where the relevant passages from ancient authors are quoted in full; Ménage, *Anatolian Studies* xiv (1964) 169–73, gives some Turkish sources.

The total number of states commemorated is thirty-one (cf. Plut. *Them.* 20. 3): Pausanias (v. 23) records twenty-seven names as engraved on the offering at Olympia, but the list was probably the same there as at Delphi, and the four omissions (Thespiae, Eretria, Leukas, and Siphnos) may be due to the negligence of the traveller or of some copyist. It is clear that the list does not refer exclusively to the battle of Plataea, though the monument was dedicated from the booty there captured, for the island-states took no part in that battle; it is best to follow the title in referring it to the whole of the Great Persian War (cf. [Dem.] lix. 97, which attributes it to Plataea and Salamis) down to Plataea but not including the campaign of Mykale, which brought in new allies. Von Domaszewski and *ATL* have attempted to sort the names into three groups, Spartan allies, Athenian allies, and Corinthian allies, an attempt which helps to illuminate the structure of the Hellenic alliance (for some qualifications, see Brunt, *Hist.* ii (1953) 146–8), but which cannot be carried through rigorously. Of the states mentioned by Herodotus as participating in the war, Kroton (viii. 47), Pale in Kephallenia (ix. 28, 31), Seriphos (viii. 46, 48) and the Opuntian Lokrians (vii. 203, 207; viii. 1-2) are unaccountably absent. Mantinea was presumably omitted because, though 500 Mantineans joined Leonidas at Thermopylae, they retired before the final struggle there (vii. 202, 222) and the Mantinean force arrived too late for the battle of Plataea (ix. 77); it is true that the Eleans, who do appear, arrived even later (ibid.), but their control of Olympia perhaps won them special consideration. The Tenians were added to the list later (see critical note); their inclusion was in recognition of the service rendered to the Greek cause by a Tenian trireme (Hdt. viii. 82. 1). We now find that this is also true for the Siphnians (see critical note); presumably the Athenians supported their claim, though not the precisely equivalent claim of Seriphos (perhaps cf. Plat. *Rep.* i. 329 e).

It is uncertain where Pausanias engraved the boastful epigram

Ἑλλήνων ἀρχηγὸς ἐπεὶ στρατὸν ὤλεσε Μήδων
Παυσανίας Φοίβῳ μνῆμ' ἀνέθηκε τόδε

(Thuc. i. 132, [Dem.] lix. 97, Plut. *De mal. Hdt.* xlii, Suidas s.v. Παυσανίας; in *Anth. Pal.* vi. 197 it appears in Doric, perhaps rightly, and in the first person, certainly wrongly), which the Spartans promptly erased (Thuc., loc. cit.; see now Fornara, *Philologus* cxi (1967) 291-4). Perhaps it was inscribed on the uppermost of the three circular limestone steps which formed the base of the monument. Diodorus (xi. 33) gives as an alleged replacement.

Ἑλλάδος εὐρυχόρου σωτῆρες τόνδ' ἀνέθηκαν
δουλοσύνης στυγερᾶς ῥυσάμενοι πόλιας,

but we doubt whether this couplet was composed soon after the battle, and have no great conviction that it was ever inscribed on the monument at all.

28 (17)

Gelo's Thank-offering for Himera: after 480 B.C.

A limestone tripod-base, north-east of the temple of Apollo at Delphi, at the head of the Sacred Way.

Syracusan alphabet in ll. 1-3, a mixed alphabet (Syracusan with Ionic delta and gamma?) in ll. 4-5 (*LSAG* 266, Western Colonies 6, against Buck, *CP* viii (1913) 137). Phot.: Marcadé, *Signatures*, i, Pl. iii. Facs.: *LSAG*, Pl. 51.

SIG 34+ ; Wilamowitz, *Gött. Nachr.* 1897, 313 ff.; Taccone, *Atti Torino* xli. 795 ff.; Pomtow–Schober, *RE* Suppl. v. 80 f.; *DGE* 144 (1); Marcadé, *Signatures*, i. 9; Pouilloux, *Choix*, 43.

Γέλον ὁ Δεινομέν[εος]
ἀνέθεκε τὸπόλλονι
Συραρόσιος.
τὸν : τρίποδα : καὶ τὲν : Νίκεν : ἐργάσατο
5 Βίον : Διοδόρο : υἰὸς : Μιλέσιος.

Diodorus (xi. 26. 7, probably following Timaeus) tells us that Gelo dedicated to Apollo at Delphi a golden tripod of sixteen talents' weight as a thank-offering for his victory at Himera in 480. Athenaeus (vi. 231 f) cites Phainias of Eresos and Theopompus (*FGH* 115 F 193) as stating that the Pythian sanctuary was adorned by Gelo and Hiero, τοῦ μὲν τρίποδα καὶ Νίκην χρυσοῦ πεποιημένα ἀναθέντος καθ' οὓς χρόνους Ξέρξης ἐπεστράτευε τῇ Ἑλλάδι, τοῦ δ' Ἱέρωνος τὰ ὅμοια. Further tripod-offerings by their brothers are perhaps attested by the couplet

φημὶ Γέλων', Ἱέρωνα, Πολύζηλον, Θρασύβουλον,
παῖδας Δεινομένευς, τοὺς τρίποδας θεμέναι

(Schol. Pind. *Pyth.* i. 152; cf. Suidas s.v. Δαρετίου, *Anth. Pal.* vi. 214). Bacchylides (iii. 17 ff.) reminds Hieron in 468 of his offerings at Delphi :

λάμπει δ' ὑπὸ μαρμαρυγαῖς ὁ χρυσὸς
ὑψιδαιδάλτων τριπόδων σταθέντων
πάροιθε ναοῦ.

At least Hiero's base can also be identified (*SIG* 35 c; *RE* Suppl. v. 81–4; Courby, *FD* ii, *La Terrasse du Temple*, 249–54); in all probability it celebrated his victory at Kyme (cf. No. 29).

Whether this dedication was completed before Gelon's death in 478 cannot be certainly affirmed. In the event, even if not in intention, it formed a pendent to the golden tripod dedicated by the Spartans and their allies for their victory over the Persians (No. 27), and Gelo, representing himself as a private citizen without title (cf. Berve, *Robinson Studies*, ii. 547), asserted that his victory over Carthage was as important to Apollo and to Greece as that victory.

Bion, the Milesian metal-worker and sculptor, is distinguished by Diogenes Laertius (iv. 58) from an earlier namesake mentioned by Hipponax, who was a native of Chios or Clazomenai.

29 (22)

Hiero's Victory at Kyme: 474 B.C.

Etruscan bronze helmet, discovered at Olympia in 1817; presented to the British Museum in 1823 by King George IV.
Archaic Syracusan letters, *LSAG* 275 (7). Phot.: *LSAG*, Pl. 51. 7; Guarducci, *Epigrafia Greca*, i. 346 fig. 175. Facs.: *Olympia*, v. 249.
SIG 35 Ba; *BMI* 1155; *Olympia*, v. 249.

> ἱάρον ὁ Δεινομένεος
> καὶ τοὶ Συρακόσιοι
> τôι Δὶ Τυράν' ἀπὸ Κύμας.

In the late sixth century the Carthaginians and Etruscans were co-operating against the Greeks of the west. Gelo's crushing defeat of the Carthaginians at Himera was followed in 474 by Hiero's great naval victory over the Etruscans who were attacking Kyme. He dedicated part of the spoils at Olympia and at Delphi, but the latter were lost by shipwreck (*SIG* 35 Bb). A second Etruscan helmet was found in the River Alpheios in 1959 (*BCH* lxxxiv (1960) 721) with a slightly different third line: τôι Δὶ Τυρρανὸν ἀπὸ Κύ[μας]. Our example has been generally thought to be metrical, two choriambic dimeters followed by a paroemiac (Wilamowitz, *Griechische Verskunst*, 381 f.). Daux, in reporting the second helmet, suggested that the seemingly poetic Τυράν' of l. 3 (= Τυρρανά; Attic, Τυρσηνά) might be a mistake for Τυρανὸν; it is not a natural mistake to make.

30 (23)

Public Imprecations at Teos: c. 470 B.C.

Two fragments from one or two stelai found in a cemetery at Araka near the site of Teos; copied by Sherard in 1709 and 1716 and by Lisle in 1716, and first edited by Chishull in 1728 (*Antiquitates Asiaticae*, 96 ff.). A alone was rediscovered and copied by P. Le Bas in 1844, but is now lost (Le Bas–Wadd. iii. 59).

Developed Ionic letters, except mu; the text is divided by cola (:) into words or words-with-conjunction-and-preposition. The letter Τ is found in early inscriptions in several east Greek cities. It is used for xi and double sigma and was probably borrowed from the Phrygian (*AJA* lxvi (1962)

405, n. 5) or possibly the Carian alphabet. It has not yet been found, apart from the numeral system, after 450 (*LSAG* 38 f.). Facs.: *IGA* 497.

CIG 3044; *IGA* 497; *SIG* 37, 38; *DGE* 710; Bannier, *Rh. Mus.* lxxiv (1925) 285–8; Buck 3.

A

Ὅστις : φάρμακα : δηλητή-
ρια : ποιοῖ : ἐπὶ Τηίοισι-
ν : τὸ ξυνὸν : ἢ ἐπ᾽ ἰδιώτηι, : κ-
ἔνον : ἀπόλλυσθαι : καὶ α-
5 ὐτὸν : καὶ γένος : τὸ κένο :
ὅστις : ἐς γῆν : τὴν Τηίην : κ-
ωλύοι : σῖτον : ἐσάγεσθαι :
ἢ τέχνηι : ἢ μηχανῆι : ἢ κατ-
ὰ θάλασσαν : ἢ κατ᾽ ἤπειρο-
10 ν : ἢ ἐσαχθέντα : ἀνωθεοίη, :
ἀπόλλυσθαι : καὶ αὐτ-
ὸν : καὶ γένος : τὸ κένο.

B

- - απονοσ - -
ξύοι : ἐν αὐτῶι - -
ὅστις : Τηίων : ε[ὐθ]ύνωι
ἢ αἰσυ[μ]νήτηι : . . . . ηι : ἢ
5 ἐπανισταῖτο : . . . 6 . . .
. . 5 . . . : ἀπόλλυσθαι : καὶ
αὐτὸν : καὶ γένος : τὸ κείν-
ο : ὅστις : τὸ λοιπὸ : αἰσυμ-
νῶ⟨ν⟩ : ἐν Τέωι : ἢ γῆι τῆι Τη-
10 ίηι : . . . . οσαν : κ. σα. . τ-
ένει [. . 3–4 . .] αρον : να[- - εἰδ]-
ὼς : προδο[ίη . . .] τὴ[ν] πό-
λ[ιν καὶ γῆν] τὴν Τηί-
ων : ἢ τὸ[ς] ἄνδρας [: ἐν ν]-
15 ήσωι : ἢ θα[λάσσηι :] τὸ
μετέ[πειτ᾽ : ἢ τὸ] ἐν
Ἀρο[ί]ηι : περιπό[λιον : ἢ τὸ]
λοιπὸ : προδο[ίη : ἢ κιξα]-
λλεύοι : ἢ κιξάλλας : ὑπο-

20   δέχοιτο:ἢ ληίζοιτο:ἢ λ-
     ηιστὰς:ὑποδέχοιτο:εἰ-
     δὼς:ἐκ γῆς:τῆς Τηίης:ἢ [θ]-
     αλάΤης:φέροντας:ἤ [τι κ]-
     ακὸν:βολεύοι:περὶ Τ[ηί]
25   ων:τὸ ξυνὸ:εἰδὼς:ἢ π[ρὸς]
     Ἕλληνας:ἢ πρὸς βαρβάρο-
     υς:ἀπόλλυσθαι:καὶ αὐ-
     τὸν:καὶ γένος:τὸ κένο:
     οἵτινες τιμοχέοντες:
30   τὴν ἐπαρὴν: μὴ ποιήσειε-
     ν:ἐπὶ Δυνάμει:καθημέν-
     ο τὠγῶνος:Ἀνθεστηρίο-
     ισιν:καὶ Ἡρακλέοισιν:
     καὶ Δίοισιν: ἐν τῆιπαρῆ-
35   ι:ἔχεσθαι:ὃς ἂν ταστήλ-
     ας:ἐν ἧισιν ἡπαρὴ:γέγρ-
     απται:ἢ κατάξει:ἢ φοιν-
     ικήια:ἐκκόψε[ι:] ἢ ἀφανέ-
     ας ποιήσει:κένον ἀπόλ-
40   λυσθαι:καὶ αὐτὸν:καὶ γ-
     ένος [τὸ κένο].

A. 10–11. Roehl and all subsequent editors add (after ἀνωθεοίη) κέν|ον,
from Le Bas. The word was not in the early copies (CIG 3044) and
would make the line three letters longer than any other line.

B. Bannier suggests in ll. 3–6 ὅστις Τηίων ε[ὐθ]ύνωι | ἢ αἰσυ[μ]νήτηι [βοηθ]ῆι
ἢ | ἐπανισταῖτο ἢ δι[αδέ]|χηται, and in ll. 8–12 ὅστις τὸ λοιπὸ αἰσυμ|νῶι
ἐν Τέωι ἢ γῆι τῆι Τη|ίηι [ἢ πλέ]οσαν κ[ὸ]σα[ν] ἐσ]τ|ένει [κυδ]άρον να[ῦν
εἰδ]|ὼς προδο[ίη].

When, after the fall of Sardis, Cyrus' general Harpagus was re-
ducing the Greek cities on the coast, the Teians abandoned their city
and settled at Abdera in Thrace. According to Strabo (xiv. i. 30,
p. 644) some of them returned later and there were said to be seventeen triremes from Teos at Lade (Hdt. vi. 8). Teos appears regularly
in the Athenian tribute-quota lists and was probably an original
member of the Athenian Alliance of 478–7. These fragments record
curses to be publicly pronounced each year by certain magistrates
(B. 29–35) on those who endanger the interests of the community.
ταστήλ|ας (B. 35) shows that more than one stele was used.

The text of A is complete. Curses are invoked against:

(a) poisoners (1–5); ξυνόν = κοινόν, accusative of respect;
(b) those who prevent the import of corn or re-export it when it has been imported (6–12). Since the curses are to be renewed on three occasions each year (B. 29–34) the clause reflects not an extraordinary famine but a permanent dependence on imported corn, which may have encouraged the establishment of the Teian colony Phanagorea in the Euxine.

The text of B. 1–18 is very uncertain. The stone was probably very badly worn and the copies are unsatisfactory. Nothing can be made of the first two lines and it is idle to speculate what offenders are covered; nor can we restore the standard formula of A. 11 f., B. 27 f., 39–41. In ll. 5–6 copies differ: one suggests, after ἐπανισταῖτο:, τ[ῶ]ι αἰ|[συμ]νήτηι, which would indicate the restoration in l. 4 of a verb such as [ξυνί]ηι. The offence in this case would be collusion with the chief magistrates or revolt against the *aisymnetes*. The alternative copy suggests ἢ δι[αμά]|χηται. The offence in this case would be opposition to the magistrates, and in l. 4 it would be necessary to restore another magistrate or officer, such as [κρίτ]ηι. In ll. 8–28 a number of offences are grouped together, and the intention seems to be to check abuse of power by the αἰσυμνήτης. The αἰσυμνήτης is described by Aristotle as a αἱρετὴ τυραννίς (*Pol.* 1285ᵃ31), but, since he is here (l. 3) co-ordinate with the εὔθυνος, he is more probably a regular magistrate, as he is at Miletus (*SIG* 57. 1). In ll. 10 f. [ἀποκ]τ|ένει[ε has been restored, a warning against arbitrary execution. Then follows the betrayal of city, suburb, or citizens, the encouragement of brigands or pirates, the deliberate misleading of the community in its relations with Greeks or barbarians (presumably Persians are intended). Provision is next made for the public pronouncing of the curse at the Anthesteria, and at the festivals of Herakles and Zeus by οἱ τιμουχέοντες (29), who are almost certainly not office-holders in general but τιμοῦχοι, who are found later at Teos, as in *SIG* 578. 60 (second century B.C.), performing a similar function: ἀναγγελλέτωσαν δὲ οἱ ἑκάστοτε γινόμενοι τιμοῦχοι πρὸς τῆι ἀρᾶι. For other appearances of the title at Teos and elsewhere, see Gottlieb, *Timuchen* (*Sitzb. Heidelberg* 1967). In l. 31 ἐπὶ Δυνάμει, 'by the statue of Dynamis', cf. *SIG* 57. 29, rather than ἐπὶ δυνάμει, 'to the best of their power'. Finally (ll. 35–41) the curse will apply to anyone who breaks these stelai, cuts out the letters, or makes them unreadable. For φοινικήϊα (ll. 37 f.) = letters, reflecting the Phoenician origin of the Greek alphabet, see Hdt. v. 58. ἀφανέας (ll. 38 f.): letters would be regarded as unreadable if the red paint were removed; cf. Thucydides' ἀμυδροῖς γράμμασι (vi. 54. 7) of the letters on the altar of Pisistratus (No. 11).

The date we can only guess from letter forms and content. All the letters except mu seem to have their developed form, which would almost certainly rule out a date earlier than 500: the letters together with the form of punctuation suggest the first half of the fifth century. The content would be less appropriate to a time when Teos was firmly controlled by Persia. It would suit the re-establishment of independence after the battle of Mykale, or a date not much later.

For other examples of public imprecations see Ziebarth, *Hermes* xxx (1895) 57–70, and, for a good discussion of their implications, cf. Vallois, *BCH* xxxviii (1914) 256–71 (commenting on a Delian inscription).

31 (32)

Athenian Relations with Phaselis: 469–450 B.C.

A marble stele, once in the monastery of St. John the Baptist on Mount Hymettus; now in EM.

Ionic writing, stoichedon 22. Phot.: *Ἀρχ. Ἐφ.* 1922, 63.

IG i². 16+; Photiades, *Ἀρχ. Ἐφ.* 1922, 62–5, 79; Wilhelm, *Sitzb. Wien*, ccxvii (5), 60 f.; Hopper, *JHS* lxiii (1943) 39–45; Hignett, *History of the Athenian Constitution*, 397; Wade-Gery, *Essays*, 180–92; *Staatsverträge* 149+; De Ste Croix, *CQ* xi (1961) 100–8; Sealey, *CP* lix (1964) 16–17; Mattingly, *Proc. Afr. Class. Ass.* vii (1964) 37–9; Seager, *Hist.* xv (1966) 508 f.

$$
\begin{aligned}
&[\check{\epsilon}\delta o]\xi\epsilon\nu\ \tau\hat{\eta}\iota\ \beta o\lambda\hat{\eta}\iota\ \kappa\alpha\grave{\iota}\ \tau\hat{\omega}\iota\ \delta[\acute{\eta}]\text{-}\\
&[\mu\omega\iota,\ A]\kappa\alpha\mu\alpha\nu\tau\grave{\iota}s\ [\acute{\epsilon}]\pi\rho\upsilon\tau\acute{\alpha}\nu\epsilon\upsilon\epsilon,\\
&[.\,]\rho\acute{\alpha}\sigma\iota\pi\pi\sigma s\ \acute{\epsilon}\gamma\rho\alpha\mu\mu\acute{\alpha}\tau\epsilon\upsilon\epsilon,\ N\epsilon\text{-}\\
&[\ldots.]\delta\eta s\ \acute{\epsilon}\pi\epsilon\sigma\tau\acute{\alpha}\tau\epsilon\iota,\ \Lambda\acute{\epsilon}\omega[\nu\ \epsilon]\hat{\iota}\text{-}\\
5\quad&[\pi\epsilon\cdot\ \tau o\hat{\iota}]s\ \Phi\alpha\sigma\eta\lambda\acute{\iota}\tau\alpha\iota s\ \tau\grave{o}\ \psi[\acute{\eta}\phi]\iota\text{-}\\
&[\sigma\mu\alpha\ \grave{\alpha}\nu]\alpha\gamma\rho\acute{\alpha}\psi\alpha\iota\cdot\ \check{o}\ \tau\iota\ \check{\alpha}\mu\ \mu\grave{\epsilon}[\nu]\ A\theta\text{-}\\
&[\acute{\eta}\nu\eta\sigma\iota\ \xi]\upsilon[\mu\beta]\acute{o}\lambda\alpha\iota o\nu\ \gamma\acute{\epsilon}\nu\eta\tau\alpha\iota\\
&[\pi\rho\grave{o}s\ \Phi]\alpha\sigma\eta\lambda\iota\tau[\hat{\omega}]\nu\ \tau\iota\nu\alpha,\ A\theta\acute{\eta}[\nu]\eta\text{-}\\
&[\sigma\iota\ \tau\grave{\alpha}s\ \delta]\acute{\iota}\kappa\alpha s\ \gamma\acute{\iota}\gamma\nu\epsilon\sigma\theta\alpha\iota\ \pi\alpha\rho\text{-}\\
10\quad&[\grave{\alpha}\ \tau\hat{\omega}\iota\ \pi o]\lambda\epsilon\mu\acute{\alpha}\rho\chi\omega\iota,\ \kappa\alpha\theta\acute{\alpha}\pi\epsilon\rho\ X\text{-}\\
&[\acute{\iota}o\iota s,\ \kappa\alpha\grave{\iota}]\ \check{\alpha}\lambda\lambda o\theta\iota\ \mu\eta\delta\grave{\epsilon}\ \grave{\alpha}\mu\acute{o}\cdot\ \tau\hat{\omega}\text{-}\\
&[\nu\ \delta\grave{\epsilon}\ \check{\alpha}\lambda\lambda\omega]\nu\ \grave{\alpha}\pi\grave{o}\ \xi\upsilon\mu\beta o\lambda\hat{\omega}\nu\ \kappa\alpha\tau\text{-}\\
&[\grave{\alpha}\ \tau\grave{\alpha}s\ \check{o}\sigma\alpha s]\ \xi\upsilon\mu\beta o\lambda\grave{\alpha}s\ \pi\rho\grave{o}s\ \Phi\alpha\text{-}\\
&[\sigma\eta\lambda\acute{\iota}\tau\alpha s]\ \tau\grave{\alpha}s\ \delta\acute{\iota}\kappa\alpha s\ \acute{\epsilon}\nu[\alpha]\iota\cdot\ \tau\grave{\alpha}s\\
15\quad&[\ldots7\ldots]\tau o[s]\ \grave{\alpha}\phi\epsilon\lambda\hat{\epsilon}\nu.\ \grave{\epsilon}\grave{\alpha}\nu\ \delta\acute{\epsilon}\ \tau\text{-}\\
&[\iota s\ \check{\alpha}\lambda\lambda\eta\ \tau\hat{\omega}]\nu\ \grave{\alpha}\rho\chi\hat{\omega}\nu\ \delta\acute{\epsilon}\xi\eta\tau\alpha\iota\ \delta\text{-}
\end{aligned}
$$

[ἴκην κατὰ] Φασηλιτῶν τινὸς
[....8...., ε]ἰ μὲν καταδικάσ-
[ει, ἡ καταδίκ]η ἄκυρος ἔστω. ἐ-
20 [ὰν δέ τις παραβ]α[ί]νηι τὰ ἐψη-
[φισμένα, ὀφ]ε[λέτ]ω μυρίας δ[ρ]-
[αχμὰς ἱερ]ὰς τῆι Ἀθηναίαι· τ-
[ὸ δὲ ψήφισ]μα τό[δε] ἀναγραψά-
[τω ὁ γραμμ]ατεὺς ὁ τῆς βολῆς
25 [ἐστήληι λιθί]νηι καὶ καταθ-
[έτω ἐμ πόλει τ]έλεσι τοῖς τῶ-
[ν Φασηλιτῶν.] vacat
vacat

The older restorations are fully discussed by Hopper. Wade-Gery's text is mostly followed here. In ll. 3–4 ['O]νγάσιππος or [M]γάσιππος; Wade-Gery suggests Νε‖[λωνί]δης, but the division ἐγραμμάτευεν, E‖[....]δης is also possible. ('E‖[πιμή]δης Leonardos; 'E‖[πι]μήδης Hiller, perhaps by a slip.) In l. 13 for ὅσας (Bannier) cf. No. 94, l. 18; πρὶν (Koehler), Χίων (Sauppe). In l. 15 no alternative to Dittenberger's [δὲ ἐκκλή]το[ς] has yet been found. In l. 18 we would put [παρὰ τόδε] (Photiades), [Ἀθήνησιν] (Wilhelm), [παρόντος] (Kirchner), in that order of probability.

The Ionic lettering, no doubt reflecting the fact that the Phaselites paid for the stone themselves (ll. 26–7; cf. Nos. 47. 38, 52. 60, 87. 36(?), 89. 43, and BSA xlix (1954) 23), misled nineteenth-century editors into dating the decree in the fourth century, until Wilhelm pointed out that the letters themselves were characteristic of the mid-fifth century. (Mattingly's attempt to date it 425–4 because of its short datives is unconvincing.) Phaselis, on the coast of Lycia, not far from the frontier of Pamphylia, by the mediation of the Chians (cf. l. 10) entered the Delian League just before the battle of the Eurymedon (Plut. *Cimon* 12. 3–4). Its merchants carried on a vigorous trade alike with the ports of the Levant and with Greece (cf. Thuc. ii. 69) and were still well known at Athens in the fourth century ([Dem.] xxxv. 1 ff., though the *ex parte* denunciations of their shiftiness and chicanery need not perhaps be taken too seriously).

The inscription occupies a central place in discussions both of inter-state juridical relations and of the history of the Athenian courts. The main provision is clearly that of ll. 6–11. Though interpretations of it based on translating ξυμβόλαιον as 'contract' still survive, roughly giving the meaning that breach of contracts made at Athens must be tried at Athens, Hopper and De Ste Croix rightly argue for a broader meaning, 'cause of action'. The subsidiary doubt is whether the emphasis in ll. 8–10 lies on Ἀθήνησι, or παρὰ τῶι πολεμάρχωι, or both. It is agreed that a privilege must be involved here, since Chios, one of Athens' most important allies, is cited as a model. The apparent emphasis on the repeated Ἀθήνησι has caused difficulty, since compelling a distant ally to come to Athens does not look like a privilege, but Seager shows that, in cases arising at Athens, which are the only ones in question, no real hardship would arise. The emphasis on Ἀθήνησι, then, can be accepted as genuine and a formalization of procedure, but the positive privilege must lie in παρὰ τῶι πολεμάρχωι, always the Athenian court for favoured aliens, perhaps because they needed no special representation there (Wade-Gery), perhaps because of its speed (De Ste Croix) (cf. also Kahrstedt, ·atsgebiet, 281). Translate, then, 'Whatever cause of action arises at Athens involving a Phaselite, the case shall be tried at Athens, in the polemarch's court, just as for the Chians, and nowhere else; other cases shall be tried on treaty terms according to the existing treaty with Phaselis.' For δίκαι ἀπὸ ξυμβολῶν see the passages collected in Hill, *Sources*², Index III. 6. 3 and the articles of Hopper and De Ste Croix.

To this last provision ll. 14–15 make some qualification, extremely obscure even with Dittenberger's restoration. There follow provisions against the breach of the privilege conferred, and the usual publication formula. The important point here lies in the word καταδικάσ|[ει. Wade-Gery argues from it, with some subsidiary support from παρὰ τῶι πολεμάρχωι in ll. 9–10, which he thinks slightly more likely to mean 'at the polemarch's tribunal' than 'in the polemarch's court', that in this inscription Athenian magistrates are still actually giving judgement themselves rather than merely acting as presiding magistrates on the classical pattern, the first evidence for which is perhaps the part played by Athena in the trial in the *Eumenides* (458 B.C.). (Sealey denies this inference from καταδικάσ[ει, citing Plato, *Laws* xii. 958 c, but the whole stress on the magistrate here seems against him.)

In Wade-Gery's view the change by which the magistrates lost this power must have been part of the reforms of Ephialtes, and accordingly he dates the decree between 469 and 462. Hignett had in fact taken the same point earlier, but saw no reason to attribute the reform to Ephialtes, though he admitted that it could not be more than a very few years later. This argument for dating the decree seems sound. It must take precedence over, though it is not necessarily incompatible with, the argument that the full classical decree-prescript of ll. 1–5 presupposes a reorganization of the Council by Ephialtes, a reorganization which has no literary support, and, in our judgement, no particular intrinsic probability (Haggard, *TAPA* lvii (1926) xxxi f.; Kahrstedt, *Klio*, xxxiii (1940) 10). The argument of Oliver

(*Hesp.* ii (1933) 496 f.) that the decree is to be dated *c.* 450 on the identification of its proposer Leon with the [Λ]έον who proposed *SEG* x. 15 (Hill, *Sources*[2], B 29, *Staatsverträge*, 150, hardly more closely datable than 460–450) carries little weight. That the decree is later than the entry of Phaselis into the League seems certain, but we see no reason to deny that the earlier agreement of l. 13 could have been of longer standing; συμβολαί do not presuppose alliance.

32 (25)

Halicarnassian Law concerning disputed Property: (?) 465–450 B.C.

A marble stele, copied at Halicarnassus (Budrum) by the Earl of Charlemont in 1749. Later it was cut in half vertically to be used for the jambs of a window, and in the process two to four letters were lost from the middle of each line. There was another inscription on the right-hand side of the stele, but only a few letters are legible. Rediscovered by Sir Charles Newton, the stele is now in the British Museum.

Ionic letters. T is used for σσ in ll. 2, 6, 16 and probably in 7; for this letter sampi see introduction to No. 30. It is probably going out of use in Halicarnassus; contrast l. 2 with l. 41. O has a dot in the centre, as has Ω in ll. 41–5. To distinguish it from O the dot in theta may have been coloured. Phot.: *Pal. Soc. Facs.*, Series 2, Pl. 62; facs.: *Imag.* 23, 14. Facs. of Charlemont's copy, *BMI* iv, p. 50.

BMI 886 (iv, p. 49); *SIG* 45; Ruehl, *Philol.* xli (1882) 54–71; Valeton, *Mnem.* xxxvi (1908) 289–334, xxxvii (1909) 60–6; *DGE* 744; Buck 2.

```
        τάδε ὁ σύλλο[γ]ος ἐβολεύσατο
        ὁ ἈλικαρναΤέ[ω]ν καὶ Σαλμακι-
        τέων καὶ Λύγδαμις ἐν τῆι ἱερῆ[ι]
        ἀγορῆι, μηνὸς Ἑρμαιῶνος πέμ-
   5    πτηι ἰσταμένο, ἐπὶ Λέοντος πρυ-
        ταν[εύον]τος τô ᾽ΟαΤαΤιος κα-
        [ὶ] Σα[ρυΤ]ώλλο τô Θεκυίλω νε-
        [ωπ]οί[ο, πρ]ὸς μνήμονας· μὴ παρ[α]-
        δίδο[σθαι] μήτε γῆν μήτε οἰκ[ί]-
   10   [α] τοῖς μνήμοσιν ἐπὶ Ἀπολλω-
        νίδεω τô Λυγδάμιος μνημονε-
```

υοντος καὶ Παναμύω τô Κασβώ-
λλιος καὶ Σαλμακιτέων μνη-
μονευόντων Μεγαβάτεω τô Ἀ-
15 φυάσιος καὶ Φορμίωνος τô Π[α]-
νυάΤιος. ἢν δέ τις θέληι δικάζε-
σθαι περὶ γῆς ἢ οἰκίων, ἐπικαλ[έ]-
τω ἐν ὀκτωκαίδεκα μησὶν ἀπ᾽ ὅτ[ε]
ὁ ἄδος ἐγένετο· νόμωι δὲ κατάπ[ε]-
20 ρ νῦν ὀρκῶ{ι}σ⟨α⟩ι τὸς δικαστάς· ὅ τ[ι]
ἂν οἱ μνήμονες εἰδέωσιν, τοῦ ᾽
καρτερὸν ἔναι. ἢν δέ τις ὕστερον
ἐπικαλῆι τούτο τô χρόνο τῶν
ὀκτωκαίδεκα μηνῶν, ὅρκον ἔναι τ-
25 ῶι νεμομένωι τὴν γῆν ἢ τὰ οἰκ-
[ί]α, ὁρκôν δὲ τὸς δικαστὰς ἡμί-
[ε]κτον δεξαμένος· τὸν δὲ ὅρκον εἶ-
[ν]αι παρεόντος τô ἐνεστηκότος. κ-
αρτερὸς δ᾽ εἶναι γῆς καὶ οἰκίων οἵτινες
30 τότ᾽ εἶχον ὅτε Ἀπολλωνίδης καὶ Πανα-
μύης ἐμνημόνευον, εἰ μὴ ὕστερο-
ν ἀπεπέρασαν. τὸν νόμον τοῦτον
ἢν τις θέληι συγχέαι ἢ προθῆτα-
[ι] ψῆφον ὥστε μὴ εἶναι τὸν νόμο-
35 ν τοῦτον, τὰ ἔοντα αὐτô πεπρήσθω
καὶ τὠπόλλωνος εἶναι ἱερὰ καὶ α-
ὐτὸν φεύγεν αἰεί· ἢν δὲ μὴ ἦι αὐτῶι ἄξια δέκα στατήρων, αὐτὸν [π]-
επρῆσθαι ἐπ᾽ ἐξαγωγῆι καὶ μη[δ]-
40 αμὰ κάθοδον εἶναι ἐς Ἁλικαρν-
ησσόν. Ἁλικαρνασσέων δὲ τῶς σ-
υμπάντων τούτωι ἐλεύθερον ἔ[ἶ]-
ναι, ὃς ἂν ταῦτα μὴ παραβαίηι κατό-
περ τὰ ὅρκια ἔταμον καὶ ὡς γέγραπτ-
45 αι ἐν τῶι Ἀπολλω[νί]ωι, ἐπικαλῆν.

l. 7: Ὀεκυῖλω is a possible alternative (*Berl. Phil. Woch.* viii. 1469).
In ll. 8–10, many editors prefer οι[ο τ]ὸς μνήμονας μὴ παρα|διδό[ναι] μήτε
γῆν...; but after οι Charlemont marked three letter-spaces and the space

on the stone requires them. Hirschfeld rightly insisted on παρα|διδο[σθαι]; three letters only would be too widely spaced.   l. 18: At the end of the line there is room for only one missing letter.   l. 19: ἄδος, from ἀνδάνω, equivalent to Latin *placitum*.   l. 20: On the stone ΟΡΚΛΙΣ...Σ; Charlemont, ΟΡΚΟΙΣΙΤΟΣ. Hirschfeld and Bannier read ὀρκῶ{ι}σι; with Dittenberger, Tod, and most editors we prefer ὀρκῶ{ι}σ⟨α⟩ι. l. 22: καρτερὸν = κύριον; the more normal sense in l. 29, κ|αρτερὸς γῆς.

This measure, variously called βούλευμα (l. 1), ἄδος (l. 19), νόμος (l. 32), provides a change, temporary or permanent, in legal procedure concerning property disputes. The first clause provides that no land or houses shall be handed over to a board of *mnemones* in the year of Apollonides, who presumably are either about to enter or have just entered office. Existing procedure, however, in which the *mnemones* play a decisive part, may be used for a period of eighteen months, and in these cases the jurors are to take an oath that 'what the *mnemones* know shall be binding'. When the eighteen months have expired those who held the property in the year of Apollonides are to be regarded as the legal owners, and if their title is disputed they are only required to substantiate their claim by an oath. Strong penalties are laid down against anyone who by constitutional or unconstitutional methods tries to reverse this law, and any Halicarnassian who abides by this law may bring a case, according to oath taken and agreements recorded in the temple of Apollo.

The law was passed by the 'joint meeting of citizens from Halicarnassus and Salmakis, together with Lygdamis'. Salmakis was probably a Carian settlement subsequently merged in Halicarnassus, but at the time of this document each of the two communities had its own officers. Together, however, they were Ἁλικαρνασσεῖς οἱ σύμπαντες (l. 41). Suidas (s.v. Ἡρόδοτος) says that Lygdamis was grandson of the colourful Artemisia who commanded a small contingent in Xerxes' fleet at Salamis. Herodotus, who opposed Lygdamis, had to leave Halicarnassus in exile, and his uncle, the epic poet Panyassis, was put to death. Later Herodotus helped to expel the tyrant, but he fell out of favour and joined the Athenian colony of Thurii (established in 443). It is naturally tempting to associate our inscription with these events, and this was even easier when ἄδος (l. 19) was thought to be part of κάθοδος. The Lygdamis of the prescript was clearly the tyrant of Herodotus' day, and he could also be the father of Apollonides the *mnemon* (l. 10); Panyassis, the father of Phormio, another *mnemon* (ll. 15 f.), could be Herodotus' uncle, giving representation to supporters and opponents of tyranny in the office. Various inferences were drawn on such assumptions: that the law reflected the pending expulsion of Lygdamis, that it gave substance to an amnesty, that it marked the defeat of his opponents by Lygdamis.

Ruehl emphasized the weaknesses of some of these assumptions. Panyassis was a common name in Halicarnassus (cf. *SIG* 46), nor was Lygdamis rare. There was nothing, he thought, in the inscription to suggest a settlement after political crisis. The law referred not to any special category of property but to all property. Ruehl's conclusion, supported by Dittenberger (*SIG* 45), is not persuasive. If a permanent change of procedure is intended, eliminating the role of the *mnemones* in property disputes, why is provision made for one year only, and why is there such emphasis on penalties for any attempt to reverse the law? Valeton seems nearer the mark in inferring that opponents of Lygdamis have gone into exile and that their properties left ownerless are in the hands of the *mnemones*. This law is to discourage any attempt to recover their lands. The main function of *mnemones* according to Aristotle (*Pol.* 1321^{b}39) was to act as registrars, but παραδίδοσθαι in ll. 8–9 cannot mean merely the handing over of details for registration; it is reasonable to believe that in certain circumstances they had charge of ownerless property. On any interpretation the phrasing of the decree is obscure: 'the circumstances were too well known to the legislators to call for precise and detailed formulation' (Tod).

Only an approximate date can be given. It has been widely held that the tyranny must have ended not later than 454, for Ἁλικαρνασσεῖς are recorded in the tribute-quota list of 454–3. This entry, however, is not necessarily inconsistent with Lygdamis' being in control, nor should we regard tyranny as being incompatible with membership of the Athenian alliance (two Carian tyrants, Tymnes and Pigres, are specifically named, *ATL* i. 446). Lygdamis' accession also is difficult to date. If Artemisia's son was too young to command at Salamis (Hdt. vii. 99. 1), her grandson could hardly have become tyrant before 460. More probably Suidas is wrong and Lygdamis was either nephew or son.

Though the immediate historical context must remain uncertain, several interesting inferences are secure. The Ionic script discredits Suidas' statement that Herodotus adopted the Ionic dialect in Samos, and the proper names show that there was a strong admixture of Carian blood in Halicarnassus. Megabates son of Aphyasis (ll. 14 f.) suggests personal links with Persians. It was easier for Herodotus than for most Greeks to be φιλοβάρβαρος.

33 (26)

Casualty-list of the Erechtheid Tribe:
460 or 459 B.C.

Marble stele (the 'Nointel Marble') from Athens; now in the Louvre.
Attic letters, ΒꚂRϟY. Ll. 62–70 are added in another hand: Ρ 62, 66;
Ρ 68, 69; Ѵ 64; Υ 65, 68. Φρῦνος (ΦΡΣ) is added in a hand different from
that of l. 67. Ll. 127–9, which are inscribed in larger letters than the rest,
form a single entry. Stoichedon. Facs.: *IG* i. 433 (not completely reliable).
IG i². 929.

'Ε   ρ   ε   χ   θ   ε   ι̌   δ   ο   ς

ḥοίδε ⋮ ἐν τῶι ⋮ πολέμοι ⋮ ἀπέθανον ⋮ ἐν Κύπροι ⋮ ἐν Αἰγ[ύ]-
πτοι ⋮ ἐν Φοινίκει [⋮] ἐν Ἁλιεῦσιν [⋮] ἐν Αἰγίνει ⋮ Μεγαροῖ

τ   ὁ   α   ὐ   τ   ὁ   ἐ   ν   ι   α   υ   τ   ὁ

5	[σ]τ[ρα]τεγὸν		Φάνυλλος	130	Ἄκρυπτος
	Φ[....]χος		Χ[..]νιος		Τιμοκράτες
	Π[αντ]αλέον		Ε[ὐγ]είτον		Ἀρχέλας
	Πολύστρατος		Ἄλ[κ]ιππος		Εὐθυκράτες
	[Δρ]ακοντίδες	75	Λυ[σ]ικλῆς		Πατροκλείδε[ς]
10	..μόστ[ρ]ατος		Κέ[λ]ευσος	135	Ἀλκμεονίδες
	..μέας		Εὐ[θ]ύδεμος		Γλαύκον
	..κλείδες		Δίκαιος		Δεμόνικος
	..κράτες		Φιλ[ί]νος		Ἀναχσίδορος
	[Χα]ιρέδεμος	80	Καλλικλῆς		Γλαύκον
15	..εσίας		Ναυσικλῆς	140	Προκλῆς
	..έσανδρος		Τ[ι]μεσίθεος		Ἀντιφὸν
	[Λυ]κόφρον		[Μν]εσιγένες		Ἀναχσίλα[ς]
	[Ἀ]πολλόδορος		Π[ο]λυκλῆς		Ἀρχέπολι[ς]
	Ἀριστοτέλες	85	Ἀλ[ε]χσίας		Καλλέας
20	[Π]ροτίας		Ἀμύδριππος	145	Θαλίαρχο[ς]
	Δράκαλος		Ἀπολλόδορος		Φιλόνιχο[ς]
	Μεχανίον		Γοργίας		Εὐκλείδε[ς]
	Φιλιστίδες		Νόθαρχος		Διόδορος
	Τιμογένες	90	Παρμον[ί]δες		Νίκαρχος
25	Χαρίσανδρος		Βάκον	150	'Επιτέλες

	Col 1		Col 2		Col 3
	[Μ]ενέκλες		Πίθον		Κύβον
	[Μ]ελάνοπος		Λυσίας		Χ[α]ιρίας
	Κλεόνβροτος		Σόστρατος		Δεμέτριος
	Ἀριστοκλείδες	95	Φιλῖνος		Ἀρκεσίλας
30	Θοκυδίδες		Φίλαιθος	155	Εὔθοινος
	Εὐθύδεμος		Φιλέταιρος		Δεμέτριος
	[Κ]αλλικράτες		Σοτέλες		Γόργον
	Ἀφσέφες		Λυσίας		Στράτ[ο]ν
	[Ἀ]ριστείδες	100	Ἀριστογένες		Ἀρισ[τ]οφάνε[ς]
35	[Φ]ιλόδεμος		Φιλῖνος	160	Γλαύκον
	[Κ]εφ[ι]σόδοτος		Διότιμος		Φυσ[ον]ίδες
	[Σ]όφιλος		Καλλονίδες		hαγ[ν]όδεμος
	[Ἀ]ντιμένες		Καλλίχσενος		Διο[κ]λês
	['Ε]παίνετος	105	Δεινίας		Φανόστρατο[ς]
40	'Εργαῖος		Σμίκυθος	165	Εὐμένιος
	Διογένες		Τιμόδεμος		Θε[ό]δορος
	Φρῦνος		Λῦσις		[Εὐρ]ύλεος
	[Κ]τεσιάδες		Ἀκεσίας		[Κέ]ρδον
	[Κ]όροιβος	110	'Επιχάρες		['Επ]ιχάρες
45	[Κ]ράτυλλος		hιερόνυμος	170	Ε[ὔ]δοχσος
	[Σ]υνφέρμιος		Ἀναχσίλας		Π[ο]λύζελος
	[Ν]ικίας		Χαιρίας		Γ[λ]αυκίας
	Λυσικλείδες		hερακλείδες		'Επιγένες
	Φρούραρχος	115	Ἀγασικλês		Ἀντιχάρες
50	Χαρ[ίσ]ανδρος		Ἀλκâς	175	Φιλιστίδε[ς]
	'Ο[λυμ]πιάρατος		Κεφισόδοτος		Ἀμφικλείδ[ες]
	Σ[. . . .]ος		Καλλικλês		Φροῦρος
	Μνε[σ]ίφιλος		Κεφισόδορος		Τίτον
	Σοσίας	120	Νομένιος		Εὔβιος
55	Ἀρχῖνος		Χσενόφιλος	180	Καλλίβ[ιος]
	Λυκῖνος		hυπέρβιος		Σμίκρο[ς]
	Καλλίας		hάγνον		Νεαῖος
	Μνεσιγένες		Πολύχσενος		'Εργοτέ[λες]
	Σίκον	125	'Ερχσιμένες		Φοκίον
60	Ἀμφικέδες		Νίκον	185	Ἄραιθ[ος]
	Χσένυλλος		*vacat*		*vacat*
	vacat				

στρατεγός: ἐν Αἰγύπτοι
  ἱπποδάμας
  Εὐθύμαχος: Τελένικος
65 Εὔμελος: μάντις
  Ἀνδροσθένες
  τοχσόται: Φρῦνος
  Ταῦρος
  Θεόδορος
70 Ἀλεχσίμαχος

ll. 5–6: Bradeen suggests $[\sigma]\tau[\rho a]\tau\epsilon\gamma\grave{o}\nu \mid \phi[\acute{v}\lambda a\rho]\chi os$, a phylarch who died while acting as general. The restoration generally accepted in l. 6 is $\Phi[\rho\acute{v}\nu\iota]$-$\chi os$; $\Phi[\acute{v}\lambda a\rho]\chi os$ is also possible.

Normally the casualties of all ten tribes are inscribed on the same stele or on a series of adjoining stelai with a common title (*Hesp.* xxxiii (1964) 26). This exceptional record of a single tribe is probably due to the exceptional number of its casualties, emphasized in the heading ($\tau\hat{o}$ $a\dot{v}\tau\hat{o}$ $\dot{\epsilon}\nu\iota a\upsilon\tau\hat{o}$); as in other casualty lists, the period covered is almost certainly the campaigning season rather than the archon's year. At this time the Athenians were fighting on two fronts, against the Persians and against the Peloponnesians. The last three engagements are recorded in chronological order (cf. Thuc. i. 105); it is a reasonable inference that this applies also to the first three, but it would be less safe to assume that all six engagements were in true sequence. The date is controversial, but the most likely year for fighting to occur successively in Cyprus, Egypt, and Phoenicia is the first year of Athens' support of the Egyptian revolt led by Inaros. Thucydides tells us that the Athenians had already dispatched 200 ships to Cyprus when they accepted Inaros' appeal for help. The Athenians then left Cyprus and proceeded to Egypt (Thuc. i. 104. 2: $\mathring{\eta}\lambda\theta o\nu$ $\mathring{a}\pi o\lambda\iota\pi\acute{o}\nu\tau\epsilon s$ $\tau\mathring{\eta}\nu$ $K\acute{v}\pi\rho o\nu$). No literary source mentions fighting in Phoenicia at this time, but if, as many think, the main part of the fleet returned from Egypt after winning control of the Nile, a raid on Phoenicia is easy to accept. If the main fleet stayed in Egypt, the raid on Phoenicia could have been made by a small detachment. Accepting 454, the year of the transference of the treasury from Delos to Athens, as the year of the final disaster in Egypt, the first year will be 460, or possibly 459 (for discussions of the chronology see *ATL* iii. 174 f.; P. Salmon, *La Politique égyptienne d'Athènes*, 156 ff.).

The list includes two generals (ll. 5–6, 63). Hippodamas may have succeeded Ph[ryni]chos in the summer, or they may have been elected together (double representation of a tribe being not uncommon later;

Hignett, *Athenian Constitution*, 348–53). Ph[ryni]chos is described as στρατηγῶν rather than στρατηγός, which is unexpected. It may be that he had an acting command though not formally general for the year. A better suggestion is that στρατηγῶν is genitive (Bannier, *Berl. Phil. Woch.* xxxvii. 351). There is one seer (ll. 128–9), four citizen archers (ll. 67–70: see Wernicke, *Hermes*, xxvi (1891) 71) and 170 others.

These men died ἐν τôι πολέμοι. In a casualty list of the forties, men were listed as dying ἐν τοῖς ἄλλοις πολέμοις, a number of separate wars (No. 48). Did the Athenians consider or want others to consider that the campaigns in Egypt and in Greece were both parts of a single war, in which they were fighting the Peloponnesians to defend themselves against the stab in the back while they championed Greeks against barbarians?

For the Athenian casualty-lists see A. Brueckner, *Ath. Mitt.* xxxv (1910) 183 ff.; Bradeen, *Hesp.* xxxiii (1964) 16–62.

34

Samians fight in Egypt: 460–454 B.C.

White marble block, apparently a statue-base, found in the Heraion at Samos, and now in the excavation-house there.

Developed Ionic letters, not stoichedon. Phot.: *Klio* xxxii (1939) 290, whence *LSAG*, Pl. 63. 21.

Peek, *Klio* xxxii (1939) 289–306; *LSAG* 331, no. 21; Kienitz, *Die politische Geschichte Ägyptens*, 72; Salmon, *La Politique égyptienne d'Athènes*, 149 f.

> [...] ἔργο πολλοὶ [- - - - traces - - - -]
> [Μέμ]φιος ἀμφ' ἐρατῆς νηυσὶν ἔθηκ[ε μάχην]
> [θο]ῦρος Ἄρης Μῆδων τε καὶ Ἑλλήν[ων, Σάμιοι δὲ]
> [νῆ]ας Φοινίκων πέντε τε καὶ δ[έκ' ἕλον·]
> 5 [...] Ἡγησα[γ]όρην Ζωϊλότο καὶ [- - -]
> - - - - - - - - - - - - - - - - - - traces - - - - -

The traces in l. 1 are consistent with Peek's preferred restoration [τόδ'] ἔργο πολλοὶ πάρα [μάρ]τυρε[s, εὖτ' ἐπὶ Νείλωι].   l. 5: [ἀλλ'] Peek.

Peek argues convincingly that this inscription is of the middle of the fifth century and that the only likely location for a Samian victory over Phoenician ships which will fit the beginning of l. 2 is Memphis,

attested by Thuc. i. 104. 2 (καὶ ἀναπλεύσαντες ἀπὸ θαλάσσης ἐς τὸν
Νεῖλον τοῦ τε ποταμοῦ κρατοῦντες καὶ τῆς Μέμφιδος τῶν δύο μερῶν πρὸς
τὸ τρίτον μέρος ὃ καλεῖται Λευκὸν τεῖχος ἐπολέμουν) as a centre of the
operations of Athens' Egyptian expedition. A sea-fight in the early
stages of the expedition is attested by Ktesias, 63 (Gilmore): ἐνίκησεν
Ἴναρος καὶ κατὰ θάλατταν, Χαριτιμίδου εὐδοκιμήσαντος, ὃς τῶν ἐξ
Ἀθηνῶν τετταράκοντα νεῶν ἐχρημάτιζε ναύαρχος, καὶ πεντήκοντα Περσῶν
νῆες, αἱ μὲν εἴκοσι αὐτοῖς ἀνδράσιν ἐλήφθησαν, αἱ δὲ τριάκοντα διεφθάρησαν.
If the reference to Memphis is sound, the battle recorded in our
epigram would have been actually on the Nile (τοῦ τε ποταμοῦ κρατοῦντες, Thuc.) and Peek may be right to explain the fact that
Ktesias has lower numbers for the Greek fleet than Thucydides'
implied 200 ships by supposing that not all the force had sailed up
the Nile, even if it had all left Cyprus. The question of the size of
the Athenian force in Egypt and its losses has often been discussed,
most recently by Salmon, op. cit. 151–8. Kienitz is doubtful about
this interpretation of the inscription and Salmon refuses to accept it,
but we see no other occasion for our text which is remotely probable.
There certainly were Athenian allies on the expedition (Thuc., loc.
cit.). Though they were here still fighting against the Persian Empire,
and not against Greeks as in No. 36, the League was sharing the
varied strains of Athens' commitments.

We cannot be sure of Hegesagoras' part in the epigram. Peek's
suggestion that he played a particularly glorious role in the battle
and was portrayed by a statue, as his countryman Maiandrios seems
to have been for his services at Eurymedon (Hill, Sources², B 123), is
at least fairly probable. Ζωΐλοτος is a known Samian name, here
allowed to cut across the metre.

35 (28)

Argives killed at Tanagra: (?) 458 B.C.

Fourteen marble fragments from a pedimental stele: *a* and *b* were found
on the Acropolis, *f*, *g*, *h*, *i*, *j*, *k*, *l*, and *n* in the Agora, *m* in the Kerameikos.
a, *b*, *d*, and *f–n* are in EM, *c* in the British Museum, *e* in private possession
in Athens.

Early Argive writing (see *LSAG* 164, Argos, 30), stoichedon except the
epigram. Photographs of *a–f*, *i*, *m* in *Kerameikos*, iii, Pl. 10–11; of *c*, *f–l*, in
Hesp. xiv (1945) 139–43; of *n* in *Hesp.* xxi (1952) Pl. 89. Facsimile of the
upper part in *Hesp.* xxi, 354 (whence *LSAG*, Pl. 29, 30).

Meritt, *Hesp.* xiv. 134–47+; *Hesp.* xxi. 351–5; *GVI* 15.

n

Ἀργε[ίον·]

[τοί]δ' ἔθ[ανον Ταν]άγραι Λακ[εδαιμο]-
[νίον hυπὸ χερσ]ί, πένθο[ς δ' ἔτλασα-

f		*a*		*d*		
hυλλεês		35 [.]έτριος	70 [...7....]ος		Ἀντ[- -]	
[Π]όλλιχος		[Ἀ]ριστίον	- - - - -		Θε[- -]	
5 [Ἀλ]κισθένες		[Σ]φενδονίον	- - - - -		E[..]λ[..]s	
[...7....]ος		[Λ]υκῖνος	- - - - -	115	Φοῖνιξ *c*	
- - - -		ϝαναξίλας	- - - - -		[Φ]αλέας	
lacuna	40	[Δ]έρκετος	75 - - - - -		[Β]ράχας	
		['Εχ]εμένες	- - - - -		Τελέσστας	
		[..5...]ις	- - - - -		Δαμοφάνες	
		- - - -	[- - -]ος	120	Θυμάρες	
		lacuna	- - - - -	*g*	Δαῑκλês	
			80 - - - - -		Σύλιχος	
			[- - -]s		Δέρκετος	
			lacuna		Λυροδόρκας	
				125	Κλέον	
					Κρατιάδας	
					[Ἀ]ισχύλος	
					[Εὐ]αρχί[δ]ας	
					lacuna	

We print here only those fragments of which the relation to the top is certain.

Among the Athenian allies who fought at Tanagra were a thousand Argives (Thuc. i. 107. 5). Those of them who fell in the battle were buried in the Kerameikos (Paus. i. 29. 8). Earlier editors assigned some or all of these fragments to the Cleonaeans who accompanied them and were buried separately (Paus. i. 29. 7), but Meritt has shown that we have here a single stele, commemorating the Argives who fell, perhaps up to 400 in number, listed by the four Argive tribes (l. 3), and cut by a stone-cutter who miscalculated the space available for the epigram. For πένθο[ς δ' ἔτλασαν] cf. Pind. *Isthm*. vii. 51, perhaps said of the Thebans who fell in this same battle.

36 (27)

Thank-offering for the Victory of Tanagra: (?) 458 B.C.

Three contiguous fragments of a marble stele found at Olympia; now in the Olympia Museum.

Corinthian letters, *LSAG* 129 f., 132 (38). Phot.: *LSAG*, Pl. 21. 38, Guarducci, *Epigrafia Greca*, i. 470 fig. 243; facs.: *Imag.* 44. 11.

Ol. v. 253; Heiberg, *Hermes* xlvi (1911) 458–60; Hitzig–Blümner, *Pausanias*, ii. 321; Guarducci, *Rend. Pont. Acc.* xii. 125–32, *Epigrafia Greca*, i. 469–72.

[Ναὸς μὲν φιάλαν χρυσέα]ν ἔχει, ἐγ δὲ [Τανάγρας]
[τοὶ Λακεδαιμόνιοι συμ]μαχία τ' ἀν[έθεν]
[δῶρον ἀπ' Ἀργείων καὶ Ἀθα]ναίων καὶ ['Ιάνων],
[τὰν δεκάταν νίκας εἴν]εκα τοῦ πο[λέμου].
5 - - - - - - - - - - - - - - - - - - Κορ[ινθ]ι - - - - - -
- - - - - - - - - - - - - - - - - ρ - - - - - - - -

After speaking of the Nike and the akroteria which crowned the eastern pediment of the temple of Zeus at Olympia (cf. No. 74), Pausanias proceeds: ὑπὸ δὲ τῆς Νίκης τὸ ἄγαλμα ἀσπὶς ἀνάκειται χρυσῆ, Μέδουσαν τὴν Γοργόνα ἔχουσα ἐπειργασμένην. τὸ ἐπίγραμμα δὲ τὸ ἐπὶ τῇ ἀσπίδι τούς τε ἀναθέντας δηλοῖ καὶ καθ' ἥντινα αἰτίαν ἀνέθεσαν. λέγει γὰρ δὴ οὕτω . . . (v. 10. 4). The fragments can be restored from Pausanias' text, but there are differences. Pausanias has in l. 4 the Doric genitive τῶ πολέμω where our text, in Corinthian script, has the ου diphthong; and Pausanias does not quote the last two lines of our text. The easiest explanation is that there were two inscriptions, one 'on the ἀσπίς' (a much more natural translation of ἐπὶ τῇ ἀσπίδι than 'relating to', accepted by Tod), which was set up over the pediment, the other on a free-standing stele. The ἀσπίς was a gilded convex shield with apotropaic Medusa's head, bowl-like in form and so sometimes called φιάλη (for this interchange see Athenaeus, x. 433c). The relevance of the last two lines is not clear. There is not room for a list of Sparta's allies, and the fact that the surviving text is in Corinthian, whereas the text on the shield which Pausanias copied presumably was not, should be significant. Heiberg suggested that there was a contrast between the general dedication by the alliance of a gold bowl within the temple and a Corinthian dedication of a gilded shield on the temple. This might be a tenable hypothesis if Pausanias had not apparently seen only a four-line epigram. Guarducci is more persuasive in regarding the shield as the general dedication and inferring a separate dedication also by the Corinthians.

Argives fought with Athens at Tanagra (see No. 35). The Ionians of the epigram are contingents from Athens' allies (Thuc. i. 107. 5: καὶ τῶν ἄλλων ξυμμάχων ὡς ἕκαστοι).

37 (31)

Alliance of Athens with Egesta: (?) 458–7 B.C.

Two fragments of a marble stele found on the Acropolis; now in EM.

Developed Attic letters except Ϟ, Ρ. Stoichedon 48, but the letters of the title in l. 1 are larger than the rest. Phot.: *Hesp.* xvii (1948) Pl. 24 (larger fragment); *TAPA* lxxv (1944) 13, *Κώκαλος* vi (1960) Pl. 17–18 (smaller frag.).

IG i². 19, with 20, ll. 1, 2; Raubitschek, *TAPA* lxxv (1944) 10–12; Woodhead, *Hesp.* xvii (1948) 59 f.; *Staatsverträge* 139; E. Roos, *Opuscula Atheniensia*, iv (1962) 8–29; Mattingly, *Hist.* xii (1963) 267 f.

a　[φιλία καὶ χσυνμαχία Ἀθεναίον καὶ] Ἐγεσταί[ον]
　　[ἔδοχσεν τῆι βολῆι καὶ τ]ο͂[ι δέμοι, ...6...ὶς] ἐ[π]ρυτάνευε, [....]
　　[- - - - ἐγραμμάτευε, - - - -]ο[....ἐπεστάτε, ἅβρ]ον ἔρχε, Ἀρ[χέ]δε-
　　[μος εἶπε·...............32................] ταὐτὸ / [...]
5　[.........19..........]ιο[.........18.........]α [hοίτινες]
　　[ἐχσορκόσοσι ἀφικόμενοι ἐς Ἔγεσταν hελέσθα]ι τὸ[ν] δ[ἐ͂μον δἐ]-
　　[κα ἄνδρας αὐτίκα μάλα· π]ερ[ὶ δὲ τ]ο....π.. [h]ιερὰ hόσομ[περ..]
　　[.........19..........]ὸν hό[ρκ]ο[ν ὀμνύ]ρα[ι. hόπ]ος δ' ἂν ὁμό[σοσ]-
　　[ιν hάπαντες, hοι στρατ]εγοὶ ἐπιμελεθέν[τον παρ]αγγ[ελ..5...]
10　[.......14......μετὰ τ]ὸν ho[ρ]κοτὸν hόπ[ος....]ς Ἐγ[εσταιο.]
　　[.....11......τὸ δὲ φσέ]φισμα τόδε καὶ τὸν [hόρκ]ο[ν] ἀνα[γράφσα]-
　　[ι ἐστέλει λιθίνει ἐμ π]όλει τὸν γραμματέα τἐς βολἐς· [hοι δὲ π]-
　　[ολεταὶ ἀπομισθοσάντ]ον· ho[ι] δὲ κολακρέται δό[ν]το[ν τὸ ἀργύρ]-
　　[ιον· καλέσαι δὲ καὶ ἐπ]ὶ χσένια τὲν πρεσβείαν τὸν Ἐ[γεσταίον]
15　[ἐς πρυτανεῖον ἐς τὸν] νομιζόμενον χρόνον. ꟾ Εὔφε[μος εἶπε· τὰ]
　　[μὲν ἄλλα καθάπερ τῆι β]ολἐι· το δὲ λοιπὸν ἐπειδὰν π[ρέσβες ἔλ]-
　　[θοσιν ἀπ' Ἐγεσταίον ho κ]ἐρυχς προσαγ[έτο.......15........]
　　[...........22...........τὸ]ς π[ρέσβες - - οτ π[ρυτάνες
　　　　　　　　　　　　lacuna
b　[πρέσβες] Ἐγεσταί[ον hοίδε τὸν hόρκον ὄμοσαν......12......]
　　[...7....]ικίνο Ἀπ[.................34.................]
　　　　　　　　　　　vacat

　　The larger fragment, the surface of which is extremely worn, gives the main part of a decree concerning alliance with Egesta, and the beginning of an amendment. A smaller fragment, previously thought to be from a different stele, was shown by Raubitschek in 1943 to belong: it gives parts of the names of Egestan envoys and, below a vacant space, the beginning of another decree concerning Halikyai (*Hesp.* xii (1943) 18 n. 29; more fully in *TAPA* lxxv (1944) 10–12; Woodhead, *Hesp.* xvii (1948) 59 f.; Manni Piraino, Κώκαλος vi (1960) 58–70), in a different and later hand.

The details of the Egesta decree cannot be recovered, but provision is almost certainly made for the exchange of oaths, and for the setting up of a stele on the Acropolis recording 'this decree and the oath' (cf. No. 52, ll. 57–8). The amendment starts before the terms of the oath are given; they were probably recorded separately, on another stele, or after the end of the decree and before the envoys' names.

The date of Athens' alliance with Egesta is controversial, depending on the restoration of an archon's name which ends in *ON* (l. 3). Until recently 454–3, when Ariston was archon, was generally accepted; for under that year Diodorus (xi. 86. 2) records a war in which Egesta was engaged. The text is unsatisfactory and has been emended to refer to a war between Egesta allied with Halikyai and Selinus: κατὰ δὲ τὴν Σικελίαν Ἐγεσταίοις καὶ Ἁλικυαίοις (for mss. Λιλυβαίοις, Λιλυβαίταις) ἐνέστη πόλεμος ⟨πρὸς Σελινουντίους⟩. Raubitschek, however, in 1944 (*TAPA* lxxv, 10 n. 3), recalling Köhler's tentative report of a curving stroke before omicron, and noting on his squeeze a vertical stroke in the preceding space, restored ἡά]βρον. These readings were challenged by Pritchett (*AJA* lix (1955) 58 f.), who found no trace of a curving stroke and claimed that the vertical stroke was wrongly placed to be part of beta, and was more probably not part of a letter. Meritt supported Raubitschek's interpretation of the vertical (*BCH* lxxxviii (1964) 413–15). Meanwhile Mattingly (*Hist.* xii (1963) 268 f.) had advocated an entirely different context, restoring Ἀντ]ιφῶν, archon of 418–17, shortly before the great expedition against Syracuse, which was partly instigated by Egesta. We have not been able to confirm a curving stroke, and we still feel doubtful whether the vertical is part of a letter. Of the three dates we would rule out 418–17, because we know of no dated Ϟ after 445, and no Ρ after 438–7 (Meiggs, *JHS* lxxxvi (1966) 92). It is also unlikely that Thucydides would have failed to mention it in his introduction to the Sicilian expedition, had Egesta exchanged oaths with Athens so recently. Diodorus' evidence for the dates of battles is not reliable, and even if Egesta became involved in 454–3 this would not be inconsistent with the making of an alliance with Athens four years earlier. On broad historical grounds Athens is more likely to have accepted commitments in Sicily in the early fifties, when the war against the Peloponnesians and the Egyptian expedition were running strongly in her favour, than in 454–3 when the Athenian and allied forces in Egypt, if not already overwhelmed, had at least been driven from Memphis and blockaded on Prosopitis. We prefer ἡάβρ]ον. Athens' motives in making an alliance so early with Egesta can only be guessed. It may have been merely the dynamism of over-confidence, seizing opportunities whenever they appeared; perhaps Athens was interested in Sicilian corn, to enter the market for herself, or to deny it to the Peloponnese (cf. later, in 427, Thuc. iii. 86. 4: βουλόμενοι δὲ μήτε σῖτον ἐς τὴν Πελοπόννησον ἄγεσθαι αὐτόθεν). For this purpose the Ionian cities of east Sicily would have been more important. Athens may have made alliances with them at about the same time (but we would not date the alliances with Rhegion and Leontinoi of Nos. 63 and 64 as early as the fifties).

Roos, while accepting a date in the fifties for the decree, argues that it was not an alliance but a mere treaty of friendship, and that Egesta did not become an ally of Athens until she appealed to the Athenian Assembly in 415. We know of no such limited agreements from the fifth century, and the heading seems to require the restoration of χσυνμαχία.

38 (37)

Victory of Selinus: fifth century B.C.

On a block of reddish limestone from Temple G at Selinus; now in the Palermo Museum.

Local alphabet, not stoichedon. Phots. and facs.: Calder, op. *infra* cit., Pl. 1–3.

Calder, *The Inscription from Temple G at Selinus* (Greek, Roman and Byzantine Monographs, no. 4) +, *Gk. Rom. Byz. Stud.* v (1964) 113–19.

> [δι]ὰ τὸς θεὸς τό[σ]δε νικόντι τοὶ Σελινόγ[τιοι.]
> [δι]ὰ τὸν Δία νικôμες καὶ διὰ τὸν Φόβον [καὶ]
> δ[ιὰ] hερακλέα καὶ δι' Ἀπόλλονα καὶ διὰ Π[οτ]-
> ε[ιδᾶ]να καὶ διὰ Τυνδαρίδας καὶ δι' Ἀθ[α]-
> 5 ναίαν καὶ διὰ Μαλοφόρον καὶ διὰ Πασι[κ]-
> ρά[τ]ειαν καὶ διὰ τὸς ἄλλος θεός, διὰ δ[ὲ] Δία
> μάλιστα. φιλία[ς] δὲ γενομένας ἐν χ[ρ]υσ-
> έο[ι] ἐλά[σα]ντα[ς καὶ] ὀνύματα ταῦτα κολ-
> άψαντ[ας εἰς] τὸ Ἀ[π]ολλόνιον καθθέμε-
> 10 ν, τὸ Διὸ[ς 2–3]γρά[ψ]αντες. τὸ δὲ χρυσίον
> ἐξέκ[οντα τα]λάντον [ἔ]μεν.

l. 10: Though Calder prints and discusses ἐν]γρά[ψ]αντες, comparison of his p. 17 shows that προ]γρά[ψ]αντες (Holm–Benndorf) is equally possible.

The occasion of this inscription cannot be fixed. Epigraphically, any date between *c.* 460 and the destruction of Selinus in 409 might be accommodated, and the popularity, before Calder, of a date *c.* 450 has rested on the attraction of importing Selinus into the war of Diod. xi. 86. 2, on which see the commentary to No. 37. Calder hesitantly suggests the defeat of the Athenian expedition in 413 as the cause for the celebration.

The inscription falls into two halves. In ll. 1–7 the gods responsible for Selinus' victory are named. Phobos is best regarded as the war-god of Selinus rather than specifically thought of as the son of Ares. Μαλοφόρος, probably the Apple-bringer rather than the Sheep-bringer, is Demeter, one of the principal deities of Selinus' ultimate mother city Megara. The position of Πασικράτεια suggests that she is the Selinuntine Persephone. Calder argues, to us, at any rate, unconvincingly, that ll. 2–7 are in choriambic dimeters and form a 'Zeus-song'.

Ll. 7–11 with their infinitives have generally been taken as an extract from a decree; we doubt if the possibility of an oracle can be completely excluded. Now that peace has come, something is to be beaten out in gold, and the names of the gods are to be inscribed (properly 'pecked', 'put in in dots') on it, and it is to be put in the Apollonion (Temple G itself?); the 'Zeus-song' is to be written up (Calder) *or* the name of Zeus is to be written first (Holm). The gold object is to be of 60 talents. Calder argues that the object was probably to weigh 60 talents and, chiefly from the usage of ἐλά[σα]ντα[ς], that it should be a shield; others have preferred a statue or statues or a gold plate. A solid gold shield weighing 60 talents would have been a dedication as costly as Pheidias' Athena Parthenos (No. 54) and we find it a shade unlikely. Other interpretations are possible, and we slightly prefer Schubring's view (*Arch. Zeitung*, i (1873) 102 f.) by which 60 talents would be the cost in silver of the gold object (see Woodward, *JHS* lxxxvi (1966) 297).

39 (30)

Athenian Tribute: 454–3 to 432–1 B.C.

When in 478–7 the grand alliance was formed under Athenian leadership, the sacred island of Delos was chosen as the centre for league meetings and the payment of tribute. In 454 the league treasury was moved to Athens, and in and from 454–3 the allies were required to bring their tribute to Athens. There it was received by the *helleno-tamiai* (an Athenian board from the first) under the general control of the Boule. From the tribute a sixtieth of each city's payment was reserved for Athena (these first-fruits may until 454 have been paid to Delian Apollo), and the *hellenotamiai* had to submit their list of these *aparchai* to the public auditors and then have them inscribed and publicly displayed. The procedure is summarized in the heading of the first list, which is considerably fuller than its successors: [*haíde ἀπαρχαὶ τêι θεôι παρεδέχθησαν παρ]ὰ τὸν ἑλλ[ενο]ταμιôν hoî[s . . . 7 . . . .| . . . ἐγραμμάτευε καὶ τοῖς λογιστêσι τοῖς] τριάκο[ντα ἀπ]εφάνθεσαν [ἀπὸ τô φό|ρο hὸν hαι πόλες ἀπέγαγον ἐπὶ Ἀρίστονος] ἄρχοντος Ἀ[θεν]αίοις μνâ ἀ[πὸ τô ταλ|άντο*].

The heading of the second list is reduced to a single line, merely giving the name of the secretary, the number of the list in the series, and a reference to the thirty (auditors): [*ἐπὶ τês ἀρχês τê]s δευτέρ[α]s hêι Λ[έον ἐγραμμάτευε : τοῖς τριάκοντα*]. The third heading follows the second (and *τοῖς τριάκοντα* is preserved), but in the fourth and subsequent lists the thirty drop out, and the deme of the secretary to the *hellenotamiai* is added.

The form of the lists is also gradually standardized. In the first list the *aparche* follows the name of the city, separated from it by a colon(:); in the second list the figures precede the name but are not carefully aligned; in the third and subsequent lists the first figures of the *aparchai* are in line, presenting a much tidier pattern. The lists of the first fifteen years were inscribed on a large block of marble (3·663 m. × 1·109 m. × 0·385 m.), with a slight downward taper of the stele on the obverse and reverse faces. The first list is set out in six columns, and for the only year in the series a summary is added, on the right side; the second list has seven columns on the obverse, but three further columns are added on the right side. All subsequent lists are confined to a single side. The first six lists are inscribed on the obverse, the next list completes the right side; the reverse is next used for five lists, and the last two lists are on the left side. Pritchett has maintained, on the evidence of the surface of the top, that there was a crowning member on the stele (*Hist.* xii (1964) 120–34). At first he thought that there might have been a relief which would have provided room on the back for a tribute list. When he was able to examine the evidence more closely, he modified his views considerably, but still thought that there was a finial on top (*Gk. Rom. Byz. Stud.* vii (1966) 123–7, viii (1967) 113–19). We do not find the evidence convincing and are inclined, following Meritt (*Hesp.* xxxv (1966) 134–40), to believe that the first stele had no crowning member. From 438–7 a second and smaller stele is used for the lists down to 432–1. Subsequent lists seem to have been inscribed on separate stelai.

The cities are usually expressed by the ethnic (e.g. *Κυμαῖοι, Ἀκάνθιοι*), more rarely by the place-name (e.g. *Περκότε, Τυρόδιϲα*),

and very occasionally the name of the local ruler is given (e.g. Κᾶρες
ͱὸν Τύμνες ἄρχει, Πίκρες Συαν[γελεύς : further examples in *ATL* i. 446).
Sometimes a group of states unite in a single payment (for *syntelies*
see *ATL* i. 446–9).

For the first eight years there is rarely any sustained geographical
order, but in some lists it may be possible to distinguish late payers.
It cannot be coincidence that the first nine names preserved in the
second list are Carian cities, none of which is found in the surviving
fragments of the first year (and the first nine names, which are not preserved, were also probably Carian). We can accept the inference that
these payments were collected from defaulters by an Athenian task-
force and represent payments which should have been made in 454–3
(*ATL* iii. 7–9). Significantly the letter-forms of the first column differ
from those of the rest of the list. Similarly in the fifth list (450–49)
the last column seems to be composed, mainly at least, of late payments and complements of incomplete payments (see No. 50). In the
list of 446–5 there is a tendency towards geographical grouping, but
this is less pronounced in the two following years. In the list of 443–2,
however, and in all subsequent lists the cities are grouped under
district headings: Ἰονικός, ͱελλεσπόντιος, ἐπὶ Θράικες (sometimes ἀπὸ
Θράικες or Θραικικός), Καρικός, Νεσιωτικός; but soon, probably from 438,
the Ionian and Carian districts are merged under the heading Ἰονικός.

The pseudo-Xenophontic oligarchic pamphlet tells us that tribute
was normally reassessed at four-year intervals ([Xen.] Ἀθ. Πολ. 3. 5).
This is confirmed by the lists that survive. It is clear from changes in
tributes that there were assessments in 450, 446, 434, and these were
years of the Great Panathenaia (see also No. 69, ll. 26–33); only one
extraordinary assessment is known before the Peloponnesian War, in
443–2. It has been suggested that this assessment was brought forward
a year to clear the decks for a specially grand celebration of the great
Panathenaia in 442 (*ATL* iii. 306); it is more probable that 443 was
a year of reorganization. It is the first year in which the cities are
listed under district headings, though this is not a major matter; it is
more significant that for the first time an assistant secretary is recorded in the heading, and the same man remains in office for a second
year, suggesting that there is more work than usual for the *hellenotamiai*. There is also another new feature in the list of 443–2, which
is more permanent. The name and deme of one of the *hellenotamiai* is
included; he may be the chairman of the board. In all this there is
perhaps a hint of some financial reorganization following the ostracism
of Thucydides son of Melesias. According to Plutarch (*Per.* 14), in
the last phase of their political struggle Thucydides was attacking
Pericles for his extravagant wasting of the city's finances. And at
some time in or near the forties a whole board of *hellenotamiai* was

condemned to death on a charge that subsequently proved groundless (Antiphon, v. 69).

Within an assessment period changes in tribute were made only in exceptional circumstances, as, for instance, when land was taken for Athenian settlers in the Chersonese and the tribute of the peninsula was reduced from 18 T. to less than 2 T. But in assessment years all tributes were reviewed in the light of economic and political conditions, and the extent of revision varied considerably. In 450 there is a significant pattern only in the islands, where there were 6 reductions, only 1 increase. In 446 the islands were unchanged; in the four other districts there were at least 25 reductions, only 2 (possibly 3) increases. The general pattern suggests a policy of concessions by Athens after the dangerous crisis of 446, when a decisive defeat by the Boeotians at Koroneia was followed by the revolt of Megara and Euboea and a Peloponnesian invasion. In the thirties the Athenian mood seems to stiffen. In 439 for the first year payments of ἐπιφορά are recorded, something in addition to the normal tribute, and possibly to be explained as the interest charged for late payments (*ATL* i. 450-3, but see Eddy, *AJP* lxxxix (1968) 129-43). Eight cities are concerned in 439, and entries appear in the following years. But too little of the lists down to 434-3 is preserved to estimate the number of payments; in the list of 433-2, which has few gaps, there are only two cases.

In 433 two new headings appear at the end of the list. Eleven cities are described as πόλες αὐταὶ φόρον ταχσάμεναι, and only three have been previously recorded, as ἄτακτοι. They are all small states; seven of them in the Thraceward area, Kallipolis in the Chersonese, the Eteokarpathians of the island of Karpathos and the small islands of Amorgos and Kasos. The inclusion of these cities has by some been thought to be the result of *apotaxis*, the separation of small communities from larger, but for this there is no evidence and some of the small states are not near any important neighbours on whom they might be dependent. The natural translation of the heading is 'cities who got their own assessment'. Formally they themselves determined what they should pay, but this is not inconsistent with the gentleness of pressure. The second category are described as πόλες hὰς hοι ἰδιōται ἐνέγραφσαν φόρον φέρεν. There are thirteen of them, and they too are small and unimportant cities; the individuals who enrolled them are more probably members of the cities than Athenians. That these two groups of new members were not freely joining the empire through good will towards Athens is strongly suggested by their record later. When war broke out few of them continued to pay. (For a detailed discussion, F. A. Lepper, *JHS* lxxxii (1962) 25-55.)

These two groups added twenty-four cities to the empire, but financially they were of little significance: together they contributed less than 6 T. This is a useful warning that the count of the number of states in each list can be misleading if pressed too hard. 140 states may produce more tribute than 160, and when the total jumps by 10 it may mean no more than that two or three *syntelies* have been broken up into their constituent parts. Some broad conclusions, however, can be drawn. The average length of the lists of the first period is the shortest of all those for the pre-war periods, and the first list is the shortest of all; the relative shortness of these lists of the late fifties seems largely to be accounted for by the absence of many of the islands which are later included. Two explanations are possible. The more commonly held view is that most of the islands were contributing ships down to 450 (*ATL* iii. 267 f., based on West, *Am. Hist. Rev.* xxxv (1929–30) 267–75). The alternative view is that the shortness of these lists, especially the first, reflects the reaction of the allies to the disaster in Egypt and the transfer of the league's centre from Delos to Athens, which the islanders may have resented more than others (Nesselhauf, *Untersuchungen zur Geschichte der delisch-attischen Symmachie*, 12; Meiggs, *JHS* lxiii (1943) 31–3, *Harv. Stud.* lxvii (1963) 6–9). The striking fluctuation in numbers during the second period from 450 to 446 must also be significant; but these lists raise special problems which will be separately discussed (No. 50).

While from a count of lines we can know, at least approximately, the number of cities contributing each year, it is much more difficult to estimate the total amount of tribute received by Athens. No list is completely preserved and in the lists of the middle thirties only a few names survive. In some of the lists of the forties, however, there are not many large gaps, and other evidence provides a rough control. Thucydides leads us to expect totals rising by 431 to 600 T., from an original assessment of 460 T. (ii. 13. 3: θαρσεῖν τε ἐκέλευε προσιόντων μὲν ἑξακοσίων ταλάντων ὡς ἐπὶ τὸ πολὺ φόρου κατ᾽ ἐνιαυτὸν ἀπὸ τῶν ξυμμάχων: original assessment, i. 96. 2). On the other hand, Tod's estimate for 443–2 is 349 T. 1,140 dr., or, if Thasos is restored in that year in place of Serme, 379 T. 640 dr.; and for 433–2, 388 T. 390 dr. Sufficient survives of these two lists to give confidence that in such estimates the margin of error must be less than 20 T. Two other pieces of evidence need to be taken into account. In the first year, 454–3, the total of the year's *aparchai* is recorded and separate figures are given for silver and electrum. However, the surface of the stone is very badly worn and the text is insecure; our own observations do not agree entirely either with *ATL* or with Pritchett, *Gk. Rom. Byz. Stud.* vii (1966) 127–9. See now McGregor, ibid. viii (1967) 103–12. The basis for assessing the amount of electrum is inadequate, but several figures of the silver total survive: [τὸ] ἀργυρίο: [κεφάλαιον ἐν]|[. .]XXHHHΔΔ[. There are two possible restorations for the two first figures [ᴈT] or [ᴈX]. The first gives a total of 383 talents paid in silver, the second 333 talents, and to these figures must be added the electrum total, almost certainly not exceeding the equivalent of 30 T. of silver. There may also be a rather better clue to the tribute total for 443 in the Parthenon building-account for 444–3 (*IG* i². 342. 36). In the record of receipts the payment to the commissioners by the treasurers of Athena is followed by a payment by the *hellenotamiai*; on the analogy of the Propylaia accounts (see No. 60) this payment probably represents the *aparchai* of the year: [....]XXᴈHᴈΔΔᴦIIIII. The vital first figures are missing, but if this does represent the *aparchai* we can be reasonably certain that the total tribute was not less than 300 T., giving an *aparchai* total of 30,000 dr. The first three figures will be MMM; for the fourth, M, ᴈ, X are all formally possible, giving tribute totals of 426+T., 376+T., and 336+T. Of these the most likely is 376+T. It is very doubtful whether the tribute in any year before 433 exceeded 400 T., and when revolt broke out in Chalkidike in 432, more than 20 talents a year were lost. These figures cannot easily be reconciled with the strict meaning of Thucydides' words. The easiest solution is to assume that Thucydides was using φόρος in an extended sense to include payments that were not strictly tribute, such as the annual indemnity from Samos; such reconciliation would be still easier if, as *ATL* (iii. 132) suggests might be the case, φόρου is an editor's addition or a gloss, and not written by Thucydides.

Of the first stele 180 fragments have been found; of the second, 73. The earliest stages in their reconstruction are reflected in *IG* i. 226–72 (Kirchhoff, 1873). Important studies by Busolt (*Phil.* xli (1882) 652–718), Pedroli (in Beloch's *Studi di storia antica*, i. 101–207), Larfeld (*Handbuch der griech. Epigraphik*, ii (1898) 20–43), Wilhelm (*Wien. Anz.* 1909, 41–58), and others contributed to much improved texts in *IG* i². 191–231 (Hiller von Gaertringen, 1924). In the following ten years more impressive advances were made in a number of detailed studies by West and Meritt, and revised texts were published by them in *SEG* v (1931). On West's untimely death in 1936 Meritt was joined by Wade-Gery and McGregor, and their combined views are set out in the four volumes of *The Athenian Tribute Lists* (1939–53). The first volume analyses, with ample illustration, the evidence of the fragments and revises the texts of *SEG* v, adding some relevant decrees. It also includes a register giving the tribute record of all cities whose names have survived, and a gazetteer in which the evidence for their sites is discussed. In vol. ii the texts of the tribute-lists are reprinted with improvements, together with an expanded collection of related texts. The history derived from them provides the main substance of vol. iii; vol. iv, in addition to indexes, includes a general bibliography. Among reviews, see Dow, *TAPA* lxxii (1941) 70–84; Klaffenbach, *Deutsche Lit. Zeit.* lxxi (1950) 33–7; Meiggs,

Eng. Hist. Rev. lv (1940) 104–6, *CR* lxiv (1950) 33–7, lxvi (1952) 97–100; Pritchett, *CP* xlvii (1952) 261–3.

Of other general studies, Nesselhauf, *Untersuchungen zur Geschichte der delisch-attischen Symmachie* (*Klio*, Beiheft xxx (1933)) is still valuable; Schwahn, s.v. φόρος, in *RE* zw. r. xx. 1 (1941) 545–644, is interesting but unreliable. A tabular record of the tribute from 453 to 431 is given in Hill, *Sources*², 403–26.

We give an extract from the last three columns (the best-preserved) of the first list, ll. 5–12 from the text in *ATL*:

IV

[Μαρ]ονῖται: ΗΡ̣̅
[Λί]νδιοι: ΓΗΗΗΔΔΔΔΓ
[Οἰ]ναῖοι ἐν ᾿Ι-
κάροι: ΗΔΔΔΗΗΙΙ
῎Εσσιοι: Η
Νεάνδρεια: ΔΔΔΗΗΗ[ΙΙ]
Λαμπόνεια: ΔΓΗΙΙΙ[Ι]

V

5 haβ[δερί]ται: ΧΗΗΡ̣̅ΔΔΔΓΙΙ
᾿Ολύνθ[ιοι]: Σκα-
βλαῖο[ι: Ἀσ]σε-
ρῖται: Η[ΗΡ̣̅ΔΓ]ΗΙΙΙΙ
Σερμυλ[ιὲς]: ΓΗΗΗΡ̣̅ΔΔΗ
10 Μεκυπερ[να]ῖοι vacat
Στόλιοι: Π[ολ]ι-
χνῖται: ΗΗΔ[Δ]ΔΗΙΙ

VI

5 Ναρ[ι]σ[βαρὲς: ΔΓΗΙΙΙΙ]
Μυδ[ο]νὲs[: ΔΔΓ]
Κια[ν]οί: Δ[ΓΗΙΙΙΙ]
Ἀρτακενο[ί: ΔΔΔΗΗΙΙ]
Νεάπολις
10 [ἐ]ν [Θ]ράικει: ΔΓ[ΗΙΙΙΙ]
Βερύσιοι hυπὸ
τêι ῎Ιδει: ΔΓΗΙΙΙΙ

In col. iv the six cities are in the following districts: Thrace, Caria, Ionia, Ionia (but once in the Hellespont), Hellespont, Hellespont. The eight of col. v are all in Thrace. In col. vi the order is Caria, Caria, Hellespont, Hellespont, Thrace, Hellespont.

40 (29)

Regulations for Erythrai: (?) 453–2 B.C.

A marble stele copied by ?Fauvel on the Acropolis, near the Erechtheum; now lost.

Early Attic letters, ΒΡΦ. Facs.: *CIG*, *ATL* ii. 38.

CIG i, addenda 73*b*, p. 891; *IG* i². 10; Highby, *Klio* Beiheft xxxvi (1936); Schaefer, *Hermes* lxxi (1936) 129–50; de Sanctis, *RF* lxv (1937) 299–309; Kolbe, *Hermes* lxxiii (1938) 249–68; Meiggs, *JHS* lxiii (1943) 21–33; Meritt, *Hesp.* xv (1946) 246–9; *ATL* ii. D 10.

[ἔδοχσεν τε͂ι βολε͂ι καὶ το͂ι δέμοι - - - - - - - - ἐπρυτάνευε - - - - -]

[. . . .] ἐπεστάτε, Λ[. . .]ι[- 'Ερ]-

[υθραί]ος ἀπάγεν σ[ῖ]το[ν ἐς] Παναθέναια τὰ μεγά[λα ἄ]χσ[ιον μὲ ὀ]-

[λέζον]ος ἒ τριο͂ν μνο͂ν καὶ ν[έ]μ[ε]ν 'Ερυθραίον [τ]ο[ῖ]ς παρο͂σι

5 [- - - - -] hιεροπο[ι]ὸς - - - - - - - - - - - - - ἐὰν δὲ ἀπαγ[—

[- - - -] ἄχσι[ον] ἒ τριο͂[ν] μν[ο͂ν] κατὰ τὰ [. . . .]εν[- - - -]α πρί⟨α⟩σθαι σῖ[το]-

[ν - - - -] τὸν [δὲ δε͂]μον -

- τo͂ι βολομένοι 'Ερυθραίον. [ἀ]π-

[ὸ κ]υάμο δ[ὲ] βολὲν [ἒ]ναι ε[ἴ]κο[σ]ι καὶ [h]έκατον ἄνδρας· τὸν δὲ

10 [- - - - -] ἐν τε͂ι βολε͂ι καὶ [μὲ χ]σέ[ν]ον ἔναι βολε[ύεν]

[με]δ' ὄλεζον ἒ τρ[ι]άκοντα ἔτε γεγονό[τ]α· δίοχσιν δ' ἔναι [κατ]-

[ὰ τ]ο͂[ν] ἐλε[γ]θέν[τ]ο[ν]. βολεύεν δὲ μὲ ἐντ[ὸ]ς τεττάρον ἐ{ι}το͂ν - - - -

κυαμεῦσα[ι δ]ὲ καὶ κατασ[τ]ε͂σαι [τ]ὲν μὲν ν[ῦ]ν βολὲν [τ]ὸς [ἐπισκ]-

[όπ]ος καὶ [τὸν] φρ[ό]ραρχον, τὸ δὲ λοιπὸν τὲν βολὲν καὶ τὸν [φρόρ]-

15 αρχον, μὲ ὄλε[ζ]ον ἒ τριάκοντα ἐμ[έ]ρας π[ρὶ]ν ἐχσιέναι [τὲν βολ]-

ὲν· ὀμνύναι [δὲ Δ]ία καὶ Ἀπό[λλ]ο καὶ Δέμε[τρα] ἐπαρομένο[ς ἐχσό]-

[λ]ειαν ἐφ[ιορκο͂σι - - - - κ]αὶ παι[σ]ὶν ἐχσό[λεια]ν[- - - - - - - - -]

[- - - -] κατὰ [h]ιερὸν [- - - -] τ[ὲ]ν δὲ βολὲν μὲ ὄλ[ε]ζον [κ]ατα[καί]-

[εν - - - - - ἐὰν] δὲ μέ, ἔναι ζεμιο͂σαι [χι]λ[ία]σ[ι] δρα[χμε͂σ]-

20 [ι⌐ - - - - - - - - - - - - - - - - - - τ]ὸν δε͂μον κατακαίεν μὲ ὄλεζον·

ὀμν[ύ]ναι [δὲ τά]δε [τὲν] βολέν· βολεύσο hος ἂν [δύ]νο[μ]α[ι] ἄριστ[α κα]-

[ὶ] δ[ι]κα[ιότα]τα 'Ερυθραίον το͂ι πλέθει καὶ Ἀθεναίον καὶ τον [χσ]-

[υ]νμά[χ]ον [κ]αὶ οὐκ [ἀποσ]τέσομαι Ἀθεναίον το͂ π[λ]έθος οὐδὲ [τ]-

[ο͂ν] χσυνμάχον τον Ἀθεναίον οὔτ' αὐτὸς ἐγὸ ο[ὔ]τ' ἄ[λ]λοι πε[ί]σομ[αι]

25 [οὐ]δ - - - - - - - - - - - οὔτ' αὐτὸς ἐγὸ οὔτ' ἄλλο[ι π]εί[σομαι - - - - -]

[- - - -] τὸν φ[υγά]δον [κατ]αδέχσομαι οὐδ[ὲ] hένα οὔτ[- - - - - - - -]

[ἄλλο]ι πείσο[μ]α[ι τὸν ἐς] Μέδος φε[υ]γό[ντο]ν ἄνευ τε͂[ς] βο[λε͂ς τε͂ς]

[Ἀθε]ναίον καὶ το͂ [δέ]μο [ο]ὐδὲ τὸν μενόντον ἐχσελο͂ [ἄ]ν[ευ] τε͂ς β[ο]-

[λε͂ς] τε͂ς Ἀθεναίον καὶ [τὸ] δέμο· ἐὰν δέ τ[ι]ς ἀποκτ[ε]ίνε[ι 'Ερυθρα]-

30 [ί]ος hέτερον 'Ερ[υ]θρ[αῖο]ν τεθ[ν]άτο ἐὰν [γν]οσθε͂ι [- - - - - - - - - -]

[- - - -] γ[ν]οσθε͂ι φευγέτο [h]άπασαν τὲ[ν] Ἀθεναίον χσυνμαχ[ί.. κ]-

[αὶ τ]ὰ χρέματα δεμόσ[ια ἔσ]το 'Ερυθραίον· ἐὰν δέ [τ]ις [- - - - - - - - -]

[- - - -] το[ῖ]ς τυράννοις [- - - -] 'Ερυθραί[ον] καὶ [- - - - - - - - -]

[- - - -] τεθνάτο [- - - -] παῖδε[ς h]οι ἐχς ἐκέν[ο - - - - - - - - -]

35 [- - - - - - - - - - - - - - - hοι] παῖδες [h]οι ἐχς [ἐ]κέν[ο - - - -]

[- - - -] 'Ερυθραίο[ν] καὶ [- - - -] Ἀθεναίον [- - - - - - -]τὰ δὲ χρέματα[-]

[- - - -] κατα[θ]έντ[.]ς

ll. 37–46 are too uncertain to be restored.

All texts are based on Boeckh's publication in *CIG* of a copy probably made by Fauvel; both the stone and the original copy are now lost. Since the copy sometimes omitted letters and occasionally gave more letters than can have been on the stone, no precise figure is given for the number of letter-spaces available where no restoration is offered. Letters are dotted where the letter given by Fauvel could be mistaken for the letter that the sense seems to require. For a more adventurous restoration of the text see *ATL* D 10.   l. 2: Λ[υσι]κ[ράτες ἔρχε· γνόμε τὸν χσυγγραφέον] Meritt. For alternatives see below. In the regulations for Miletus of 450–49 (D 11) the formula is [τάδε ℎοι χ]συνγγραφ[φὲς χσυνέγραφσαν. It would be a little surprising to find the shortened formula so early.   l. 3: Though Boeckh noted that σ and ο in σ[ί]τον were marked as uncertain in the copy, other restorations depart much further from the copy. Probably the Erythraians were required to bring corn to the Great Panathenaia. ll. 9 f.: τὸν δὲ κ[υα|με]υθέντα ἐλ[έ]γχέν *ATL*; one would expect δοκιμάζεν. Neither is close to the copy, which has TONΔEΘ|..YOENSΑΘE.ΘE.ΟN. ll. 13 f.: The copy has Α...|ΘΟΟS, but we accept [ἐπισκ]ό[π]ος, because these officials are concerned with the appointment of the first Boule but not of its successors. As contrasted with ἄρχοντες and φρούραρχοι, ἐπίσκοποι are travelling commissioners who help to deal with constitutional issues; they do not remain in the cities they visit (see Hill, *Sources*[2], Index, p. 356: Busolt, *Gr. St.* 1355).   l. 17: The copy indicates 14 letter-spaces after EO(= EΦ). ll. 17 f.: τὸ]ν δὲ ℎό[ρ]κον ὀ[μνύ|ναι] κατὰ [ℎ]ιερὸν [κ]αιομένον; *IG* i[2], *ATL*.   l. 20: καὶ ℎ]ό[τ]αν ℎο δέμος ὀμνύει *ATL*. This restoration keeps close to the copy, but to introduce the people's oath so indirectly would be odd. See below.   ll. 32 f.: ἐὰν δέ τις [ℎα]λô[ι προ|διδ]ὸς το[ῖ]ς τυράννοις τὲμ πόλ[ιν τ]ὲν Ἐρυθραί[ο]ν *IG* i[2], *ATL*. This seems to be required by the sense, but the copy has, after τυράννοις, TEMNΑΜ.ΟS.

It is clear that Fauvel found the stone very difficult to read, but he recorded what he thought he saw and not what he thought he ought to see. The opening and closing sections of his text make no sense and attempts at detailed restoration are unprofitable. The central section was apparently much less worn; Fauvel's text is intelligible and needs considerably less modification.

All that can safely be said of the opening section (ll. 2–8) is that it concerns the obligations of Erythrai to the Great Panathenaia. In the early forties Athens required all members of the Delian League to bring standard offerings of cow and panoply to this greatest of Athenian festivals (No. 46, ll. 41 f., but the date is disputed). The Erythraian regulations are less simple and represent an early stage in the conversion of an Athenian into an Empire festival. The central section (ll. 8–29) lays down the main terms of the political settlement. A democratic council is to be installed on the Athenian model; the number, 120, is considerably smaller than Athens' 500, and, while an Athenian could serve only twice, it seems that the Erythraian was only debarred from being a member twice within four years. The first new democratic council is to be installed by the Athenian ἐπίσκοποι in co-operation with the φρούραρχος (garrison commander); in future by the φρούραρχος acting with the outgoing council. Councillors on entering office are required to take an oath of loyalty to the new Erythraian democracy, to the Athenian democracy, and to the allies of Athens, and there are to be no more political expulsions or restorations without the authority of Athens. Those who may not be restored are 'those who have taken refuge with the Medes' (l. 27), and later there is probably a warning against 'betraying the city to the tyrants' (l. 33). We infer that Athens has forcibly intervened to expel a small medizing faction, and set up a democracy. She has installed a garrison which will remain to safeguard the settlement and protect Erythrai from medizers. The following section (ll. 29 ff.) opens with the provision that murder shall be punished by death, but these cases are not, as later, subject to Athenian control, and if an Erythraian is exiled he is automatically outlawed from all cities of the Athenian alliance. Any attempt to betray the city to the tyrants also incurs the death penalty. In the last five lines restorations become increasingly insecure.

Modern discussion of this important decree was reopened by Highby's detailed re-examination of its text, date, and historical significance. Highby, in contrast to most earlier commentators, emphasized the implied friendliness of Athens, the reality of the Persian menace, and the degree of independence left to Erythrai in contrast with later Athenian settlements with other cities. He concluded that the decree marked the original entry of Erythrai into the Delian League when Athens drove out a medizing faction and liberated the town, probably in the sixties. Highby was right in pointing the contrast with later settlements (note that the Delian League is still called a χσυνμαχίς or χσυνμαχία (l. 31), not yet πόλες hὸν Ἀθεναῖοι ἄρχοσι); but had Erythrai been outside the league up to this point, the decree would have opened with a declaration of alliance. The more natural interpretation is that Erythrai had temporarily revolted from the league and had been restored to loyalty by Athenian armed intervention.

A proper appreciation of the decree's significance depends on its date. From the letter-forms as printed in *CIG* the date cannot be more narrowly set than c. 470-450. A more precise date, however, can be given if certain assumptions are accepted. Two independent fragments in London and Athens (*IG* i². 11, 12/13a) also concern an Athenian settlement with Erythrai. The first mentions ἐπίσκοποι and φρούραρχος and deals with legal cases whose nature is not clear; the second contains an oath of loyalty to Athens and her allies and marks the close of a decree. These two fragments, whose letter-forms and spacing are very similar, probably come from the same stele (Meiggs, op. cit.,

p. 34, accepted by Meritt, *Hesp.* xv (1946) 246-9). Their letter-forms suggest a date not earlier than 460 and not later than 445. They can be restored to give a stoichedon line of forty-seven letters, which without undue strain can be applied also to the lost inscription. It is a tempting economy with Meritt to regard these two fragments as part of the same decree that Fauvel copied. Meritt finds the essential link in l. 20 of Fauvel's text, where he restores: [καὶ h]ό[τ]αν ho δῆμος ὀμνύει τὸν δῆμον κατακαίειν μὲ ὄλεζον; the oath of the Athens fragment will be the people's oath to which this line refers. Meritt further restores in the prescript an archon's name, Λ[υσι]κ[ράτες ἔρχε], so dating the document in 453-2. This date would provide an admirable historical context. The tribute-lists suggest that Erythrai was not paying tribute in 453-2, since Boutheia, which is normally listed with the other small cities of the Erythraian peninsula, paid separately, and considerably more than her normal payment. We can accept the conclusion of *ATL* (i. 487) that Boutheia remained loyal while Erythrai revolted. The tribute-lists illustrate similar trouble at Miletus at this same time. Miletus, almost certainly absent from the list of 454-3, is paying again in 452-1. An Athenian force could have recovered both Erythrai and Miletus in the summer of 452.

The main issues are not, however, settled beyond dispute, for there are serious difficulties in linking the two surviving fragments with Fauvel's stone: (1) The form of rho in *CIG* is consistently Ρ; in the surviving fragments it is consistently P. In *CIG* there is sometimes confusion between Ρ and R, but no instance of P being printed as Ρ. There is also some confirmation from Fauvel's text that the *CIG* form is correct; Fauvel's .IEKON of l. 18 probably reflects HIERON. (2) If the oath of the Athens fragment (*IG* i². 12/13a) is an oath to be taken by the people in addition to the council's oath, it should be directly introduced. In Meritt's text the first mention of it is 'and when the people takes its oath' (l. 20). These two fragments may therefore be from a separate decree, and their datable letter-forms will not necessarily help towards the dating of Fauvel's decree. There would remain only the restored archon's name, and Λυσανίας (466-5) would fit equally well the vertical stroke that survives. Nor is an archon's name essential or even normal in fifth-century inscriptions before the Peace of Nicias. Such a restoration as Λ[έον] ε[ἶπε is also possible. We prefer to think that Athens had to intervene more than once at Erythrai, as at Miletus, and that the surviving fragments are later than Fauvel's decree and reflect a tightening up—towards the end of the fifties; in which case the lost decree might be from the early fifties or even earlier; or the lost decree might be from 453-2 and the surviving fragments from 450-49, when Athens intervened for a second time at Miletus (*ATL* ii. D 11).

Four further fragments (*IG* i². 12/13b + *Hesp.* xiv. 82-3) have been in the past associated with *IG* i². 11 and 12/13a, but were rejected by Meritt, *Hesp.* xv. 246-7, since their thicknesses were different. We are doubtful whether the thicknesses are original; these fragments need further consideration.

41 (36)

Civil Laws of Gortyn: about 450 B.C.

Twelve columns engraved on the inner surface of a circular wall, which supported the cavea of a theatre constructed about the first century B.C. or later: the wall had previously formed part of a much earlier building. One detached fragment in the Louvre, the rest *in situ* at ancient Gortyn.

Archaic Cretan writing, boustrophedon. The columns follow in sequence from right to left. Digamma (F) is in use, but not koppa: κ serves for κ and χ, π for π and φ, κσ for ξ; there is no aspirate sign. Full phots. and facs.: *IC* iv. 72, Willetts, *The Law Code of Gortyn*.

IC iv. 72+(Guarducci) and Willetts, op. cit. (1967), are fundamental with full translation and commentary. Other important editions are Bücheler and Zitelmann (*Rh. Mus.* xl (1885) suppl.); *IJG* i. 352 ff.; Köhler and Ziebarth (1912); Buck 117. An elementary introduction to the Code as a whole, G. Smith, *Acta Congressus Madvigiani*, i. 235-49. English translations: Merriam, *AJA* i (1885) 324-39, ii (1886) 24-37 (whence Botsford and Sihler, *Hellenic Civilization*, 275-88); Roby, *Law Quarterly Review*, ii (1886) 135 ff. See also Willetts, *Aristocratic Society in Ancient Crete, passim*; Diamond, *Primitive Law*, 54 f., 303, 309, 364-7.

We republish one section only (iv. 23-vi. 1).

Col. iv. 23: τὸν πατέρα τὸν | τέκνον καὶ τὸν κρεμάτον κ‖αρτερὸν ἔμεν
τᾶδ δαίσιος | καὶ τὰν ματέρα τὸν Fὸν αὐ|τᾶς κρεμάτον. ἆς κα δόοντι, |
30 μὲ ἐπάνανκον ἔμεν δατέ|θθαι· αἰ δέ τις ἀταθείε, ἀποδ‖άτταθθαι τõι
ἀταμένοι ᾶ|ι ἔγρατται. ἒ δέ κ' ἀποθάνει τις,|(σ)τέγανς μὲν τὰνς ἐν πόλι
35 κ' ᾶ|τι κ' ἐν ταῖς (σ)τέγαις ἐνει, αῖ|ς κα μὲ Fοικεὺς ἐνFοικει ἐπ‖ὶ κόραι
Fοικίον, καὶ τὰ πρόβατα κα|ὶ καρταίποδα, ἆ κα μὲ Fοικέος ει, | ἐπὶ τοῖς
υἱάσι ἔμεν, τὰ δ' ἀλ|λα κρέματα πάντα δατέθθα|ι καλõς καὶ λανκάνεν
40 τὸς μ‖ὲν υἱύνς, ὁπόττοι κ' ἰοντι, δύ|ο μοίρανς Fέκαστον, τὰδ δ|ὲ
θυγατέρανς, ὁπότται κ' ἰον|τι, μίαν μοῖραν Fεκάσταν. δ|ατέθ[θ]αι δὲ
45 καὶ τὰ ματρόια, ἒ ‖ κ' ἀποθά[νε]ι, ἇιπερ τὰ [πατρõ]ι' | ἔγ[ρατ]ται. αἰ
δὲ κρέματα μὲ εἴ|ε, στέγα δέ, λακὲν τὰ̀δ θ[υ]γατέ|ρας ἀι ἔγρατται. αἰ
50 vacat αἰ δέ κα λε|ι ὁ πατὲρ δοὸς ἰον δόμεν τᾶ|‖ι ὀπυιομέναι, δότο κατὰ
τ|ὰ ἐγραμμένα, πλίονα δὲ μέ. vacat | ὀτείαι δὲ πρόθθ' ἔδοκε ἒ ἐπέσ|πενσε,

ταῦτ' ἔκεν, ἄλλα᾿ δὲ μὲ | ἔτι τὸν π[α]τρόι[ο]ν [κ]ρέ[ματ'] | Col. v:
ἀπολαν[κά]νεν. γυνὰ ὅ[τ]εία κ|ρέματα μὲ ἔκει ἒ [πα]τρὸδ δό|ντος ἒ
5 ἀ[δ]ελπιõ ἒ ἐπισπέν|σαντος ἒ ἀπολά[κ]ονσα ἅ||ι ὄκ' ὁ Αἰθ[α]λεὺς
(σ)ταρτὸς ἐκόσ|μιον οἱ σὺν Κύ[λ]λοι, ταύτ|ας μὲν ἀπολανκάνεν, ταῖ|δ
δὲ πρόθθα μὲ ἔ[ν]δικον ἔμεν.

10 Leaf ἒ κ' ἀποθάνει ἀνὲρ ἒ γυν||ά, αἱ μέν κ' ἐι τέκνα ἒ ἐς τέ|κνον
τέκνα ἒ ἐς τούτον τέ|κνα, τούτος ἔκε[ν] τὰ κρέμα|τα. palm αἰ δέ κα
15 μέτις ἐι τούτο|ν, ἀ[[α]]δελπιοὶ δὲ τõ ἀποθανόν||τος κ' ἐκς ἀδε[λ]πιõν
τέκν|α ἒ ἐς τούτον τέκνα, τούτ|ος ἔκεν τὰ κρέματα. palm αἰ δέ κα | μέτις
20 ἐι τούτον, ἀδευπιαὶ δ|ὲ τõ ἀποθανόντος κ' ἐς ταυτ||ᾶν τέκνα ἒ ἐς τõν
τέκνον τέ|κνα, τούτος ἔκεν τὰ κρέμα|τα. palm αἰ δέ κα μέτις ἐι τούτον, |
25 οἶς κ' ἐπιβάλλει ὀπõ κ' ἐι τὰ κρ|έματα, τούτος ἀναιλέθθα||ι. palm αἰ
δὲ μὲ εἶεν ἐπιβάλλοντε|ς τᾶς Ϝοικίας, οἵτινές κ' | ἴοντι ὁ κλᾶρος τούτονς
ἔ|κεν τὰ κρέματα. vacat

30 αἰ δέ κ' οἱ | ἐπιβάλλοντες οἱ μὲν λεί||οντι δατέθθαι τὰ κρέματ|α οἱ δὲ
μέ, δικάκσαι τὸν δι|καστὰν ἐπὶ τοῖλ λείονσι δ|ατέθθαι ἔμεν τὰ κρέματα
35 π|άντα πρίν κα δάττονται. vacat || αἰ δέ κα δικάκσαντος τõ δ|ικαστᾶ
κάρτει ἐνσείει ἒ ἅ|γει ἒ πέρει, δέκα στατέραν|ς καταστασεῖ καὶ τὸ
40 κρέι|ος διπλεῖ. vacat τνατõν δὲ καὶ καρ||πõ καὶ Ϝέμας κ' ἀντιπιδέμας κ' |
ἐπιπολαίον κρεμάτον αἴ κα μ|ὲ λείοντι δατέθ[θαι, τὸ]ν δ|[ικαστ]ὰν
45 ὀμνύντα κρίνα|ι πορτὶ τὰ μολιόμενα. vacat [α]ἰ [δ]||έ κα κρέματα δατιό-
μενοι| μὲ συνγιγνόσκοντι ἀν|πὶ τὰν δαῖσιν, ὀνὲν τὰ κρέμ|ατα κ' ὂς κα
50 πλεῖστον διδ|õι ἀποδόμενοι, τᾶν τιμᾶν || δια[λ]ακόντον τὰν ἐπαβο|λὰν
Ϝέκαστος. palm δατιομέ|νοιδ δὲ κρέματα μαίτυρα|νς παρέμεν δρομέανς
ἐλε|υθέρονς τρίινς ἒ πλίανς.| Col. vi: θυγατρὶ ἒ διδõι, κατὰ τὰ αὐτ|ά.

For the Cretan dialect the standard works on Greek dialects may
be consulted (e.g. Buck, pp. 169–72), together with J. Brause, *Laut-
lehre der kretischen Dialekte*. For the language of the Code cf. Schick, *RF*
lxxxiii (1955) 373–6.

We find frequent references in antiquity to the publication of laws
by means of their inscription upon tablets or on the walls of public
buildings (Wilhelm, *Beitr.* 264–71), but this is the best example of
their preservation to our times in this form. Not that we have before
us a complete and ordered code, comparable to that of Hammurabi
or of the XII Tables. The 'Code' of Gortyn is rather the result of
a revision, more or less thoroughgoing and systematic, of earlier laws
by the Gortynian legislative body, in which some important questions
are dealt with only cursorily, while others are wholly neglected. It

contains frequent references to previously existing law, the knowledge and practice of which are throughout assumed.

Crete was famous for its early laws and lawgivers, and in this respect Gortyn had a specially high reputation (cf. Strabo, x. 4. 17, p. 481). The site is rich in other legal texts, both earlier than (*IC* iv. 1–71) and nearly contemporary with (*IC* iv. 73–140) the 'Code'. No fifth-century Cretan inscriptions are at all firmly dated, and attempts to date this text tend to be subjective. Guarducci (*RF* lxvi (1938) 264–73) has argued for the years 480–460; this is probably a little too early (Shoe, *Profiles of Greek Mouldings*, i. 18, Pl. 8. 5; Carpenter, *AJA* xxxvii (1933) 24; Kirsten, *Die Insel Kreta im fünften und vierten Jahrhundert*, 44).

The following translation may help the understanding of this difficult text:

'The father shall have power over the division of the property among the children, and the mother over that of her property. As long as they live, they have no obligation to divide it; but if one (of the children) is fined, a division shall be made for the one who has been fined, as is written. But if a man dies, the houses in the city and whatever is in the houses, unless they are occupied by a serf living on the land, and the sheep and the cattle, which do not belong to a serf, shall belong to the sons, and the other property shall be fairly divided and the sons, as many as there are, shall take two shares each, and the daughters, as many as there are, one share each. The mother's property too, if she dies, shall be divided in the same way as is prescribed for the father's property. But if there is no property but a house, the daughters shall take their share as is prescribed. If a father while alive wishes to make a gift (to a daughter) on marriage, let him give it, as is prescribed, but no more. To whatever woman a gift was made or promised before (this legislation), she shall keep it, but take no further share (of the inheritance). A woman who has no property, either by gift or by promise of a father or brother, or by inheritance, at the time when the *startos* of the Aithaleis, Kullos and the others, were *kosmoi*, they shall take their share, but there shall be no proceedings against those (who received property) before.

'If a man or woman dies, if there are children or children's children or their children, these shall have the property. But if there are none of these, but brothers of the dead or children of the brothers or their children, these shall have the property. But if there are none of these, but sisters of the dead or their children or their children's children, these shall have the property. But if there are none of these, the next relations, from wherever the property descends, shall have the property. But if there are no relations of the family, those who are the *kleros*, they shall have the property.

'If of the heirs [ἐπιβάλλοντες is here used more generally than in v. 25], some wish to divide the property and others do not, the *dikastes* shall rule that the property be managed by those who wish to divide until it is divided. If, after the *dikastes* has made his ruling, anyone enters on the property by force or leads any thing off or takes it, he shall pay ten staters and double the value of the object. And for living things, fruits, clothing, ornaments and furniture, if they do not want to divide them, the *dikastes* having sworn shall judge the contentions advanced. And if in dividing property they do not agree about the division, they shall sell the property to whoever offers most to buy it and each one shall take the proper share of the price. When they are dividing property, there shall be present three or more witnesses of age and free. If a man makes a gift to a daughter, the same shall apply.'

It is sometimes held (see, e.g. Woodhouse, *Solon the Liberator*, 77) that κρέματα in this text does not include land, which remains a possession of the family group rather than of an individual. This can hardly be so. v. 39–47 seems to make a distinction between other property and real property, and other passages (e.g. ii. 48–50, viii. 42–4) make it clear that κρέματα are capable of producing καρπός and undergoing Ϝεργασία. See Ruschenbusch, *Acta Congressus Madvigiani*, i. 250.

Father and mother remain in control of their property while they live; note that the woman's property is not merged with her husband's. The general principle (see vi. 2–11) is that the child cannot incur claims on what is his father's property, but this is qualified in iv. 29–31 by the provision that an heir's future share can be used to pay a fine. Otherwise the parent has complete control of the division of his property. Even the paying of dowries is optional while he lives (iv. 48–51).

The general lines of succession to the dead are clear. There is no trace of wills. The property is divided into two sections, one of which goes only to the sons, while the other falls to be divided among the sons and daughters. The first section is apparently limited by the fact that serfs and property associated with them have to go with the main share of the property. It would seem clear that only town houses belong to the first section, and not even those if they have some connection with the serfs and hence with the rural estate. On the Cretan Ϝοικέες see Finley, *RIDA* vii (1960) 168–72; Lotze, Μεταξὺ ἐλευθέρων καὶ δούλων, 4–25. On iv. 31–7 see also Willetts, *Klio* xxxix (1961) 45–7; we cannot, however, accept his view that the town houses are referred to, but not their contents, and the contents of country houses, but not the houses themselves. For the proportions of sons' and daughters' shares cf. Ephorus *FGH* 70 F 149, *ap.* Strabo, x. 4. 20, p. 482: φερνὴ δ' ἐστίν, ἂν ἀδελφοὶ ὦσι, τὸ ἥμισυ τῆς τοῦ ἀδελφοῦ μερίδος.

Even if there is no rural property, the daughters get some share (iv. 46–8). The contrast between Gortyn and Athens, where daughters got nothing of right, if there were sons, and were only vehicles for transmitting the property, if there were not, is notable. Women have had property before this law (iv. 52–v. 9), even by inheritance (v. 4). That no legal proceedings are allowed against those who have already acquired their property (v. 7–9) suggests that they may have acquired more than this law allows, and the provision forbidding dowries larger than the legal share of inheritance (iv. 46–8) certainly suggests a tendency to restrict female control of property. However, it should be noted that it is hard to find any trace of such growing restriction in the treatment of the heiress (vii. 15–ix. 24), who by Athenian standards is very generously treated.

The order of succession (v. 9–28) is rather more simple, on the surface, than that of classical Athens. In Athens, of course, there is an absolute priority for the males in any particular remove; father and mother, here not mentioned at all, rank between children and brothers, and there is a sharp distinction between ἀδελφοὶ ὁμοπάτριοι and ὁμομήτριοι. The further relationships are more closely defined than in Gortyn, where we are left in total darkness as to whether the ἐπιβάλλοντες are only of the paternal family or on both sides. Nor does Gortyn tell us whether grandchildren, for example, receive *per stirpes* or as individuals. Notice that succession moves only three steps from the deceased. It might be tempting to say that this is accidental or that great-great-grandchildren are an unlikely contingency, but it is not obvious why the deceased is more likely to possess great-grandchildren than his brother or sister, and there are many parallels from other societies where close kinship is only thought to extend so far. The most difficult part of this section is the last (v. 25–8). Most editors have punctuated after ἐπιβάλλοντες and translated τᾶς Ϝοικίας οἵτινές κ᾽ ἴοντι ὁ κλᾶρος as 'those who form the inheritance of the house', sc. the serfs. We find it very hard to believe that the serfs inherit the estate in any circumstances, and prefer to follow de Sanctis (*Storia dei Greci*, i. 508) and Guarducci in seeing some reference here to other free families connected with that of the deceased in the property-pattern of the land by kinship or neighbourhood. (So also Lotze, op. cit. 12–14, but he denies that κρέματα includes land.)

A few words on legal procedure. The importance of witnesses is marked throughout the 'Code', but in this section they only appear at the division of an estate or at the logically connected occasion of the bestowal of a dowry (v. 51–vi. 2). Decisions are made in three ways. The first two are automatic, following directly from the application of the law to the facts. Either there is a fine, expressed in the future indicative (e.g. v. 38) or the *dikastes*, of whose method of appointment we know nothing, faced with clear facts, is said to δικάκσαι (v. 31). In a more complex situation, he has to use his own judgement, first swearing (that he will do so honestly), ὀμνύντα κρίναι (v. 43–4). See Diamond, op. cit. 364–7.

The *kosmoi*, the best-known Cretan magistrates, appear only at v. 3–6, and merely as a date. We cannot see any reason to support the view of Willetts (*Aristocratic Society*, 98 f.) that the ᾱ ὄκ' clause dates previous legislation, and it seems to us much more likely that it dates the legislation before us. Dates by *kosmoi* sometimes just give the names of the *kosmoi* or their principal member. At Gortyn they are more often in the form ἐπὶ τῶν Δυμάν[ων κ]ορμιόντων τῶν σὺν Καρταιδάμαι τῶ 'Ονυμάρ[χω] (*IC* iv. 182. 21–2). The form we find here is unique, though it may have recurred at *IC* iv. 142. 2. There is a clear inference that at Gortyn at this time the *kosmoi* of one year all came from a single group, no doubt with rotation between groups; this cannot always have been so, since it makes nonsense of the regulation *IC* iv. 14, *g–p*, 2 (quoted above, p. 3). Hesychius defines σταρτοί as αἱ τάξεις τοῦ πλήθους, and it is doubtless a form of στρατός. If we translate it roughly as 'clan', there is no more difficulty in saying that such and such a clan were *kosmoi* than in the Attic Αἰαντὶς ἐπρυτάνευε, where only fifty members of the whole tribe are in fact concerned. This apparently straightforward conclusion does not, however, easily fit *IC* iv. 80. 4–7, on which see Guarducci (ad loc., and *Historia* ix (1935) 443–5) and Willetts (op. cit. 111–13).

42 (33)

Relations between Argos, Knossos, and Tylisssos: about 450 B.C.

(*A*) The most substantial, with top and bottom preserved, of five fragments of poros from the boundary wall of a temenos of Artemis at Tylissos; now in the Heraklion Museum. (*B*) Two joining fragments of a stele of greyish limestone found at Argos; now in the Argos Museum.

(*A*) Argive letters (cf. No. 35) with both earlier and later forms than *B*, in three columns, each stoichedon 22, save in l. 22 which has 23 letters. (*B*) Argive letters, stoichedon 37, with some irregularities in ll. 42–8. The lettering of both seems slightly later than that of No. 35; koppa has disappeared. There is some difference of lettering in *B*, l. 43 ff.: V is replaced by Y from l. 43; omicron loses its central dot and ⊙ becomes Φ

from the middle of l. 44. See *LSAG* 165 (Argos 39). Phots. of (*A*): Ἀρχ.
'Εφ. 1914, 94–8; *IC* i. 307. Of (*B*): *BCH* xxxvii (1913) Pl. iv; Vollgraff
(below) Pl. i–ii.

Vollgraff, 'Le Decret d'Argos relatif à un pacte entre Knossos et Tylissos'
(*Verh. d. Kon. Ned. Ak. v. Wet., afd. Let.*, N.S. li. 2) +; Buck 85 (*B*); *Staats-
verträge* 147–8+; *LSAG*, loc. cit.; Graham, *Colony and Mother City in Ancient
Greece*, 154–60, 235–44.

A

Col. i　[....ἰαρὰ παρ]εχόντο τοὶ πα-
　　　　[ρὰ τὸν Ἀργεί]ον, δέρματα δὲ φ-
　　　　[ερόσθο hοι Κν]όhιοι. πρὸ Ταυ-
　　　　[ροφονίον θύε]ν ἐν Τυλισοῖ F-
　　5　[άρνα...6..., ἀμ]νὰν δὲ καὶ δι-
　　　　[.....11......]· σπονδὰς νεοτ-
　　　　[έρας] μὲ τιθέσθαι μεδατέρο-
　　　　[νς, αἰ] μὲ συνδοκοῖ τοῖ πλέθε-
　　　　[ι, συνβ]άλλεσθαι δὲ τὰν τρίτ-
　　10　[αν αἶσ]αν τὸς Ἀργείος τὰν ψά-
　　　　[φον· καὶ] τινας τὸν εὐμενέον

Col. ii　δυσμενέας τιθείμεθα καὶ τ-
　　　　ὸν δυσμενέον εὐμενέας, μὲ θ-
　　　　έσθαι, αἰ μὲ συνδοκοῖ τοῖ πλ-
　　15　έθει, συνβάλλεσθαι δὲ τὸνς
　　　　ἐκ Τυλισὸ τὰν ψάφον τὰν τρί-
　　　　ταν αἶσαν. αἰ δὲ μάχα γένοιτ-
　　　　ο μὲ παρέντον τὸν ἀτέρον, σπ-
　　　　ονδὰνς θέσθο 'ν τοῖ δεομένο-
　　20　ι πέντε ἀμέρανς. αἰ στρατήα
　　　　ἐνσ[ιείε] ἐνς τὰν γᾶν τὰν Κνο-
　　　　hίαν, [Τυλισίονς] ὀφελῆν παντ-

Col. iii　ι σθένει [.....10..... σῖτον]
　　　　παρεχόν[το hοι Κνόhιοι τοῖ]-
　　25　ς Ἀργείο[ις Κνοhοῖ, τοὶ δ' Ἀργ]-
　　　　εῖοι τοῖ[ς ἐν Τυλισοῖ..5...]
　　　　ιεν στρα[τήαν τριάκοντα ἀμ]-
　　　　ερᾶν· αἰ δ[ὲ......14......]
　　　　ἱμεν τὰν [.......15........]
　　30　ς. κὲν Τυλ[ισοῖ.....11......]

ε κα Ϝαρθ[......15........]
-πάγεσθα[ι.......14.......]
να. αἴ κ' ἔνθ[......14.......]
- - - - - - -

B

νες[.....10.....]
[...........23............] τὸν χ̑ο[ρον τὸ]ν Ἀ[χ]α-
[ρναίον τοῖ Τυλισίοι ἐξε͂μ]εν ξύλλεσθαι πλὰ[ν] τ-
[ὰ μέρε τὰ Κνοσίον συν]τέλλοντα ἐνς πόλιν. ἡό τ[ι]
5   [δέ κα ἐκ δυσμενέ]ον ℎέλομες συνανφότεροι, δα[σ]-
[μο͂ι τὸν κὰτ γ]ᾶν τὸ τρίτον μέρος ἔχεν πάντον, τ[ο͂]-
[ν δὲ κὰτ] θάλασαν τὰ ℎέμισα ἔχεν πάντον· τὰν δὲ [δ]-
[εκ]άταν τὸνς Κνοσίονς ἔχεν, ℎό τί χ' ἔλομες κοι[ν]-
[ᾶ]ι· τὸν δὲ φαλύρον τὰ μὲν καλλ⟨ι⟩στεῖα Πυθόδε ἀπ[ά]-
10   γεν κοινᾶι ἀμφοτέρονς, τὰ δ' ἄλλα τοῖ [Ἄρει Κνοσ]-
οῖ ἀντιθέμεν κοινᾶι ἀμφοτέρονς. ἐξ[αγογὰν δ' εἶ]-
μεν Κνοσόθεν ἐνς Τυλισὸν κὲκ Τυλι[σο͂ Κνοσόνδ]-
ε· α[ἰ] δὲ πέρανδε ἐξάγοι, τελίτο ℎόσσα[περ ℎοι Κν]-
όσιοι· τὰ δ' ἐκ Τυλισο͂ ἐξαγέσθο ℎόπυ[ί κα χρε͂ι. το͂]-
15   ι Ποσειδᾶνι το͂ι ἐν Ἰυτο͂ι τὸν Κνοσίο[ν ἰαρέα θύ]-
εν. τᾶι ℎέραι ἐν Ἐραίοι θύεν βο͂ν θέλει[αν ἀμφοτ]-
έρον[ς κ]οινᾶι, θύεν δὲ πρὸ Ϝακινθ[ίον....8....]
.κο[...]κ[- - - - - - - - - - - - - - - - - - -

two lines lost

21   [......14.......]ανοντο[.......14.......]πρ[α]-
τομενίαν ἄγεν κατὰ ταὐτ[ὰ κατὰ τὸ δόγμα] τὸ ἀμ[φ]-
οτέρον. χρέματα δὲ μὲ 'νπιπασκέσθο ℎο Κνόσιο[ς]
ἐν Τυλισοι, ℎο δὲ Τυλίσιος ἐν Κνοσοι ℎο χρείζ[ο]-
25   ν. μὲ δὲ χόρας ἀποτάμνεσθαι μεδατέρονς μεδ' ἅ[π]-
ανσαν ἀφαιρῖσθαι. δροι τᾶς γᾶς· ℎυὸν ὄρος καὶ Ἀ-
ιετοὶ κάρταμίτιον καὶ τὸ το͂ Ἀρχο͂ τέμενος κα[ὶ]
ℎο ποταμὸς κὲλ Λευκόπορον κἀγάθοια, ℎᾶι ℎύδο-
ρ ῥε͂ι το͂μβριον, καὶ Λᾶος. ℎῖ κα το͂ι Μαχανεῖ θύομ-
30   ες τὸνς Ϝεξέκοντα τελέονς ὄϝινς, καὶ τᾶι ℎ⟨έ⟩ραι
τὸ σκέλος Ϝεκάστο διδόμεν το͂ θύματος. αἰ δὲ συμπλέονες πόλιες ἐκ πολεμίον ἕλοιεν χρέματα,
ℎόπαι συνγνοῖεν ℎοι Κνόσιοι καὶ τοὶ Ἀργεῖοι,

 hούτο ἔμεν. τôι Ἄρει καὶ τἀφροδίται τὸν Κνοσί-
35 *ον ἱαρέα θύεν, φέρεν δὲ τὸ σκέλος Fεκάστο. τὸν Ἄ-*
 ρχὸν τὸ τέμενος ἔχεν τὸν Ἀχάρναι· τοῖς θύονσι
 ξένια παρέχεν τὸνς Κνοσίονς, τὸνς δ' Ἀργείονς
 τôι χόροι. ἐν Τυλισôι αἴ κα καλêι ho Κνόσιος πρ-
 εσγέαν, hέπεσθαι hόπυί κα δέεται, καὶ χὸ Τυλίσ-
40 *ιος, τὸν Κνόσιον κατὰ ταὐτά· αἰ δὲ μὲ δοῖεν ξένι-*
 α, βολὰ ἐπαγέτο ῥύτιον δέκα στατέρον αὐτίκα ἐ-
 πὶ κόσμος, κὲν Τυλισôι κατὰ ταὐτὰ ho Κνόσιος. v
 ha στάλα ἔσστα ἐπὶ Μελάντα βασιλέος. ἀFρέτευ-
 ε Λυκοτάδας hυλλεύς. v ἁλιαίαι ἔδοξε τᾶι τôν v
45 *ιαρôν· v ἀ(Fρέτευε) v βολᾶς v Ἀρχίστρατος Λυκοφρονίδας·*
 τοὶ Τυλίσιοι ποὶ τὰν στάλαν ποιγραψάνσθο τάδε·
 αἴ τις ἀφικνοῖτο Τυλισίον ἐνς Ἄργος, κατὰ ταὐτά
 σφιν ἔστο hαιπερ Κνοσίοις· vacat
        vacat

A. Vollgraff suggests *hερμᾶι, ἀμ]νὰν δὲ καὶ δί*|[*δομεν Δαίραι* for ll. 5–6.
In l. 23 he has *κὰτ τὸ δύνατον*, which is two letters too long. In ll. 25–6
he suggests *σιταρ*]|*κὲν*, but the first letter of 26 is a certain iota. For 28 ff.
he suggests *αἰ δ[έ κ' ἀποστήλοντι, ἀπ*]|*ίμεν τὰν* [*στρατήαν ἐπ' οἴκον*]|*ς.*
κὲν Τυλ[*ισôι κὰτ ταὐτά. hî δ*]|*έ κα Fαρθ*[*αίαι ὄFιν θύομεν, ἀ*]|*πάγεσθα*[*ι*
καὶ τἀπόλλονι Fάρ]|*να. αἴ κ' ἔνθ*[*ει τις Κνοσίον ἐν*|*ς Ἄργος,*]
B. l. 9: The iota was omitted. In l. 30 we should perhaps allow the ⊟ to
stand for *hε*, rather than say that epsilon was omitted. In l. 38 most texts
have punctuation after, rather than before, *ἐν Τυλισôι*. Ll. 46–7 both have
two extra letters in the margin.

 We have omitted four small fragments from Tylissos. One of them,
Vollgraff's (I), may be restored as the prescript of an Argive decree,
and Vollgraff claims that his (III) overlaps with the text of *B*, ll. 34–5.
This last is by no means certain (see Jeffery, *LSAG*, loc. cit.), and
formal proof is therefore lacking that these texts really form part of
a single document, of which copies were set up in both Argos and
Tylissos. Some difficulty may also be felt about the letter-forms of
the Tylissian copy. Nevertheless, though it might be possible to construct a scheme of events by which on two occasions fairly close in
date Argos intervened in the affairs of Knossos and Tylissos, there
is no hint in the documents that they reflect different circumstances,
and it seems highly probable that the two texts belong together.
 A. '(1–6). The representatives from the Argives shall provide the
sacrifice, and the Knossians shall receive the skins. Before the Tauro-
phonia, sacrifice in Tylissos a sheep (to Hermes?) and give (?) a lamb

(to Daira?). (7–20). Neither party shall make any new treaty, save with the assent of the federal assembly, and the Argives shall cast the third part of the votes. And if we make any friend an enemy and any enemy a friend, we shall not do so, save with the assent of the federal assembly, and the representatives from Tylissos shall cast the third part of the votes. But if a battle takes place with the other party not present, it shall be lawful to make a truce in necessity for five days. (21–8). If any army enters the land of the Knossians, the Tylissians shall help ($\delta\phi\epsilon\lambda\epsilon\hat{\iota}\nu = \dot{\omega}\phi\epsilon\lambda\epsilon\hat{\iota}\nu$; cf. Thuc. v. 23. 1) with all their strength as far as possible. The Knossians shall provide food for the Argives at Knossos, but the Argives for forces at Tylissos. An army shall be fed (?) for thirty days.' These provisions for the conduct of joint expeditions seem to continue at least as far as l. 30.

B. '(2–4). The Tylissian may pillage ($\xi\dot{\upsilon}\lambda\lambda\epsilon\sigma\theta\alpha\iota = \sigma\kappa\dot{\upsilon}\lambda\lambda\epsilon\sigma\theta\alpha\iota$) the territory of the Acharnaeans [cf. l. 36, perhaps the modern Archanes, south of Knossos], except those parts which belong to the city of the Knossians. (4–11). Whatever we both together take from the enemy, (the Tylissian) shall in a division take a third of all which is taken by land, and half of everything which is taken by sea, and the Knossians shall keep the tithe of whatever we take jointly; and of the spoils [$\phi\alpha\lambda\dot{\upsilon}\rho\sigma\nu$ is probably not an engraver's error, but a by-form of $\lambda\alpha\phi\dot{\upsilon}\rho\sigma\nu$ produced by metathesis] both shall send the finest jointly to Delphi, and the rest both shall dedicate jointly to Ares at Knossos. (11–14). There shall be export from Knossos to Tylissos and from Tylissos to Knossos; but if any (Tylissian) export goods beyond, he shall pay as much as the Knossians pay; and goods from Tylissos may be exported whither he may desire. (14–17). The priest of the Knossians [cf. l. 34] shall sacrifice to Poseidon at Iytos [perhaps the modern Mt. Iuktas]; both shall sacrifice jointly a cow to Hera in the Heraion [the famous Argive Heraion is more probable than a Cretan temple] and they shall sacrifice before the Hyakinthia - (21–3). They shall keep the first day of the month at the same time according to the decision of both. (23–5). The Knossian may not possess real property ($\dot{\epsilon}\nu\pi\iota\pi\dot{\alpha}\sigma\kappa\sigma\mu\alpha\iota = \dot{\epsilon}\gamma\kappa\tau\dot{\alpha}\sigma\mu\alpha\iota$) at Tylissos, but the Tylissian who wishes (may do so) at Knossos. (25–9). Neither party shall cut off any of the land or take it all away. The boundaries of the land: Swine's Mount and the Eagles and the Artemision and the precinct of Archos and the river [perhaps the Platyperama], and to Leukoporos and Agathoia following the course of the rainwater [cf. ᾇ ὕδωρ ῥεῖ, *GDI* 5016. 12, 5075. 51, etc.; ὡς ὑδάτων ῥοαί, *Inschr. Priene*, 37. 107] and Laos. (29–31). When we sacrifice to Machaneus [see *RE* xiv. 141 f. and Vollgraff ad loc., who identifies Machaneus with Castor] the sixty full-grown rams, to Hera too shall be given the leg of each victim. (31–4). If several cities together capture property

from the enemy, as the Knossians and Argives agree, so shall it be.
(34–5). The priest of the Knossians shall sacrifice to Ares and Aphrodite, and shall receive the leg of each victim [Ares and Aphrodite are
linked in many Cretan documents, and also at Argos; Paus. ii. 25. 1].
(35–8). Archos shall keep the precinct at Acharna; the Knossians shall
provide gifts to the sacrificers, and the Argives to the chorus. (38–42). If
the Knossian calls for an embassy in Tylissos, it shall follow wherever
he wishes, and if the Tylissian (call the Knossian), the Knossian
shall follow likewise. [Vollgraff regards this as machinery for emending
the arrangements between Knossos and Tylissos, and takes the next
sentence closely with it, but the usual view, which makes the clause
bind both parties to support the embassies of the other, is probably
preferable.] If they should not offer hospitality, let the Council forthwith impose a fine [for ῥύτιον see Wilhelm, *Jahresh.* xiv (1911) 197 ff.]
of ten staters on the *kosmoi*, and the Knossian similarly at Tylissos.
(43–4). The stele was erected (ἔσστα = ἐστάθη) when Melantas was
king [Vollgraff's attempt to identify him with Meltas, last king of
Argos according to Paus. ii. 19. 2, is certainly wrong; he is a mere
eponymous official] and Lykotadas of the tribe Hylleis was in office
[despite Amandry, *Hesp.* xxi (1952) 217, Lykotadas is a personal
name here and not a phratry; see Wörrle, *Untersuchungen zur Verfas-
sungsgeschichte von Argos* (Diss. Erlangen, 1964), 19 n. 41, 50 n. 26].
(44–8). Resolved by the assembly concerned with sacred business;
Archistratos of the Lykophronid phratry was president of the Council;
let the Tylissians add to the stele these words: if any Tylissian comes
to Argos, he shall have the same rights as the Knossians.'

The situation here envisaged is complex, but the text seems to imply
a federal structure in which Argos, Knossos, Tylissos, and perhaps
other states (see especially *B*, 31–2) are linked, in which physical
intervention by Argos in Crete is thought possible (*A*, 24–6), and
within which special arrangements are made to govern the relations
of Knossos and Tylissos, many of them clearly designed to protect
the position of Tylissos against her stronger neighbour. These arrangements seem to incorporate the result of previous negotiations between
Knossos and Tylissos themselves, to judge by the frequent use of the
first person. The alternative view, proposed by Kahrstedt (*Klio*, xxxiv
(1941) 72–91) and followed by Gschnitzer (*Abhängige Orte*, 44–7) by
which we have here a treaty between Argos and Knossos, in which
Tylissos only appears as a dependency of Argos, seems to us nearly
impossible. It makes better sense of *B*, 4–7, where the Argives become
the subject of the verbs ἔχεν, but creates confusion everywhere else.
It is satisfactorily refuted by Graham, 239–44, but we do not find his
own statement of the position entirely convincing, since he puts the
reason for Argive intervention almost entirely on her unattested,

though quite likely, position as mother city of these Cretan states, and plays down the indications of a federal structure.

The text is later than No. 35, but not by much, and it seems safe to put this remarkable extension of Argive interests around the year 450 or a little earlier.

The language is Argive in both texts, in fact more Argive in the Tylissian than in the Argive text, for in *A* Argive intervocalic *h* is preserved even in Κνόhιοι, while *B* has Κνόσιοι throughout and the Cretan hοι in l. 33 to go with it; for the Argive dialect see Bechtel, *GD* ii. 437 ff., Buck, pp. 162–4.

43 (35)

Political Expulsions from Miletus:
between 470 and 440 B.C.

On a marble base, which once bore a stele, found *in situ* in the North Market at Miletus.

Ionic letters, stoichedon 44, but blank spaces are left at the end of lines or final letters are inscribed on the right-hand side of the base in order that each line may end with a word or the preposition of a compound verb. Phot.: *Milet* i. 6. 101.

SIG 58; *Milet*, i. 6. 100–4; Glotz, *CRAI* 1906, 511–29; Meiggs, *JHS* lxiii (1943) 26; Barron, *JHS* lxxxii (1962) 1–6.

[. . . . . . . 15 . . . .]σ[. . . . . τ]ὸ[. Ν]υμφαρήτο καὶ Ἀλκι[μον]
[καὶ Κ]ρεσφόντην [τὸ]⟨ς⟩ Στρατώνακτος φεύγεν τὴν ἐπ' αἴμ[ατ|ι]
[φυγὴν] καὶ αὐτὸς [κα]ὶ ἐκγόνος, καὶ ὃς ἄν τινα τούτων κατ[α]-
[κτείνε]ι, ἑκατὸν [στ]ατῆρας αὐτῶι γενέσθαι ἀπὸ τῶν
5 [χρημά]των τῶν Νυμ[φαρή]το· τὸς δ' ἐπιμηνίος, ἐπ' ὦν ἂν ἔλθωσ|ιν
[οἱ κατα]κτείναντες, ἀποδοῦναι τὸ ἀργύριον· ἢν δὲ μή, αὐτὸ|[ς]
[ὀφε]ίλεν. ἢν δὲ ἡ πόλι[ς ἐ]γκρατ⟨ὴ⟩ς γένηται, κατακτέναι
[αὐ]τὸς τὸς ἐπιμηνίος [ἐ]π' ὦν ἂν λαφθέωσιν· ἢν δὲ μὴ κατα-
[κτ]είνοσιν, ὀφείλεν ἕ[κ]αστον πεντήκοντα στατῆρας.
10 τὸν δὲ ἐπιμήνιον, ἢν μὴ προθῆι, ἑκατὸν στατῆρας ὀφείλε[ν]
καὶ τὴν ἐσιῶσαν ἐπιμηνίην αἰ ποιεῖν κατὰ τὸ ψήφισμα·
ἢν δὲ μή, τὴν αὐτὴν θωιὴν ὀφείλεν.

In l. 1 either τ]ὸ[ν or τ]ὸ[ς. In l. 2 [τό]ν and in 7 ἐ]γκρατές are errors by the mason.

In this Milesian decree three men (and perhaps more) and their descendants are outlawed. A price is put on their heads, and if they are captured the ἐπιμήνιοι in office are to put them to death or pay heavy fines. The surviving inscription is on a base which originally supported a stele. Twenty letters are missing at the beginning of the first line, but this gives insufficient room for the preamble to the decree, which probably therefore began on the stele. Since such a division of the text is extremely awkward it is reasonable to infer that the stele was already inscribed when this decree was passed, and that our decree was added because it was of the same nature.

Most interpretations derive from an ingenious analysis by Glotz (op. cit.). He pointed out that the inclusion of the descendants in the sentence showed that the crime was treason, and he interpreted the monument in the light of a passage from Nicolaus of Damascus (*FGH* 90 F 53), which echoed some of the phrases of our decree. The passage describes the events in Miletus leading to the overthrow of the Neleids, apparently at the end of the monarchy. Glotz, noting that Alkimos and Kresphontes are good Neleid names, suggested that the original inscription on the stele recorded an expulsion of the Neleids in the sixth century, and that in a similar situation when Neleids were again expelled in the fifth century the record was inscribed on the same stele. Glotz associated the expulsion with the Athenian decree of 450–49 providing for the closer control of Miletus by a board of five Athenian officials (*ATL* ii. D 11). He assumed that this decree marked the imposition of democracy by Athens, when their attempt to work with oligarchs, alluded to by the Old Oligarch ([Xen.] *Ἀθ. Πολ.* 3. 11), had failed. Recent discussion has modified this picture of Athenian relations with Miletus. The Athenian decree of 450–49 implies that Athens still wishes to co-operate with a Milesian oligarchy (Meiggs, *JHS* lxiii (1943) 27), and the tribute-lists may suggest a date for its later suppression. Barron has shown that Neleids were in office in 450–49 and in 446–5 (op. cit.) and he reinforces the view developed by A. J. Earp (*Phoenix* viii (1954) 142–7) that Miletus was in revolt from 446 to 443 (when she does not appear in any fragment of the tribute-lists). The Milesian expulsion decree in their view should follow the suppression of the oligarchy in 443 or 442.

This dating depends largely on the inference by Glotz that the Milesian decree recorded the expulsion of the Neleids. The evidence barely justifies the conclusion. We do not know how many names preceded those that survive, but since (*a*) 100 staters are to be paid to anyone who kills any of the persons named, and the property of Nympharetos will apparently suffice, and (*b*) room has to be left on the stele for an earlier inscription, it is unlikely that the text was long. Not enough Neleid names can be identified to speak of a Neleid

oligarchy in control. Nor need this decree mark the final suppression
of oligarchy. The fact that rewards are to be paid from the property
of Nympharetos implies that he is only recently dead, probably killed
in political *stasis*. In an Athenian decree laying down regulations for
Erythrai (No. 40, l. 33) a penalty is specified for anyone who is found
betraying the city to 'the tyrants' (τοῖς τυράννοις) and these are probably to be identified with those who have taken refuge with the Medes
(τὸν ἐς] Μέδος φευγό[ντο]ν, l. 27). Nympharetos and Stratonax may
(perhaps with a few others) have been 'the tyrants' in Miletus; they
may have been killed or expelled when Athens first intervened, probably in 452. The final suppression of the oligarchy would probably
have been accompanied by more sweeping expulsions. It is also doubtful whether this Milesian decree reflects a democracy of the Athenian
pattern. A Milesian decree of 380–79 has a prescript in the Athenian
mould with Epistates, and Prytany with Athenian tribal name (Wiegand, *Sitzb. Berl.* 1901, 911). It is likely that this Athenian model was
introduced before Athens collapsed, and the natural context is the
suppression of oligarchy. But in our decree ἐπιμήνιοι seem to fulfil
the function of Prytany. The word is used in that sense in an early
fifth-century inscription from Eretria (*IG* xii, suppl. 549, Μεκισστ[ίδ]|ος
φυλῆς: ἐπιμεν[ι]ούρες), but it is also used for religious officials (*RE*,
s.v. ἐπιμήνιοι) and this might be the meaning here. Rehm considered
that the letter-forms suggested a date 'fairly early in the fifth century'
(*Arch. Anz.* 1906, 16); we share this view, but there are too few dated
fifth-century inscriptions from Ionia to rely on letter-forms. It would
be wise to exclude neither the forties nor the sixties.

44 (40)

Appointment of a Priestess and building of a Temple of Athena Nike: (?) 450–445 B.C.

Marble stele found on the north slope of the Acropolis, with a cutting for
another stone on top closely fitted by scarf joint. A second decree is on the
back (No. 71); now in EM.

Developed Attic letters except Ϛ. Stoichedon 29. Phot.: Kern 14; Ἀρχ.
Ἐφ. 1897, Pl. 11; Guarducci, *Epigrafia Greca*, i. 141 fig. 32.

Kabbadias, Ἀρχ. Ἐφ. 1897, 174–94; *SIG* 63; *IG* i². 24; Welter, *Jahrb.*,
Anz. liv (1939) 1–22; Schlaifer, *Harv. Stud.* li (1940) 257–60; Meritt,
Hesp. x (1941) 307–15; Papademetriou, Ἀρχ. Ἐφ. 1948/9, 146–53;
Mattingly, *Hist.* x (1961) 169 f.; Meritt and Wade-Gery, *JHS* lxxxiii
(1963) 109–11.

[. . . . . 18 . . . . τὸ]ι [δέ]μο[ι . . .]

[. . . . . 17 . . . .]αικος εἶπε· [τει]

[Ἀθεναίαι τει Νί]κει hιέρεαν hὲ ἀγ[. .]

[. . . . . . 12 . . . . .] ἐχς Ἀθεναίον hαπα[σō]-

5 [ν καθίστα]σθαι καὶ τὸ hιερὸν θυρōσα-
ι καθότι ἂν Καλλικράτες χσυγγράφσ-
ει· ἀπομισθōσαι δὲ τὸς πολετὰς ἐπὶ τ-
ες Λεοντίδος πρυτανείας· φέρεν δὲ τ-
ὲν hιέρεαν πεντέκοντα δραχμὰς καὶ

10 τὰ σκέλε καὶ τὰ δέρματα φέρεν τὸν δε-
μοσίον· νεὸν δὲ οἰκοδομεσαι καθότι
ἂν Καλλικράτες χσυγγράφσει καὶ βο-
μὸν λίθινον.

hεστιαῖος εἶπε· τρες ἄνδρας hελέσθ-

15 αι ἐγ βολες· τούτος δὲ μετ[ὰ] Καλλικρά-
[το]ς χσυγγράφσαντας ἐπ[ιδεῖχσαι τε]-
[ι βολ]ει καθότι ἀπομ[ισθοθέσεται . .]

[. . . . . .]ει τοσ[- - - - - - - - - - - - -]
- -

Meritt infers that the main decree was inscribed on the upper stone and
that the lower stone which survives carried amendments (see below),
of which one starts on the upper stone [τὸς δὲ πρυτάνες χρεμ- and continues
on the lower stone (ll. 1 f.) [ατίσαι περὶ τούτου ἐν τō]ι [δέ]μο[ι ἐν τ|ει
πρότει hέδραι υ Γλ]αῦκος εἶπε. l. 2: Possible alternatives for the proposer's
name are Πατ]αικός and Φαλ]αικός.   ll. 3–5: The epitaph of the first
priestess (SEG xii. 80, see below) shows that she was appointed by lot: hὲ
ἀ[ν δι|ὰ βίο hιεράτα]ι ἐχς Ἀθεναίον hαπα[σō|ν κλερόσα]σθαι Papademe-
triou; hὲ ἀγ [κλ|ερομένε λάχε]ι ἐχς Ἀθεναίον hαπα[σō|ν καθίστα]σθαι
Meritt and Wade-Gery.

The surviving text provides for (a) the appointment for life, by lot,
of a priestess of Athena Nike, and all Athenian women are to be
eligible (it is to be a democratic priesthood, not confined to an
aristocratic family as so many of the traditional priesthoods had been);
(b) the construction of a door for Nike's hιερόν according to Kalli-
krates' design, and the placing of the contract; (c) the payment to the
priestess of an annual salary of 50 dr., together with the legs and
hides from public sacrifices; (d) the building of a temple to be designed by Kallikrates and an altar of stone (marble). An amendment
(though the normal amendment formula, τὰ μὲν ἄλλα καθάπερ, is
omitted) was carried by Hestiaios, ensuring a more democratic pro-

cedure. Three members of the Boule are to be elected to co-operate with the architect in drawing up the specification for the contract (for the door), and they are to submit their recommendations to the Boule.

These terms are clear on the stone, but the date and context are uncertain. The three-barred sigma without other early letter-forms points to a date between *c.* 450 and 445 (Meiggs, *JHS* lxxxvi (1966) 92), but the Ionic temple of Nike was not built on the bastion flanking the entrance to the Acropolis on its south side until the twenties (Dinsmoor, *The Architecture of Ancient Greece*³ (1950) 185 f.), when work on the Propylaia had been broken off. Before the bastion and temple were dismantled in 1936 there were still some who maintained that the temple was built before the Propylaia; this position is no longer tenable (G. Welter, *Jahrb.* liv (1939), *Anz.* 1–22). There might be more specific evidence for the date if Dinsmoor and others are right in attributing *IG* i². 111 to the beginning of the building of the temple, and if the *epistates* of that decree, Σμίκυθος, is to be identified with the *epistates* of *IG* i². 60, which concerns the settlement with Mytilene after her revolt in 427. The last three letters correspond, but the number of letters is not known. Even if this evidence is dismissed a date in the twenties is probably right. Mattingly, distrusting the letter-form criterion, dates our decree to the twenties in order to associate it directly with the actual building of the temple. In support he emphasizes that we now know that the first priestess died towards the end of the fifth century (for her epitaph see J. Papademetriou, Ἀρχ. Ἐφ., 1948/9, 146; *SEG* xii. 80) which, he thinks, makes her appointment in the early forties very unlikely. The purely epigraphic evidence for the date of the epitaph would not necessarily point to the last years of the century. The widespread intrusion of Ionic letters, though extremely rare in public inscriptions before the last decade of the fifth century, is not uncommon earlier in private inscriptions, and the lettering would not be out of place as early as 430 (phot.: *BSA* l (1955) 2). The identification, however, of Myrrhine, Nike's first priestess, with the Myrrhine of Aristophanes' *Lysistrata*, suggested by Papademetriou, and further elaborated by Lewis in *BSA* l (1955) 1–7, has been generally accepted, and requires a date for her death after 411 when the play was produced. But, as Meritt and Wade-Gery have pointed out (*JHS* lxxxiii (1963) 110, where other objections also are given to Mattingly's dating), the priestess of Hera at Argos, who served for 56½ years (Thuc. ii. 2. 1 and iv. 133), makes a tenure of some 45 years for the first priestess of Nike acceptable (an even longer period of office, 64 years, is attributed to Lysimache, priestess of Athena, by the elder Pliny, *NH* xxxiv. 76, Lewis *BSA* l. 4–6). The early date for the decree is easier to accept if we associate the decision to build a temple to Athena Nike with the end of the fighting against

Persia and a Peace of Kallias. This is at least a reasonable inference if the scenes on the north and south sides of the frieze depict, as is generally thought, fighting between Greeks and Persians. This interpretation seemed more compelling when it was thought that the mover of the decree was Hipponikos, son of Kallias (*IG* i². 24. 4; ἱππόν]ικος), but Dinsmoor and West made it clear that the traces on the stones were incompatible with the restoration (*Hesp.* Suppl. v. 159, n. 337). It may also be significant that in a later decree, almost certainly concerned with the temple, the allies as well as the Athenians are allowed a hearing (*IG* i². 88. 9–11: ἐ δὲ βολὲ μὲ ἀ[πολαμ-βανέτο πλὲν | ἐὰ]ν κ[ρι]θἔι π[ερὶ τού]το πρ[ό]τ[ερον ὑπὸ τὸν βολο|μέ]νο[ν Ἀ]θεναί[ον] καὶ τὸν χσυμ[μάχον - -). It seems unlikely that the allies would be encouraged to express proposals concerning a temple or sanctuary with which they had no concern. If Nike's temple was particularly associated with the end of fighting against Persia it would be sound Athenian policy or propaganda to give them a hearing.

There is a further complication. If the decree began on the lower stone there is room in the first two lines, before the speaker's name, for only one of the three normal elements of a prescript (prytany, secretary, president). If this is the beginning of a decree the two missing elements should be on a separate stone. There was, indeed, another stone fitted to our surviving stone by a splice or scarf-joint, sloping down towards the back, designed to provide as close a fit as possible. Dinsmoor argued that this joint was quite unsuited to receive the bottom moulding of an *akroterion* or relief, such as might crown a decree (*AJA* xxvii (1923) 319), and Meritt pointed out that the top line comes too close to the top of the stone to be the beginning of the inscription, but that the distance is exactly one-half of the normal interspace between lines (*Hesp.* x (1941) 312). His conclusion was that the decree began at the top of the upper stone, running on to the third line of the lower stone, where the first amendment began. Subsequently, with Wade-Gery, he argued that such an important amendment presupposes a substantive decree of major importance. 'Its main subject-matter was almost surely the architectural reorganization of the western approach to the Acropolis' (*JHS* lxxxiii (1963) 109), and the delay between plan and execution was to be explained by a conflict of interest involving the south-west wing of the Propylaia and the precinct of Athena Nike, which led to a very considerable alteration in the original plan of the Propylaia. This is an exciting hypothesis, but there are difficulties. On any interpretation the decree concerns matters of considerable importance. Why should the mason have chosen to set out his inscription on two stones carefully jointed together rather than on a single stele? He begins the 'second amendment (l. 14) on a new line; why does he begin the 'first' and more important one in the middle of a line? Would one understand from the wording or the order of clauses that the building of a temple was highly controversial? If the amendment represents religious forces protesting against the secular, would they have chosen Kalli-krates, who seems to have been deeply committed to Periclean building policies? He supervised the building of the middle long wall (Plut., *Per.* 13. 7), was entrusted with strengthening the security of the Acropolis against runaway slaves and footpads (*IG* i². 44), and collaborated with Iktinos on the Parthenon.

It is perhaps less difficult to believe that the upper stone carried a relief and the name of the prytany and the secretary. Normally when the secretary's name was recorded above a decree it was also included in the text of the decree itself, but the Chalkis decree is an exception (No. 52). Above that decree and another affixed on its left was an upper stone, probably with a relief and the name of the γραμματεύς; no secretary is recorded below in the text of the decree. In a decree of 410–09 (*IG* i². 109 = *ATL* ii. D 9) both secretary and tribal prytany are recorded above the decree. For the closeness of the first line to the top of the stone cf. *IG* i². 81, below a relief (phot.: *AM* xix (1894) Pl. 7).

Perhaps too little attention has been paid to the actual terms of the decree and the order in which they are formulated. The first injunction is not to build a temple, but to appoint a priestess in a democratic manner. The second is to provide a door for τὸ ἱερόν, whether that be the whole precinct or the 'Cimonian' shrine below the actual temple. Provision is made for the leasing of the contract for this work, and then for the payment of the priestess. It is only after this that the temple is mentioned, and the emphasis on providing a doorway for the ἱερόν surely implies that the temple will not be built until later.

45 (67)

Athenian Decree enforcing the use of Athenian Coins, Weights, and Measures: (?) 450–446 B.C.

Seven fragments: two of local limestone from Syme, one each of marble from Aphytis, Cos, and Siphnos. One of marble was copied at Smyrna and is now lost; another was recently identified in Odessa Museum (*SEG* xxi. 18).

All fragments in Ionic script except the Cos fragment, which has de-veloped Attic letters except Ϛ. Phot.: *ATL* ii, Pl. 5, 6, 7; of the Cos frag-ment, also *BCH* lxxxix (1965) 438–9.

ATL ii. D 14, with full bibliography (1949); Tod, *JHS* lxix (1949) 104 f.;

E. S. G. Robinson, *Hesp.* Suppl. viii (1949) 324–40; Cavaignac, *Rev. Num.* xv (1953) 1–7; Mattingly, *Hist.* x (1961) 148–69, *Proc. Afr. Class. Ass.* vii (1964) 48, *CQ* xvi (1966) 187–90; Meritt and Wade-Gery, *JHS* lxxxii (1962) 67–74; Meritt, *Gk. Rom. Byz. Stud.* viii (1967) 126–9.

[(1) - - - - - -]ολε[- - - - - - - - - - - - - -c. 27- - - - - - - - - - - - -]αι τὰ γ[
- - - - - - - - -c. 19- - - - - - - - - - ἄρχ]οντε[ς ἐν ταῖς π]όλεσι ἢ ἄρ[χοντες
- - - - - - - - - - -c. 22- - - - - - -(2) οἱ] δὲ ἑλληνοταμ[ίαι - - - - - - - - - - -
c. 24 - - - - - - - - -ἀ]ναγραφόντων· ἐὰ[ν δὲ μὴ - - - - - - - - - - - - - - - -
π]όλεών τινος, ἐσα[γέτω ὁ βουλόμενος αὐτίκα μάλα εἰς τ]ὴν ἡλιαίαν τὴν
τῶ[ν θεσμοθετῶν τοὺς ἠδικηκότας· ο]ἱ δὲ θεσμοθέ[τ]αι πέ[νθ' ἡμερῶν
δό]ντων [δίκας τοῖς φήν]ασι ἕκαστον. (3) ἐὰν δὲ [ἄλλος ἔξω τ]ῶν ἀρχόν-
[των ἐν τ]αῖς πόλεσι μὴ ποιῆι κα[τὰ τὰ ἐψηφισ]μένα ἢ τῶν [πολι]τῶν
ἢ τῶν ξένων, [ἄτ]ιμ[ος ἔστω καὶ τὰ χρή]ματα [αὐτοῦ] δημόσια [ἔσ]τω
καὶ τῆς θεοῦ τ[ὸ ἐπιδέκατον. (4) καὶ εἰ μ]ή εἰσι[ν] ἄρχοντες Ἀθηναίων,
ἐ[πιτελεσάντων ὅσα ἐν τῶι ψ]ηφίσματι οἱ ἄρχοντε[ς οἱ ἑκάστης τῆς
πόλεως· καὶ] ἐὰμ μὴ ποιῶσι κατὰ τ[ὰ ἐψηφισμένα, ἔστω κατὰ τῶν
ἀρχ]όντων τούτων περὶ [ἀτιμίας δίωξις Ἀθήνησι· (5) ἐν δὲ τῶ]ι ἀργυρο-
κοπίωι τὸ ἀργύ[ριον δεξαμένους κόψαι μὴ ἔλα]ττον ἢ ἥμυσυ καὶ ἀ[- - -
- - - - - - - - - -c. 29- - - - - - -]ι αἱ πόλεις· πράττ[εσθαι δὲ ἀεὶ τοὺς
ἐπιστάτας τρεῖς] δραχμὰς ἀπὸ τῆς μν[ᾶς· τὸ δὲ ἄλλο ἥμυσυ. . 5. . .μηνῶν
κατ]αλλάττειν ἢ ἐνόχο[υς εἶναι - - - - - -c. 12 - - - - - -· (6) ὃ δὲ ἂν
περιγ]ίγνηται ἀργυρίο[υ τοῦ πεπραγμένου κόψαι καὶ ἀποδό]σθαι ἢ τοῖς
στρατ[ηγοῖς ἢ τοῖς - - - - - - -c. 15 - - - - - - -· (7) ἐπε]ιδὰν δὲ ἀπο-
δοθῆι, [- - - - - - - - - - -c. 29- - - - - - -]αι καὶ τῶι Ἡφαίσ[τωι- - - -
c. 14 - - -(8) καὶ ἐάν τι]ς εἴπ[ηι ἢ] ἐπιψηφίσηι περ[ὶ τούτων ἐξεῖναι
ξενικῶι νομίσμα]τι χρῆσθαι ἢ δανε[ίζειν, ἀπογραφέσθω αὐτίκα μάλα
πρὸς] τοὺς ἕνδεκα· οἱ δ[ὲ ἕνδεκα θαν]άτωι ζ[ημιωσάντων· ἐὰν] δὲ ἀμφι-
σβητῆι, εἰσ[αγαγόντων εἰς τὸ δικαστήρι]ον· (9) κήρυκας δὲ ἑλέσθαι
τὸ[ν δῆμον - -c. 25 - -τὰ ἐψηφισμ]ένα, ἕνα μὲν ἐπὶ Νή[σους, ἕνα δὲ
ἐπὶ Ἰωνίαν, ἕνα δὲ ἐφ' Ἑλλήσπο]ντον, ἕν[α] δὲ ἐ[πὶ τὰ ἐπὶ Θραίκης·
το[ύτοις δὲ τὴν πορείαν ἑκάστωι συγγράψαντες οἱ στρατηγοὶ ἀ]ποστει-
λάντ[ων· εἰ δὲ μή, καθ' ἕνα ἕκαστον εὐθυ]νόσθων [μ]υρ[ίαις δραχμαῖς·
(10) καταθεῖ]ναι δὲ τὸ ψήφισμα τ[όδε τοὺς ἄ]ρχοντα[ς τ]οὺ[ς ἐ]ν ταῖς
πόλεσιν [ἀναγράψαντας ἐν στήληι λιθίνηι ἐν τῆι ἀγορᾶι τῆ[ς πό]λεως
[ἑκάστης] καὶ τοὺς ἐπιστ[άτας ἔμπροσθεν] τοῦ ἀργυροκοπίου· ταῦτα δὲ
ἐπ[ιτελέσαι Ἀθηναίους, ἐ]ὰμ μὴ αὐτοὶ βούλωνται· (11) δεηθῆναι δὲ
αὐτῶ[ν] τὸγ κήρυκα τὸν ἰόντα ὅσα [κ]ελεύου[σιν] Ἀθηναῖοι· (12) προσγρά-

ψαι δὲ πρὸς τὸν ὅρκον [τ]ὸν τῆς βουλῆς τὸν γραμματέα τὸν τῆς [βουλῆς
εἰς τὸ λοιπὸν τα]δί· ἐάν τις κόπτηι νόμισ[μα] ἀργυρίου ἐν ταῖς πό[λεσι
κ]αὶ μὴ χρῆται νομ[ίσμασιν τοῖς Ἀθηνα]ίων ἢ σταθμοῖς ἢ μέτ[ροις,
ἀλλὰ ξενικοῖς νομίσμασι]ν καὶ μέτροις καὶ σταθμοῖς, [τιμωρήσομαι
κα]ὶ ζ[ημιώσω κατὰ τὸ πρότε]ρον ψήφισμα ὃ Κλέαρχ[ος εἶπεν· (13)
ἐξεῖναι δὲ καὶ ὁτωιοῦν ἀποδιδόν]αι τὸ ξενικὸν ἀργύριον [ὃ ἂν ἔχηι καὶ
καταλλάττειν κατὰ ταὐτὰ ὅ]ταμ βούληται· τὴν δὲ πό[λιν ἀνταποδοῦναι
αὐτῶι νόμισμα ἡμεδαπόν·] αὐτὸν δὲ τὰ [ἑ]αυτοῦ ἕκαστ[ον κομίζειν
Ἀθήναζε καὶ θεῖναι εἰς τὸ ἀργυ]ροκόπιον· (14) ο[ἱ δὲ] ἐπιστάτ[αι ἅπαντα
τὰ παρ' ἑκάστων ἀποδοθέντα ἀνα]γράψαντες κατα[θέντων στήλην
λιθίνην ἔμπροσθεν τοῦ ἀργυροκο]πίου σκοπεῖν τῶι βου[λομένωι· ἀνα-
γραψάντων δὲ καὶ ξύμπαν τὸ νόμισμα τὸ] ξενικόν, χω[ρὶς τό τε ἀργύριον
καὶ τὸ χρυσίον, καὶ ξύμπαν τὸ ἡμεδαπὸ]ν ἀργύρι[ον - - - - - - - - - - -
- - - - - - - - - - - - - - - - - - -].

This composite text follows, with minor exceptions, *ATL*, though some
restorations we have confined to our notes. In (8) we accept Tod's criticism
(*JHS* lxix (1949) 104 f.) of *ATL*'s ἐπιψηφίσηι περ[ὶ τούτων, ὅτι ἔστι and
adopt his alternative. In (14) we have included Tod's suggestion in place
of *ATL*'s ἀνα]γράψαντες κατα[θέντων παρὰ τὴν στήλην. In (2) *ATL* has οἱ]
δὲ ἑλληνοταμ[ίαι τὰ ἀργυροκόπια ἐν ταῖς πόλεσι ἀ]ναγραφόντων· ἐὰ[ν δὲ
μὴ ὀρθῶς ἀναγραφῆι τὸ ἐκ τῶν π]όλεων τινός, in (5) μὴ ἔλ]αττον ἢ ἥμυσυ
καὶ ἀ[ποδόσθαι ὡς ἂν νόμισμα ἱκανὸν ἔχωσ]ι αἱ πόλεις. For the minting
fee πέντε] δραχμὰς is also possible, but seems too high. (6) στρατ[ηγοῖς ἢ
τοῖς ἀποδέκταις εὐθύς *ATL*. (7) [ψηφίσασθαι καὶ περὶ τῶν τῆι Ἀθηναί]αι
καὶ τῶι Ἡφαίσ[τωι ὀφειλομένων] *ATL*. (9) κήρυκας δὲ ἑλέσθαι τὸ[ν δῆμον
καὶ πέμψαι εἰς τὰς πόλεις κατὰ τὰ ἐψηφισ]μένα *ATL*; [ἀπαγγέλλοντας or
ἀπαγγελοῦντας τὰ ἐψηφισ]μένα, Tod.

The decree requires all members of the Athenian Alliance to use
Athenian coins, weights, and measures. Independent silver coinages
are banned and local mints closed; electrum issues are not mentioned,
and Kyzikene staters remained plentiful and popular. In the clauses
that survive no exceptions are made. It is generally assumed that the
decree would not apply to Chios, Lesbos, and Samos, which might
still regard themselves as autonomous, but there is no firm evidence
(see below). Responsibility for carrying out the decree is to rest with
Athenian officials in the cities (ἄρχοντες τῶν Ἀθηναίων), and if there
are none, with local officials (4). The masters of the mint at Athens
are to convert foreign currencies, belonging to states or individuals,
into Attic coin, and a minting fee (? 3 drachmae in the mina) is probably specified (5). Heralds are to be sent to the various districts of

the empire under the supervision of the generals to report the decisions of the Assembly, and every city is to set up a copy of the decree in its Agora; at Athens a copy is to be set up in front of the mint. The importance attached to the decree is shown by the heavy penalties threatened against the executive if they fail to carry out instructions, the specification of summary arrest and death for anyone who proposes the repeal of the decree, and, above all, by the inclusion of a special clause in the Bouleutic oath. In future every member of the Boule must bind himself by oath to take action against and punish any offenders against the decree 'as prescribed by the earlier decree moved by Klearchos'.

While the main lines of the decree are firmly established, many details are uncertain. We do not know the precise terms of exchange (5). Hephaistos, and probably with him Athena, are mentioned in a context which we do not understand (7). If the *ATL* restoration is sound and a vote is to be taken about debts to these gods, we do not know when they were incurred. The duty laid on the *hellenotamiai* in (2) may not be, as restored, the drawing up of a list of local mints. Nor can we identify 'the former decree of Klearchos' (12). We cannot, with *ATL* ii. 67, believe that the words refer to our decree on the ground that 'for the future swearer the decree would be "earlier" than his oath'; such a superfluous addition of πρότερον would be very un-Greek. It is probably, but not necessarily, to be inferred that the present decree was also moved by Klearchos, and the subject of the former decree is probably related to the present decree rather than to a different subject. It may have set out the main lines of policy, to be followed by these detailed elaborations.

More important is the uncertainty of date. When Tod published his text in 1933, scholars' views ranged between 430 and 415. Aristophanes clearly parodied the decree in a passage of his *Birds* (1040 f.), in which the decree-monger offers for sale among his 'new laws': χρῆσθαι Νεφελοκοκκυγιᾶς τοῖσδε τοῖς (τοῖς αὐτοῖς Cobet) μέτροισι καὶ σταθμοῖσι καὶ ψηφίσμασι (Bergk unnecessarily wished to emend to νομίσμασι) καθάπερ 'Ολοφύξιοι. A date not far from 414 when the play was produced seemed to be required. It was also widely thought that the imperialistic tone of the decree reflected the spirit of Cleon and his associates. Hiller thought that this dating suited the scripts of the various fragments, and this too was the opinion of D. M. Robinson when he published a new fragment from Aphytis in 1935 (*AJP* lvi (1935) 149–54). The broad consensus, however, was badly shaken when in 1938 Segre published a small new fragment from Cos (*Clara Rhodos*, ix (1938) 151–78). Previous fragments had been in Ionic; the new text from Dorian Cos was in Attic letters and, according to Segre, on Pentelic marble. Since the decree seemed to provide for the setting up of copies by the Athenians in cities that were recalcitrant (10), it was reasonable to infer that the Cos copy had been cut at Athens and could be dated by comparison with dated Athenian documents. The crucial letter-form was the early three-barred sigma (Ϟ), which, by a generally accepted criterion, had become obsolete by 445. Segre did not hesitate to date the decree in the early forties.

The new dating has met with considerable opposition. Tod (*JHS* lxix (1949) 105) urged a later date, even if not later than 439, and pointed out that the early sigma was also found on Samian *Horoi* usually associated with the Samian revolt of 440–39 (but see Barron, *JHS* lxxxiv (1964) 35–48). Cavaignac (*Rev. Num.* xv (1953) 1 ff.) argued for a return to the later date primarily on historical grounds; Athens had not, he thought, reached such open imperialism in the forties. Mattingly (*Hist.* x. 148–69) made the decree a launching pad for a wide-spreading attack on dating by letter-forms, and proposed sharply revised dates for several important decrees hitherto dated before 445 on these grounds. Pritchett (*BCH* lxxxvii (1963) 20–3) suggested a compromise that might, he hoped, be acceptable to epigraphists and historians. If the marble was an island marble and not Pentelic, and if the cutter had come from Athens to Cos in the forties and stayed there, he might have used the forms with which he was familiar when he left Athens. The rigorous examination of the stone with samples from various different quarries by a highly experienced Greek mineralogist has in fact revealed that the marble was almost certainly not Pentelic (A. N. Georgiades and W. K. Pritchett, *BCH* lxxxix (1965) 400–40). On the present evidence, though the marble is not securely identified (Georgiades, followed by Pritchett, thinks that it is probably Parian), it is perhaps more likely to have been inscribed in Cos than in Athens. But why should a mason, whether Coan or Athenian, working in Cos use an Attic sigma that had been obsolete for more than twenty years, when none of his other letters suggests that he was old-fashioned? The epigraphic argument may be a little weakened, but it remains strong.

The coins themselves may ultimately give the decisive answer, but at present the numismatic evidence is as ambiguous as the epigraphic. Already by 1913, when Gardner surveyed the coinage of the Athenian empire, it was clear that most of the islands, apart from Samos, Chios, and Lesbos, though they minted freely in the sixth century, had closed their mints by, or soon after, 450 (and in 1913 no one suggested that Athens had tried to enforce the use of her own coins on all the allies as early as that). In the other districts of the empire the evidence was much more obscure; in Asia Minor there seemed little evidence of independent minting after the Persian wars, but the big towns of Thrace, Abdera, Maroneia, and Ainos seemed to have minted freely without any obvious sign of a break (P. Gardner, *JHS* xxxiii (1913) 147–88). When E. S. G. Robinson carried out a similar review in 1949, the Cos fragment had been found and the question Robinson set out to answer was: 'Is the evidence of the coins compatible with the early date (*c.* 449) that the Cos fragment seems to demand for the Coinage decree?' (*Hesp.*, Suppl. viii (1949) 324–40). He had more coins to work from than Gardner, and thirty years of numismatic research and controversy had led to many modifications. He concluded that the coins tended to support the early date, though they also showed how difficult the decree was to enforce. But this conclusion cannot be pressed too far, for the evidence is inadequate. Before expecting a more decisive answer from the numismatists we need considerably more dated hoards. Style alone in such small-scale designs is a vulnerable criterion, as the coinage of Samos illustrates.

Barron, by a detailed examination of die-links, has put the study of Samian silver coinage on much firmer foundations. The coins that most concern us are the series marked with letters from B to Ξ, each letter almost certainly covering a year, and the whole series extending, therefore, over fifteen years. For Gardner this series probably began in 428. When the Samian revolt was crushed in 439 Athens will have imposed a democracy, but by 412 the oligarchs are in power (Thuc. viii. 21). Gardner inferred that the democracy was overthrown in 428, when the Mytilenean oligarchs revolted, and that the lettered series represented a period of oligarchy (op. cit. 160 f.). Robinson, without discussing the political implications, inferred that the series started rather earlier, 'surprisingly soon after the crushing of the revolt'. Barron's more detailed argument is more convincing; with him we believe that the lettered series lasted from 454 to 439 and represented an oligarchic interlude in Samos. But in accepting the early date for the Coinage decree Barron is basing his argument on other factors than the coins. The dating of this series from 454 to 439 is quite compatible with the later dating of the Coinage decree. It does not help us to date the Coinage decree, nor help us to decide whether the so-called autonomous allies were excluded from its provisions, though Barron infers from the language of the decree, and particularly of the Bouleutic oath, that no exceptions were made. (Barron, *The Silver Coins of Samos* (1966) 50–93.)

Finally Chios. It has long been realized that Chios minted freely through most at any rate of the fifth century, and at some point changed from a coinage consisting only of didrachms and tetrobols to one of tetradrachms, drachms, and smaller fractions. Stylistically, there is a clear break between the two issues, and in the interval between them must be placed a unique electrum stater in Berlin.

Boardman has dated this stater from the form of its bulbous-necked amphora to the middle of the fifth century (*BSA* liii–liv (1958–9) 308, with 300 n. 3). The Chian coins included in the inventory of the Other Gods for 429–8 (*IG* i². 310. 112–13) are from the new silver issue (Barron, op. cit. 86). It is a reasonable hypothesis that the electrum stater is the Chian reaction to a ban on silver issues other than Athenian, and that later (perhaps after the Samian revolt) the Athenians allowed Chios to resume minting.

46

Tightening-up of Tribute Payment: (?) 447 B.C.

Four fragments of a marble stele; three in EM, one in the British Museum. Attic letters, stoichedon 23 (ll. 1–14), 40 (ll. 15–77). In the right top corner a rectangle is reserved, perhaps for a painting (cf. *IG* ii². 2496, which has a relief in this position). Phots.: *ATL* i. 121 f. (frs. 1, 2, 3); *ATL* ii, Pl. 2 (frs. 1 and 4); *DAT* 44 (fr. 1), 46 (fr. 2), 48 (fr. 3).

IG i². 66; *DAT* 43–60; Woodward *JHS* lviii (1938) 108 f.; Raubitschek, *AJP* lxi (1940) 477–9; Meritt, *Epigraphica Attica* (1940) 38; Hill and Meritt, *Hesp.* xiii (1944) 1–15; Wade-Gery, *Hesp.* xiv (1945) 216 f., 226–8; *ATL* ii. D 7; Mattingly, *Hist.* x (1961) 150–69; Meritt and Wade-Gery, *JHS* lxxxii (1962) 67–74; Meiggs, *Harv. Stud.* lxvii (1963) 22; Mattingly, *CQ* xvi (1966) 188 f.; Meiggs, *JHS* lxxxvi (1966) 97.

Θεοί
ἔδοχσεν τêι βολ[êι καὶ τôι] δέμοι, Οἰνεῖς ἐπρυ[τάνευε, Σπ]ου-
δίας ἐγραμμάτε[υε...6...]ον
5 ἐπεστάτε, Κλενί[ας εἶπε· τὲ]μ β-
ολὲν καὶ τὸς ἄρχ[οντας ἐν] τêσ-
ι πόλεσι καὶ τὸς [ἐπισκό]πος ἐ-
πιμέλεσθαι hόπ[ος ἂν χσ]υλλέ-
γεται ho φόρος κ[ατὰ τὸ ἔ]τος h-
10 έκαστον καὶ ἀπά[γεται] Ἀθένα-
ζε· χσύμβολα δὲ π[οιέσα]σθαι π-
ρὸς τὰς πόλες, hό[πος ἂ]μ μὲ ἐχσ-
êι ἀδικὲν τοῖς ἀ[πάγο]σι τὸμ φ-

ὅρον· γράφσασα δ[ὲ ℎε] πόλις ἐς

15 γραμματεῖον τὸ[μ φό]ρον, ℎόντιν' ἂν ἀποπέμπει, σεμε-
ναμένε τῶι συμβ[όλο]ι ἀποπεμπέτω Ἀθέναζε· τὸς δὲ ἀ-
πάγοντας ἀποδο͂[ναι] τὸ γραμματεῖον ἐν τῆι βολῆι ἀ-
ναγνο͂ναι ℎόταμ[πε]ρ τὸμ φόρον ἀποδιδο͂σι· ℎοι δὲ πρυτάνες μετὰ Διο[νύ]σια ἐκκλεσίαν ποιεσάντον τοῖ-

20 ς ℎελλενοταμία[σι ἀ]ποδεῖχσαι Ἀθεναίοις τὸμ πόλεον τὰς ἀποδόσα[ς τὸμ φόρον ἐ]ντελε͂ καὶ τὰς ἐλλιπό-
σας χορίς, ℎόσαι [ἂν . . . . 9 . . . . . . Ἀθ]εναίος δὲ ℎελομέ-
νος ἄνδρας τέττ[αρας ἀποπέμπεν ἐπὶ] τὰς πόλες ἀντ-
ιγραφσομένος τ[ὸμ φόρον τὸν ἀποδοθέντα κα]ὶ ἀπαι-

25 τέσοντας τὸμ μὲ [ἀποδοθέντα παρὰ τῶν ἐλλιποσ]ο͂ν, τ-
ὸ μὲν δύο πλε͂ν ἐπ[ὶ τὰς ἐπὶ Νέσον καὶ ἐπ' Ἰωνίας ἐπὶ] τ-
ριέρος ταχείας, [τὸ δὲ δύο ἐπὶ τὰς ἐφ' Ἑλλεσπόντο κα]-
ὶ ἐπὶ Θράικες· ἐ[σάγεν δὲ ταῦτα τὸς πρυτάνες ἐς τὲμ]
βολὲν καὶ ἐς τὸ[ν δῆμον εὐθὺς μετὰ Διονύσια καὶ βο]-

30 ·λεύεσθαι περὶ τ[ούτον χσυνεχο͂ς ℎέος ἂν διαπραχθ]-
ε͂ι· ἐὰν δέ τις Ἀθ[εναῖος ἒ χσύμμαχος ἀδικε͂ι περὶ τὸ]-
ν φόρον ℎὸν δεῖ [τὰς πόλες γραφσάσας ἐς γραμματεῖ]-
ον τοῖς ἀπάγοσ[ιν ἀποπέμπεν Ἀθέναζε, ἔστο αὐτὸν γ]-
ράφεσθαι πρὸς [τὸς πρυτάνες τῶι β]ολομένο[ι Ἀθενα]-

35 ίον καὶ τὸν χσ[υμμάχον· ℎοι δὲ πρυτά]νες ἐσαγ[όντον]
ἐς τὲμ βολὲν [τὲν γραφὲν ℎέν τι]ς ἂγ γράφσετα[ι ἒ εὐθ]-
υνέσθο δόρο[ν χιλίαισι δραχμ]ε͂σ[ι ℎ]έκαστος· [ℎο͂ δ' ἂν]
καταγνο͂ι ℎ[ε βολέ, μὲ τιμᾶν αὐτ]ο͂ι κυρία ἔστο [ἀλλ' ἐσ]-
φερέτο ἐς τ[ὲν ἐλιαίαν εὐθύ]ς· ὅταν δὲ δόχσει [ἀδικε͂]-

40 ν, γνόμας πο[ιέσθον ℎοι πρυ]τάνες ℎό τι ἂν δοκ[ε͂ι αὐτ]-
ὸμ παθε͂ν ἒ ἀ[ποτεῖσαι· καὶ ἐ]άν τις περὶ τὲν ἀπα[γογὲ]-
ν τε͂ς βοὸς ἒ [τε͂ς πανℎοπλία]ς ἀδικε͂ι, τὰς γραφὰ[ς ἔνα]-
ι κατ' αὐτὸ κ[αὶ τὲν ζεμίαν κ]ατὰ ταὐτά· τὸς δὲ [ℎελλεν]-
ο[ταμίας ἀναγράφσαντας ἐ]ς πινάκιον λελ[ευκομέν]-

45 [ον ἀποφαίνεν καὶ τὲν τάχσι]ν τὸ φόρο καὶ [τὰς πόλες]
[ℎόσαι ἂν ἀποδο͂σιν ἐντελε͂ κα]ὶ ἀπογ[ράφεν . . . 7 . . . .]

c. 10 lines lost

[. . . . . 24 . . . . τὲμ] βολὲν τὲν ἐσι[ο͂σ]-
[αν περὶ τὸν ἀπαγόντον τὸμ φόρον· ℎ]όσοι δὲ τὸν ἀπα[γ]-
[όντον Ἀθέναζε ἐς τὸ πινάκιον ἂν]αγεγράφαται ὀφέ-

60 [λοντες . . . . . . 18 . . . . ἐπ]ιδεῖχσαι τôι δέμ-
[οι . . . . 20 . . . . ἐὰν δ]έ τις τôμ πόλεον ἀ-
[μφισβετêι περὶ τô φόρο τês ἀποδ]όσεος, φάσκοσα ἀπ-
[οδεδοκέναι . . . . 16 . . . .]θαι τὸ κοινὸν τês
[πόλεος . . . . 20 . . . .]ας τὰς πόλες καὶ τ-
65 [. . . . . 20 . . . . γράφεσ]θαι δὲ μὲ ἐχσêναι
[. . . . . 25 . . . .]τος ὀφελέτο ho γρ-
[αφσάμενος . . . . 17 . . . .] τὲν δὲ γραφὲν ἔνα-
[ι πρὸς τὸν πολέμαρχον μενὶ Γαμε]λιôνι· ἐὰν δέ τις ἀ-
[μφισβετêι . . . . 17 . . . .] κλέσες, hε βολὲ βο-
70 [λευσαμένε . . . . 17 . . . .] ἐσαγόντον δὲ hοι
[ἐσαγογês ἐς τὲν ἑλιαίαν τὸς Ἀθε]ναίοις τὸμ φόρον
[ὀφέλοντας hεχσês κατὰ τὸμ πίνα]κα τês μενύσεος· ἐ-
[. . . . . 21 . . . . τô νέο] φόρο καὶ τὸ περυσ-
[ινô . . . . . . 12 . . . . . . τὲν δὲ βολὲν π]ροβολεύσασαν ἐχ-
75 [σενεγκên . . . . 18 . . . .] πέρι τêι hυστερα-
[ίαι ἐς τὸν δêμον . . . . . . 12 . . . . . . τ]ês hαιρέσεος χρε-
[ματίσαι - - - - - - - - - - - - - - -] vacat.

l. 22: ἐλλιπôσιν R. G. Thomas, τινες ôσιν ATL.   l. 24: τὸν
ἀποδοθέντα A. Griffin, τêσι ἀποδόσεσι ATL.   l. 37: We prefer χιλίαισι
to μυρίαισι (ATL), cf. No. 69. 30.   l. 40: πο[ιέσθον P. J. Rhodes
(cf. Thuc. iii. 36. 2), πο[ιόντον ATL.   l. 57: [. . . . 9 . . . . . χρεματίσαι
δὲ καὶ τὲμ] βολὲν ATL.   l. 60: ὀφέ[[λοντες ἐν τêι βολêι τὲμ βολὲν
ἐπ]ιδεῖχσαι ATL.   l. 61: [οι κατὰ τὲν πόλιν hεκάστεν ATL.
ll. 66–7: τὸ δὲ γραφέν]τος ὀφελέτο ho γρ|[αφσάμενος τὲν τιμὲν ἐὰν φεύγει·]
ATL.

The fluctuations in the number of cities in the annual quota lists,
and the recurrence of incomplete and double payments in the early
forties show that Athens could not rely on receiving every year all
the tribute that was due to her. This decree is an attempt to improve
discipline, and the measures approved by the Assembly are to be the
responsibility of the Boule, with the co-operation of Athenian officials
overseas—travelling commissioners (ἐπίσκοποι) and resident officials
(ἄρχοντες), both of whom are found in other decrees of the fifties
and forties (No. 40, ATL ii. D 11).

I (11–18): Identification-seals are to be agreed with each city so
that the couriers shall have no opportunity to defraud. The amount of
tribute is to be recorded on a sealed tablet before dispatch, so that
the money actually handed over by the carrier may be checked
against the record. We infer that previously some cities, credited with

only partial payments, had protested that the balance must have been lost in transit. 2 (18–22): An Assembly is to be convened after the Dionysia (when the tribute was due, Schol. Ar. *Ach.* 504) to hear a report from the *hellenotamiai* on the response by the cities. 3 (22–31): The Assembly will then each year elect four men to travel in pairs and give receipts to the cities that have paid, and demand their tribute from defaulters. 4 (31–41): Offenders against this decree, Athenian or ally, may be prosecuted by any Athenian or ally. The case shall be brought before the Boule by the prytany on duty, but the Boule has no authority to decide the penalty. After a preliminary hearing it must send the case, with a recommendation, to a popular court. 5 (41–3): At this point there is an unexpected digression. If anyone commits an offence in regard to the dispatch of cow and panoply, the procedure and penalty shall follow the same line. We infer from the concise phrasing that this subject is topical and that Athens' allies have only recently been required to send these offerings to the great Panathenaia. After this interruption provision is made for the publication on a whitened tablet of the tribute record, but the details are lost and there follows a gap in the text. The remaining fragment preserves an average of only twelve letters from a forty-letter line, an inadequate basis for restoration.

This decree has a strongly imperial flavour; its date is important but controversial. Until recently a date in the early twenties was generally accepted, for it seemed to be closely related to, and a pre-cursor of, a decree moved by Kleonymos in 426, providing for the appointment of tribute collectors in the allied cities (No. 68). More-over, the imperial tone was thought to fit a period when Cleon and those like him were becoming increasingly influential in Athenian politics. Woodward, however, suggested that epigraphically the interval between the two decrees might be substantial (*JHS* lviii. 108 f.) and in 1939 Raubitschek proposed a date in the forties, on the strength of letter-forms (*AJP* lxi (1940) 477 f.); but it is doubtful whether his redating would have received much encouragement had not a large new fragment been published in 1944 (Hill and Meritt, *Hesp.* xiii (1944) 1–15). It was this fragment which revealed the mover's name, and the best-known Kleinias (not a common name) was the father of Alcibiades, who died at the battle of Koroneia in 447 or 446. Wade-Gery suggested that 447 would in fact prove a very suitable date, coming between the short tribute list of 447, with its absentees and part-payments, and the long list of 446, recording complements for the previous year as well as the current year (*Hesp.* xiv (1945) 226–8), but this interpretation of the tribute lists has been abandoned in *ATL* iii. 59 f. Neither of these arguments is decisive. We know too little about the many prominent Athenians to feel confident in the identification of this Kleinias; and if the lists of the early twenties were better preserved we might find ample evidence of partial payments in them. Many historians still feel that the tone is too imperialistic for the forties (Mattingly, *Hist.* x. 187 f.).

The only objective argument is provided by the letter-forms. Raubitschek emphasized the angle at which the loop of the rho closes against the vertical, and the curved lines of upsilon, as signs of an early date. Similar rhos may be found into and beyond the twenties, but, with very rare exceptions indeed, curved upsilons are not found after 430 (Meiggs *JHS* lxxxvi (1966) 97 n. 43). Epigraphically the twenties are too late, but the thirties cannot be ruled out. The main attractions of 447 are still the mover's name, the evidence of the quota lists (see p. 135), and the temper of the years following the Peace of Kallias (Meiggs, *Harv. Stud.* lxvii (1963) 1 ff.). The spirit of Kleinias' decree strongly resembles that of the Coinage decree, and for that decree also we accept a date in the early forties (No. 45). To them we add the decree alluded to by Kleinias, which required not only Athenian colonies but all her allies to bring standard offerings of cow and panoply to the Great Panathenaia (ll. 41 f.). Erythrai had earlier been required to bring offerings to the Great Panathenaia (No. 40), but Erythrai could be regarded as a colony of Athens, and the offerings were not yet standardized.

Previously the earliest record of this obligation on all allies was in the short decree that was carried after the Assessment decree of 425 (No. 69, ll. 55–8). Thoudippos, who had proposed the assessment, later proposed that all the cities assessed should bring a cow and panoply to the Great Panathenaia and [escort them in the procession like colonists]. Mattingly (*Hist.* x (1961) 153) regards this as the decree referred to by Kleinias and would date the Kleinias decree shortly afterwards. If, however, Thoudippos' decree marked the introduction of the policy we should expect a longer formulation; his short decree is more intelligible if he was merely extending an existing obligation to cities which were being assessed for the first time, or after a long interval (see Meritt and Wade-Gery, op. cit.).

47

Athenian Treaty with Kolophon: (?) 447–6 B.C.

Four fragments, of which two join, from a marble stele; now in EM.

A poor script strongly influenced by Ionic (paid for by the Kolophonians, ll. 38 f.) The aspirate is consistently dropped, of the Ionic double letters psi certainly (37, 40) and xi almost certainly (53, where ἐχσόλες for ἐξόλες would give too long a line) are used, but not eta or omega. The letter-forms are inconsistent rather than evidence of two hands. For dating Ϟ is the most significant. Non-stoichedon 39–42. Phot.: *ATL* ii, Pl. 8; Hondius, *Novae Inscriptiones Atticae*, Pl. 2 and 3 (frags. 2, 3, 4); facs. frag. 2, p. 8.

IG i². 14/15; Hondius, *NIA* (1925) 7–21; Schaefer, *Hermes*, lxxi (1936) 136 f. = *Probleme der Alten Geschichte*, 19 f.; Kolbe, *Hermes*, lxxiii (1938) 256–9; *ATL* ii. D 15, iii, pp. 282–4; Mattingly, *Hist.* x (1961) 175, xii (1963) 266; *Staatsverträge* 145; Meiggs, *Harv. Stud.* lxvii (1963) 26 f.; Meritt and Wade-Gery, *JHS* lxxxiii (1963) 102 f.; Mattingly, *Ehrenberg Studies*, 210–12.

```
      [ἔδοξεν τêι βολêι καὶ τôι δέμοι...7....ἐπρυτάνε]-
      [νε....8....ἐγ]ρα[μμάτευε, - - ἐπεστάτε - - - - - - -]
      [...]ς εἶπε· Ϟ[ο]λ[ο]φο[ν - - - - - - - - - - - - - - - - - - - - -]
  5   [...7....]σ[- - - - | ....]ες Ἀθ[ε]να[- - - - ||....]ον[...]
      αὐτο[- - - - |...]αι δὲ ταῦτα π[- - - -|....]ς ἄλλες πόλε̣[ος - - - -|
      .Ϟ]ολ[ο]φόνιοι πο[- - - -| lacuna
 10   [........15.......]αι Τρι̣οπίο ε[- - - - - - -]
      [....8....ψέφ]ισμα γένεται, ὅς [- - - - - - - - - - - - - -]
      [..5...ἐν τούτ]οι τôι χρόνοι δε/[- - - - - - - - - - - -]
      [....9.....Ϟο]λοφονίον καὶ τô[ν - - - - - - - - - -]
      [.....10.....] Ἀθενôν μεδεόσ[ες - - - - - - - - - - -]
 15   [.....10.....]α δ' ἐκένο τôι ε[- - - - - - - - - - - - - -]
      [.....10.....] Ϟολοφονίον π[- - - - - - - - - - - - - - -]
      [.....11......] δὲ γένεται ἐπ[- - - - - - - - - - - -]
      [..5...Ἀθεν]αîοι ἐὰμ μέ τις αὐ[το - - - - - - - - - -]
      [....8....·] οἱ δ' αἱρεθέντες πέ[ντε οἰκισταὶ οἱ ἐς Ϟο]-
 20   [λοφôνα τ]ά τ' ἐψεφισμένα φρα̣[ζόντον τêσι πόλεσι κα]-
      [ὶ ἐπιμελ]εθέντον, ὅπος ἂν [- - - - - - - - - - - - - - - - -]
      [οἱ οἰκέτ]ορες μετὰ τô δέ[μο - - - - - - - - - - - - - - - -]
      [...7....] ἱερὸν τôν παρ' α[ὐτοîς· τôν δὲ αἱρεθέντον λα]-
      [μβανέτο] ἔκαστος τês ἐμ[έρας ἑκάστες ἐς ἐφόδια δρ]-
 25   [αχμέν· τὸ] δὲ ἀργύριον ὀφε[λόντον Ϟολοφόνιοι καὶ Λ]-
      [εβέδιο]ι καὶ Διοσιρîται κ[- - - - - - - - - - - - - - - - - -]
      [...6... Ϟ]ολοφονίον μ[- - - -|...γέν]εται ὅ [τ]ι ἂν δί[καιον - - -
 30   - -|...6...μ[.]ε[.] ἑκαστο̣ [- - - - - -||...6...] ὅταν δὲ γέ[νεται - - -|
      ...τὰ ὀ]νόματα [- - - -|.... το]îς δὲ Ϟ[ολοφονίοις - - - |
 35   ....8....]οι[- - - - - - - - | lacuna [...6...]οι̣ν[- - - -||Ϟολοφ]ôνι
      αρο[- - - - |....]νας λε[- - - - - - |
```

[τὸ] δὲ ψέφισμ[α τόδε καὶ τὸν ὅρκον ἀναγραψάτο ὁ γραμ]-
[μα]τεὺς ὁ τῆς β[ολῆς ἐστέλει λιθίνει ἐμ πόλει τέλεσ]-
[ι τ]οῖς Κολοφο[νίον· Κολοφῶνι δὲ ταῦτα καὶ τὸν ὅρκ]-
40 [ον] ἀναγράψαν[τες ἐστέλει λιθίνει οἱ ἐς Κολοφῶνα]
οἰκισταὶ κατα[- - - - - - - - - - - - - - - - - - - -]
ονιονονομοσ[- ἐ]-
ρô καὶ βολεύσο [ὅ τι ἂν δύνομαι καλὸν καὶ ἀγαθὸν πε]-
ρὶ τὸν δέμον τ[ὸν Ἀθεναίον . . . . 21 . . . .]
45 [ο]ν καὶ οὐκ ἀποστ[έσομαι τô δέμο τô Ἀθεναίον οὔτε]
[λ]όγοι οὔτ' ἔργ[οι οὔτ' αὐτὸς ἐγὸ οὔτ' ἄλλοι πείσομαι]
[κ]αὶ φιλέσο τὸ[ν δέμον τὸν Ἀθεναίον καὶ οὐκ αὐτομο]-
[λ]έσο καὶ δεμο[- - - - - - - - - - -24–6- - - - - - - - - - - οὔτ' α]-
ὑτὸς ἐγὸ οὔτ' ἄ[λλοι πείσομαι -]
50 μενος πόλιν ο[- ὅρκ]-
ον ἀλεθê [τ]αῦτ[α - νὲ τὸν]
[Δ]ία καὶ τὸν Ἀπό[λλο καὶ τὲν Δέμετρα, καὶ εἰ μὲν ταῦτ]-
[α] παραβ⟨α⟩ίνοιμ[ι ἐξόλες εἴεν καὶ αὐτὸς ἐγὸ καὶ τὸ γ]-
[έ]νος τὸ ἐμὸν [ἐς τὸν ἄπαντα χρόνον, εὐορκôντι δὲ εἴε]
55 μοι πο[λ]λὰ καὶ [ἀγαθά].

l. 14: Ἀθενôν μεδεόσ[ες is to be preferred to *ATL*'s Ἀθενôν μεδὲ ὅσ[ες. For the cult of Ἀθηνᾶ Ἀθηνῶν μεδέουσα see Barron, *JHS* lxxxiv (1964) 35–48; for other examples Hill, *Sources*², p. 319, and p. 50, here.   ll. 41–3: κατὰ [τάδε Κολοφονίος ὁμόσαι, καθ' ἃ Κολοφ]|ονίον ὁ νόμος [κελεύει κατὰ ἱερôν καιομένον· κατε]ρô καὶ βολεύσο Kolbe; κατα[θέντον ἐν ἀγορᾶι τέλεσι τοῖς Κολοφ]|ονίον ⟨ον⟩· ὁμοσ[άντον δὲ Κολοφόνιοι τάδε· δράσο καὶ ἐ]|ρô καὶ βολεύσο *ATL*.   l. 44: For the main clause of the oath see below.   l. 48: δέμο[ν οὐ καταλύσο τὸν Κολοφονίον...] is perhaps to be preferred to *ATL*'s δεμο[κρατίαν οὐ καταλύσο Κολοφôνι....   ll. 49–51: οὔτ' ἐς ἄλλεν ἀφιστά]|μενος πόλιν ο[ὔτ' αὐτόθι στασιάζον, κατὰ δὲ τὸν ὅρκ]|ον ἀλεθê [τ]αῦτ[α ἐμπεδόσο ἀδόλος καὶ ἀβλαβôς *ATL*.

The clear traces of oath formulae show that this inscription belongs to the series including Erythrai (No. 40), Chalkis (No. 52), and Samos (No. 56) that record Athenian settlements with cities which have revolted and been recovered. Letter-forms suggest a date near the mid century, and before 445, for the older sigma (ϟ) is retained while all other letters, though poorly inscribed, are in the developed style. From the tribute-quota lists we know that Kolophon was at least outwardly loyal in the late fifties, for her tribute payment is preserved in all four years of the first period. No record, however, survives in any of the three comparatively well-preserved lists of the second period (449–446). It is at least probable that this decree dates from 447–6 (*ATL*).

The first fragment comes from the opening of the decree, but so little is preserved in its nine lines that even their general sense is beyond the range of rational guessing. The second fragment is little better, but there are tantalizing clues. The small neighbouring cities of Dios Hieron and very probably Lebedos are mentioned (ll. 25 f.). In l. 19 there may be a reference to οἰκισταί (οἱ δ' αἱρεθέντες πέ[ντε οἰκισταὶ οἱ ἐς Κο|λοφῶνα]); they are certainly mentioned in l. 41. These οἰκισταί should be men sent out from Athens to establish a settlement, and perhaps the settlers are mentioned in l. 22 ([οἱ οἰκέτ]ορες). Was this to be a colony of Athenians at or near Kolophon? This is the view of the authors of *ATL*, who point to the reductions in the tribute of Kolophon, Lebedos, and perhaps Dios Hieron (for which there is no evidence in the assessment period 446–443). They further think that Athens adopted a policy of planting colonies in Ionia to compensate for the withdrawal of garrisons, which in their view Athens undertook to remove by the terms of the Peace of Kallias. By restoring the inscription on a dedication from the Acropolis, τῆς ἀποι[κίας] τῆς ἐς Ἐρ[ύθρας], a close parallel to Kolophon is found in Erythrai (*ATL* iii. 282–4): 'the lowered quotas of Erythrai and of its neighbour Hairai justify the assumption that there was a colony in the southern part of the Erythraian peninsula.' This case is not compelling. There is clear evidence of a reduction in the tribute assessment of Hairai from 3 T. to 1 T. in 446, but no evidence of a reduction at Erythrai. In the second period she was required to pay 9 T. on behalf of the peninsula; in 446 Erythrai was assessed at 7 T., but the small states normally in her syntely paid separately. Polichna paid 4,000 dr., Elaius 100 dr.; Boutheia, Pteleus, and Sidus may well have paid 1 T. 900 dr. between them. For the Erythraians the argument that we hear nothing in our literary sources of Athenian colonies or cleruchies in Ionia carries little weight; but the detailed narrative in Thucydides of the troubles at Kolophon and Notion in the early years of the Archidamian War is difficult to reconcile with Athenian colonization. Had an Athenian settlement been established at or near Kolophon as recently as 447 or 446 there should be some trace of it in Thucydides (iii. 34). The colony which made the dedication on the Acropolis could be Eretria, and the settlement implied by the οἰκισταί sent to Kolophon could have resembled the settlement of Kolophonian refugees at Notion which Athens established when fresh trouble broke out at Kolophon in 430–427 (Thuc. iii. 34. 4: καὶ ὕστερον Ἀθηναῖοι οἰκιστὰς πέμψαντες κατὰ τοὺς ἑαυτῶν νόμους κατῴκισαν τὸ Νότιον, ξυναγαγόντες πάντας ἐκ τῶν πόλεων, εἴ πού τις ἦν Κολοφωνίων).

The remaining two fragments, which join, provide glimpses of the oath to be taken by the Kolophonians, but one of the most important questions remains in doubt. *ATL* restores the oath of loyalty to include the allies as well as the Athenians: (ll. 42–6) δράσο καὶ ἐ]|ρô καὶ βολεύσο [ő τι ἂν δύνομαι καλὸν καὶ ἀγαθὸν πε]|ρὶ τὸν δῆμον τ[ὸν Ἀθηναίον καὶ περὶ τὸς ξυμμάχος αὐτ|ô]ν καὶ οὐκ ἀποστ[έσομαι τô δέμο τô Ἀθεναίον οὔτε | λ]όγοι οὔτε ἔργ[οι οὔτ' αὐτὸς ἐγὸ - - -. This text is vulnerable. If the allies were mentioned in the positive clause they should, as in the Erythrai oath (No. 40, l. 24) and in the Samian oath (No. 56, l. 19) also be mentioned in the negative clause, and there is no room for οὔτε τὸν ξυμμάχον here. Nor in ll. 44 f. is [περὶ τὸς ξυμμάχος αὐτ|ôν] persuasive; we should expect περὶ τὸς ξυμμάχος τὸς Ἀθεναίον as in the Erythraian and Samian oaths. Kolbe's restoration, which omits the allies but includes with the Athenian demos the demos of Kolophon, is perhaps to be preferred (*Hermes*, lxxiii (1938) 257): πε]ρὶ τὸν δέμον τ[ὸν Κολοφονίον καὶ τὸν δέμον τὸν Ἀθεναί|ο]ν, though the Athenian demos should precede the demos of Kolophon, and the forty-three letters required would make this longer than any other line. The same gods are invoked for the Kolophonian oath (l. 52) as for the Erythraian oath (No. 40, l. 16).

Mattingly's invitation (*Hist.* x (1961) 175) to refer the decree to the situation at Kolophon and Notion in the early years of the Archidamian War described by Thucydides should be rejected. The three-barred sigma remains a strong argument against such a late date (Meiggs, *JHS* lxxxvi (1966) 92). Moreover, in this decree Athens seems to control Kolophon, and the record of Kolophonian tribute shows that this control was maintained into the thirties. When Athens settled Kolophonians at Notion in 427 she did not control Kolophon (see also Meritt and Wade-Gery, *JHS* lxxxiii (1963) 102 f.; Meiggs, *Harv. Stud.* lxvii (1963) 26 f.).

IG i². 34, an unrelated fragment referring to a settlement (συνθέκα[s, l. 8) also concerns Kolophon and has ϟ; on the back (*IG* i². 35) is a later decree (Σ), implying good relations with Athens.

48 (48)

Athenian Casualty-list: (?) 447 B.C.

Marble stele; now in EM.

Developed Attic letters; ll. 15, 18, 19, 35, 36, 67, 72 (Ἀρχέπολις), and perhaps the epigram (45–8) seem to be later additions. The need for space for such additions had been foreseen (Dow, *Harv. Stud.* liii (1942) 97).

Phot.: A. Conze, *Die attischen Grabreliefs*, 1427, Pl. 293A. Facs.: Kirchhoff, *Hermes*, xvii (1882), folded at end of vol.
IG i². 943; Kirchhoff, op. cit. 623–30; Meiggs, *Harv. Stud.* lxvii (1963) 17 f.

Col. i

ἐγ Χερρονέσοι
Ἀθεναίον : hοίδε
ἀπέθανον·
'Επιτέλες : στρατεγός
5 'Ερεχθεῖδος
Πυθόδορος
Ἀριστόδικος
Τέλεφος
Πυθόδορος

10 Αἰγεῖδος
'Επιχάρες
Μνεσίφιλος
Φαιδιμίδες
Λάχες
15 Νικόφιλος

Πανδιονίδος
Λυσικλῆς

Λεοντίδος
Χαιρῆς

20 Οἰνεῖδος
'Ροδοκλῆς
Εὐρύβοτος
Πολίτες
'Εροκλεῖδες

25 Κεκροπίδος
Ἀρίσταρχος
Καρυστόνικος
Θεόμνεστος
Ἀρίσταρχος

Col. ii

ἐμ Βυζαντίοι
50 Ἀθεναίον : hοίδ[ε]
ἀπέθανον

'Ερεχθεῖδος
Νικόστρατος
Φιλόκομος

55 Αἰγεῖδος
Χίονις

Πανδιονίδος
Φιλιστίδες

Λεοντίδος
60 Λυσίμαχος

Ἀκαμαντίδος
Καλλισθένες

Οἰνεῖδος
Κάλλιππος

65 Κεκροπίδος
Κνίφον
Δεμοτέλες

hιπποθοντίδος
hαίσον

70 Αἰαντίδος
Νικόδεμος

Ἀντιοχίδος
Φανίας

Col. i   Col. ii

30 Εὐκράτες
    Νικόμαχος

    hιπποθοντίδος
    Σοτελίδες
    Ποσείδιππος

35 Αἰαντίδος
    Δίφιλος

    Ἀντιοχίδος
    Κράτον
    Ἀντικράτες
40 Εὔδοχσος

    hοίδε : ἐν τοῖς ἄλλοις

    πολέμοις : ἀπέθανον

    Ἐρεχθεῖδος
    Λυσανίας

Col. ii

    Πανδιονίδος
75 Σιμονίδες
    Αἰσχύλος Ἀρχέπολις
    Σμικρίον
    Χαροπίδες
    Ναχσιάδες
80 Λεοντίδος
    Φίλον
    Εὔδεμος
    Ἀκαμαντίδος
    Πρόταρχος
85 Κεκροπίδος
    Χαιρίας
    Ἀστυάναχς
    Λυσίστρατος
    hιπποθοντίδος
90 Τιμόνοθος
    Ἀντιφάνες
    Αἰαντίδος
    Κλένοθος
    Φίλιος
95 Καλλικλῆς
    Ἐλευθεράθεν
    Σεμιχίδες

45 hοίδε παρ' hελλέσποντον ἀπόλεσαν ἀγλαὸν hέβεν
    βαρνάμενοι, σφετέραν δ' εὐκλέϊσαμ πατρίδα
    hόστ' ἐχθρὸς στενάχεμ πολέμο θέρος ἐκκομίσαντας,
    αὐτοῖς δ' ἀθάνατον μνêμ' ἀρετêς ἔθεσαν.

The casualties of a single year are here listed according to the areas in which they fought, in the Chersonese (ll. 1–40), Byzantium (ll. 49–73), and 'the other wars' (ll. 41–4, 74–97), and below the lists, running across the stele, is an epigram commemorating those who died by the Hellespont. In each area the names are listed under their tribal headings, arranged in the official order of the tribes. Note that Eleutherai (l. 96), listed last, fell outside the tribal organization, though part of Attica. In laying out his text the mason left extra space in each tribal entry, apparently anticipating that more names would be reported. There are indeed additions in a later hand (cf. No. 33), and it seems that when he originally designed his layout he did not expect his third list, which is very much more crowded. It was probably also not in the mind of the man who composed the epigram. The verses could cover Byzantium as well as the Chersonese, but hardly 'the other wars'.

Kirchhoff dated this list to the last phase of the Peloponnesian War, on the ground that only in that period did we know of important fighting in the area of the Hellespont: he assumed that the epigram was relevant to all three lists and that 'the other wars' must also all be in or near the Hellespont. This assumption was unwarranted, and it is now generally agreed that the letters and general style of the inscription must be substantially earlier. The name Καρυστόνικος (i. 27) must have been chosen to commemorate the conquest of Karystos *c.* 472; by 412 such a man would be very unlikely to be on active service. Ναχσιάδες (i. 75) has similarly been associated with the reduction of Naxos (*c.* 467), but such a name would be appropriate at any date in a family that had links with Naxos. More recently 440 or 439, when Byzantium joined Samos in revolt, has been generally accepted (e.g. Tod, p. 102). It is, however, almost inconceivable that in either of the two years of the Samian revolt Samos should be included among 'the other wars', with fewer casualties than Byzantium or the Chersonese. We therefore prefer 447, when Pericles led an expedition to protect the Chersonese from Thracian invaders and resettle it with Athenians (Plut. *Per.* 19. 1). The date is inferred from the tribute lists, *ATL* iii. 289 f. The casualties at Byzantium (ἐμ Βυζαντίοι need not mean inside the town, cf. *IG* i². 949. 40, 44, 50, 52) will have been in fighting Thracians threatening the town or in crushing a revolt. The 'other wars' will be minor actions carried out by small task forces at various points in the Aegean, where there was probably widespread discontent against Athens in the years immediately following the Peace of Kallias.

It is not clear why Epiteles, general, is not included within his tribal list, unless, perhaps, it is to emphasize that the generals were not merely commanders of tribal contingents. If, however, he is to be identified with Epiteles, son of Soinautes, who made a dedication of a marble basin on the Acropolis near the mid century (*DAA* 384), his tribe in fact is Erechtheis. Another Epiteles, also from Erechtheis, was killed in the year when the tribe lost men on six battlefields (No. 33, l. 150).

49 (44)

Athenian Colony at Brea: *c.* 445 B.C.

Two fragments of a marble stele found in the Erechtheum; now in EM. The stone was cut in half before being reworked as two column-bases in the Byzantine period (cf. Paton, *The Erechtheum*, 497–500). Text B was inscribed on the right-hand side of the top half, the inscribed face of which was deleted, but which had room for thirty-eight lines, a maximum figure which is probably an over-estimate, since there could well have been a more widely spaced prescript. A third small fragment, with eleven letters only in four lines, found in the Agora, still retains its left edge, which the two main fragments have lost in reworking, and now does not join (*Hesp.* xiv (1945) 86 f., xxi (1952) 380); we omit it here.

Developed Attic letters, except Ρ. A stoichedon 35, B stoichedon 17. Phot.: *Hesp.* xiv (1945) 88 (squeeze of A).

IG i². 45; Wilhelm, *Sitz. Wien.* 217. 5 (1939) 11–17; Meritt, *Hesp.* x (1941) 317–19; Woodhead, *CQ* ii (1952) 57–62; Mattingly, *CQ* xvi (1966) 172–86.

30–35 lines missing

A (face)

................ε πρὸς hὲν ἂν φα[ίνει ἔ]
[γράφεται, ἐσ]αγέτο. ἐὰν δὲ ἐσάγει ἐνεχ[..5...]
[...7....] hο φένας ἒ hο γραφσάμενος. πο[..5...]
[...6...]ν αὐτοῖς παρασχόντον hοι ἀπ[οικιστ]-
5 [αὶ καλλ]ιερέσαι hυπὲρ τὲς ἀποικίας, [hοπόσα]
[ἂν αὐτο]ῖς δοκεῖ. γεονόμος δὲ hελέσθ[αι δέκα]
[ἄνδρας,] ἕνα ἐχ φυλὲς· hοῦτοι δὲ νεμάντ[ον τὲν]
[γὲν. Δεμ]οκλείδεν δὲ καταστὲσαι τὲν ἀ[ποικί]-
[αν αὐτο]κράτορα, καθότι ἂν δύνεται ἄ[ριστα. τ]-
10 [ὰ δὲ τεμ]ένε τὰ ἐχσειρεμένα ἐὰν καθά[περ ἐστ]-
[ί, καὶ ἄλ]λα μὲ τεμενίζεν. βοῦν δὲ καὶ π[ανhοπλ]-
[ίαν ἀπά]γεν ἐς Παναθέναια τὰ μεγάλ[α καὶ ἐς Δ]-
[ιονύσι]α φαλλόν. ἐὰν δέ τις ἐπιστρα[τεύει ἐπ]-
[ὶ τὲν γὲ]ν τὲν τὸν ἀποίκον, βοεθὲν τὰ[ς πόλες h]-
15 [ος ὀχσύ]τατα κατὰ τὰς χσυγγραφὰς hα[ὶ ἐπὶ..]
[...6...]το γραμματεύοντος ἐγένον[το περὶ τ]-
[ὸν πόλε]ον τὸν ἐπὶ Θράικες. γράφσαι δ[ὲ ταῦτα]
[ἐν στέλ]ει καὶ καταθὲναι ἐμ πόλει· πα[ρασχόν]-
[τον δὲ τ]ὲν στέλεν hοι ἄποικοι σφὸν α[ὐτὸν τέ]-
20 [λεσιν. ἐ]ὰν δέ τις ἐπιφσεφίζει παρὰ τὲ[ν στέλ]-
[εν ἒ ῥρέ]τορ ἀγορεύει ἒ προσκαλὲσθα[ι ἐγχερ]-
[εῖ ἀφαι]ρὲσθαι ἒ λύεν τι τὸν hεφσεφι[σμένον],
[ἄτιμον] ἔναι αὐτὸν καὶ παῖδας τὸς ἐχς [ἐκένο]
[καὶ τὰ χ]ρέματα δεμόσια ἔναι καὶ τὲς [θεὸ τὸ ἐ]-
25 [πιδέκα]τον, ἐὰμ μέ τι αὐτοὶ hοι ἄποικ[οι....]
[....δέ]ονται·· hόσοι δ' ἂν γράφσοντα[ι ἐποικ]-
[έσεν τὸ]ν στρατιοτὸν, ἐπειδὰν hέκοσ[ι Ἀθένα]-

[ζε, τριά]κοντα ἐμερôν ἐμ Βρέαι ἔναι ἐπ[οικέσ]-
[οντας. ἐ]χσάγεν δὲ τὲν ἀποικίαν τριάκ[οντα ἐ]-
30 [μερôν. Α]ἰσχίνεν δὲ ἀκολουθôντα ἀπο[διδόνα]-
[ι τὰ χρέ]ματα. *vacat*

B (side)

[Φ]αντοκλês εἶπε· περὶ
[μ]ὲν τês ἐς Βρέαν ἀποι-
[κ]ίας καθάπερ Δεμοκλ-
35 [ε]ίδες εἶπε· Φαντοκλέ-
[α] δὲ προσαγαγên τὲν ᾽Ε-
[ρ]εχθεîδα πρυτανεία-
[ν] πρòς τὲν βολὲν ἐν τê-
[ι] πρότει hέδραι· ἐς δὲ
40 [Β]ρέαν ἐχ θετôν καὶ ζε-
[υ]γιτôν ἰέναι τòς ἀπο-
[ί]κος.

l. 1: hε δὲ ἀρχ]έ Wilhelm.   ll. 2–3 ἐνέχ[υρα ἄχ|σια θέτο] ho φένας Wil-
helm; ἐνεχ[υραζέ|το αὐτόν] *IG* i².   ll. 3–4: We prefer Meritt's πό[ρον δ᾽ ἐ|ς
θυσία]ν to π⟨ρ⟩ό[βατα ἐ|ς θυσία]ν which Wilhelm proposed in place of
πο[ίμνια | δὲ αἰγô]ν (*IG* i²).   l. 15: We prefer ἐπὶ . . | . . . . . .]το γραμματεύ-
οντος (with name only of secretary) to ἐπὶ . . | . . .πρό]το γραμματεύοντος.
l. 20: *IG* i² restored [στέλ|λεν ἐ ῥέ]τορ to avoid Kirchhoff's ῥhέ|τορ; the
spelling ῥρέ]τορ creates no problem.   ll. 25–6: περὶ?| σφôν δέ]ονται *IG* i²;
?hεαυ|τοîς δέ]ονται. Much of B (ll. 31–7 and part of 38) has now been lost.

We know of more than a dozen settlements, colonies, and cleruchies
sent out by Athens in the fifth century, and of most of them we know
when they were sent, where they were sent, and, in outline, how they
fared. It is a strange irony that the only settlement for which we
have good contemporary evidence is the colony of Brea, whose date
and site are uncertain and which for us has no history. Apart from
this decree it is mentioned for certain only by Stephanus of Byzantium
(Βρέα, πόλις ⟨Θράκης⟩, εἰς ἣν ἀποικίαν ἐστείλαντο Ἀθηναῖοι. . . .), by
Hesychius (Βρέα· Κρατῖνος μέμνηται τῆς εἰς Βρέαν ἀποικίας . . .) and
by Theognostos (Cramer, *Anecdota Graeca Oxon.* ii. 102).

The opening lines (*c.* 30–35) will have included more than the
decision to establish the colony and the number of settlers. After
three fragmentary lines relating to legal procedure, our text continues:

1 (3–6). [The cost of the] sacrifice on behalf of the colony is to be
provided by the ἀποικισταί, who are apparently the adjutants of the

οἰκιστής, and may correspond to the ten men sent to Thurii : τοὺς εἰς Θούριον πεμφθέντας ἐπὶ τὸ κτίσαι αὐτήν. ἐπέμφθησαν δὲ δέκα ἄνδρες (Schol. Ar. *Clouds* 332). The word does not occur elsewhere.

2 (6–8). Ten γεωνόμοι are to be elected, one from each tribe, to allocate the land; cf. Phryn. *Praep. Soph.*, p. 57 (ed. de Borries) : γεωνόμης μὲν ὁ διανέμων ἐν ταῖς ἀποικίαις ἑκάστῳ τὸν κλῆρον, γεωμέτρης δὲ ὁ μετρῶν τοὺς κλήρους.

3 (8–9). Demokleides is to establish the colony at his discretion, without further reference to the authorities at home.

4 (9–11). The sites reserved for the gods are to remain reserved, but their number is not to be increased. (These reservations are much more likely to be sites chosen for the gods of the new community than native cult places preceding the colony.)

5 (11–13). The colonists are to send a cow and panoply to the Great Panathenaia in the mother city, and a phallos to the Dionysia. That a cow and not a bull was to be sent, in spite of Schol. Ar. *Clouds* 386 (ἐν τοῖς Παναθηναίοις πᾶσαι αἱ ὑπὸ τῶν Ἀθηναίων ἀποικισθεῖσαι πόλεις βοῦν τυθησόμενον ἔπεμπον), we now know from No. 46, ll. 41–2. For these offerings see p. 121.

6 (13–17). If the colonists' land is attacked, the cities (of the district) are to come to their aid as sharply as possible according to the agreements concerning the cities of the Thraceward district carried when [e.g. Demostratos] was secretary (of the Boule, probably in the current year). The χσυγγραφαί would have been based on recommendations by a commission (cf. *ATL* ii. D 11 ; τάδε hοι χ]συγγρα[φὲς χσυνέγραφσαν].

7 (17–20). This decree is to be inscribed and set up on the Acropolis at the expense of the colonists.

8 (20–6). Anyone who proposes the reversal of the decree, or any modification of any of its clauses shall with his children lose the rights of a citizen and his property shall be confiscated, unless the colonists themselves have some request to make for themselves.

9 (26–9). Any troops who enrol in the colony when they return to Athens must arrive in Brea within thirty days.

10 (29–31). The colony is to be led out within thirty days and Aeschines shall go with the colonists and give them their money (cf. Libanius on Athenian cleruchs: ἐλάμβανον πεμπόμενοι ὅπλα τ' ἐκ τοῦ δημοσίου καὶ ἐφόδιον, *Arg. Dem.* viii).

It is extremely unlikely that the first thirty lines of our text come from an amendment. Demokleides presumably moved the decree in the Assembly and proposed autocratic powers for himself. The form of the amendment (not having τὰ μὲν ἄλλα καθάπερ τῆι βολῆι) strongly suggests that the decree was not based on a *probouleuma*. There may have been differences of opinion in the Boule; it is even possible that

Demokleides was not himself a member. He is perhaps to be identified with the mover of an amendment in *IG* i². 152 (? after 430), and might be the general from Aegeis in 439–8 (No. 56, l. 28, Δεμ-[οκλείδες]), but many other restorations are there possible.

Phantokles moved an amendment to Demokleides' decree, by which he was guaranteed access to the Boule; he is to be introduced by the prytany of Erechtheis, which, since the name of the next prytany is not known until the very end of the prytany, or, by elimination, in the ninth prytany, will either be the tenth or the current prytany. Perhaps Phantokles had made a long speech implying strong suspicions, and was told that such details did not involve principles and were better dealt with by the Boule. He also had it explicitly established that the colonists should be drawn from the two lowest classes. We infer that the decree of Demokleides either did not restrict membership at all, or, less probably, confined it to the zeugitai or the thetes; and since στρατιῶται (l. 27) are to be included it would have been the thetes who were excluded.

The only clues to the date are the mention of the colony by Cratinus (though he covers a long span); the form of the rho (P), which is not uncommon near the middle of the century, but has not been found in any dated inscription known to us after 438–7 (see Meiggs, *JHS* lxxxvi (1966) 92); and the coincidence with fighting just terminated. On epigraphic grounds the decree, to take extreme limits, should fall between 450 and 430; Mattingly's suggested dating in the tenth prytany of 426–5 should therefore (apart from other weaknesses in his argument) be ruled out (*Hist.* xii (1963) 258–61). Woodhead's dating *c.* 438 is epigraphically acceptable but we cannot accept his site. Following Bergk he emends the text of Thuc. i. 61. 4 from Βέροιαν to Βρέαν. The colony of Brea, he thinks, was established between Therme and Strepsa as a barrier against any encroachment by Perdikkas into Chalkidike from the north-west. When it proved ineffective the colonists were perhaps absorbed by Potidaea, after it had been occupied by Athens in 429. Edson, however, has given good reasons for retaining Βέροιαν (*CP* l (1955) 169–90; but see Alexander, *AJP* lxxxiii (1962) 265–86). We prefer the more traditional association with Plutarch's 1,000 settlers sent out to live with the Bisaltai (*Pericles*, 11. 5), a tribe that bordered on Argilos. Supporting evidence may perhaps be seen in the reduction at the assessment in 446 of Argilos' tribute, and the trouble that preceded the foundation, giving rise to the χσυγγραφαί of our decree (l. 15), may be reflected in the payment by Abdera in 446 of one talent of her tribute to Eion at the mouth of the Strymon, List 8, col. i. 105: Η ἐς ['Ε]ιόνα hαβδερῖ. The military expedition, from which the troops, eligible for inclusion in the colony, are expected to return, will be the reduction of Euboea in

446 (see also *ATL* iii. 287 f.). The most likely date for the colony is 446–5; Brea may have been abandoned when the strategically more valuable Amphipolis was founded in 437–6.

50 (38)

Athenian Tribute quota-lists of the Second Assessment Period: 449–446 B.C.

The tribute lists of this period are the most interesting and controversial of the series. Until 1933 there seemed to be no special problem. The first list of the 450 assessment, 450–49, was numbered and secure; below it, at the bottom of the front face of the stele, was an unnumbered list: ἐπὶ τê[ς ἀρχês h]êι Μενέτ[ιμο]ς ἐγραμμάτευε Λαμ-[πτρεύς], contrasted with ἐπὶ τês ἀρχês τê[ς] πέμπτες h[êι - - - of the list above. This list was assumed to be the list of 449–8 and the next year was thought to follow at the top of the right side face; it was a very short list indeed. Below it a much longer list was assumed to be the list of 447–6 and its prescript was restored as the eighth year. The top list on the back of the stele was for 446–5, the ninth, though only two letters of its prescript were thought to survive. Below it, clearly numbered, was the tenth list, for 445–4.

In 1935 Wade-Gery published a fragment hitherto overlooked (*BSA* xxxiii. 101). It joined a fragment from the top of the right face, and the result of this discovery was to dissolve the seventh list. What had been the prescript of this list was shown to be part of a summary of the *aparchai* received in the first year; the list of cities was seen to be a continuation of the second list. There were now three lists for four years and ample scope for speculation. The potential clues were not many:

1. The list below that of 450–49 was not numbered.
2. The number of the following list had to be restored. Meritt at first argued that ὀγδόες, the eighth year (447–6) was the only possible restoration (*DAT* 67 f.). Gomme and Dow, we think, were right in insisting that epigraphically, since the text was not strictly stoichedon, either hεβδόμες or ὀγδόες was possible (Gomme, *CR* liv (1940) 65–9; Dow, *CP* xxxviii (1943) 20–7); and hεβδόμες invited a more probable restoration for the secretary's name; ὀγδόες compelled the very rare Διοδές; hεβδόμες allowed the very common Διόδορος or Διόδοτος.
3. The list on the right face included payments which completed partial payments in the list at the bottom of the front face; it also

closely followed the order of cities in that list. It is virtually certain that it records the payments of the year immediately following.
4. The ninth list begins some distance below the top of the stele. No fragment has been identified from the area above it.

Those who thought that a missing list was out of the question had to believe that the space at the top of the reverse of the stele was occupied by a very short list containing not more than seventy cities (the next lowest number known being 140 in 453). The list would even be a little shorter if, as has been suggested by Lewis (*BSA* xlix (1954) 25-9), the letters assumed to be part of the prescript of list 9 belong to cities (McGregor, *Phoenix*, xvi (1962) 267 f., favours *ATL*; Pritchett, *Hist.* xiii (1964) 132 f., *AJA* lxviii (1964) 400 f. with Pl. 128 A, inclines towards Lewis's suggestion). If list 8 came above list 9 the list on the right face could conveniently be the seventh, and the number will have been omitted from the sixth list by a careless accident. Historically the reconstruction makes sense—a short list in 449-8, followed by a tightening-up of collection in 448-7; and then a large-scale withholding of tribute as a reaction to the defeat of Athens at Koroneia and the crisis of 446. There are, however, two serious objections. The complete absence of fragments from the assumed list of 447-6 would be very surprising. Tribute-list fragments are easy to identify; there is no area of corresponding size on either of the first two stelai from which no fragment survives. One would also expect a sensationally short list in 447-6 to be reflected in the list of 446-5, but list 9 is a very normal list, suggesting neither strain nor pressure.

Those who accepted the force of this argument and inferred that one year's record was missing were divided in choice between 449-8 and 447-6. A gap for the latter year could mean that the collection was so poor that it was decided not to inscribe it (Gomme, *CR* liv (1940) 66), or (much less probably) that Athens, faced with the crisis which followed Koroneia, gave up her claim for the year (Accame, *RF* lxvi (1938) 413). Wade-Gery (*Hesp.* xiv (1945) 212-15), followed by *ATL* (iii. 281), believing firmly in a Peace of Kallias in 449, interpreted the missing list as a moratorium for 449-8 while Pericles invited the Greeks to a congress at Athens in order to discuss the new situation arising from the peace. When Sparta led the way in holding aloof, the congress was not held and tribute was reimposed.

A new element was introduced into the argument when Pritchett maintained that the 'missing' list was probably inscribed on the back of a block which crowned the stele. We do not believe that there was such a block (see p. 84). Even if there were, it is not likely to have been more than a small architectural feature. The complete absence of fragments from the top of the stele would still be difficult to explain.

We prefer to believe that no list of cities was inscribed for 449–8, and that this is why no numeral was inscribed for the list at the bottom of the obverse; we are, however, doubtful whether Pericles would have taken the risk of remitting tribute even temporarily. It is possible, as Meritt once suggested (*The Greek Political Experience* (Studies in Honor of W. K. Prentice), 53; cf. Gomme, *CR* liv (1940) 67), though later he changed his mind, that the entire tribute of the year was given to some particular project. Athena Nike, for whom a temple was voted at about this time (see No. 44), would have been a suitable recipient.

The main difference between the lists of the second and the first assessment periods is the evidence in the second of partial and complementary payments. It used to be thought that the list of 450–49 had some twenty more paying cities than any of the four lists of the first period, and various explanations, such as the conversion in 450 of ship contributions to tribute, were found. A closer analysis in *ATL* (iii. 30–2) makes it highly probable that there was no significant increase in tribute-payers; the list was much larger because it included many cities whose tribute was paid in two instalments. The last column of the list in fact seems to be composed of complementary payments and late payments. In list 7 (of *ATL*) the number of cities has fallen by some 15, from *c.* 165 to 150, and several payments are incomplete. Above the last nine names in the list was a separate heading, of which only one letter survives. These were probably cities who paid late in the year: $M[\epsilon\tau\grave{\alpha}\ \Delta\iota o\nu\acute{\upsilon}\sigma\iota\alpha]$. Complements for the partial payments of list 7 are included in list 8 and the explanation is controversial. *ATL* (iii. 59 f.) believe that these complements were levied by generals on campaign before the tribute was sent to Athens. The money was paid early in 447, but it was not reported by the generals until they returned to Athens after midsummer 447 and was therefore recorded by the next year's board of *hellenotamiai*. This seems an exceedingly unbusinesslike procedure. Why should generals, when there were ample reserves at home, finance their forces from small levies at numerous points? Wade-Gery's earlier view is to be preferred, that partial payments are a sign of discontent (*Hesp.* xiv. 226–8; Meiggs, *Harv. Stud.* lxvii (1963) 16–18). Wade-Gery tentatively explained the considerable improvement in collection by the decree of Kleinias, which was designed to check abuses connected with tribute. The dating of this decree in 447 between lists 7 and 8, though by no means certain, remains an attractive hypothesis (see No. 46). The long list of 447–6 will then be a witness to the successful emergence of Athens from a period of acute crisis. In 446 a new assessment was made and a large number of tributes were reduced (p. 86). Having regained firm control of her empire after a period of strain Athens was wise to make concessions.

Prescripts of Lists [7 and 8]

[7]. [ἐπ]ὶ τε̑[s ἀρχε̑s h]ε̑ι Μενέτ[ιμο]s : ἐγρα[μμάτ]ευε Λαμ[πτρεύs]

[8]. ἐπὶ τε̑s ἀ[ρχε̑s τε̑s—εs] | hε̑ι Διοδ[—ἐγραμμάτευε] | [Π]αιονί[δεs]

[7] col. iv. 9–17		[8] col. i. 94–101	
[ΗΗΔΔΔ]ΔΓⱶ	Θάσιοι	𐌐ⱶⱶⱶ	Θάσιοι
[- -]IIII	Ἀβυδενοι	𐌐ΔΔⱶⱶ	Κυζικε[νοί]
[𐌐]Η	Ἐρετριε̑s	ΔΔΔΓⱶ	Ἐφαισσ[τιε̑s]
[ΔΓⱶ]IIII	Βρ[υ]νχειε̑s	ΔΔΔⱶⱶII	Λιμν⟨α⟩ῖο[ι]
[ΗΗ]Η	[Σίφν]ιοι	[.]ΔΔIIII	Ἀβυδεν[οί]
ΔΓⱶ[IIII]	[Διδ]υμοτε⟨ι⟩χ[ῖται]	𐌐ⱶⱶⱶ	Δαρδα[νε̑s]
Δⱶⱶⱶ	['Ἰᾱτα]ι	𐌐	Ἐλαιό[σι]οι :
𐌐ΗΗ𐌐ΔΔΔΔIIII	[Τορο]ναῖοι	ⱶⱶⱶ	Σιγει[έ]s :
Δ[Δ]ΔΔΓⱶ	[Δαρδ]ανε̑s		

The restored quota of Thasos in list 7 (246 dr.), with the payment in list 8 (54 dr.), together represent the normal Thasian quota before 446, 300 dr. from a tribute of 3 T. Similarly the payments of Dardanos here recorded (46 dr. in list 7, 54 in list 8) together represent the normal quota of 100 dr. from a tribute of 1 T.

[7] col. i. 2–15		[8] col. i. 4–17	
[ΔΓⱶ]IIII	Ναρ[ισβα]ρ[έs]	[Δ]ΓⱶIIII	Ναρισ[βαρε̑s]
[..?..]ⱶⱶⱶII	Τεν[έδι]οι	[Η]Η𐌐ΔΔΔΓ[ⱶⱶⱶ]	Τενέδ[ιο]ι
[Γⱶⱶⱶ]II	Γε[ντ]ίνιοι	[Δ]ΓⱶIIII	Σταγί[ρῖ]ται
[ΔΓ]ⱶIIII	Σ[ταγ]ιρῖτα[ι]	Γ[ⱶⱶ]ⱶII	Γεντί[ν]ιοι
[Η𐌐]	[Κερα]με̑s	Η𐌐	Κεραμ[έ]s
[𐌐ΗΗΗΗ]	[Καμιρ]ε̑s	𐌐ΗΗΗΗ	Καμι[ρ]ε̑s
[ΗΗ]	[hαλικ]αρν[άσσ]ιοι	ΗΗ	hαλικαρνάσσιοι
[Η]	[Μυριναῖοι]	Η	Μυριναῖοι
[Η]	[Μεκυπερναῖοι]	Η	Μεκυ[πε]ρναῖοι
[ΔΔΔ]ⱶⱶⱶII	Π[λαδασε̑s]	[Δ]ΔΔⱶⱶⱶII	Πλαδαϑε̑s
[Η]	[Πεδασε̑s]	Η	Πεδα[σ]ε̑s
[𐌐]ΗΗΗΗ	[Κυμαῖοι]	[𐌐]ΗΗΗΗ	Κυμαῖοι
[Δ]ΓⱶIIII	[Πιταναῖοι]	[Δ]ΓⱶIIII	Πιταναῖοι
ΔΓⱶIIII	Γρυ[νειε̑s]	[Δ]ΓⱶIIII	Γρυνειε̑s

The order of the cities in these two lists corresponds so closely that the restorations in list 7, even when no trace of figure or name survives, are justified.

51 (41)

Athenian Expedition to Megaris: 446 B.C.

Found by Fauvel among the graves near the Acharnian Gate of Athens. The main fragment, most of which has been erased with a claw-chisel, is in the EM; a chip from the left-hand edge, found in the American excavations of the Agora, in the area of Fauvel's house, has now also been transferred there.

Ionic letters of the third quarter of the fifth century, not stoichedon.

IG i². 1085 + ; Allen, *Pap. Am. School*, iv (1885–6) 100; Peek, *Ath. Mitt.* lxvii (1942) 83, no. 138; Gomme, *HCT* i. 340; *SEG* x. 411+.

> μνῆμα τ[όδ' ἐστ' ἐ]πὶ σάματι κείμενον ἀνδρὸς ἀρίστο.
> Πυθίων | ἐγ Μεγάρω⟨ν⟩ δαιώσας ἑπτὰ μ⟨ὲ⟩ν ἄνδρας,
> ἑπτὰ δὲ ἀπορρή⟨ξ⟩ας λ|όγχας ἐνὶ σώματι ἐκείνων
> εἵλετο τὰν ἀρετὰν πατέρα εὐκ|λείζων ἐνὶ δήμωι.
> 5 οὗτος ἀνήρ, ὃς ἔ⟨σ⟩ωισεν Ἀθηναίων τρ|ὲς φυλὰς
> ἐκ Παγᾶν ἀγαγὼν διὰ Βοιωτῶν ἐς Ἀθήνας,
> εὔκλ|εισ' Ἀνδοκίδαν δισχίλοις ἀνδραπόδοισιν.
> οὐδέ{δε}να | πημάνας ἐπιχθονίων ἀνθρώπων
> ἐς Ἀίδα κατέβα πᾶσιν μα|καριστὸς ἰδέσθαι.
> 10 φυλαὶ αἴδ' εἰσίν· Πανδιονίς, Κεκρ|οπίς, Ἀντιοχίς.

l. 1: σάματι Fauvel, σώματι Bekker. l. 2: The nu of Μεγάρων and the epsilon of μέν were omitted. δαίξας Koehler, but the reading of Fauvel and Koumanudes seems correct. l. 3: ἀπορρήσας seems to have been on the stone. l. 5: The first sigma of ἔσωισεν was omitted. l. 7: εὔκλεισ' Allen, εὐκλέϊσ' vulgo.

Like many other inscriptions in Ionic lettering, this suffered from early attempts to give it a context in the fourth century. Koehler, however, was surely right to place the circumstances described in 446 (*Hermes*, xxiv (1889) 92–100; Beloch, *Hermes*, xxiv. 479; Busolt, *GG* iii. 426; *CAH* v. 89; Beloch gives no reasons for his doubts, *GG* ii². 1. 182). The text supports Diodorus (xii. 5) in his statement that the Athenians reacted to the revolt of Megara (Thuc. i. 114) by sending a force into the Megarid, and not merely by returning from Euboea to Athens, as Thucydides implies; and adds the detail that the force consisted of three tribal regiments under the command of Andokides (for whom see p. 41). The need for Pythion's guidance must have been caused by the northward march to Eleusis of the Spartan king Pleistoanax. For the route followed see Hammond, *BSA* xlix (1954)

113. A garrison evidently remained in Pegai, for it was in Athenian hands at the conclusion of the Thirty Years' Peace (Thuc. i. 115. 1, iv. 21. 3).

52 (42)

Athenian Relations with Chalkis: 446–5 B.C.

A marble stele found built into the south wall of the Acropolis: now in the Acropolis Museum. Cuttings show that another stone was affixed on the left and that the two were surmounted by a third stone, probably adorned with a relief and bearing the name of the γραμματεύς the omission of which is otherwise remarkable.

Attic letters (but in l. 77 H = η), stoichedon 32, except in ll. 1, 2. P and P, L and ∠, Ͷ and Ʌ, Σ. Phot.: *ATL* ii, Pl. 10.

Foucart, *RA* xxxiii (1877) 242–62; *SIG* 64; *IG* i². 39; E. Meyer, *Forsch.* ii. 141–8; *ATL* ii. D 17 and iii. 297; Mattingly, *JHS* lxxxi (1961) 124–32, *Ehrenberg Studies*, 201 f.

  ἔδοχσεν τê[ι β]ολêι καὶ τôι δέμοι, Ἀντιοχὶς ἐ[πρυτ]-
  άνευε, Δρακ[ον]τίδες ἐπεστάτε, Διόγνετος εἶπε·
  κατὰ τάδε τὸν hόρκον ὀμόσαι Ἀθεναίον τ-
  ὲν βολὲν καὶ τὸς δικαστάς· οὐκ ἐχσελô Χα-
 5 λκιδέας ἐχ Χαλκίδος οὐδὲ τὲν πόλιν ἀνά-
  στατον ποέσο οὐδὲ ἰδιότεν οὐδένα ἀτιμ-
  όσο οὐδὲ φυγêι ζεμιόσο οὐδὲ χσυλλέφσο-
  μαι οὐδὲ ἀποκτενô οὐδὲ χρέματα ἀφαιρέ-
  σομαι ἀκρίτο οὐδενὸς ἄνευ τô δέμο τô Ἀθ-
 10 εναίον, οὐδ' ἐπιφσεφιô κατὰ ἀπροσκλέτο
  οὔτε κατὰ τô κοινô οὔτε κατὰ ἰδιότο οὐδ-
  ὲ ἑνός, καὶ πρεσβείαν ἐλθôσαν προσάχσο
  πρὸς βολὲν καὶ δêμον δέκα ἑμερôν hόταν
  πρυτανεύο κατὰ τὸ δυνατόν. ταῦτα δὲ ἐμπ-
 15 [ε]δόσο Χαλκιδεῦσιν πειθομένοις τôι δέ-
  [μ]οι τôι Ἀθεναίον. hορκôσαι δὲ πρεσβεία-
  [ν] ἐλθôσαν ἐχ Χαλκίδος μετὰ τôν hορκοτô-
  ν Ἀθεναίος καὶ ἀπογράφσαι τὸς ὀμόσαντας. hόπος δ' ἂν [ὀ]μόσοσιν hάπαντες, ἐπιμελ-
 20 όσθον hοι στ[ρ]ατεγοί. vacat
  κατὰ τάδε Χαλκιδέας ὀμόσαι· οὐκ ἀπο[σ]τέ-

σομαι ἀπὸ τὸ [δ]έμο τὸ Ἀθεναίον οὔτε τέ[χ]ν-
ει οὔτε μεχανεῖ οὐδεμιᾶι οὐδ' ἔπει οὐδὲ
ἔργοι οὐδὲ τοῖ ἀφισταμένοι πείσομαι, κ-
25 αὶ ἐὰν ἀφιστεῖ τις κατερὸ Ἀθεναίοισι, κ-
αὶ τὸν φόρον ηυποτελῶ Ἀθεναίοισιν, ηὸν
ἂν πείθο Ἀθεναίος, καὶ χσύμμαχος ἔσομα-
ι ηοῖος ἂν δύνομαι ἄριστος καὶ δικαιότ-
ατος καὶ τοῖ δέμοι τοῖ Ἀθεναίον βοεθέσ-
30 ο καὶ ἀμυνῶ, ἐάν τις ἀδικεῖ τὸν δῆμον τὸν
Ἀθεναίον, καὶ πείσομαι τοῖ δέμοι τοῖ Ἀθεναίον. ὀμόσαι δὲ Χαλκιδέον τὸς ηεβῶντ-
ας ηάπαντας· ηὸς δ' ἂμ μὲ ὀμόσει, ἄτιμον αὐτὸν ἔναι καὶ τὰ χρέματα αὐτῶ δεμόσια καὶ
35 τὸ Διὸς τὸ Ὀλυμπίο τὸ ἐπιδέκατον ηιερὸ-
ν ἔστο τὸν χρεμάτον. ηορκῶσαι δὲ πρεσβείαν Ἀθεναίον ἐλθῶσαν ἐς Χαλκίδα μετὰ τ-
ὸν ηορκοτὸν τὸν ἐν Χαλκίδι καὶ ἀπογράφσαι τὸς ὀμόσαντας Χαλκιδέον.

vacat

40 Ἀντικλῆς εἶπε· ἀγαθεῖ τύχει τεῖ Ἀθεναίον ποέσθαι τὸν ηόρκον Ἀθεναίος καὶ Χαλκιδέας, καθάπερ Ἐρετριεῦσι ἐφσεφίσατ-
ο ηο δῆμος ηο Ἀθεναίον· ηόπος δ' ἂν τάχιστ-
α γίγνεται, ἐπιμελόσθον ηοι στρατεγοί.
45 ηοίτινες δὲ ἐχσορκόσοσι ἀφικόμενοι ἐ-
ς Χαλκίδα, ἑλέσθαι τὸν δέμον πέντε ἄνδρας αὐτίκα μάλα. περὶ δὲ τὸν ηομέρον ἀποκ-
ρίνασθαι Χαλκιδεῦσιν, ηότι νῦμ μὲν Ἀθεναίοις δοκεῖ ἐᾶν κατὰ τὰ ἐφσεφισμένα· η-
50 όταν δὲ δοκεῖ βολευσάμενοι ποέσοσι τέ-
ν διαλλα[γ]έν, καθότι ἂν δοκεῖ ἐπιτέδειο-
ν ἔναι Ἀθεναίοις καὶ Χαλκιδεῦσιν. τὸς δ-
ὲ χσένος τὸς ἐν Χαλκίδι, ηόσοι οἰκῶντες
μὲ τελῶσιν Ἀθέναζε, καὶ εἴ τοι δέδοται η-
55 υπὸ τὸ δέμο τὸ Ἀθεναίον ἀτέλεια, τὸς δὲ ἄ-
λλος τελῶν ἐς Χαλκίδα, καθάπερ ηοι ἄλλο-
ι Χαλκιδέες. τὸ δὲ φσέφισμα τόδε καὶ τὸν

ℎόρκον ἀναγράφσαι, Ἀθένεσι μὲν τὸν γραμμ[α]τέα τῆς βολῆς ἐστέλει λιθίνει καὶ κ-
60 αταθῆναι ἐς πόλιν τέλεσι τοῖς Χαλκιδέον, ἐν δὲ Χαλκίδι ἐν τῶι ℎιερῶι τῶι Διὸς τὸ
Ὀλυμπίο ℎε βολὲ Χαλκιδέον ἀναγράφσασ-
α καταθέτο. ταῦτα μὲν φσεφίσασθαι Χαλκιδεῦσιν. υυυυ τὰ δὲ ℎιερὰ τὰ ἐκ τῶν χρεσμ-
65 ὸν ℎυπὲρ Εὐβοίας θῦσαι ὁς τάχιστα μετὰ
ℎιεροκλέος τρῆς ἄνδρας, ℎὸς ἂν ἕλεται ℎ-
ε βολὲ σφὸν αὐτὸν· ℎόπος δ' ἂν τάχιστα τυθ-
ε͂ι, ℎοι στρατεγοὶ συνεπιμελόσθον καὶ τ-
ὸ ἀργύριον ἐς ταῦτα [π]αρεχόντον. vacat
70 Ἀρχέστρατο[ς] εἶπε· τὰ μὲν ἄλλα καθάπερ Ἀ-
ντικλῆς· τὰς δὲ εὐθύνας Χαλκιδεῦσι κατ-
ὰ σφὸν αὐτὸν ἔναι ἐν Χαλκίδι καθάπερ Ἀθ-
ένεσιν Ἀθεναίοις πλὲν φυγῆς καὶ θανάτ-
ο καὶ ἀτιμίας· περὶ δὲ τούτον ἔφεσιν ἔνα-
75 ι Ἀθέναζε ἐς τὲν ℎελιαίαν τὲν τῶν θεσμοθετῶν κατὰ τὸ φσέφισμα τῶ δέμο· περὶ δὲ φυ-
λακῆς Εὐβοίας τὸς στρατηγὸς ἐπιμέλεσ-
θαι ℎος ἂν δύνονται ἄριστα, ℎόπος ἂν ἔχε-
ι ℎος βέλτιστα Ἀθεναίοις.
80   ℎόρκος

Euboea, which had been encouraged to revolt by the decisive
defeat of the Athenians at Koroneia, was recovered by Athens in the
late summer of 446. The Hestiaians had put to death the crew of an
Athenian ship and received no mercy; their city was destroyed and
they were forced to evacuate. The rest of the island came to terms
(Thuc. i. 114. 3: τὴν μὲν ἄλλην ὁμολογίᾳ κατεστήσαντο). This stele
concerns the settlement with Chalkis; it does not, however, record
the main terms which will have been set out in a decree on the stele
which was originally attached to the left. Our stele refers to this
earlier decree and is a corollary to it: τὰ ἐφσεφισμένα l. 49, possibly
τὸ φσέφισμα in l. 76 (but see below), and the article in τὸν ℎόρκον of
l. 3. It contains the oaths to be taken at Athens and Chalkis and a
decree which answers representations made by the Chalkidians for
a reconsideration of some of the terms of the settlement. The tone is
polite but very firm.

The Athenian oath (3–16) is to be taken by the members of the

Boule and the full panel of 6,000 jurors. They undertake, so long as
Chalkis remains obedient, not to treat Chalkis like Hestiaia but to
preserve the city. They will not have recourse to martial law but will
follow the normal processes of justice, and any deputation coming from
Chalkis will be given a hearing by the Boule and Assembly. These
are no generous concessions, and in the Chalkidian oath of loyalty
and obedience which follows (21–32) the status of Chalkis as the
subject of an imperial power is made explicit. In the declaration of
loyalty there is no mention of Athens' allies as in the Council's oath
at Erythrai (No. 40, ll. 23 f.) and perhaps in the Kolophonian oath
(No. 47, l. 44), and the declaration has to be more comprehensive:
22–4, οὔτε τέχνει οὔτε μεχανεῖ οὐδεμιᾶι, οὐδ' ἔπει οὐδὲ ἔργοι; in Kolophon's oath, ll. 45–6, οὔτε λόγοι οὔτ' ἔργοι without further qualification.
More serious is the undertaking, found here for the first time, to de-
nounce to Athens any attempt to stir up revolt (25). The Chalkidians
also have to promise to pay to the Athenians φόρον . . . hὸν ἂν πείθο
Ἀθεναῖος (26 f.). This might mean one of two things: either that
Chalkis at each assessment would be able to make representations
about her assessment (according to the procedure set out in the assessment decree of 425, No. 69) and then pay regularly; or the reference
might be to the new assessment to be made after the crushing of the
revolt. No figure survives for Chalkis in the lists of 445–443. Before
the revolt she was required to pay 5 T. (*ATL* i, p. 36); after it she
pays only 3 T. (the name is restored in 441 and 439; both figure and
name survive in 432 and 429). For τὸν φόρον hὸν ἂν πείθο cf. Thuc.
i. 101. 3, of the Thasians after they had capitulated in 463: χρήματά
τε ὅσα ἔδει ἀποδοῦναι αὐτίκα ταξάμενοι καὶ τὸ λοιπὸν φέρειν. Chalkis
must also promise help to the Athenian demos if it is attacked, and
must obey the Athenian demos; the emphasis throughout is not on
Athens but more specifically on the Athenian demos. The importance
still attached to such oaths as these is reflected in the provision for
making lists of those who swear, 6,500 in Athens, and in Chalkis all
adult males (18, 38 f.).

A vacant space is left below the oaths and the arrangements for
administering them. There follows a decree, moved by Antikles, returning chilly answers to Chalkidian pleas for concessions, and it
was presumably passed at the same meeting of the Assembly as the
oaths, for there is no prescript with the names of prytany and secretary.
So far as the hostages are concerned, for the present, matters will
rest according to the decision already taken by Athens, but when
the time is ripe the Athenians will make the διαλλαγέ after joint con-
sultation (see below). Athens has no intention to prevent Chalkis'
collecting taxes from foreign residents, but she must still insist on
exemption for those who, while living at Chalkis, pay dues to Athens,

and any to whom Athens has granted exemption from dues (52–7, but the interpretation is controversial; see below). Antikles' decree closes with a public recognition of oracles (64–9): 'The sacrifices required by the oracles are to be carried out as soon as possible by Hierokles and three members to be elected from the Boule; and the generals are to give any help that is needed and provide the money.' Antikles has not covered all the ground; Archestratos, in an amendment, confirms the rulings already given about judicial control (ll. 71–6). While Chalkis may continue to decide in her own courts the normal run of cases, those which involve the major penalties of exile, death, or loss of rights are to be subject to appeal to Athens. Finally Archestratos requires the generals to take such measures as are necessary for the security of Euboea.

Within this well-preserved text several points are obscure or controversial. l. 4: The oath at Athens is to be taken by the Boule and jurors. Do they represent the whole people, or merely themselves? Probably the latter, for they are the two most vital organs of control, and the Assembly itself must remain unfettered (so Meyer, loc. cit. 144 f.). Note that not every clause of the oath is appropriate to both categories. ll. 4 ff.: οὐκ ἐχσελô Χαλκιδέας .... This clause is not impossible to reconcile with Plutarch's statement (*Per.* 23. 4) that the *hippobotai* were driven out. The expulsion of those who were naturally most opposed to Athenian domination could have been taken immediately after the end of fighting; the oaths were part of a settlement that was formulated later. Probably the primary intention is to assure Chalkis that she will not be treated like Hestiaia. Neither this passage nor any other on the stele can be safely used as an argument for or against an Athenian cleruchy at this time. ll. 12–14: The promise to give a hearing to any deputation from Chalkis could be of practical value; [Xen.] *Ἀθ. Πολ.* 3. 1 emphasizes the delays and difficulties of foreigners' getting an audience in Athens. l. 42: We now know, from the identification of a large fragment, that the oath imposed on Eretria was identical with the Chalkidian (Schweigert, *Hesp.* vi (1937) 317–19; *ATL* ii. D 16). l. 51: τὲν διαλλαγέν is usually taken as 'arrangement', which does not adequately explain the article. Y. Garlan, *BCH* lxxxix (1965) 332–8, basing his argument on André Aymard's studies of the problems of hostages in the ancient world, plausibly suggests that the Chalkidians, having failed to secure the release of their hostages, are pleading that the hostages should later on be changed; the Athenians undertake to negotiate the change when they think that the right time has come. ll. 52–7: τὸς δὲ χσένος ... Though this clause may not be strictly grammatical the meaning is clear. Tod translates: 'But the aliens at Chalcis, save those who, resident there, pay taxes to Athens and any one who has received from the Athenian people a grant of exemption, shall in all other cases pay taxes to Chalcis as do also the Chalcidians.' *ATL* iii. 295–7 revives the view, once widely held, that the ξένοι are Athenian cleruchs settled on the land of the expelled *hippobotai* in the Lelantine plain. Meyer's arguments against this thesis (op. cit. 146 f.) are still compelling. An Athenian decree would not call Athenians ξένοι; they would be either Ἀθηναῖοι or κληροῦχοι; nor could the Chalcidians have expected to receive dues from Athenian cleruchs. The reference is surely to non-Athenians. l. 71: εὐθύνας here clearly means punishments in general rather than the examination of magistrates at the end of their year of office (as held by Gomme in *HCT* i. 342); Athens would not wish her control to be limited to magistrates; discontented oligarchs in particular had to be watched. Control by Athens is exercised by specifying the penalty rather than the nature of the offence, for the latter would provide an easy means of evasion (see G. E. M. de Ste Croix, *CQ* xi (1961) 270). l. 74: ἔφεσις has sometimes been taken to mean compulsory reference in the first instance (e.g. Gomme, *HCT* i. 342). Attic usage, however, is consistent: ἔφεσις and ἐφίημι always imply a second hearing. Tod refers to *SIG* 921. 30, 38, 96, 101; Arist. Ἀθ. Πολ. 9. 1, 45. 2, etc. (see also Wade-Gery, *Essays* (1958) 192–5). Since no qualification is added, appeal should be open to both prosecution and defence. Athens needed to ensure not only that friends of Athens were not condemned as a result of national prejudice but also that anti-Athenian elements were not wrongly acquitted. l. 76, κατὰ τὸ φσέφισμα τὸ δέμο might refer either to the decree which detailed the main settlement with Chalkis (equivalent to κατὰ τὰ ἐφσεφισμένα of l. 49), or to a general decree concerning jurisdiction in the empire.

Some of the Athenians named on this stone may be identifiable. Drakontides, who presided over the Assembly, may be the general of 433–2 (No. 61, l. 20; *PA* 4551); Antikles (l. 40) may be the general of 440–39 (Thuc. i. 117. 2; *PA* 1051) or the Antikles who was first assistant secretary and then secretary of the Parthenon Commission (see p. 164; *PA* 1052). Hierokles (l. 66) is almost certainly ὁ χρησμολόγος οὑξ Ὠρεοῦ of Ar. *Peace* 1047 (cf. Eupolis fr. 212, Kock i, p. 316 = Edmonds I, p. 389: Ἱερόκλεες βέλτιστε χρησμῳδῶν ἄναξ), *PA* 7473. Perhaps he served in the field as a μάντις and was given a holding at Oreus, which replaced Hestiaia and was populated from Athens.

Mattingly (*JHS* lxxxi (1961) 124–32) has revived a view that had some currency in the nineteenth century. He argues that this settlement with Chalkis follows the expedition to Euboea in 424–3, recorded by Philochorus (*FGH* 328 F 130) according to a scholiast on Aristophanes (*Wasps* 718). The Athenians named fit better, he thinks, into the twenties than the forties; he points out close parallels between passages on this stele and decrees of the twenties, and argues that the imperial attitude displayed by Athens suggests Cleon rather than Pericles. Some of his individual points are attractive, but two objections are decisive. (1) R, which occurs commonly with P on this stele, is not infrequent near the mid century; we know of no example later than 438-7 (Meiggs, *JHS* lxxxvi (1966) 92, 94). (2) The terms of the decree imply a major upheaval, after which Athens imposed stringent terms on Chalkis and Eretria. This would cause no surprise after the crushing of the serious revolt of 446, but a large-scale campaign in 423 would be very difficult to accept. Thucydides' silence would be very puzzling indeed.

53

Accounts of Nemesis of Rhamnous: *c.* 450–440 B.C.

Marble stele found at Rhamnous; now in EM.
    Letter forms vary: Ϟ (I); Ϛ (II–V). V (I, III, IV); Υ (II). Rho and phi have the developed forms (Ρ, Φ) consistently. Ionic Η and Ω in II, IV, V. τοῖσι in I; τοῖς in III (ἱεροποιοῖς in V). Phot.: Ἀρχ. Ἐφ. 1934-5, 128.
    Stavropoullos, Ἀρχ. Ἐφ. 1934-5, 128-32; Wilhelm, *Jahresh.* xxxii (1940) 200-14; M. I. Finley, *Studies in Land and Credit in Ancient Athens*, 284 f.; Pouilloux, *La Forteresse de Rhamnonte* (1954), no. 35, pp. 147-50.

I   Ἐπ' Αὐτοκλείδ-
      ο δεμαρχõντο-
      ς: τõ τẽς Νεμέσ-
      εος ἀργυρίο: κ-
    5 εφάλαιον: τõ π-
      αρὰ τοῖσι τὰς
      διακοσίας δρ-
      αχμὰς ὀφέλοσι
      ΜΜΜⴑ:ΧΧ: τõ δὲ ἄ-
   10 λλο ἀργυρίο: ⊢-
      õ τẽς Νεμέσεο-
      ς: κεφάλαι{:}ον: Μ
      ΧΧⴑΗΗΔ́ΔΓⵕⵕ
      ⊢ΙΙΙ.

II

  15 'Επὶ Μνησιπτολέμ-
ο ἄρχοντος κεφάλ-
αιον παντὸς τô ἱε-
ρô ἀργυρίο ⋮ ⊢ΧΗ
ΗΗ⊠ΔΔΔΔΓⱵⱵΙΙΙΙ.

III

  20 'Επὶ Ναυσιμένος ἄρχοντος κεφάλαιον τô ἱ-
ερô ἀργυρίο τô πα-
ρὰ τοῖς τὰς διακοσί-
ας ἔχοσι ⋮ ΜΜΜ⊠ΧΧ
  25 τô δ' ἄλλο ⋮ ΜΧⱵΗΗΔΔⱵⱵ
ΙΙ.

IV

    'Επ' Εὐαινέτο ἄρχον-
τος κεφάλαιον τρι-
ακοσιοδράχμων
  30 ΜΧΧΧⱵ ⋮ παντὸς δὲ
⊢⊢ⱵΗΗΔⱵⱵΙ.

V

    'Επὶ Δημοφάνος δημάρ-
χο παρὰ ἱεροποιοῖς κε-
φάλαιον ⋮ ⊠ΗΗΓⱵΙΙΙΙ
  35 τριακοσιοδράχμων
ΜΧΧΧΧΗΗΗΗ ⋮ διακοσι-
οδράχμων ⋮ ΜΜΜ⊠ΧΧ
παντός ⋮ ⊢⊢Χ ⱵΗΓⱵΙΙΙΙ.

On this stele are recorded annual accounts of the financial resources, in reserve or on loan, of the cult of Nemesis of Rhamnous. Five years, probably consecutive, are covered in a single column and dated by the demarch. The deme of Rhamnous was on the coast of Attica, north-east of Athens, in a rather isolated situation, and the central settlement, including the temple of Nemesis, was strongly fortified (Pouilloux, op. cit.).

These accounts are an extreme example of the unsystematic character of most Greek records. There are three different forms of the dating formula. Whereas the first two accounts give the total on loan and the balance in hand, the third gives only the combined total. When in the fourth year a new form of loan is recorded, the older form is not specified but merely included in a grand total. The ἱεροποιοί who are in control of finances are mentioned only in the last year, and there are other minor anomalies.

It was normal for Greek temples to lend their money at interest. The fullest illustration comes from Delos (No. 62); on the other hand, the large-scale lending of Athena's reserve to finance the Peloponnesian War (No. 72) seems to have been an exceptional measure, and, as a loan to the state rather than to individuals, stands on rather a different footing. The loans from the money of Nemesis do not, on the face of it, appear to vary according to the need of the borrower, but are in standard sums, 200 and 300 dr. Finley has doubted this interpretation of τοῖσι τὰς διακοσίας δραχμὰς ὀφέλοσι (I = τοῖς τὰς διακοσίας ἔχοσι in III) on the ground that the number of borrowers (185) would be too large. But, as Pouilloux points out (op. cit. 149), one man might 'take up several shares'; the cult of Nemesis at Rhamnous was also of more than local importance. The temple that was built for her not long after 440 was very probably by the same architect as the temples of Hephaistos and Ares at Athens (the temple of Ares was probably originally at Acharnai, and only moved to Athens in the Augustan period), and of Poseidon at Sounion (Dinsmoor, *Hesp.* ix (1940) 1–52, esp. 47; Plommer, *BSA* xlv (1950) 66–109). These accounts, to judge from their letter-forms, were probably earlier than this temple; if Nemesis' own resources were of the order of 9–10 T. (l. 38), the temple will have needed some subvention.

Nemesis of Rhamnous is not listed in the surviving fragments from the inventory of the 'other gods' set up in 428 (*IG* i². 310), nor is she among the 'other gods' from whom money was borrowed in 423–2 (No. 72). It is virtually certain that her treasures were not moved when the treasures of the temples of Attica and the lower city were concentrated for security on the Acropolis shortly before the Peloponnesian War (No. 58). They were considered safe within the strong walls of Rhamnous.

54 (47)

Accounts of Pheidias' Statue of Athena: 447–438 B.C.

A: 440–39 B.C.

Upper portions of two marble stelai, found on the Acropolis; now in EM. The stelai were uniform in cross-section (28 × 11 cm.) and probably also in height, but 1, never used, lacks the cutting for a T-clamp visible on 2.

Developed Attic writing: 1 not stoichedon, 2 stoichedon. Phots.: Austin, Pl. 8; (2 only) *BCH* xci (1967) 69.

IG i². 355, 355a+; Austin, 62 f.; Donnay, *BCH* xci. 68–71.

(1)

     θεοί ⋮ Ἀθενᾶ ⋮ Τύχε
     Κιχέσιππος ⋮ ἐγραμμά-
     τευε ⋮ ἀγάλματος ⋮ ἐπι-
     στάτεσι ⋮ Μυρρινόσιος
5   λêμμα ⋮ παρὰ vacat
             vacat

(2)

     Κιχέσιππος ἐγ[ρ]-
     αμμάτευε: ἀγάλ[μ]-
     ατος: ἐπιστάτε[σ]-
     ι: Μυρρινόσιος: λ-
5   êμμα: παρὰ ταμιδ-
Η ν: hοῖς Δεμόστρα-
     τος: ἐγραμμάτευ-
     ε: Χσυπεταόν: ταμ-
     ίαι: Κτεσίον: Στ[ρ]-
10   οσίας: Ἀντιφάτ[ε]-
     ς: Μένανδρος: Θ[υμ]-
     οχάρες: Σμόκορ[δ]-
     ος: Φειδελείδ[ες.]
     vacat

𐅆ΔΔΔ χρυσίον: ἐονέθ-
15 𐅆ΤΤΧ ε, σταθμὸν: 𐅆ΤΧ𐅆Η̣
   ΧΧΧ𐅆 τιμὲ τούτο ΔΓΗΗΗΙ
   Η𐅆ΗΗ ΙΙΙΙΙ vacat
     vacat
   ΤΤ𐅆Η ἐλέφας ἐονέθε
   ΗΔΔΔ vacat
20 ΔΗΗΗ vacat
   - - - - - -

A 1 was rejected and uncompleted, perhaps because the contractors had stipulated for a stoichedon text (Austin), perhaps also because the stone-cutter realized he had left no room for a column of figures (Meritt, *CP* xxxiv (1939) 384). For the end of l. 16 Dinsmoor (*AJA* xvii (1913) 76) suggested ΔΓΗΗΗ[C], but the reading seems clear, though Donnay makes the last figure Τ.

B. 438 B.C.

Two joining fragments of a marble stele, preserving the left edge and top.

Developed Attic writing, save for R, stoichedon. Facs.: Ἀρχ. Ἐφ. 1937. 509. Phot.: Cavaignac, *Études*, xlix, Fig. 12, *BCH* xci. 72.

IG i². 354+; Dinsmoor, Ἀρχ. Ἐφ. 1937, 507–11; Donnay, op. cit., 71–5.

```
        ἐπιστά[ται - - - - - - -]
        τάδε ἔλ[αβον - - - - - ἀργ]-
        ύριον vacat [vacat        ]
        ⟦ΠΗΗ [- - - - - - - - - - -]
    5   ΠΔΔ [- - - - - - - - - - -]

        χρυσι[ο - - - - - - - - - -]
        ετο: ΗΗ[- - - - - - - -]
        Κάλλα[ισχρος - - - - - ἀνέ]-
        θεκεν [- - - - - - - - - - - -]

   10   ἀναλό[ματα - - - - - - - - -]
        . Η[- - - - - - - - - - - - - -]
        ⟦Α⟧ΔΔ [- - - - - - - - - - -]
        ἀπεργα[σία - - - - - - - - - -]
        ΠΗΗΑΔΔ[- - - - - - - - -]

   15   καταβλ[εμα - - - - - - - - - -]
        ΔΔΔ[- - - - - - - - - - - - -]
        ΗΗΗ[- - - - - - - - - - - - -]
        χρυσιο [- - - - - - - - - - ἀγά]-
        [λ]ματι π[- - - - - - - - - - -]
```

Dinsmoor restores ll. 1–12 ἐπιστά[ται ἀγάλματος χρυσõ‖ τάδε ἔλ[αβον παρὰ ταμιõν ἀργ]‖ύριον vacat | ⟦Π⟧ΗΗ[Η4444ΠΤΤ]‖⟦Π⟧ΔΔ[- - -] | χρυσί[ο δὲ σταθμὸν περιεγέν]‖ετο: ΗΗ[....τõ ἀναθέματος hò]‖ Κάλλα[ισχρος Ἀφιδναῖος ἀνέ]‖θεκεν [vacat] | ἀναλό[ματα vacat]‖ [⟦Π⟧]Η[ΗΗΠ XXXXΗΗ]‖⟦Π⟧ΔΔ and l. 18 χρυσίο [περιτμέματα τõι ἀγά]-. See Donnay.

The ἄγαλμα in question (called ἄγαλμα χρυσõν in *IG* i². 358 and χρυσοτὸν ἄγαλμα ibid. 359) is Pheidias' chryselephantine statue of Athena, the cult-image of the Parthenon. Philochorus (quoted by the scholiast on Ar. *Peace* 605) states that, in 438–7 (reading Θεοδώρου for the scholiast's Πυθοδώρου), τὸ ἄγαλμα τὸ χρυσοῦν τῆς Ἀθηνᾶς ἐστάθη εἰς τὸν νεὼν τὸν μέγαν, ἔχον χρυσίου σταθμὸν ταλάντων μδʹ (44), Περικλέους ἐπιστατοῦντος, Φειδίου δὲ ποιήσαντος (*FGH* 328 F 121; cf. Thuc. ii. 13. 5, who gives the weight of gold as 40 T., Diod. xii. 39, who gives it as 50 T., Plut. *Per*. 13).

This weight of gold suggests that the statue cost at least 616 T., and, if Dinsmoor is right, as he surely must be, in identifying our B as the final summation of all the accounts, the total cost was between 700 and 1,000 T. The arrangement of the extant accounts has been discussed by Meritt, *AFD* 30–41, Dinsmoor, *Harv. Stud.*, Suppl. i. 158–65, and Donnay. Factors which they have not taken into account lead us to prefer the following arrangement, which Lewis will justify elsewhere: *IG* i². 360, 447–6(?); *IG* i². 361, 446–5; *IG* i². 359, 444–3; *Hesp.* xxx (1961) 262, no. 74, 443–2 or 441–0; *IG* i². 358, 442–1; *IG* i². 355, 440–39; *IG* i². 356, 439–8; *IG* i². 354, 438. (*IG* i². 357 and 362 do not belong to the series.) In these documents all receipts come from the treasurers of Athena, the largest annual receipt yet known is for 160 T., no payment except for gold and ivory has yet been identified, and there is as yet no trace of money being carried from year to year. The ἐπιστάται spent what they received. In our text A they received 100 T. from the treasurers, of whom only seven are named, paid 87 T. 4,652 dr. 5 ob. for gold weighing 6 T. 1,618 dr. 1 ob. (giving the ratio of gold to silver as 14:1; cf. No. 59, ll. 21–3) and 2 T. 743 dr. for ivory; the account then breaks off.

55 (50)

Expenses of the Samian War: 440 and 439 B.C.

Two fragments of a marble stele, found on the Acropolis; now in EM.
Developed Attic writing, stoichedon 65 (?). Phot.: Meritt, *AFD* 43.
IG i². 293+; Meritt, *AFD* 42–8 (with a 93-letter line), *AJP* lv (1934) 365–6 (with a 64-letter line).

```
. . 5 . . . εκ - - - - - - - - - - - - - - - - - - - - - - - - -
. . . . εσε - - - - - - - - - - - - - - - - - - - - - - - - -
. . . σοσι - - - - - - - - - - - - - - - - - - - - - - - - -
. . . Φρεά[ρριος - - - - - - - - - - - - - - - - - - - -
5   ΗϞϞϞϜΤΤΤ[- - - - - - - - - - - - - - - - - - - - -
```

Ἀθεναῖοι ἀ[νέλοσαν ἐπὶ Τιμοκλέος καὶ ἐπὶ Μορυχίδο ἀρχόντον Ἀθεναίοισι, ἐς τὸν]
πρὸς Σαμίο[ς πόλεμον τάδε· τάδε ἐν τοῖν δυοῖν ἐτοῖν hοι ταμίαι
παρέδοσ]α[ν τὸν τῆς]
Ἀθεναίας Π[ολιάδος στρατεγοῖσι τοῖς πρὸς Σαμίος· ἀνάλομα παρὰ
ταμι]ὸν ἐ[κ πόλεο]-

ς, ho͂ις Φυρό[μαχος ἐγραμμάτευεν, ἐπὶ τε͂ς βολε͂ς, he͂ι......12......
προ͂τ]ος ἐ[γραμμά]-
10 τευε· ταμία[ι...................... 45 ....
Εὐ]βο[λίδες ἐ]-
χς Οἴο Ναυσ[- -]
ͱͱͱͱ⊩ᚦᚱΤΤΤ[- -]
παρὰ ταμιο͂[ν ἐκ πόλεος, ho͂ις Δεμόστρατος ἐγραμμάτευεν, ἐπὶ τε͂ς
βολε͂ς, he͂ι 'Επιχαρ]-
ῖνος Περαι[εὺς προ͂τος ἐγραμμάτευε, στρατεγοῖσι τοῖς πρὸς Σαμίος
ἀνάλομα δεύτ]-
15 ερον· hoίδε [ταμίαι ἐσαν - - - - - - - - - - - - - - - - -]
Ἀφιδναῖος[- -]
⊩ͱͱͱͱ⊩ΤΤΤ[- -]
χσύμπαντο[ς κεφάλαιον τὸ ἐς Βυζαντίος καὶ ἐς Σαμίος ἀναλόματος - -]
⨯ͱ[ͱ]ͱͱ[- -]
- - - - - - -

The small fragment, first assigned to this inscription by Meritt, *AJA* xxxviii (1934) 69, is here placed in ll. 7–10, after an unpublished suggestion by Wade-Gery.

The restorations, and even the line-length, must be considered very uncertain. The starting-point for Meritt's revisions was his conviction that the secretary of the treasurers for 440–39 was not Phyromachos (l. 9), but Demostratos (l. 13), and this observation, based on the accounts of the gold and ivory statue (No. 54), still seems good.

But we should not lose sight of another possibility. It is conceivable that ll. 1–5 represent the end of the account of the conciliar year 441–0, and that ll. 6–17 record two payments made during the conciliar year 440–39, made by different boards of treasurers because Hekatombaion 28, the end of the treasurers' year of office, fell between them (cf. No. 61). We retain the outlines of Meritt's solution largely because we do not readily see how our alternative can be expressed in lines long enough to accommodate reasonably full boards of treasurers in ll. 10–11, 15–16.

L. 7 of this text leaves no doubt that we are dealing with events of the year 440, when Samos, which, with Chios and Lesbos, still contributed ships rather than money, challenged the right of Athens to intervene in her war with Miletus. Pericles seems to have thought that political intervention in Samos would settle the matter (Thuc. i. 115. 2–3), but his actions provoked a revolt in which Byzantium joined, and the Samians won some initial successes before the deployment of Athens' full resources settled the matter (see No. 56).

The first three sums of money on this stele (ll. 5, 12, 17) add up to

the fourth (l. 19). On Meritt's reconstruction of the text, ll. 1–5 give
the expense, 128 T. +, of the subjugation of Byzantium, and ll. 6–17
give the expense of the war against Samos, 368 T. + in 441–0 and
908 T. + in 440–39. The total of these last, 1,276 T. +, corresponds
well enough with the figure of 1,200 T. for the cost of the war given
by Nepos (*Timoth.* 1), and probably to be restored in Isocrates (xv.
111, reading ἀπὸ διακοσίων [νεῶν] καὶ χιλίων ταλάντων) and Diodorus
(xii. 28, reading ⟨χιλίων⟩ διακοσίων).

Several points of importance are here raised about Athenian
financial history. The inscription appears only to give the amounts
spent on the war by the treasurers of Athena out of their reserves.
Did the Athenians spend a proportion or all of their current revenue
as well? Does the fact that Athena's money was called on imply
that there was no other reserve, whether in the hands of the *helleno-*
tamiai or in the Athenian δημόσιον? This is the view, for example of
G. H. Stevenson, *JHS* xliv (1924) 1 ff., followed by *ATL* iii. 337,
but it is denied by Gomme, *Hist.* ii (1953) 16 f., *HCT* ii. 31–2. It is
part of the general thesis of the authors of *ATL* (iii. 118–31, 338;
Meritt, *Hesp.* xxiii (1954) 185–93) to support the reading in Thucydides ii. 13. 3, ὑπαρχόντων δὲ ἐν τῇ ἀκροπόλει αἰεί ποτε ἀργυρίου ἐπισήμου
ἑξακισχιλίων ταλάντων. Is this implication of a steady balance compatible with the heavy drain shown by this inscription? This, too, is
denied by Gomme, *HCT* ii. 30. Finally, there is the question of the
Samian indemnity. According to Thucydides (i. 117. 3) the Samians
agreed χρήματα τὰ ἀναλωθέντα ταξάμενοι κατὰ χρόνους ἀποδοῦναι.
Epigraphical evidence which may refer to these repayments is collected in Hill, *Sources*², 306–7 (see also No. 68 here). The view of *ATL*
(iii. 334–5) is that the indemnity was paid off in annual instalments
of 50 T., and that the 26th and possibly last instalment was paid in
414–13. Gomme argues (*Hist.* ii. 18–19, *HCT* ii. 33) that the indemnity could have been and was paid off before 431.

56

Athenian Treaty with Samos: 439–8 B.C.

Four fragments of a marble stele, only two of which join, found on the
Acropolis; now in EM.

Developed Attic letters. Stoichedon 35. Phot.: *AFD* 51–3; *ATL* ii, Pl. 11.
IG i². 50; Wade-Gery, *CP* xxvi (1931) 309–13; Meritt, *AFD* 48–56;
ATL ii. D 18; *Staatsverträge* 159.

a — ο — | — απι — | — ικε — | — Λεμνο — | — ι καθάπ[ερ — |
— οι κατα — | — Πελο]ποννεσ — | — δὲ ἐν τε͂[ι — | — ϙοι δὲ
κα[— | — χρόνο ὑπα — | — α]ὐτὸς Ἀθεν — | — α]ὐτόν· hοσ —
| — ν ἀποδ — | — σ — |

lacuna

15 [- δρ]-
[άσο καὶ ἐρο͂ καὶ βολεύσο τοῖ δέμοι τοῖ Ἀθενα]-
b [ίον hό τι ἂν δύνομαι καλὸν κ]αὶ ἀ[γ]αθόν, [οὐδὲ ἀ]-
[ποστέσομαι ἀπὸ το͂ δέμο το͂ Ἀ]θεναίον οὔτε λ[ό]-
[γοι οὔτε ἔργοι οὐδὲ ἀπὸ τον] χσυμμάχον τὸν Ἀ-
20 [θεναίον, καὶ ἔσομαι πιστὸς τ]οῖ δέμοι τοῖ Ἀθ-
[εναίον· Ἀθεναῖος δ' ὀμόσαι· δρ]άσο καὶ ἐρο͂ καὶ
[βολεύσο καλὸν τοῖ δέμοι τοῖ] Σαμίον hό τι ἂν
[δύνομαι καὶ ἐπιμελέσομαι Σα]μίον κατὰ hὰ [.]
[. . . . . 25 . . . .] Ἀθεναίον [. .]
25 [. . . . . 26 . . . .] κρατε[. . . .]
[-] λ[. . . 6 . . .]

lacuna

c [στ]ρατεγ[οὶ ὄμνυον τὸν hόρκον· Σοκράτες Ἐρε]-
χθεῖδος· Δεμ[- - - - - - Αἰγεῖδος· - - - - - - Πα]-
νδιονίδος· Χ[. . . . . 10 . . . . . Λεοντίδος· Περικλ]-
30 ε͂ς· Γλαύκον Ἀ[καμαντίδος· Καλλ]ί[σστρατος Οἰ]-
d νεῖδος· Χσε[νοφο͂ν Κεκροπίδ]ος· Τλεμπ[όλεμος]
[Αἰαντίδος· . . . . Ἀντιοχίδο]ς· βολὲ ἐρχε [. . . .]
[. . . . . 16 . . . . προ͂τ]ος ἐγραμμάτευε Ῥα-
[μνόσιος vacat]   vacat

ll. 23–6: ἐπιμελέσομαι Σα]μίον κατὰ hὰ [h]|[ομολόγεσαν hοι στρατεγοὶ
hοι] Ἀθεναίον [κα]|[ὶ hοι ἄρχοντες hοι Σαμίον· Καλλι]κράτε[ς εἶπ]|[ε ATL.
ATL infers a lacuna of 14 lines after l. 26, but this is based on the assumed
tapering of the stele. It is, however, doubtful whether the back of the stele,
from which the inference is made, is original. For l. 28 see below. ll. 32–3:
Lolling reported ιυ after ἐρχε. τὸ[ν ἐ|νιαυτὸν hότε (Meritt AFD) satisfies
the traces but is unconvincing. hό[τε (IG i², ATL ii) requires a patrony-
mic or an improbably long name. ATL iv. x suggests Ἀθ[εν|αίοις hε͂ι
. . . . 8 . . . . .

After a stubborn resistance Samos surrendered in the ninth month.
Thucydides records the main penalties imposed: the Samians had to
pull down their walls, surrender their fleet, and repay the cost of the
operations in instalments (Thuc. i. 117. 3). The future relations

between Athens and Samos had also to be defined; these fragments give part of a decree in which they were recorded.

Not more than seven letters from a probable 35 survive in any of the 14 lines of the first fragment, an inadequate basis for restoration. Lemnos, where the original Samian hostages were deposited, is mentioned (l. 4) and, almost certainly, the Peloponnesians (l. 7, Πελο]πον-νεσ[—]). This recalls the Corinthian claim in Thucydides to have opposed intervention when the Peloponnesian League met to discuss help for Samos (Thuc. i. 40. 5). The second fragment contains what survives of the oaths to be taken by Samos and Athens, and by comparison with other oaths the general sense at least can be restored. The most striking feature is the apparent generosity of Athens, especially when compared with her attitude to Chalkis in 446–5 (No. 52). The oath of loyalty is once again, as at Erythrai, to the allies as well as the Athenians. More important, whereas the Athenian oath to Chalkis merely repudiates the use of force, there is a positive undertaking to look after the interests of the Samian demos. Athens (and perhaps we could say Pericles) seems to have decided that the wisest policy was to pin her faith on a democratic government at Samos; this perhaps helps to explain why the Samian democrats remained faithful to the bitter end.

The last two fragments come from a list of the ten generals who took the oath. Sokrates was general from Erechtheis in 441–0 (Androtion, FGH 324 F 38). For Aegeis Wade-Gery suggested Δεμ[οκλείδες], who established the colony of Brea (No. 49), but names with this beginning are very common. Wade-Gery's full restoration of the line, however, neatly fills the space: Δεμ[οκλείδες Αἰγείδος : Φορμίον Πα]∥νδιονίδος. If correct it would confirm that Phormio not only had an estate in Paiania (Paus. i. 23. 10) but was also registered in Paiania's tribe, Pandionis. This in turn would mean that Pericles' tribe was not the only one to have two representatives on the generals' board in this period: on at least two occasions (440–39 and 430–29) Phormio and Hagnon will both have represented Pandionis. But other restorations are possible. Lewis suggests Καλλίας (Καλλιάδο), who died in 432 while general at the siege of Potidaea (Thuc. i. 61. 1, 63. 3); a Kallias, son of Kalliades, of the tribe Pandionis is attested in the late fourth century (for this suggestion and the problem of double representation, see Lewis JHS lxxxi (1961) 118–23). Glaukon (son of Leagros) represented Akamantis together with Pericles in 441–0 and 433–2 (see table in Hill, Sources², pp. 401–3). Wade-Gery suggests for the general from Oineis Καλλ]ί[οστρατος, who was on the board in 441–0, but the surviving part of a letter might be from tau. For Antiochis (l. 32) Andrewes and Lewis suggest Λέον, who may have represented the tribe in taking the oath to the Peace of Nikias (JHS lxxvii (1957) 179). Since the revolt of Samos began in 441–0 and the siege ended in the ninth month (Thuc. i. 117. 3) and the record of expenditure covers only two years (No. 55), we should expect these generals to be the board of 440–39. They do not, however, include some of the generals of that year known from Thucydides; this must be the board of 439–8.

57 (49)

Victory of Taras over Thurii: soon after 440 B.C.

On three of the four faces of a bronze spear-butt, found at Olympia; now in Berlin. There are two others with the same text (*Olympia* v. 255–6) still at Olympia.

Laconian–Tarentine writing (see *LSAG* 279) avoiding curved strokes. Facs.: *LSAG*, Pl. 53. (Phot. of *Olympia* v. 256, *Olympische Forschungen*, i, Pl. 63 b.)

SIG 61+; *DGE* 58; *LSAG* 282 (Taras 10).

σκῦλα ἀπὸ Θουρίον Ταραν-
τῖνοι ἀνέθεκαν Διὶ ’Ολυ-
μπίοι δεκάταν.

The foundation of Thurii (for the form of the name see Tod, *Γέρας Κεραμοπούλλου*, 197–205) in 443 was followed by a long and bitter struggle with Taras for the possession of the territory and town of Siris. After about ten years it was agreed συνοικῆσαι μὲν κοινῇ, τὴν δ’ ἀποικίαν κριθῆναι Ταραντίνων (Strabo vi. 1. 14, p. 264 = Antiochus *FGH* 555 F 11). The dedication of these spear-butts doubtless commemorates the Tarentine success. See further Grote, pt. 2, ch. 47; Beloch, *GG* ii². 1. 199–201; Busolt, *GG* iii. 529–37; Meyer, *GA* iv. 20 ff.; Meloni, *Rend. Linc.* v (1950), 574 ff.

58 (51)

Financial Decrees moved by Kallias: 434–3 B.C.

A marble stele of which a portion at the foot has been cut away. Face A is otherwise complete, and since, when the stone was later used as an altar-piece in the Attic village Charvati, it was laid face down, the text is well preserved. Face B has suffered considerably. Its margins have been decorated with a Christian design at the cost of 9–10 letters at the beginning and end of each line; the two ends have been bevelled, involving the loss of a line at the top and the bottom; and a channel has been cut down the centre removing 5–7 letters; also the surface of ll. 2–16 is very worn; now in the Louvre.

A and B are cut by the same stone-cutter; developed Attic letters, stoichedon 54(A), 51(B). The use of the aspirate is inconsistent in both (A 4 *há* : A 5 *ἅ*; A 22 *καθ' ἕκαστον* : A 23 *ἑκάστοι*. B 8 [ο]*ἱ* : B 27 *h*[ο]*ι*). Phot.: of A and B, *ATL* i. 210 f.; A and B with facs. of B, *JHS* li (1931) Pl. 1–3.

IG i². 91, 92; Kolbe, *Thukydides im Lichte der Urkunden* (1930) 50–91 (= *Sitzb. Berl.* 1927, 319 ff.; 1929, 273 ff.); Wade-Gery, *JHS* li (1931) 57–85; Meritt *AJP* lv (1934) 263–74; West, *AJA* xxxviii (1934) 389–407; S. Accame, *RF* lxiii (1935) 468–96; Dinsmoor *AJA* li (1947) 127–40; Wade-Gery and Meritt, *Hesp.* xvi (1947) 279–86; Mattingly, *Proc. Afr. Class. Ass.* vii (1964) 35–55.

A

[ἔδ]οχσεν τῆι βολῆι καὶ τῶι δέμοι, Κεκροπὶς ἐπρυτάνευε, Μνεσίθεος ἐ-
[γ]ραμμάτευε, Εὐπείθες ἐπεστάτε, Καλλίας εἶπε· ἀποδôναι τοῖς θεοῖς
[τ]ὰ χρέματα τὰ ὀφελόμενα, ἐπειδὲ τῆι Ἀθεναίαι τὰ τρισχίλια τάλαντ-
[α] ἀνενένεγκται ἐς πόλιν, ἃ ἐφσέφιστο, νομίσματος ἑμεδαπô. ἀποδι-
[δ]όναι δὲ ἀπὸ τôν χρεμάτον, ἃ ἐς ἀπόδοσίν ἐστιν τοῖς θεοῖς ἐφσεφισμ-
[έ]να, τά τε παρὰ τοῖς ἑλλενοταμίαις ὄντα νῦν καὶ τἆλλα ἅ ἐστι τούτον
[τô]ν χρεμάτον, καὶ τὰ ἐκ τῆς δεκάτες ἐπειδὰν πραθῆι. λογισάσθον δὲ h-
[οι λ]ογισταὶ hοι τριάκοντα hοίπερ νῦν τὰ ὀφελόμενα τοῖς θεοῖς ἀκρ-
[ιβô]ς, συναγογὲς δὲ τôλ λογιστôν ἑ βολὲ αὐτοκράτορ ἔστο. ἀποδόντον
10 [δε τ]ὰ χρέματα hοι πρυτάνες μετὰ τῆς βολῆς καὶ ἐχσαλειφόντον ἐπει-
[δὰν] ἀποδôσιν, ζετέσαντες τά τε πινάκια καὶ τὰ γραμματεῖα καὶ ἐάμ π-
[ο ἄλ]λοθι ἐι γεγραμμένα. ἀποφαινόντον δὲ τὰ γεγραμμένα hοί τε hιερ-
[ὲς κ]αὶ hοι hιεροποιοὶ καὶ εἴ τις ἄλλος οἶδεν. ταμίας δὲ ἀποκυαμεύε-
[ν τό]υτον τôν χρεμάτον hόταμπερ τὰς ἄλλας ἀρχάς, καθάπερ τὸς τôν hι-
15 [ερô]ν τôν τῆς Ἀθεναίας. hοῦτοι δὲ ταμιευόντον ἐμ πόλει ἐν τôι Ὀπισθ-
[οδό]μοι τὰ τôν θεôν χρέματα hόσα δυνατὸν καὶ ὅσιον, καὶ συνανοιγόν-
τον καὶ συγκλειόντον τὰς θύρας τô Ὀπισθοδόμο καὶ συσσεμαινόσθο-
ν τοῖς τôν τῆς Ἀθεναίας ταμίαις. παρὰ δὲ τôν νῦν ταμιôν καὶ τôν ἐπισ-
τατôν καὶ τôν hιεροποιôν τôν ἐν τοῖς hιεροῖς, hοὶ νῦν διαχερίζο[σι]-
20 ν, ἀπαριθμεσάσθον καὶ ἀποστεσάσθον τὰ χρέματα ἐναντίον τῆς βολ[ὲ]-
ς ἐμ πόλει, καὶ παραδεχσάσθον hοι ταμίαι hοι λαχόντες παρὰ τôν νῦ[ν]
ἀρχόντον καὶ ἐν στέλει ἀναγραφσάντον μιᾶι ἅπαντα καθ' ἕκαστόν τε
τôν θεôν τὰ χρέματα hοπόσα ἐστὶν ἑκάστοι καὶ συμπάντον κεφάλαιο-
ν, χορὶς τό τε ἀργύριον καὶ τὸ χρυσίον. καὶ τὸ λοιπὸν ἀναγραφόντον h-
οι αἰεὶ ταμίαι ἐς στέλεν καὶ λόγον διδόντον τôν τε ὄντον χρεμάτον

καὶ τὸν προσιόντον τοῖς θεοῖς καὶ ἐάν τι ἀ[π]αναλίσκεται κατὰ τὸν ἐ-
νιαυτόν, πρὸς τὸς λογιστάς, καὶ εὐθύνας διδόντον. καὶ ἐκ Παναθεναίον ἐς Παναθέναια τὸλ λόγον διδόντον, καθάπερ hοι τὰ τὲς Ἀθεναίας τ-
[α]μιεύοντες. τὰς δὲ στέλας, ἐν αἷς ἂν ἀναγράφσοσι τὰ χρέματα τὰ hιερ-
30 [ά, θέ]ντον ἐμ πόλει hοι ταμίαι. ἐπειδὰν δὲ ἀποδεδομένα ἐι τοῖς θεοῖς
[τὰ χρ]έματα, ἐς τὸ νεόριον καὶ τὰ τείχε τοῖς περιδσι χρέσθαι χρέμασ-
[ιν- -]

B

[ἔδοχσεν τὲι βολὲι καὶ τὸι δέμοι, Κεκροπὶς ἐπρυτάνευε, Μνεσίθε]-
[ος ἐγραμμάτευε, Ε]ὐπ[ε]ίθες [ἐπεστάτε, Κ]αλλίας εἶπ[ε· . . . . .11. . . . . .]
[. .5. . . τὰ λί]θινα καὶ τὰς Νί[κας τὰς χ]ρυσᾶς καὶ τὰ Προ[πύλαια· . . . .]
[. . . .9. . . . .]εθὲι παντελὸς [. . .7. . . .]σει χρέσθαι ἀπ[. . . . .11. . . . . .]
5 [. . . .9. . . . .] κατὰ τὰ ἐφσεφι[σμένα], καὶ τὲν ἀκρόπολιν [. . . . .10. . . . .]
[. . . .9. . . . .]ργμένα καὶ ἐπι[σκευά]ζεν δέκα τάλαντα ἀ[ναλίσκοντα]-
[ς τὸ ἐνιαυτ]ὸ hεκάστο hέος [ἂν. . . .]θει καὶ ἐπισκευα[σθὲι hος κάλ]-
[λιστα· συνε]πιστατόντ[ο]ν δ[ὲ τὸι ἔρ]γ[ο]ι [ο]ἱ ταμίαι καὶ [οἱ ἐπιστάτα]-
[ι· τὸ δὲ γράμ]μα τὸν ἀρχιτέκ[τονα ποι]ὲν [ὅ]σπερ τὸμ Προ[πυλαίον· hού]-
10 [τος δὲ ἐπιμ]ελέσ[θο] μετὰ τὸ[ν ἐπιστ]ατὸν hόπος ἄρισ[τα καὶ εὐτελέ]-
[στατα. .5. . .]έσεται hε ἀκρ[όπολις] καὶ ἐπισκευασθέ[σεται τὰ δεό]-
[μενα· τοῖς δ]ὲ ἄλλοις χρέμα[σιν τοῖ]ς τὲς Ἀθεναίας το[ῖς τε νῦν δσι]-
[ν ἐμ πόλει κ]αὶ hάττ' ἂν τ[ὸ] λο[ιπὸν ἀν]αφέρεται μὲ χρὲσ[θ]α[ι
                                                        μεδὲ ἀπα]-
[ναλίσκεν ἀ]π' αὐτὸν ἐ[ς] ἄλλο μ[εδὲν ἒ] ἐς ταῦτα hυπὲρ μυ[ρ]ί[ας
                                                        δραχμὰ]-
15 [ς ἒ ἐς ἐπισκ]ευὲν ἐάν τι δέε[ι· ἐς ἄλλ]ο δὲ μεδὲν χρὲσ[θ]α[ι τοῖς χρέμα]-
[σιν ἐὰμ μὲ τ]ὲν ἄδειαν φσεφ[ίσεται] ὁ δέμος καθάπερ ἐ[ὰμ φσεφίσετ]-
[αι περὶ ἐσφ]ορᾶς· ἐὰν δέ τις [εἴπει ἒ] ἐπιφσεφί[σ]ει μὲ ἐ[φσεφισμένε]-
[ς πο τὲς ἀδεί]ας χρὲσθαι το[ῖς χρέμ]ασιν τοῖ[ς] τὲς Ἀθε[ναίας ἐνεχέ]-
[σθο τοῖς α]ὐτοῖς hοῖσπερ ἐά[ν τι ἐσ]φέρεν εἴπει ἒ ἐπιφ[σεφίσει· θε]-
20 [οῖς δὲ πᾶσ]ιν κατατιθέναι κ[ατὰ τὸ]ν ἐνιαυτὸν τὰ hεκά[στοι ὀφελό]-
[μενα παρὰ τ]οῖς ταμίασι τὸν [τὲς Ἀθ]εναίας τὸς ἑλλενο[ταμίας· ἐπε]-
[ιδὰν δ' ἀπὸ] τ[ὸ]ν διακοσίον τα[λάντο]ν hὰ ἐς ἀπόδοσιν ἐφ[σεφίσατο h]-
[ο δέμος τοῖ]ς ἄλλοις θεοῖς ἀ[ποδοθ]ὲι τὰ ὀφελόμενα, τα[μιευέσθο τ]-
[ὰ μὲν τὲς Ἀθ]εναίας χρέματα [ἐν τὸι] ἐπὶ δεχσιὰ τὸ 'Οπισ[θοδόμο, τὰ
                                                                δ]-
25 [ὲ τὸν ἄλλον θ]εὸν ἐν τὸι ἐπ' ἀρ[ιστερ]ά.

[ℎοπόσα δὲ τō]ν χρεμάτον τōν [ℎιερō]ν ἄστατά ἐστιν ἒ ἀν[αρίθμετα ℎ]-
[οι ταμίαι] ℎ[ο]ι νῦν μετὰ τὸν τε̣[ττάρο]ν ἀρχōν ℎαὶ ἐδίδο[σαν τὸν λόγ]-
[ον τὸν ἐκ Πα]ναθεναίον ἐς Παν[αθένα]ια ℎοπόσα μὲγ χρυ[σᾶ ἐστιν αὐ]-
[τōν ἒ ἀργυρᾶ] ἒ ὑπάργυρα στε[σάντον, τὰ δ]ὲ̣ ἄλλ[α ἀριθμεσάντον...]

B. ll. 2-3 [ἐκποιε͂ν τἀγά|λματα τὰ λί]θινα ATL; [ἐκποιε͂σαι τὰ | βάθρα τὰ
λί]θινα Gomme, Mattingly. ll. 3-4: [καὶ ἐ|πειδὰν ποι]εθε͂ι παντελōς
IG i²; [ℎέος | δὲ ἂν ἐκποι]εθε͂ι ATL; [ℎόπο|ς δ' ἂν ἐκποι]εθε͂ι Wilhelm.
ll. 4-6: [διασκέφ]σει χρε͂σθαι ἀπ[αναλίσκοντα|ς ἐς τὸ δέον] ..καὶ τὲν ἀκρό-
πολιν [ℎέρχσαι ℎόσ|α μέ ἐστι ℎε]ργμένα..., l. 7: ℎέος [ἂν ℎερχ]θε͂..,
ll. 10-11: ℎόπος ἄριστ[α καὶ ἀσφαλέ|στατα ℎερχθ]έσεται Wilhelm.
ll. 4-6: [ἀπαναλό]σει χρε͂σθαι ἀπ[ὸ τōν χρεμάτο|ν Ἀθεναίας] κατὰ τὰ
ἐφσεφι[σμένα], καὶ τὲν ἀκρόπολιν [νέμεν πλὲν ε|ἰ μὲ τὰ ἐχσε]ργμένα,
l. 7: ℎέος [ἂν νεμε]θε͂ι, ll. 10-11: ℎόπος ἄριστ[α καὶ εὐτελέ|στατα
νεμεθ]έσεται ATL.

Few decrees of the fifth century have provoked more continuous
controversy than these two important financial decrees. The margin
of error, however, was considerably reduced when in 1931 Wade-Gery
(*JHS* li (1931) 57-85) demonstrated that both decrees were almost
certainly moved by the same man at the same meeting of the Assembly.

The content of A is secure apart from its end, which has been cut
away. 1 (2-7). Now that the 3,000 T. voted by the Assembly have
been brought up to Athena on the Acropolis the state is to repay its
debts to the other gods, as already voted, from the money held by
and due to the *hellenotamiai*. 2 (7-13). The public auditors now
in office are to check the debts under the supervision of the Boule,
after any records of the debts that priests or other temple officers
hold have been presented, and the *prytaneis* are to hand over the
money. 3 (13-18). Treasurers of these other gods are to be selected
by lot at the normal election times and they are to keep the treasures
in the Opisthodomos, sharing responsibility for security with the
treasurers of Athena. 4 (18-27). These treasurers are to take over
the treasures of the other gods and record on a stele to be set up on the
Acropolis a regular inventory each year, listing the property of each
god separately, together with the income and expenditure of the year.
5 (27-30). Like the treasurers of Athena their year of office is to begin
on the day of the Panathenaia (Hekatombaion 28, Athena's day).
6 (30-31). When the debts have been repaid to the other gods; any
money left over is to be used on the dockyard and walls.

The detail of B is much less certain. 1 (2-3). The opening clause
refers to the golden Victories and the Pro[pylaia], but no convincing
restorations have been found. 2 (3-12). There follows provision for

supplementary work on the Acropolis, perhaps concerned primarily
with security (see Wilhelm's restorations above) at a cost of 10 T.
a year. The architect (of the Propylaia) is to make the plan and the
work is to be supervised by the treasurers (of Athena) and the commissioners (of the Propylaia). 3 (12–19). Apart from this expenditure
no sum above 10,000 dr. may be drawn from Athena's reserve without a special sanction. 4 (19–25). [? The *hellenotamiai* are to deposit in
the course of the year the moneys due to the other gods (as they
become available; later in the year they will be handed over to the
treasurers of the other gods).] When these debts have been repaid
from the 200 T. voted by the people, Athena's treasury is to be on
the right of the Opisthodomos, that of the other gods on the left.
5 (26–9). The treasurers of Athena are to complete the weighing and
counting of Athena's treasure with the co-operation of the four boards
of the past Panathenaic period [and presumably they are to publish
inventories].

The historical interpretation of these texts depends largely on their
date. They come after the beginning of the Propylaia (mentioned
almost certainly in B 3 and 9), in a year of the Great Panathenaia
(B 27), before the election of the treasurers of the other gods, and
almost certainly before the outbreak of war (for the treasures of the
other gods have only just been centralized). The Propylaia were
begun in 437–6 (*IG* i². 363); the first record of treasurers of the other
gods comes from an inventory of 429–8 which refers to the previous
year's board (*IG* i². 310); inventories of Athena's treasures begin in
434–3 (*IG* i². 232). There is little doubt that Kallias moved his decrees
in 434–3. We may perhaps be a little more precise and suggest that
it was after the Great Panathenaia of 434 (B 27) and shortly before
the elections (? in the spring) of 433 (A 14). If this date is approxi-
mately right these decrees precede Athens' acceptance of Corcyra's
appeal for help against Corinth in the summer of 433. Thucydides says
that the ten ships sent by Athens, to be followed by a second squadron
of twenty, sailed soon after the Assembly's decision (i. 45. 1: οὐ πολὺ
ὕστερον). The payments by the treasurers of Athena for the two
squadrons were made in the first prytany of 433–2, not earlier than
1 July (No. 61). The decrees of Kallias confirm Thucydides' judgement that when Athens made her defensive alliance with Corcyra
the people had already been convinced that war with the Peloponnese
was imminent: ἐδόκει γὰρ ὁ πρὸς Πελοποννησίους πόλεμος καὶ ὡς
ἔσεσθαι αὐτοῖς (Thuc. i. 44. 2). Decree A of Kallias shows that the
decision had already been taken to concentrate the treasures of
the temples of the rural demes and the lower city for security on the
Acropolis (A 18–22). Such a drastic step would not have been taken
had not the Assembly been persuaded that there was a serious risk of

war. (Had Pericles at this stage said that he 'already saw war approaching from the Peloponnese' (Plut. *Per.* 8. 7)?)

The decrees also provide important evidence for the reconstruction of the history of Athenian finance during the Periclean period, but in this field it is much easier to ask the questions than to answer them. When were the debts of the other gods incurred? Some at least not recently, because a search has to be made for the records (A 11–13); perhaps in the first Peloponnesian War, perhaps even as early as the Persian Wars? How are we to interpret the 3,000 T.? As the main payments for buildings and expeditions in the forties and early thirties had been made by the treasurers of Athena (Nos. 54, 55, 59, 60), it is extremely unlikely that there was in 433 any large reserve in a public treasury below the Acropolis (*pace* Gomme, *HCT* ii. 31). We should not, therefore, think of a single transfer in 433, but of a series of instalments paid over several years. Are we to identify the 200 T. of B 22 with these instalments? This is suggested by *ATL* (iii. 326–8; see also *Hesp.* xxvi (1957) 182–8); the authors believe that, following the Peace of Kallias, it was resolved, in view of the heavy expenditure contemplated on rebuilding, to set aside 200 T. each year: 'from 448 the estimated reserves, at the rate of 200 T. a year, were being contributed systematically to the chest of the treasurers of Athena.' The last payment was made in 434–3 and so the 200 T. of 433–2 were available for the other gods. This simple solution is most attractive and should perhaps be accepted; but logically it would be easier to believe that the decision to pay 3,000 T. to Athena was taken in 443 as part of a financial reorganization consequent on the ostracism of Thucydides, son of Melesias. It is also possible that the 200 T. of B is not the repetition of what has been an annual payment. It is a little strange, if it was known that the annual reserve of 200 T. was to be used, that the sum from which the debts are to be repaid should be expressed in A 6–7 in such a cumbersome way. It is not impossible that the figure was first introduced as a second (now lost) amendment in A, intended perhaps to set a limit to the amount that should be repaid. For a reconstruction of Athenian financial history, based partly on these decrees, see *ATL* iii. 118–32; Gomme, *Hist.* ii (1953) 44–63 (summarized in *HCT* ii. 26–33).

Against a general consensus in favour of 434–3 Mattingly has revived arguments used by Beloch and others for a later date. Beloch advocated the period of the Peace of Nikias, but these years were excluded when it was realized that a board of ten treasurers of the other gods was attested for 421–0 (*IG* i². 370. 7–9); Mattingly proposes 422–1, a date which Wade-Gery once supported, though he later withdrew his support in favour of 434–3 (*JHS* liii (1933) 135).

Mattingly, like Beloch, stresses the use of the later form of the first declension dative plural in A: ἑλλενοταμίαις, ταμίαις, αἷς in ll. 6, 18, 28, though B 21 has ταμίασι. Wade-Gery, reviewing the evidence systematically, concluded that the change began about 422 and was complete about 418. He noted, however, that the later form was used in two tribute lists assigned to the early years of the Archidamian War. These two lists Meritt then dated to 429 and 425; the revised view of *ATL* assigns them to 429 and 428 (lists 25 and 26). Mattingly still holds to the dates he proposed in 1961, 426 and 425 (*Hist.* x (1961) 166 ff. and *CQ* xi (1961) 155–60; answered by Meritt and Wade-Gery in *JHS* lxxxii (1962) 73 f.). 'Thus there is, I believe, good reason for claiming that the form -αις first appears epigraphically in spring 426. From then on we have a fairly continuous series.' Meiggs hopes to support Meritt's revised dating elsewhere; these two lists form an adequate bridge. Mattingly also follows Beloch in appealing to the absence of any recorded vote of ἄδεια until after the Peace of Nikias. B 12–19 had enacted that for any expenditure from Athena's reserve over 10,000 dr. a preliminary vote of ἄδεια was to be recorded. In the borrowings from Athena in 433 for the Corcyra expedition (No. 61) there is no record of such a vote; it is first found in the accounts of Athena's treasurers for 418–17 (No. 77, l. 15). This needs explanation, but if it marks the first application of the restriction imposed by decree B, why is it not applied in the earlier payments of 418–17? Mattingly also appeals to the isolated definition of a payment made from Athena's funds in 425–4 as ἐχς Ὀπισθο]δόμο (No. 72, l. 20). He argues that before 422–1 only part of Athena's reserve was kept in the Opisthodomos, and that it was only when the 3,000 T. were handed over to her that all her funds were concentrated 'there. It would still remain extremely odd that only one payment should be so specified. But the decisive argument against Mattingly remains the argument used by Kolbe against Beloch. The inventory of the other gods' treasurers for 429–8 (*IG* i². 310) shows them well established in office; only five are listed. This may reflect deaths from the plague, but even in No. 54 only seven treasurers of Athena are listed. Nor does Mattingly satisfactorily explain why only 200 T. were set aside to repay the 766 T. known from the report of the logistai (No. 72) to be owing to the other gods in 422. For the two important decrees of Kallias 434–3 may be regarded as a firm date. Their mover is probably the son of Kalliades, general in 433–2, for whom see pp. 153, 173.

There remain other obscurities:

1 (6–7). The debts of the other gods are to be repaid from moneys now in the hands of the *hellenotamiai* καὶ τἆλλα ἅ ἐστι τούτον | [τό]ν χρεμάτον, καὶ τὰ ἐκ τἔς δεκάτες ἐπειδὰν πραθἔι. The first two sources

may be tribute received and tribute still to come, but other imperial moneys might also be included (φόρος would more probably have been used if only tribute were concerned). We do not know the source or scope of the δεκάτη. Antiphon used the word δεκατευταί in his speech against the general Demosthenes (Harpokration s.v.) but that does not carry us further. Mattingly accepts identification with the δεκάτη imposed in 410 by Alcibiades at Chrysopolis on merchantmen sailing out of the Euxine (Xen. *Hell.* i. 1. 22), but Polybius (iv. 44. 4) implies that Alcibiades was the first to impose the tax; we consider also that a 10 per cent tax, compared with the normal 2 or 2½ per cent import duty, is exceptionally high and would be barely explicable in peace-time. Tod alternatively suggests that it might be a charge of 10 per cent on the produce of state lands in the occupation of private citizens, but such a source would be a very odd companion to funds handled by the *hellenotamiai*. The problem remains unsolved.

2. The identification of the Opisthodomos (A 15–17) is uncertain. We prefer to follow those who think that it was the western end of the Doerpfeld temple.

3. The annual date of the election of magistrates (A 14) is not recorded. The generals were elected in the first prytany after the sixth that was favourable (Arist. *Ἀθ. Πολ.* 44. 4). It seems likely that the elections of the archons and other magistrates were held at roughly the same time. There will at least have been a significant interval, as at Rome, between election and entry to office in midsummer (to allow for δοκιμασία).

4. In A 18–19 παρὰ δὲ τὸν νῦν ταμιὸν refers to the local treasurers of the temples. The distinction is between the local officers now responsible and the state officials who will be responsible after centralization.

5. The golden Nikai of B 3 are statues of a standard form, derived from the Nike on the hand of Pheidias' Parthenos, weighing 2 T. Those referred to here were probably the first of the series and are possibly to be identified with those recorded in a fragment from the Agora (Schweigert, *Hesp.* ix (1940) 309). For a detailed discussion of these golden Nikai see D. B. Thompson, *Hesp.* xiii (1944) 173–209.

6. (B 19). The first εἰσφορά known to us was levied in 428 (Thuc. iii. 19. 1); Thucydides says of it τότε πρῶτον, but he is probably implying only that it was the first of many during the war. There may be a reference to εἰσφορά in a decree concerning Hestiaia, *c.* 445–435 (*IG* i². 42. 22 f.).

59 (52)

Building-accounts of the Parthenon:
434-3 B.C.

On the right-hand side of a marble stele, originally set up on the Acropolis; now in EM.

Developed Attic letters. Slightly irregular stoichedon, Austin, 61 f. Phot.: ll. 1-9 (squeeze), Cavaignac, *Études*, lv, Fig. 18.

IG i². 352; Dinsmoor *AJA* xvii (1913) 53-80, xxv (1921) 233-45. Cf. A. H. Smith, *JRIBA* xxxiv (1926) 131 f.; A. Burford, 'Parthenos and Parthenon' (*Greece & Rome*, Suppl. to vol. x) 23-35.

> τοῖς ἐπιστάτεσι, hοῖς
> Ἀντικλῆς ἐγραμμάτευ[ε],
> ἐπὶ τῆς τετάρτες καὶ δε-
> κάτες βολῆς, hῆι Μετα-
> 5 γένες πρῶτος ἐγραμμ-
> άτευε, ἐπὶ Κράτετος ἄρχ-
> οντος Ἀθεναίοισιν,
> λέμματα τὸ ἐνιαυτὸ
> τούτο τάδε·
> 10 ΧΗΗΗ   περιγενόμενομ
> Η𐅈ΔΔ   μὲν ἐκ τὸ προτέρο
>   ἐνιαυτὸ
>
> ___
>
>   𐅈𐅉𐅉   χρυσῶ στατῆρες
>   [𐅉𐅉𐅉𐅉]   [Λαμφσ]ακενοί
> 15 𐅉𐅉𐅈𐅉𐅉   [χρυσῶ] στατῆρες
>   hέκτε: Κ[υζικεν]οί
>
> ___
>
>   πα[ρὰ ταμι]ῶν [hοὶ τὰ]
>   ΜΜ𐅈: τῆς θεῶ [ἐτ]αμίευ[ον],
>   hοῖς Κράτες ἐγρ[α]-
> 20   μμάτευε Λαμπτρε[ύς]
>
> ___
>
>   ΧΗΗΗ   χρυσίο πραθέ[ντος]
>   𐅈ΔΔⱵⱵ   σταθμὸν 𐅈ΔΔΔ[Δ]Γ[ⱵⱵⱵ]
>   τιμὲ τούτο
>
> ___

XΗΗΗ   ἐλέφαντος [πρα]θ[έν]-
25   ΓΙΙΙΙ   τος σταθμὸ[ν Τ]ΤΤ

ᚹΔ: τιμὲ τ[ούτο]

ἀναλόμα[τ]α

[...]ΗΗ:
[--]ⱵⱵӏ: ὀνεμάτο[ν]

μισθομ[άτον]

---

30   Χ[ᚹ[ΗΗ   h]υπορ[γοῖς Πεντελê]-
ΗΗΔ[Δ   σι καὶ λίθος ἀνατιθ]-
ΓⱵΙΙ   ἐ[σι ἐπὶ τὰ κύκλα]

MᚹΧΗΗ
ΗᚹΔΔΔ   ἀγ[αλματοπο]ιοῖς
ΔⱵⱵ   ἐνα[ιετίον μι]σθός

35   [Χ]ᚹΗΗΗ
[..]ΔⱵΙΙ   καταμ[ενίο]ις

[- - -]   περ]ιε[γέν]ετο

[- - -]   τô ἐνιαυτ]ô τού[το]

[ᚹ᚜᚜   χρυσô στατêρες]

[᚜᚜᚜᚜   Λαμφσακενοί]

40   [᚜᚜ᚐ᚜᚜   χρυσô στατêρες]

[hέκτε: Κυζικενοί]

The change in the number of Lampsakene staters (ll. 14, 39) arises from a new fragment to be added by Woodward to *IG* i². 340. L. 22 has a new reading confirming Dinsmoor's restoration (*AJA* xvii (1913) 75). We have given l. 25 the minimum restoration, which even so makes ivory three times cheaper than in fourth-century Delphi (*FD* iii. 5. 25. 5); no doubt the *epistatai* were selling off waste. There is no line vacant after l. 29. The restoration of the figure in l. 30 is new, replacing XX[- -]; we see the bottom of a vertical, not a diagonal, in the second space. The two-line figure in l. 35 is partly new.

When the Assembly decided to build a new temple for Athena Parthenos the application of democratic principles to public building was already firmly established. The essential features of the Parthenon accounts are anticipated in the accounts of the Promachos (*SEG* x. 243), and of another unknown public work which was spread over eight years (*IG* i². 335).

A board of annually changing commissioners with its own secretary was elected by the people for each project. They were responsible for general supervision and for the keeping of accounts, which had to be inscribed and exposed to scrutiny, normally on the Acropolis. The first Parthenon account covers 447-6, the last 433-2. The accounts of these fifteen years were recorded year by year on the four sides of a marble stele, the first six lists in three columns on the obverse, followed by seven lists on the reverse; the fourteenth year was added on the right side, and the final year on the left side.

The accounts for 434-3 are the best preserved and their form is typical. The heading gives the date, by the number in the series, the first secretary of the Boule, and the archon (the names of the commissioners, recorded down to 438-7, are no longer given). Antikles, the secretary, had been assistant secretary to the board since 443-2 (possibly from the commencement; but the restoration of the name in *IG* i². 340, l. 39 (446-5) is very doubtful, and it is probably significant that in 443-2 an assistant secretary was first recorded for the *hellenotamiai* (list 12, l. 36)). Antikles became secretary, without an assistant, from 436-5 to the end, and is perhaps to be identified with the mover of a decree concerning Chalkis in 446-5 (No. 52, l. 40). The accounts begin with the balance inherited from the previous year, only 1,470 dr. of silver and a supply of Lampsakene and Kyzikene electrum staters which had remained untouched since they were given to the first year's board. Presumably contractors and workmen wanted their wages in good Attic coin; electrum might be more difficult to change. Next follows the year's income of the board. As usual the main grant comes from Athena's treasurers, but this year it is little more than 4 T., as the work is nearing its end. Roughly the same amount is realized by the sale of surplus gold (the ratio to silver is 14:1). The year's expenses are divided between purchases, monthly salaries (for architects, commissioners, and their secretaries), day wages for men working in the Pentelic marble-quarries and loading the marble on to wagons (τὰ κύκλα, restored from *IG* i². 350, l. 47, are probably little more than platforms on wheels, corresponding to our bolster wagons), and pay to sculptors working on the figures of the pediments. The accounts close with the year's surplus in silver and electrum.

Plutarch in a colourful passage of his *Pericles* (12. 2) implies that the Parthenon and its great chryselephantine cult-statue were paid for from the allies' tribute. This cannot be proved from the accounts, but the fact that the main paymasters seem to be the treasurers of Athena and that by the time of the Peloponnesian War Athens' main reserve is in the keeping of Athena, ἱερὰ χρήματα, gives some support to Plutarch. In the same context Plutarch speaks of 'thousand-talent temples', encouraging estimates. R. S. Stanier, in the most detailed calculations known to us (*JHS* lxxiii (1953) 68–76), has applied the known costs of the various operations in the building of the fourth-century temple of Asklepios at Epidaurus to the Parthenon. Making allowances for the difference between limestone and marble, and for the fall in the value of money, Stanier estimates the cost at just under 470 T. In his calculations, however, there are too many uncertain factors in the comparison, insufficient allowance is made for wastage in the very stringent selection of the finest-quality marble, and the language of Plutarch implies a considerably higher figure. In two widely separated years, 447–6 and 442–1, a balance of more than 33 talents was handed over by the commissioners of the year to their successors (*IG* i². 340, l. 41 ; 345, l. 9: $\begin{smallmatrix}\Delta\Delta\\MM\end{smallmatrix}$ — ? —): such figures are not easy to reconcile with a total of less than 500 T. Heliodoros (*ap.* Harpocration, s.v. Προπύλαια ταῦτα) recorded the cost of the Propylaia as 2,000 T. (see Keaney, *Hist.* xvii (1968) 507 f.). Stanier's figures are sufficient to show that this is quite unacceptable, but it is a credible figure (as Cavaignac suggested in *Études*, 102 f.) for the combined cost of the Parthenon, the cult-statue, and the Propylaia, allowing some 700–800 T. for the Parthenon.

60 (53)

Building-accounts of the Propylaia:

434–3 B.C.

Two fragments from the back of a marble stele, originally on the Acropolis; now in EM. The stele has rough patches; like the building, it was never finished.

Developed Attic letters. Slightly irregular stoichedon, Austin 63.
IG i². 366.

[θεοί : Ἀ]θεναία [: Τύχε]

[ἐπὶ τὲς τετ]άρτες ἀρχὲς, ἑι Διογέ[νες ἐ]γρ[αμμάτευε]

[....9.....], ἐπὶ τὲς βολὲς, ἑι Μετα[γένες] πρ[ότος ἐγραμ]-

[μάτευε, ἐπι]στάται· Ἀρί[στυλ]λος Μ[ελιτεύς], Μ_|[....8....]

5 [....8....]s, Δίκτυς Κο[ι]λεύ[s], Τιμ[όστρατος] Κε[...7....]

[....8....Θ]οραιεύς· τούτοις λ[έμματα τ]ὸ ἐνια[υτὸ τάδε]·

]ΗΗΗΔΓΗΗΗ   παρὰ τὸμ πρ[ότερον ἐ]πιστατ[ὸν, hοῖς]

Ἐπικλὲς ἐγρα[μμάτευ]ε Θορίκ[ιος].

παρὰ ταμιὸν, hο[ὶ τὰ τὲ]s θεὸ ἐτα[μίευον],

10   hοῖς Κράτες ἐγρ[αμμά]τε[υ]ε Λαμπ[τρεύς].

[π]αρὰ ℎελλενοταμ[ιôν, ℎ]οῖς Προτόγ[ικος]

- - -   [ἐγραμ]μάτευε Κερ[αμε]ύς, τô χσυμ[μαχ]-

[ικô φόρο μ]νᾶ ἀπὸ τô [τα]λάντο.

[παρὰ ταμ]ιôν ℎεφα[ισ]τικô ἀπὸ Λ[αυ]ρ[είο

15 - - -   ....8....ο. το[..τ]ôμ πέντε μ[ε]ρô[ν].

[παρὰ ℎελλενοταμôν ἀ]πὸ στρατιᾶς ΤΙ[..]

- - -   - - - - - - - - - - - - - - ϙιππο Ἀγρυλêθε[ν]

- - - - - - - - - - - - - - - πα]ρὰ Τιμοσθένο[ς]

In 438–7 Pheidias' great statue of Athena in the Parthenon was dedicated (see No. 54), and now that the temple was nearing completion the main labour force could be transferred to Mnesikles' Propylaia. The first year's accounts cover 437–6, the last 433–2. Presumably the work was then abandoned owing to the imminence of war; it was never completed. The accounts follow the same general pattern as those of the Parthenon, but with minor differences. In the heading of each year Athena and Fortune are invoked (extant only for 437–6 and 434–3); the dating prescript omits the archon's name (as did the early years of the Parthenon accounts). The mina in the talent contributed by the *hellenotamiai* represents Athena's *aparche*; before the Propylaia were begun it was probably paid to the Parthenon (a payment by the *hellenotamiai* in 444–3 (*IG* i². 342. 36) has been plausibly restored as the *aparche* on a tribute of 376 T. 4,550 dr., No. 39, p. 88). The *hellenotamiai* in 434–3 made a second contribution (ll. 16–18), parallelled also in 435–4 and 433–2. These payments probably represent money in hand from grants allocated for routine patrols by small forces (*ATL* iii. 329–32, proposing for ll. 16–18: [ἀ]πὸ στρατιᾶς τ⟨ε⟩[ς μετὰ . . . c. 6 . . . παρὰ . . c. 4 . .]ϙιππο Ἀγρυλêθε[ν]. The missing names would be those of the general in charge of the expedition and the *hellenotamias* who made the transaction.). A contribution from a Laurium mine was also made to the Parthenon commissioners in 439–8, and possibly in other years also.

The figures that survive from the Propylaia accounts throw less light than those of the Parthenon on the scale of expenditure. The volume of marble is considerably smaller and there was less need for precious materials, but in any estimate of cost the particularly fine quality of the marble needs emphasis. It is significant that when Demosthenes refers with pride to the Periclean buildings he mentions the Propylaia first (Dem. xxii. 13: οἱ τὰ Προπύλαια καὶ τὸν Παρθενῶν' οἰκοδομήσαντες ἐκεῖνοι), not because it was grander than the Parthenon, but because it was grander in relation to its function. Grandeur in a temple need cause no surprise. Such magnificence in a secular building was a splendid extravagance.

61 (55)

Expenses of the Squadrons sent to Corcyra:

433 B.C.

Marble stele, found on the Acropolis; now in EM.
Developed Attic alphabet. The aspirate is not used in ἐμέραι (ll. 11, 22). Stoichedon, but the syllabic division of the words is observed. Phot.: *AJA* xxxiii (1929) 399, Meritt, *AFD* 70. Facs.: ibid. 71.

IG i². 295+; J. Johnson, *AJA* xxxiii. 398–400; Meritt, *AFD* 68–71; Oguse, *BCH* lix (1935) 416–20.

$$[Ἀθεναῖοι\ ἀνέλ]οσαν\ ἐς\ Κόρκυρα[ν\ τάδε·\ ἐπὶ\ Ἀ]-$$

[φσεύδος ἄρχο]ντος καὶ ἐπὶ τες βολες ει Κρ[ι]-
[τιάδες Φαένο] Τειθράσιος πρōτος ἐγραμμά-
[τευε, ταμίαι h]ιερōν χρεμάτον τες Ἀθεναία[ς]
5   [...6...ἐκ Κερ]αμέον καὶ χσυνάρχοντες, hοῖς
[Κράτες Ναύ]πονος Λαμπτρεὺς ἐγραμμάτευε,
[παρέδοσα]ν στρατεγοῖς ἐς Κόρκυραν τοῖς
[πρότοις ἐκ]πλέοσι Λακεδαιμονίοι Λακιά-
[δει, Προτέαι] Αἰχσονεῖ, Διοτίμοι Εὐονυμεῖ
10 [ἐπὶ τες Αἰαν]τίδος πρυτανείας πρότες πρυ-
[τανευόσες, τ]ρες καὶ δέκα ἐμέραι ἐσελελυ-
[θυίαι ἐσαν, ΔΔ] ⊢Τ *vacat*
[ἐπὶ Ἀφσεύδος] ἄρχοντος καὶ ἐπὶ τες βολες
[ει Κριτιάδες] Φαένο Τειθράσιος πρōτος ἐ-
15 [γραμμάτευε, τα]μίαι hιερōν χρεμάτον τες Ἀ-
[θεναίας Προνάπ]ες Ἐρχιεὺς καὶ χσυνάρχον-
[τες, hοῖς Εὐθίας Αἰ]σχρονος Ἀναφλύστιος
[ἐγραμμάτευε, παρέ]δοσαν στρατεγοῖς ἐς Κόρ-
[κυραν τοῖς δευτέρ]οις ἐκπλέοσι Γλαύκονι
20 [ἐκ Κεραμέον, Μεταγ]ένει Κοιλεῖ, Δρακοντί-
[δει Θοραιεῖ ἐπὶ τες] Αἰαντίδος πρυτανείας
[πρότες πρυτανευόσε]ς τει τελευτ[αίαι ἐμέ]-
[ραι τες πρυτανείας ⊢] *vacat*

The new restoration in l. 16 is derived from a new fragment added to *IG* i². 232–3 by W. E. Thompson, *Hesp.* xxxiv (1965) 32.

This stele only contained the payments made by the treasurers of

Athena to the two squadrons sent to Corcyra in the summer of 433, a first squadron of ten ships (Thuc. i. 45) and a reinforcing squadron of twenty ships (Thuc. i. 50–1). If any other payments, e.g. for Macedon, were made in 433–2, they were recorded on another stele, now lost.

The restoration πρότες in l. 22 is almost certain and carries with it Aἰαν]τίδος in l. 10. The alternatives are to read τρίτες, ὀγδόες, or ἐνάτες in l. 22 and Λεον]τίδος in l. 10, but in that case the interval between the departures of the two squadrons will have been nearly three months at the least and the whole winter at the most, which is not compatible with Thucydides' narrative. On these facts, it is now agreed that the battle of Sybota was fought in August 433 (Hubbell, *CP* xxiv (1929) 218 f.; Jacoby, *Gött. Nachr.* 1929, 16 f. (= *Abhandlungen zur Griechischen Geschichtschreibung*, 222); Kolbe, *Thukydides im Lichte der Urkunden*, 30 f.; Gomme *HCT* i. 196 f.).

The alternative to 𐆐𐆐]𐅂T in l. 12 is 𐅁𐆐]𐅂T, but 66 T. seems an improbably large sum; as the amount recorded in l. 23 occupied only one space, 𐅁 is an almost certain restoration.

The boards of treasurers making the payments (ll. 4–6, 15–18) differ because the Panathenaia, at which the treasurers laid down office, falls between the two payments.

The names of the generals in command of the first squadron are the same on the stone as in Thucydides (i. 45), though the latter follows his usual practice of using the patronymic in place of the demotic. But with regard to the reinforcing generals (ll. 19–21) there is a marked discrepancy, for Thucydides speaks of αἱ εἴκοσι νῆες . . ., ὧν ἦρχε Γλαύκων τε ὁ Λεάγρου καὶ Ἀνδοκίδης ὁ Λεωγόρου (i. 51. 4), while the stone names Glaukon, Metagenes (for the restoration see Müller–Strübing, *Aristophanes u. die hist. Kritik*, 600), and a Drakon or Drakontides. Whether Thucydides himself was at fault or an early copyist we cannot determine: the manuscripts are unanimous and Pseudo-Plutarch evidently had the same text (*Vit. X Orat.* 834 c). The best explanation is probably that of Stahl (*Rh. Mus.* xl (1885) 439), that this Drakontides was son of Leogoras of the deme of Thorai (*RE* v. 1663 f., *PA* 4551) and might therefore be confused with Andocides son of Leogoras Κυδαθηναιεύς, who had been στρατηγός in 441–0 (Androtion *FGH* 324 F 38). If that is right, this Drakontides may well have been the ἐπιστάτης from the tribe Antiochis of No. 52, l. 2, and have taken part later in the attack on Pericles (Plut. *Per.* 32. 3), but he must be distinguished from his namesake of Aphidna, who figures among the Thirty Tyrants (Arist. Ἀθ. Πολ. 34. 3, Xen. *Hell.* ii. 3. 2). For the difficulty in general and the principles of historical criticism involved see Gomme, *HCT* i. 31, 85, 188–90.

62 (54)

Accounts of the Delian Temples: 434–432 B.C.

Fragment of a marble stele, the left side preserved, found in Athens, now lost.

Ionic letters: the numerals are slightly larger than the remaining letters. Only ll. 1–6 stoichedon.

IG i². 377+; Kahrstedt, *Gött. Nachr.* 1931, 182–3; West, *AJA* xxxviii (1934) 1–9; Meritt, *Hesp.* v (1936) 378–80; *SEG* x 303+.

.a

Διοφ[

Ξανθῆς

Βολακλῆς

5   Δημοθαλῆς

Ἀναξιδῆμος

[- - - - - - - - - - - - - - - -παρ]ὰ Δηλίων ὀφελόντ[- -

[- - - - - - - - - - - - - - - - -]εγένετο καὶ αἱ παρα[- - - - - - - - - - - - - - - - -]

[..c. 4.. κεφάλαιον ἀργυρίο] σύμπαν ⊞ ⊡ΗΗΗΗΔ[- - - - - - - - - - - - - -]

10 [. . . . . . . .c. 17. . . . .]σιον τὸ βαλανεῖον ὤρισαν τ[- - - - - - - - - - - - -]

[. . . .c. 8. . . .ὠικοδ]όμησαν, τὴν Ῥήνειαν ὤρισαν αν[- - - - - - - - - - - - - -]

[. . . . .c. 11. . . . . .] ἐδάνεισαν ⊞ΤΤΤΤΔΔ꞉ἐπιδε[κάτοις τόκοις πέντε

ἔτη, ὥστε ἀπο]-

[διδόναι τὸ]ς δανεισαμένος ⟨ΤΤΤΧΧΧΔ[ΔΔ τό τε ἀρχαῖον καὶ τὸς

τόκος ὧν]

[ἐδα]νείσαντο. χρόνος ἄρχει Μεταγειτνιὼν μὴν Ἀθήν[ησιν ἄρχοντος

Ἀψεύδος],

15 [ἐν] Δήλωι δὲ Βουφονιὼν μὴν ἄρχοντος Εὐπτέρος. [τὴν γῆν τὴν ἐν

Δήλωι τὴν]

[ἱ]ερὰν ἐμίσθωσαν καὶ τὸς κήπος καὶ τὰς οἰκίας καὶ [..c. 4.. δέκα

ἔτη. χρόνος ἄρ]-

[χ]ει Ποσιδηιὼν μὴν Ἀθήνησι ἄρχοντος Κράτητος, ἐ[ν Δήλωι δὲ

Ληναιὼν μ]-

[ὴ]ν ἄρχοντος Εὐπτέρος, ὥστε ἀποδιδόναι τὴμ μίσθωσ[ιν ἀπάντων

τούτων τὸς με]-

[μ]ισθωμένος κατὰ τὰς ξυγγραφάς. μισθώσεως κεφ[άλαιον τὸ μὲν

πρῶτο ἔτος]

20 ꟼΗΗΔΓⱵ : τῶν δὲ ἄλλων ἐτῶν: ꟼΗΗΗ[...c. 7....τὴν γῆν τὴν ἐν
'Ρηνεί]-
αι τὴν ἱερὰν ἐμίσθωσαν δέκα ἔτη. χρόνος [ἄρχει - - - - - - - - - - - - -]
μὴν ἄρχοντος Ἀψεύδος, ἐν Δήλωι Ἱερὸς [μὴν ἄρχοντος - - - - - - - - - -]
ρο, ὥστε ἀποδιδόναι τὸμ μεμισθωμέ[νον τὸ ἔτος ἑκάστο τὴμ μίσθ]-
ωσιν: ΤΧΗΔ: τὴν θάλατταν τὴν πο[- - - - - - - - - - - - - - - - - - - -]
25 ..4..τὴν ἐν 'Ρηνείαι ἐμίσθωσαν δέκα [ἔτη] - - - - - - - - - - - - - - -]

The loss of the stone and attested variations of spacing make it impossible
to be confident about the length of lines. But it is unlikely that the gap in
l. 16 can have been much longer than τἆλλα. We have preferred τὸ ἔτος
ἑκάστο to the traditional ἑκάστο τὸ ἔτος in l. 23. For the chronological
restorations, see below.

Accounts of the administration of Delos in the periods of Athenian
hegemony in the fifth and fourth centuries have been found at both
Athens and Delos (cf. Tod, vol. ii, no. 125). This, the earliest of the
series, lacks its heading, and we cannot tell by what board it was set
up, though the dating by Athenian as well as Delian archons indicates
that it was at least partly Athenian. The board dealt not only with
property on Delos, which, though not tribute-paying, clearly from
its archon retains the framework of a state, but also with property on
Rheneia, which did pay tribute as a distinct unit. Whether it already
possessed the title of Ἀμφικτύονες, when it first came into existence
or acquired Athenian members we do not know. We have no other
evidence between the removal of the treasury of the Delian league
to Athens in 454 and the winter of 426–5, when the Athenians
purified the whole island. In the following spring they organized
a quadrennial festival there with musical, gymnastic, and equestrian
contests (Thuc. iii. 104: cf. Stengel, RE iv. 2433 ff.). Early in 422 they
expelled all the Delians from the island (Thuc. v. 1, Diod. xii. 73),
but in 421 they allowed them to return, at the behest of the Delphic
oracle, after the conclusion of the Peace of Nikias (Thuc. v. 32. 1,
Diod. xii. 77). In 410–09 we find the sanctuary in the control of
four Athenian Ἀμφικτύονες with some Delian νεωκόροι in a subordi-
nate capacity, but in 408–7 the accounts were drawn up jointly by
Athenian Ἀμφικτύονες and Delian ἐ]π[ίσκ]οποι, perhaps as a result
of some measure of conciliation (Coupry, BCH lxi (1937) 364–79).
After the fall of Athens the Spartans temporarily freed Delos (cf. Tod,
vol. ii, no. 99; new fragment, Inscriptions de Délos, 88).
The text before us falls into seven sections: (a) the end of a list of
names, probably Delians rather than Athenians, officials or debtors

(we cannot tell whether this was the only column of names) (ll. 1–6);
(*b*) a mutilated clause apparently dealing with the recovery of debts
amounting to 55,410+ dr. = 9 T. 1,410 dr. (ll. 7–9); (*c*) a statement
about building and demarcation of sacred property (ll. 10–11);
(*d*) the record of a loan of 9 T. 20 dr., slightly less than the amount
recovered under (*b*), for five years at 10 per cent interest (ll. 12–15)
(it is interesting that Apollo's money was invested in loans in a way
in which Athena's never was); (*e*) a lease of temple property in [Delos
for ten years] (ll. 15–20); (*f*) a lease of sacred land in Rheneia for
ten years at an annual rent of 1 T. 1,110 dr. (the annual tribute of
Rheneia was 300 dr.) (ll. 20–4); (*g*) a lease of fishing rights on Rheneia
for ten years (ll. 24–5). The θάλαττα is probably a pond or lagoon
rather than the open sea (cf. Strabo xiv. 1. 26, p. 642 for sacred
ponds; and for a parallel lease of a λίμνη see Pleket, *Epigraphica*, i,
no. 40, A. 35).

The correspondences between the Athenian and Delian calendar
have given some trouble, which has no clear solution and is slightly
complicated by the fact that the Delian year ran, roughly, from winter
solstice to winter solstice, whereas the Athenian, equally roughly, ran
from summer solstice to summer solstice. Since the Delian Bou-
phonion normally corresponded with the Athenian Boedromion, it is
clear that the equation in ll. 14–15 shows the Delian calendar one
month in advance of the Athenian. West has shown that the loan
of ll. 12–15 follows rather than precedes the lease of ll. 15–20, and
rightly restores Ἀψεύδος in l. 14 and Ληναιὼν in l. 17. The correct
restoration of l. 21 remains a puzzle. West, restoring χρόνος [ἄρχει
Ἀθήνησιν Γαμηλιών], argued that 433–2 was an ordinary year at
Athens. Meritt, restoring χρόνος [ἄρχει ἐμβόλιμος Ποσιδηιών], argued
that this inscription offered no obstacle to the belief he has always
held, on other grounds, that 433–2, the year traditionally associated
with Meton's calendar reforms, was an intercalary year at Athens.

63 (58)

Alliance between Athens and Rhegion:

433–2 B.C.

Marble stele broken at left and bottom; now in the British Museum.

Attic letters. The original prescript has been erased and a longer text
by a different hand substituted, involving an extra line and the closer
spacing of the letters. There is very little difference in the letter-forms of

the two hands. They could be, but need not be, contemporary. Stoichedon 34 (ll. 1–8), 33 (from l. 9). Phot.: Austin, Pl. 6.

Bauer, *Klio*, xv (1918) 188–91; *IG* i². 51; Accame, *RF* lxiii (1935) 73–5; Gomme, *HCT* i. 198; Meritt, *CQ* xl (1946) 85–91; Accame, *RF* lxxx (1952) 127–35; *Staatsverträge* 162; Mattingly, *Hist.* xii (1963) 272.

[θεοί: πρέσβες ἐκ 'Ρεγίο h]οὶ τὲν χσυμμαχίαν
[ἐποέσαντο καὶ τὸν hόρκ]ον Κλέανδρος Χσεν-
[. . . . . .19. . . . .]τίνο, Σιλενὸς Φόκο,
[. . . . . . .14. . . . . . ἐπὶ Ἀφ]σεύδος ἄρχοντος κ-
5   [αἰ τὲς βολὲς hεῖ Κριτιά]δες πρõτος ἐγραμμ-
[άτευε υυ ἔδοχσεν τῆι βο]λῆι καὶ τõι δέμοι, Ἀ-
[καμαντὶς ἐπρυτάνευε, Χ]αρίας ἐγραμμάτευ-
[ε, Τιμόχσενος ἐπεστάτ]ε, Καλλί-vacat
[ας εἶπε· χσυμμαχίαν εἶν]αι Ἀθεναίοις καὶ
10 ['Ρεγίνοις· τὸν δὲ hόρκο]ν ὀμοσάντον Ἀθενα-
[ῖοι hίνα ἐ̣ι hάπαντα πι]στὰ καὶ ἄδολα καὶ h-
[απλᾶ παρ' Ἀθεναίον ἐς ἀί]διον 'Ρεγίνοις, κα-
[τὰ τάδε ὀμνύντες· χσύμ]μαχοι ἐσόμεθα πισ-
[τοὶ καὶ δίκαιοι καὶ ἰσ]χυροὶ καὶ ἀβλαβὲς
15 [ἐς ἀίδιον 'Ρεγίνοις καὶ] ὀφελέσομεν ἐ[άν τ]-
[ο δέονται - - - - - - - - - - - - - - - - - - -]

At the end of l. 8 there are ten unfilled letter-spaces. It is virtually certain that the mason has left out γραμματεύς from l. 4 (cf. its inclusion in the Leontinoi treaty, No. 64, ll. 6–7). He chose to leave two spaces vacant between prescript and decree rather than have them at the end, as in the Leontinoi treaty.

In the year of Apseudes, 433–2, Leontinoi and Rhegion each sent four envoys to Athens, and at the same meeting of the Assembly both cities were accepted by Athens into alliance. Very little is preserved of the texts of the agreements: provision is made for the Athenians to take an oath, and, after Meritt's rigorous examination of the stones, we can be almost certain that the alliance with Rhegion at least, and probably with both cities, was agreed for all time: ἐς ἀί]διον in l. 12, where previous editors had accepted Ἀθεν]αίον, a reading determined by assumed sense; the delta is clear and had been reported long ago. The approach to Athens by Rhegion and Leontinoi in 433–2 is easy to understand. When Athens openly decided to intervene in Corcyra in the summer of 433 it must have been clear to the Greek world that war between Athens and the Peloponnesian

League might be imminent. Against this background the Ionian cities of Sicily might well fear that Syracuse would take advantage of Athens' preoccupation to try to swallow them. That Sicily was closely watching the mainland is confirmed by Thucydides' statement that when war broke out Sparta sent for aid to Sicily, 'to those who *had* chosen the Spartan side', with a demand for ships (Thuc. ii. 7. 2 : τοῖς τἀκείνων ἑλομένοις).

There is, however, a major complication. As Bauer first pointed out (op. cit.) the prescripts of both decrees are inscribed on erasures, replacing prescripts that were a little shorter. The two decrees are cut by different hands, and in the Leontinoi decree at least the main text is by a different hand from that of the prescript. The evidence of Thucydides has also to be taken into account. He tells us (iii. 86. 3) that in 427 Leontinoi and her allies sent to Athens for help κατὰ παλαιὰν ξυμμαχίαν. The inference has been generally accepted (e.g. by Bauer, Tod, and Meritt) that the 433-2 agreements represented a renewal of alliances made earlier, and that the lettering of the texts confined possible dates to the forties (*c.* 448, Meritt; after 446, Tod and others). These alliances of the forties were renewed, it was thought, in 433-2, and the record of the renewal was provided by changing the original prescript to give the new date and the names of the envoys. The proposer was a Kallias, and the authors of *ATL* suggest that this was the author not of the renewal but of the original treaties, Kallias son of Hipponikos, who negotiated peace with Persia in 449 and with Sparta in 446 (iii. 277). In this they were following the suggestion made by Wade-Gery (*Essays*, 206) that when the Persian Peace of Kallias was renewed in 424-3 the record of the original terms remained, but the prescript was erased and a new one substituted in Ionic letters (so deceiving Theopompus).

Lewis has pointed out that it seems unlikely that 'the prescript of an Athenian decree can have a live archon, a live grammateus, a live epistates, living ambassadors, and a dead proposer' (*JHS* lxxxi (1961) 118, n. 8). The Kallias of 433-2 was probably the son of Kalliades who died at the siege of Potidaea and may have already proposed the two surviving financial decrees of 434-3 (No. 58). Others have found more radical objections. Accame (in the fuller statement of his views in *RF* lxxx (1952) 127-35) suggested that the text of the Leontinoi treaty dated back to the fifties, reflecting Athenian alliances with the Ionian cities of east Sicily at the same time as an alliance was made with Egesta in the west (No. 37). The old stone was retained and the prescript erased because there was a relief on a second stone above the inscription. The new preamble was, he thinks, cut by the same mason who cut and then recut the Rhegion prescript. The text of the Rhegion treaty, however, according to Accame, is of

the same date, and probably cut by the same mason as the second prescript. An erasure was necessary because he had made two mistakes.
He had omitted οἳ τὲν χσυμμαχίαν ἐποιέσαντο καὶ τὸν hόρκον (thirty-
seven letters), and he had inscribed the Leontinoi ambassadors instead of the four from Rhegion, which would have been two letters
longer. So Accame explains the difference of thirty-nine letters between the new and the old prescripts. This is a neat solution, but one
cannot believe that a mason could make two such mistakes. Accame,
however, has rightly emphasized an important point which is often
ignored. There is no doubt that the text of the Leontinoi alliance
looks substantially earlier than that of the prescript. While the latter
has letter-forms that are typical of the thirties, the text of the alliance
has the V-shaped upsilon which is increasingly rare after 450, and a nu
in which the second and third strokes are considerably shorter than
the first. On the other hand, as Meritt points out: 'so far as the general
character of the lettering can determine, the later prescripts in the
erasures may well be the work of one man' (*CQ* xl. 86). This is probably not the mason who cut the text of the Rhegion alliance, for
there are small but significant differences in the letters; but there is so
little difference that they could be close contemporaries.

Mattingly attempted a simpler solution. He argued that it was uncommon to include the archon's name in the prescript before the
Peace of Nicias, and that the elaborate date formula was not included
in the texts of 433-2, which were not renewals, but the original
alliances. 'For some reason their prescripts were re-inscribed in the
420's, presumably to give greater chronological precision by adding
the name of the archon and the first secretary of Council.' This simple
explanation cannot be accepted as it stands. The change would have
added fifty-eight letters, whereas the number actually added was
thirty-nine (for a detailed analysis of the prescripts see Meritt, op. cit.
85 f.).

It is doubtful whether the language of Thucydides quoted above
(κατὰ παλαιὰν ξυμμαχίαν) is a decisive argument for regarding the
decrees of 433-2 as renewals of older alliances, for παλαιός in Thucydides covers a wide range and sometimes seems to refer to short
periods (as in iii. 13. 1 and iv. 79. 2, both quoted by Mattingly). We
may also agree that the implied procedure is extremely anomalous;
what we should expect is a short note below the original text recording
the renewal, or a new short record on a separate stone. But the established view that these two inscriptions record renewals of alliances
made in the forties should be accepted, unless and until a solution is
found which both satisfies 'common sense' and adequately explains
the changes in the number of letters in the two prescripts.

The alliances were 'for ever'. This was once thought to be a development of the fourth century, but Meritt draws attention to Hermo-krates' speech to the Sicilians at Gela: καὶ αὐτοὶ μάλιστα μὲν ἐς ἀίδιον ξυμβῶμεν (Thuc. iv. 63. 1), and the conception is now known to go much further back (see No. 10).

One of the Rhegine envoys, Silenos, died at Athens and was publicly buried, IG ii². 5220:

> εὐρύχοροί ποτ' ἔθαψαν Ἀθῆναι τόνδε τὸν ἄνδρα
> ἐλθόντ' ἐκ πάτρας δεῦρ' ἐπὶ συμμαχίαν·
> ἔστι δὲ Σιληνὸς παῖς Φώκο, τόμ ποτ' ἔθρεψεν
> Ῥήγιον εὔδαιμον φῶτα δι[κ]αιότατον.

Despite the Ionic letters, there is no real ground for supposing this text to have been set up later.

64 (57)

Alliance between Athens and Leontinoi:

433–2 B.C.

The upper part of a marble stele found between the Theatre of Herodes and the Theatre of Dionysos; now in EM.

As in the record of the alliance with Rhegion the original prescript has been erased and a longer text substituted, involving an extra line and the closer spacing of the letters. There is a marked difference between the two hands; the original text has Ⱶ, V (but Σ). Stoichedon 18 (1–15), 17 (16–32).
IG i². 52; Staatsverträge 163; see No. 63.

> [θ]εοί: πρέσβες ἐγ Λεον[τ]-
> ίνον hοὶ τὲγ χσυμμαχί-
> αν ἐποέσαντο καὶ τὸν h-
> όρκον Τιμένορ Ἀγαθοκ-
> 5 λέος, Σῶσις Γλαυκίο, Γέ-
> λον Ἐχσεκέστο, γραμμα-
> τεὺς Θεότιμος Ταυρίσ-
> κο ἐπ' Ἀφσεύδος ἄρχοντ-
> ος καὶ τὲς βολὲς hε̂ι Κρ-
> 10 ιτιάδες ἐγραμμάτευε,
> ἔδοχσεν τε̂ι βολε̂ι καὶ
> το̂ι δέμοι, Ἀκαμαντὶς ἐ-

πρυτάνευε, Χαρίας ἐγρ-
αμμάτευε, Τιμόχσενος
15 ἐπεστάτε, Καλλίας ἐ- υυ
ῖπε· τὲμ μὲν χσυμμαχία-
ν εἶναι Ἀθεναίοις καὶ
Λεοντίνοις καὶ τὸν ὅ[ρ]-
κον δōναι καὶ δέχσασ-
20 [θαι. ὀμόσ]αι δὲ Ἀθεναί-
[ος τάδε· σύ]νμα[χ]οι ἐσόμ-
[εθα Λεοντ]ίν[οις ἀί]διο-
[ι ἀδόλος κ]αὶ [ἀβλα]βōς·
[Λεοντίνο]ς ὅ[μōς ὀ]μόσ-
25 [αι· σύνμαχοι ἐσόμ]εθα
[Ἀθεναίοις ἀίδιοι] ἀδό-
[λος καὶ ἀβλαβōς· π]ερὶ
- - - - - - - - - - - - - - μπο
- - - - - - - - - - - - - - ενα
30 - - - - - - - - - - - - - δεε
- - - - - - - - - - - - - σθ
- - - - - - - - - - - - - οπ

In the prescript πρōτος is omitted in l. 10, probably deliberately; its inclusion would have entailed either a second extra line or squeezing an extra letter into four of the lines. See No. 63 and commentary.

65 (61)

Athenian Relations with Methone and Macedon: 430 B.C. and later

A marble stele, broken at the bottom, found in the Theatre of Dionysos. Above the inscription is a relief (upper part missing) showing Athena seated, holding out her hand to a standing figure in a short *chiton*, behind whom stands a hound (Binnebössel, no. 3); now in EM.

Attic letters, but Ionic gamma in l. 51 and eta in ll. 41, 52; the aspirate is frequently dropped. Stoichedon 41. Phot.: Kern 15, *ATL* ii. Pl. 1. *SIG* 75; *IG* i². 57; West, *AJA* xxix (1925) 440–4; *ATL* ii. D 3–6, iii. 133 ff.; Mattingly, *CQ* xi (1961) 154–65, xvi (1966) 183.

Μεθοναίον ἐκ Πιερ[ίας]

[Φ]αίνιππος Φρυνίχο ἐγραμμάτ[ευε]

[ἔδ]οχσεν τêι βολêι καὶ τôι δέμοι, 'Ερεχθεῖς ἐπρ[υτάν]-

[ευε], Σκόπας ἐγραμμάτευε, Τιμονίδες ἐπεστάτε, Δ[ιοπ]-

5 [εί]θες εἶπε· δι[α]χειροτονêσαι τὸν δêμον αὐτίκ[α πρὸ]-

[ς Μ]εθοναίος εἴτε φόρον δοκεῖ τάττεν τὸν δêμο[ν αὐτ]-

[ίκ]α μάλα ἒ ἐχ[σ]αρκêν αὐτοῖς τελêν ὅσον τêι θε[ôι ἀπ]-

[ὸ τ]ô φόρο ἐγίγνετο ἑὸν τοῖς προτέροις Παν[αθ]ε[ναίο]-

[ις] ἐτετάχατο φέρεν, τô δὲ ἄλλο ἀτελὲς ἔνα[ι· τὸν δὲ ὀφ]-

10 [ει]λεμάτον ἃ γεγράφαται τôι δεμοσίοι τ[ôι τὸν Ἀθε]-

[να]⟨ί⟩ομ Μεθοναῖοι ὀφείλοντες, ἐὰν ὄσι ἐπιτ[έδειοι Ἀ]-

[θε]ναίοις ὅσπερ τε νῦν καὶ ἔτι ἀμείνος, ἐπι[χορêν ἀπ]-

[ότ]αχσιν περὶ τêς πράχσεος Ἀθεναίος, καὶ ἐὰν [κοινὸ]-

[ν] φσέφισμά τι περὶ τôν ὀφειλεμάτον τôν ἐν τê[ισι σα]-

15 [νί]σι γίγνεται μεδὲν προσηεκέτο Μεθοναίο[ις ἐὰμ μ]-

[ὲ χ]ορὶς γίγνεται φσέφισμα περὶ Μεθοναίον· π[ρέσβε]-

[ς δ]ὲ τρêς πέμφσαι ηυπὲρ πεντέκοντα ἔτε γεγον[ότας]

[ho]ς Περδίκκα[ν], εἰπêν δὲ Περδίκκαι ηότι δοκε[ῖ δίκα]-

[ιο]ν ἔναι ἐâν Μεθοναίος τêι θαλάττει χρêσθα[ι μεδὲ]

20 [ἐχσ]êναι ηορίσασθαι, καὶ ἐὰν εἰσεμπορεύεσθ[αι καθ]-

[άπε]ρ τέος ἐ[ς] τὲν χόραν καὶ μέτε ἀδικêν μ[έ]τε [ἀ]δ[ικêσ]-

[θαι] μεδὲ στρα[τ]ιὰν διὰ τêς χόρας τêς Μεθ[ο]ναίον [διά]-

[γεν ἀ]κόντομ [Με]θοναίον, καὶ ἐὰμ μὲν ὁμολ[ο]γôσιν [ηεκ]-

[άτερ]οι χσυ[μβι]βασάντον ηοι πρέσβες, ἐὰν δὲ μέ, [πρεσ]-

25 [βεί]αν ἑκάτ[ερ]ο[ι] πεμπόντον ἐς Διονύσια, τέλος [ἔχον]-

[τας] περὶ ηô[ν] ἂν διαφ⟨έ⟩ρονται, πρὸς τὲν βολὲν κα[ὶ τὸν]

[δêμ]ον· ε[ἰ]πêν δὲ [Π]ερδίκκαι ηότι ἐὰν ηοι στρατι[ôται]

[ηοι] ἐμ Ποτειδ[ά]αι ἐπαινôσι γνόμας ἀγαθὰς ηέ[χσοσι]

[περὶ] αὐτὸ Ἀθε[ν]αῖοι. ἐχειροτόνεσεν ηο δêμος [Μεθον]-

30 [αίο]ς τελêν η[όσο]ν τêι θεôι ἀπὸ τô φόρο ἐγίγνε[το ηὸν]

[τοῖ]ς προτέρο[ις] Παναθεναίοις ἐτετάχατο φ[έρεν, τô]

[δὲ ἄ]λλο ἀτε[λὲς ἔ]ναι. υ ἔδοχσεν τêι βολêι καὶ [τôι δέμ]-

[οι, h]ιπποθο[ντὶς ἐ]πρυτάνευε, Μεγακλείδες [ἐγραμμά]-

[τευ]ε, Νι[κ]ο[..5... ἐ]πεστάτε, Κλεόνυμος εἶπε· Μ[εθοναί]-

35 [οις] ἔν[αι ἐχ]σα[γο]γὲν ἐγ Βυζαντίο σίτο μέχ[ρι....α]-

[κισχ]ιλίον μεδίμνον τô ἐνιαυτô ἑκάστο, ηοι [δὲ ηλλε]-

[σπ]οντοφύλακες μέτε αὐτοὶ κολυόντον ἐχσάγεν μ[έτ]-

[ε ἄλ]λον ἐόντον κολύεν, ἒ εὐθυνέσθον μυρίαισι δρ[αχ]-
[μεῖσ]ιν ἕκαστος· γραφσαμένος δὲ πρὸς τὸς ἑλλεσπ[ον]-
40 [το]φύλακας ἐχσάγε[ν] μεχρὶ τô τεταγμένο· ἀζέμιος [δὲ]
[ἔσ]το καὶ ἑ ναῦς ἑ ἐχσάγοσα· hό τι δ' ἂν κοινὸν φσήφ[ισμ]-
[α π]ερὶ τôν χσυμμάχο[ν] φσεφίζονται Ἀθεναῖοι πε[ρὶ β]-
[οε]θείας ἒ ἄ[λ]λο τι προ[σ]τάττο[ν]τες τêσι πόλεσι ἒ [περ]-
[ὶ σ]φôν [ἒ] περὶ τôν πόλεον, hό τι ἂν ὀνομαστὶ περὶ τ[ês π]-
45 [όλε]ος τê[s] Μεθοναίον φσεφίζονται τοῦτο προσέ[κεν]
[αὐτοῖ]s, τ[ὰ] δὲ ἄλλα μέ, ἀλλὰ φυλάττοντες τὲν σφετ[έρα]-
[ν αὐτôν ἐ]ν τôι τεταγμένοι ὄντον· hὰ δὲ hυπὸ Περδ[ίκκ]-
[ο ἀδικêσ]θαί φασι βουλεύσασθαι Ἀθεναῖος hό τι ἂ[ν δο]-
[κ]êι [ἀγαθ]ὸν εἶναι περὶ Μεθοναίον ἐπειδὰν ἀπαν[τέσ]-
50 [ο]σι ἐ[ς τὸ]ν δêμον hοι πρέσβες [h]οι παρὰ Περδίκκο [οἵ τ]-
ε μετ[ὰ Πλ]ειστίο οἰ[χ]όμενοι καὶ hοι μετὰ Λεογό[ρο· τê]-
[σ]ι δὲ [ἄλλ]εσι πόλε[σι χ]ρηματίσαι ἐπειδὰν ἐσέλ[θει ἑ]
[π]ρυ[ταν]εία ἑ δευτ[έρα] μετὰ τὰς ἐν τôι νεορίοι ἕ[δρας]
[ε]ὐθ[ὺς] ἐκκλεσίαν [πο]έσαντες· συν[ε]χôς δὲ ποὲν τ[ὰς ἐκ]-
55 [ε]ῖ ἕ[δρα]s ἕος ἂν δι[απρ]αχθêι, ἄλλο δὲ προχρεμα[τίσαι]
[το]ύ[το]ν μεδὲν ἐὰμ μέ τι οἱ στρατε[γ]οὶ δέοντα[ι. υ ἔδοχ]-
[σεν τêι] βολêι καὶ τôι δέμοι, Κεκροπὶς ἐπρυ[τάνευε,.]-
[...6...]ες ἐγραμμάτε[υ]ε, h[ι]εροκλείδες ἐ[πεστάτε,..]-
[...6...] εἶπε· ἐπειδὲ ἔ[............24.............]
60 [...6...] Ἀθεναι[..............29..............]
lacuna

[ἔδοχσεν τêι βολêι καὶ τôι δέμοι, Ἀκαμαντὶς ἐπρυτά]-
[νευε, Φαίνιππος ἐγραμμάτευε.]

Ll. 10–11: Early copies read the third letter in l. 11 as H which is impossible; Boeckh, whom we follow, restored iota, *ATL* i, p. 212 preferred τ[ôν ἀπειτε|μέ]νομ.

This stele was inscribed when Phainippos was secretary, in 423 (Thuc. iv. 118. 11), but it records a series of decrees concerning Methone, the first of which probably dates from 430 (see below). The first two decrees are very well preserved. Of the third only part of the prescript survives; the final decree (it is unlikely that there were more than four) is completely lost. The publication together of these decrees is an interesting reminder that the common provision for leasing the contract and setting up a stele is not a mere formality; even important decrees concerning relations with other states could remain in the archives unpublished.

Methone was an Eretrian colony on the west shore of the Thermaic gulf. No record survives of any tribute payment before the Peloponnesian War, but the name can and probably should be restored in 432–1 (list 23. II. 67). Methone's main importance to Athens lay in her usefulness as a base, military and diplomatic, in an area that was dominated by Macedon. These decrees record privileges granted to reward and ensure her loyalty.

In the first decree (ll. 3–32) we have, 1 (5–9): The Assembly is asked to decide at the present meeting whether Methone should be formally reassessed, or whether she should be required to pay only the *aparche* (of 1/60th) on her current assessment. A note is added at the end of the decree (29–32) that the people granted this privilege, and in list 26 Methone is recorded as paying 300 dr. under the heading *haίδε τôν πόλεον αὐτὲ[ν] | τὲν ἀπα[ρ]χὲν ἀπέγαγον* (26. II. 51 f., probably to be restored also in 25. II. 33). 2 (9–16): Her debts to Athens (probably but not necessarily unpaid tribute) will be specially considered, and no general decree about debts shall apply to Methone, unless she is specifically mentioned. 3 (16–29): Three envoys are to be sent to Perdikkas requiring him not to restrict Methone's freedom of movement by sea or land (*εἰσεμπορεύεσθαι . . . . ἐς τὲν χόραν* (ll. 20 f.), referring to Methone's trade with the interior), and not to take his forces through Methone's territory without her agreement. If the envoys cannot reconcile Perdikkas and Methone, they should both be asked to send plenipotentiaries to Athens at the time of the Dionysia to state their cases before Boule and Assembly. Perdikkas is reminded that Athenian troops at Potidaea are watching him.

Various dates between 430 and 426 have been given to this decree, and the decision rests on the dating of tribute list 26. We accept the dating of this list in 429–8, reflecting with list 25 (430–29) the assessment of 430. We also follow *ATL* (iii. 133–7) in associating the decree with the assessment of late summer 430. The reference to the former Panathenaia (l. 31) is then a reference from one Great Panathenaia to the last, from 430 to 434. Athenian troops are still besieging Potidaea, which fell in the winter of 430–29 (in ll. 27 f. *hoι στρατιôται hoι ἐμ Ποτει-δ[ά]αι* could mean an Athenian garrison in Potidaea when Athenian settlers had occupied the town; but more probably settlers would have been expected to defend themselves and they are called *ἔποικοι* in *ATL* ii. D 21. 9; cf. No. 66). In 429–8, and probably in 430–29, Methone pays only the *aparche*. She will probably have been brought into the Athenian empire in 434, and the occasion may have been the change of Athenian policy in the Thraceward area. Athens had, probably early in the thirties, formed an alliance with Perdikkas (see *ATL* iii. 313, n. 61 for the attractive hypothesis that *IG* i². 71 should be identified with this alliance). Perdikkas would reasonably resent the incorporation of

Methone in the Athenian empire, and Methone was in an uncomfort-able position. When, however, Athens appeared in strength Perdikkas came to terms again, in 431 (Thuc. ii. 29. 6); but, though formally reconciled, he remained hostile and secretly sent support to anti-Athenian forces in the north-west in 429 (Thuc. ii. 80. 7). Athens makes diplomatic protests on Methone's behalf, but is clearly anxious to avoid an open break.

The second decree (ll. 32–56) was passed in the first prytany of 426–5 (for the date see No. 72, l. 5). For Kleonymos, who moved, probably in the same year, a decree tightening up the collection of tribute (No. 68), see p. 188. 1 (ll. 34–41): Methone may import annually a limited quantity of corn from Byzantium, but must give notice to the *hellespontophylakes*. This is the only clear record of Athenian officers' controlling the shipping through the Hellespont, but they may be implied in the payments recorded in the tribute list of 429–8, and restored in that of 430–29 (lists 26, 25) by two communities in the Chersonese: $[\pi]\acute{o}\lambda\epsilon\varsigma$ $a\emph{i}[\delta]\epsilon$ $\grave{a}\rho\chi a\hat{\iota}\varsigma$ | $[\emph{e}\delta]o\sigma a\nu$ $\tau\grave{o}\mu$ $\phi\acute{o}\rho o\nu$ (26. I. 10, 25. III. 66). Possibly the establishment of special officers at this key-point on the corn-route was a war-measure; apart from helping to ensure Athenian supplies it gave her a useful hold over allies who depended for their corn on imports. A similar privilege is recorded for Aphytis (*ATL* ii. D 21. 1–6), also during the Archidamian War. It seems that reserve stocks, under Athenian control, were stored at Byzantium (l. 35). 2 (ll. 41–7): Any general decrees requiring from the cities (possibly only those of the Thraceward area) military assistance or any other service shall not apply to Methone unless she is specially named. She will be playing her proper part if she safeguards her own territory (for $\grave{\epsilon}\nu$ $\tau\hat{o}\iota$ $\tau\epsilon\tau a\gamma\mu\acute{\epsilon}\nu o\iota$ $\emph{o}\nu\tau o\nu$ cf. Xen. *Cyrop.* vi. 2. 37; *IG* ii². 116. 48). 3 (ll. 47–51): Methone's complaints against Perdikkas will be considered when the two embassies sent to Macedon report to the people. 4 (ll. 51–6): The other cities' affairs are to be discussed in the next prytany immediately after the sessions in the dockyard, and their business is to have priority unless the generals have other urgent business. This is perhaps a reference back to ll. 41–7, and may refer to special arrangements that are contemplated for the better security of the Thraceward area (Mattingly, *CQ* xi (1961) 161 f. Compare $\tau\grave{a}\varsigma$ $\chi\sigma\upsilon\gamma\gamma\rho a\phi\grave{a}\varsigma$ . . . $\pi\epsilon\rho\grave{\iota}$ $\tau\grave{o}\nu$ $\pi\acute{o}\lambda\epsilon o\nu$ $\tau\grave{o}\nu$ $\grave{\epsilon}\pi\grave{\iota}$ $\Theta\rho\acute{a}\iota\kappa\epsilon\varsigma$ at the time of the colonization of Brea, No. 49, ll. 15 ff.).

Mattingly has argued in favour of a later date for the first Methone decree, which he would place in 427–6 (loc. cit. 154–65). This has the advantage of shortening the interval between the first and second decrees, but the case depends on the redating, which we do not accept, of tribute lists 25 and 26 to 426–5 and 427–6 respectively.

66 (60)

Resettlement of Potidaea: 429 B.C.

Marble base with large cutting on top, probably for a relief, found east of the Propylaia; now in EM.
Developed Attic writing, not stoichedon. Drawing: *DAA* p. 329.
DAA 306+.

ἔποικον
ἐς Ποτείδαιαν

In the winter of 430–29 Potidaea capitulated after a siege of about two and a half years and its inhabitants evacuated the town; thereafter the Athenians ἐποίκους ἔπεμψαν ἑαυτῶν ἐς τὴν Ποτείδαιαν καὶ κατῴκισαν (Thuc. ii. 70. 4); Diodorus (xii. 46. 7) gives the number of the colonists as a thousand. This dedication falls into a group of dedications made by departing colonists, for which see *DAA* p. 325. The dedicants agree with Thucydides in describing themselves as ἔποικοι. In the view of the authors of *ATL* (iii. 285) 'apoikoi and epoikoi are the same, differing only in meaning as do our own words "emigrant" and "immigrant", and reflecting merely the point of view from which the writer envisaged the process of colonization: either from the mother city or to the new location', but Thucydides does also use ἄποικοι in a similar context (v. 116) and these colonists are still described as [τ]οῖς ἐποίκοι[s] τ[οῖς] ἐμ Ποτειδαία[ι], even after arriving at their destination (*ATL* ii. D 21. 9). For a full discussion see Ehrenberg, *CP* xlvii (1952) 143 f. (= *Polis und Imperium*, 245 f.). There are attractions in his view that ἔποικοι here may mean 'additional settlers', sent out to supplement the city's depleted population, but there is no support other than the prefix for the belief that there was any population left to supplement.

67 (62)

Contributions to the Spartan War-fund: (?) about 427 B.C.

A mutilated stele of grey marble above the door of the church of St. Basil, about 11 km. south of Sparta on the Gytheion road, perhaps originally from the shrine of Athena Chalkioikos on the Acropolis at Sparta. ·

Spartan alphabet (see *LSAG* 197 (Sparta 55)). Facs. of ll. 1–10 in *IG* v (1). 1.
CIG 1511; Fränkel, *Rh. Mus.* lvii (1902) 534–43; *IG* v (1). 1+; *SIG* 84; *DGE* 13; Adcock, *Mélanges Glotz*, 1–6.

Front

[- - - - - - - - τοῖς Λακ]εδαιμονίο[ις . .]λο[. .]
[- - - - - - - - ακα]τίος δαρι⟨κ⟩ός. Ε. . . . Α[. . . . .]
[- - - - - - - - - τοῖς Λ]ακεδαιμονίοις ποτ[τ]ὸν
[πόλεμον ἐνν]έα μνᾶς καὶ δέκα στατῆρας.

5 [ἔδοκε τοῖς Λακ]εδαιμονίοις Λυ⟨κ⟩είδα hυιὸς
[- - - - - - - - -]ος Ὀλέ[νι]ος [ἔ]δο[κε τοῖς Λακε]-
[δαιμονίοις] ποττὸν πόλεμον τριερεΓ . ΧΜ . .
[- - - ἀργυρί]ο μνᾶς δύε καὶ τριάκοντα. [ἔδον]
[- - - - - -] τὸν Χίον τοὶ φίλοι τοὶ τὸν [- -]

10 [- - - - - -] στατῆρας Αἰγιναῖος. [ἔδον τοὶ]
[- - - - - τοῖ]ς Λακεδαιμονίοις ποττὸν [πό]-
[λεμον μεδίμνος] τ[ε]τρακινχ[ε]λίος καὶ ἄλλος
[μεδίμνος τετρ]ακινχελίος καὶ ἀσταφίδος
[- - - - - τάλ]αντα.

15 [- - - - - - -] h[υ]ιὸς [ἔ]δ[ο]κε τ[οῖς Λακεδαιμο]-
[νίοις - - -] πολλὰ καὶ δαρικὸς ὀκτακατ[ίος]
[- - καὶ ἀργ]υρίο τρία τάλαντα.
[- - - - -] ἔ[δο]ν ποττὸν πόλεμον
[ἀργυρίο τάλα]ντον τριάκοντα μνᾶς [καὶ]

20 [- - - - τ]ρισχελίος μεδίμνος καὶ [ἄλλος]
[μεδίμνος - -]κοντα καὶ ἀρ[γ]υρί[ο] Ϝεξέ[κοντα]
[μνᾶς. ἔδον τ]οὶ Ἐφέσιοι τοῖς Λακεδαιμ[ο]-
[νίοις ποττὸ]ν πόλεμον χελίο{υ}ς δαρ[ικὸς].

Side

ἔδον τοὶ Μά-
λιοι τοῖς
Λακεδαι-
μονίοις
5 ἀργυρίο
Ϝίκατι
μνᾶς.
ἔδοκε ΜΟ-

ΛΟΚΡΟΣ τοῖς
10 Λακεδαιμο-
νίοις τάλαν-
τα α ἀργυρίο.
ἔδον τοὶ
Μάλιοι
15 τοῖς
[Λ]ακεδαι-
μονίο[ις]
- - -

Another fragment, from the precinct of Athena Chalkioikos (*BSA* xiv (1907–8) 135 f., *IG* v (1). 219), is added by Jeffery, *LSAG* 197, who reads: [- - -τ]οὶ Ἀπελλ[- - - | -- ἔδον τοῖς Λακεδ]αιμονίο[ις-- | --] καλ-λόσι [- - - | -- ὁ δεῖνα] ἔδοκε [ποττὸν πόλεμον? - - - | --] ἔδον ποτ[τὸν πόλεμον -- | --]ενερ[-- | --]θαι ἀρ[γυρίο? - -

We are dependent on Fourmont's copy except for ll. 1–10, and even they have suffered since he read them. Although Fränkel claimed to see *einige Schatten von Buchstaben* below l. 10 on the only face of the stone now visible, we can see nothing of ll. 11–23 on our squeezes and are puzzled about the original layout of the inscription. l. 2: There have been a variety of readings. Fourmont read ΕΦΕΙ..ΑΛ.ΨΟΙ, Fränkel read and restored ἐφέκε [Κ]αλ[λίμα|χος ἆραι, Wilamowitz suggested 'Εχε[μμ]ᾶ λ[ό]χο[ς ἔδοκε. In l. 5 Fourmont read Λυρείδα.   In l. 6 'Ολέ[ρι]ος would also be possible. In l. 7 Boeckh suggested τριέρε[σι] and Dittenberger τριέρε[σι] μ[ισθὸν]. In l. 9 τοὶ τὸν [Λακεδαιμονίον?] is the reading attested by Fourmont and Fränkel; Kolbe emended to ποττὸν [πό|λεμον]. We cannot confirm either reading. Side, ll. 8–9: Μόλο⟨β⟩ρος Boeckh (cf. Thuc. iv. 8. 9); Μό[λον] Λοκρός Wilamowitz.   l. 12 seems clearly corrupt, but it cannot be determined whether the fault is Fourmont's (reading τάλαντον) or the stonecutter's.

Peloponnesian financial weakness was noted by Pericles (Thuc. i. 141. 3) and admitted by Archidamos (i. 80. 4) and the Corinthians (i. 121. 3). One means of remedying it was to receive extraordinary contributions in cash and kind, and these are here recorded. For a similar text, see Tod, vol. ii, no. 160. The gifts include money in Aeginetan staters, darics, and perhaps other currencies; some contribute food, corn, or raisins. One gift may have been earmarked for pay to trireme crews, the remainder are merely 'for the war'.

Possible donations by Spartans themselves, individually or as a group (Front, l. 2; Side, ll. 8–9), are very far from certain. An individual foreigner certainly appears in Front, l. 6, apparently from Olenos in Achaea. A pro-Spartan party appears in Front, l. 9, translating 'the friends (of Sparta) among the Chians', and foreign states appear, Ephesus (Front, l. 22) and Melos (Side, ll. 1–7, 13 ff.).

The dating of the inscription has varied. The appearance of Melos rules out a date between 416 and 404, and the probable reference to triremes in Front, l. 7, suggests a date earlier than the loss of the Spartan fleet at Pylos in 425 (Thuc. iv. 23. 1), though Kahrstedt (*Gr. Staatsrecht*, i. 32, 336) assigns the text to 424–416. A date between 431 and 425 has therefore been most popular, perhaps exactly in 427, when Alkidas put in at Ephesus (Thuc. iii. 32. 2). A pro-Spartan party in Chios would explain Athenian suspicions of Chios in winter 425–4 (Thuc. iv. 51). This date has been argued for by Adcock and supported by Jeffery (*LSAG*, loc. cit.) from a consideration of the lettering, and the argument seems satisfying to Meiggs. The implications for relations between Melos, Sparta, and Athens have often been noted (see, e.g., de Ste Croix, *Hist.* iii (1954–5) 13).

On the other hand, Fränkel and Meyer (*Theopomps Hellenika*, 266) preferred the last years of the Decelean War, with Melos making a thank-offering for her restoration by Lysander (Xen. *Hell.* ii. 2. 9). Lewis is tempted to go a stage further. He thinks the argument from the lettering indecisive, and would draw attention to the various sums contributed in darics (Front, ll. 2, 16, 23), which he thinks unlikely to have been so widespread during the Archidamian War. Might not the inscription belong to 396–5, when Ephesus was Agesilaus' base (Xen. *Hell.* iii. 4)?

68

Appointment of Tribute Collectors: 426 B.C.

Thirteen fragments of a marble stele, the last of which, giving the ends of ll. 21–33, was only recently found, from on or near the Acropolis; now in EM. Above the inscription was a relief, the small surviving part of which shows jars and sacks in which the tribute was carried (Binnebössel, no. 4).

Attic letters, stoichedon 36. Phot. of fragments 1–11: *DAT* 4–12 (with Pl. 1, drawing), *ATL* i. 123–6; of fr. 12: *ATL* ii. Pl. 5; of fr. 13: *AJP* lxxxviii (1967) 32, Pl. i; of reconstructed stele: ibid., Pl. ii.

IG i². 65; Meritt, *DAT* 3–42; Dow, *AJA* xlii (1938) 602 f.; Raubitschek, *AJP* lxi (1940) 475–9; *ATL* ii. D 8; Meritt, *AJP* lxxxviii (1967) 29–32.

$$[- - - 5 \text{ or } 6 - - -]\epsilon\mu\alpha[- - - - - c. \text{ } 11 - - - - -]s \text{ } vv$$
$$\phi\acute{o}\rho[o]$$
$$\H{\epsilon}\delta o\chi\sigma\epsilon[\nu] \text{ } \tau\hat{\epsilon}\iota \text{ } \beta o\lambda\hat{\epsilon}\iota \text{ } \kappa\alpha\grave{\iota} \text{ } \tau[\hat{o}\iota \text{ } \delta\acute{\epsilon}\mu o\iota], \text{ } K\epsilon\kappa\rho o\pi\grave{\iota}s \text{ } \grave{\epsilon}\pi-$$

ρυτάνε[υ]ε, Πολέμαρχος [ἐγραμμά]τευε, Ὄνασος ἐ-
5 πεστάτ[ε, Κ]λεόνυμ[ος εἶπε· ηοπόσ]αι πόλες φόρο-
ν φέροσ[ι Ἀθ]ενα[ίοις ηαιρέσθον] ἐν ἑκάστει τε-
[ι] πόλει [φόρο ἐγλογέας ηόπος ἂν] ηεκασταχόθε-
[ν Ἀθε]ν[αίοις σύμπας ἐγλέγεται] ηο [φόρος] ἒ ηυπ-
[εύθυνοι ὄσι ηοι ἐγλογὲς - - -]

lacuna

10 [- - - - - - - - - - - -] ἐπ-
[άναγκες ?......13......τὲν πρυτανεία]ν ηέτ-
[ις ἂν πρυτα]νεύε[ι.....10.....μετὰ τὰ] Διονύσ-
[ια· καὶ ἀναγ]νôνα[ι ἐν τôι δέμοι τὰς πό]λες ηαίτ-
[ινες ἂν ἀπο]δôσι τ[ὸν φόρον καὶ αἴτιν]ες μὲ ἀπο-
15 [δôσιν καὶ η]αίτιν[ες ἂν κατὰ μέρε· ἒ]πὶ δὲ τὰς ὀφ-
[ελόσας πέ]μπεν πέ[ντε ἄνδρας ηίνα] ἐσπράχσον-
[ται τὸν φ]όρον· ἀναγ[ραφόντον δὲ ηοι ἑλλ]ενοτα-
[μ]ίαι ἐς σανίδι τὰς [πόλες τὰς ἐλλιπό]σας τô φό-
[ρ]ο καὶ τὸν ἀπαγόντ[ον....9.....κα]ὶ τιθέναι
20 [η]εκάστοτε πρόσθε[ν....9..... ἔ]στο δὲ καὶ Σαμίοις καὶ Θεραίοι[ς....8....]σ[.]ι[.]σ[....]ι▨[.τ]-
ὸν χρεμάτον ὁν τε χ[....8....]εν τ̂ες ηαιρέσεος
[τ]ôν ἀνδρôν καὶ εἴ τ[ις ἄλλ]ε πόλις ἐτάξατο χρ-
[έ]ματα ἀπάγεν Ἀθέν[αζε· τ]ὸ δὲ φσέφισμα τόδε ἐσ-
25 [τέ]λει ηε Κεκροπὶ[ς πρυτα]νεία θέτο ἐμ πόλει· Π
[...]κριτος εἶπε· τ[ὰ μὲν ἄλ]λα καθάπερ Κλεόνυμ-
[ος, η]όπος δὲ ἄρι[στα καὶ ῥρα]ῖστα οἴσοσι Ἀθενα-
[ῖοι τ]ὸν πόλεμ[ον, τάδε πρὸς] τὸν δêμον ἐκφέρεν
[ἐκκλε]σίαν [δὲ χσυνάγεν ἐ]οθινέν· ἔδοχσεν τêι
30 [βολêι καὶ τôι δέμοι, Κεκρ]οπὶς ἐπρυτάνευε, Πο-
[λέμαρχος ἐγραμμάτευε, η]υγιαίνον ἐπεστάτε,
[....9.....εἶπε· τὰ μὲν ἄλλ]α κατὰ τὸ πρότερο[ν]
[φσέφισμα,.......14.....]ματα εστονδ[....]

lacuna

[......12......] - [...........23...........]
35 [......12......]θα[...........22...........]
[.]ι[.]ι< [...7....]ανε[...........21...........]
ξειεο[.]λ[..]ι πλερ[...6...τ. ν δὲ....ν ἐπ]ιμελ-
ετὰς ηαιρêσθαι τô[ν ἄλλον δικôν τôν περὶ] τὸν Ἀ-

θεναίον χρεμάτον κ[ατὰ τὸ....9.....φ]σέφισ-
40 μα καὶ τὸν στρατεγὸν [ἕνα τάττεν παρέ]ζεσθα-
ι hόταν περί τινος τὸν [πόλεον δίκε δικάζετα]-
ι. ἐὰν δέ τις κακοτεχνêι [hόπος μὲ κύριον ἔστα]-
ι τὸ φσέφισμα τὸ τô φόρο [ἒ hόπος μὲ ἀπαχθέσετ]-
αι ho φόρος Ἀθέναζε γρά[φεσθαι προδοσίας αὐ]-
45 τὸν τôν ἐκ ταύτες τês πό[λεος τὸν βολόμενον π]-
ρὸς τὸς ἐπιμελετάς· ho[ι δὲ ἐπιμελεταὶ ἐσαγό]-
ντον ἔμμενα ἐς τὸ δ[ικαστέριον ἐπειδὰν hοι κ]-
λετêρες ἔκοσι· δι[πλο] î δὲ [ὄντον hοι κλετêρες]
ἒ κατὰ hôν γράφεσθαί τις β[όλοιτο· ἐὰν δέ το κα]-
50 ταγνôι τὸ [δικ]αστέριον τι[μᾶν ὅ τι χρὲ αὐτὸν π]-
αθêν ἒ ἀ[π]οτεîσαι· τὸς δὲ κέ[ρυκας hόσοι ἄν τιν]-
ες [δ]σι ὃς ἂν hοι πρυτάνες με[τὰ τês βολês hέλο]-
[ντα]ι πέμφσαι ἐς τὰς πόλες ἐ[πὶ τês Κεκροπίδο]-
[ς πρ]υτανείας hόπος ἂν αἱρε[θôσι hοι ἄνδρες h]-
55 [οι] τὸν φόρον ἐγλέχσοντες κ[αὶ ἀναγραφôσι ἐν]
[τô]ι βολευτερίοι· τὲν δὲ στέλ[εν hοι πολεταὶ ἀ]-
[πο]μισθοσάντον. vacat
[φ]όρο ἐγλο[γês τô]
[πα]ρὰ τὸν πό[λεον]

One small unplaced fragment with eight letters on three lines is omitted here.   ll. 10–11: [.τοîς δὲ ἑλλενοταμίαις ἐκκλεσίαν ποιêν]ἐπ||[ἄναγκες περὶ τôν πόλεον Meritt.   l. 12: [δέκα ἑμερôν] Meritt, DAT; [δέκα hεμέραις μετὰ] Διονύσια Mattingly (Hist. x (1961) 152 n. 22); [εἴκοσι ἑμερôν μετὰ] Διονύσια Meritt; perhaps [χρεματίζεν] or [ἐς τὸν δêμον].   l. 13: Despite the aorist infinitive, we prefer our text to Meritt's [ἐς δὲ κοι]νὸν ἀ[ποφαινόσθον hαι πό]λες.   l. 19: [τὰ ὀνόματα] Wilhelm; [τὸ ἐλλιπόν] Dow (AJA xlii (1938) 603).   l. 20:[τô Μετροίο] Meritt, DAT; [τô βέματος] or [τôν hερόον] ATL.   ll. 20–2: Meritt suggests tentatively [ἔ]στο δὲ καὶ Σα[μίοις καὶ Θ]εραίοι[ς hομοîον φ]σ[έ]φ[ι]σμ[α] περ[ὶ τ]ôν χρεμάτον ὅν τε χ[ρὲ ποêν πλ]ὲν; we do not feel confident about the traces in l. 20, and print only what we are sure of; all Meritt's readings are at least possible.   l. 26: Π||[υθό]κριτος or Π||[ολύ]κριτος.   l. 28: [ταῦτα εἰς] gives less satisfactory spelling; [γνόμεν ἐς] Meritt.   l. 29: Alternatively, [ἐκκλε]σίαν [ποέσαντας hε]οθινέν (sc. τὸς πρυτάνεις) Meritt.   l. 32: [Κλεόνυμος] Meritt.   l. 48: For the practice of requiring two witnesses to a summons see [Dem.] xl. 28.

The decree of Kleinias (No. 46) marks an earlier attempt to tighten up tribute collection. This decree, moved by Kleonymos, has a similar objective and uses similar language. The problem that Kleinias attempted to resolve was the leaking of tribute between dispatch by the ally and receipt by Athens; Kleonymos is concerned to ensure that the full tribute should be collected in the cities. The solution approved by the Assembly was the appointment of individual collectors in each city, and, though the text has to be restored (ll. 8–9), it seems clear that these collectors would be held personally responsible. It was once widely thought that they were Athenian, but Antiphon's statement quoted from his speech concerning the tribute of Samothrace is explicit: ἡρέθησαν γὰρ ἐκλογῆς παρ' ἡμῖν οἷς πλεῖστα ἐδόκει χρήματα εἶναι (frag. 52, Thalheim). This decree puts the matter beyond doubt.

Collectors are to be appointed in each city [and in the gap between the first and second fragment we may assume that their functions and responsibilities were defined]. There follow (10–25), as in the Kleinias decree, procedures to ensure that the new measure will be effective. An Assembly is to be convened every year after the Dionysia (when tribute should normally be paid) for the *hellenotamiai* to make a report on the year's response of the cities (10–15). Five men are to be sent each year to exact tribute from defaulters, and the *hellenotamiai* are to put up lists of defaulters, and of payers, on wooden boards in front of [the Metroon, the platform, or the statues of the tribal heroes in the Agora] (15–20). The decree is then applied with certain modifications to (or, on Meritt's view, instructions are given to promote a similar decree about) payments by Samos, Thera, and other cities (with similar obligations) which are not tribute payments (20–4). In the case of Samos these are probably instalments of her war indemnity (see p. 151). Meritt (*DAT* 36 f.) plausibly suggests that an indemnity was also imposed on Thera when she was brought into the empire in 431 or 430 (recorded in the list of 429–8, *ATL*, list 26. III. 22, probably to be restored in the list of 430–29, list 25. II. 24). Thera differs from Samos in paying tribute as well as indemnity. The decree is to be set up on the Acropolis by the prytany now in office (ll. 24 f.). A short rider follows, demanding another meeting of the Assembly on the next morning; the intention of the proposer was probably to ensure that the decree of Kleonymos was carried out effectively; some details may have been disputed.

A second decree is then recorded, presumably passed at the meeting required by the rider to the first decree. It may have been proposed by Kleonymos, for his name fills the space and he proposed another decree on the same day (*SEG* x. 73). The early lines are lost; what survives is concerned primarily with the judicial arrangements required to make the original decree effective. Anyone guilty of obstructing the 'tribute decree' (requiring the allies to appoint collectors) may be prosecuted by anyone from the city concerned. The case is to be reported to the ἐπιμεληταί (cf. *ATL* ii. D 11. 42) who are to take it to a heliastic court at Athens within a month from the return of the κλητῆρες (summoners), and the court is to decide the penalty (37–51). The heralds to be appointed by the *prytaneis* acting with the Boule are to be sent during the present prytany, so that collectors may be appointed and their names recorded in the Council House (51–6). The first decree had merely instructed the *prytaneis* to set up the decree on the Acropolis; formal provision is now made for the *poletai* to make the contract (56 f.). The larger letters of the two lines below the decree signify the title (cf. ὅρκος in No. 52).

The Kleonymos responsible for this decree is almost certainly to be identified with the Kleonymos who moved a decree in favour of Methone in the first prytany of 426–5 (No. 65, l. 34). It is probable that he was a member of the Boule in this year and that our decree should be dated in the second prytany of 426–5 (cf. No. 72, l. 6). We cannot, however, prove that he moved it as a probouleuma, for the only certain sign of a probouleuma in the fifth century is the amendment formula τὰ μὲν ἄλλα καθάπερ τῆι βολεῖ, which Meritt restored before l. 10 in *DAT* and *ATL*, but which he has abandoned now that the new fragment has confirmed Wilhelm's restoration in l. 26: τ[ὰ μὲν ἄλ]λα καθάπερ Κλεόνυμ|[ος; it is not, however, certain that τὰ μὲν ἄλλα καθάπερ ὁ δεῖνα was never used to amend a probouleuma. Kleonymos is one of Aristophanes' favourite targets, a coward, glutton, and liar (for references see *PA* 8680, i. 580). His politics were probably those of Cleon (see especially *Wasps*, 592 f.), and his decrees show that he deserves more serious consideration than Aristophanes' gibes would suggest.

The tribute collectors may have provided a precedent for the appointment of collectors of first-fruits in the cities for the Eleusinian Mysteries (No. 73).

69 (66)

Reassessment of the Tribute of the Athenian Empire: 425–4 B.C.

Forty-three fragments of a marble stele, now in EM, reconstructed with plaster.

Developed Attic letters. Stoichedon 70. Phot.: *The Athenian Assessment of 425 B.C.* (Meritt and West), 3–31; *ATL* i. 107–17.

IG i². 63; Meritt and West, *The Athenian Assessment of 425 B.C.*; McGregor, *TAPA* lxvi (1935) 146–64; Meritt and Wade-Gery, *AJP* lvii (1936)

377–94; *ATL* i. A 9; Meritt, *Epigraphica Attica* (1940), 131–8; *ATL* ii. A 9; Dow, *TAPA* lxxii (1941) 70–84; Béquignon and Will, *RA* xxxv (1950) 5–34; Gomme, *HCT* iii. 500–4 (1956).

Θ [ε ο ί]
τά[χσι]ς [φ]ό[ρο]
ἔδοχσεν τε̂[ι βολε̂ι καὶ τόι δέμοι,...ντὶς] ἐπρ[υτάνευε,...]\ον ἐγρα[μ-
                                                          μάτευε,...7....ἐπε]-
στάτε, Θόδι[ππος εἶπε· πέμφσαι κέρυκας] ἐκ το̂ν [....8....ὸς] ἂν
                                                          χερο[τονέσει hε βολὲ ἐς τὰ]-
5 ς πόλες δύο [μὲν ἐπ' Ἰονίαν καὶ Καρίαν] δύο δὲ ἐ[πὶ Θράικεν δύο δ]ὲ
                                                  ἐπὶ Ν[έσος δύο δὲ ἐφ' Ἑλλέσπ]-
οντον· hοῦτ[οι δὲ ἀνειπόντον ἐν τόι] κοινόι h[εκάστες τε̂ς πόλ]εος πα[ρε̂ναι
                                                          πρέσβες τὸ Μαι]-
μακτεριο̂ν[ος μενός· .....11......ἐ]σαγογέα[ς....9.....τούτ]ος δὲ
                                                          [hελέσθαι καὶ γραμμα]-
τέα καὶ χσυ[γγραμματέα ....9.....]ον· hε δὲ β[ολὲ ......12......]
                                              σθο[.....10.....δέκα ἄνδ]-
ρας· hοῦτοι [δὲ τὰς πόλες πέντε ἐμερ]ο̂ν ἀφ' ἐς ἄ[ν..............
                                  32...............ἒ τ]
10 ἐς ἐμέρας h[εκάστες χιλίας δραχμὰς] hέκαστ[ος ἀποτεισάτο· τὸς δὲ
                                                          τάκτας hορκοσάντον h]-
οι hορκοτα[ὶ τε̂ι αὐτε̂ι ἐμέραι ἐπειδὰν] τυγχ[άνοσιν hαιρεθέντες ἒ ὀφελέτο
                                                          hέκαστος τὲ]-
ν αὐτὲν ζεμ[ίαν· τὸν δὲ διαδικασιὸν hοι] ἐσ[α]γ[ογε̂ς ἐπ]ιμε[λόσθον περὶ
                                                  τὸ φόρο ἐπειδὰμ φσε]-
φίσεται hο [δε̂μος· ἐσαγογέον δὲ hο λα]χὸν κα[ὶ h]ο πολέμαρ[χος ἀνακρι-
                                                          νάντον τὰς δίκας ἐν τ]-
ε̂ι ἐλιαίαι [καθάπερ τὰς δίκας τὰς ἄλ]λας τὸ[ν ἐ]λιαστόν· ἐ[ὰν δὲ
                                  ....18.........τε̂σι]
15 πόλεσ[ι] κατ[ὰ τὰς δ]ια[δικασίας εὐθυ]νέσθο μ[υ]ρίασι δραχ[με̂σι κατὰ
                                                          τὸν νόμον hέκαστος αὐ]-
τόν· hοι δὲ [....]θέτα[ι δικαστέριον] νέον κα[θ]ιστάντον χ[ιλίος δικαστάς·
                                                          τὸ δὲ φόρο, ἐπειδ]-
ὲ ὀλέζον ἐγ[ένε]το, τὰς [νῦν τάχσες χσ]ὺν τε̂ι [βο]λε̂ι χσυντα[χσάντον
                                                          καθάπερ ἐπὶ τε̂ς τελευτ]-
αίας ἀρχε̂ς [πρὸς] μέρο[ς hαπάσας τὸ Π]οσιδε[ιο̂]νος μενός· χ[ρεματι-
                                                          ζόντον δὲ καὶ hοσεμέραι]

[ἀ]πὸ νομενί[ας κα]τὰ τ[αὐτὰ hίνα ταχθ]ε̄[ι] ho φό[ρ]ος ἐν τ̑οι Πο[σι-
δειο̑νι μενί· he δὲ βολὲ πλέθοσ]-
20 [a] χρεματι[ζέτο κ]αὶ χ[συνεχο̑ς hίνα τ]ά̣[χσ]ες γ[έ]νονται ἐὰμ [μέ τι
ἄλλο φσεφίζεται ho δε̑μο]ς· τ-
[ὸ]ν δὲ φόρο[ν ὀλέζ]ο μὲ τ[όλει νῦν ταχσάντ]ον μ[ε]δεμιᾶι ε̄ ho[πόσον
πρὸ τὸ ἐτύγχανον ἀπάγ]οντ-
[ες] ἐὰμ μέ τ[ις φαίν]εται[ι ἀπορία hόστε ὅσ]ες τ[ε̄]ς χόρας ἀδυ[νάτο μὲ
πλείο ἀπάγεν· τένδε] δὲ τ[ε̄]-
[ν γ]νόμεν [καὶ τὸ φσέ]φ[ισμα τόδε καὶ τὸμ φ]όρο[ν] hὸς ἂν ταχθ[ε̄ι τε̑ι
πόλει hεκάστει ἀνα]γρά[φσ]-
[ας] ho γρ[αμματεὺς τε̑ς βολε̑ς ἐν δυοῖν στ]έλα[ι]ν λιθίναιν [καταθέτο
τὲμ μὲν ἐν τ̑οι βο]λευ[τε]-
25 [ρ]ίοι τὲ[ν δὲ ἐμ πόλει· ἀπομισθοσάντον δὲ] ho[ι] πολεταί, τ[ὸ δὲ ἀργύριον
παρασχόντον] hοι κ[ο]-
λακρέτ[αι· τὸ δὲ λοιπὸν ἀποφαίνεν τε̑σι π]όλ[ε]σι περὶ τὸ φ[όρο πρὸ τ̑ομ
Παναθεναίον τ]ο̑μ με[γ]-
άλον· ἐσ[άγεν δὲ τὲμ πρυτανείαν hέτις ἂν] τυ[γ]χάνει πρυτ[ανεύοσα τὰς
τάχσες κατὰ Π]αναθ[έ]-
ναια· [ἐὰν δὲ hοι πρυτάνες μὲ τότε ἐσάγο]σι ε̑[ς] τὸν δε̑μον κ[αὶ τὲμ
βολὲν καὶ τὸ δικαστ]έριον
περὶ τ̑ο [φόρο μεδὲ εὐθὺς χρεματίζοσι ἐ]πὶ σ[φ]ο̑ν αὐτο̑ν, ὀφ[έλεν hεκατὸν
δραχμὰς hιε]ρὰς τε̑-
30 [ι Ἀ]θεν̣α[ίαι hέκαστον τὸμ π]ρ[υτάνεον κ]αὶ τὸ[ι] δεμοσίοι h[εκατὸν καὶ
εὐθύνεσθαι χιλί]ασι
[δρα]χμε̑[σι hέκαστον τὸμ πρ]υτά[νεον, κα]ὶ ἐάν τις ἄλλος δι[δο̑ι φσέφον
τε̑]σι [πόλεσι μ]ὲ ἔναι τ-
[ὰς] τάχσ[ες κατὰ Π]α[ναθένα]ια τὰ μ[εγάλα] ἐπὶ τε̑ς πρυτανεί[ας hέτις
ἂν πρ]ότε [πρυτα]νεύει, ἄτ-
[ι]μος ἔσ[το καὶ] τὰ χ[ρέματα αὐτο̑ δ[εμόσι]α ἔσ[τ]ο καὶ τε̑ς θεο̑ [τὸ
ἐπιδέκατ]ον· ἐχ[σενε]γκέτο δὲ τ-
αῦτα ἐς [τὸν] δε̑μον [...6...]ὶς π[ρ]υτα[νεί]α ἐπάναγκες ἐπει[δὰν hέκει
hε] στρα[τιὰ] ἐς τρίτεν ἐ-
35 μέραν [προ̑τ]ον μετ[ὰ τὰ hιε]ρά· ἐ[ὰν] δὲ [μὲ δ]ιαπ[ρ]αχθε̑ι ἐν ταύ[τει
χρεματί]ζεν πε̣[ρ]ὶ τούτο πρὸ[τ]-
ον τε̑ι [hυσ]τεραία[ι χσυνε]χο̑ς [hέ]ος [ἂν δ]ιαπ[ρ]αχθε̑ι ἐπὶ τε̑[ς 8
....]ς πρυτανείας· ἐὰν δ[ὲ μ]-
ὲ ἐχσε[νέγ]κοσι ἐς [τὸν δε̑μ]ον ε̄ [μὲ] δι[απρά]χσ[ο]σι ἐπὶ σφο̑ν α[ὐτο̑ν,
εὐθυν]έσθο μυρίασι δρ[αχμε̑]-

σιν hέ[καστ]ος τôμ [πρυτάν]εον [φό]ρο[ν hος] διακολύον ἐπιδ[ôναι ἐς
τὰ]ς στρα[τι]άς· τὸς δ[ὲ ἐς δί]-
κας πρ[οσκε]κλεμέ[νος ἀχθ]ênα̣[ι h]υπ[ὸ τôν] δεμοσίον κλετέ[ρον hίνα
h]ε βολ[ὲ δικά]σε[ι εὐθὺς ἐ]-
40 ἀμ μὲ ὀ[ρθôς] δοκôσ[ι διακο]νê[ν· τὰ]ς δ[ὲ πορ]είας τοῖς κέρυχ[σι τοῖς
ἰôσι χσυγγράφσαι κατὰ τ]-
ον hόρ[κον τὸ]ς τάκ[τας hέο]ς τ[ô πο]ρε[υθέσ]ον[τα]ι hίνα μὲ αὐ[.....
..14.......hοι δὲ κέρυκες]
τὰς τά[χσ]ες τêσι π[όλεσι ἐπ]α̣[ναγ]κα̣[σθέντ]ο[ν hό]πο ἂν δοκê[ι .....
...17........hό τι δὲ πε]-
ρὶ τôν [τ]άχσεον κα[ὶ τὸ φσεφίσμα]το[ς τêσι] π[όλεσι] χρὲ λέγ[εσθαι
περὶ τούτο τὸν δêμον φσε]φ-
ίζεσθ[α]ι καὶ ἐάν τ[ι ἄλλο ἐσάγοσι] h[οι πρυτάνες πε]ρὶ τὸ δ[έοντος·
hόπος δὲ ἂν τὸμ φόρον] ἀπά-
45 [γ]οσιν [h]αι πόλες [ἐπιμελέσθον hοι στρατεγοὶ εὐθὺ]ς hότ[αν χσυντάχσει
hε βολὲ τ]ὲν τάχσι-
[ν τὸ] φό[ρ]ο hίνα ệι [τôι δέμοι ἀργύριον hικανὸν ἐς τὸμ] πόλ[εμον· τὸς
δὲ στρατεγὸς] χρêσθαι π-
[ερὶ τô φ]όρο κατα[σκέφσει καθ' ἕκαστον ἐνιαυτὸν ἐχσετ]ά̣[σαντας κατὰ
γêν κα]ὶ θάλατταν πρ-
[ôτον πόσ]α δεῖ ἒ ἒ[ς τὰς στρ]α[τιὰς ἒ ἐς ἄλλο τι ἀναλίσκεν· ἐν δὲ τêι
hέδραι τ]ês βολês τêι πρό-
[τει περὶ] τ[ο]ύτο α̣[ἰεὶ δίκ]α̣ς [ἐσαγόντον ἄνευ τês ἑλιαίας καὶ τ]ὸν ἄλλον
δικαστερίον ἐὰμ μ-
50 [ὲ δικαστôν] προ[τον δικα]σά̣[ντον ἐσάγεν φσεφίζεται hο] δêμ[ος·] τοῖς
δὲ κέρυχσι τοῖς ἰôσι τ-
[ὸμ μίσθον] ἀποδ[όντον hο]ι κ̣[ολακρέται....9.....εἶπ]ε· τὰ μὲ[ν] ἄλλα
καθάπερ τêι βολêι· τὰς
[δὲ τάχσες] hόσαι [ἂν κατ]ὰ π[όλιν......13.......τὸς πρ]υτάνε[ς] hοὶ
ἂν τότε τυγχάνοσι πρυτ-
[ανεύοντ]ες καὶ τὸ[ν γρα]μμ[ατέα τês βολês...7....ἐς τ]ὸ δικαστέριον
hόταν περὶ τôν τάχσ-
[εον ệι h]όπος ἂν α[ὐτὰς ἀ]νθ[ομολογôνται hοι δικαστα]ί υ ἔδοχσ[εν] τêι
βολêι καὶ τôι δέμοι, Α-
55 [ἰγεῖς ἐ]πρυτάνευ[ε, Φίλ]ιπ[πος ἐγραμμάτευε,...7....]ορος ἐπεσ[τάτε],
Θόδιππος εἶπε· hοπόσ-
[εσι πό]λεσι φόρος [ἐτάχ]θ[ε ἐπὶ τ]ês [βολês hêι Πλειστί]ας πρôτός
[ἐγρα]μμάτευε ἐπὶ Στρατοκ-

[λέος] ἄρχοντος βό[ν καὶ πανhοπ]λ[ίαν ἀπάγεν ἐς Παναθ]έναια τὰ
μ[εγάλα] hαπάσας· πεμπόντον
δ[ὲ ἐν] τῆι πομπῆι [καθάπερ ἄποι]κ[οινυν κατὰ τάδε ἔτα]χσεν τὸμ φό[ρον
τῆ]σι πόλεσιν hε βολ[ὲ]
hῆι [Πλ]ειστίας π[ρῶτος ἐγραμμ]ά[τευε .....11...... ἐ]πὶ Στρατοκλ[έος ἄ]ρχοντος ἐπὶ [τό]ν [ἐσ]-
60   αγογ[έο]ν hοῖς Κα[....8 or 10....ἐγρ]α[μμάτευε...9 or 7....]ς.

Our text is based on the revision of Meritt and West's original text in
ATL ii. 40 f.; but at some points we agree with Béquignon and Will
(*RA* xxxv (1950) 5 ff.) in preferring the earlier restorations of *ATL* i. 154 f.
l. 4: πέμφσαι κέρυκας] ἐκ τόν [μισθοτόν *ATL* ii; ἐκ τόν [βολευτόν *ATL* i,
BW. Neither satisfies. Heralds form a professional class and would not be
members of the Boule; μισθοτοί is very unflattering, roughly corresponding to
'hireling' (see Gomme, *HCT* iii. 502 n. 1).   l. 7: κυαμεῦσαι δὲ ἐ]σαγογέα[ς
τριάκοντα *ATL* ii; hε δὲ βολὲ καὶ ἐ]σαγογέα[ς κλεροσάτο *ATL* i, BW.
l. 8: χσυ[γγραμματέα ἐχς hαπάντ]ον *ATL* i and ii; ἐκ σφόν αὐ]τόν BW: ἐ δὲ
β[ολὲ τὸν φόρον hελέ]σθο [hοὶ τάχσοσι δέκα *ATL*.   l. 9: ἀφ' ἐς ἄ[ν hαιρεθέντες τυγχάνοσι ἐγγραφσάντον] *ATL* i, BW; ἀφ' ἐς ἄ[ν hαιρεθόσι ὁμομο-
κότες ἀναγραφσάντον] *ATL* ii.   l. 12: hοι] ἐσ[α]γ[ογὲς ἐπ]ιμε[λεθέντον τὸ
φόρο καθάπερ ἂν φσε]||φίσεται hο [δέμος *ATL* ii; we follow *ATL* i, BW.
l. 13: ἐπάναγκες δὲ hο ἄρ]χον κα[ὶ h]ο πολέμαρ[χος χσυνδεχέσθον τὰς
δίκας] *ATL* i; hοῦτοι δὲ καὶ hο ἄρ]χον κα[ὶ h]ο πολέμαρ[χος ἀνακρινάντον
ATL ii. The restoration in the text is an improvement in *ATL* iv, p. ix,
on a suggestion by BW.   ll. 14 f.: ἐ[ὰν δὲ hοι τάκται μὲ τάττοσι τέσι] |
πόλεσ[ι *ATL* ii; ἐ[ὰν δὲ μὲ εὐθὺς χρεματίζοσι τέσι]| πόλεσ[ι *ATL* i, BW.
l. 16: [νομο]θέτα[ι neatly fills the space, but the responsibility of estab-
lishing a new court does not seem appropriate to νομοθέται (nor is the
office otherwise known at Athens until the last years of the century). We
should expect the *thesmothetai* to have been appointed. Perhaps they were, and
the mason left a letter out, ? θε⟨σ⟩μο]θέτα[ι.   l. 18: φθίνοντος τὸ Π]οσι-
δε[ιδ]νος μενός· χ[ρεματίζεν δὲ περὶ τὸ φόρο εὐθὺς *ATL* i, BW.   l. 20:
χ[συνεχὲς *ATL*.   l. 28: κ[αὶ μὲ φσεφίζονται δικαστ]έριον *ATL* ii; κ[αὶ
τὲμ βολὲν καὶ τὸ δικαστ]έριον *ATL* i, BW.   l. 30: Ἀ]θενα[ίαι τῆι Νίκει
τὸν γ]ρ[αμματέα *ATL* i, BW. For the tribe name see below.
ll. 34 and 36: We follow Bannier, *ATL* i, BW.; τὸς δ[ὲ κέρυ]|κας πρ[οσκε]κλεμέ[νος
ἀχθ]ένα[ι *ATL* ii.   l. 41: hίνα μὲ αὐ[τοὶ ἄτακτοι ἴοσι *ATL* ii; hίνα μὲ
αὐ[τοτελὲς ἀπίοσιν *ATL* i, BW.   l. 42: hό]πο ἂν δοκέ[ι τοῖς ἄρχοσι ἀνειπὲν
ATL ii; hό]πο ἂν δοκέ[ι τῶι δέμοι ἀποφαίνεν *ATL* i, BW.   l. 53: δελόσαι
ἐς τ]ὸ δικαστέριον *ATL* ii; ἐφιέναι ἐς τ]ὸ δικαστέριον *ATL* i, BW, but this
is the language of appeal. ἐσφέρεν would be more appropriate.   l. 59: καὶ
hε ἐλιαία ἐ]πὶ Στρατοκλ[έος BW following Schöll. The space, however,
is almost certainly to be filled by a demotic, both here and in the following
line.

Though more than half of this decree is missing, and though much
of the detail depends on restoration that is far from secure, the length

of the line is known and the main provisions are clear. The Athenians order a new assessment. Ten assessors are to be selected by the Boule and sworn in, and must draw up within five days the list of cities to be assessed. Heralds are to be sent out, two to each of the four districts of the empire, to announce the assessment and to require the cities to send representatives to Athens in Maimakterion (November–December). A new jury court of 1,000 is to be set up and *eisagogeis* are to be appointed to be responsible for the hearing of tribute cases. The court for hearing these cases shall be in session throughout Posideion (January–February) and must complete its work by the end of the month. The main work of assessment is theirs; the final responsibility is shared by the Boule. The decree also looks forward. In future there must be a reassessment every four years at the time of the great Panathenaia and the *prytaneis* in office at the time will be held responsible and heavily fined if this is not done. There is also a clause (46–50) probably allowing for individual changes of assessment in years when there was no general assessment. (Some controversial details will be discussed below.)

The main purpose of the decree is to raise money for the war: 'they shall not assess a smaller tribute for any city than it was previously paying, unless owing to the poverty of the territory they cannot pay more' (21–2, as restored). Below the decree the cities were listed with their new assessments and there is no doubt that this instruction dominated proceedings in Posideion. At the foot of the list the grand total was recorded, but the first letter is missing. The tribute demanded from the empire was either 960–1,000 T. or 1,460–1,500 T. (see p. 199). By 1935 sufficient evidence had accumulated to make the higher figure inevitable. Two district totals in large part survive. The Hellespontine district, whose assessment before the war was not more than 85 T., is now required to pay between 250 and 300 T. (ΗΗΗ⅍[---]); the Thracian district's total is raised from *c.* 130 T. to between 310 and 350 T. (ΗΗΗΗ⅍[--]); and the island district, complete or nearly complete, though the total is not preserved, is required to pay at least 160 T. in place of a pre-war *c.* 60 T. (omitting Aegina, occupied by Athens since 431 and no longer paying tribute). The minimum combined total for these three districts is 720 T., which, if the lower total were right, would leave a maximum of 280 T. for the Ionian/Carian district, and two new groups of cities, the Aktaian cities opposite Lesbos on the mainland and cities in the Euxine, which together were assessed at not less than 80 T. A balance of *c.* 200 T. only is left for Ionia/Caria, whose assessment before the war was not less than 150 T. Existing figures in this district show, as we should expect, that Ionia/Caria was not given such singular concessions; Kaunos for instance is raised from a pre-war ½ T. to 10 T., Pedasos from 2 to

3 T., Syme from 1,800 dr. to 3 T. The grand total must have been more than 1,460 T.

This great increase was achieved mainly by a revolutionary revision in which very few states were unaffected; most had their tributes doubled or trebled, but the wide variety in proportional increase shows that, as the decree requires, cases were individually considered. The list also contained many names that had not appeared for a very long time, such as minor Carian cities which lapsed in the forties; we may infer that all cities which had ever paid were listed. Other states were included that are not known to have been assessed before. Melos is the most conspicuous example, required to pay 15 T., though it was neutral at the beginning of the war (Thuc. ii. 9. 4), resisted Athenian aggression successfully in 426 (Thuc. iii. 91. 1–3), and fought for independence in 416. There is also, at the end of the list, a substantial group of cities in the Euxine. No tribute payment for the Euxine is recorded in the pre-war lists, but it is possible that they were included in the assessment of 428. The Aktaian cities, listed after the Hellespontine district, had been taken by Athens from Mytilene in 427 (Thuc. iii. 50. 4), and were probably specially assessed then. In the thirties the number of cities recorded in the annual lists of *aparchai* never exceeded 175. In 425 not less than 380 and possibly more than 400 were assessed.

The assessment of 425 was in more respects than its scale extraordinary. It was not in a Great Panathenaic year, and it was introduced so late that representatives could not be expected to come to Athens from the cities until the winter (Maimakterion). Some special explanation is required, and most scholars have attributed the assessment to the influence of Cleon. Gomme (*HCT* iii. 500 ff.) has emphasized that for this there is no positive evidence; the silence of Thucydides, he thinks, and even more of Aristophanes, who in 424 made Cleon a central figure in his *Knights*, is barely consistent with this view. The indirect arguments, however, remain very strong indeed. Whatever the precise date of the decree, it was passed within three months of Cleon's spectacular success on Sphakteria, when his reputation at Athens was at its height (he was still popular enough to be elected general in 424). If Meritt and Wade-Gery are right (*AJP* lvii (1936) 377–94), the influence of Cleon's capture of the Spartans was direct and immediate, but their thesis raises difficulties. In the middle of the decree (l. 34), a prytany with six letters assuming that *he* before it was spelt with the aspirate (Oineis or Aegeis) is required to bring 'this business' before the *ekklesia* and carry it through before the end of its period of office, under threat of heavy penalties; but for the prytany under which the decree was in fact passed (l. 3) seven and not six letter-spaces are available, Leontis or Aiantis. Though there is no explicit record preserved in our sources, it is virtually certain that the order of prytanies was not established at the beginning of the year and that the name of the next prytany was unknown, except by elimination in the ninth, until the end of its predecessor's term (Ferguson, *The Athenian Secretaries*, 19–27; Brillant, *Les Secrétaires Athéniens*, 23 f.). The business was to be brought before the *ekklesia* on the second day after the [return] of the expedition (34–5). Since the terms of reference imply that the prytany will be nearing the end of its term when the business is submitted to the *ekklesia*, Meritt and Wade-Gery infer that the introduction of the decree was delayed beyond the second prytany into the third. This delay they explain by Cleon's movements. They suggest that the probouleuma was drafted in the Boule immediately the news of the surrender reached Athens, but that Cleon took longer than had been expected in returning home. When the fighting was done there was less need for haste and, though he fulfilled his promise by returning to Athens within twenty days, they were three or four days out in their calculation. This is a possible explanation, but not in itself probable, and there is a further objection. If this reconstruction is right, a stele was set up on the Acropolis which said that the members of the [Oineis] prytany would be very heavily fined if they did not do what it was already known they had not done (ll. 34–8).

Other views therefore must be seriously considered. If in the two places (3 and 34) different tribes are indeed mentioned, then it is possible that the tribe of l. 3 is Leontis Pryt. II, followed by Oineis Pryt. III in l. 34, and that the decree was passed on the last day of Leontis when it was known that Oineis was to follow. This, however, though formally possible, perhaps relies too much on coincidence. An alternative is to believe that in l. 34 the mason wrote ἐ Λεοντίς, though the aspirate is not dropped elsewhere in this inscription. This possibility, however, is strengthened if in l. 36 we restore, instead of ἐπὶ τε͂[ς εἰρεμένε]ς πρυτανείας, which we do not think can mean 'the said prytany', ἐπὶ τε͂[ς Λεοντίδο]ς πρυτανείας, the more normal formulation.

If this cardinal point in the argument of Meritt and Wade-Gery is questioned we may also question the close association of the decree with Cleon's success at Sphakteria. An alternative has been urged by McGregor, who argued that the evidence pointed to Nikias' expedition against Corinth (*TAPA* 1935, 146 ff.). Though some of his arguments were convincingly refuted by Meritt and Wade-Gery, his case is worth restating in a revised form. Meritt and Wade-Gery's case rests primarily on the time-table that they have reconstructed from Thucydides; if, however, we follow Gomme (*HCT* iii. 478, 719), we shall prefer McGregor's conclusion. There is roughly a month's difference between the two time-tables, and the main reason for the discrepancy lies in the interpretation of Thucydides' indications of time at the beginning of Book IV. It is generally agreed that in the first year of the war the Spartans invaded Attica towards the end of May, when the corn was ripe (τοῦ σίτου ἀκμάζοντος, Thuc. ii. 19. 1). In 425 they invaded at roughly the same time as the Syracusans attacked Messene (ἐπιγιγνομένου θέρους περὶ σίτου ἐκβολήν, when the corn was in the ear, Thuc. iv. 1. 1). When the Spartans hastily withdrew from Attica, Thucydides says that a severe shortage of food was a contributory factor; for they had invaded early and the corn was still green (ἅμα δὲ πρῷ ἐσβαλόντες καὶ τοῦ σίτου ἔτι χλωροῦ ὄντος ἐσπάνιζον τροφῆς τοῖς πολλοῖς, Thuc. iv. 6. 1). Meritt and Wade-Gery hold that 'early' is to be taken with reference to the condition of the grain, rather than to dates by civil calendar or Julian reckoning. The Spartans invaded, they think, at roughly the normal date. Gomme is more probably right in holding that the invasion was earlier in the calendar than usual. The comparison of Thuc. iv. 2. 1 with iv. 1. 1 supports him. There is one further gain if we accept Gomme's timetable in which Cleon brings his Spartan prisoners to Athens at the end of July or the beginning of August. McGregor argued that the second decree of Thoudippos, which required all the allies included in the assessment to bring standard offerings to the Great Panathenaia, and which was passed when Aegeis was prytany, must have been later than Posideion, during which month appeals against assessments were to be heard in the special court established by the main decree. It was therefore later than Prytany IV, and the six-lettered tribe that the report of the *logistai* requires for the fourth prytany (No. 72. 18-19) must be Oineis, which should be restored in our decree at l. 34. This is the most natural way to understand the aorist in the second decree, ℎοπόσ|[εσι πό]λεσι φόρος [ἐτάχ]θ[ε; neither of the alternatives suggested by Meritt and Wade-Gery is convincing. Certainly the clause *might* refer to the preliminary assessment by the τάκται, which could be complete within a week of the decree, but it is much more likely to refer to the final assessment confirmed by the Boule after appeals have been heard. The alternative explanation—that ἐτάχθε is an epistolary aorist, 'used in relation to the time when the duties named in the main verb must be performed', is even less attractive. But though we believe that the expedition referred to in the main decree is more probably that of Nikias than that of Cleon, the date is still sufficiently near to Cleon's spectacular triumph to justify the belief that his political followers were primarily responsible for it.

The association with the followers of Cleon may also be reflected in the tone of the decree, for this is perhaps the strongest decree that has survived from the fifth century. The executive is threatened with penalties at every turn, in a manner reminiscent of, but more intensive than, the Coinage decree (No. 45) and the decree of Kleinias (No. 46). The polemical tone of most of the clauses presupposes opposition, and a strong determination to override it. This is the bullying tone that gives Aristophanes so much scope in the *Knights*. It may also be relevant to emphasize that the sequence of clauses is extremely un-systematic; one has the impression that the text was drafted by an inexperienced man. Wade-Gery and Meritt have pointed out (op. cit. 392 n. 36) that in Speech IX of Isaeus there is a Cleon, son of Thou-dippos, of the right age to be the son of our Thoudippos. Their suggestion that Thoudippos may have married a daughter of Cleon and named one of his sons after his father-in-law is attractive, for Thoudippos is a rare name.

Some of the details of the assessment procedure outlined in the decree remain uncertain, and not only because there are many gaps in our text; Athenian decrees are considerably less precise than Roman, and much that we should like to know is taken for granted and not specified. The first provision of the decree is that heralds should be sent out to the cities of the empire requiring them to send representatives to Athens in Maimakterion. Much later in the decree it is laid down that the heralds are to announce in the cities 'the making of the assessments' (τὰς τά[χσ]ες, meaning the news that there is to be an assessment, not the assessment fixed for each city, cf. ll. 31 f.), and the demos is to prescribe by vote what the heralds are to say about the assessment (a strongly democratic feature; one would have thought that the Boule would have been better suited). We infer that representatives are to come to Athens from all cities on the asses-sors' list, and not only those who wish to appeal against their assess-ment. Meanwhile, at Athens the ten assessors would first have drawn up their list of cities and then (though this is not specified in the decree) assigned assessments to each, based presumably on the rough knowledge that was available in the Boule of the cities' resources and on the general injunction to increase the figures. The cities' re-presentatives, hearing at Athens what was proposed, had the right of appeal to a special court of 1,000. A similar court, but of 1,500, is recorded in the quota-list of 429 (Lepper, *JHS* lxxxii (1962) 33 f. suggests that the heading in question refers not to the current assess-ment of 430 but to 434). It would be interesting to know when the Athenians introduced the principle of appeal against assessment to an Athenian court. It is not likely to have been in force while tribute was paid to Delos, nor immediately after the transfer of the treasury from Delos to Athens in 454. The assessment of 450 is a possible context, especially if peace was made with Persia in that year. Perhaps, however, 446 is a more likely date, when Athens, after the shocks of Koroneia and the revolts of Euboea and Megara, was prepared to make concessions to retain her hold over her 'allies' (see p. 86). This may be what is meant when the Chalkidians, after the crushing of their revolt in 446, are required to include in their oath: καὶ τὸν φόρον hυποτελô Ἀθεναίοισιν, hὸν | ἂν πείθο Ἀθεναῖος (No. 52, ll. 25–7). The decree does not make it clear that only appeal cases go to court, but common sense demands it, and the use of the term διαδικασίαι implies a decision between two claims, in this case the assessments proposed by the Athenian *taktai* and the allies' counter-proposals (for the view that all tribute went before the Heliaia, see BW, pp. 14 f.). When the assessment has been finally approved by the Boule, the generals, according to reasonable restoration, are to be at once responsible for seeing that the cities bring their tribute; it is interesting to note that Thucydides records the activities of a squadron of νῆες ἀργυρολόγοι operating in the winter of 425–4 and the summer of 424 (Thuc. iv. 50. 1, 75).

Of the next clause, the penultimate of the decree, very little is preserved. It seems to provide for extraordinary assessments of individual cities by the Boule in the light of an annual review by the generals of the anticipated military and naval expenses of the year. The procedure in these extraordinary assessments is to be simple. No *taktai*, *eisagogeis*, or special court are to be appointed; the work will be confined to the Boule unless the Assembly votes that these assessments should go first before a popular court. After a short clause dealing with the pay of the heralds a rider is added, the sense of which is controversial (ll. 51–4). It seems to be laid down that certain assessments are to be referred to the court in order that the jurors may concur. According to *ATL* (iii. 76) 'assessments which have been decided after appeal and which the Boule includes in its final list must be reported back to the court. Previously (ll. 14–16) the *taktai* have been ordered to make such assessments in accordance with the decisions of the court. The rider now gives to the court the opportunity to see that its decisions have been carried out by the *taktai*.' We think it more probable that the rider refers to the extraordinary assessments of the penultimate clause. It is a democratic insistence that the Boule shall not have the final word; their recommendations must be submitted to the popular court for their approval.

A second and substantially later decree, proposed also by Thoudippos, prescribes that all the cities that have been assessed are to bring cow and panoply to the Great Panathenaia. This requirement has been thought, by Mattingly (*Hist.* x (1961) 153) and others, to be an innovation, referred to soon after by the decree of Kleinias (No. 46, ll. 41 f.), which is primarily concerned with the tightening up of tribute collection. In our commentary on that decree we have given reason for dating it before the Peloponnesian War, and probably in the forties. The instruction in the assessment decree of 425 is better interpreted as the application of a current rule to *all* the cities on the assessment list, including many who have either never paid tribute before, or not paid for many years.

Below the decree the cities with their new assessments are listed in four columns. The districts are in a new order (Islands, Ionia–Caria, Hellespont, Thrace) and include two headings not found before. The Aktaian cities, added as an appendix to the Hellespont (col. iii. ll. 124 ff.) are on the mainland opposite Lesbos, and were taken by Athens from Mytilene when her revolt was crushed in 427 (Thuc. iii. 50. 3). No Euxine names (here an appendix to Thrace) have survived from any earlier list, but the evidence for the years from 428 to 425 is negligible; they may have been incorporated in 428. Each district list is followed by a district total, and the grand total is recorded at the bottom of the stele. There is a margin of error in calculating the number of cities now assessed. We can only roughly estimate the number of cities occupying two lines; more important, the gaps between the districts cannot be securely determined. The *ATL* text assumes eight uninscribed lines after the island total, and two other substantial gaps, after the Ionian district and after the Aktaian cities, which immediately follow the Hellespontine total. The main reason is the difficulty otherwise of filling out the Aktaian appendix. Dow, however, emphasizes that the normal practice in tribute quota-lists is to leave no such gap, and we are inclined to follow him (Dow, *TAPA* lxxii (1941) 70–84; see also *ATL* ii. 43 n.). The *ATL* text allows for *c.* 380 cities; if Dow is right, there could be up to 410. In either case there are considerably more names than the 341 otherwise known (though in no single year, so far as we know, had the number of cities recorded as paying exceeded 190).

We give the district totals, the island district, and an extract from the Ionian–Carian panel.

---

h[ελλεσποντίο φόρο
κεφ[άλαιον]
ΗΗΗ𐅄[- - -
Phot.: *ATL* i. 115, fig. 164.

[Θραικίο φόρο]
[κεφάλαιο]ν: ΗΗΗ𐅄[-
Phot.: *ATL* i. 116, fig. 167.

[κεφάλα]ιον [τ]ὸ χσύμπαντος: [𐅇]ΗΗΗΗΗ𐅄𐅄[- -
Phot.: *ATL* i. 117, fig. 170.

From col. i.

		Νεσιοτικὸς φόρο[ς]	
	𐅄𐅄𐅄	Πάρι[ο]ι	(18)
	𐅄𐅗	Νάχσ[ιο]ι	(6⅔)
	𐅄𐅗	Ἄνδρ[ιοι]	(6)
65	𐅄𐅗	Μέλιο[ι]	—
	𐅗ΤΤΤΤ	Σίφνι[οι]	(3)
	𐅄𐅗	Ἐρετρι[ες]	(3)
	𐅗	Θεραῖ[οι]	—
	𐅄	Κεῖο[ι]	(4)
70	𐅗	Καρύσ[τιοι]	(5)
	𐅄	Χαλκι[δες]	(3)
	𐅗Τ	Κύθνι[οι]	(3)
	𐅄	Τέν[ι]ο[ι]	(2)
	ΤΤ	Στ[υ]ρες	(1)
75	[ΤΤ]	Μ[υ]κόνι[οι]	(1)
	[ΤΤ]	[Σ]ερίφιο[ι]	(1)
	[Τ]	Ἰέται	(3,000 dr.)
	[Τ] vacat	Διες	(2,000 dr.)
	Τ	Ἀθενῖται	(2,000 dr.)
80	Τ	Σύριοι	(1,500 dr.)
	ΧΧ	Γρυγχες	(1,000 dr.)
	Χ	Ῥεναιες	(300 dr.)
	ΧΧ	Διακρες ἀπ[ὸ]	(800 dr.)
		Χαλκιδέον	
85	Χ	Ἀναφαῖοι	—
	vacat	Κερία Δ|||	—
	ΧΧ	Φολέγανδρος	—
	ΗΗΗ	Βέλβινα	—
	Χ	Κίμολος	—
90	Χ	Σικινεται	—
	Η	Ποσίδειον	—
		ἐν Εὐβοίαι	
	ΤΧΧ	Διά[κρ]ιοι	—
		ἐν Ε[ὐβοία[ι]	
95	vacat	[h]εφ[αισ]τι[ες]	
	ΤΤΤΤ	[h]ο[ι ἐν Λέμνοι]	(3)
	[vacat]	[Μυριναῖοι]	(1½)
	[Τ]	[Ἴμβριοι]	(1)
		[Νεσιοτικô φόρο]	
100		[κεφάλαιον]	
	[𐅅𐅗𐅄ΤΤΤΗΗΗΗΔ|||]		

Figures in brackets after the city-name are from the assessments of the thirties, and are in talents, except where stated.

From the Ionian–Carian panel, col. ii, ll. 138–57

	Χ	Καρυα[νδὲς]	(500 dr.)
	Ͱ	Βρυκόντιοι	(500 dr.)
140	Χ	Ταρβανὲς	(?)
	Χ	Μύνδιοι	(500 dr.)
		παρὰ Τέρμερα	
	ͰΤ	Ἐδριὲς Ὑμεσσὲς	
		Κυρομὲς	
145	ΤΤ	Τέλος	—
	ΤΤ	Κελένδερις	—
	ΧΧΧΧ	Ἰτύρα	—
	ΧΧΧ	Σύμε	(1,800 dr.)
	ΧΧΧ	Π⟨ε⟩δ⟨α⟩σὲς	(?)
150	ΧΧ	ἱνδαιὲς	
	Η	Ἐλαιόσιοι	(100 dr.)
		Ἐρυθραίον	
	[—]	['Ι]ερὰ παρὰ	—
		[Σι]δυμέας	
155	[—]	[Κρυὲ]ς	(2,000 dr.)
	[—]	[Ἄσπεν]δος	—
		[ἐμ Παμφ]υλίαι	

Of these cities, Πεδασὲς, ἱνδαιὲς, Ὑμεσσὲς are not recorded on any fragments of the quota-lists after 446. Of the joint payers, Ἐδριὲς are not recorded earlier. Ὑμεσσὲς had in the first two periods paid 1,200 dr.; Κυρομὲς (more commonly Ὑρομὲς) paid 2,500 dr. before 438. Among those enrolled for the first known time Kelenderis (l. 146) and Aspendos (l. 156) are east of the Chelidonian Isles, a region generally regarded as in the Persian sphere.

70

Athens honours Herakleides of Klazomenai:
424–3 B.C.

The lower part of a marble stele, found on the Acropolis; now in EM.
    Ionic letters of the early fourth century, stoichedon 31. Phot.: Pečírka, *The Formula for the Grant of Enktesis in Attic Inscriptions* (Prague, 1966), Pl. 1.
    IG ii². 8; Foucart, *BCH* xii (1888) 163–9; Köhler, *Hermes*, xxvii (1892) 68–78; West, *AJP* lvi (1935) 72; Wade-Gery, *Essays*, 208; Stockton, *Hist.* viii (1959) 74–9; Pečírka, op. cit., 22–5.

ψήφισμα τόδε κ]-
[αὶ τὸ πρότερον γενόμενον Ἡρακλείδηι]
ἀναγράψαι τὸν [γραμματέα τῆς βολῆς κα]-
ὶ θέναι ἐν πόλει.

ἔδοξεν τῆι βολῆι κ[αὶ τῶι δήμωι . . . 6 . . .]
. . ς ἐπρυτάνευεν, Σ[. . . . ἐγραμμάτευεν],
5   [Ν]εοκλείδης ἐπεστ[άτει, ... 12 . . . . . .]
[εἶ]πεν· Ἡρακλείδην [τὸν Κλαζομένιον ἀν]-
[αγρ]άψαι τὸγ γραμμ[ατέα τῆς βολῆς πρόξ]-
[ενο]ν καὶ εὐεργέτη[ν καθότι ἂν τῶι δήμω]-
[ι δο]κῆι καὶ θέναι ἐ[ν πόλει, ἐπειδὴ εὖ ἐπ]-
10 [όησ]εν τὰς Ἀθηναίω[ν πρεσβείας καὶ ἐν π]-
[ᾶσι ἀ]νήρ ἐστι ἀγαθ[ὸς εἰς τὸν δῆμον τὸν]
[Ἀθη]ναίων. Θοκυδίδη[ς εἶπε· τὰ μὲν ἄλλα κ]-
[αθά]περ τῆι βολῆι· ἐπ[ειδὴ δὲ οἱ πρέσβες]
[οἱ π]αρὰ βασιλέως ἥκ[οντες ἀγγέλλοσι Ἡ]-
15 [ρακ]λείδην συμπράτ[τεν ἑαυτοῖς προθύ]-
[μως] ἔς τε τὰσπονδὰς [τὰς πρὸς βασιλέα ἔ]-
[ς τε ἄ]λλο ὅ τι ἐπαγγέ[λειαν, ἐναι Ἡρακλε]-
[ίδηι] γῆς ἔγκτησιν κα[ὶ οἰκίας Ἀθήνησι]-
[ν καὶ ἀ]τέλειαν καθάπ[ερ τοῖς ἄλλοις πρ]-
20 [οξένο]ις· καὶ ἐάμ πο βια[ίωι θανάτωι ἀπο]-
[θάνηι, ἐναι π]ερὶ αὐτὸ τ[ὴν τιμορίαν καθ]-
[άπερ . . . . . 10 . . . . .]ΝΛΓ[

We have added letters to 3, 12, 13, 16, 20, 22.   ll. 20–1: We follow
Wilhelm, *Sitzb. Wien.* ccxvii, 5, 23 f. In 21–2 [καθ|άπερ Ἀθηναίοις ἀ]ϙα-
γ[έγραπται would fit, but is unparalleled.

At the top of the stone there survive a few letters from the end of
a decree, and below, separated by a space, a second decree honouring
Herakleides, who is to have the title of *proxenos* and benefactor for his
services to Athens. A rider mentions the King of Persia, a treaty, and
probably envoys. The lettering suggests the early fourth century,
and Foucart identified this Herakleides with Herakleides of Byzantium,
who was similarly honoured for helping Thrasybulus in 389 to recover
Byzantium (Dem. xx. 58); the treaty was the King's Peace of 387.
Köhler more convincingly advocated Herakleides of Klazomenai,
who was elected general by the Athenians (Plat. *ion* 541 d) and was

also responsible for raising Assembly pay from 1 to 2 obols (Arist. *Ἀθ. Πολ.* 41); appropriately he was nicknamed "*ὁ βασιλεύς*" (ibid.). The treaty he identified with Andocides' treaty of friendship with Persia negotiated by an embassy in which his uncle Epilykos served (Andoc. iii. 29). Herakleides was honoured for services rendered to the Athenian envoys. The fourth-century lettering Köhler explained as a copy of a fifth-century decree destroyed by the Thirty (cf. Tod, vol. ii, no. 98), added to a later decree perhaps conferring citizenship. Köhler's conclusions were considerably strengthened by Wade-Gery's further identifications. Andocides' uncle Epilykos could be the first secretary of the Boule in 424–3; the president of the Assembly that voted the decree was probably Neokleides, secretary of Aegeis in 424–3, and the mover of the rider, Thucydides, treasurer of Athena in the same year (*Essays* 207 f.). A treaty with Darius, in his first year, towards the end of 424–3 made good historical sense.

In the course of a strong attack on the Peace of Kallias, D. Stockton has revived Foucart's identification with Herakleides of Byzantium (*Hist.* viii (1959) 74 ff.), but there remain decisive objections: (1) In l. 6 the ethnic has to be added after the name; *τὸν Κλαζομένιον* gives precisely the number of letters required. Stockton suggests *τὸν ἐκ Βυζαντίου*, which must be rejected because the cutter uses o for ου in *Θοκυδίδ[ης*, in l. 12, and would almost certainly have inscribed *τὸν Βυζάντιον*. (2) Realizing that the Athenians were extremely unlikely to reward anyone for helping to secure the King's Peace, which was a humiliation to them, Stockton suggests that the king in question might have been either Seuthes or Medokos, but no Thracian king would be called *βασιλεύς* without qualification: *βασιλεύς*, standing alone, must mean the Persian King. (3) Demosthenes says that Herakleides of Byzantium was voted the title of *πρόξενος* and *εὐεργέτης* and given complete *ἀτέλεια*. These honours are recorded in our decree, but with them also is *γῆς ἔγκτησις* (see p. 263), which is not mentioned by Demosthenes.

Raubitschek, while accepting the treaty, dates it, and with it our decree, in 415 (*Gk. Rom. Byz. Stud.*, v (1964) 156); his hypothesis seems to us insufficiently strong to outweigh the evidence collected by Wade-Gery (see also Andrewes, *Hist.* x (1961) 3, n. 6).

71 (73)

Decree concerning the Priestess of Athena Nike:
424–3 B.C.

On the reverse of the stele which bears No. 44 (q.v.); now in EM.

ll. 1–6 (to κες) have developed Attic letters; the remainder, by a different hand, Ionic. Stoichedon 23. Phot.: Ἀρχ. Ἐφ. 1897, Pl. 11; Kern 14. *IG* i². 25; Meritt, *AJP* lvi (1935) 71; Wade-Gery, *Essays*, 209; Mattingly, *Hist.* x (1961) 169–71; Meritt and Wade-Gery, *JHS* lxxxiii (1963) 110 f.

> ἔδοχσεν τῆι βολῆι καὶ τῶι δέ-
> μοι, Αἰγεὶς ἐπρυτάνευε, Νεοκ-
> λείδες ἐγραμμάτευε, Ἁγνόδε-
> μος ἐπεστάτε, Καλλίας εἶπε· τ-
> 5   ῆι ἱερέαι τῆς Ἀθενάας τῆς Νί-
> κες [[Ͱ]] πεντήκοντα δραχμὰς τὰ-
> ς γεγραμμένας ἐν τῆι στήλ[ηι]
> ἀποδιδόναι τὸς κωλακρ[έτας],
> οἳ ἂν κωλακρετῶσι τô Θ[αργηλ]-
> 10   [ιῶ]νος μηνός, τῆι ἱερ[έαι τῆς Ἀ]-
> [θην]αίας τῆς Νίκη[ς....8....]

In l. 6 the first hand inscribed Ͱ, which was subsequently erased; the second hand spelt out the figure. For the punctuation in ll. 9–10 see Wilhelm, *Sitzb. Wien.* 217. 5 (1939) 63 f.

The earlier decree on the front face of the stone had specified that the priestess was to receive 50 dr. (a year). It seems that, if she was appointed in the early forties, as the earlier decree required (No. 44), her salary had not yet been paid or had been paid irregularly, or by different officials. Meritt and Wade-Gery (op. cit. 111) think it more probable that Myrrhine had been paid regularly from the beginning. 'The new decree plans something new about the cult (we can only guess what) and it begins with a recapitulation about something that will not be altered by the innovation.' This is a formally possible but rather forced interpretation. For Mattingly, who dates the earlier decree *c.* 427, there is no difficulty: 'As it [the temple] was being finished certain details about the priestess' salary were formally settled.' Still believing in the early forties as the context of the first decree we infer either that Myrrhine, for reasons we do not understand, had not yet been paid, or that she had been paid at a different time of the year. We also doubt whether the original text continued substantially further; on the front face the extant text has already reached an amendment, which does not seem to be of major importance.

'It [sc. the second decree] is doubtless consequent on the news of the treaty, being a renewal of *IG* i². 24 which itself was doubtless consequent on the news of the treaty with Artaxerxes' (Wade-Gery, *Essays* 209). This may be too confident, but the conjunction of treaty and decree is probably not coincidence. Kallias, the mover, may be the grandson of the Kallias who led the Athenian peace embassy to Susa in 450 or 449 (*PA* 7826).

The date is given by the secretary Neokleides (see No. 70, and Wade-Gery, *Essays* 208 f.).

72 (64)

Loans to the Athenian State from the Sacred Treasuries:
426–5 to 423–2 B.C.

Eighteen fragments, of which two are uninscribed, of a white marble stele, found on the Acropolis; now in EM, with the exception of *h* (ll. 108–23), which is lost. Reworking has removed four letter-spaces on the left and five or six on the right, and left bevelled edges.

Developed Attic writing, stoichedon; some irregularities must be assumed, but their extent and reason are in dispute. The aspirate sign is always omitted in the words ἐμέρα, ἕκαστος, and ἕνδεκα. Phot. of *d*, *i–p*: Meritt, *Calendar*, 6–24; of *q*: *Hesp.* iv (1935) 159; of parts of *b*: Pritchett, *Ancient Athenian Calendars*, Pl. 20, and *Hesp.* xxxiv, Pl. 57; of parts of *e* and *k*: *AJP* lxxxv (1964) 40. Facs. of all fragments except *q*: Meritt, *Calendar*, Pl. i; *AFD* Pl. xii.

Textual bibliography: *IG* i². 324+, 306. Modern study starts with Meritt, *The Athenian Calendar in the Fifth Century*. Meritt, *AFD* 128–51; Broneer, *Hesp.* iv (1935) 158 f. (fragment *q*); Meritt, *CQ* xl (1946) 60–4; *SEG* x. 227+; Pritchett and Neugebauer, *Calendars of Athens*, 94–105; Meritt, *Athenian Year*, 60–71; Pritchett, *Ancient Athenian Calendars on Stone* (Univ. Calif. Publ. Class. Arch. iv) 270–3, 290–312. Lang, *Hesp.* xxxiii (1964) 146–67; Pritchett, *Hesp.* xxxiv (1965) 131–47; Lang (with Meritt), *Hesp.* xxxiv (1965) 224–47; Lang and Meritt, *CQ* xviii (1968) 84–94.

[τάδε ἐλογίσαν]το hοι λογιστα[ὶ ἐν τοῖς τέτ]ταρσιν ἔτεσιν ἐκ Παναθεναίον
ἐς [Παναθέναια ὀφελ]-
[όμενα· τάδε hο]ι ταμίαι παρέδοσ[αν Ἀνδρο]κλês Φλυεὺς καὶ χουν-
άρχοντες hελλ[ενοταμίαις....]

[. . . . . 10 . . . . .]εῖ καὶ χσυνάρχοσι[ν στρατ]εγοῖς ℎιπποκράτει Χολαργεῖ
καὶ χσυ[νάρχοσιν ἐπὶ τῆς]
[Κεκροπίδο]ς πρυτανείας δευτέ[ρας πρυ]τανευόσες, τέτταρες ἐμέραι
ἔσαν ἐσελ[ελυθυίαι, ἐπὶ τε͂]-
5 [ς βολῆς ℎεῖ] Μεγακλείδες πρῶτο[ς ἐγραμ]μάτευε, ἐπὶ Εὐθύνο ἄρχοντος,
ΔΔ· τόκος τ[ούτοις ἐγένετο]
[ℙℾℍℙΔΔ]ΔΔΓ⊢· υ δευτέρα δόσις ἐπ[ὶ τῆς Κ]εκροπίδος δευτέρας
πρυτανευόσες, λοι[παὶ ἔσαν ℎεπτὰ ἐ]-
[μέραι] τε͂ι πρυτανείαι, ℙ· τόκος τ[ούτον υ] ΤΤΧℾℍℍℍℍℙΔΔ υ τρίτε
δόσις ἐπὶ τῆς Παν[διονίδος πρυτα]-
[νείας] τετάρτες πρυ[τ]ανευόσες, [ἐσελελ]υθυίας πέντε ἐμέρας τῆς
πρυτανείας, Δ[ΔℾΤΤΤℙℾℍΔΙΙΙⅭ· τ]-
[όκος τ]ούτον υ ΤΧℾℍℍΔΓ⊢⊢⊢⊢ΙΙ υ τ[ετάρτ]ε δόσις ἐπὶ τῆς Ἀκαμαντίδος πρυτανεία[ς ὀγδόες πρυταν]-
10 [ευόσ]ες, πέντε ἐμέρας ἐσελελυθ[υίας τε͂]ς πρυτανείας, ΔΔΔΔ[Τ]ΤΤΤ
ΧΧΧ· τόκος τούτο[ν υ ΤΧΧΧΧℾℍℍΙ υυ]
[πέμπ]τε δόσις ἐπὶ τῆς Ἀκαμαν[τίδος πρ]υτανείας ὀγδόες πρυτανευόσες
ἐσελελ[υθυίας δέκα ἐμέ]-
[ρας τ]ῆς πρυτανείας, ℍ· τόκος τ[ούτον υ]ΤΤΤℙℾℍℍℍℍΔΔΔ υ
ℎέκτε δόσις ἐπὶ τῆς Ἐρε[χθεῖδος πρυταν]-
[είας] δεκάτες πρυτανευόσε[ς, ἐσελελ]υθυίας ℎεπτὰ ἐμέρας τῆς πρυτανείας, ΔℾΤ[ΤΤΧΧΧ· τόκος τού]-
[τοις] ἐγένετο ΧΧΧΧℍℙΔΔΔ⊢⊢⟨⊢⟩[ΙΙ ΙΙ υ κεφ]άλαιον τὸ ἀρχαῖο ἀναλόματος ἐπὶ τῆς Ἀνδρ[οκλέος ἀρχῆς κα]-
15 [ὶ χσυ]ναρχόντον ℍℍℙ꜖Τℙℍ[ΔΙΙ ⅬⅭ υ τ]όκο κεφάλαιον τοῖ ἀργυρίοι
τοῖ ἀναλοθέντ[ι ἐπὶ τῆς Ἀνδροκ]-
[λέος] ἀρχῆς καὶ χσυναρχόντο[ν ΔΤℍ]ℙΔΔΔΔΓ⊢⊢⊢⊢ υυυυυ
τάδε παρέδοσαν ℎοι τα[μίαι Φοκιάδες ἐ]-
[χς Οἴ]ο καὶ χσυνάρχοντες, ἐπὶ Σ[τρα]τοκλέος ἄρχοντος καὶ ἐπὶ τῆς
βολῆς ℎεῖ Πλ[ειστίας πρῶτος υ]
[ἐγραμμ]άτευε, στρατεγοῖς περ[ὶ Πε]λοπόννεσον Δε[μ]οσθένει Ἀλκι-
σθένος Ἀφιδ[ναῖοι, ἐπὶ τῆς . . .]-
[εῖδος] πρυτανείας τετάρτες [πρυτα]νευόσες, τρίτει ἐ[μέ]ραι τῆς πρυτανείας ἐσ[ελελυθυίας, ἐχς]
20 [Ὀπισθ]οδόμο ΔΔΔ· τόκος τούτο[ις ἐγέ]νετο ℙℾℍℍℍℍΔυυ ℎετέρα
δόσις στρατεγοῖς [Νικίαι Νικεράτ]-
[ο Κυδα]ντίδει καὶ χσυνάρχο[σιν ἐπὶ] τῆς Πανδιονίδος πρυτανείας ἐνάτες
πρυτ[ανευόσες, πέμπτ]-

[ει καὶ] δεκάτει ἐμέραι τε͂ς π[ρυταν]είας ἐσελελυθυίας, Ⱶ[2]· τόκος τούτοις ἐγένε[το ΤΤΧΧΧ𐅅ΗΗΗ *vv*]
[κεφάλ]αιον τô ἀρχαίο ἀναλόμ[ατος] ἐπὶ τὲς Φοκιάδο ἀρχε͂ς καὶ χσυναρχόντον Ⱶ[⍋⍋⍋ *v* τόκο κεφάλα]-
[ιον τôι ἀ]ργυρίοι τôι ἀναλοθ[έντι] ἐπὶ τε͂ς Φοκιάδο ἀρχε͂ς καὶ χσυναρχόντον Τ[ΤΤΧΧΧ𐅅ΗΗΔ *vvvvv*]
[τάδε παρέδ]οσαν *h*οι ταμίαι Θ[οκυ]δίδες Ἀχερδόσιος καὶ χσυνάρχοντες, ἐπὶ Ἰσ[άρχο ἄρχοντος κα]-
[ὶ ἐπὶ τε͂ς βολε͂ς] *ḥ*[ε͂ι Ἐπί]λ[υ]κος [προ͂]τος ἐγραμμάτευε, *h*ελλενοταμίαις *h*ένοις Δ[.......14.......]
[...6...καὶ χσυνάρχοσι καὶ νέοις] Χαροπίδει Σκα[μβ]ονίδει καὶ χσυνάρχοσιν [ἐπὶ τε͂ς *h*ιπποθον]-
[τίδος πρυτανείας πρότες πρυταν]ευόσες, *h*έκτει καὶ εἰκοστε͂ι τε͂ς πρυτανεί[ας,......12......]
[..⍋⍋⍋ΤΤ𐅆𐅅ΗΗΗΗ𐅄ΔΔΔͰͰ· τόκος το]ύτοις ἐγένετο ΧΧΧΧ𐅅Η𐅄ΔΓI̮I̮I̮I *v* δευτέρα δ[όσις ἐπὶ τε͂ς ..5...]
[..........21...........πρυταν]ευόσες, δοδεκάτει τε͂ς πρυτανείας ⍋⍋ΤΤΤ[.......15........]
[..........21...........τρίτε δ]όσις ἐπὶ τε͂ς Ἐρεχθεΐδος πρυτανείας *h*ε[........16........]
[.............26.............]ḤΗ· τόκος τούτοις ἐγένετο 𐅅ΗΔΔͰͰIC *v* τε[τάρτε δόσις ἐπὶ τε͂ς]
[Ἀκαμαντίδος πρυτανείας ὀγδόες] πρυτανευόσες, τριακοστε͂ι τε͂ς πρυτα-ν[είας Ⱶ· τόκος...7....]
[........17.........κεφάλαιον] τô ἀρχαίο ἀναλόματος ἐπὶ τε͂ς Θοκυδίδο [ἀρχε͂ς καὶ χσυναρχόν]-
[τον Ⱶ𐅄⍋ΤΤΤ *v* κεφάλαιον τόκο τôι] ἀργυρίοι τôι ἀναλοθέντι ἐπὶ τε͂ς Θοκυδ[ίδο ἀρχε͂ς καὶ χσυναρ]-
[χόντον ΤΤ𐅆ΗΗΔ ....7.....τάδε παρ]έδοσαν *h*οι ταμίαι Τιμοκλε͂ς Εἰτεαῖος κ[αὶ χσυνάρχοντες, ἐπὶ]
[Ἀμενίο ἄρχοντος καὶ ἐπὶ τε͂ς βολ]ε͂ς *h*ε͂ι Δεμέτριος Κολλυτεὺς προ͂τος ἐγρ[αμμάτευε, ...9.....]
[...........22...........Μυρρ]ινοσίοι καὶ χσυνάρχοσι ἐπὶ τε͂ς Ἀκαμα[ντίδος πρυτανείας *vv*]
[πρότες πρυτανευόσες δοδεκάτε]ι τε͂ς πρυτανείας 𐅄𐅈ΤΤΤΤΧΧΧΧ𐅅ΗΗΔΔ τό[κος τούτοις ἐγένετον]
[ΧΧΧΧΗΗΔΔΔΔͰͰͰͰIIIII *v* δευτέρ]α δόσις ἐπὶ τε͂ς Πανδιονίδος πρυτανεί[ας τρίτες πρυτανευ*vv*]-

[ὅσες, δοδεκάτει τῆς πρυτανείας] ΤΤℙℙ· τόκος τούτοις ἐγένετο
ΗℙΔⱵⱵⱵⅢⅢ[Ι υ τρίτε δόσι]ς [ἐπὶ τε̑ υ]-
[ς...6...ῖδος πρυτανείας τετά]ρτες πρυτανεύοσες, τετάρτει τῆς
πρυτα[νείας, παρὰ] Σαμ[ίον ⊄Τ υ]
[ΧΧΧΗΗΗ· τόκος τούτοις ἐγένετο] ℙℙΔΔΔⱵⱵ υ τετάρτε δόσις ἐπὶ
τῆς Αἰαντ[ίδος πρυτ]ανεί[ας ὀγδό]-
[ες πρυτανεύοσες, τετάρτει καὶ] εἰκοστε̑ι τῆς πρυτανείας Ⱶ· τόκος
τούτο[ις ἐγέν]ετο ΧℙΗ[Ηυυυυ]
45 [πέμπτε δόσις ἐπὶ τῆς Λεοντίδο]ς πρυτανείας δεκάτες πρυτανεύοσες
τ[εῖ τρίτ]ει τῆς πρ[υτανεί]-
[ας ⊄ℙΤΤΤΗΔΔⱵⱵΙΙϹ· τόκος τούτον] ΗΔΔⱵⱵΙΙϹ υ κεφάλαιον τὸ
ἀρχαῖο ἀναλό[ματος] ἐπὶ τῆς Τι[μοκλέο]-
[ς ἀρχε̑ς καὶ χσυναρχόντον ΗℙⰛⰛ]ⰛⰛΤΤΧℙΗΔΔΔΔⱵⱵΙΙϹ υ κεφάλαιον τόκο τ[οῖς ἀ]ναλοθε̑σι χρ[έμασι υ]
[ἐπὶ τῆς Τιμοκλέος ἀρχε̑ς καὶ χσυ]ναρχόντον ΤℙΗΗΗΔⱵⱵϹ υ κεφά-
λαι[ον ἀν]αλόματος χσύ[μπαντ- υ]
[ος Ἀθεν]αίας ἐν τοῖ[ς] τέ[τταρσιν ἔ]τεσιν ἐκ Παναθεναίον ἐς Παν-
αθέν[αια ℙ̅͞³̅]ⱵⱵΗⰛⰛⰛⰛℙΤΤΧ[ΗΗℙⱵⱵυ]
50 [κεφά]λαιον τόκο χσύμπαν[τος Ἀθε]ναίας ἐν τοῖς τέτταρσιν ἔτεσιν
ἐ[κ Παν]αθεναίον ἐς Πα[ναθέν- υ]
[αια ⊄]ℙΤΤΤΧΧΧℙΗΗΗΗΔΔΔℙ[...5... τάδε] Ἀθεναίας Νίκες
ἐ[πὶ τε̑ς .....10.....]ς πρυτανείας [...6...]
[...πρ]υτανεύοσες, τετάρτε[ι τῆς πρυτα]νείας Τιμοκ[λε̑ς Εἰτεαῖος καὶ
χσυ]νάρχοντες πα[ρέδοσα]-
[ν ℙΤ· τόκος] τούτοις ἐ[γ]ένετο Η[------] vacat
[τάδε ἐλογίσα]ντο [hοι] λογιστ[αὶ ὀφελόμ]εν[α τοῖς ἄλλοις θεοῖς ἐν τοῖς
τέττ]αρσιν ἔτ[εσιν ἐκ Παν]-
55 [αθεναίον ἐς Παναθέν]αια.[τάδε παρέδοσ]αν h[οι ταμίαι τὸν ἄλλον θεὸν
Γόργο]ινος Ο[ἰνεῖδο Ἰκαρι]-
[εὺς καὶ χσυνάρχοντες ἐκ τὸν ἑκάστο χ]ρεμάτο[ν ἐπὶ Ἀμενίο ἄρχοντος
στρατ]εγοῖ[ς.....11......]
[....8...., ἐπὶ τῆς βολε̑ς hε̑ι Δεμέτρι]ος πρῶτ[ος ἐγραμμάτευε, ἐπὶ τε̑ς
Ἀκαμαντ]ίδ[ος πρυτανείας]
[πρότες πρυτανευόσες, hεκατομβαιῶ]νος ὀγ[δόει φθίνοντος, πέμπτει καὶ
εἰκοστε̑ι τῆς πρυτανε]-
[ίας ἐχς Ὀπισθοδόμο. υ Ἀρ]τέμι[δος Ἀγρ]οτέρα[ς.................
..40...................]

60 [.........18........., τό]κος τ[ούτο ΗΗ]Η𐅃Δ[...................
.....................42....................]
[.............29...............]Η, τό[κος τούτο.........18...
......] 𐅄 𐅃𐅄ΔΔ [......12......]
[.........17......... Ποσειδόν]ος ἐπὶ Σο[υνίοι 𐅄ΧΧ.....10.....,
τόκ]ος τούτο ΗΗΗ𐅄ΔΔ[....9.....]
[..........21..........., τόκο]s τούτο [...6... Ἀρτέμιδος Μουι-
χί]⟨α⟩σι ΤΧΧΧΧ𐅃𐅄ΗϹ, τό[κος τούτο]
[........................52...........................] ΗΗΔΔ
ΓΗ, τόκο[s το]ύτ[ο...6...]
65 [..4..]ο Χ𐅃ΗΗΗΗ𐅄ΔΔΓΗͰ[...................36.........
...] ΔͰͰͰͰͰΙΙΙΙ, τόκο[s το]ύτ[ο..5...]
[..4..]ΙΙϹ. Ἀφροδίτες ἐν ἱππολυ[τείοι ....24.............]
ͰͰͰͰΙΙΙΙϹ v Μοσ[ὸν 𐅃...., τόκο]-
[s τού]το ΓͰΙΙ v Ἀπόλλονος Ζοστῆ[ρος..........21...........
Ἀδρασ]τείας 𐅄ΔΔΔΓͰ, τ[όκος τούτο Ͱ]
[Βενδ]ῖδος 𐅄ΔΔΔΓͰ, τόκος τού[το Ͱ ....29........
.....] ΙϹϽ. v Ἀπόλλον[ος....8....]
[..4..] τούτο τόκος ΓͰͰͰ v[...................36...............
..] ἑρακλέος ἐν [Κυνοσάργε]-
70 [ι ΔΔ, τ]ούτο τόκος ΙϹ v ἑ[...........22...........Δεμ]οφόντος
[...6...], τόκος τούτ[ο....9.....]
[Ἀθενα]ί[ας ἐπὶ] Παλλ[ενίδι Τ𐅄ΗΗ....11......, τόκο]s τούτο ΗΔΔ
ΓͰͰͰͰΙΙΙϹϽ. v Ἀπόλλο[νος....8....]
[..........20.......... Ἀρτέμιδος Βραυρονία]s ΧΗΗΗ𐅄ΔΔΔΔΓ
ͰΙΙΙΙ, τόκος τούτο Δ[ΓͰ....10.....]
[....9.....]ΧΗΔ[.............24.............Ἀθ]εναίας ἐπὶ Παλλα-
δίοι Δεριονέοι [𐅃ΗΗΗ𐅄..5...]
[τόκος το]ύτο ΔͰ[.....11......Χ]𐅃Η[Η...8..., τό]κος τούτο
ΔΔϹ v Ποσειδόνος Καλαυρε[άτο..5...]
75 [τόκο]s τούτο [..4.. κεφάλαιον τ]ὸ ἀ[ρχαίο ἀναλό]ματος τὸν ἄλλον θεὸν
τῆς πρότες [δ]όσεο[s τῆς ἐπὶ]
[Γοργ]οίνο [ἄρχοντος 𐅂𐅂𐅂𐅄𐅃ΗΗ]ΗΗ[𐅄ΔΔΔΔ v κεφάλ]αιον τόκο
τούτοι τὸι ἀναλόματι ΧΧΗΔΔ[...7....]
[δευτ]έρ[αν δόσιν παρέδοσαν] ἑοι τα[μίαι τὸν ἄλ]λον θεὸν Γόργοινος
Οἰνείδο Ἰκαριεὺς [καὶ χσυν]-
[άρχοντες καθ' ἕκαστον θεὸν] ἀπὸ τὸ[ν χρεμάτον] ἐπὶ τῆς Λεοντίδος
πρυτανείας δεκάτε[s πρυταν]-

[εὐόσες, Σκιροφοριῶνος ὀγ]δόει φθ[ίνοντος, εἰ]κοστεῖ τês πρυτανείας v
                Ἀρτέμιδος Ἀγρ[οτέρας]

80 [ΤΤΤΤΧ⌐ΗΗΗΗ⌐, τόκος τοῦτο] ΔⱵⱵⱵⱵ||[||C v Ἀφροδί]τες ἐν
        Κέποις ΤΤ⌐Η⌐ΔΔΓ|, τόκος τοῦτο Γ⊢[ⱵⱵⱵ|||C]

[........16........ΧΧ[⌐Η]ΗΗΔΔΔΔ[...5..., τοῦτο] τόκος Ⱶ||C⊃ v
        Διονύσο ΗΗΗ⌐Γ⊢|, τόκος το[ῦτο |C v]

[.........19........., τ]όκος το[ῦτο..v Ποσε]ιδῶνος ἐπὶ Σουνίοι
        ΤΤΤΤΧ⌐ΔΔΓⱵⱵ|||C, τό[κος τοῦ]-

[το ΔⱵⱵⱵ||C⊃ v ..5... ΧΧ]ẌΧ⌐ΗΗΔΔ[ΔΔΓⱵⱵⱵ|||, τ]όκος
        τοῦτο ⱵⱵ|||C v Ἀρτέμιδος Μονιχίας[ι...6...]

[........17.........]⊢|| v Θεσέο[ς ⌐ΗΗΗΓⱵⱵⱵ|]|||C, τόκος τοῦτο
        ||C⊃ v hιλισô ΗΗΗΗⱵ⊢|, τόκ[ος τοῦτο]

85 [|C.......14......, τ]όκος τοῦ[το . v hεφαίσ]το ΤΧ⌐ΗΗΔΔΔΔΓ
        ⱵⱵⱵ, τόκος τοῦτο ⱵⱵⱵ|||C v Ἀφ[ροδίτε]-

[ς ἐν hιππολυτείοι..]⊢||, τόκο[ς τοῦτο ..5...] v Μοσôν ⌐²ΔΔⱵ, τόκος
        τοῦτο |C⊃ v θεô χσενικô [..5...]

[......13......, τόκο]ς τοῦτ[ο... v hερακλέ]ος ἐν Κυνοσάργει
        ⌐ΔΔΔ, τόκος τοῦτο C v Δεμο[φôντο]-

[ς ....17.........] v Ἀθε[ναίας ἐπὶ Παλλ]ενίδι ΧΧΧΗΗΗΗΔΓ
        ⱵⱵⱵ|, τόκος τοῦτο ⱵⱵ|||C v Ἀ[πόλλο]-

[νος.......15........τ]όκο[ς...6... v Ἀρτέ]μιδος Βραυρονίας ΗΗΗ
        ⌐ⱵⱵⱵ|C, τόκος τοῦτο |[C v ...]

90 [..................34.................]⊃ v Ἀθεναίας ἐπὶ Παλλα-
        δίοι ⱵⱵ|C, τόκος τοῦτ[ο ..4..]

[................30.............ΗΔΔΔ]ΔⱵⱵⱵⱵ|||, τόκος τοῦτο
        C v Μετρὸς ἐν Ἀγρας ΗΗ[...6...]

[................35.............]⊢Ⱶ, τοῦτο τόκος C v Ἀθε-
        ναίας Ζοστερίας Η[...7...]

[................30.............ΗΗΗΗ]ΔΔΓⱵⱵ, τόκος τοῦτο |C
        vvv κεφάλαιον τô ἀρχ[αίο ἀνα]-

[λόματος τôν ἄλλον θεôν τês δευ]τέρ[ας δόσε]ος ἐπὶ Γοργοίνο ἄρχοντος
        v ⟨⟩⟨⟩ΤΤΤ⌐⌐ΗΗΗΗ[⌐ΔΔΔΔ]-

95 [ΓⱵⱵⱵ vvvv κεφάλαιον τόκο τού]τοι [τôι ἀργ]υρίοι ⌐ΔΔΔⱵⱵvv
        κεφάλαιον ἀναλόματος τô ἀ[ρχαίο]

[ἐπὶ Γοργοίνο ἄρχοντος v ⌐ΤΤ]ΤΤ⌐[⌐ΙΗΗΗ]⌐ΔΔΔΓⱵⱵⱵ vvv
        κεφάλαιον τόκο χσύμπαντος το[ύτοι]

[τôι ἀργυρίοι ΧΧΗΗ - -] vacat

[τάδε ἐλογίσαντο ℎοι λογιστ]αὶ ἐν τ[οῖς τέτ]ταρσιν ἔτεσιν τόκον τοῖς τε͂ς
θεο͂ ℎὰ ℎοι πρό[τεροι]

[λογισταὶ λελογισμένα παρέ]δοσαν [ἐν τοῖς ℎε]πτὰ ἔτεσιν τόκον τετρα-
κισχιλίοις ταλά[ντοις]

100 [ταλάντοι τετρακισχιλίαι]ς πεντα[κοσίαις εἴ]κοσι δυοῖν δραχμαῖν·
τούτοις τόκος ἐγέ[νετο]

[ⵂⵀ𐅅𐄂𐄂𐄂𐄂𐅅Χ𐅆ΗΗΔⵏⵏⵏΙΙΙ] vacat

[τόκον ἐλογίσαντο τοῖς ἄλ]λοις θεο[ῖς ἐν τοῖς τέ]τ̇ταρσιν ἔτεσιν ℎὰ
ℎοι πρότεροι λογι[σταὶ]

[λελογισμένα παρέδοσαν ἐ]ν τοῖς ℎεπ[τὰ ἔτεσιν πε]ντακοσίοις ταλάντοις
διακοσίοις τ[αλάντ]-

[οις ℎεχσέκοντα ταλάντοι]ς ℎὲχς ταλ[άντοις χιλί]αις ἐνενέκοντα δραχμαῖς
πέντε δραχ[μαῖς]

105 [τέτταρσι δραχμαῖς ἐν τοῖ]ς τέτταρσ[ιν ἔτεσιν 𐅄]𐄂𐄂𐅆ΤΤΧΧΗΗΗΔΔ
Δ𐅆ⵏⵏⵏΙⅭ vacat

[τόκον ἐλογίσαντο καὶ τοῖ]ς Ἀθεναία[ς τε͂ς Νίκες ἐ]ν τοῖς τέτταρσιν
ἔτεσιν ℎὰ ℎοι πρότ[εροι]

[λογισταὶ λελογισμένα π]αρέδοσαν ἐ[ν τοῖς ℎεπτὰ] ἔτεσιν εἴκοσι ταλάντοις δυοῖν ταλ[άντο]-

[ιν τρισχιλίαις ἐνενέκον]τα δραχμ[αῖς] ὀκτὸ [δραχ]μαῖς δυοῖν ὀβολοῖν
Τ𐅆ⵀ𐄐ΔΔΔⵏⵏΙΙ[ΙΙΙ vacat]

[τόκον ἐλογίσαντο τοῖς τὸ] ℎερμο͂ ἐν [τοῖ]ς τέτ[ταρσι]ν ἔτεσιν ℎὰ ℎοι
πρότεροι λογισταὶ λ[ελογι]-

110 [σμένα παρέδοσαν ἐν τοῖς ℎε]π[τὰ ἔ]τ[εσι]ν ταλάν[τοι τ]ετρακοσίαις
ἐνενέκοντα δραχμαῖς [. . 5 . . .]

[- - - ΗΗΗΔ𐅆ⵏ - -] vacat

[Ἀθεναίας Νίκες ἀρχαῖον ὀφέλοσιν ἐν] ἕνδεκα ἔτεσιν ⦂⟨𐄂𐄂⟩𐅆ΤΤΤΧΧ
Χ𐅆ΔΔΔΔ𐅂ⵏⵏΙΙ vacat

[Ἀθεναίαι Νίκει τόκος ἐγένετο⦂𐅆. . .]ΔΔΔⵏΙⅭ vacat

[Ἀθεναίας Πολιάδος ἐν ἕνδεκα ἔτεσιν] τὸ ἀρχαῖον [ὀ]φέλοσιν⦂ 𐅇 𐅇 𐅇 𐅇
𐅆ΗΗ𐄂𐄂𐄂𐄂𐅆ΤΤΤ𐅆𐅆Η[Η𐅅ΔΔ𐅂]

115 [Ἀθεναίας Πολιάδος τόκος ἐγένετο ἐν] ἕνδεκα ἔτεσ[ιν⦂]𐅇ΗΗ𐄂𐄂𐄂𐄂
ΤΤΤΧΧΧ𐅆ΗΗΗ ⵏⵏⵏⵏ vacat

[ἐν ἕνδεκα ἔτεσιν Ἀθεναίας Νίκες καὶ] Πολιάδος⦂ [𐅇 𐅇 𐅇 𐅇]𐅆ΗΗ
𐅆⟨𐄂⟩𐅆ΤΤΧΧΧΗΗ[ΗΔΔⵏⵏΙΙ]

[ἐν ἕνδεκα ἔτεσιν κεφάλαιον τὸ Πολιά]δος καὶ Νίκ[ες τόκ]ο ⦂ 𐅇ΗΗ
𐄂𐄂𐄂𐄂𐅆ΤΤΤ[- - -]

[- - - - *vacat*] *vacat*

[τοῖς ἄλλοις θεοῖς ἀναλόματος τὸ ἀρχ]αῖο ἐν ἔνδεκα [ἔτεσιν κεφάλαιον :

ΓΗΗΗΗ૪૪ΤΧΡΔΔΔΓΗΗ]

120 [τοῖς ἄλλοις θεοῖς τόκο χσύμπαντος ἐ]ν ἔνδεκα ἔτεσ[ιν κεφάλαιον :

- - - - - -]

[- - - - *vacat*] *vacat*

[ἀρχαῖον χσύμπαν ἐν ἔνδεκα ἔτεσιν ἅπ]ασι τοῖς θε[οῖς : ΡΓΗΡ૪૪૪

૪ΓΤΤΤΤΧΧΧΧΓΗΗΗΗ - -]

[τόκο χσύμπαντος ἅπασι τοῖς θεοῖς ἐν] ἔνδεκα ἔτεσ[ιν κεφάλαιον :

- - - - - - - -]

[- - - -] *vacat*

The reconstruction of the text in Meritt, *Calendar*, 'a veritable triumph of acumen and industry' (Tod), remains fundamental to Pritchett and Lang, despite their divergent approaches, and to this slightly more conservative text. In l. 8 the restoration of the total is, as the record stands, necessary, and follows from the year-total of l. 15 and the quadrennium-total of l. 49; it is not, however, in conformity with the interest recorded in l. 9, which seems to have been calculated on a sum 2,000 dr. smaller. (Lang, *Hesp.* xxxiv (1965) 227–9, suggests recasting these items on the assumption that the interest figure in l. 46 was wrongly added into the total for 423–2 (l. 47), but that this error was not transferred to the total for the quadrennium (l. 49) or for the eleven years (ll. 114, 116, 122). The true total for 423–2 would then be 192 T. 1,520 dr., and the quadrennium total should be assumed to have stood on the stone as ΓΗΗΗ૪૪ ૪૪ΓΤΤΧ[ΗΡΔΔΔΓ]. The total for 426–5 will then have been ΗΗΡ ૪ΤΡΓΗ[ΡΔΓ] (l. 15), and the payment in l. 8 ૪[૪ΓΤΤΤΡΓΗΡ ΔΓ], the interest again being calculated on a figure too small by 2,000 dr.) In l. 10 ἐσελελυθ[υίας] is a possible alternative. The restorations in ll. 10 and 14 are interlocking. The spacing justifies Lang's correction in l. 14; Meritt wrote ΤΧΧΧΧΓΗΗΗΗ in l. 10 and ΧΧΧΧΗΡΔΔΗΗ|ΙΙΙ in l. 14. In ll. 18–19 the alternatives are Αἰγεῖδος and Οἰνεῖδος; Οἰνεῖδος would be eliminated, if it held the second prytany this year as *ATL*'s view of No. 69 demands (see pp. 194 f.). In ll. 21–2 Pritchett (*Calendars of Athens*, 102) prefers ὀγδόν|ει and ΤΤΧΧΧΓΗΗΔΔΔ, with slight crowding at the end of l. 22. This seems a shade less satisfactory (cf. Meritt, *Athenian Year*, 68). The uncertainty has repercussions: it affects the total of interest in Year 2 (l. 24) and thus that in Year 3 (l. 36; cf. l. 51), with consequences on the dates of individual payments in Year 3. Meritt wrote πέμπτ|ει, but ΤΤΧΧΧΓΗ ΗΗΡΔ, with appropriate consequences; this is only a possibility if Year 2 had 368 days (see commentary). The same applies to ll. 28–9, where Meritt read [στρατεγοῖς ἐς | τὰ ἐπὶ Θράικες ૪૪૪ΤΤΤΓΗΡ. We follow Pritchett and Lang (1964) on the figure; Pritchett suggests ἐχς Ὀπισθοδόν|μο before it. Meritt and Lang now prefer [ἐχς Ὀπισθοδόμ|ο ૪૪૪ΤΤΡΓΗΗΗΗ ΡΔΔΔΗΗΙΙ]. In l. 30 the prytany was the third (Meritt, Pritchett) or

the fourth (Lang); in view of the uncertainty, we suppress the restorations.
In l. 31 the prytany was the sixth (Lang) or seventh (Meritt, Pritchett).
Again we suppress the restorations, which in this case involve a difference
of reading. Though the last figure of the payment has always been read as
Η since Rangabé and Ross (cf. Meritt, *Calendar*, 27, *Hesp*. xxxiv (1965)
236–9), Pritchett has argued for the possibility of ⊔ (*Ancient Athenian
Calendars*, 270–3). In ll. 33–4 the figure to be restored is close to 1½ T.,
but there is some doubt about the introductory formula, and we prefer
to make no restoration. In l. 36 our partial restoration depends on following Lang in ll. 21–2; if one follows Pritchett there, this figure must
be 60 dr. higher. For ll. 37–8 Wade-Gery (*CQ* xxiv (1930) 33–9) suggested
[στρατεγου|ῖς ἐπὶ Ἰονίας (or ἐς Σκιόνεν) Εὐρυμέδοντι], and has been fol-
lowed, with variations, by Meritt and Lang; see, however, Gomme, *HCT*
iii. 627 f., Lewis, *JHS* lxxxi (1961) 119. In ll. 40–1 the first interest figure
may be ½ ob. smaller and the second ½ ob. larger. Ll. 41–2: if one fills out
l. 41 τῆς, as would seem more natural, 11 letters are left for the tribe in
prytany, yet the two possibilities, Ἀκαμαντίδος and Πανδιονίδος, are al-
ready accounted for (ll. 38–40). To explain the break τῆυ|ς, Lang follows
a suggestion of Meritt that the edge of the stone was damaged in ll. 37–51,
and the irregularities of line-ending which seem to be necessary are thereby
explained. The situation is complicated by the tempting possibility that
the payment of ll. 51–3 belongs to the same day, but there again the tribe
has 11 letters. Pritchett prefers to assume that a 10-letter tribe was written
in 11 spaces in l. 42, as Meritt had already assumed for l. 52. Lang (1964)
discounted l. 52 and wrote [Πανδιονίδος] and [τρίνυ|τες] there. There
are perhaps still other possibilities. The wrong tribe-name may have been
written in error (cf. *IG* ii². 1672. 1, 37 and *BSA* xlix (1954) 32), or we might
write [|C νυ τρίτε δό]σ[ις ἐπὶ τ|ῆς..5...ίδος]. In l. 42 πρὸς] Σαμ[ίος is epi-
graphically possible. For ll. 46–9 see above on l. 8. Ll. 51–3: see on ll. 41–2;
the uncertainty of date makes the interest uncertain. The figure in l. 51 is
underlined on the stone. In ll. 55–6 Meritt (*AFD* 132) restores Νικίαι καὶ
χσ|υνάρχοσι, comparing Thuc. iv. 129. 2. In l. 58 the restoration of the date
by month is sound, despite Pritchett, *AJP* lxxxv (1964) 46–8. For the
demonstration that the payments were outstanding for 342 days see Lang
(1965) 231–4. In l. 63 we prefer our reading to Meritt's Μονιχί⟨α⟩ς ⟨Τ⟩Τ,
as requiring the assumption of less error, but the crossbar was certainly
omitted from the alpha, and where there is one error, there may well be
two (cf. l. 83). In l. 79 the theta has been lost since it was seen by Rangabé
and Velsen, and the phi never received its vertical; however, the doubts
about reading and restoration expressed by Pritchett (*AJP* lxxxv (1964)
40–50) are unjustified (cf. Meritt, *AJP* lxxxv (1964) 412–16). New restorations in ll. 91, 93 are by Pritchett (*Ancient Athenian Calendars*, 306). For
ll. 98–123 we have in general followed Meritt, *CQ* xl (1946) 60–4 and Meritt
and Lang (1968), though one cannot place conviction in the literal accuracy
of the summation-formulae and we have not made the changes in ll. 114,
116, 122 which follow from their revised view of the true total for 423–2.
In l. 105 we prefer our restoration to Kubicki's π|έντε ὀβολοῖς τόκον and
Meritt's τέτταροιν ὀβολοῖς, as giving a more accurate calculation; we have

made consequential minor changes in, ll. 110–11, 119, 122. In ll. 112 and 116 the vertical stroke of Ϙ is three times omitted; more seriously, it appears that in l. 112 the ⊓ is a mistake for ⊿, committed by the auditors themselves and transferred to the totals in l. 116 and (doubtless) in 122 (cf. Meritt, *Calendar*, 49 f.). There is a minor difficulty about the text of l. 113, where the stone is lost; Meritt and Lang now prefer Dodwell's reading Δ Δ Δ ⊓ ΙΙC to that of Gell printed here.

This text falls into the following sections:

I. Ll. 1–2. Heading of the whole document, which was drawn up by the λογισταί, for whom cf. Nos. 39, 58.

II. Ll. 2–51. Loans from Athena Polias in four successive 'conciliar' years, with interest reckoned to the close of the quadrennium.

Lines	Year	Number of loans	Total loans	Interest due
2–16	426–5	6	261 T. 5,610$\frac{7}{12}$ dr.	11 T. 199$\frac{1}{8}$ dr.
16–24	425–4	2	130 T.	[3 T. 3,710 dr.]
25–36	424–3	4	163 T.	[2 T. 5,210+dr.]
36–48	423–2	5	192 T. 1,642$\frac{5}{12}$ dr.	1 T. 813$\frac{1}{4}$ dr.
48–51	Quadrennium	17	747 T. 1,253 dr.	18 T. 3,935+dr.

III. Ll. 51–3. Loan in 423–2 from Athena Nike, 6 T.; interest 100+dr.

IV. Ll. 54–97. Two loans in 423–2 from the Other Gods, amounting to 54 T. 5,988 dr.; interest, over 2,200 dr. The share of each individual god is recorded, together with the interest due in respect of it. The order of the gods is the same in both loans (Meritt, *Calendar*, 22).

V. Ll. 98–111. Interest due for the quadrennium, 426–5 to 423–2, on loans made during the years 433–426.

Lines	Lender	Loan	Interest
98–101	Athena Polias	4,001 T. 4,522 dr.	[195 T. 1,713$\frac{1}{2}$ dr.]
102–5	Other Gods	766 T. 1,09[9] dr.	37 T. 2,338$\frac{5}{12}$ dr.
106–8	Athena Nike	22 T. 3,098$\frac{1}{2}$ dr.	1 T. 592$\frac{5}{8}$ dr.
109–11	Hermes	1 T. 490(?+) dr.	[316 (?+) dr.]

VI. Ll. 112–23. Totals for eleven years, 433–2 to 423–2.

Lines	Lender	Loan	Interest
112–13	Athena Nike	28 T. 3,548$\frac{1}{3}$ dr.*	At least 5 T. 31$\frac{5}{12}$ dr.
114–15	Athena Polias	4,748 T. 5,775 dr.	1,243 T. 3,804 dr.
116–17	Nike and Polias	4,777 T. 3,323$\frac{1}{4}$ dr.*	1,248–1,250 T.
119–20	Other Gods	821 T. 1,08[7] dr.	?
122–3	Grand total	5,599 T. 4,900(?) dr.*	?

The asterisked items are all 450 dr. too high; see end of critical note. As the funds of Hermes were apparently administered by the treasurers of Athena and not by those of the Other Gods (*IG* i². 301. 12, 69; cf. Wade-Gery, *Num. Chron.* 1930, 37), we may suppose that the loan from Hermes was not reckoned with those from the Other Gods, but was included in the grand total.

In these accounts the following points call for notice.

1. Interest is reckoned at the rate of one drachma *per diem* for 5 T. i.e. slightly over 1⅙ per cent per annum. One must not, however, expect all calculations to work out completely accurately. Meritt and Pritchett have assumed various forms of fractional approximation to account for minor divergences; Miss Lang has made a promising start in showing how the calculations could have been made with an abacus, which is *a priori* most probable. The charging of interest is more probably to be attributed to normal practice or piety than interpreted as a means of restraint (against Gomme, *HCT* ii. 435). The interest is very small; before this quadrennium it seems to have been five times as high (Wade-Gery, *CR* xliv (1930) 163–5; West, *TAPA* lxi (1930) 234 f.).

2. The accounts are based on the 'conciliar' year, a year approximating to the solar year and beginning somewhere near the summer solstice. The four years of our quadrennium, it is agreed, comprised 1,464 days. Meritt long maintained that the four years could not have had precisely 366 days each. This was denied by Pritchett and Neugebauer, and Lang has also found it possible to make restorations on a basis of equal years. However, the argument of Meritt (*Athenian Year*, 202–7) that some conciliar years between 422 and 411 did not have 366 days still seems powerful. These conciliar years were divided into ten prytanies of 37 or 36 days. Pritchett and Neugebauer have, comparing Arist. Ἀθ. Πολ. 43. 2, maintained that the first six prytanies always had 37 days and the last four 36; Meritt and Lang have argued against this view. Two other types of year must be distinguished: the civil or 'festival' year beginning on Hekatombaion 1, lunar in character, with 12 or 13 months of 29 or 30 days; and the year which ran 'from Panathenaia to Panathenaia' (ll. 1, 54), i.e. from Hekatombaion 28 in one festival year to Hekatombaion 27 in the next; this was the term of office of the treasurers of Athena and the treasurers of the Other Gods (No. 58A, l. 28) and probably of the *hellenotamiai*. Athenian terminology is, however, loose; our quadrennium, though really comprising the conciliar years 426–422, is sometimes equated with the corresponding Panathenaic quadrennium (ll. 1, 49, 50), and the archon-years are equated with the conciliar years (e.g. ll. 5, 17, 25, 37). Less readily intelligible to us is the way in which loans appear to be attributed to the treasurers who held

office for the greater part of a conciliar year, even though they fell
before the Panathenaia and should have been made by their pre-
decessors (ll. 25–9, 55–9), but the fact seems inescapable.

3. The dates of the loans here registered are expressed in terms of
the conciliar year, i.e. by the name of the tribe in prytany, its number
in the year, and the day of the prytany. Only in the records of the
Other Gods is the date by the festival calendar added (ll. 58, 79;
cf. Notopoulos, *AJP* lxvi (1945) 411–14, who explains this as a concession to rural conservatism, and No. 81).

4. Only in a few cases is the purpose of the loan expressly indicated
in this record. Hippokrates and his colleagues (l. 3) received 20 T.
in the late summer of 426, possibly for an invasion of Megaris (cf.
Thuc. iv. 66); the old view that it can be inferred that Hippokrates
was in some sense 'chairman' of the board of generals is untenable
(Dover, *JHS* lxxx (1960) 66; Lewis, *JHS* lxxxi (1961) 120). In the
autumn of 425 a sum of 30 T. was paid στρατεγοῖς [is this an error for
στρατεγōι?] περὶ Πελοπόννεσον Δεμοσθένει (l. 18), probably for the
consolidation of the position at Pylos. Some precision, now lost, was
added in ll. 28–9, 37–8; these may relate to the destination of the
loan or to its source (cf. ἐχς | ’Οπισθ]οδόμο, ll. 19–20, and [παρὰ]
Σαμ[ίον, l. 42, for which cf. Nos. 68, l. 21 and 77, l. 18). Other associa-
tions of loans with operations recorded by Thucydides may be guessed
at (cf. Wade-Gery, *CQ* xxiv (1930) 33–9 for the year 423). We call
attention to the important notes by Gomme, *HCT* ii. 433–6, iii. 487 f.,
504 f., 592 f., 627 f., 630.

5. One group of payments calls for special comment. Every spring
during the quadrennium the treasurers of Athena paid out 100 T.
(ll. 12, 22, 33, 44). These payments should roughly coincide with the
Dionysia, the time of the year when tribute came in (No. 39) and
when one would expect the *hellenotamiai* to be in no need of loans.
It was held by Gomme (*HCT* ii. 433 f.) that this undermined what
would seem to be the obvious and natural view of Athenian war
finance, that the Athenians spent all their income as it came in, and
only borrowed from the gods the amount necessary to make up the
deficit, i.e. that total Athenian expenditure was simply the sum of the
total Athenian income (whatever that was) and the loans before us.
He was led to develop a theory by which the Athenians will have
spent only a previously earmarked part of the tribute directly, and
paid the remainder into Athena's treasury, borrowing it again when
necessary and charging themselves with interest on it. This view seems
to us untenable. Our inscription has no trace of repayments, which
these payments to Athena would surely have been, and one would
expect these 100 T. payments to be less regular in amount and date
and later in the campaigning season. We prefer the simple view,

supposing only that Athena regularly made a token 100 T. contribution to the war at the beginning of the campaigning season.

6. We learn from ll. 98–111 that in the years 433–426 the Athenians
had borrowed over 4,001 T. from Athena Polias and over 766 T.
from the Other Gods, besides 24 T. or so from Athena Nike and
Hermes. Simple division by seven will tell us that the average annual
drain on the reserve in this period ran well over three times higher
than in the quadrennium 426–422, but we can go a stage further
than that. Inspection of the interest figure in l. 115 shows that the
weight of the borrowing must be placed before the midpoint of the
seven years, and mainly in the years 432–429 (West, *TAPA* lxi (1930)
234–6; *ATL* iii. 341–4). We give *ATL*'s table of loans for 433–422,
without claiming literal accuracy for it.

433–2	76 T. (Cf. No. 61)	427–6	100 T.
432–1	1,145	426–5	261
431–0	1,370 (Cf. *SEG* x. 226)	425–4	130
430–29	1,300	424–3	163
429–8	600	423–2	253
428–7	200		

Some uncertainty is introduced by the loss of the interest figure for
the Other Gods. The computation assumes that the reduction of
interest (see above) was precisely at the beginning of 426–5; if it
was earlier, the weight of the loans must be pushed back further still.
The financial worries referred to in Thuc. ii. 70. 2, iii. 19. 1 are thus
amply attested.

The evidence for the drain on the reserve can be pursued with
greater uncertainties into an investigation of the size of the reserve
at various times, and in particular at the Peace of Nikias, which lies
beyond our immediate scope. *ATL* iii. 326–48 and Gomme, *HCT* iii.
687–9 will be found the most helpful introductions to the problems.

73 (74)

Athenian Decree regulating the Offering of First-fruits at Eleusis: (?) *c.* 422 B.C.

Complete marble stele found near the church of S. Zacharias at Eleusis,
and a small fragment of the Athenian copy (cf. lines 51–2) found in the
Plaka area north of the Acropolis; both now in EM.

Developed Attic writing, stoichedon (fifty letters to the line, with occa-
sional irregularities); the aspirate sign is omitted eight times (lines 3, 15, 18,
20, 24, 31, 32, 47). Phot. of the Athens fragment: *Jahresh.* vi (1903) 10.

LGS ii. 4+; *IG* i². 76+; *SEG* x. 110+; Guillon, *BCH* lxxxvi (1962)
467-75.

[Τιμο]τέλ[ε]ς Ἀχαρνε[ὺς] ἐγραμμάτευε.
[ἔδοχσ]εν τῆι βολῆι καὶ τῶι δέμοι, Κεκροπὶς ἐπρυτάνευε, Τιμοτέ-
[λες ἐ]γραμμάτευε, Κυκνέας ἐπεστάτε· τάδε οἱ χσυγγραφῆς χσυνέ-
[γρ]αφσαν· ἀπάρχεσθαι τοῖν θεοῖν τὸ καρπὸ κατὰ τὰ πάτρια καὶ τὲ
5 ν μαντείαν τὲν ἐγ Δελφῶν Ἀθεναίος ἀπὸ τὸν ἑκατὸν μεδίμνον [κ]-
ριθῶν μὲ ἔλαττον ἒ ἑκτέα, πυρῶν δὲ ἀπὸ τὸν ἑκατὸν μεδίμνον μ-
ὲ ἔλαττον ἡμιέκτεον· ἐὰν δέ τις πλείο καρπὸν ποιῆι ἒ τ[οσοῦτο]-
ν ἒ ὀλείζο, κατὰ τὸν αὐτὸν λόγον ἀπάρχεσθαι. ἐγλέγεν δὲ [τὸς δ]εμ-
άρχος κατὰ τὸς δέμος καὶ παραδιδόναι τοῖς ἱεροποιοῖς τοῖς
10 Ἐλευσινόθεν Ἐλευσινάδε. οἰκοδομέσαι δὲ σιρὸς τρῆς Ἐλευσῖν-
ι κατὰ τὰ πάτρια ηόπο ἂν δοκεῖ τοῖς ἱεροποιοῖς καὶ τῶι ἀρ[χ]ιτ-
έκτονι ἐπιτέδειον ἔναι ἀπὸ τὸ ἀργυρίο τὸ τοῖν θεοῖν. τὸ[ν δὲ κα]-
ρπὸν ἐνθαυθοῖ ἐμβάλλεν ηὸν ἂν παραλάβοσι παρὰ τὸν δεμάρ[χον],
ἀπάρχεσθαι δὲ καὶ τὸς χσυμμάχος κατὰ ταὐτά. τὰς δὲ πόλες [ἐγ]λ[ο]-
15 γέας ηελέσθαι τὸ καρπὸ, καθότι ἂν δοκεῖ αὐτέσι ἄριστα ὁ καρπὸ-
[ς] ἐγλεγέσεσθαι· ἐπειδὰν δὲ ἐγλεχθεῖ, ἀποπεμφσάντον Ἀθέναζε·
τὸς δὲ ἀγαγόντας παραδιδόναι τοῖς ἱεροποιοῖς τοῖς Ἐλευσινόθεν Ἐλευσινάδε. ἐ[ὰ]ν δὲ μὲ παραδέχσονται πέντε ἑμερῶν νννν
ἐπειδὰν ἐπαγγελεῖ, παραδιδόντον τὸν ἐκ τὲς πόλεος ηόθεν ἂν [ἒ]-
20 [ι] ὁ κα[ρπ]ός, εὐθυνόσθον ηοι ἱεροποιοὶ χιλίαισιν ͵υ δραχμέσι [η]-
[έκασ]τος· καὶ παρὰ τὸν δεμάρχον κατὰ ταὐτὰ παραδέχεσθαι. [κέρ]υ-
[κα]ς δὲ ηελομένε ηε βολὲ πεμφσάτο ἐς τὰς πόλες ἀ[γ]γέλλον[τ]ας [τὰ]
[νῦν] ηεφσεφισμένα τῶι δέμοι, τὸ μὲν νῦν ἔναι ηος τάχιστα, τὸ δὲ [λ]-
οιπὸν ηόταν δοκεῖ αὐτεῖ. κελευέτο δὲ καὶ ηο ηιεροφάντες καὶ [ὁ]
25 δαιδὸχος μυστερίοις ἀπάρχεσθαι τὸς ηέλλενας τὸ καρπὸ κατὰ
τὰ πάτρια καὶ τὲν μαντείαν τὲν ἐγ Δελφῶν. ἀναγράφσαντες δὲ ἐ[μ]
πινακίοι τὸ μέτρον τὸ καρπὸ τὸ τε παρὰ τὸν δεμάρχον κατὰ τὸ[ν δ]-
[έ]μον ηέκαστον καὶ τὸ παρὰ τὸν πόλεον κατὰ τὲν πόλιν ηεκάσ[τεν]
[κ]αταθέντον ἔν τε τῶι Ἐλευσινίοι Ἐλευσῖνι καὶ ἐν τῶι βολ[ευτ]ε-
30 [ρ]ίοι. ἐπαγγέλλεν δὲ τὲν βολὲν καὶ τῆσι ἄλλεσι πόλεσιν [τ]ε͂[σι] ηε-
[λ]λενικε͂σιν ἁπάσεσι, ηόποι ἂν δοκεῖ αὐτεῖ δυνατὸν ἔναι, λ[έγο]ν-
τας μὲν κατὰ ηὰ Ἀθεναῖοι ἀπάρχονται καὶ οἱ χσύμμαχοι, ἐκέ[νοι]-
[ς] δὲ μὲ ἐπιτάττοντας, κελεύοντας δὲ ἀπάρχεσθαι, ἐὰν βόλονται,
[κ]ατὰ τὰ πάτρια καὶ τὲν μαντείαν τὲν ἐγ Δελφῶν. παραδέχεσθαι δ-
35 ὲ καὶ παρὰ τούτον τὸν πόλεον ἐάν τις ἀπάγει τὸς ηιεροποιὸς κα-

τὰ ταὐτά. θύεν δὲ ἀπὸ μὲν τὸ πελανὸ καθότι ἂν Εὐμολπίδαι [ἐχσηϵ]-
[γὸ]νται, τρίττοιαν δὲ βόαρχον χρυσόκερον τοῖν θεοῖν hεκα[τέρ]-
[αι ἀ]πὸ τὸν κριθὸν καὶ τὸν πυρὸν καὶ τὸι Τριπτολέμοι καὶ τὸι [θε]-
ὸι καὶ τε͂ι θεᾶι καὶ τὸι Εὐβόλοι hιερεῖον hεκάστοι τέλεον καὶ
40 τε͂ι Ἀθεναίαι βο͂ν χρυσόκερον· τὰς δὲ ἄλλας κριθὰς καὶ πυρὸς ἀπ-
οδομένος τὸς hιεροποιὸς μετὰ τε͂ς βολε͂ς ἀναθέματα ἀνατιθέν-
αι τοῖν θεοῖν, ποιεσαμένος hάττ᾽ ἂν τὸι δέμοι τὸι Ἀθεναίον δοκε͂-
ι, καὶ ἐπιγράφεν τοῖς ἀναθέμασιν, hότι ἀπὸ τὸ καρπὸ τε͂ς ἀπαρχε͂-
ς ἀνεθέθε, καὶ hελλένον τὸν ἀπαρχόμενον· [τοῖ]ς δὲ ταῦτα ποιο͂σι
45 πολλὰ ἀγαθὰ ε͂ναι καὶ εὐκαρπίαν καὶ πολυκαρπία[ν, hοί]τινες ἂν
[μ]ὲ ἀδικο͂σι Ἀθεναίος μεδὲ τὲν πόλιν τὲν Ἀθεναίον μεδὲ τὸ θεό. v

[Λ]άμπον εἶπε· τὰ μὲν ἄλλα καθάπερ αἱ χσυγγραφαὶ τε͂ς ἀπαρχε͂ς τὸ
καρπὸ τοῖν θεοῖν· τὰς δὲ χσυγγραφὰς καὶ τὸ φσέφισμα τόδε ἀναγ-
ραφσάτο hο γραμματεὺς hο τε͂ς βολε͂ς ἐν στέλαιν δυοῖν λιθίναι-
50 ν καὶ καταθέτο τὲν μὲν Ἐλευσῖνι ἐν τὸι hιερο͂ι, τὲν δὲ hετέραν [ἐ]-
μ πόλει· hοι δὲ πολεταὶ ἀπομισθοσάντον τὸ στέλα· hοι δὲ κολ[ακρ]-
έται δόντον τὸ ἀργύριον. ταῦτα μὲν πε[ρ]ὶ τε͂ς ἀπαρχε͂ς τὸ καρ[π]ὸ͂ [τ]-
οῖν θεοῖν ἀναγράφσαι ἐς τὸ στέλ[α], μένα δὲ ⋮ ἐμβάλλεν hεκατονβ-
αιῶνα τὸν νέον ἄρχοντα. τὸν δὲ βασ[ι]λέα hορίσαι τὰ hιερὰ τὰ ἐν τ[ὸ]-
55 ι Πελαργικὸι, καὶ τὸ λοιπὸν μὲ ἐνhιδρύεσθαι βομὸς ἐν τὸι Πελαργικὸι ἄνευ τε͂ς βολε͂ς καὶ τὸ δέμο, μεδὲ τὸς λίθος τέμνεν ἐκ τὸ [Π]-
ελαργικὸ, μεδὲ γε͂ν ἐχσάγεν μεδὲ λίθος. ἐὰν δέ τις παραβαίνει v
τ ⋮ οὕτον τι, ἀποτινέτο πεντακοσίας δραχμάς, ἐσαγγελλέτο δὲ h-
[ο] βασιλεὺς ἐς τὲν βολέν. περὶ δὲ τὸ ἐλαίο τε͂ς ἀπαρχε͂ς χσυγγράφ-
60 σας Λάμπον ἐπιδειχσάτο τε͂ι βολε͂ι ἐπὶ τε͂ς ἐνάτες πρυτανείας·
hε δὲ βολὲ ἐς τὸν δε͂μον ἐχσενενκέτο ἐπάναγκες.

It is generally held that at the close of line 18 the engraver wrote ἐπει and then deleted the letters when he realized that he had repeated them at the beginning of line 19; we see no trace of erasure on the stone; the Athenian copy does not seem to have had these four extra letter-spaces. The punctuation marks in ll. 53 and 58 seem to cover erasures. The Athenian copy has parts of ll. 15–21; it can be shown also to have had fifty letters to the line; it had εὐθυνέσθον in l. 20 and must have had some other minor discrepancies (Wilhelm, *Jahresh.* vi. 13 f.).

However complete a text may be, its full importance may be impossible to determine, if we cannot date it. This is a frustrating example.

The prescript is normal, save that the motion had been formulated by a body of ξυγγραφεῖς (l. 3) and could be described as αἱ ξυγγραφαί (l. 47). Such drafts, normally on complicated matters, could be confided to an individual (ll. 59–61, Andoc. i. 96), but were normally produced by a committee. The earliest known example is from 450–49 (*ATL* ii. D 11 ; Hill, *Sources²*, B 30), the best-known ξυγγραφεῖς are those of 411 (Thuc. viii. 67 ; Arist. Ἀθ. Πολ. 29. 2, 30. 1) ; cf. also No. 49, l. 15; *ATL* ii. D 9. 8; Swoboda, *Rh. Mus.* xlv (1890) 302 f. ; Busolt, *Gr. St.* 459 ff. ; Hignett, *History of the Athenian Constitution*, 242.

All Athenian farmers must set aside not less than $\frac{1}{600}$ of their barley and $\frac{1}{1200}$ of their wheat to be collected and delivered at Eleusis by their respective demarchs 'in accordance with ancestral custom and the oracle from Delphi' (ll. 4–10). For the ratio of barley to wheat in Attic agriculture, see Jardé, *Les céréales dans l'antiquité grecque*, 36 ff. The ἱεροποιοὶ οἱ Ἐλευσινόθεν (ll. 9, 17) are to be distinguished from the ten ἱεροποιοὶ οἱ κατ' ἐνιαυτόν (No. 84, l. 6; Arist. Ἀθ. Πολ. 54. 7). They are the older board of Eleusinian officials (cf. Hill, *Sources²*, B 8 (*SEG* x. 6), l. 120), who were gradually replaced by the ἐπιστάται Ἐλευσινόθεν first appointed c. 450 (Hill, *Sources²*, B 41 (*SEG* x. 24) ; see *JHS* lxxxiii (1963) 111–14 for the date), but who make no appearance in our text.

The first-fruits are to be stored in σιροί (ll. 10–13). The word is normally used of underground granaries, which hardly seem likely here; for the nature and position of the Eleusinian σιροί see Noack, *Eleusis*, 193–201.

Similar first-fruits shall be collected by ἐκλογεῖς in all the allied cities and delivered at Eleusis to the ἱεροποιοί, who must accept them without delay (ll. 14–21) and keep an official record of the offering made by each several deme and city (ll. 26–30). The clause (ll. 21–4) providing for the prompt notification of the allies seems misplaced, while that (ll. 24–6) relating to a Panhellenic invitation would be more appropriately inserted in the following section. Laqueur (*Epigraphische Untersuchungen*, 98–101) attributes this disorder to amendments made to the original ξυγγραφαί in the course of debate, but his attempt to dismember the decree is sufficiently answered by Billheimer (*AJA* xxxvi (1932) 471–3) and the incoherence is probably rightly attributed by Guillon to committee-work (op. cit. 470, n. 1). The ἐκλογεῖς τοῦ καρποῦ (ll. 14–15) in the allied cities are parallel to the ἐκλογεῖς τοῦ φόρου whose appointment was ordered in 426 by No. 68. Dittenberger proposed to read καὶ Ἐλευσῖνι for Ἐλευσῖνι καὶ in l. 29, to make the text refer to the Eleusinion at Athens; the text has been most recently defended by Rubensohn, *Jahrb.* lxx (1955) 11–16.

All other Greek cities shall, so far as possible, be invited to make similar offerings (ll. 30–6). Here too, as in the exhortation of the ἱεροφάντης and the δᾳδοῦχος (ll. 24–6), appeal is made to ancestral custom and the Delphic oracle. Isocrates (iv. 31) speaks of ἀπαρχαὶ τοῦ σίτου as annually offered by most cities, and of the Pythia as ordering defaulters to comply with the practice.

Ll. 36–44 order the disposal of the first-fruits thus deposited at Eleusis for sacrifices and votive offerings. The πελανός (l. 36) is flour made from the choicest corn, both wheat and barley (*LGS* ii, pp. 25 f.; Stengel, *Opferbräuche*, 66–72). The γένος of the Eumolpidai (ll. 36–7) enjoyed the hereditary and exclusive right of ἐξήγησις at Eleusis (Jacoby, *Atthis*, 26 f. and *passim*). The τρίττοια βόαρχος (l. 37; cf. *IG* i². 5. 5, 844 B 6) was a sacrifice of three victims, of which the first was a bull (*LGS* ii, p. 10). The God and the Goddess (ll. 38 f.) are generally identified with Plouton and Persephone (Farnell, *Cults of the Greek States*, iii. 136 ff.); for Euboulos (Eubouleus) see Frazer's *Pausanias*, ii. 118, and Jessen in *RE* vi. 864–9.

Ll. 44–6 invoke blessing and prosperity on those who thus honour the Eleusinian goddess and act fairly towards Athens.

Ll. 47–61 comprise a rider moved by Lampon, certainly the noted prophet whose activity extended at least from 443, when he took a leading part in the foundation of Thurii (Wade-Gery, *Essays*, 257), until 414 (Ar. *Birds* 521, 988). He was the first Athenian signatory of the Peace of Nikias and the alliance with Sparta which followed (Thuc. v. 19. 2, 24. 1). He is called ἐξηγητής by Eupolis (F 297 K.) and by the scholiast on Ar. *Clouds* 332. The rider provides:

(*a*) For the publication of the decree in two copies (ll. 47–53).

(*b*) That the archon of the next year shall intercalate a second Hekatombaion (ll. 53–4). Usually the month duplicated in an intercalary year was Posideion, but we know of a doubling of Gamelion (*IG* ii². 1487. 54) and of Anthesterion (ibid. 844. 33). Here Hekatombaion, the first month of the Attic civil year, is duplicated, presumably in order to give longer notice of the date at which first-fruits must be delivered at Eleusis, probably (though this is not expressly stated) during the Eleusinia in the month Boedromion.

(*c*) That the sanctuaries in the Pelargikon shall be delimited, the erection of unauthorized altars there prevented, and the removal of stones or earth therefrom stopped (ll. 54–9). For the delimitation of sacred precincts cf. *IG* i². 94. 7, τὸς ὁριστὰς ἐπιπέμφσαι ὁρίσαι τὰ hιερὰ ταῦτα. For the Pelargikon as a hunting-ground for stones or earth see Pollux, viii. 101 and Lucian, *Pisc.* 47. Thucydides (ii. 17. 1) contrasts it with the Acropolis, the Eleusinion, and εἴ τι ἄλλο βεβαίως κλῃστὸν ἦν.

(*d*) That Lampon shall draft a regulation regarding the first-fruits of olive oil and lay it before the Council, which must perforce submit it to the Assembly (ll. 59–61).

The course of the discussion about the date is well summarized by Guarducci (*RF* lxxxix (1961) 283–95), though her own solution, spring 424, is quite impossible (Meritt, *Classical World*, lvi (1962) 39–41). The first editors were influenced by the Panhellenic tone of the decree in associating it with Pericles' Congress decree (Plut. *Per.* 17) and placing it in the 440s (so, last, Cloché, *L'antiquité classique*, xiv (1945) 102 f.). A variant of this view, placing the main decree in the 440s and Lampon's amendment and the publication of the whole at the time of the Peace of Nikias (Will, *REG* lxi (1948) 1–18), should not have survived J. and L. Robert's destruction of it (*REG* lxii (1949) 102 f.), but cf. Accame, *RF* lxxxiii (1955) 153–63. Recent discussion has leant heavily on Wilhelm's view of the letter-forms (*Jahresh.* vi. 15, *Wien. Anz.* 1922, 45), though his comparison with documents of 420 and 415 has received more notice than his comparison with No. 61 of 432. The strongest epigraphic argument for a late date, 422–415, lies in the frequent omission of the aspirate, but we are not convinced that a date even as early as 435 is formally impossible. Objective, internal arguments are hard to come by. As we have seen, Lampon's career is too long to be helpful. The extant accounts of the moneys received by the Eleusinian ἐπιστάται from the ἱεροποιοί in 422–1 to 419–18 ἀπὸ τô σίτο τês ἀπαρχês (*IG* i². 311; cf. *SEG* x. 211 for undatable, more complex parallels) do suggest a *terminus ante quem*; Ziehen (*LGS*, loc. cit.; see also Mattingly, *Proc. Afr. Class. Ass.* vii (1964), 53–5) has argued for 423–2, Guillon (op. cit.) for 422–1. However, they are not quite conclusive, since the amounts they record are small, and cannot be said to disprove Körte's dating (in Noack, *Eleusis*, 313–17) to the spring of 418 or Dinsmoor's dating (*Archons of Athens*, 338–40, supported by Meritt, *AFD* 172, n. 3) to the spring of 415, both times when one might hold that the ambition of Alcibiades led the Athenians to adopt grandiose schemes. The best argument would lie in the discovery of a year with the peculiar calendar-scheme ordered in ll. 53–4. The relative attractions of 423–2 and 422–1 as dates for the decree then turn on whether 422–1 was an intercalary year, as Meritt used to hold (*Calendar*, 101–4; *Athenian Year*, 218), or ordinary, as was maintained by McGregor (*AJP* lix (1938) 145–68), now joined by Meritt (*Phoenix* xxi (1967) 88 f.). The next intercalary year was probably 419–18, but it can be excluded here as the intercalary year ordered by the decree because its second month was not a second Hekatombaion, but Metageitnion (Antiphon vi. 44; for the date, see most recently Meritt, *Year*, 210–12). It is hard to make Körte's date fit any plausible pattern of intercalary years, and it has lost popularity for that reason. Dinsmoor's date can certainly be made to fit, but his key **argument, that Kekropis held the eighth prytany both in this decree** and in 416–15, relies on restorations of No. 77, ll. 47, 49, which are by no means certain. We should not be in the least surprised if new discoveries assigned the decree to, say, 435, though the passage of Thucydides quoted above offers some evidence against a date before the Peloponnesian War.

This decree was not in operation as such in the fourth century, having been replaced at a date unknown by a law of Chairemonides to which an amendment was passed in 353–2 (*IG* ii². 140). The accounts of the receipts from the ἀπαρχαί for 329–8 survive, arranged by the ten Attic tribes and outlying Athenian possessions, and distinguishing wheat and barley (*IG* ii². 1672. 263–96). The survival or revival of the custom in the age of Hadrian is attested by two dedications (*IG* ii². 2956–7), the second of which reads οἱ ἐπὶ Φλαουίου Ἀμφικλέους ἄρχοντος Πανέλληνες ἐκ τῆς τοῦ Δημητρίου καρποῦ ἀπαρχῆς (but not, as is sometimes said, by Aelius Aristides, *Eleus.*, p. 417, *Panath.*, pp. 167 f., ed. Dindorf, who is referring to the past).

74 (65)

Thank-offering of the Messenians and Naupaktians:

c. 421 B.C.

Near the foot of the lofty triangular basis of Parian marble which supported the Nike of Paionios at Olympia (for which see, for example, Lullies, *Griechische Plastik*, no. 176, p. 61). Discovered in 1875 near the south-east corner of the temple of Zeus; now in the Olympia Museum.

Ionic letters: ll. 3–4 are much smaller than ll. 1–2. For the arrangement of the letters see Harder, *Jahrb.* lviii (1943) 128 f. (= *Kleine Schriften*, 120 f.). Phot.: Berve, *Das neue Bild der Antike*, Fig. 5, opp. p. 97; Harder, *Kleine Schriften*, abb. 56. (The facsimiles, e.g. *LSAG*, Pl. 71. 33, are correct in showing four-bar sigma in l. 1, denied in earlier impressions of this book; see Mitchel, Φόρος Meritt (1974), 107–9.)

SIG 80+; Buck, *CP* viii (1913), 137; *DGE* 65; Pomtow, *Jahrb.* xxxvii (1922) 81; Harder, *Festschrift B. Schweitzer*, 192–201 (= *Kleine Schriften* 125–36).

Μεσσάνιοι καὶ Ναυπάκτιοι ἀνέθεν Διὶ
'Ολυμπίωι δεκάταν ἀπὸ τῶμ πολεμίων.
Παιώνιος ἐποίησε Μενδαῖος,
καὶ τἀκρωτήρια ποιῶν ἐπὶ τὸν ναὸν ἐνίκα.

Pausanias says (v. 26. 1) that the Messenians who had been settled by the Athenians at Naupaktos erected a statue of Nike at Olympia

to commemorate, in his view, their war with Acarnania and Oiniadai
(*c.* 455; cf. Paus. iv. 25), but that they themselves connected it
with the aid they had rendered to the Athenians at Sphakteria in
425 (cf. Thuc. iv. 9. 1, 36. 1, 41. 2), explaining the use of the indeter-
minate phrase ἀπὸ τῶν πολεμίων as due to fear of the Spartans.

Pausanias' own view is unlikely epigraphically and the Nike itself
cannot possibly be so early. The Messenian view gives the right approximate date, but their inference from ἀπὸ τῶν πολεμίων can hardly
have been more than a bad guess, since such phrases occur not infrequently on early dedications (cf., e.g., No. 25). It seems best to
refer the dedication to all the Messenian operations in support of the
Athenians during the Archidamian War (so Frazer, *Pausanias*, iii.
643 ff.; cf. also Hitzig–Blümner, *Pausanias*, ii. 442 f.).

For a very similar parallel monument at Delphi, of which the inscription is only very badly preserved, see Pomtow, *SIG* 81, *Jahrb.*
xxxvii. 55–112; *RE* Suppl. iv. 1308 ff.; Colin, *FD* iii. iv. 1–5, 163–5;
Courby, *FD* ii, *La Terrasse du Temple*, 297–302.

The Athenians also, it may be noted, dedicated two statues of Nike
about the same time on the Acropolis, one [ἀπὸ] Ἀμπρακιωτῶν κα[ὶ
τῆ]ς ἐν [᾿Ολπαις στρατι]ᾶς καὶ τῶν ἐπαν[αστ]άντ[ων τῶι δήμωι τ]ῶι
Κερκυραίων [καὶ ἀπ'] Ἀν[ακτορίων] (*IG* ii². 403, *SIG* 264), and the
other ἐς μνήμην τῶν ἐν τῇ Σφακτηρίᾳ (Paus. iv. 36. 6).

L. 1 shows that the Messenians, settled in Naupaktos under
Athenian auspices at the close of the Helot Revolt (Thuc. i. 103. 3),
combined with some of the previous inhabitants of the town, for whom
see No. 20. (See now Mastrokostas, Ἀρχ. Δελτ. xix. 2 (1964) 295.)

The dedication, both at Olympia and at Delphi, is in the Doric
dialect. The artist's signature and note are in Ionic and Attic, save
for the word ναόν. Harder's comments on the relationship of the two
inscriptions are of interest. The view that Paionios was a native not
of the well-known Mende on the peninsula of Pallene but of an
Ionian city of that name north of Ainos in Thrace (Paus. v. 27. 12),
though accepted by Jeffery, *LSAG* 365, rests on the belief that Ionic
was not the alphabet of Chalcidic Mende, which, on her showing
(ibid. 363), seems unlikely; we do not believe in Pausanias' second
Mende. L. 4, as Harder has shown, is not, as Pomtow thought, a
slightly later addition to the original inscription. Paionios' success in
a competition for designing the ἀκρωτήρια must refer to the bronze-
gilt Nike which crowned the temple pediment and the λεβῆτες at its
extremities (Paus. v. 10. 4); Pausanias must have misunderstood the
word ἀκρωτήρια when he attributed the sculptures in the eastern pediment to Paionios (v. 10. 8). They can hardly be by him. See Ashmole
and Yalouris, *Olympia; The Sculptures of the Temple of Zeus*, 8.

75

Athenian Tribute quota-list:
(?) 418–17 B.C.

Four fragments of a marble stele, with no joins. The position of three is established, and the approximate position of the fourth; now in EM.

Developed Attic letters; in two of four instances the aspirate is dropped. Stoichedon 50 (prescript). Phots. of frags. 1 and 3: *Hesp.* viii (1939) 54; frag. 2: *ATL* i. 100 f.; frag. 4: *Hesp.* xvii (1948), Pl. 8 and *ATL* ii. 37.

ATL i, list 33; Meritt, *Hesp.* viii (1939) 54–9; *AJP* lxii (1941) 10; *Hesp.* xvii (1948) 31 f.; *ATL* ii, list 33; *ATL* iii (1950) 357; Meiggs, *CR* lxiv (1950) 63 f.; Mattingly, *Proc. Afr. Class. Ass.* vii (1964) 47.

[ἐπὶ τêς βολêς εἰ...7.... Ἀ]φιδναῖος πρōτ[ος ἐγραμμάτευε, ἔρχε]
[δὲ Ἀθεναίοις Ἀντιφōν Σκ]αμβονίδες ἐπὶ τê[ς ἑβδόμες καὶ τρια]-
[κοστês ἀρχês ἑλλενοταμί]αι ἐσαν hοῖς Ἀντ[........16........]
[........16........ Περγ]ασêθεν Μνεσίθεο[ς Ἀραφένιος...6...]
5 [........16........ Εὐπυ]ρίδες Αἰσχίνες Π[εριθοῖδες...7....]
[Θυμαιτ]άδε[ς Ἐργοκλês Βεσ]αιεύς vacat
[πόλες h]αἶδε [ἀπέδοσαν ἀπα]ρχὲν τêι θεōι μνᾶ[ν ἀπ]ὸ τō ταλάντ[ο vv]

	I			II	
	Νεσιοτ[ικός]			hελλε[σ]πόντιο[ς]	
	----------Ἀναφ[αῖοι]		Η	Σι[γε]ιês	
10	----------Θερα[ῖοι]		ΧΧ	Κυ[ζι]κενοί	10
	----------Σερίφ[ιοι]		ⅭΔ[ΓΗΙΙΙΙ][Ἀρτα]κενοί		
	----------Ἰêτα[ι]		-------[....]οί		
	----------Τένιο[ι]		[Βυσβ]ικενοί		
	----------Σίφνιο[ι]		[Προκ]οννέσιοι		
15	----------Ἄνδριο[ι]		[Παρια]νοί	15	
	[ΔΓΗΙΙ]ΙΙ	Σικινê[ται]		[Χαλχεδ]όνι[οι]	
	----------Κύθνι[οι]				
	lacuna			*lacuna*	
	[--------]		[.]ε[--------]		
	[ΗⅭΔΓΗΙΙ]ΙΙ		Χε[ρρονεσῖται]		
			ἀπ'[Ἀγορâς]		
	[------]vv		Κ[αλλιπολῖται]		

Col. ii. 12. *ATL* restore [Κιαν]οί; [Ἀζει]οί is also possible.

The style of the preamble is very close to list 34 (421–0), and two archons near to the Peace of Nikias have the required number of letters, Ἀλκαῖος in 422–1 and Ἀντιφῶν in 418–17. The date is important for the light it may throw on Athenian assessment policy. Meritt has wavered between the two dates and in *ATL* decided on 422–1, largely influenced by the scale of the few tributes that have been preserved. Sigeum, which before the war paid only 1,000 dr., now pays 1 T. Kyzikos now pays 20 T.; before the war she paid 9 T. Such figures are barely reconcilable with the established view that the final list of the assessment following 425 was not drawn up until peace had been made in the spring of 421, and that this assessment reflected the conciliatory mood of the peace terms. The foundation of the view is a substantial article by West published in 1925 (*AJA* xxix (1925) 135–51). West thought that this was a necessary conclusion from the figures that survived, combined with arguments from probability. His conclusion that the peace assessment could reasonably be regarded as a return to Aristides was accepted in *ATL* (iii. 347 ff.), but there are serious objections: (1) The assessment decree of 425 (No. 69, ll. 26–33) had threatened severe penalties if any Great Panathenaia passed without a new assessment; at the time of the festival in 422 there was no good reason for postponement. The year's armistice made in spring 423 had not led to peace, Mende and Scione had revolted after the armistice had been agreed, and by the end of the summer Cleon was again militant and was himself to lead an expedition to recover Amphipolis. This was no time for a soft assessment. (2) The Hellespontine total for this assessment is in part preserved, but the crucial first figure is missing; the total must be either *c.* 96 T. or *c.* 196 T. If, as in the Hellespontine total of 425 which was 250+T. (see p. 199), the numeral is indented one letter-space the restoration would give *c.* 196 T.: [v ͰΗ]ΡΔΔΔΔΡΡ̤ΗΗΗΗ̣—(phot.: *ATL* i, Figs. 164 and 173). Epigraphically this is to be preferred. (3) List 33 is better placed in 418–17 than in 422–1 (as in *ATL*): (*a*) the last *hellenotamias* in the prescript of list 33, presumably of the last tribe in the official list, Antiochis, is [.....11......]αιευς; Ἐργοκλῆς Βεσ]αιεύς, *hellenotamias* in 418–17 (No. 77, l. 10) precisely fills the gap. (*b*) If we restore the archon of 422–1 we have to assume syllabic division at the end of l. 2: τριανυ|κοστές, and this in the fifth century is very rare indeed; the numeral required for 418–17, ℎεβδόμες, exactly fills the space. (*c*) The first secretary of the Boule in list 33 was from the deme Aphidna; the first secretary of 418–17 is also from Aphidna (*IG* i². 370. 14). It is true that in one case the name has seven letters, in the other apparently only six, but that is not a fatal objection. In list 33 we can restore ἐι rather than ℎει (*ATL*), although ℎοῖς is used in l. 3; there is a good parallel in No. 58, which has ℎά in l. 4, but ἁ in

l. 5; similarly No. 84 has ἑλλενοταμίαις in l. 10, but ηελλενοταμίαις in l. 11.

On this evidence we prefer to date list 33 in 418–17, reflecting the assessment of 418 rather than 425; and since such little evidence as we have, together with the comparative failure of Athenian policies, suggests that the 418 assessment was probably close to its predecessor, we think that the Hellespontine figures of the list confirm our restoration of the Hellespontine total there. Several figures from the two assessments that follow 425 do show a return to pre-war levels or near, but our evidence is mainly from the island district and the islands on whom Athens probably depended, more than on the rest of the empire, for her crews may have been ᴐre favourably treated than the other districts. And even in the islands there are exceptions (see *ATL* iii. 348 f. for a table of all the figures preserved from the period of the Peace of Nikias). Kythnos was raised from pre-war 3 T. to 6 T. in 425, and was still assessed at 6 T. in 418; Ceos, assessed at 10 T. in 425, was reduced to 6 T. in 418, but before the war she had paid only 4 T. Similarly Naxos at 9 T. was paying less than in 425 (15 T.), but more than pre-war (6⅔ T.). We hold that the new assessment after 425 was completed in 422, that its main feature was a moderate scaling down of 425 figures, many of which had probably proved in practice too high to collect, a reduction of the total from 1,460+T. to perhaps rather less than 1,000 T.

Meritt and McGregor (*Phoenix* xxi (1967) 85 f.) now accept this dating, and produce further arguments for it.

76 (70)

Inventory of Treasures in the Hekatompedos: 418–17 B.C.

On two halves of a marble stele, found on the Acropolis; one is now in the British Museum, the other in the Cabinet des Médailles of the Bibliothèque Nationale.

Developed Attic writing, stoichedon 71. Phot. (Paris fragment): Robert, *Collection Froehner*, Pl. xlviii.

IG i². 268+ ; Meritt, *AJP* lix (1938) 501.

τάδε παρέδοσαν ηαι τέτταρες ἀρχαί, ηα[ὶ ἐδίδοσαν τὸν λόγον ἐκ
                                        Παναθεναίον ἐς Πανα]θ[ένα]-
ια, τοῖς ταμίαις Πυθοδόροι ηαλαιεῖ [καὶ χσυνάρχοσι, οἷς Φορμίον
                                        Ἀριστίονος Κ]υδαθενα[ι]-

εὺς ἐγραμμάτευε· hοι δὲ ταμίαι, hοῖς Φο[ρμίο]ν Ἀ[ριστίονος Κυδαθε-
ναιεὺς ἐγραμμάτε]νε, π[α]-
ρέδοσαν τοῖς ταμίαις Ἀναχσικράτει Λα[μπ]τρε[ῖ καὶ χσυνάρχοσιν
⟨οἷς⟩ Εὔχσενος Εὐφάνο]ς Προσ-
5 πάλτιος ἐγραμμάτευεν, ἐν τōι νεōι τōι h[εκατ]ομπέδ[οι· φιάλαι χρυσαῖ ⫶⫶⫶,
σταθμὸν τούτ]ον ΧΧ⌐
ΔΔΔΔⱵⱵⱵⱵ. κόρε χρυσ͡ε ἐπὶ στέλες, ἄσταθ[μος. ἀποραντέριον ἀργυρὸν, ἄσταθμον. στεφά]νο χρυ-
σὸ ⌐[⌐], σταθμὸν τούτοιν ⌐ΔΔΔ. σ[τ]έφανος χρ[υσὸς, h]ὸ[ν ἐ Νίκε
ἔχει, σταθμὸν τοῦτο ⌐Δ. φιάλαι ἀρ[γ]-
υραῖ ⌐⫶⫶, σταθμὸν τοῦτον ⌐ΗΗ[Η.] καρχέσιο[ν ἀργυρὸν, σταθμὸν τοῦτο
ΗΗ. καρχέσιον ἀργυ]ρὸν Δ[ι]-
ὸς Πολιὸς, σταθμὸν τοῦτο ΗΗ. στέφανος [χρυσὸς, σταθμὸν τοῦτο . . .
ⱵⱵⱵ⫶⫶. στεφά]νε χ[ρυ]σ͡ε, σταθ-
10 μὸν ταύτες ⌐ΔⱵⱵⱵ. στέφανοι χρυσοῖ ⌐[⌐]⫶⫶, σ[ταθμὸν τούτων ΗΔΔΔ
⌐⫶⫶. στέφανος χρυσ]ὸς, σταθμὸν τ-
οῦτο Δ⌐ⱵⱵⱵ⫶⫶⫶. χρυσίδε ⫶⫶, σταθμὸν τούτοι[ν ΗΗ⌐ΔΔΔΔⱵⱵⱵ⫶⫶⫶.
χρυσίς, σταθμὸν] ταύ[τε]ς ΗΔΔΔ⌐ⱵⱵⱵ[⌐].
χρυσίς, σταθμὸν ταύτες ΗΔ⌐ⱵⱵⱵⱵ. στέφ[ανος χρυσὸς, σταθ]μ[ὸν τοῦτο
ΔΔ⌐Ⱶ⫶⫶. ἀρ[γ]υρίς, σταθμὸν
ταύτες Η⌐ΔΔΔΔⱵⱵ. θυμιατέριον ἀργυ[ρὸν, σταθμὸν τοῦτο Χ. ἐπέτεια ἐπεγέν]ετο· [στ]έ[φα]νος χ[ρ]-
υσὸς, σταθμὸν τοῦτο ΧΗΗ⌐. στέφανος χρ[υσὸς, σταθμὸν τοῦτο.. Ⱶ.
στέφανος] χρυσὸς, σταθμὸν τ-
15 [ο]ύτο ΔΔΔ⌐.

We have had help from a text prepared by W. E. Thompson.

The stones presumably join, but the right-hand (London) half is badly
worn. We have abandoned some letters in l. 1, which rest only on Visconti's
observation. Either the stonecutter omitted something in l. 4, presumably
οἷς, or we should read συνάρχοσι hοῖς (Thompson); conformity in spelling
with l. 2 is not possible.

The lists which the second Kallias Decree (No. 58 B, ll. 25 ff.)
ordered the treasurers of Athena to draw up began in 434–3, and
were organized in three series, for the Pronaos, the Hekatompedos,
and the Parthenon, i.e. for the porch, east cella, and west cella of the
building we call the Parthenon (for the term ὁ ναὸς ὁ Ἑκατόμπεδος
and its origin see Doerpfeld, *Ath. Mitt.* vi (1881) 297–302; Dinsmoor,
AJA li (1947) 123 ff.). Though these *traditiones* or inventories were

drawn up annually and ἐκ Παναθεναίον ἐς Παναθέναια refers to the
annual term of each board, the four boards of the expiring quadrennium seem to have co-operated in setting up their inventories at the
time of the Great Panathenaia. The stele before us carried on one
side the inventories of the years 422–418 and on the other those of the
years 418–414.

Of the objects before us only two gold *phialai*, the golden *kore* on
a stele, and the ἀπορραντήριον were in the Hekatompedos in 434. The
rest represent an accumulation which, except in the first three years
of the Archidamian War, seems to have been remarkably steady. The
'gold crown, which the Nike has' (l. 7) is listed more fully later (e.g. in
IG ii². 1386. 12–14, 401–400 B.C.) as στέφανος χρυσός, ἡ Νίκη ἔχει ἐπὶ
τῆς κεφαλῆς ἡ ἐπὶ τῆς χερὸς τὸ ἀγάλματος τὸ χρυσὸ, i.e. ᴜne chryselephantine Athena of Pheidias (cf. No. 54), and was first listed in 428–7,
but the Nike itself is not inventoried before the end of the Peloponnesian War. It is noteworthy that among the additions of this
year (ἐπέτεια) there appears the most valuable single item, a gold
crown weighing 1,250 dr. This was dedicated by cleruchs (Ferguson,
Treasurers, 50 n. 1, 52), apparently celebrating the Great Panathenaia
of 418, the first true peace-time Great Panathenaia for sixteen years,
with a particularly splendid offering.

For Pericles (Thuc. ii. 13. 4) the sacred treasures represented an
iron reserve. The objects listed here, assuming a 12:1 gold–silver
ratio, were worth little more than 10 T., and insignificant beside the
eight gold Nikai weighing 2 T. apiece (i.e. worth 192 T.) which seem
to have existed at this time (Woodward, Ἀρχ. Ἐφ. 1937, 159 ff.;
Thompson, *Hesp.* xiii (1944) 173–209). Nevertheless, few of them (the
καρχήσιον of Zeus Polieus is a notable exception) survived the melting
operations of the end of the war. See, in general, Ferguson, *Treasurers*,
85–103.

77 (75)

Payments from Athena's Treasury for
public purposes: 418–414 B.C.

Six fragments of a marble stele, found on the Acropolis; now in EM, save
one (containing the left-hand portions of ll. 63–81) in the British Museum.

Developed Attic writing, stoichedon (with slight irregularities): in the
first three years the normal line has eighty-five letters, in the fourth year
ninety-six. There is some inconsistency in the use of the aspirate, and
χσυνάρχοντες (-οσι) does not always have initial chi. Phot. and facs.: *AJA*
xxxiv (1930) 126 ff.; Meritt, *AFD* 124–9 and Pl. xiii.

IG i². 302; West and McCarthy, *AJA* xxxii (1928) 346–52 (ll. 2–35); West, *AJA* xxix (1925), 3–10, xxxiii (1929) 37–40 (both on ll. 49–60); Meritt, *AJA* xxxiv (1930) 125–52, *AFD* 160–74 (both on the whole, with new fragment of ll. 46–9); Bannier, *Phil. Woch.* xlvii. 669 (l. 17); Ferguson, *Treasurers*, 23 n. 1, Kahrstedt, *Untersuchungen zur Magistratur*, 125 n. 1 (both on ll. 53, 55, 57); Meritt, *Hesp.* v (1936) 382 (l. 79); Meritt, *AJP* lviii (1937) 180 f., Giffler, *Hermes* lxxv (1940) 222, Meritt, *CQ* xl (1946) 45 f. (all on ll. 18, 27).

<pre>
      [θ   ε   ο]   ι
418– [Ἀθεναῖοι ἀνέλοσαν ἐπὶ Ἀντιφôντος ἄρχοντος καὶ ἐπὶ τês βολês, hêι
17B.C.
             ...7.... πρôτος ἐγραμμάτευε, τ]αμίαι h-
      [ιερôν χρεμάτον τês Ἀθεναίας Πυθόδορος Ἀλαιεὺς καὶ συνάρχοντες hοῖς
                    Φορμίον Ἀριστίονος Κ]υδαθεναιε-
      [ὺς ἐγραμμάτευε παρέδομεν hελλενοταμίαις Ἐργοκλêῖ Ἀριστείδο
                    Βεσαιεῖ καὶ συ]νάρχοσι καὶ παρέδροις h-
   5 [ιεροκλêῖ Ἀρχεστράτο Ἀθμονεῖ καὶ συνάρχοσι ἐπὶ τês...6...ίδος
                    πρότες πρυτα]νευόσες καὶ hεμέραι δευτ-
      [έραι ....60....................
                    .....]ος τοῖς μετὰ Δεμοσθένος. ἔ-
      [δοχσεν τôι δέμοι κατὰ τὸ...6...]ίρ [φσέφισμα τὸ ἀργύριον τὸ παρα-
                    δοθὲν ἀποδôνα]ι τὸς hελλενοταμίας καὶ [τ]-
      [ὸς παρέδρος τοῖς ταμίαις τês] θεô Πυθ[οδόροι Ἀλαιεῖ καὶ χσυνάρχοσι
                    καὶ τὸς τα]μίας τês θεô πάλιν παραδ[ν]-
      [αι τοῖς hελλενοταμίαις κ]αὶ τοῖς παρέδ[ροις, τούτος δὲ δôναι στρατεγοῖς
                    ἐπὶ Θ]ράικες Εὐθυδέμοι Εὐδέμο [υ]
  10 [.. not more than 21 ..] *vacat*
      [ἐπὶ τês ...6...ίδος πρυτα]νείας δευτέρας [πρυτανευόσες hελλενο-
                    ταμίαις Ἐρ]γοκλêι Ἀριστείδο Βεσαιεῖ [υ]
      [........17......... Αἰχ]σονεῖ καὶ συνάρχο[σι καὶ παρέδροις
                    hιεροκλêι Ἀρχε]στράτο Ἀθμονεῖ καὶ συν[ά]ρχ[ο]-
      [σι......13......κοστê]ι τês πρυτανείας π[αρέδομεν ....14....
                    .. χρυσί]ο Κυζικενô στατêρας ΧΧΧΧ[..]
                                                        ¿¿¿¿
      [..........21..........]· ἀργύριον τούτον [γίγνεται 20
                    ....]ⅠⅠⅠ· τοῦτο τὸ χρυσίον παρέδομ[ε]-
  15 [ν τοῖς τριεράρχοις ἐπὶ Ἄ]ργος τοῖς μετὰ Δεμ[οσθένος φσεφισαμένο τô
                    δέμο τὲν] ἄδειαν. *vacat*
      [ἐπὶ τês ....14.......]ες πρυτανευόσες ὀ[γδόει εἰκοστêι hεμέραι
                    τês πρυ]τανείας στρατεγοῖς παρέδομ-
</pre>

[εν ....18.........]δει Αὐτοκλεῖ Ἀναφλ[υστίοι .. not more
                                                     than 20 ..] vacat

[ἐπὶ τῆς Πανδιονίδος ἐνά]τες πρυτανευόσες τ[ρίτει καὶ δεκάτει ἡμέραι
                                    τῆς π]ρυτανείας παρέδομεν τὸ ἐχσ-

[άμο κατὰ τὸν ἐνιαυτὸν ἐ]πελθόντος ἑλλενοτ[αμίαις Ἐργοκλεῖ
                            Ἀριστείδο Βεσ]αιεῖ καὶ χσυνάρχοσι καὶ παρ-

20 [έδροι ἑλλ]ενο[ταμιôν ἱ]εροκλεῖ Ἀρχεστράτο [Ἀθμονεῖ.. · ℏοῦτοι δὲ
                                ἔδοσαν στρ]ατ{ρατ}εγοῖς Νικίαι Νικεράτ-

[ο Κυδαντ]ίδει Καλ[λιστρ]άτοι Ἐμπέδο ℏοέθεν Κ[.. not more than
                                                     26 ..] vacat

[κε]φάλα[ι]ον ἀναλ[όματος τὸ] ἐπὶ τε̑

17–   [ἀ]ρχε̑ς 𐅄𐅄ΤΧΓΗΗΗ[....8....]ΙΙ vacat
B.C. Ἀθεναῖοι ἀνέλοσαν ἐ[πὶ Εὐφέμο ἄρ]χοντος καὶ [ἐπὶ τῆς βολῆς ℏε̑ι
                          ....9..... πρ]ο̑τος ἐγραμμάτευε, ταμίαι ℏιε-

25 ρὸν χρεμάτον τῆς Ἀ[θεναίας Ἀναχσικράτες Λαμπτρεὺς καὶ χσυν-
                      άρχοντες ℏοῖς] Εὔχσενος Εὐφάνος Προσπάλτ-

ιος ἐγραμμάτευε π[αρέδομεν ....28.............. στρα-
                        τεγοῖς ἐς] τὰ ἐπὶ Θράικες κα[ὶ] Ῥίνονι Χ-

αρικλέος Παιανιε[ῖ ἐπὶ τῆς ...εῖδος ...6...πρυτανευόσες καὶ ἡμέραι
                              δευτέ]ραι καὶ εἰκοστε̑ι τῆς πρυτα-

νείας [φ]σεφισαμέν[ο τὸ δέμο τὲν ἄδειαν .. not more than 32 ..]
                                                     vacat

ἐπὶ τῆς Αἰαντίδο[ς ...6... πρυτανευόσες παρέδομεν στρατεγοῖς ἐς
                        Μέλον Τεισί]αι Τεισιμάχο Κεφαλε̑θεν ν

30 Κλεομέδει Λυκο[μέδος Φλυεῖ ....18......... τῆς πρυτανείας
                        φσεφισαμέν]ο τὸ δέμο τὲν ἄδειαν 𐅅 νννν

ἐπὶ τῆς Ἀντιοχί[δος . 2–3 ..άτες πρυτανευόσες ℏελλενοταμίαις
                  παρέδομεν .... 7–8 ....]οι Α[ὐρ]ίδει Τιμάρχοι Παλ-

λενεῖ καὶ στρα[τεγοῖς ἐς Μέλον Τεισίαι Τεισιμάχο Κεφαλε̑θεν Κλεομέδει
                        Λυκομέδ]ος Φλυεῖ τρίτει καὶ δεκ-

άτε[ι τε̑]ς [πρυτανείας φσεφισαμένο τὸ δέμο τὲν ἄδειαν .. not more
                                                     than 22 ..] vacat

[κεφάλαιον ἀναλόματος τὸ ἐ]πὶ τε̑ς

35 [ἀρχε̑ς -]vacat

6–   [Ἀθεναῖοι ἀνέλοσαν ἐπὶ Ἀριμνέστο ἄρχοντος καὶ ἐπὶ τῆς βολῆς ℏε̑ι
B.C.   Ἀρ...6... προ̑τος] ἐγραμμάτευε ταμίαι [ℏ-]

[ιερὸν χρεμάτον τῆς Ἀθεναίας Δεχσίθεος Φυλάσιος καὶ χσυνάρχοντες
                  ℏοῖς Λυσικλε̑ς Δ]ρακοντίδο Βατε̑θ[εν]

[ἐγραμμάτευε ....61......................
.............] Παλλενêι [..5...]

lacuna of unknown length

46 [......13.......]ΔΔ *vacat*
[ἐπὶ τῆς Κεκρο]πίδος [............................... 69
....]

[....11.....]ονει[.....................45...................
...]οι [...........23...........]

[ἐπὶ τῆς Κεκροπ]ίδος [..................37..............
ἡμέραι] τῆς πρυτανεία[ς στρατε]γο[ῖς Ἀλ]-

50 [κιβιάδει Κλειν]ί[ο Σκαμβονίδει Λαμάχοι Χσενοφάνος hοêθεν Νικίαι
Ν]ικεράτο Κυδαντίδει καὶ παρέδρο[ις]

[......................55...................]ΗΗΗ
vacat

[ἐπὶ τῆς ....36................ ἡμέραι στρ]ατεγοῖς
ἐς Σικελίαν Ἀλκιβιάδει Λαμάχο[ι]

[Νικίαι καὶ ....38.............. Ἀντ]ιμάχοι
hερμείοι Ⳑ[ⳤ]ⳤ *vaca·*

[ἐπὶ τῆς..................36................ἡμέρα]ι στρατεγοῖς
ἐς Σικελ[ί]αν Ἀλκιβιάδει Λαμάχοι

55 [Νικίαι καὶ..................38..............] Ἀντιμάχοι
hερμείοι ⳐΤΤΤΤΧ[.]ΗΗΗ *vacat*

[ἐπὶ τῆς ....36............... ἡμέρ]αι στρατεγοῖς ἐς Σικελίαν Ἀλκιβιάδει Λαμάχο[ι]

[Νικίαι καὶ ....38..............] Ἀντιμάχοι
hερμείοι χρυσίο Κυ[ζ]ικενô στατêρ-

[ας ....44..................]ΗΗΙΙΙC *vacat*
[κεφάλαιον ἀναλόμα]τος τô ἐπὶ τῆς

60 [ἀρχês .....11......]ΔΓΗΙΙΙΙ *vacat*

[Ἀθεναῖοι ἀνέλοσαν ἐπὶ Χαρίο ἄρχοντος καὶ ἐπὶ τῆς βολês hêι ..5...]ίδες
πρôτος ἐγραμμάτευε, ταμίαι hιερôν χρεμάτον υ

[τῆς Ἀθεναίας Λεοχάρες .....11...... καὶ χσυνάρχοντες hοῖς Τελέα]ς
Τελενίκο Περγασêθεν ἐγραμμάτευε παρέδοσαν στρ-

[ατ]εγοῖς Τελεφόν[οι ..5... καὶ χσυνάρχοσι καὶ hελλενοταμίαι καὶ]
παρέδροι Φερεκλείδει Πειραιεῖ φσεφισαμένο τô δέμ-

[ο] τὲν ἄδειαν ἐπὶ τῆς Αἰαντίδος τρί[τες πρυτανευόσες ...6... hεμ]έραι
τῆς πρυτανείας ⳐΤΧΧΧ𐅅[Η]Η𐅅ΔΔΔΓΗΗΙΙΙC τε καὶ χρυσίο

65 Κυζικενô ⳤⳤⳤⳤⳤⳤⳤ𐅐ℝℝℝℝ τιμὲ τούτον γίγν[εται .. not more than
16 ..] *vacat*

ℎελλενοταμίαις καὶ παρέδροις ἐδανείσα[μεν.......15........] Ἀρι-
στοκράτει Εὐονυμεῖ καὶ χσυνάρχοσι 𐅄ΤΤΤΤ, οὗτοι δ-
ὲ ἔδοσαν ἀθλοθέταις ἐς Παναθέναια Ἀμέμπτο[ι.....ΙΙ......καὶ]
χσυνάρχοσι ἐπὶ τὲς Ἐρεχθεῖδος δευτέρας πρυτανευόσε-
ς εἰκοστῆι ἡμέραι τὲς πρυτανείας. vacat
ἐπὶ τὲς Κεκροπίδος τετάρτες πρυτανευόσες ℎέ[κτει ἡμέραι τ]ὲς πρυτανείας ℎελλενοταμίαις καὶ παρέδροις Ἀριστοκρ-
70 άτει Εὐονυμεῖ καὶ χσυνάρχοσι στρατιόταις ἐ[μ Μέλοι ...7....]ΔΔ
vacat
ἐπὶ τὲς Ἀντιοχίδος ὀγδόες πρυτανευόσες δεκά[τει ℎε ΄οαι τὲς] πρυτανείας ℎελλενοταμίαις καὶ παρέδροις Ἀριστοκρ[ά]-
τει Εὐονυμεῖ καὶ χσυνάρχοσι στρατιόταις ἐμ Μ[έλοι ....9.....]𐅄Δ
vacat
ἐπὶ τὲς Ἀντιοχίδος ὀγδόες πρυτανευόσες τρίτε[ι ἡμέραι τὲς πρυ]τανείας
ℎελλενοταμίαις καὶ παρέδροις Ἀριστοκρ[άτ]-
ει Εὐονυμεῖ καὶ χσυνάρχοσι ΗΗΗ, ℎοῦτοι δ' ἔδοσαν [τῆι ἐν Σικελίαι
σ]τρατιᾶι. vacat
75 ἐπὶ τὲς Ἀντιοχίδος ὀγδόες πρυτανευόσες εἰκοσ[τῆι ἡμέραι τὲς πρ]υτα-
νείας ℎελλενοταμίαις καὶ παρέδροις Ἀριστοκρ[ά]-
τει Εὐονυμεῖ καὶ χσυνάρχοσι ἐς τὰ⟨ς⟩ ναῦς τὰς ἐς Σι[κελίαν ἐσκομισάσα]ς
τὰ χρέματα ΤΤΤΤΧΧ vacat
ἐπὶ τὲς Ἀντιοχίδος ὀγδόες πρυτανευόσες δευτέ[ραι ἡμέραι τὲς πρυτα]-
νεία[ς] ℎελλενοταμίαι καὶ παρέδροι Φιλομέ[λοι Μ]-
αραθονίοι καὶ στρατεγοῖ ἐν τῶι Θερμαίοι κόλπο[ι.........18........
καὶ τ]ῆι αὐτῆι ἡμέραι ℎελλενοταμίαι κ[αὶ παρέ]-
δροι Φιλομέλοι Μαραθονίοι καὶ στρατεγοῖ ἐν Ἐφ[έσοι .. not more
than 23 ..] vacat
80 κεφάλαιον ἀνα[λόματος τ]ὸ ἐπὶ τ[ὲς]
ἀρχὲς ΗΗΗΗ𐅄ΤΤΤ - - - - - - - - - -
vacat

We have followed the line-numbers of Meritt's *AFD* text to avoid con-
fusion, but there is no means of determining the length of the lacuna. The
new fragment (ll. 46–9 left) is certainly placed in relation to the left margin,
but its vertical position is not certain. For the restorations in ll. 2, 25 cf.
No. 76. l. 6: καὶ εἰκοστῆι or τριακοστῆι τὲς πρυτανείας; the argument in
Meritt, *Calendar* 117, is not valid; ℎόστε δõναι τοῖς τριεράρχοις ἐς Ἄργ]ος
Dittenberger (ἐπὶ Ἄργ]ος Tod, cf. l. 15), ℎόστε δõναι τριεράρχοις ᾿ἐπὶ
Ἐϊόν]ος West–McCarthy; there must be a sum of money in the lacuna.

l. 7: Our restoration is perhaps preferable stylistically to ἐ‖[δοχσεν τῆι βολῆι καὶ τῶι δέμοι· .]ιọ[. . . .9. . . . . εἶπε· τὸ ἀργύριον τοῦτο παραδõνα]ι (Meritt) or earlier suggestions. ll. 13–14: Meritt thinks a sum of money in silver preceded the reference to Kyzikene electrum and fills the first gap in l. 14 with a reference to ʰεκταί; we judge it slightly more probable that more than one type of gold or electrum was referred to here (see also Bogaert, *Ant. Class.* xxxii (1963) 107 f.; W. E. Thompson, *Num. Chr.* 1963, 2 f.). l. 17: [Ἀλκιβιάδει Σκαμβονί]δει Meritt, but other names might also fit. l. 18: Meritt rightly, despite Giffler's objections. ll. 18–19: τὸ ἐχς‖[Σάμο κατὰ ὁμολογίαν ἀ]πελθόντος West, but see Tod, *AJP* lxvii (1946) 333. l. 20: There is some error, and this seems psychologically more probable than . . .5.. ʰοῦτοι δὲ ἔδοσαν] ⟨σ⟩τρατεγοῖς. l. 21: The only known general beginning with Κ who is possible is Kleomedes (ll. 30, 32). l. 26: Can πάρεδροι have dropped out before 'Ρίνονι (Tod)? l. 27: πρότες or τρίτες, not Αἰγεῖδος πρότες (Giffler). l. 29: ὀγδόες or ἐνάτες. l. 31: ἐνάτες or δεκάτες. l. 36: Ἀρ. . .6.'.., the first two letters from *ATL* ii, list 39, l. 1. ll. 46–58: The restorations possible are very various; see below. In ll. 51, 53, 55, 57 Meritt restores πάρεδροις, followed by name-demotic, name-demotic, occupying twenty-nine letters; Ferguson, regarding l. 51 as irrelevant, not altogether plausibly, restores in 53, 55, 57 τῶι ταμίαι τῶι χσυμπλέοντι μετὰ τῆς στρατίας (?cf. No. 78 Second stele, frag. *a*, l. 10), and Kahrstedt has πάρεδροι τῶι συνεκπλέοντι κατὰ τὸ φσέφισμα throughout (presumably a misprint for χσυνεκπλέοντι). l. 76: The sigma was omitted.

This text records the payments made by the treasurers of Athena in the Panathenaic quadrennium 418–414. The word describing these payments is παρέδομεν or παρέδοσαν (l. 62), except in l. 66 where ἐδανείσαμεν is used, probably indicating an abnormal payment (Lewis, *Hesp.* xxviii (1959) 246, against Meyer, *Forschungen*, ii. 135, n. 1; for another explanation, see Davison, *JHS* lxxviii (1958) 31 f.); probably all the payments were technically loans. To five items the phrase φσεφισαμένο τõ δέμο τὲν ἄδειαν is added (ll. 15, 28, 30, 33, 63); the second Kallias decree (No. 58, l. 16) tells us that this was to be routine procedure, and it is surprising that this is the first text which uses such a phrase (cf. p. 160), though we should not follow Ferguson (*Treasurers*, 162) in seeing in it a sign of protest by the *tamiai*. Ferguson believed that there was no room in our text for large payments by the *tamiai* for the Sicilian expedition, and held that the Athenians created a separate war fund after the Peace of Nikias, out of which major war expense could be met without borrowing from Athena (*Treasurers*, 159–62). There seems little ground for this view (see *ATL* iii. 354–8). The πάρεδροι frequently mentioned here are assessors or assistants of the *hellenotamiai*, save possibly in ll. 50 ff.

In 418–17 four payments were made, amounting in all to between 58 T. 1,829 dr. and 58 T. 1,996 dr. (1) The first (ll. 2–10) was originally intended for a squadron operating under Demosthenes, of whose movements in summer 418 Thucydides tells us nothing, either off Argos or at the mouth of the Strymon (see critical notes) ; by a decree, part of which is quoted, the payment was transferred to Euthydemos (for whom see Thuc. v. 19, 24, vii. 16, 69, Plut. *Nic.* 20, Diod. xiii. 13) and others for Thracian operations of which Thucydides has nothing to say. (2) In the second prytany, close in time to the battle of Man-tinea (Thuc. v. 57 ff.), Demosthenes does receive a payment (ll.11–15), largely if not all in electrum, for operations off Argos, perhaps con-nected with the blockade of Epidauros (Thuc. v. 75. 5; cf. *AJA* xxxii (1928) 350). (3) The third payment (ll. 16–17) has sometimes been used as evidence that Alcibiades, who was certainly not a general at the time of Mantinea (Thuc. v. 61. 2; Diod. xii ·9), was elected at a by-election later in the year (Wade-Gery, *CQ* xxiv (1930) 34 n. 2) ; the restoration is not certain, and we do not know who was the colleague of Autokles (general in 424–3, Thuc. iv. 53, 119) or what they were doing. (4) The fourth payment (ll. 18–21), in late spring 417, was to Nikias, Kallistratos (who fell in Sicily, Paus. vii. 16. 4, [Plut.] *Vit. X Orat.* 844b), and perhaps K[leomedes], presumably for Nikias' campaign to Chalkidike and Amphipolis (Thuc. v. 83–4) ; the money apparently came from Samos and has been used as evidence that Samos was still paying off her indemnity (see No. 55) as late as this (*ATL* iii. 334 f.).

In 417–16 three payments are recorded, the first (ll. 26–8) to one or two generals operating in Thrace and to Rhinon (for whom see Wade-Gery, *CQ* xxiv (1930) 35 n. 1), the second and third (ll. 29–33) to Teisias and Kleomedes for the Melian expedition (Thuc. v. 84).

The account for 416–15 is unfortunately the worst preserved. It is probably a false inference from the fact that Alcibiades, Lamachos, and Nikias were listed with demotics in ll. 49–50 only that this was the first of only four payments for the Sicilian expedition. There may have been more; certainly the two payments preserved in a relatively complete condition (ll. 52–3, 54–5) are for relatively small sums, 30 T. and 14 T. 1,000 dr. Nor are we in any better condition for the dates of the payments, the relation of which to the mutilation of the Hermae has been much discussed (West, *AJA* xxix. 3–16, xxxiii. 37–40; Meritt, ibid. xxxiv. 131–49; Dinsmoor, *Archons,* 337–41; Meritt, *AFD* 165–73, *Hesp.* iv (1935) 574 f.; Hatzfeld, *REG* l (1937) 293–303; Macdowell, *Andokides On the Mysteries,* 186–9) ; in our belief the inscription offers no certain fact to supplement the literary evidence, and the possibilities for restoration are too various to discuss here.

The record of 415–14 is much better preserved, and shows a total expenditure of between 353 and 355 T. (l. 81). The payments are not registered strictly in order of date, but according to the purposes to which they are applied. Of Telephonos (l. 63) and of the operation conducted by him and his colleagues we know nothing. The 9 talents granted to the ἀθλοθέται for the Lesser Panathenaia of 415 (ll. 66–8) may represent a specially luxurious celebration after the troubles of the summer; we do not accept Davison's view (*JHS* lxxviii (1958) 32) that they are an advance payment for the Great Panathenaia of 414. The next two payments (ll. 69–72), in autumn 415 and spring 414, are apparently to an occupation-force in Melos. Then follow two items connected with the Sicilian expedition (ll. 73–6): 300 T. sent on Nikias' urgent appeal (Thuc. vi. 93. 4, 94. 4; Diod. xiii. 8), and 4 T. 2,000 dr. to defray the expenses of the squadron (consisting, according to Meritt's conjecture, of eight vessels) which took this money and a cavalry force to Sicily. As seventeen days elapsed between these two payments, Meritt thinks that the expenses of the squadron were not paid until after its return from the west, and therefore substitutes ἐσκομισάσα]ς for the διακομίσα]ς of previous editors; however, the horse-transports may have taken seventeen days to prepare. Finally, two payments of unknown amount are made on the same day (ll. 77–9) in spring 414, one to a general in the Thermaic Gulf, possibly Euetion, who attacked Amphipolis in the summer (Thuc. vii. 9), the other to a general at Ephesos, presumably operating in support of Pissouthnes and Amorges (Meritt, *Hesp.* v (1936) 382; Andrewes, *Hist.* x (1961) 5).

The accounts of the Sicilian expedition were continued for the year 414–13 on the reverse of a large stele which already contained the accounts for 432–1 and probably 431–0 (see no. 81). For the text see Meritt, *AFD* 86–93. Connected with these texts is a fragmentary account assembled by Meritt, *Hesp.* xxvi (1957) 198–200, on which contributions to the campaign by Sicilian allies seem to have been recorded.

78 (77)

Decrees relating to the Sicilian Expedition:

415 B.C.

Eight fragments of at least two marble stelai (for fragment *g*, which has no preserved back, is thicker than fragment *c*, which has) found on the Acropolis; now in EM.

Developed Attic writing, stoichedon. The aspirate is rarely omitted.

IG i². 98, 99+ ; *SEG* x. 107+.

First Stele (?)

Fragment b

[- - - - - - -]ναν [. . . .]ν[. . . . . 10. . . . .]νι̣ [. . . .]οι̣ο [. . .5. . .]
[- διαχεροτονε̂σαι τὸν δε̑μ]ον αὐτίκα μάλα εἴτε δοκε̂ι hένα στρατ[εγ]-
[ὸν- - - - - - - h]ελέσθαι τύχει ἀγαθε̂ι νυνὶ hοίτινε[ς] ἀ-
[- - - - - - - -]το[.] τὸς πολεμίος hος ἂν δύνονται πλει-
5 [στ - - - - - -]ο̣σθον δὲ καὶ τὸν χσυμμάχον hοποσ-
[- - - - - - - - π]όλες ἐς τὲμ βολὲν τὲν Ἀθεναίο[ν]
[- - - - - - - - - h]εχσέκοντα νεο̂ν hόταμπερ[. . .]
[- - - - - - -]αις ἂμ βόλοντ[αι. . . . 9. . . . .]
[- - - - - - -]λλο [. . . . . . . .16. . . . .]
- -

Fragment c

[. . .] βολὲν καθότι ἄριστα κ̣[- - - - - - ἐά]-
ν τε ἀπὸ το̂ τιμέματος δοκε̂ι [- - - - - - - - ἐάν]
τε τὲμ πόλιν ἀναλο̂ν hόσον α[- - - - - - - τὰ]-
ς hεχσέκοντα να̂υς ἐὰμ προσ[- - - - - - - -]
5 μενον ε̣ι ἐσφέρεν hόταν δεε[- - - - - - ἐκκ]-
λεσίαν ποιεσάντον δέκα hε[μερο̂ν - - - - - π]-
ερὶ ἄλλο μεδενὸς πρότερον [- - - - - - - -]
ε ἐκκλεσίαν ποιε̂ν τὸς πρυτ[άνες - - - - - -]
αι τοι̂ς στρατεγοι̂ς τὸν νεο̂ν [- - - - - - - -]
10 οις· περὶ δὲ το̂ ἔκπλο τὸν νεο̂ν [- - - - - - ἐ]-
πανορθο̂σθαι ἐν το̂ι δέμοι hο[- - - - - - - ἐ]-
κκλεσίαν ποιόντον hόταν κε[- - - - - - -]
ον καὶ τε̂ς ἄλλες hυπερεσίας [- - - - - -]
καὶ ἀργυρίο ἐς καλλιέρεσιν [- - - - - -]
15 [.] hεχσακοσίον [καὶ] χιλίον [- - - - -]
- -

Second Stele (?)

Fragment a

[ἔδοχσεν τε̂ι βολε̂ι καὶ το̂ι δ]έμοι̣ [- - - - - -
[. . . . . .20. . . . . εἶ]πε· τύχε[ι ἀγαθε̂ι - - -
[. . . . . .22. . . . .]μένας μισ[θ - - - - - -
[. . . . . .21. . . . . .τ]ετταράκον[τα - - - -
5 [. . . . . .19. . . . . .πελ]τάσταις χρ[- - - - - - -

[..........22..........τ]οχσότας π[------
[...........23...........]δεει ἐκ το[------
[..........21..........τ]έτταρας ὀβο[λὸς ----
[.......17.........κυβε]ρνέτας δὲ καὶ [----
10 [........19..........τ]αμίαν δὲ χσυμπ[----
[..........20..........] hε βολὲ hόταμ με̣[---
[.......16.......τοῖ]ς τριεράρχοις κα[----
[..........21..........] τὸμ πολεμίον λ[----
[..........22..........]λλον hότι αν[----
- - - - - - - - - - - - - - - - - -

Fragments *d* and *g*

[- - - - - - - - - - - - - - - -]ι̣ο̣ [..5...]
[- - - - - - - - - - - - -]σοτοντ[.]
[----]α̣ι̣ ἒ φρορο̂σι τὲ[μ πόλιν ἒ τὲ]ν χόραν τ-
[-----]ν hὸς ἂν μὲ περιπο[λε̂ι μεδὲ μ]ισθοφορε̂-
5 [ι----]το πλὲν hοπόσοις [...7....h]ε βολὲ καὶ
[------ ἔ]νοχον ἔναι ζεμία[ι ...6...]αι μέτε τον
[----- πρ]υτάνες· λῦσαι δὲ [...7....]αι τὸ φσέφι-
[σμα - - - τ]ὸ ἔκπλο τὸν ἐχσέ[κοντα νεο̂]ν hέος ἂν ἠ̣
[----- ἐ]π' ἄλλο ἔργον με[δ' ἐπ' ἄλλεν σ]τρατιὰν
10 [----- τ]ρισχιλίον· ἐ[ὰν δέ τις εἴπει] ἒ ἐπιφσ-
[εφίσει ----]ς ἐχσαιρ[.......14.......]ον μ[.]
[------]ογι̣τ [..........20..........]
- - - - - - - - - - - - - - - - - -

Unknown Stele

Fragment *e*

]▨ιιΟΣ[
]τε̑ι Ἀθεναι κ[
στρα]τιόταις διανε[μ
]εν̣αι τὸν νεο̂ν [
5   ]ρχσοσι[
- - -

Fragment *f*

]τεγκ[...7....]
hεκ]ατὸν τριέρε̣[ς .]
] πολέμιοι hότι

]ạστέσασθαι το
5   ἐπιτ]έδειον ἔναι h-
]αμ ποι χρεσ-
]ς ναυσὶν
πρυ]τανε-
]ντ-
- - -

Fragment h

]αν[
]ιτο[
]ος χσυμμάχος α[
]ς κ[αὶ] τομ φορον [
5   ]σθαι τ[
]ος[
- -

Less conservative texts have been current since Kirchhoff, but, since it is impossible to define the length of line more closely than 50–70 letters, we print no restoration. Our text is based, with very slight variations, on that prepared by K. J. Dover for the *Historical Commentary on Thucydides*, which he has generously placed at our disposal. The top of *a*, the right margins of *b, f*, and *g*, and the left margin of *c* are preserved. In *b* l. 3 εἴτε πλείος or εἴτε τρês seems inevitable.

In the spring of 415 the Athenians, after hearing a report from the envoys they had sent to Egesta and from representatives of that city, resolved to dispatch a fleet of sixty vessels to Sicily under the command of Alcibiades, Nicias, and Lamachos as στρατηγοὶ αὐτοκράτορες (Thuc. vi. 8. 2). Four days later (vi. 8. 3) another Assembly was held, to speed up the preparation of the fleet and vote any additional provision the generals might require. At it, Nicias, emphasizing the difficulties of the undertaking, estimated the force needed as not less than 100 ships (not including Athenian and allied transports), not less than 5,000 Athenian and allied hoplites, and a proportionate number of light troops (vi. 25. 2). The Assembly forthwith voted the generals full powers with regard to the size of the expedition and the whole voyage (vi. 26. 1). There were doubtless later Assemblies, one of which we hear of in Andoc. i. 11. The expedition eventually consisted of 136 ships (100 Athenian), 5,100 hoplites (2,200 Athenian), and 1,300 light-armed (vi. 43).

Of the fragments before us, *b* certainly refers to the first Assembly. It still regards the number of generals as an open question (ll. 2–3); that there was ever any possibility of entrusting the expedition to one general is a matter on which the literary sources are silent. For the procedural formula used here, cf. No. 65, ll. 5 ff. Jones (*Athenian Democracy*, 112–14) regards such formulae as a sign that the decree was drafted in the Assembly, but we think it more likely that they are a sign of disagreement in the formulation of a probouleuma by the Council. Worth notice too is the language of l. 4, which seems to have been part of instructions stronger in language than anything in Thuc. vi. 8. 2.

Fragment *c* seems firstly (ll. 2–3) to be raising problems about the financing of the expedition, possibly on the lines of the distinction between public and private effort which runs through Thuc. vi. 31. 3–5, but there is no obvious parallel for the way in which τίμημα is used here. In ll. 4–12 the holding of further Assemblies, priority for their business, and the amendment of something are contemplated. The number of ships concerned is still sixty. We incline to attribute this text too to the first Assembly, looking forward to the second.

In fragment *a* we have reached a stage of detailed planning, with precise numbers, categories of light-armed, and pay. In l. 10 τ]αμίαν or ℎελλενοτ]αμίαν δὲ χουμπ[λὲν is a tempting restoration; he may perhaps be identified with Antimachos Ἑρμειος who appears beside the generals in No. 77, ll. 53, 55 (cf. Kahrstedt, *Untersuchungen zur Magistratur*, 125 n.).

In fragments *d* and *g* ll. 7–8 the revocation of a previous decree, presumably that of the first Assembly, is certainly in question. In l. 9 the diversion of certain resources elsewhere seems to be forbidden. L. 10 has generally been thought to define these resources as 3,000 T. (Ferguson, *Treasurers*, 160 f., *ATL* iii. 356 n. 40). It is tempting to interpret ll. 10–11 as a prohibition on touching the reserve fund of 1,000 T. established in 431 (Thuc. ii. 24. 1, viii. 15. 1).

79 (79 and 80)

Confiscated Property of the Hermokopidai:
414 B.C.

A

Excerpt from a stele of yellowish-grey marble, of which fifteen fragments survive, found in various places in Athens; now in EM and the Agora Museum.

The text was laid out in four columns (we give col. i only). There was no general heading, and the text must have been continued from another

stele. Developed Attic writing, partly stoichedon. Phot.: *Hesp.* xxii (1953)
Pl. 67–9, 72.
Pritchett, *Hesp.* xxii (1953) 240–9+, xxv (1956) 276–81, xxx (1961)
23–5 (three new fragments).

6 lines lost

- -	- - -	[. . .6. . .]ς
- -	- - -	[. .5. . .]ε
- -	- - -	[παῖς Π]εισίστρατος Κάρ
10		[κεφάλαιο]ν Ἐφαιστοδόρο
		[. . . .8. . . .]ⱶⱶΙΙΙC.
		[Ἀλκιβιάδο τ]ô Κλεινίο
		[Σκαμβωνίδ]ο σκεύε τάδε ἐπρά[θ]ε·
- -	- - -	[. . . .]τια
15 - -	- - -	[χύτ]ρα χαλκê
- -	- - -	[χύτ]ρα χαλκê
- -	- - -	[χύτρ]ạ χαλκê
- -	- - -	[. .5. . .]ς χαλκôς
		lacuna
- -	.Δ - -	.| - - -
20 [Ι]ΙΙ	ΔΓⱶⱶⱶ	ἐπικαρπί̣[α]
		Θρίαι
[Ι]ΙΙ	ΔΔ	ἐπικαρπία
		Ἀθμονοῖ.
		κεφάλαιον σὺν ἐπονίο[ις]
25		ΧΧΧΧ𐅅ΗΗΔΔⱶⱶⱶΙΙΙΙΙ.
		Πολυστράτο τô Διο[δόρο]
		Ἀγκυλêθεν·
ⱶΙ	ΗΗⱶⱶ	Πίστος
[ⱶ]	ΔΔΔΔⱶⱶ	ἐπικαρπία Ἀγ-
30		κυλêσι.
		κεφάλαιον σὺν ἐπονίο[ις]
		ΗΗΔΔΔΔΓⱶⱶΙ.
		Κεφισοδόρο μετοίκο ἐμ Περα[ιεῖ]·
ⱶⱶ	Η𐅂ΔΓ	Θρâιττα
35 ⱶΙΙΙ	ΗΔΔΔΓ	Θρâιττα
[ⱶ]ⱶ	Η𐅂ΔΔ	Θρâιξ
ⱶⱶΙΙΙ	ΗΗΔΔΔΔ	Σύρος

[Ͱ]ΙΙΙ	ΗΓ	Κάρ
ͰͰ	ΗℙΔͰ	ἱλλυριός
40 ͰͰΙΙΙ	ΗΗΔΔ	Θρᾶιττα
ͰΙΙΙ	ΗΔΓ	Θρᾶιξ
ͰΙΙΙ	ΗΔΔΔΔͰͰͰ	Σκύθες
ͰΙΙΙ	ΗΔΔͰ	ἱλλυριός
ͰͰ	ΗℙͰͰ	Κόλχος
45 ͰͰ	ΗℙΔΔͰͰͰ	Κὰρ παῖς
Ͱ	ℙΔΔͰͰ	Καρικὸν παιδίον
[Ͱ]ͰͰΙ	ΗΗΗͰ	Σύρος
[Ͱ]Ͱ	ΗℙͰ	Μελιττ[ενός or ενέ]
Ͱ	ℙΔΔΔΓ..Ι	Λυδέ

- -

Enough stone is preserved to the right of the lacuna to make it clear that the items listed were short ones. In l. 29 the figure restored for the sales-tax is certain, but represented an overcharge (Pritchett, *Hesp.* xxii, 229, 246). In l. 49 the figure is a new reading.

B

Eight joining fragments of white marble, found at various places in Athens; now in EM and the Agora Museum. Nine other fragments probably belong to the same stele.

Developed Attic writing, generally stoichedon, with considerable variations in spacing. Phot.: *Hesp.* viii (1939) 71, xxii, Pl. 78; *AJA* lvi (1952), Pl. 5.

Meritt, *Hesp.* viii (1939) 69–76+; Pritchett, *Hesp.* xxii (1953) 268–79, xxx (1961) 28 (another fragment).

50 - -	- - -	[....] καὶ ἔ[γγονα τούτον].
		vacat
		vacat
		[Ἀδειμάν]το τô Λε[υκ]ολοφίδο Σκα[μβονίδο]·
- -	..	ἀνὲρ [Ἀρ]ιστόμαχος
55		ἀγρὸς [ἐν] Θάσοι ἐν Ἰ[- -]
		καὶ οἰκ[ία]·
- -	[...]ΗΗℙ	ἔπεστιν [πίθ]οι ἐνγ[- - -]
		ἡγιὲς ΔƉ[..σ]αθρο[ι̣ - -]
		ἐπιθέμα[τα ἔχοντες].
		οἴνο ἀμφο[ρê]ς [- - -]
60 - -	[..]ΗℙΔΔΔ	ℾℙ̣ΔΔΔΔ τρ[ê]ς χόε[ς].

		vacat
	[Π]αναιτίο·	
65 - -	[.]ΔΔ	οἶνο ἀμφορ[έ]ς Ἀττι[κô]
		καθαρô ΗΙΙΙΙ ἐ[π]τὰ χό[ες]
[ΗΗΗ]	[Η]ΗᴾΔ	σμένε ἐν τôι [ἀ]γρ[ôι]
		τôι ἐν 'Ισ[...6...]ΔΓ[- -]
[ΗΙ]	[Η]	βόε ἐρ[γάτα δ]ύο ἐν Ἀρ - -
[Η]	[ᴾ]ΔΔ	βόε [δύο]
70 - -	- - -	β[όε]ς τέτταρες καὶ μό[σχοι - -]
		πρόβατα ᴾΔΔΔΙΙΙΙ
- -	- - -	καὶ ἔκγονα τούτον
[ΓΗΗΙΙΙ]	[ᴾΗΗ]Δ	αἶγες ᴾΔΓΙΙ καὶ ἔγγον[α τούτον].
		vacat
75	[Πολυστρά]το τô Διοδόρο Ἀγκυλέος·	
		οἰκία ἐγ Κυδαθεναίο[ι, ἐι πρόθυρον]
		τὸ δίκιον, ἐι γεῖτόν ἐ[στι τὸ hιερὸν]
- -	[....]ᴾ	Ἀρτέμιδος τês Ἀθμον[όθεν]
		Ἀμαρυσίας
80	- - -	χόριον Ἀγκυλêσι νο[τόθεν]
		τô λόφο hίνα τὸ hιε[ρὸν - -]
	3 lines vacant	
85	Νικίδ[ο τô] Φοινικί[δο Μ]ελιτ[έος]·	
	Η ᴾΗΗ	ἐκχαλ[- - - - -
		vacat
	Εὐφιλέτο τô Τ[ιμοθέο Κυδαθεναιέος]·	
	περὶ ἀμφότερα· οἰκ[ία - - -]	
90	ΔΓ ΧΓᴾ	ἀπ[- - - -]
	2 lines vacant	
	Φερεκλέος τô Φε[ρεν]ικα[ίο Θεμακ]έο[ς]·	
	περὶ ἀμφότερα· οἰκ[ία ἐ]μ Βατêι [καὶ] χορίον	
95		*vacat*
		hέτ[ερον] χορίον [...]αλαν[- -]
		ετ[..5...] *vacat*
		χορί[ον π]αρὰ τὸ Πύθ[ιον.]ΙΟ[
		vacat
100 ΔΗΗ	ΧΗΗ	[ο]ἰκό[πε]δον [ἔ]λὺ [κ]αὶ χέρ[ρον]
		παρ[ὰ τὸ Π]ύθιον

ἑτε[ρον] χορίον παρὰ τ[ὸ]
ἡερά[κλε]ιον
ὀργά[δος] τὸ ἥμισυ τῆς ἐ[ντὸς τὸ]

105   Πυθ[ίο υ κ]αὶ διανόμο τὸ ἀπὸ [τὸ ἱερὸ]
[τὸ δὲ ἄλλ]ο ἥμισυ ἐγ Κυκάλει·
τα̣[ῦτα ἐπ]ράθε συνλέβδεν ἅπαν[τα].

        2 lines vacant

110   μισθόσες ἡαίδε κ[ατε]βλέθεσαν
τὸν ἀσεβεσάντο[ν περὶ] τὸ θεό·
Φαῖδρο τὸ Πυθο[κλέος] Μυρρινοσίο
     ⊓Δ   ο[ἰκίας μ]ίσθοσις κατεβλέθε
           [γῆς Μυρρ]ινόντι μίσθοσις

115   Ṇ   ΗΗΗ⊓   [κατεβλέ]θε
    İ   ἐκ τὸν Ἀδειμ[άντο τὸ Λ]ευκολοφίδο Σκαμβονίδο
     Χ⊓ΗΔΔΔⱵΗΙΙΙΙ [...7....]ΟΙ.ΡΕΣ
     ἐκ τὸν Ἀχσιόχ[ο τὸ Ἀλκιβιάδο Σ]καμβονίδ[ο]
     Χ⊓ΗΔΔΔⱵΗΗΙΙΙC[- - - - - - - -]

120   ΗΗ⊓   [- - - - - - - -]
     Η⊓ΔⱵΗΙΙΙΙ   [- - - - - - - -]
     ἐκ [τὸν -]
     -

l. 57: ἐνγ[έα ἀμφορέον] Pritchett.   ll. 60–5: These wine prices are discussed by Pritchett, *Hesp.* xxv (1956) 199–203; [⊓]ΔΔ is very probable in l. 64.   l. 67: Ἰσθ[μόι] edd., but the theta seems very uncertain.   ll. 68–73: We follow Pritchett's suggestions (*Hesp.* xxv. 257–60), except for his [τούτον] at the end of l. 70.   l. 86: The current restoration is ἐκχαλ[κόματα]; perhaps ἐκ Χαλ[κίδος ἐπικαρπία vel sim. (*Ehrenberg Studies*, p. 191, n. 56).   ll. 89, 94: περὶ ἀμφότερα was added later in both these lines.   l. 93: Φι[λοδ]ικα[ίο (Raubitschek) is a more convincing name, but Φε[is slightly more probable epigraphically.   l. 96: π[αρ]ὰ Λαν[or ἐ[ν.]αλαν[.   l. 98. A new reading, which we cannot explain.   ll. 104–5: τῆς ἐ[πὶ τόι]||Πυθ[ίοι κ]αὶ (Meritt) fills the space but leaves the case of διανόμο unexplained.   ll. 116–17: Traces of another column to the left.

Ἐν δὲ ταῖς Ἀττικαῖς στήλαις αἱ κεῖνται ἐν Ἐλευσῖνι, τὰ τῶν ἀσεβησάντων περὶ τὼ θεὼ δημοσίᾳ πραθέντα ἀναγέγραπται (Pollux, x. 97). The two excerpts given here come from a large number of fragments, assigned by Pritchett to ten or eleven stelai (whether Stele XI belongs to the series is doubtful) and published or republished by him, *Hesp.* xxii (1953) 225–99 (some additional fragments, ibid. xxx (1961) 23–9), supplemented by important commentaries by him and Amyx, ibid. xxv (1956) 178–317, xxvii (1958) 163–310. The fragments were found over a wide area, but by far the largest number come from the south-east corner of the Agora, the site of the Eleusinion, for which see Wycherley, *The Athenian Agora: Testimonia*, 74–85. Nothing of the kind has been found at Eleusis, and we must either follow Boeckh in emending Pollux's text to Ἐλευσινίῳ, which is unlikely, since ἐν τῷ Ἐλευσινίῳ is the standard phrase, or assume a simple confusion in Pollux or his source (so Pippin, ibid. xxv. 324 f.).

The condemnation of the Hermokopidai and the confiscation of their property was placed by Philochorus in 415–14 (*FGH* 328 F 134). Pritchett's Stele X, certainly the latest of the series, can be dated to late winter 414–13 with virtual certainty, and references (A 20, 22, 29) to ἐπικαρπία, crops not yet harvested, show that Stelai I–II belong to a September. Pritchett, ibid. xxii. 232–4, thought this more likely to be September 414 than September 415, but it seems not unlikely that the whole process took a considerable time (Lewis, *Ehrenberg Studies*, 181 ff.).

Pollux's words and the place of exhibition of the stelai suggest that they were primarily thought of as exhibiting the property of those who had profaned the Mysteries (Pollux, B 111), but since this case was inextricably confused with the affair of the Hermokopidai and many of the accused were involved in both, our documents recognize the confusion, though perhaps the recognition was delayed, as the later addition of περὶ ἀμφότερα to B 89, 94 suggests (in Stele X, 13, however, τὸμ περὶ ἀμφότερα was inscribed from the first). See Lewis, op. cit. 187.

Of the thirty-three names given by Andocides, i. 12–18, as having been denounced for profaning the Mysteries, twelve have so far appeared on the stelai (two changes in Andocides' text, Νικίδης for Νικιάδης and Οἰωνίας for Ἰωνίας in i. 13 must now be made). Of the twenty-two names given by him (i. 35, 67) for the mutilation of the Hermai, four have so far appeared. His lists appear then to be substantially accurate. Though Euphiletos, listed as περὶ ἀμφότερα here, B 89, and in Stele X, 13–14, does not appear in his list of those who profaned the Mysteries, he may well be included in τοὺς ἄλλους of And. i. 17 (see Pritchett, ibid. xxii. 230–2; Macdowell, *Andokides On The Mysteries*, 71 f.).

Of the names before us, Hephaistodoros (A 10) was denounced by Teukros (And. i. 15); Alcibiades (A 12–13) needs no comment here; Polystratos (A 26, B 75) was denounced by Andromachos and executed at an early stage in the proceedings (And. i. 13); Kephisodoros (A 33; we should perhaps consider restoring ἐμ Πέρα[ιεῖ οἰκῶντος], the normal designation of a metic) was denounced by Teukros (And. i. 15; Macdowell, op. cit. 211, suggests identifying him with the comic dramatist); Adeimantos (B 53, 116), a friend and fellow demesman of

Alcibiades, was denounced by Agariste and went into exile (And. i. 16), shared Alcibiades' rehabilitation, and became general in 407, but was not affected by his second fall, and survived to be general at Aigospotamoi and to be accused of contributing to that defeat by treachery (Xen. *Hell.* i. 4. 21, 7. 1, ii. 1. 30, 32; Lys. xiv. 38; *PA* 202); Panaitios (B 63) is presumably, since he lacks περὶ ἀμφότερα, the Panaitios denounced by Andromachos for the Mysteries (And. i. 13), and not the one denounced by Andocides himself for the Hermae (And. i. 52, 67, rightly distinguished by Macdowell, op. cit. 72; Pritchett apparently identifies them); Nikides (B 85) was denounced by Andromachos (And. i. 12–13); Euphiletos (B 89; see above) was denounced by Teukros and Andocides for the Hermae (And. i. 35, 51, 56, 61–4); Pherekles (B 93) was denounced by his own slave (And. i. 17) for having the Mysteries performed in his house in Themakos (apparently not listed in B 94 ff.) and also by Teukros for the Hermae (And. i. 35); Phaidros (B 112), denounced by Teukros (And. i. 15), is shown by the appearance of his full name in this text to be the friend of Socrates, after whom Plato's dialogue is named, and his later poverty (Lys. xix. 15) is now explained (cf. Hatzfeld, *REA* xli (1939) 313–18); Axiochos, also the eponym of a Socratic dialogue and uncle of Alcibiades (for the *stemma*, see Vanderpool, *Hesp.* xxi (1952) 6), was denounced by Agariste and went into exile (And. i. 16), returning to move the second decree of No. 89 and speak in the debate after Arginusai ([Plat.] *Axiochos* 369 a).

Even more important, however, than their political interest is the social and economic evidence that these texts provide. They throw some light on what possessions a fifth-century Athenian might have and what they were worth. The prices should be taken with some reserve, since they are the product of a forced sale, with perhaps some taint of impiety about the goods as well as the owners. The texts deserve study as a whole, and our excerpts are misleading to the extent that household utensils and furniture are relatively uncommon in them.

Real property. The scatter of land-holdings is interesting. A 20–4 shows an owner of crops both at Thria and Athmonon. Polystratos, besides land in his own deme of Ankyle (A 29, B 80), has a town house in Kudathenaion with a two-column porch (B 76). Adeimantos has a farm outside Attica altogether, in Thasos, fully equipped with storage-pithoi, sold as part of the farm (B 55 ff.; cf. Amyx, *Hesp.* xxvii (1958) 168–70. Other texts show property in Oropos, Euboea, and Abydos.); Pherekles, besides his house in his own deme of Themakos (And. i. 17), has a property at Bate and other miscellaneous lots (B 95 ff.); Phaidros was apparently not living in his own deme of Myrrhinous at all, but leasing his property there for 410 dr. (a year?

B 113–15; a town house of his may be referred to in Lys. xxxii. 14). Adeimantos and Axiochos seem each to have had an income from leases four times as great (B 116 ff.). For the various terms for real property in these texts, see Pritchett, *Hesp*. xxv. 261–9. For ἐλύ (B 100), cf. Hesych. εἰλύ· μέλαν, but there may be a connection with ἰλύς.

Slaves (*Hesp*. xxv. 276–81, xxx. 27). The total of slaves found in these texts is now 45. The largest single preserved holding is that of the metic Kephisodoros (A 34 ff.), who had at least 16; Adeimantos had at least 8 (Stele VI, 18 ff., 54 (= B 54 here), X, 3), Axiochos at least 7 (Stele X, 7, 9; *Hesp*. xxx. 26). Since these last two have more than one entry, it is unsafe to assume that Polystratos had only the one slave recorded in A 28. Twenty-four prices are preserved, averaging 170–80 dr. The median price is slightly lower, 157 dr., since the average is substantially increased by a Carian goldsmith and a Macedonian woman, who fetched 360 and 310 dr. (Stele II, 77 ff.), and the Syrian here (A 47). No variation in price between men and women or between nationalities can be detected, except that the two Syrians are high; Pritchett's view that παῖς and παιδίον here (A 45–6) denote children is hardly safe, since the words are regularly used of slaves of all ages. Of the 35 slaves whose origins can be ascertained, 12 are Thracian, 7 Carian, 3 Scythian, 3 οἰκογενεῖς, 2 Syrian, 2 Illyrian, with 1 each from Colchis, Lydia, Macedonia, Phrygia, Messenia, and Cappadocia (interpreting Μελιττ[, A 48, as referring to Melitene, rather than to Malta or the Illyrian island of Melite).

These documents were doubtless drawn up by the πωληταί, whose duties included that of selling confiscated property (Arist. Ἀθ. Πολ. 47. 2, 52. 1). The left-hand column records the ἐπώνιον on each sale, and the second column the price paid. The ἐπώνιον (A 24, 31) was not an exact 1 per cent, but determined by a scale on which, for example, for every amount from 100 dr. to 104 dr. 5 ob. the buyer paid 1 dr. 1 ob. additional tax (Pritchett, *Hesp*. xxii. 226–30). In the early fourth century a similar scale worked to a base of 2 per cent (Pritchett, *CP* li (1956) 100–2), but the tax was halved again later.

80

An Oligarchic Decree: 411 B.C.

Fragment of a marble stele, with the left edge preserved, found on the south slope of the Acropolis; now in EM.

Ionic script, stoichedon 30. The last four lines are in another, more deeply cut, hand. Phot.: *IIA* 44.

IG ii². 12+ ; Wilhelm, *Jahresh.* xxi/xxii (1922–4) 147; *IG* i². p. 297; Ferguson, *CP* xxi (1926) 73–4; Weston, *AJP* lxi (1940) 345–6, 356–7; Kahrstedt, *Klio*, xxxiii (1940) 12; Lenschau, *Rh. Mus.* xc (1941) 24–30; de Ste Croix, *Hist.* v (1956) 17–19.

```
      [....8....]ην[..........20.........]
      [...6...]ηι ην τε[.........18........]
      [...6...]άτης ᾿Ικα[ριεὺς ἐγραμμάτευεν.]
      [βολῆ]ς ἐπεστάτε[........17.........]
 5    [...κ]αὶ μετ᾿ αὐτὸ π[........16........]
      [.Ξυ]πεταιών, Διωπ[........16........]
      [..] Κεφαλῆθεν, Καλ[........16........]
      [.᾿Ι]ππομένης εἶπε· [........16........]
      στίωι, ἐπειδὴ πρόξ[ενός ἐστι ᾿Αθηναίω]-
10    ν καὶ εὐεργέτης κ[αὶ εὖ ποεῖ ὅ τι δύνατ]-
      αι τὴν πόλιν τὴν ᾿Αθ[ηναίων καὶ τὴν...]
      στίων τὸ ψήφισμα τ[ὸ προψηφισμένον α]-
      ὑτῶι ἀναγράψαι ἐν σ[τήληι λιθίνηι τὸ]-
      ν γραμματέα τῆς βολ[ῆς τὸν νῦν γραμμα]-
15    τεύοντα καὶ καταθεῖν[αι ἐν πόλει. τὰ δὲ]
      χρήματα, ἅ ἐστιν Πυθοφά[νει ᾿Αθήνησιν]
      ἢ ἄλλοθί πο ὧν ᾿Αθηναῖοι κ[ρατῶσιν, καὶ]
      περὶ τῆς νεὼς ἃ λεγει καὶ [περὶ τῶν χρη]-
      [μ]άτων, μὴ ἀδικῆν μηδένα κ[αὶ ἀσυλίαν ἐ]-
20    ναι αὐτῶι καὶ τοῖς χρήμα[σι αὐτὸ καὶ ἀ]-
      νίοντι καὶ ἀπίοντι. ταῦτ[α μὲν ἔστω ἐψ]-
      ηφισμένα ὅσης ᾿Αθηναῖοι [κρατῶσι πᾶσ]-
      ι τοῖς Πυθοφάνος κατὰ τα[ὐτά· ὅπως δ᾿ ἂν]
      ταῦτα γίγνηται, τοὺς στ[ρατηγὸς τὸς α]-
25    [ἰ]εὶ στρατηγῶντας ἐπιμ[έλεσθαι καὶ τ]-
      [ὴ]ν βολὴν τὴν αἰεὶ βολεύ[οσαν. προσανα]-
      [γ]ράψαι δὲ καὶ τόδε τὸ ψή[φισμα ἐς τὴν α]-
      [ὐ]τὴν στήλην τὸγ γραμμ[ατέα τῆς βολῆς.]
      υυ ἐπὶ ᾿Αριστοκράτος ἄ[ρχοντος υυυυυ]
30    [ἔδ]οξ[εν] τῆ[ι] β[ολ]ῆι, Κεκρ[οπὶς ἐπρυτάνε]-
      [υε, ...7.... ἐγρα]μμάτε[υεν, ᾿Αριστοκρά]-
      [της ἦρχε, ...7....]ς ἐπε[στάτε, - - - -]
      - - - - - - - - - - - - - - - -
```

L. 2 : τ|ῆι γνώμ]ηι ἦν Τε[ισάμενος εἶπεν vac.] Wilhelm; [ἔδοξεν | τῆι βολ]ῆι·
ἦν τε[τάρτη τῆς πρυτανείας] Lewis *ap.* de Ste Croix.   l. 4: Wilhelm. Restoring a name creates overwhelming difficulties.   l. 5: π[ρόεδρευον or π[ρόεδροι
ἦσαν Wilhelm; π[ρυτάνες] or π[ρυτάνες ἦσαν Kahrstedt.   ll. 8 and 11:
That the honorand is from Karystos seems never to have been doubted,
but τήν τε Καρυ]|στίων in ll. 11–12 is stylistically impossible and καὶ τὴν
Καρυ]|στίων (Wilhelm) is one letter too long. Epigraphical anomalies are
eliminated by restoring καὶ τὴν Φαι]|στίων in ll. 11–12, and in l. 8 εἶπε[ν·
Πυθοφάνει τῶι Φαι]|στίωι for the vulgate εἶπε· [Πυθοφάνει τῶι Καρυ]|-
στίωι.   l. 15: [τὰ δὲ] Leonardos, Lenschau; [vvvv] Wilhelm.   l. 18:
[περὶ ἐμπολη|μ]άτων Wilamowitz.   ll. 31–2: our restoration.

The decree itself (ll. 8–28) is regular enough. Pythophanes, presumably a merchant and already an Athenian *proxenos*, receives in
return for his continued good services the inscription of a previous
decree in his honour (presumably this stood higher up the stone and
may end in ll. 1–2; the suggestion of Weston that *IG* ii². 73 is yet
another decree for him is unconvincing) and security for his trading
operations. The Athenian Empire is still in being (ll. 17, 22). The
prescript, however, has no epigraphical parallel whatsoever. Wilhelm
pointed out that there was space for five names in ll. 4–7, and, comparing Arist. Ἀθ. Πολ. 30. 4, κληροῦν δὲ τὴν βουλὴν τοὺς ἐννέα ἄρχοντας,
τὰς δὲ χειροτονίας κρίνειν πέντε τοὺς λαχόντας ἐκ τῆς βουλῆς, καὶ ἐκ
τούτων ἕνα κληροῦσθαι καθ' ἑκάστην ἡμέραν τὸν ἐπιψηφιοῦντα, attributed
ll. 3–28 to the year 411. This is certainly right, but opinion remains
divided as to whether the decree comes from the regime of the Four
Hundred or that of the Five Thousand. Ferguson maintained the
latter and it sustained him in his belief that Ἀθ. Πολ. 30 was not
merely an advance programme but the actual constitution of the
Five Thousand; the former view was advocated by Lenschau and
de Ste Croix, who, accepting the restored reference to Karystos,
pointed out that it was in revolt during the regime of the Five
Thousand (Thuc. viii. 95. 7) and that the Four Hundred did have five
proedroi (Thuc. viii. 67. 3), and the name suggests that they presided
over as well as enrolled the Four Hundred. The placing of this decree
is complicated by the problems of reconciling it with the other known
decree of the period, [Plut.] *Vit. X Orat.* 833 d, ἔδοξεν τῇ βουλῇ,
μιᾷ καὶ εἰκοστῇ τῆς πρυτανείας· Δημόνικος Ἀλωπεκῆθεν ἐγραμμάτευε,
Φιλόστρατος Παλληνεὺς ἐπεστάτει, Ἄνδρων εἶπε, equally alien to the
normal democratic formulae. Lewis's restoration of ll. 1–2 of this
decree brings the two prescripts into line, but is probably wrong, in
default of a parallel for his dating formula; it does, however, have
the advantage of finding room for the clause ἔδοξεν τῆι βολῆι, the
absence of which is otherwise surprising.

Ll. 29–32 start a further decree passed in 399–8, presumably also for Pythophanes. The observation that they are in a second hand disposes of the argument that the fourth-century democracy would not have reinscribed a decree of the Four Hundred. For ἔδοξεν τῆι βολῆι without mention of the δῆμος, in this period, for simple renewals of earlier honours, cf. Tod, vol. ii, no. 98.

81 (81)

Expenditure of the Treasurers of Athena: 411 B.C.

On the left side of a stele, not yet fully reconstructed, on the front of which were the accounts of 432–1 (Meritt, *AFD* 80–3) and probably also of 431–0 (ibid. 84–5), and on the back the accounts of 414–13 (ibid. 88–9) and probably also of 413–12 and 412–11 (now only represented by *IG* i². 307). Below this text was almost certainly the account of 411–10 (under the regime of the Five Thousand), of which there survives only a very small unpublished fragment on the right-hand side of *IG* i². 307. All the fragments, save a tiny scrap of the accounts of 432–1 from the Agora (*Hesp.* xxx (1961) 241), are in EM.

Ionic letters, but Attic lambda, not stoichedon (cf. Austin 52 f.). Phot.: Meritt, *AFD* 91; facs.: ibid. Pl. i.

IG i². 298; Meritt, *AFD* 93; Ferguson, *Treasurers*, 145–6.

[Ἀθηναῖ]οι ἀνήλω[σαν ἐπὶ]
[Μνασιλ]όχου ἄρχο[ντος]
    vacat
[ταμί]αι ἱερῶν χ[ρημάτ]-
5 [ων τῆ]ς Ἀθηναία[ς Ἀσω]-
[πόδω]ρος Κυδαθ[ηνα]-
[ιεὺς] καὶ συνάρχο[ντ]-
[ες] οἷς Εὔανδρος Ἐ[ρ]-
[ι]θαλίωνος Εὐωνυμ-
10 [ε]ὺς ἐ[γρ]αμμάτευεν
παρέδοσαν ἑλληνο-
ταμίαις Ἀντισθέν-
ει Ἑρμείωι καὶ συν-
άρχοσιν ψηφισαμέ-
15 νης τῆς βολῆς Ἑκατ-
[ο]μβαιῶνος ἐνάτει

[φθί]νοντος ἀπὸ τῶν
[χρημάτ]ων Ἀθηναίας
[Πολιά]δος: ϞϞ⋔ΤΤΧΧ
20 [.. 4–5 ..] ⋔ΔΔⱵⱵⱵⱵΙΙΙΙ τῆ-
[ς Νίκης Ἀ]θηναίας ἀπὸ
[.. c. 9 ..]ων ⋔ΗΔΔΔΔ
- - - - - - - - - - - - - - - - -

We follow Meritt's text, save in l. 22, where the last numeral was read
by Lolling, apparently rightly, and the restoration [τῶν χρημάτ]ων (Lolling
and Kirchhoff) would be unparalleled. Perhaps [τῶν ἐπετεί]ων; cf. ἐκ τὸν
ἐπετείον in No. 84, l. 3.

This record dates from the rule of the Four Hundred in the summer
of 411. Mnasilochos (l. 2; for the Doric form of the name, see Keil,
Hermes, xxix (1894) 39 n. 1), one of their number, ἦρξεν . . . . δίμηνον
ἐπὶ Θεοπόμπου ἄρχοντος, ὃς ἦρξε τοὺς ἐπιλοίπους δέκα μῆνας (Arist.
Ἀθ. Πολ. 33. 1); he reappears later as one of the Thirty (Xen. *Hell.*
ii. 3. 2). The oligarchs use ψηφισαμένης τῆς βολῆς (l. 14) instead of the
democratic ψηφισαμένο τὸ δέμο (No. 77 *passim* and No. 84, l. 3). They
also date by month and day (ll. 15, 17) without reference to prytany,
though they had prytanies of some sort (Thuc. viii. 70. 1): according
to Meritt's reckoning 21st or 22nd Hekatombaion = 14 or 15 August
411 (*Athenian Year* 218). They use Ionic letters for the first time in
these texts, perhaps on principle.

82 (82)

Eretria revolts from Athens: 411 B.C.

White marble stele, found at Eretria; now in the museum there.
Ionic writing, with angular Ƀ and Ρ and dotted omikron (for the circular
letters, see *BSA* lvii (1962) 3 n. 27). Ll. 2–10 stoichedon. Phot.: *IG* xii. 9,
Pl. i (part).
IG xii. 9. 187 A+; *SIG* 105; *DGE* 804; Buck 13.

θεοί.
ἔδοξεν τεῖ βουλῆι· Ἡγέλοχον
τὸν Ταραντῖνον πρόξενον εἶναι καὶ εὐεργέτην καὶ αὐτὸν
5 κ[α]ὶ παῖδας, καὶ σίτηριν εἶνα-

ι καὶ αὐτῶι καὶ παιρίν, ὅταν ἐ-
[π]ιδημέωριν, καὶ ἀτελέην καὶ
προεδρίην ἐς τὸς ἀγῶνας ὡς σ-
υνελευθερώραντι τὴμ πόλιν
10 ἀπ' Ἀθηνάων.

l. 2: All editions cited, save Buck, have βολῆι, wrongly.

The defeat of thirty-six Athenian ships under Thymochares by the
Spartan admiral Agesandridas off Eretria in the summer of 411 was
immediately followed by the revolt of that city (Thuc. viii. 95).
Agesandridas' forty-two ships included some from Taras (Thuc. viii.
91. 2), and Hegelochos may have been in command of them. For the
revolt and its background see Wallace, *The Euboian League and its
Coinage*, 1–4. The omission of any reference to the δῆμος in l. 2 (contrast *IG* xii, suppl. 549) suggests that Eretria was under an oligarchy
when this decree was passed. Below this decree there stands on the
stone a similar decree of later date in honour of another Tarentine
(*SIG* 106), with the democratic formula ἔδοξεν τε̑ι βουλε̑ι καὶ τῶι δέμοι.

The substitution of rho for intervocalic sigma is characteristic of
Eretria and Oropos. Plato's assertion (*Crat.* 434 c) that the Eretrians
substitute rho for final sigma has as yet no epigraphic support. See
Buck, p. 57.

83

Rewards for Informers at Thasos:
(?) 411–409 B.C.

Block of white marble with raised edge round the inscription, found in the
Agora at Thasos; now in the museum there.

Parian alphabet, but with Ξ, uniquely in this script. The letters of the
second law are smaller and more closely spaced, but show no other difference from the first. Phot.: Pouilloux, *Recherches*, Pl. 13. 1; *LSAG*, Pl. 58.

Pouilloux, *Recherches sur l'histoire et les cultes de Thasos*, i. 139–62, no. 18;
Salviat, *BCH* lxxxii (1958) 212–15; Chamoux, *REG* lxxii (1959) 351–6;
Pouilloux, *Choix*, 31; *LSAG* 303, no. 76; Pleket, *Hist.* xii (1963) 75–7.

I. ὃς ἂν ἐπανάστασιν βολευομένην ἐπὶ Θάσωι κατείπηι καὶ φανῆι
ἐόντα ἀληθέα, χιλίος στατῆρ|ας ἐκ τῆς πόλεως ἰσχέτω· ἢν δὲ δο̑λος
κατείπηι, καὶ ἐλεύθερος ἔστω· ἢμ πλέος ἢ εἷς κατείπωσι, | τριηκόσιοι
κρινόντων δίκην δικάσαντες· ἢν δέ τις τῶν μετεχόντων κατείπηι, τό τε

ἀργύριον | ἰσχέτω καὶ κατώμοτος κατ' αὐτô μὴ ἔστω μηδὲ δίκη μηδεμία
5 μήτε ἱρὴ μήτε βεβήλη περὶ τότων ‖ μηδὲ ἐν τῆι ἐπαρῆι ἔστω πλὴν ἑνός,
τô πρῶτο βολεύσαντος· ἄρχει εἰνάτη ἀπιόντος Ἀπατορι|ῶνος, ἐπὶ
Ἀκρύπτο, Ἀλεξιμάχο, Δεξιάδεω ἀρχόντων. |

II. ὃς ἂν ἐν τῆις ἀποικίησιν ἐπανάστασιν βολευομένην κατείπηι, ἢ
προδιδόντα τὴν πόλιν Θασίων | τινὰ ἢ τῶν ἀποίκων, καὶ φανῆι ἐόντα
ἀληθέα, διηκοσίος στατῆρας ἐκ τῆς πόλεως ἰσχέτω· ἢν δὲ τὰ | χρήματα
ἦι τô ἐπανισταμένο πλευνὸς ἄξια διηκοσίων στατήρων, τετρακοσίος
10 στατῆρας ἐκ τῆς πόλεως ‖ ἰσχέτω· ἂν δὲ δόλος κατείπηι, τό τε χρῆμα
ἰσχέτω καὶ ἐλεύθερος ἔστω· ἤμ πλέος ἢ εἷς κατείπωσι, τριηκόσιοι |
κρινόντων δίκην δικάσαντες· ἢν δέ τις τῶν μετεχόντων κατείπηι, τό
τε ἀργύριον ἰσχέτω καὶ κατώμοτος | κατ' αὐτô μὴ ἔστω μηδὲ δίκη
μηδεμία μήτε ἱρὴ μήτε βεβήλη περὶ τότων μηδὲ ἐν τῆι ἐπαρῆι ἔστω
πλὴν ἑνός, τô | πρῶτο βολεύσαντος· ἄρχει τῆι ῥήτρηι τρίτη ἱσταμένο
Γαλαξιῶνος, ἐπὶ Φανοδίκο, Ἀντιφάνεος, Κτησίλλο | ἀρχόντων.

I. For information about a plot against Thasos, the city will pay
1,000 staters (the equivalent of 1,600 Attic drachmae). A slave will
get his freedom as well. If there is more than one informer, 300 men
will hear the issue and decide (their priority). [Chamoux infers from
the aorist that this will be the court which has judged the conspirators,
but this is not a necessary inference; in any case judging would have
to precede decision.] If it is one of the conspirators who lays the
information, he will get the money, no charge based on an oath,
either religious or secular, may be brought against him, and he
will be exempt from the curse incurred (for ἐπαρή cf. No. 30 and
Tod, vol. ii, no. 191, l. 26), but this amnesty shall not apply to the
initiator of the plot.

II. The second law extends the reward to plots formed in 'the
colonies'. (It is possible that Neapolis, cf. No. 89, is included in this
term.) The reward is here only 200 staters, unless the estate of the
plotter is worth more, in which case the reward will be doubled,
otherwise there is no essential difference in the formulae.

For encouraging informers against possible disturbance of the
status quo cf. No. 52, l. 25. Abdera (BCH lxvi–lxvii (1942–3) 189, no. 3)
provides the closest parallel for rewards for such information; rewards
for prospective tyrant-slayers are attested at Athens (Ar. Birds 1074–5),
Miletus (No. 43) and Ilion (OGIS 218).

Most of our parallels come from democracies ensuring their own
safety. Pouilloux has argued that here we have documents of the
Thasian oligarchy which came or returned to power in the summer of

411 (Thuc. viii. 64). He rightly notes that the lettering appears somewhat later than any other Thasian text in the Parian alphabet, and
later than several texts in Ionic to which dates of 430–425 can be
plausibly assigned; and suggests that the Parian alphabet was deliberately revived by the oligarchs, a phenomenon perhaps paralleled
on the coins and amphora-stamps. He suspects that the absence of any
reference to the need to preserve the demos or democracy indicates
an oligarchic regime, an argument from silence which is perhaps
stronger than Chamoux allows, but which is clearly not decisive. The
argument to which he and Pleket attach most weight lies in the references to τριηκόσιοι. A law from much earlier in the century (Pouilloux, op. cit., p. 37, no. 7, 7–8) has a similar reference: ἀπεγγυάτω ὁ
[κατειπὼν τὴ|ν ἀπεγγύην] παρὰ τριηκοσίοισιν κατάπερ τῶν βιαίωμ. A
text of the same period as ours (IG xii. 8. 263) listed men who had
their property confiscated κατὰ τὸν ἅδον τῶν τριηκοσίων, 'according to
the decision of the Three Hundred'. These included an Apemantos, and
it has been generally and probably rightly held that sons of his are to
be found at Athens, having been exiled from Thasos ἐπ' ἀττικισμῶι
and receiving proxeny and ἀτέλεια at Athens (see Tod, vol. ii, no. 98,
with commentary). Pouilloux therefore argues that the Three Hundred was the oligarchic instrument of government early in the century,
revived by the anti-Athenian oligarchs in 411. We can only agree
with Chamoux that the absence of an article before τριηκοσίοισιν and
τριηκόσιοι in the early law and in our text is fairly strong evidence
against their referring to a fixed organ of government, and is much
more consonant with the view that the size of the appropriate jury
panel is being fixed. We are less sure that he is right in suggesting that
IG xii. 8. 263, where we do find the article, can be explained away
similarly; in the fourth century there certainly was a body called οἱ
ἑξήκοντα καὶ τριηκόσιοι (IG xii. 8. 276, 3–5). However, the absence of
the article does break Pouilloux's link between our text and the probably anti-Athenian board of IG xii. 8. 263, and there is much to be
said for Chamoux's caution in refusing to date our text more closely
than 430–400, though he has not convinced Pleket.

Pouilloux at first argued that the article was missing because the
Three Hundred was not yet formally organized. This was just possible,
though difficult, on his original chronology. Observing that Apatourion
(l. 5) was an autumn month and Galaxion (l. 13) fell in the spring (see
now for the Thasian calendar Salviat, op. cit., pp. 216 f.), but that
the boards of archontes were different in the two laws, he suggested
that the change of archontes fell at the winter solstice and that the
first law was of October 411, the second of March 410. Salviat has,
however, now made it probable that Apatourion was the first month
of the Thasian year, which means that the two laws, of different

years, must be at least seventeen months apart; Pouilloux's explanation of the absence of the article will not stand. The chronology of the Thasian oligarchy remains obscure; Pouilloux holds that it was continuous from summer 411 until Thrasyboulos recovered Thasos for Athens in the summer of 407 (Xen. *Hell.* i. 4. 9; Diod. xiii. 72. 1–2), Chamoux that Thrasyboulos had already interrupted it in winter 411–10. This is a question which turns entirely on whether Xen. *Hell.* i. 1. 12 implies a capture of Thasos by Thrasyboulos, and whether ἐν Θάσῳ is the correct reading in Xen. *Hell.* i. 1. 32 (see also Andrewes, *JHS* lxxiii (1953) 6–8); the inscriptions as yet do not solve it.

The reward offered even in the first law is not large and the second law is markedly less generous; Pouilloux attributes this fact to the oligarchs' deteriorating finances.

84 (83)

Expenditure of the Treasurers of Athena:
410–9 B.C.

On the obverse of a marble stele, sometimes called the 'Choiseul Marble', brought from Athens to Paris by Choiseul-Gouffier; now in the Louvre. Above the inscription is a relief representing Athena armed, an olive-tree, and Erechtheus (phot.: *Ath. Mitt.* xxxv (1910) Pl. iv). The reverse has the accounts of 407–6 (see below). See Ferguson, *Treasurers*, 28 f.

Developed Attic writing (the aspirate is sometimes omitted), not stoichedon. Phot. and facs.: Meritt, *AFD*, Pl. ii–vi.

IG i². 304 A+; Meritt, *AFD* 62, 94–108; *SEG* x. 232+; Andrewes, *JHS* lxxiii (1953) 5 f.

Ἀθεναῖοι ἀνέλοσαν ἐπὶ Γλαυκίππο ἄρχοντος καὶ ἐπὶ τῆς βολῆς ἕι
            Κλεγένες ἁλαιεὺς πρῶτ[ος]

ἐγραμμάτευε· ταμίαι hιερõν χρεμάτον τῆς Ἀθεναίας Καλλίστρατος
            Μαραθόνιος καὶ χσυνάρχο[ν]-

τες παρέδοσαν ἐκ τõν ἐπετείον φσεφισαμένο τõ δέμο ἐπὶ τῆς Αἰαντίδος
            πρότες πρυτανευόσες· he[λλ]-

[ε]νοταμίαις παρεδόθε ⠆ Καλλιμάχοι hαγνοσίοι ⠆ Φρασιτελίδει Ἰκαριεῖ ⠆
            hίπποις σῖτος ἐδόθε ⠆ Ἀθεναίας Πολ[ιά]-

5   [δ]ος ⠆ ΤΤΤΧΧΧΗΗΔΔΔΓΗΗ⊢C ⠆ Νίκες ⠆ ⊞ΔΔΔΔ⊢III⊃ ⠆ ἐπὶ τῆς
            Αἰγεῖδος δευτέρας πρυτανευόσες ⠆ ἀθλοθέταις παρεδ[ό]-

θε ἐς Παναθέναια τὰ μεγάλα ⠆ Φίλονι Κυδαθεναιεῖ καὶ συνάρχοσιν
            Ἀθεναίας Πολιάδος ⠆ ⊞Χ ⠆ hιεροποιοῖς κατ' [ἐ]-

νιαυτὸν : Διύλλοι ἑρχιεῖ καὶ συνάρχοσιν ἐς τὲν ἑκατόμβεν : ⱶΗΔⱶ
ⱵⱵⱵ : ἐπὶ τῆς Οἰνεῖδος τρίτες πρυταν[ε]-
υόσες : ℎελλενοταμίαις παρεδόθε : Περικλεῖ Χολαργεῖ καὶ συνάρχοσιν :
ℎίπποις σῖτος ἐδόθε : ΤΤⱵΗΗΗΗΔΔ[:]
ἕτερον τοῖς αὐτοῖς ℎελλενοταμίαις ℎίπποις σῖτος ἐδόθε : ΤΤⱵΗΗΗΗ :
ἕτερον τοῖς αὐτοῖς ℎελλενοταμία[ις]
10 ℎέρμονι ἐδόθε ἄρχοντι ἐς Πύλον : ⱵΤ : ἕτερον : τοῖς αὐτοῖς ἑλλενοταμίαις ἐς τὲν διοβελίαν : ΤΤ : ἐπὶ τῆς Ἀκ-
αμαντίδος τετάρτες πρυτανευόσες : ℎελλενοταμίαις παρεδόθε : Περικλεῖ
Χολαργεῖ καὶ συνάρχοσιν : σ[ῖ]-
τος ⟨ℎί⟩πποις ἐδόθε : ΤΤΤ : ἕτερον τοῖς αὐτοῖς ℎελλενοταμίαις ἐς τὲν
διοβελίαν ἐδόθε : ⱵΤΤΤΧΗΗΗⱵΓ : ἐπὶ τ[ε]-
ς Κεκροπίδος πέμπτες πρυτανευόσες : ℎελλενοταμίαις παρεδόθε :
Περικλεῖ Χολαργεῖ καὶ συνάρχοσιν ἐ[ς]
τὲν διοβελίαν : ΤΤΤΤΧΧΗΗ : ἐπὶ τῆς Λεοντίδος ℎέκτες πρυτανευόσες :
τρίτει ἑμέραι τῆς πρυτανείας
15 ἑλλενοταμίαις παρεδόθε : Διονυσίοι Κυδαθεναιεῖ καὶ συνάρχοσιν :
ΧΗΗⱵΔΔΔⱵⱵⱵ : ἐνάτει τῆς πρυτανε[ί]-
ας ℎελλενοταμίαις Θράσονι Βουτάδει καὶ συνάρχοσιν : ΤΤΤΧⱵΔΔΔ
ⱵⱵⱵΙΙ : ℎενδεκάτει τῆς πρυτανείας ℎε-
λλενοταμίαις παρεδόθε Προχσένοι Ἀφιδναῖοι καὶ συνάρχοσιν στρατεγδι
ἐχς Ἐρετρίας : Εὐκλεῖδει ἀνομολόγ-
εμα : ΧΧΧⱵΗΗΔΔΔΔΙϽ : τρίτει καὶ δεκάτει τῆς πρυτανείας ℎελλενοταμίαις Περικλεῖ Χολαργεῖ καὶ συνάρχοσιν : [.]
ΧΧΧΧⱵΗΗΗΗΓⱵ : ὀγδόει καὶ εἰκοστεῖ τῆς πρυτανείας : ℎελλενοταμίαις : Σπουδίαι Φλυεῖ καὶ συνάρχοσιν : ΤΤΧΧ[.]
20 Η : τριακοστεῖ τῆς πρυτανείας τὰ ἐχσάμο ἀνομολογέθε : ℎελλενοταμίαι :
Ἀναίτιοι Σφεττίοι καὶ παρέδροι [Π]-
ολυαράτοι Χολαργεῖ : ⱵⱵΤΤΧ : ἐπὶ τῆς Ἀντιοχίδος ἑβδόμες πρυτανευόσες : πέμπτει τῆς πρυτανείας παρεδ[ό]-
θε Διονυσίοι Κυδαθεναιεῖ καὶ συνάρχοσιν ἐς τὲν διοβελίαν : Τ : ἑβδόμει
τῆς πρυτανείας ℎελλενοταμίαις Θρ[ά]-
σονι Βουτάδει καὶ συνάρχοσιν ἐς τὲν διοβελίαν : ΤΧΗΗΔΔΔⱵⱵΙΙΙϽ :
τεῖ αὐτεῖ ἑμέραι ℎελλενοταμίαις Φαλάνθοι [Ἀ]-
λοπεκέθεν καὶ συνάρχοσιν σῖτος ℎίπποις : ΤΤΤΤ : ℎέκτει καὶ δεκάτει
τῆς πρυτανείας ℎελλενοταμίαις Προ[χσέ]-
25 νοι Ἀφιδναῖοι καὶ συνάρχοσιν : ΧⱵΔΔΔⱵⱵⱵⱵΙΙΙ : τετάρτει καὶ εἰκοστεῖ
τῆς πρυτανείας ℎελλενοταμίαις Εὐπόλι[δι Ἀ]-

φιδναῖοι καὶ συνάρχοσιν : ⋈ΗΗΗΗ : ἑβδόμει καὶ εἰκοστεῖ τὲς πρυτανείας
        ἑλλενοταμίαις Καλλίαι Εὐονυμ[εῖ κ]-
αὶ συνάρχοσιν : ΤΧΧ⋈🅿ΔΓΙΙΙC : ἐπὶ τὲς ἱπποθοντίδος ὀγδόες
        πρυτανευόσες δοδεκάτει τὲς πρυτανείας : ἑλ[λενο]-
ταμίαις παρεδόθε Προχσένοι Ἀφιδναῖοι καὶ συνάρχοσιν : ΤΤΤ⋈ΗΔΔ
        ΔΗΗΗΙΙΙΙ : τετάρτει καὶ εἰκοστεῖ τὲς πρ[υτα]-
νείας ἑλλενοταμίαις ἐδόθε Διονυσίοι Κυδαθεναιεῖ καὶ συνάρχοσιν :
        ΤΤΤΧΧΧΧΗΗΗΔΓΗΗΙC : ἑέκτει καὶ τριακοσ[τεῖ]
30 τὲς πρυτανείας ἑλλενοταμίαις ἐδόθε Θράσονι Βουτάδει καὶ συνάρχοσιν :
        ΤΧΧΧΗΗΗΔΔΓΗΗΗΙΙΙ : ἐπὶ τὲς Ἐρεχθεῖδ[ος]
ἐνάτες πρυτανευόσες δοδεκάτει τὲς πρυτανείας : ἑλλενοταμίαις ἐδόθε
        Προχσένοι Ἀφιδναῖοι καὶ συνάρχοσιν [:]
ΧΧΗ🅿ΔΔΔΓΗΗΗΙ : τρίτει καὶ εἰκοστεῖ τὲς πρυτανείας : ἑλλενο-
        ταμίαις ἐδόθε Διονυσίοι Κυδαθεναιεῖ καὶ συνάρχοσ[ιν]
[.]ΤΤΤ⋈ΗΗ🅿ΔΔΔΔΗΗΗΙΙΙ : ἑέκτει καὶ τριακοστεῖ τὲς πρυτανείας :
        ἑλλενοταμίαις ἐδόθε Θράσονι Βουτάδει καὶ σ[υν]-
[ά]ρχοσιν ΤΤΧΧΧ⋈ΗΗΗ🅿ΙΙC : ἕκτει καὶ τριακοστεῖ τὲς πρυτανείας
        τὰ ἐχσάμο ἀνομολογέσα[ντο ℎοι σύ]μμαχ[οι]
35 [: το]ῖς στρατεγοῖς ἐς Σάμοι Δεχσικράτει Αἰγιλιεῖ : ᛒᛒΤΧ : Πασιφõντι
        Φρεαρρίοι : ⋈Τ : Ἀριστοκρά[τει....8....]ι : ⋈ : Ε[...]
[....] Εὐονυμεῖ : ⋈ΧΧΧ⋈ΗΗΗ🅿ΔΔΔΔΓΗ : Νικεράτοι Κυδαντίδει
        τριεράρχοι : ΧΧΧ : Ἀριστοφάνει Ἀνα[φλυστίοι τριε]ράρ[χοι]
[...6... :] ἐπ[ὶ] τὲς Πανδιονίδος δεκάτες πρυτανευόσες ἐνδεκάτει τὲς
        πρυτανείας ἑλλενο[ταμίαις ἐδόθε] Προ[χσ]-
[ένοι Ἀφιδναῖοι] καὶ συνάρχοσιν : ⋈ΗΗΗΗΔΔΔΔΗΗΙΙΙΙΙ : τρίτει καὶ
        εἰκοστεῖ τὲς πρυτανείας ἑλλεν[οταμίαις ἐδόθε....]
[..c. 14..καὶ συνάρχοσι]ν : ΤΤ🅿ΔΔΔΔΙΙΙ : ἕκτει καὶ τρια-
        κοστεῖ τὲς πρυτανείας ℎελ[λενοταμίαις ἐδόθε...]
40 [..c. 19..καὶ συνάρχ]οσιν : ⋈ΧΧΧΧ⋈Η🅿ΓΗΙΙΙΙ : υυ κεφάλαιον
        ἀργυρίο σύμπαν ℎὸ Κ[αλλίστρατος Μαραθόνιος]
[καὶ συνάρχοντες παρέδοσαν..c. 5...] vacat

In l. 12 the stone has ΙΗΓΓΟΙΣ; the cutter joined the wrong pair of ver-
ticals. At the beginning of l. 33 Meritt (*BSA* xlvi (1951) 205 n. 5) now prefers a numeral to the [:] of his published text. This is surely right, but leaves
l. 35 as the only possible example of punctuation at the beginning of a line,
and we agree with Wade-Gery, *JHS* liii (1933) 136, that this is suspicious.
Meritt's restoration of ll. 40–1 leaves so little space for the total figure that
we should perhaps consider omitting the demotic. For ἐχσάμο in ll. 20, 34 see

Tod, *AJP* lxvii (1946) 333. In l. 35 J. K. Davies suggests to us Ἀριστοκρά[τει Τρινεμεε]ῖ; if he is rightly identified with the well-known Aristokrates, this is apparently the only demotic from his tribe which fits. In ll. 35–6 Bradeen (*Hesp.* xxxiii (1964) 49 n. 65) restores Ἐ[ὐμ|άχοι].

These accounts, practically complete, of the payments made in 410–9 by the treasurers of Athena are as usual based on the conciliar year. Since a change of *hellenotamiai* and the payments of ll. 5–7 indicate that the Panathenaia, celebrated on Hekatombaion 28, fell in the second prytany, we can infer, with Meritt, that at least some portion of the first prytany fell in the previous archon-year 411–10. If we compare the decree quoted by Andocides, i. 96–8, it becomes clear that the transition from the regime of the Five Thousand to full democracy took place within 411–10. (See also *TAPA* xcv (1964) 210 f.)

Meritt's analysis of the *hellenotamiai* listed here shows that the two mentioned in l. 4 belong to the Panathenaic year of 411–10. They remain undisturbed, and further evidence of the peacefulness of the restoration of democracy comes from an observation of the tribal affiliations of the other nine *hellenotamiai* of the document. Two pairs of them, Pericles and Anaitios from Akamantis, Proxenos and Eupolis from Aiantis, come from the same tribe, and Meritt is certainly right to deduce that the proposal recorded in Arist. Ἀθ. Πολ. 30. 2 to have twenty *hellenotamiai* was put into effect by the Five Thousand and maintained by the democracy. This conclusion is confirmed by the fact that the *kolakretai* (cf. Nos. 31, 69, 71, 73), who have no place in Ἀθ. Πολ. 30, disappear henceforth from our documents, their functions being performed by the *hellenotamiai*. (Meritt's interpretation is doubted by Kahrstedt, *GGA* cxcvii. 45–7, *Untersuchungen zur Magistratur*, 99–101, on which see Meritt, *AJP* lvi (1935) 319 f.; and by Pritchett, *BCH* lxxxviii (1964) 474–9.) We do not accept the view of *ATL* iii. 364 that the *kolakretai* were restored in 410, purely to pay juries. We see no reason why the *hellenotamiai*, whose accounts we do not have, should not have paid juries as they paid for the setting-up of stelai.

It would appear that all these payments were made ἐκ τῶν ἐπετείων (l. 3), from the annual income of Athena Polias and Athena Nike. Unless, surprisingly, there was a separate stele for payments from capital account, the conclusion would seem to follow that the restored democracy inherited an empty treasury. In the late summer signs of a firm hand on Athenian finances appear. Presumably at the Panathenaia, the normal time, the decision was taken to reimpose tribute to replace the 5 per cent tax levied since 414 (Thuc. vii. 28. 4) and we possess fragments of the assessment (*ATL* ii. A 13). From the third prytany we have a fragment of a decree (*ATL* ii. D 9) which contemplates the repayment of the debt to Athena, i.e. the re-establishment of a capital reserve; what measures were taken we do not know, but there seems to have been more money available in 409-8. Counterbalancing this, our inscription shows in the third prytany the first of many payments for the *diobelia* (see below). See, in general, Ferguson, *Treasurers*, 33-7, *ATL* iii. 363-6.

The money passing through these accounts was at least 180 T., but it is unlikely that it was much more. The problem of determining what the money was spent on is not easy to resolve, since, except for isolated cases, the treasurers stopped recording the destination of the money after the fifth prytany. Andrewes suggests that the *hellenotamiai* came to have specialized functions, and that payments to Dionysios and Thrason are for the *diobelia*, and payments to Eukleides are for military purposes. Such an assumption would give a total of over 34 T. for the *diobelia*, over 6 T. for the Great Panathenaia, and over 22 T. for fodder for the horses, leaving all or nearly all the rest for military purposes.

In the three items described by the noun ἀνομολόγημα, or the verb ἀνομολογεῖσθαι (ll. 17, 20, 34), we seem to have pure book-transactions, in which the recipients took money that had been collected at Eretria or Samos directly and reported their use of what was in theory money due to the goddess. There seems no reason to see in τὰ ἐχσάμο (ll. 20, 34) anything but the importance of Samos as a base for operations; reference to Samos' debt from her revolt (cf. Nos. 55, 68, 72, 77) here seems unlikely. These accounts cover only Athens, Eretria, Pylos, and Samos, and Andrewes deduces that the Hellespont fleet under Alcibiades and Theramenes lay outside the Athenian financial system. The Samian collections may have been spent on Thrasyllos' Ionian expedition (Xen. *Hell.* i. 2. 1), the city's major effort of the year. The money at Eretria (l. 17) ought to be connected with an attempt to recover Euboea, in revolt from Athens (see Wallace, *The Euboian League and its Coinage*, 5 n. 13). Pylos (l. 10) was not recovered by the Spartans till the following year (Diod. xiii. 64). The entry in ll. 27-8 is to be identified with the payment to Oinobios in No. 89, l. 47.

Of the men mentioned here, Pericles (ll. 8, 11, 13, 18), is the son of Pericles and Aspasia, who received Athenian citizenship, was στρατηγός in 406, and was executed after the battle of Arginusae (Plut. *Per.* 37; Xen. *Hell.* i. 5. 16, 7. 2; Eupolis F. 98); Hermon (l. 10) had commanded the περίπολοι at Mounychia in 411 and joined the revolt against the Four Hundred (Thuc. viii. 92. 5); Proxenos (ll. 17, 24, 28, 31, 37) was a descendant of the tyrannicide Harmodios (Isaeus v. 46-7); Eukleides (l. 17) and Anaitios (l. 20) may be those of the name who appear among the Thirty (Xen. *Hell.* ii. 3. 2); Aristokrates

(l. 35) is generally identified with the son of Skellias (Thuc. viii. 89, 92; Arist. Ἀθ. Πολ. 33; Xen. *Hell.* i. 7. 2, 34); Pasiphon (l. 35) was killed shortly after this as ἄρχων τοῦ ναυτικοῦ (*Hesp.* xxxiii (1964) 44, 48); Nikeratos (l. 36), the son of Nikias, was one of the victims of the Thirty (Xen. *Hell.* ii. 3. 39; Lys. xviii. 6, xix. 47).

The διωβελία, which appears here as a major object of expenditure, is not to be identified either with the θεωρικόν (cf. Sandys on Arist. Ἀθ. Πολ. 28. 3) or with the pay for juries or the Assembly (Beloch, *Rh. Mus.* xxxix (1884) 239 ff.; *GG* ii². 1. 398). The most probable theory is that which sees in it a measure of poor relief instituted by the state during the closing years of the Peloponnesian War, when the loss of Euboea and the Spartan occupation of Decelea brought widespread ruin to Athenian citizens (Wilamowitz, *Ar. u. Ath.* ii. 212–16); it was, Aristotle tells us (Ἀθ. Πολ. 28. 3), introduced by Cleophon, and was administered in 406 by Archedemos, another popular leader (Xen. *Hell.* i. 7. 2). Beloch's objection (*GG*, loc. cit.) that such a system would involve an annual outlay of at least 240 T. is based on the assumption that every citizen could and did claim this dole, and this is probably untrue.

The following guide to the accounts of the treasurers for the rest of the war may be helpful. 409–8: *IG* i². 301; Wade-Gery, *Num. Chron.* 1930, 16–38, 333–4; Ferguson, *Treasurers* 16–37; Meritt, *AFD* 61–3; *SEG* x. 233. 408–7: lost. 407–6 (on the reverse of the stele before us): *IG* i². 304 B; Meritt, *AFD* 116–27; Tod, *GHI* 92; *SEG* x. 234; Pritchett, *Ancient Athenian Calendars on Stone*, 286–9; *BCH* lxxxviii (1964) 455–88 (with important new readings and suggesting, wrongly, we think, that it has parts of the accounts of 408–7 and 407–6), Meritt, *TAPA* xcv (1964) 204–12. 406–5: *IG* i². 305; *SEG* x. 235. 405–4: Meritt, *Hesp.* xi (1942) 275–8; Woodward, ibid. xxv (1956) 109–21. 404–3 (?): Woodward, *Hesp.* xxxii (1963) 144–55.

85 (86)

Phrynichus' Assassins honoured: 409 B.C.

Five joining fragments, and one placed by its text, of a marble stele, found on the Acropolis; now in EM.

Developed Attic writing, use of aspirate inconsistent. Ll. 3–47 stoichedon 36.

IG i². 110+.

I

[ἐπὶ Γλαυκί]ππο ἄ[ρ]χον[τ]ος.

[Λόβον ἐκ] Κεδὸν ἐγραμμάτευε.

[ἔδοχσεν τεῖ] βολεῖ καὶ τοῖ δέμοι, ἱπποθοντὶ-

[ς ἐπρυτάνε]υε, Λόβον ἐγραμμάτευε, Φιλιστίδε-

5 [ς ἐπεστάτε,] Γλαύκιππος ἔρχε : Ἐρασινίδες εἶπ-

[ε· ἐπαινέσα]ι Θρασύβολον ὅς ὄντα ἄνδρα ἀγαθὸ-

[ν περὶ τὸν δεμ]ον τὸν Ἀθεναίον καὶ πρόθυμον π-

[οιεν ηό τι δύνα]ται ἀγαθόν· καὶ ἀντὶ ὄν εὖ πεπο-

[ίεκεν τέν τε πόλιν] καὶ τὸν δεμ[ο]ν τὸν Ἀθεναίο-

10 [ν στεφανοσαι αὐτὸν χρυσδι στε]φάνοι, ποιεσα-

[ι δὲ τὸν στέφανον ἀπὸ χιλίον δρ]αχμον· ηοι [δὲ η]-

[ελλενοταμίαι δόντον τὸ ἀργύρι]ον. καὶ [ἀνειπ]-

[εν τὸν κέρυκα Διονυσίον ἐν τοῖ] ἀγονι ηον ηέν-

[εκα αὐτὸν ηο δεμος ἐστεφάνος]ε : Διοκλες εἶπε·

II

15 [τὰ μὲν ἄλλα καθάπερ τεῖ βολεῖ·] εἶναι δὲ Θρασύ-

[βολον Ἀθεναῖον, καὶ φυλες τε κ]αὶ φρατρίας ηο-

[ν ἂν βόλεται γράφσασθαι αὐτό]ν· καὶ τἀλλα τὰ ἐ-

[φσεφισμένα τοῖ δέμοι κύρια ε]ναι Θρασυβόλο-

[ι· εναι δὲ αὐτοῖ εὑρίσκεσθαι π]αρὰ Ἀθεναίον κ-

20 [αὶ ἄλλο ηό τι ἂν δοκεῖ ἀγαθὸν π]ερὶ ηον εὐεργέ-

[τεκεν τὸν δεμον τὸν Ἀθεναίον.] καὶ ἀναγραφσά-

[το ηο γραμματεὺς τὰ ἐφσεφισμ]ένα· ηελέσθαι δ-

[ὲ ἐγ βολες πέντε ἄνδρας αὐτί]κα μάλα, ηοίτινε-

[ς] δι[κάσοσι Θρασυβόλοι τὸ μέ]ρος τὸ γιγνόμεν-

25 ον. τὸς [δὲ ἄλλος, ηόσοι τότε εὖ ἐ]ποίεσαν τὸν δε-

μον τὸν Ἀθε[ναίον, ... 10 . . . . .]ιν καὶ Ἀγόρατο-

ν καὶ Κόμονα [καὶ . . . 6 . . .]ο[.]ο[. . . .] καὶ Σίμον κα-

ὶ Φιλῖνον κα[ὶ . . . . 8 . . . .]α, εὐεργέ[τα]ς [ἀ]ναγράφ-

σαι ἐμ πόλε[ι ἐν στέλει λ]ιθίνει τὸν γραμ[μα]τέ-

30 α τες βολες. [καὶ ἔγκτεσι]ν εἶναι αὐτοῖς ὅμπερ

Ἀθεναίοις, [καὶ γεπέδο]ν καὶ οἰκίας, καὶ οἴκεσ-

ιν Ἀθένεσι, [καὶ ἐπιμέλ]εσθαι αὐτον τὲν βολὲν

τὲν αἰεὶ β[ολεύοσαν κα]ὶ τὸς πρυτάνες, ηόπος ἄ-

ν μὲ ἀδι[κονται. τὲν δὲ σ]τέλεν ἀπομισθοσάντο-

35 [ν ηοι πολεταὶ ἐν τεῖ βο]λεῖ· τὸς δὲ ηελλενοταμ-

[ίας δοναι τὸ ἀργύριον]. ἐὰν δὲ δοκεῖ αὐτὸς καὶ

[ἄλλο εὑρίσκεσθαι, τὲν] βολὲν προβολεύσασαν

III　　[ἐχσενεγκε͂ν ἐς τὸν δε͂μ]ον· Εὔδικος εἶπε· τὰ μὲν
　　　　[ἄλλα καθάπερ Διοκλε͂ς· περὶ] δὲ τὸν δοροδοκεσ-
40　　[άντον ἐπὶ το͂ι φσεφίσματι], ὃ ἐφσεφ[ί]σθε Ἀπολλ-
　　　　[οδόροι, τὲν βολὲν βολεῦσ]αι ἐν τε͂ι πρότει ἑέδ-
　　　　[ραι ἐν το͂ι βουλευτερί]οι, καὶ κολάζεν, τὸν [δ]ορο-
　　　　[δοκεσάντον καταφσ]εφιζομένεν καὶ ἐς δικασ-
　　　　[τέριον παραδιδο͂σα]ν, καθότι ἂν δοκε͂ι αὐτε͂[ι]· τ-
45　　[ὸς δὲ βολευτὰς τὸς] παρόντας ἀποφαίνεν ἁ[ττ']
　　　　[ἂν εἰδο͂σιν, καὶ ἐάν] τίς τι ἄλλο εἰδε͂ι περὶ τ[ού-]
　　　　[τον· ἐχσε͂ναι δὲ καὶ] ἰδιότει, ἐάν τις βόλετα[ι. v]
　　　　　　　　　　vacat

The restorations are not all certain, and those adopted here often differ
from those in *IG*. l. 9: βολέν is also possible. ll. 12–13: καὶ [ἀνειπ|ε͂ιν
Διονυσίον τὸν ἐν ἄστει το͂ι] ἀγο͂νι *IG*. l. 16: The normal fourth-century
formula φυλε͂ς καὶ δέμο καὶ φρατρίας is two letters too long here and is not
yet known in full in the fifth century. l. 23: [ἐ τὸν δε͂μον τρε͂ς ἄνδρας
Michel. l. 36: αὐτὸς = αὐτούς; ἐὰν δὲ δοκε͂ι αὐτὸς καὶ | [ἄλλο ἄχσιος
ἀγαθο͂ *IG*. l. 44: So Lipsius, *Attische Recht*, 184 n. 23; αὐτὸς ἐσάγε]ν *IG*.
l. 45: παρόντας imperfect, 'those who were present when the decree was
initiated'; τ[ὸς δὲ πέντε ἄνδρας] παρόντας Bannier (*B. Phil. Woch.* 1922, 835),
IG. Valeton, *Hermes*, xliii (1908) 481 ff. has restorations of ll. 42, 45 which
transfer the investigation to the Areopagus.

The assassination of Phrynichus upon his return from a mission to
Sparta in the autumn of 411 heralded the fall of the Four Hundred.
Thucydides states (viii. 92) that he was struck down in the Agora near
the Council House by one of the περίπολοι, who made his escape; his
accomplice, an Argive, when caught and tortured, refused to divulge
the names of the conspirators but maintained that they were numerous.
Lysias says (xiii. 71): Φρυνίχῳ . . . . κοινῇ Θρασύβουλός τε ὁ Καλυδώνιος
καὶ Ἀπολλόδωρος ὁ Μεγαρεὺς ἐπεβούλευσαν· ἐπειδὴ δὲ ἐπετυχέτην αὐτῷ
βαδίζοντι, ὁ μὲν Θρασύβουλος τύπτει τὸν Φρύνιχον καὶ καταβάλλει
πατάξας, ὁ δὲ Ἀπολλόδωρος οὐχ ἥψατο, ἀλλ' ἐν τούτῳ κραυγὴ γίγνεται καὶ
ᾤχοντο φεύγοντες. By Lycurgus, eighty years later (*Leocr.* 112), the
deed is unequivocally assigned to both Thrasyboulos and Apollodoros.

Lysias in the first years of the fourth century (xiii. 70–2) quotes
two decrees to refute the claim of Agoratos (l. 26) to have killed
Phrynichus and been made a citizen for it. The first, he says, made
Thrasyboulos and Apollodoros citizens, but not Agoratos. Agoratos
and others had got themselves put on the stele as εὐεργέται by paying
money to an orator. He cited a second decree to prove that this assertion was true. It is not easy to reconcile these statements with the

decree before us. This was passed in the eighth prytany (cf. No. 84, l. 27) of Glaukippos' archonship, i.e. in the spring of 409, already some nineteen months after the assassination, and falls into three parts: (I) a proposal, originating probably in the Council (l. 15), by Erasinides, almost certainly the general executed after the battle of Arginusae in 406 (Xen. *Hell.* i. vi. 29, vii. 2, 34; Philochoros *FGH* 328 F 42), praising Thrasyboulos for his loyalty to the δῆμος, and granting him a golden crown to be proclaimed at the Dionysia, now, we may calculate, imminent (Meritt, *Calendar* 98 n. 1; Dinsmoor, *Archons* 346 n. 6; Meritt, *AFD* 105 n. 3); (II) an amendment by Diokles, granting Thrasyboulos citizenship, the confirmation of privileges previously bestowed, a prospect of further benefits, and a share in some property or award; to seven or eight of his fellow conspirators, among them Agoratos, lesser honours and rights are awarded; (III) a second amendment by Eudikos orders an inquiry into the bribery alleged to have been used to secure a decree in favour of Apollodoros.

It does not seem that any part of our decree, except possibly ll. 25–30, corresponds with those quoted by Lysias. It is clear that some decree or decrees in favour of Thrasyboulos and Apollodoros have preceded ours. To save Lysias' credit, we must assume that the inquiry ordered in III rehabilitated Apollodoros' claims and resulted in his receiving the citizenship, and also that it cast some doubts on the claims of Agoratos and the minor conspirators. That the assumption is true at any rate as far as Apollodoros is concerned is perhaps supported by the fact (Lys. vii. 4) that Apollodoros received as a reward a plot of ground which had belonged to Peisander and retained it until shortly before the rule of the Thirty, as well as by his posthumous reputation attested by Lycurgus. It therefore seems unlikely that our decree represents the final state of the rewards for the assassination. As far as the true facts, as opposed to the official decision, are concerned, the variant story of Thucydides must be borne in mind.

The grant of ἔγκτησις (ll. 30–2), i.e. the right of a non-citizen to own real property in Attica, is among the earliest known (cf. No. 70). Fine (*Hesp.*, Suppl. ix. 204–5) argued from the circumstances of this affair that the privilege was originally necessarily linked with an actual grant of land as a reward for public services. The evidence certainly does not impose this view, which we think improbable. See J. and L. Robert, *REG* lxv (1952) 141, and Pečírka, *Geras Thomson* (Prague, 1963), 193–201, who analyses the evidence about the origin of the privilege. See also Pečírka, *The Formula for the Grant of Enktesis in Attic Inscriptions*, 18–21.

86 (87)

Republication of Draco's Law of Homicide: 409–8 B.C.

Marble stele, formerly near the cathedral at Athens; now in EM.
Developed Attic script; the aspirate is omitted, except in ll. 11–26.
Stoichedon 50, except ll. 1, 2, 10, 56, which are in larger letters.
IG i². 115+; Bonner and Smith, *The Administration of Justice from Homer to Aristotle*, i. 111–25+; Hignett, *History of the Athenian Constitution*, 305–11.

Διόγν[ε]τος Φρεάρριος ἐγραμμάτε[υε].
Διοκλῆς ἔρχε.

ἔδοχσεν τῆι βουλῆι καὶ τῶι δέμοι, Ἀκα[μ]αντὶς ἐπ[ρ]υτάνευε, [Δ]ιό[γ]-
νετος ἐγραμμάτευε, Εὐθύδικος [ἐ]πεστάτε, [..]ε[..φ]άνες εἶπε· τὸ[ν]
5 Δράκοντος νόμον τὸμ περὶ τὸ φό[ν]ο ἀναγρα[φ]σά[ν]τον οἱ ἀναγραφές-
ς τὸν νόμον παραλαβόντες παρὰ τὸ β[α]σ[ι]λέ[ος με]τ[ὰ τὸ γραμμ]ατέο-
ς τῆς βουλῆς ἐστέλει λιθίνει καὶ κα[τ]α[θ]έντ[ον πρόσ]θε[ν] τῆς στο-
ᾶς τῆς βασιλείας· οἱ δὲ πολεταὶ ἀπομι[σθο]σ[άντον κατὰ τὸν ν]όμο-
ν· οἱ δὲ ἑλλενοταμίαι δόντον τὸ ἀρ[γ]ύ[ρ]ι[ον].
10 πρῶτος ἄχσον.

          καὶ ἐὰμ μὲ 'κ [π]ρονοί[α]ς [κ]τ[ένει τίς τινα, φεύγ]ε[ν· δ]ι-
κάζεν δὲ τὸς βασιλέας αἴτιο[ν] φόν[ο] ε........17........ε [β]ολ-
εύσαντα· τὸς δὲ ἐφέτας διαγν[ό]ν[α]ι. [αἰδέσασθαι δ', ἐὰμ μὲν πατὲ]ρ ἒ-
ι ἒ ἀδελφὸ[ς] ἒ hυές, hάπαντ[α]ς, ἒ τὸν κο[λύοντα κρατὲν· ἐὰν δὲ μὲ] hοῦ-
15 τοι ὄσι, μέχρ' ἀνεφ[σι]ότετος καὶ [ἀνεφσίο, ἐὰν hάπαντες αἰδέσ]ασ-
θαι ἐθέλοσι, τὸν κο[λύ]ον[τα κρατὲν· ἐὰν δὲ τούτον μεδὲ hὲς ἒι, κτ]έ-
νει δὲ ἄκο[ν], γνῶσι δὲ ho[ι πε]ντ[έκοντα καὶ hὲς hοι ἐφέται ἄκοντ]α
κτέναι, ἐσέσθ[ο]ν δὲ h[οι φ]ρ[άτορες, ἐὰν ἐθέλοσι, δέκα· τούτος δ]ὲ ho-
ι πεντέκο[ν]τ[α καὶ] hὲς ἀρ[ι]στ[ίνδεν hαιρέσθον. καὶ hοι δὲ πρ]ότε[ρ]-
20 ον κτέ[ν]α[ντ]ε[ς ἐν] τό[ιδε τῶι θεσμῶι ἐνεχέσθον. προειπὲν δ]ὲ τῶι κ-
τέναν[τι ἐν ἀ]γορ[ᾶι μέχρ' ἀνεφσιότετος καὶ ἀνεφσιο· συνδιόκ]εν
δὲ [κἀ]νεφσ[ιὸς καὶ ἀνεφσιὸν παῖδας καὶ γαμβρὸς καὶ πενθερὸ]ς κ-
αὶ φρ[ά]τ[ο]ρ[ας ....36................]αἴτι-
ος [ἒι] φό[νο ....26............ τὸς πεντέκοντ]α καὶ
25 hένα ....42....................φόνο
hέλοσ[ι ....35................ ἐὰν δ]ὲ [τ]ις τ-
ὸ[ν ἀν]δρ[οφόνον κτένει ἒ αἴτιος ἒι φόνο, ἀπεχόμενον ἀγορᾶ]ς ἐφο-

ρί[α]ς κ[α]ὶ [ἆθλον καὶ ἱερὸν Ἀμφικτυονικὸν ὅσπερ τὸν Ἀθεν]αῖον κ-
[τένα]ν̣[τα ἐν τοῖς αὐτοῖς ἐνέχεσθαι, διαγιγνόσκεν δὲ τὸς] ἐ[φ]έτα[ς].

The remainder is nearly illegible, except at the beginnings and ends of lines. ll. 30–1 : τε̑ι ἐμεδ|[απε̑ι (cf. Dem. xxiii. 28).   ll. 33–4 : ἄρχον]τα χε[ρ]|ὸν ἀ[δίκον (cf. Plato, *Laws* ix. 869 c).   ll. 34–5 : τ]ὸν ἄδικον κ|τέ[νει.   ll. 35–6 : διαγιγνόσκ]εν δὲ τὸς ἐ|[φέτ]ας.   ll. 36–9 :]εις ἒ ἐλεύθ|ε[ρ]ος ἒι κα̣[ὶ ἐὰν ἄγοντα ἒ φέροντα βίαι ἀδικο̑ς εὐθὺς] ἀμυνό-μενο|ς κτέ[ν]ει ν[εποινὲ τεθνάναι . . . . 20 . . . .]ΣΕΧΟΝ-ΤΟΒ|ΙΑΝ . . Ạ (cf. Dem. xxiii. 60).   At l. 56 [δεύτ]ε̣ρος [ἄχσον] is distinguishable, and thereafter there are traces of four lines before the stele breaks off.

We owe our text to the generosity of R. S. Stroud, who will shortly republish the whole. Though the stone is extremely worn, substantial restorations are possible with the aid of documents contained in Demosthenes xxiii and xliii. In l. 4 at least four other names are possible besides the current [Χσ]ε[νοφ]άνες. In l. 6 the current anachronistic restoration παρὰ τὸ κ[ατὰ πρυτανείαν γραμμ]ατέο|ς is impossible. In l. 12 most texts have αἰτ[ι]ο̑[ν] φό[νο] ἒ [ἐάν τις αἰτιᾶται hος βουλ]ε̣ύσαντα, which seems difficult. Wolff, *Traditio* iv (1946) 71–8, argues for αἰτ[ι]ο[ν] φό[νο] ἒ [τὸν αὐτόχερα ἒ τὸν βου]λ̣|εύσαντα, which seems right in principle, though not quite reconcilable with the new readings. For ll. 13–14, 16–20 cf. Dem. xliii. 57, where the order is different and ll. 14–16 are omitted. In l. 16 τὸν hό[ρκ]ον [ὀμόσαντας] is generally, but wrongly, read. For ll. 26–9 cf. Dem. xxiii. 37.

After the fall of the Four Hundred the Athenians embarked on a revision of their laws, and in our texts we find both συγγραφεῖς, presumably primarily concerned with the revision, and ἀναγραφεῖς, presumably primarily concerned with publication, though it is doubtful whether the distinction should be pressed too far. Among the latter was Nicomachos, of whom Lysias asserts that προσταχθὲν . . . αὐτῷ τεττάρων μηνῶν ἀναγράψαι τοὺς νόμους τοὺς Σόλωνος, ἀντὶ μὲν Σόλωνος αὐτὸν νομοθέτην κατέστησαν, ἀντὶ δὲ τεττάρων μηνῶν ἐξέτη τὴν ἀρχὴν ἐποιήσατο, καθ' ἑκάστην δὲ ἡμέραν ἀργύριον λαμβάνων τοὺς μὲν ἐνέγραφε, τοὺς δὲ ἐξήλειφεν (xxx. 2; cf. 17, 25). Of this first stage we now have fairly copious epigraphical evidence; two stelai, that before us and *IG* i². 114 (revised by Wade-Gery, *BSA* xxxiii (1932–3) 113–22; νόμοι βουλευτικοί), and the earlier sides, in Attic script, of several fragments of opisthographic walls or multiple stelai. At the restoration of the democracy in 403 Teisamenos carried a decree, πολιτεύεσθαι Ἀθηναίους κατὰ τὰ πάτρια, νόμοις δὲ χρῆσθαι τοῖς Σόλωνος, καὶ μέτροις καὶ σταθμοῖς, χρῆσθαι δὲ καὶ τοῖς Δράκοντος θεσμοῖς, οἷσπερ ἐχρώμεθα ἐν τῷ πρόσθεν χρόνῳ (Andoc. i. 83), and went on to order further revisions, represented for us by the later sides, inscribed in Ionic script, of the 'walls'.

For the growth of the epigraphic evidence, and for recent work on the two phases of the revision, see the bibliography by Dow, *Hist.* ix (1960) 292 f., to which add Dow, *Hesp.* xxx (1961) 38–53.

From the decree on our stele we learn that Draco's law of homicide was to be obtained from the *basileus*, though we do not know in what form he preserved it, and exhibited in front of the stoa named after his title (for which see Wycherley, *The Athenian Agora: Testimonia*, 21–5). For the exhibition of laws there see in particular Andoc. i. 82, Arist. *Ἀθ. Πολ.* 7. 1. The cost of the stele is to be met by the *hellenotamiai* (see p. 258).

Aristotle states that under Solon the Athenians τοῖς Δράκοντος θεσμοῖς (cf. l. 20 and Kahrstedt, *Klio*, xxxi (1938) 18 f.) ἐπαύσαντο χρώμενοι πλὴν τῶν φονικῶν (*Ἀθ. Πολ.* 7. 1; cf. Plut. *Solon* 17. 1). There would appear from our text to have been some further revision, since it seems to begin (l. 11) in the middle and has no reference to premeditated murder. Presumably, Draco's legislation on this had been repealed before 409, although in the fourth century all homicide laws, even those on premeditated murder, could still, probably loosely, be ascribed to Draco (Dem. xxiii. 51, cf. xx. 157–8; see Hignett, op. cit. 307). One may doubt whether changes were confined to simple omission.

Stroud's convincing reading [δεύτ]ερος [ἄχσον] in l. 56 shows that Draco's laws on homicide were arranged and presumably originally inscribed on at least two *axones*. This would seem to imply that Draco's *axones* were distinct from Solon's in numbering, contrary to some recent opinion (Dow, *Proc. Mass. Hist. Soc.* lxxi (1953–7) 28 f.; Ruschenbusch, Σόλωνος Νόμοι, 27, 70–6). Harrison's ingenious explanation (*CQ* xi (1961) 3–5), by which πρῶτος ἄχσον would have referred, not to the text which follows, but to a separate text on voluntary homicide, appears to fall to the ground.

Whatever Draco's reputation, the text before us would seem to be largely devoted to ameliorating the plight of the involuntary homicide. The basic penalty is exile, after a pronouncement (on Wolff's interpretation) by the βασιλεῖς (l. 12; this term probably includes both the ἄρχων βασιλεύς and the φυλοβασιλεῖς), resting on a decision by the fifty-one ἐφέται. The homicide may, however, be pardoned by the unanimous vote of the nearest kinship-categories available, and this concession is retrospective (ll. 13–20; ἐσέσθον (l. 18) = 'admit', 'allow to enter Attica'). Even though ll. 21 ff. are concerned with prosecution, ll. 26–9 guarantee the exile some immunity by threatening the punishment of his murderer. The relevance of our text to these matters and the other evidence on them is discussed by Ruschenbusch, *Hist.* ix (1960) 129–54, and Macdowell, *Athenian Homicide Law in the Age of the Orators*, 117–25.

For the complex questions surrounding the Ephetai see Hignett, loc. cit., and MacDowell, op. cit. 48–57.

87 (88)

Athens ratifies a Treaty with Selymbria: 407 B.C.

Five fragments of a marble stele, found on the south slope of the Acropolis; now in EM. At the bottom, a semicircular stump for insertion into a base.

Attic writing, with frequent lapses into Ionic (Ω occurs three times, H = η five times, with three other occasions where it is corrected to E, Λ = λ three times, Ⅼ = γ once (!; l. 34; cf. *Hesp.* xxii (1953) 265, l. 9). Inaccurate stoichedon (Austin, 51 ff.), with a basic 36-letter line.

IG i². 116+ ; *Staatsverträge* 207+.

    [.............31..............]ε̣ροσα
    [.............30.............]αι Ἀθεν-
    [.............30.............]ε̣χσαγο
    [.............31.............]νκ..ιε
5 [...............34...............]σε̣
    [.........23.........]ελλ[...] Ἀθεν...
    [.........22......... κ]ατάλογον κατ..
    [.........21......... ὁ]μέρος δὲ ℎὸς ἔχο[σ]-
    [ιν Ἀθεναῖοι ἀποδο̑ναι, τὸ δὲ] λοιπὸμ μὲ λαμβάν-
10 [εν, καταστέσασθαι δὲ Σελυμ]βριανὸς τὲμ πολι-
    [τείαν αὐτονόμος τρόποι ℎ]ότοι ἂν ἐπίστοντ-
    [αι ....17......... ὄφ]ελε τὸ κοινὸν τὸ Ση-
    [λυμβριανὸν ἒ ἰδιοτὸν τι]ς Σελυνβριανὸν τοι
    [.........18.........] ε̣ἴ το [χ]ρέματα ἐδεδέμε-
15 [υτο ἒ εἴ τις τόι κοινόι] ὄφελεν ἒ εἴ τις ἐτίμοτ-
    [ο ....20.........] φεύγοσι Σελυμβριανὸν
    [.......15.......]ος πολεμίος δὲ καὶ φιλίος
    [......14......] ἃ δὲ ἀπόλετο ἐν τόι πολέμοι
    [χρέματα Ἀθεναί]ον ἒ τὸν συμμάχον ἒ εἴ τι ὀφελ-
20 [όμενον ἒ παρακ]αταθέκεν ἔχοντός το ἔπραχσα-
    [ν οἱ ἄρχοντες,] μὴ ἔναι πρᾶχσιν πλὲγ γὲς καὶ οἰ-
    [κίας· ὅσα δὲ ἄ]λλα χσυμβόλαια προτο̑ ἐν τοῖς ἰ-
    [διόταις πρ]ὸς τὸς ἰδιότας ἒ ἰδιώτει πρὸς τὸ κ-

[οινὸν ἒ κο]ινôι πρὸς ἰδιότεν υ ἒ ἐάν τι ἄλλο γίγ-
25 [νεται, δια]λύεμ π[ρ]ὸς ἀλλέλος· ὅ τι δ' ἂν ἀμφισβη-
[τôσι, δίκας] ἔναι ἀπὸ χσυμβολôν. τὰς δὲ χσυνθέκ-
[ας ἀναγράφ]σαντας ἐ[ς] στέλεν θêναι ἐς τὸ hιερὸ-
[ν τὸ ... 7 ....]ς. ὤμοσαν Ἀθεναίον οἱ στρατεγοὶ
[καὶ οἱ τριέραρχ]οι καὶ hοι hοπλîται καὶ εἴ τι-
30 [ς ἄλλος Ἀθεναίον] παρῆν καὶ Σελυμβ[ρ]ιανοὶ π-
[ά]ντε[ς. υ Ἀλ]κιβ[ιάδες] εἶπε· καθὰ χσυνέθεντο Σε-
[λυμ]βρια[ν]οὶ πρ[ὸς Ἀθ]εναίος, κατὰ ταῦτα ποιêν,
κ̣αὶ καταθêναι ἐγ̣ [πόλ]ει ἀναγράφσαντας τὸστ-
[ρ]ατε⟨γ⟩ὸς [τ]ὰ̣ς συνθέ[κ]α̣ς μετὰ τô γραμματέος τ-
35 [ἐς] βολês [[.........18........]] ἐν στέλει λιθί-
[ν]ει τέλεσι τοῖς αὐτôν̣ καὶ τὸ φσέφισμα τόδε.
[Ἀπο]λλόδορον δὲ τὸν Ἐμπέδο ἐπαινέσαι καὶ ἀφêν-
[α]ι̣ αὐτὸν τês ὁμερέας καὶ [ἐ]χσαλείφσαι τὰ ὀνόμα-
[τα] τὸν ὁμέ[ρ]ον τὸν Σελυμ[β]ριανὸν καὶ τὸν ἐγγυε-
40 [τὸν α]ὐτôν [α]ὔριον τὸν γραμ[ματ]έα τês βολês [ὅ]πο
[ἐσὶ ἀν]αγεγ[ρ]αμμένο̣ι̣ ἐναντίον τῶμ πρυτάνε-
[ων· ....]όμ[α]χον δὲ τὸν Σελυμβ[ρια]νὸν ἀναγρά-
[φσαι ἐν τ]êι [αὐ]τêι στέλει πρόχσε[νον Ἀθ]εναίον·
[ἔναι δὲ καὶ] Ἀπολλοδόροι τὲμ προ[χσε]νίαν κα-
45 [θάπερ τôι] π̣ατρὶ αὐτô· τὸς δὲ πρέσβ[ες καὶ] Ἀπολ-
[λόδορον κ]αλέσαι ἐς πρυτανεῖον ἐπ[ὶ χσέν]ια ἐ-
[ς αὔριον.] vacat

Current restorations go back to Wilhelm *apud* Michel 1437. We do not
find them all satisfactory, but the inaccuracy of the stoichedon makes
attempts to replace them hazardous, and we prefer to interpret by commentary. We have in several places read rather more than earlier editors.
l. 12: [δίκας δὲ ἔναι περὶ ôν] and (ll. 13–14) τοî[ς πρόσθε ἐν τêι πόλει ἒ],
with a stop after ἐτίμοτο (=ἠτίμωτο) Wilhelm; this seems excessively vague
and the sense will overlap with ll. 22–5. ll. 16–18: [κάθοδον δ' ἔναι τοῖς]
φεύγοσι Σελυμβριανôν | [ἐγομένοις τὸς αὐτ]ὸς πολεμίος δὲ καὶ φιλίος | [τοῖς
ἐν τêι πόλει] (Wilhelm). We would prefer νομίζοσιν, but do not understand
the use of δέ. l. 24: τôι κοινôι is three letters too long. l. 28: Ἀπόλλονο]ς
is one letter too long. We have thought of Ἑρακλέος, but the coins (*BMC
Thrace*, 170, nos. 2–4) which prompted the guess have been reassigned to
Dikaia (*Num. Chr.* 1965, 3 f.). l. 35: Wilhelm's second thoughts (*Sitzb.
Wien*, ccxvii (5) 89) were mistaken and have misled Bengtson. The readings
on the stone are clear, and so is the erasure (Meritt, *Hesp.* x. 327 f.). Whether
the stone-cutter erased καὶ τὸν Σελυμβριανὸν (Wilhelm), or καὶ τὸ φσέφισμα

τόδε (Meritt), hardly matters.   ll. 40–1 : [ὁ]π[ό]σοι εἰσ]ὶ γεγ[ρ]αμμένοι
Kirchhoff; we have no great confidence in our view.   ll. 44–6. The last
few letters of these lines are now lost.

Selymbria (the modern Silivri, on the north shore of the Propontis)
appears in the tribute quota-lists from 451–0 to 430–29, normally
as a fairly high payer (5 to 9 T.), but abnormally in 435–4 and
433–2 with a mere 900 dr., which probably indicates a sensitive
border-line position between Athenian and Odrysian power (*ATL* iii.
310 ff.). By 410 it is in revolt from Athens, refusing to admit Alcibiades,
but paying him a sum of money (Xen. *Hell.* i. 1. 21). In 408 (for the
chronology here adopted, see Ferguson, *CAH* v. 483–5, *Treasurers*,
38–45) he recaptured the town, aided by treachery within, but showing great personal courage and powers of conciliation. His willingness
to restrain his Thracian allies seems to have helped him, without
bloodshed, to induce Selymbria to accept an Athenian garrison and
pay him money (Plut. *Alc.* 30; Xen. *Hell.* i. 3. 10; Diod. xiii. 66. 4).

The conciliatory nature of the settlement appears more clearly in
this document, which falls into two parts: (1) the settlement at the
capitulation (1–31), of which the beginning is lost, (2) its ratification
at Athens in 407 (31–47).

  1. The settlement: (*a*) (8–10) restoration of hostages, perhaps from
410, and an undertaking to take none in future; (*b*) (10–12) a guarantee of Selymbrian autonomy; (*c*) (12–14), possibly, a cancellation of
debts to the Athenian state; (*d*) (14–18), apparently, a general restitu-
tion of civil rights for the disenfranchised and exiles; (*e*) (18–22) an
abandonment of Athenian and allied claims to property lost in Selymbria, except for real property; (*f*) (22–6) all other causes of dispute
(not 'contracts'; see De Ste Croix, *CQ* xi (1961) 102) to be settled by
agreement or, failing that, by δίκαι ἀπὸ ξυμβολῶν (cf. No. 31 ; Hopper,
JHS lxiii (1943) 47–8, argues that here, at any rate, there is evidence
for such ξυμβολαί containing provisions for cases purely internal to
one city, but the reference is more probably to individuals of the two
states) ; (*g*) (26–8) provision for recording the settlement; (*h*) (28–31)
record of the oaths taken by all Selymbrians and Athenians on the
spot.

  2. An Athenian decree, proposed by Alcibiades in 407, ratifies the
settlement (cf. No. 88), orders its publication, apparently at the
generals' expense (but, if Wilhelm was right in his guess about what
was deleted, it could have been intended that the Selymbrians should
pay), and the deletion of the names of the Selymbrian hostages and
their sureties, and confers honours on individual Selymbrians.

  For fuller discussion of the decree in its historical background see
Hatzfeld, *Alcibiade*, 283–4; Andrewes, *JHS* lxxiii (1953) 8.

88 (89)

Athenian Treaty with the Clazomenians at Daphnus
407 B.C.

Two fragments of a marble stele found on the north slope of the Acropolis; now in EM.

Ionic writing, stoichedon 34. Phot. of upper fragment: Ἀρχ. Ἐφ. 1898, Pl. i.

The upper fragment: *IG* i². 117+; *SEG* x. 139+. Another fragment, *IG* ii¹. 99, was assigned to the stele by Wilhelm, *Ath. Mitt.* xxviii (1903) 446, but not republished; we do not feel entirely confident that he was right.

> ἔδοξεν τῆι βολῆ[ι καὶ τῶ]ι δήμ[ωι, ...6...ις ἐ]-
> πρυτάνευε, Κράτη[ς] ἐγραμμ[άτευε, Ἐπιγέν]-
> ης ἐπεστάτε, Ἀλκιβιάδης εἶπ[ε· τὰς ξυνθήκα]-
> ς, ἃς ξυνέθεντο οἱ στρατηγοὶ [τοῖς οἰκίσασ]-
> 5 ι Δαφνόντα, εἶναι αὐτοῖς κατὰ [τὰ ξυγκείμε]-
> να, ἐπειδὴ ἄνδρες ἐγένοντο ἀγ[αθοί, καὶ ἀνα]-
> γράψαι τὸγ γραμμα[τέα τῆς βολῆς ἐν στήληι]
> λιθίνηι ἐν [πόλει τάς τε ξυνθήκας καὶ τὸ ψή]-
> [φισμα τόδε - - -

Wilhelm's fragment, preserving part of nine lines and of the right edge, may have mentioned Ἀλκι[βιάδης, but nothing can be made of it.   l. 1: Ἐρεχθηίς, Κεκροπίς, and Ἀντιοχίς are the possibilities. Ἐρεχθηίς, which held office in the last prytany of 408–7 and the second of 407–6, is the most likely, but we do not know which tribe held office in the first prytany of 407–6.   l. 2: Κρατ is cut over six letter-spaces and ΕΠΙΓΕ[Ν] is faintly visible below it. The chances are high that the stone-cutter at first confused the names of the secretary and the *epistates*.

This decree, moved by Alcibiades on his return to Athens in the summer of 407, confirms the treaty made by the Athenian generals with the Clazomenians settled at Daphnus. It is thus a close parallel to No. 87.

In the early summer of 412 Alcibiades and Chalcideus brought about the defection of Clazomenae from Athens (Thuc. viii. 14. 3), but the city was soon recovered and the instigators of the revolt moved to Daphnus (ibid. 23. 6). Shortly afterwards Astyochos invited the Clazomenians to move to Daphnus themselves and adhere to Sparta, but his overtures were rejected and his subsequent attack proved fruitless (ibid. 31. 2–3). Clazomenae was still in alliance with Athens in

410 (Xen. *Hell.* i. 1. 10–11) and in 407–6, when it was being attacked by exiles (Diod. xiii. 71. 1).

In what circumstances the Athenian generals came to make this treaty with the settlers at Daphnus, and whether there had been any change in the composition of the settlement, we have no means of telling. The exiles of 407–6 need not necessarily be the settlers at Daphnus. For further trouble at Clazomenae cf. Tod, vol. ii, no. 114, and commentary. For the topography of the area and the secessions see J. M. Cook, Ἀρχ. Ἐφ. 1953–4, ii. 149–57.

89 (84)

Athens honours Neapolis in Thrace:

409–407 B.C.

Eight fragments (of which one cannot be assigned to its position and is here omitted) of a marble stele, found in or on the south slope of the Acropolis; now in EM. Above the inscription is a partly preserved relief (Binnebössel, 38–40, no. 15. Phot.: Svoronos, *Ath. Nat. Mus.*, Pl. 204; *Jahrb.* xlii (1927) 70). Athena, her left arm resting on a shield, holds out her right hand. A similar relief over a mid fourth-century decree concerning Neapolis (Tod, vol. ii, No. 159; Svoronos, Pl. 107) shows that her hand was held out to a smaller figure representing the local goddess Parthenos (the name is inscribed above the figure on the later stele).

In the first decree, which is not stoichedon, the use of eta and the consistent dropping of the aspirate reflect Ionic influence ; the only other Ionic form is Λ (lambda), once in l. 44. The second decree's letters are consistently Attic; ου is used for o consistently in the first decree, occasionally in the second; stoichedon 73. Phot.: *BSA* xlvi, Pl. 23.

IG i². 108; Wilhelm, *Sitzb. Wien* 217. 5 (1939) 91–6, no. xl; Meritt and Andrewes, *BSA* xlvi (1951) 200–9; Pouilloux, *Recherches sur l'histoire et les cultes de Thasos*, i. 155–60.

First hand

[Θ   ε]   ο   [ι]
[N]   ε   ο   [π]   ο   λ   ι   τ   δ   [ν]
[τ]   δ   μ   π   α   ρ   ὰ   Θ   ά   σ [ο ν]
[ἔ]δοχσεν τῆι β[ο]υ[λῆι] καὶ τôι δήμοι, Λεοντὶς ἐπρυτά[νευεν,]
5 Σιβυρτιάδ[ης ἐγρα]μμάτευεν, Χαιριμένης ἐπεστ[άτει, Γλ]-
αύκιππος ἦρχ[ε, ...]θεος εἶπεν· [ἐπ]αινέσαι τοῖς Νεοπ[ολίταις]
παρὰ Θάσον [πρôτον μ]ὲν ⌈ὅτι ἄποικοι ὄντες Θασίον⌉ [καὶ πολιο]-

ρκόμενοι [ὑπ' αὐτὸν] καὶ Πελο[πονν]ησίον οὐκ ἠθ[έλησαν ἀ]-
[πο]στῆνα[ι ἀπ' Ἀθηναί]ον, ἄνδ[ρες δ' ἀ]γαθοὶ ἐγένο[ντο ἔς τε τὴ]-
10 [ν στρα]τ[ιὰν καὶ τὸν δῆ]μον τ[ὸν Ἀθηναίον κα]ὶ το[ὺς χσυμμά]-
[χους - - - - c. 13 - - - - -] ∩ [- - - - - c. 16 - - - - -]Ε[- - - c. 8 - - -]

lacuna

[- - - - - - - - - - c. 26 - - - - - - - - - - - Ἀ]θηνα[ιο - - - - - c. 13 - - - - -]
[- - - - - - - c. 27 - - - - - - - - - -] χρήματα [- - - - c. 11 - - - - -]
[- - - - - - - c. 25 - - - - - - - - - -]νηι Ἀθηναίον [- - - c. 9 - - - -]
[- - - - - - - c. 24 - - - - - - - - - -]ιασιν εἶναι Νεοπο[λιτ - - c. 4 - -]
25 [- - - - - - - c. 22 - - - - - - - -]ον καὶ χρῆσαι ΤΤΤΤΧΧ [- - c. 7 - - -]
[- - - - - - - - - - c. 22 - - - - - - - - - - -]ον ἐδέοντο ὅπος ἂν ἔχο[σιν ἐς]
[τὸν πόλεμον· - - - - c. 8 - - - - πο]ιεˆσθαι αὐτοῖς ἐκ τοˆγ χρημ[άτον.]
[- - - - - c. 10 - - - - - τῆς Νέας Π]όλεος ἐκ τοῦ λίμενος, τοὺς ἐν [Θάσοι]
[στρατηγὸς ἑκάστο τὸ ἐ]νιαυτοˆ ὃς ἀφειληφότας παρὰ [σφοˆν γρα]-
30 [φσαμένος ἕος ἂν ἐντελ]ὲ ἀποδοθῆι· ποιεˆν δὲ ταῦτα ἕ[ος ἂν αὐ]-
[τοῖς ὁ πόλεμος ἦι ὁ πρὸς] Θασίος· ὁ δὲ διδόασι ν[ῦν Νεοπολῖτ]-
[αι - - - - - c. 11 - - - - -]ς καὶ βο[υ]λόμενοι καὶ ἐθελοντ[αὶ ἔδοσαν τοῖς]
[ἑλληνοταμ]ίαις ⊢ΧΧΧΧ⊢ΗΗΗ καὶ πρόθυμοί εἰσ[ι ποιεˆν ὅ τι δύν]-
[ανται ἀγ]αθὸν αὐτοὶ ἐπαγγειλάμενοι καὶ λ[όγοι καὶ ἔργοι ἐς τ]-
35 [ὴν πόλ]ιν τὴν Ἀθηναίον, καὶ ἀντὶ τῆς εὐεργε[σίας ταύτης τὸ νῦ]-
[ν εἶ]ναι καὶ ἐν τοˆι λοιποˆι χρόνο[ι] παρ' Ἀθηναί[ον - - - - c. 12 - - - - αὐ]-
[τ]οῖς ὃς ἀνδράσιν οὖσιν ἀγαθο[ῖ]ς καὶ τὴ[ν] πρόσοδον εἶναι αὐτ]-
οῖς πρὸς τὴμ βουλὴν καὶ τὸν δῆ[μ]ον π[ρότοις μετὰ τὰ ἱερὰ ὃς]
εὐεργέταις οὖσιν Ἀθηναίον· το[ὺς δὲ πρέσβεις τὰ ὑπομνήμα]-
40 τα τούτον ἃ οἱ Νεοπολῖται ἔδο[σαν πάντα παραδοῦναι τοˆι γρ]-
αμματεῖ τῆς βουλῆς χορὶς μὲν [τὰ νῦν δεδομένα χορὶς δὲ τἆλ]-
λα, καὶ τὸ φσέφισμα τόδε ἀναγρά[φσας ὁ γραμματεὺς ὁ]
τῆς βουλῆς ἐστήληι λιθίνηι καταθ[έτο ἐμ πόλει τέλεσι τοῖ]-
ς Νεοπολιτοˆν· ἐν δὲ Νέαι Πόλει αὐτοὶ [ἀναγράφσαντες καταθ]-
45 έντον ἐν τοˆι ἱεροˆι τῆς Παρθένο ἐστήλ[ηι λιθίνηι· καλέσαι δὲ καὶ]
ἐπὶ χσένια τὴμ πρεσβείαν ἐς τὸ πρυτα[νεˆιον ἐς αὔριον υυυυ]

Second hand

Οἰνοβίοι Δεκελεεῖ στρατεγοˆι ΤΤΤ⊓Η[ΔΔΔ⊢⊢⊢⊢ΙΙΙΙ]

Third hand

Ἀχσίοχος εἶπε : ἐπαινέσαι τοῖς Νεοπολίταις τοῖς ἀπὸ [Θράικες ℎος
ὁσιν ἀνδράσιν ἀγαθοῖς]

ἔς τε τὲν στρατιὰν καὶ τὲμ πόλιν τὲν Ἀθεναίον καὶ hότ[ι ἐς Θάσον
ἐστρατεύοντο χσυμπολιορ]-
50 κέσοντες μετὰ Ἀθεναίον : καὶ hότι χσυνναυμαχόντ[ες ἐνίκον] καὶ [κατὰ
γὲν χσυνεμάχον τὸν πά]-
ντα χρόνον καὶ τὰ ἄλλα hότι εὖ ποιôσιν Ἀθεναίο[ς καὶ ἀντὶ τ]ούτον
[........ 16 .... παρὰ Ἀ]-
θεναίον εἶναι αὐτοῖς καθάπερ ἐφσέφισται τ[ôι δέμο]ι : [κα]ὶ hόπος ἂμ
μ[ὲ ἀδικôνται μεδὲν μέτ]-
ε ὑπὸ ἰδιότο μέτε ὑπὸ κοινô πόλεος τός τε σ[τρατεγὸ]ς hοὶ ἂν hεκάστοτε
ἄ[ρχοσι πάντας ἐπιμέ]-
λεσθαι αὐτôν hό τι ἂν δέονται : καὶ τὸς ἄρχ[ο]ν[τ]ας τοὺς Ἀθεναίον hοὶ
ἂν hεκ[άστοτε .... 9 .....]
55 ον τὲμ πόλιν Νεοπολίτας φυλάττοντα[ς] καὶ προθύμος ὄντας ποιὲν
hό τι ἂν [....... 15 ....]
καὶ νῦν hευρίσκεσθαι αὐτὸς παρὰ τ[ô δ]έμο τô Ἀθεναίον hό τι ἂν δοκêι
ἀγαθ[ὸν .... 9 ..... : περὶ]
δὲ τês ἀπαρχês τêι Παρθένοι h[έπερ κ]αὶ τέος ἐγίγνετο τêι [θε]ôι ἐν τôι
δέμο[ι πράχσαι πρὸς αὐ]-
τός· ἐς δὲ τὸ φσέφισμα τὸ πρό[τερον ἐ]πανορθôσαι τὸν γραμματέα
τês βολês : κ[αὶ ἐς αὐτὸ μεταγρ]-
[άφ]σαι ἀντὶ τês ἀποικί[ας τês Θασί]ον hότι συνδιεπολέμεσαν τὸμ
πόλεμον μ[ετὰ Ἀθεναίον : πρέ]-
60 [σβεσι δὲ ..]αι : καὶ Π[...7....καὶ...]οφάντοι : ἐπαινέσαι hάτε νῦν
λέγοσιν κ[αὶ πράττοσιν ἀγα]-
[θὸν hυπὲρ Ἀθε]ν[αίον τô δέμο καὶ hότι] πρόθυμοί εἰσι ποιὲν hό τι
δύνανται ἀ[γαθὸν ἐς τὲν στρα]-
[τιὰν καὶ τὲμ πόλιν ἐς τὸ λοιπὸν καθά]περ τὸ πρότερον· καλέσαι
δὲ καὶ ἐπὶ χ[σένια ἐς αὔριον υ]
[...7.... εἶπε: τὰ μὲν ἄλλα καθάπερ τêι] βουλêι· τêι δὲ Παρθένοι
ἐχσαιρε[σθαι τὲν ἀπαρχὲν κα]-
[θάπερ τὸ πρότερον .... 15 .... hο δ]έμος ε[ὔ]χσεται.

Our text follows, with very minor divergencies, that of Meritt and Andrewes. They corrected several readings that had been generally accepted, and in particular showed that in the second decree current texts had lines that were six letters too long.

The first decree praises the people of Neapolis for their support, military and financial, of Athens and her forces in the fighting against

Thasos and her Peloponnesian allies. They will receive the honour due for their services and have priority of access to the Athenian Boule and Assembly. [? Their envoys are to hand over the records of their gifts to the secretary.] This decree was passed in the sixth prytany of 410–9 (cf. No. 84, l. 14). The line following was added later. It records a payment to the Athenian general Oinobios, probably the man who is said to have carried the proposal for Thucydides' recall (Paus. i. 23. 9). The sum is identified by Meritt and Andrewes (p. 203) with a payment in the eighth prytany recorded in the accounts of Athena's treasurers for 410–9 (No. 84, l. 28).

The second decree praises Neapolis for her continued loyalty and implies that the war with Thasos is ended. The Neapolitans are promised protection by Athenian generals and Athenian officials [? resident in Neapolis]. Their representations about their Virgin Goddess are to be considered in the Assembly, and in a rider their request is granted (see below). The explicit reference to Neapolis as a colony of Thasos is to be erased from the first decree. Their envoys are praised and invited to public hospitality.

Neapolis (the modern thriving port of Kavalla) is on the Thracian coast opposite Thasos, commanding an easy route to the rich economic resources of the interior. She was probably closely controlled in her early history by her mother city Thasos (in the same way that Mytilene controlled the coastal cities of the mainland opposite Lesbos). When Thasos revolted from Athens in 465 her ἐμπόρια on the mainland were one of the causes of dispute (Thuc. i. 100. 2). The terms imposed by Athens when Thasos surrendered included the loss of control of her mainland colonies. Neapolis, not necessarily against her will, was incorporated in the Athenian Alliance and appears regularly in the tribute-lists with an assessment of only 2,000 dr. (perhaps kept low by Athens to ensure goodwill in an economically vital area). When after the Sicilian disaster Thasos revolted again, Neapolis showed her loyalty to Athens by active help in the struggle to regain control, and her hostility to Thasos may also be reflected in a contemporary Thasian decree (No. 83). Thasos was recovered by Thrasyboulos in 407 (Xen. Hell. 1. 4. 9; Diod. xiii. 72. 1), and it was probably in this year that Axiochos (presumably the uncle of Alcibiades; see p. 246) moved the second decree. He had been exiled in 414 for complicity in the desecration of the Mysteries (Andoc. i. 16; for his name in the sale-lists of confiscated property see No. 79). He probably returned with Alcibiades in 407.

In l. 7 the correction required by the second decree (ll. 58 f.) was made, and it involved a small consequent change in l. 8. The revisions were made with the lettering of the second decree: παρὰ Θάσον [πρῶτον μ]ὲν ὄ{υ}τι

συνδιεπο[λέμε]σαν τὸν πόλεμον μετὰ Ἀθεναίο[ν καὶ πολιο]|ρκό-
μενοι ὑ[πὸ Θασίον] καὶ Πελο[ποννη]σίον οὐκ ἠθ[έλησαν ἀ][πο]στῆνα[ι].
l. 25: The 4+ T. of this line seem to be a loan, and the 5+ T. of l. 33
a gift.   l. 54: ἄρχοντες τῶν Ἀθεναίον, political residents, often in charge
of small garrisons, were widely distributed in the Athenian Empire (see
Nos. 45, 46). Here the reference is probably to the Athenian official(s)
at Neapolis rather than such officials throughout the empire (as Tod and
others).   l. 56: hó τι ἂν δοκεῖ ἀγαθ[ὸν τεῖ βολεῖ Meritt and Andrewes;
ἀγαθ[ὸν hô δεôνται P. J. Rhodes.   l. 64: IG i², widely accepted, has [ἐπειδὰν
ho κêρυχς εὐ]φέμος ε[ὖ]χσεται, but there is no trace of φ on the stone. Meritt
and Andrewes suggest hὲν ἂν Νεοπολιτôν ho δ]êμος ε[ὖ]χσεται. It is not
certain what privilege the envoys of Neapolis were requesting for their
Virgin. Tod inferred that τεῖ [θε]ôι in l. 57 referred to Athena and that
Neapolis was asking that the *aparche* previously paid to Athena might now
be paid to her own goddess. Meritt and Andrewes (p. 209) think that such
a request would hardly be in keeping with the mutual goodwill manifest
in the decree. Their alternative hypothesis that Neapolis was asking Athens
to agree to the restoration of her first-fruits to the Virgin, which had lapsed
in the emergency, is less satisfactory, for, as Dittenberger (*SIG* 107), quoting
Kirchhoff, noted, that was a question which Neapolis could decide for
herself. And on an Athenian inscription ἡ θεός should be Athena (cf. No. 45,
clause 3). A goddess Parthenos, distinct from Athena, is also found at
Halicarnassus (*SIG* 46. 3). For the remains of her Neapolis temple see
BCH lxxxvi (1962) 830–40, Ἀρχ. Δελτ. xvii b (1961/2) 235–8.

90 (90)

Athens honours Oiniades: 408–7 B.C.

A marble stele, found on the Acropolis; now in EM.
Ionic letters, stoichedon 23. Phot.: Kern 18; *IIA* 41.
IG i². 118.

Θ   ε   ο   ι
ἔδοξεν τῆι βολῆι καὶ τῶι δήμωι, Ἀντιοχὶς ἐπρυτάνευε, Εὐκ-
λείδης ἐγραμμάτευε, Ἱεροκλ-
5 ῆς ἐπεστάτε, Εὐκτήμων ἦρχε· υ
Διειτρέφης εἶπε· ἐπειδὴ ἀνή-
ρ ἐστι ἀγαθὸς Οἰνιάδης ὁ Παλ-

αισκιάθιος περὶ τὴν πόλιν τ-
ὴν Ἀθηναίων καὶ πρόθυμος πο-
10 ιεῖν ὅ τι δύναται ἀγαθόν, καὶ ε-
ὖ ποιεῖ τὸν ἀφικνόμενον Ἀθηναίων ἐσκίαθον, ἐπαινέσαι τ-
ε αὐτῶι καὶ ἀναγράψαι αὐτὸν
πρόξενον καὶ εὐεργέτην Ἀθη-
15 ναίων καὶ τὸς ἐκγόνος αὐτô, κ-
αὶ ὅπως ἂν μὴ ἀδικῆται ἐπιμέ-
λεσθαι τήν τε βολὴν τὴν ἀεὶ β-
ολεύοσαν καὶ τοὺς στρατηγὸς καὶ τὸν ἄρχοντα τὸν ἐν Σκι-
20 άθωι ὃς ἂν ἦι ἑκάστοτε· τὸ δὲ ψ-
ήφισμα τόδε ἀναγράψαι τὸν γ-
ραμματέα τῆς βολῆς ἐν στήλη-
ι λιθίνηι καὶ καταθῆναι ἐμ π-
όλει. καλέσαι δὲ αὐτὸν καὶ ἐπ-
25 ὶ ξένια ἐς τὸ πρυτανεῖον ἐς α-
ὔριον· υ Ἀντιχάρης εἶπε· τὰ μὲ-
ν ἄλλα καθάπερ τῆι βολῆι, ἐς δ-
[ὲ τ]ὴγ γνώμην μεταγράψαι ἀντ-
[ὶ τô "Σ]κιαθίο", ὅπως ἂν ἦι γεγρα-
30 [μμένο]ν, "Οἰνιάδην τὸν Παλαισ-
[κιάθιον"].

Though more than thirty fifth-century decrees conferring the title of *proxenos* or commending *proxenoi* have in part survived, this decree is the only completely preserved example. The title of *proxenos* was widely spread among Greek states and was useful for trading and political reasons. In return for the honorary title, and sometimes other privileges (see No. 70), the *proxenos* was expected to look after the interests of the city honouring him and its citizens. Skiathos, though a small island in the northern Sporades and thinly populated, had a good harbour which was important to Athenian ships sailing to and from Thrace and/or the Euxine. Oiniades, apart from his general loyalty to Athens, 'helps Athenians who come to Skiathos', an important qualification for the office. When the Athenian *episkopos* comes to keep a watchful eye on the establishment of Cloudcuckoobury his first question is *ποῦ πρόξενοι;* he needs to know what is going on, and the local friends of Athens are the people to tell him (Ar. *Birds*, 1021). Oiniades is perhaps a little touchy; he wants to make it clear on the stone that he comes from the old town. The Boule in framing the probouleuma had not realized the subtle distinction; an Athenian friend has the necessary amendment carried in the Assembly. The change is made before the text is inscribed, but it is still made clear that an amendment was needed.

91 (91)

Athens honours Archelaos of Macedon: 407–6 B.C.

Two joining fragments of a marble stele, from the Acropolis; now in EM. Attic letters, stoichedon 31. Phot.: *Jahresh.* xxi–xxii (1922–4) 123.

IG i². 105; Wilhelm, *Jahresh.* xxi–xxii (1924) 141; Meritt *AFD* 107–15; de Sanctis, *RF* lxiii (1935) 209; Meritt, *Class. Stud. presented to Edward Capps*, 246–50.

[ἔδοχσεν τῆι βολῆι καὶ τῶ]ι δέμοι, Ἀκα[μα]-
[ντὶς ἐπρυτάνευε, Φελ]λεὺς [ἐγρ]αμ[μ]άτ[ευ]-
[ε, Ἀντιγένες ἔρχε, Σιβ]ύρτιο[ς ἐ]πεστά[τε,]
[Ἀλκιβιάδες εἶπε· ἐς τ]ὲν πο[ίε]σιν τὸν [νε]-
5 [ὸν δανεῖσαι τὸς στρα]τεγὸς τ[ὸ]ς μετὰ Π[ε]-
[ρικλέος ἀργύριον παρ]ὰ τὸν ν[ῦ]ν ὄντον ἀ-
[ποδεκτῶν τοῖς ναυπεγ]οῖς· ho δ' ἂν δανεί-
[σοσιν, ἀποδόντον αὐτο]ῖς πάλιν hοι τρι-
[εροποιοί· τὸς δὲ τεταγ]μένος πλὲν ἐπὶ τ-
10 [ὲν πλέροσιν τὸν νεῶν h]ος τάχιστα ἀποσ-
[τελάντον hοι στρατεγ]οί· εἰ δὲ μέ, ἐσαγό-
[σθον προδοσίας ἐς τὸ δ]ικαστέριον· ho[ι]
[δὲ στρατεγοὶ περὶ τὸ μ]ὲ ἐθέλοντος ἀπι-
[έναι ἐσαγόντον· τὲς δὲ] κομιδὲς τὸν νε[ὸ]-
15 [ν, hὰς ἂν hοι ναυπεγοὶ ἐ]γ Μακεδονίας σ[τ]-
[έλλοσι, τὲν βολὲν ἐπιμ]ελ[ε]θῆναι, hόπος
[ἂν σταλῶσιν hος τάχισ]τα Ἀθέναζε καὶ π-
[λεροθῶσι καὶ ἐπὶ Ἰονί]αν κομίζεται hε

[στρατιὰ φυλάχσοσα φυ]λακὲν τὲν ἀρίστ-
20 [εν· ἐὰν δέ τις μὲ ποέσει] κατὰ ταῦτα, ὀφέλ-
[εν . . . ίας δραχμὰς αὐτὸ]ν ηιερὰς τêι Ἀθ-
[εναίαι· τôι δὲ πρότοι ἐλθ]όντι καὶ κομ[ι]-
[σαμένοι ναῦν δôναι δορεὰν κ]αθά[περ ἔδ]-
[οχσεν τôι δέμοι· ἐπειδὲ δὲ Ἀρχέλας καὶ]
25 [νῦν καὶ ἐν τôι πρόσθεν χρ]ό[ν]οι ἐσ[τὶν ἀν]-
[ὲρ ἀγαθὸς περὶ Ἀθεναί]ος τός τε ἐκπ[λεύ]-
[σαντας ναυπεγὸς ἀνέλ]αβεν καὶ ἐς τὸ [. .]
[. . . . . .18. . . . .] ἀπέπεμφσεν κα[ὶ]
[. . . . . .18. . . . .]ο στρατόπεδον κ-
30 [αὶ ἔδοκεν αὐτοῖς χσύλ]α καὶ κοπέας καὶ
[ἄλλα ηόσον ἐδέοντο παρ'] αὐτô ἀγαθά, ἐπα-
[ινέσαι Ἀρχέλαι ηος ὄν]τι ἀνδρὶ ἀγαθôι
[καὶ προθύμοι ποιêν η]ό[τι] δύναται ἀγαθ-
[όν, καὶ ἀνθ' ὃν εὐεργέτε]κεν τέν τε πόλιν
35 [καὶ τὸν δêμον τὸν Ἀθεναί]ον ἀναγράφσα-
[ι αὐτὸν καὶ παῖδας προχσένο]ς καὶ ε[ὐερ]-
[γέτας ἐμ πόλει ἐστέλει λιθίνει] κ[αὶ ἐπι]-
[μέλεσθαι αὐτὸν - - - - - - - - - - - - - - - -]-

Ll. 11–12: ἐσαγό||[ντον ηοι ἔνδεκα Mattingly, *Ehrenberg Studies*, 200.
ll. 27–9: καὶ ἐς τὸ [νε|όριον τὸ ἐν. . . .9. . . . .] ἀπέπεμφσεν κα[ὶ | κατέστεσεν
ἐς τὸ ηαυτ]ô στρατόπεδον Meritt.

The last surviving lines of this decree include familiar formulae (cf.
No. 90, ll. 6–15). In them a non-Athenian is being praised for services
which are briefly described. The main clue lies in the reference to
timber for oars (κοπέας, l. 30) which at once suggests Macedon, and
since Macedon is mentioned earlier in the decree (l. 15) and the
name Archelaos provides a restoration in l. 32 which precisely fills the
available space, we may reasonably infer that Archelaos, King of
Macedon, is receiving from Athens the titles πρόξενος καὶ εὐεργέτης.
The Athenian fleet, especially after the loss of Amphipolis, depended
primarily on Macedonian timber, and timber in Macedon was a royal
monopoly. So Andocides can boast that in 411 he supplied oars to the
Athenian fleet at Samos owing to his inherited friendship with
Archelaos: ὄντος μοι Ἀρχελάου ξένου πατρικοῦ καὶ διδόντος τέμνεσθαί τε
καὶ ἐξάγεσθαι ὁπόσους ἐβουλόμην (Andoc. ii. 11). Similarly Archelaos'
predecessor, Perdikkas, in an alliance with Athens included in the
terms of his oath: καὶ οὐδένα κο]πέας ἐχσάγεν ἐάσο ἐὰμ μὲ Ἀθε[ναίοις
(*IG* i². 71. 22 f.; *SEG* x. 86).

The details of the first part of the decree are considerably more uncertain and they depend in part on the date. It cannot be earlier than
the accession of Archelaos (between 414 and 410; Beloch, *GG*² iii. 2. 55)
but the only specific clue is the number of letters (9) available for the
archon's name. In *IG*. i² Wilhelm's restoration of Theopompos, archon
in 411–10, was accepted, but this date rested largely on the restoration
of Pydna in l. 28, which seemed to associate the decree with the
operations of Theramenes in 411–10. Theramenes helped the Macedonian army before Pydna (Diod. xiii. 49. 1; Xen. *Hell.* i. 1. 2); it
was reasonable to infer help given by Archelaos to Athens. However,
the prescript of this decree implies the restoration of full democracy,
and, although it can be shown that the democracy was restored before
the end of the archon-year 411–10, the democratic prytanies at the
end of 411–10 were Aiantis and possibly part of Aigeis, not Akamantis
(l. 1) (cf. No. 84; Andocides i. 96–8; Meritt, *AFD* 106–10). We
follow Meritt in his restoration of Ἀντιγένες, epigraphically equally
suitable, archon in 407–6.

Any restoration of the full text must be very hypothetical but in
what survives, ἐγ Μακεδονίας (15), Ἀθέναζε (17), κομιδὲς τὸν νε-
[?ὸ|ν] (14 f.), there is some support for Meritt's suggestion that the
decree provides for the dispatch of shipwrights (ναυπεγοί, though the
word has to be restored) to Macedon to build triremes and send
them as quickly as possible to Athens, and to man them and dispatch
them as quickly as possible to Ionia (restored). If Meritt's interpretation is correct the decree becomes considerably more interesting. The
name of the proposer has ten letters, and though there are many
ten-letter names it is tempting with Meritt (*Class. Stud. presented to
Edward Capps*, 249) to restore Ἀλκιβιάδες. The decree would illustrate
the boldness and originality of Alcibiades. From 410 to 407 he had
swung the war, which had seemed lost at Syracuse, in Athens' favour,
but the fleet was not strong enough to maintain decisive control of
the sea. Athenian resources after the destruction of the fleet at Syracuse
were severely strained and only small detachments of triremes could
be sent from Athens to their base at Samos. In 406 the situation was
again critical. Alcibiades had been dismissed and Conon was blockaded
in Mytilene. Only substantial reinforcements could restore the
position. In the summer of 406 no less than 110 ships were dispatched
from Athens (Xen. *Hell.* 1. 6. 24). Is this, in part at least, the result
of the emergency measures that Alcibiades had taken in 407 by this
decree? To import timber in large quantities when Athens no longer
had secure control of the sea routes was dangerous; heavy timber
cargoes, whether towed or carried on board would mean slow sailing,
and slow-moving merchantmen would be very vulnerable. Did
Alcibiades resolve the problem by having the much-needed triremes

built where the timber was cut in Macedon? New triremes would move fast and should be safe from attack.

Ll. 4–9 are important for the history of Athenian financial procedure. A mention of the *apodektai* seems fairly certain. These officials, said, probably wrongly, by Androtion (*FGH* 324 F 5) to have been instituted by Kleisthenes, make their first certain appearance in 417 (*IG* i². 94. 16–17). In the fourth century their function is to receive the state revenues and to distribute them to the various boards of magistrates in fixed, legally budgeted amounts (Jones, *Athenian Democracy*, 102 f.). It is not clear how far this system is already in operation here, but it seems that the *trieropoioi* have exhausted their vote and that a decree is necessary before the *apodektai* can advance the money against later repayment.

92

Athens and Carthage: 406 B.C.

Two fragments of a marble stele, one (*a*) found in the Nike-bastion; both now in EM.

Developed Attic writing, stoichedon (probably 36). Phot.: *Harv. Stud.*, Suppl. i. 248.

Meritt, *Harv. Stud.*, Suppl. i. 247–53; Luria, *Vestnik Drevnej Historii*, 1947, 3, 122–5; Stroheker, *Hist.* iii (1954) 163–71; *Staatsverträge* 208.

(*a*)   [ἔδοχσεν τῆι βο]λῆι κ[αὶ τôι δέμοι, . . c. 6 . . ἐπρυ]-
           [τάνευε, . . c. 6 . .]ς Ἀφιδ[ναῖος ἐγραμμάτευε, . . .]
           [. . . . . . 12 . . . . . .]ς ἐπεσ[τάτε, - - - εἶπε· - -]
           [. . . . . 11 . . . . . .]κανκα[. . . . . 19 . . . .]
       5   [. . . . . . 12 . . . . .]ονοτα[. . . . . 19 . . . .]
           [. . . . . 11 . . . . . . ἀ]ναγρά[φσαι δὲ Καρχεδονίος εὐ]-
           [εργέτας Ἀθενα]ίον τὸν [γραμματέα τês βολês ἐ]-
           [μ πόλει ἐστέλ]ει λιθίν[ει· . . . . 16 . . . .]
           [. . . . . 11 . . . . . .] ἐς Σικελ[ίαν πέμφσαι πρὸς στρα]-
      10   [τεγὸς Ἀννίβα]ν Γέσκον[ος καὶ Ἱμίλκονα Ἄννον]-
           [ος . . . . 9 . . . . .]ς αὐτὸς [. . . . . 20 . . . .]
           [. . . . . . 13 . . . .]τα̣[. . . . . 21 . . . .]
                              lacuna

(*b*)   π]-
           [ρὸς στρατεγὸς Ἀννίβαν Γέσκονος καὶ Ἱμ]ίλκο-

15 [να Ἅννονος· ἐπαινέσαι δὲ καὶ τὸς κέρυκα]ς τὸς
    [Ἀθέναζε ἀφιγμένος ὅτι εἰσὶν ἄνδρες ἀγ]αθοὶ
    [περὶ τὸν δῆμον τὸν Ἀθεναίον· καλέσαι δὲ] καὶ ἐ-
    [πὶ χσένια ἐς τὸ πρυτανεῖον ἐς αὔριον vv] vacat
    [.............29..............Ἀνν]ίβας
20 [................34.................]υτ
    -

Meritt suggests for ll. 3–6: [κέρυ|χσι μέν, ὃς ἀφέ]καν Κα[ρχεδόνιοι, πρόσοδον ἐν|αι πρὸς τὸν δῆμ]ον, ὅτα[μπερ πρότον ἐκκλεσία κ|υρία γένεται]. Luria prefers τὸς ἥκοντας for Καρχεδονίος in l. 6.   ll. 8–9: [κέρυκας δὲ Ἀθεναίο|ν αὐτίκα μάλα] Meritt.   In l. 11 a trace after αὐτός may be the top of phi, which would make αἰτέσοντα]ς αὐτὸς φ[ιλίαν καὶ χσυμμαχίαν not unattractive.   In l. 19 we read an iota for the first time, which elimi-nates Meritt's σύμ]βασ|[ις, and opens the way to his alternative [Καρχεδονίον οἵδε ὄμνυον τὸν ὅρκον]. Since there is some possibility that l. 14 duplicates ll. 10–11, Meritt suggests that an amendment formula has been lost.

It seems clear that Hannibal and Himilkon were both referred to in a context which has to do with Sicily. This seems to point clearly to the first half of 406, when they were together in Sicily (Diod. xiii. 80. 1–2) until Hannibal died before Akragas at the beginning of summer (ibid. xiii. 86. 3). The fact that both secretary and *epistates* were given their demotics (ll. 2–3) also points to the last years of the Peloponnesian War. It seems clear that Carthaginian representatives are present in Athens, and that Athenians are to go to Sicily. The only reason for supposing that any arrangement was ultimately arrived at lies in the apparent presence of Hannibal's name in a post-script.

Despite suggestions (Thuc. vi. 15. 2, 34. 2, 90. 2) that the Athenian expedition of 415 was aimed at Carthage as well as at Syracuse, it had in fact in 414 sent a trireme to Carthage περὶ φιλίας (Thuc. vi. 88. 6). Our sources give us no further information about relations between Athens and Carthage, but Stroheker has shown that Carthage adopted some of the Athenian methods of dividing Sicily against Syracuse, and her messengers, though they can hardly have expected any material help from Athens in 406, may well have been interested in her diplomatic support. That Athens should have grasped at any friend in this year, particularly one who was diverting the attention of Syracuse from the war in the Aegean, is not surprising. Luria calls attention to the possible relevance of Euripides, *Phoenissae*, from which Radermacher (*Neue Jahrb.* cli (1895) 236 f.) had already in-ferred Athenian interest in Carthaginian activities in this period.

93 (93)

Monument of a Lycian Dynast: late fifth century B.C.

On the northern face of the monolithic shaft of a limestone monument at Xanthus in Lycia, commonly called the 'Xanthian Stele'. The shaft supported a tomb-chamber with an elaborate frieze, crowned by a seated statue (Demargne, *Fouilles de Xanthos*, i. 79–105, with Pl. xxvi–xlii).
    Ionic writing. Stoichedon, except at the ends of the longer lines. Iota does not always have its own space. Facs.: *TAM* i, p. 41.
    TAM i. 44+; Hicks–Hill 56; Nachmanson, *HGI* 26; Geffcken 98; Hiller *H. Gr. Ep.* 56; König, *Die Stele von Xanthos*, i. 79–81.

$[ε]ξ$ οὗ τ᾽ Εὐρώπην $[Ἀ]σίας$ δίχα πόν$[τ]ος$ ἔνεμ$[ε]ν$,
$[ο]ὐδείς$ πω Λυκίων στήλην τοιάνδε ἀνέθηκ⟨ε⟩ν
$[δ]ώδεκα$ θεοῖς ἀννγοράς ἐν καθαρῶι τεμένει,
$[. .]εων$ καὶ πολέμου μνῆμα τόδε ἀθάν⟨α⟩τον.
5 $[. . . .]ις$ ὅδε Ἁρπάγο υἱὸς ἀριστεύσας τὰ ἄπαντα
$[χε]ρσὶ$ πάλην Λυκίων τῶν τότ᾽ ἐν ἡλίκιαι,
$[πο]λλὰς$ δὲ ἀκροπόλεις σὺν Ἀθηναίαι πτολιπόρθωι
$[π]έρσας$ συνγενέσιν δῶκε μέρος βασιλέας·
ὧν χάριν ἀθάνατοι οἱ ἀπεμν⟨ή⟩σαντο δικαίαν.
10 ἑπτὰ δὲ ὁπλίτας κτεῖνεν ἐν ἡμέραι Ἀρκάδας ἄνδρας,
Ζηνὶ δὲ π⟨λ⟩έστα τροπαῖα β⟨ρ⟩οτῶν ἔ[στ]ησεν ἀπάν⟨τ⟩ων,
καλλίστοις δ᾽ ἔργοις Κα[ρ]ίκα γένος ἐστεφάνωσεν.

Letters are omitted in ll. 2, 4, 9, 11. A fault in the stone was avoided in l. 3. The normal restoration $[νικ]έων$ in l. 4 requires that nu and iota were written in one space, but this seems unlikely at the beginning of the line.

The monument was both tomb and victory-memorial. The Greek inscription was a relatively trivial part of it, for it was preceded by a Lycian inscription of 138 lines on the southern and eastern faces and above it, and followed by another Lycian text, apparently in a different dialect, of 105 lines, below it and on the western face. The Lycian texts are not yet decipherable (see König, *Die Stele von Xanthos*; Meriggi, *Germanen und Indo-Germanen*, *Festschrift für Hermann Hirt*, ii. 277–81; Friedrich, *Entzifferung verschollener Schriften und Sprachen²*, 86–90 = *Extinct Languages* 104–9), but certain names can be read in the text which precedes the Greek epigram: Spartans, Athenians, Ionians, Melesandros (who in 430–29 sailed to Caria and Lycia with six ships to collect money for the Athenians and to protect commerce, but was defeated and killed by the Lycians, Thuc. ii. 69),

Amorges (Thuc. viii. 5, 19, 28, 54), Darius and Artaxerxes, presumably Darius II (424–405) and Artaxerxes II (405–359), Hieramenes (Thuc. viii. 58), and Tissaphernes. All these names point to the last fifteen years of the fifth century, except that of Melesandros, and there is something to be said for the view of W. E. Thompson (*Hesp.* xxxvi (1967) 105 f.) that we should read the name Melesandros which appears in the Athenian expense-accounts for 414–13 (Meritt, *AFD* 88, l. 3) in the dative instead of the genitive and assume a second Athenian general of the name. This would considerably shorten the duration of the events described in the Lycian text. The Lycians were added to the Delian League by Cimon and still paid tribute in 446–5 (*ATL* ii, list 9, col. iii, 30), but probably fell away soon afterwards. The vigour of their native dynasty is best represented by their coins (for which see *B.M. Cat. Coins*, Lycia, xxv–xliv; Head, *HN*² 688–93; Babelon, *Traité*, ii. 172–343; Jenkins, *Num. Chr.* 1959, 32–41). The subject of this monument was named at the beginning of l. 5. [Κόρρ]ις was suggested by Imbert, *REG* vii (1894) 271, as representing the native name ↓∧ΡΧΕ, of whom a long series of coins exists. The dynasty is referred to as Κα[ρ]ίκα γένος in l. 12, and the Lycian equivalent appears both in the Lycian text here and on coins.

The dialect of the poem seems to be Attic; the poet, though not without vigour, had a memory better than his technique. L. 1 repeats the first line of an epigram (*Anth. Pal.* vii. 296, Diod. xi. 62) assigned (probably erroneously) to Simonides, which was associated in antiquity with the Battle of the Eurymedon (defended by Wade-Gery, *JHS* liii (1933) 82–6. Meyer, *Forsch.* ii. 94 preferred Cyprian Salamis); the τ' is meaningless in the new context. For l. 3 see Tritsch, *JHS* lxii (1942) 41 f.; Picard, *BSA* xlvi (1951) 137 f.; Martin, *Recherches sur l'agora grecque*, 169–74. τόδε in l. 4 refers to the monument in general, ὅδε in l. 5 to the crowning statue. For ll. 5–6 cf. Soph. *Trach.* 488; πάλην certainly means 'wrestling', and is not another form of βαλήν or βαλλήν 'king' (Aesch. *Pers.* 657, Soph. fr. 472 Nauck). L. 7 recalls the Athena common on Lycian coins. In l. 8 βασιλέας = βασιλείας. For l. 9 cf. Hesiod, *Theog.* 503. L. 10 is curiously reminiscent of No. 51, ll. 2–3; the Arcadians may have been mercenaries in the service of Amorges or of the Spartans (Thuc. viii. 28. 4).

94 (96)

Athens honours the Samians: 405 B.C.

Four fragments of a marble stele, found on the Acropolis, now in the museum there. Above the inscription is a relief representing Athena and

Hera, the patron goddesses of Athens and Samos, standing with right hands clasped (Binnebössel, No. 22).

Ionic letters, stoichedon, but sometimes observing the syllabic division of words, 57–61. The letters of ll. 1–4 are much larger than the rest. ΑΕΘ are frequently inscribed ΛΕΟ. Phot.: *ΠΑ* 19; Kern 19.

IG ii². 1; P. Foucart, *REA* i (1899) 181–99; *SIG* 116.

Κηφισοφῶν Παιανιεὺς | ἐγραμμάτευε. |
Σαμίοις ὅσοι μετὰ τõ δήμο τõ Ἀθηναί|ων ἐγένοντο.
5 ἔδοξεν τῆι βολῆι καὶ τῶι δήμωι, Κεκροπὶς ἐπρυτάνευε, Πόλυμνις
Εὐωνυμεὺς
ἐγραμμάτευε, Ἀλεξίας ἦρχε, Νικοφῶν Ἀθμονεὺς ἐπεστάτει· γνώμη
Κλεσόφο
καὶ συνπρυτάνεων· ἐπαινέσαι τοῖς πρέσβεσι τοῖς Σαμίοις τοῖς τε
προτέρο-
ις ἥκοσι καὶ τοῖς νῦν καὶ τῆι βολῆι καὶ τοῖς στρατηγοῖς καὶ τοῖς
ἄλλοις
Σαμίοις ὅτι ἐσὶν ἄνδρες ἀγαθοὶ καὶ πρόθυμοι ποιὲν ὅ τι δύνανται
ἀγαθόν,
10 καὶ τὰ πεπραγμένα αὐτοῖς ὅτι δοκõσιν ὀρθῶς ποιῆσαι Ἀθηναίοις
καὶ Σαμί-
οις· καὶ ἀντὶ ὧν εὖ πεποιήκασιν Ἀθηναίος καὶ νῦν περὶ πολλõ ποιõνται
καὶ
ἐσηγõνται ἀγαθά· δεδόχθαι τῆι βολῆι καὶ τῶι δήμωι, Σαμίος Ἀθηναίος
ἔναι,
πολιτευομένος ὅπως ἂν αὐτοὶ βόλωνται· καὶ ὅπως ταῦτα ἔσται ὡς
ἐπιτηδειό-
τατα ἀμφοτέροις, καθάπερ αὐτοὶ λέγοσιν, ἐπειδὰν ἐρήνη γένηται, τότε
περὶ
15 τῶν ἄλλων κοινῆι βολεύεσθαι. τοῖς δὲ νόμοις χρῆσθαι τοῖς σφετέροις
αὐτῶν
αὐτονόμος ὄντας, καὶ τᾶλλα ποιὲν κατὰ τὸς ὅρκος καὶ τὰς συνθήκας
καθάπερ
ξύνκειται Ἀθηναίοις καὶ Σαμίοις· καὶ περὶ τῶν ἐνκλημάτων ἃ ἂγ
γίγνηται
πρὸς ἀλλήλος διδόναι καὶ δέχεσθαι τὰς δίκας κατὰ τὰς συμβολὰς τὰς
ὅσας.
[ἐ]ὰν δέ τι ἀναγκαῖογ γίγνηται διὰ τὸν πόλεμον καὶ πρότερον περὶ τῆς
πολι-

20 [τ]είας, ὥσπερ αὐτοὶ λέγοσιν οἱ πρέσβες, πρὸς τὰ παρόντα βολευομένος
ποιὲν

[ἧ]ι ἂν δοκῆι βέλτιστον ἔναι. περὶ δὲ τῆς ἐρήνης, ἐὰγ γίγνηται, ἔναι
κατὰ ταὐτὰ

[κ]αθάπερ Ἀθηναίοις, καὶ τοῖς νῦν οἰκôσιν Σάμον· ἐὰν δὲ πολεμὲν δέηι,
παρασκ-

[ε]υάζεσθαι αὐτὸς ὡς ἂν δύνωνται ἄριστα πράττοντας μετὰ τῶν
στρατηγῶν.

[ἐὰ]ν δὲ πρεσβείαν ποι πέμπωσιν Ἀθηναῖοι, συμπέμπεν καὶ τὸς
ἐξάμο παρόντας,

25 [ἐά]ν τινα βόλωνται, καὶ συνβολεύεν ὅ τι ἂν ἔχωσιν ἀγαθόν. ταῖς δὲ
τριήρεσι

[ταῖς] ὅσαις ἐς Σάμωι χρῆσθαι αὐτοῖς δôναι ἐπισκευασαμένοις καθότι
ἂν αὐ-

[τοῖς δ]οκῆι· τὰ δὲ ὀνόματα τῶν τριηράρχων, ὧν ἦσαν αὗται αἱ νῆες,
ἀπογράψαι

[τὸς πρέσ]βες τῶι γραμματεῖ τῆς βολῆς καὶ τοῖς στρατηγοῖς, καὶ
τούτων εἴ πό

[τί ἐστι ὄφλημ]α γεγραμμένον ἐν τῶι δημοσίωι ὡς παρειληφότων τὰς
τριήρες,

30 [ἄπαντα ἐξαλειψά]ντων οἱ νεωροὶ ἀπανταχόθεν, τὰ δὲ σκεύη τῶι
δημοσίωι ἐσ-

[πραξάντων ὡς τάχιστα κα]ὶ ἐπαναγκασάντων ἀποδôναι τὸς ἔχοντας
τούτων

[τι ἐντελῆ· γνώμη Κλεσόφο καὶ] συνπρυτάνεων· τὰ μὲν ἄλλα καθάπερ
τῆι βολῆι,

[ἔναι δὲ τὴν δωρειὰν Σαμίων τοῖς ἥ]κοσιν, καθάπερ αὐτοὶ αἰτôνται, καὶ
νέμαι

[αὐτὸς αὐτίκα μάλα ἐς τὸς δήμος καὶ τὰ]ς φυλὰς δέκαχα· καὶ τὴν
πορείαν παρα-

35 [σκευάσαι τοῖς πρέσβεσι τὸς στρατηγὸς ὡ]ς τάχιστα καὶ Εὐμάχωι
καὶ τοῖς

[ἄλλοις Σαμίοις πᾶσι τοῖς μετὰ Εὐμάχο ἥκοσ]ι ἐπαινέσαι ὡς ὀσιν
ἀνδράσιν

[ἀγαθοῖς περὶ τὸς Ἀθηναίος· καλέσαι δ' Εὔμ]αχον ἐ[πὶ δ]εῖπνον ἐς τὸ
πρυτανέον

[ἐς αὔριον. ἀναγράψαι δὲ τὰ ἐψηφισμένα τ]ὸγ γραμμ[ατέα τῆς βο]λῆς
μετὰ τῶν

[στρατηγῶν ἐστήληι λιθίνηι καὶ κατα]θεναι ἐς πόλι[ν, τὸς δὲ
ἑλλην]οταμίας
40 [δõναι τὸ ἀργύριον· ἀναγράψαι δ' ἐς Σά]μωι κατὰ ταὐτὰ τέ[λε]σι [τοῖς
ἐκέ]νων.

The Samian oligarchy which revolted from Athens in 440 (Nos. 55, 56) was replaced by a democracy; but by 412 oligarchs were again in power (probably having taken advantage of Athenian failure at Syracuse). They hoped with Peloponnesian help to revolt from Athens but they were crushed by the Samian demos. Athens now conferred autonomy on the democracy (Thuc. viii. 21 with *IG* i². 101, revised by Lewis, *BSA* xlix (1954) 29–31), and Samos remained loyal even after the decisive disaster at Aigospotamoi in 405. In the uneasy interval between the destruction of the Athenian fleet and the capitulation of Athens the Athenians showed by this decree their gratitude to Samos:

1 (1–12). The Samian envoys now present and a previous embassy are praised, together with the generals and the people of Samos, for their loyalty.

2 (12–15). In recognition of their loyalty all Samians shall have Athenian citizenship, but their form of government shall be their own concern. When peace comes details can be discussed.

3 (15–18). Samos shall retain the autonomy granted by Athens in 412, and the judicial agreements shall remain without change.

4 (19–25). Samos and Athens shall act together about issues of war, peace, and negotiation.

5 (25–32). The Samians may use the Athenian triremes left at Samos (presumably by Conon and Philokles before Aigospotamoi, Diod. xiii. 104). The envoys are asked to send a list of the trierarchs to whom these ships were assigned. Any debts in their name shall be cancelled, but equipment must be collected.

A rider (31–40), perhaps following a speech in the Assembly by Eumachos, their leader, provides that the Samian envoys now in Athens shall have Athenian citizenship and shall be divided equally between the ten tribes by the archons (cf. Hdt. v. 69, emended by Lolling: δέκαχα δὲ καὶ τοὺς δήμους κατένειμε ἐς φυλάς). Eumachos is invited to δεῖπνον (37) as a citizen and not to ξένια, the normal hospitality for foreign envoys. Finally, instructions are given for the inscribing and display of the decree, the money to be provided by the *hellenotamiai*, who from 411 had absorbed the duties of the *kolakretai* (see No. 84). If a stele was set up at once it was destroyed under the Thirty, for the copy that survives was inscribed in 403–2 (when

Cephisophon was secretary). With it were two other decrees confirming and extending the privileges granted in 405 (Tod, vol. ii, No. 97).

The proposals in the decree were put before the Assembly by 'Kleisophos and his fellow *prutaneis*', a unique formula, to emphasize that the proposal was unanimous; they also moved the amendment to show that this too was non-controversial.

95 (94 and 95)

Thank-offering for the Victory of Aigospotamoi:

405 B.C.

On thirteen blocks of grey limestone with prints of the feet of bronze statues. Ten of the blocks were found at the south-east corner of the sacred precinct at Delphi, close to the main gate by which the Sacred Way enters it. Reconstruction in Pouilloux and Roux, *Énigmes à Delphes*, p. 57.

Ionic writing. Roughly stoichedon, except *c* (see Austin, 78). Facs.: *FD* iii. 1, pp. 30 ff. Phots. of *b*, *c*: ibid. Pl. ii. 1–2; of *b*: *BCH* xc. 432; of *a*: *BCH* lxxxiii (1959) 176; of the top of *b*: *BCH* xc. 436.

FD iii. 1. 50–68; *SIG* 115+; Pomtow, *RE* Suppl. iv. 1209–14; La Coste-Messelière, *BCH* lxxvii (1953) 182–9; Pouilloux and Roux, op. cit. 55–60; Bousquet, *BCH* xc (1966) 428–40.

Front Row

(*a*)   – ⏑⏑ – ⏑⏑]ον θεῶν ἱερὸν δάπεδον·

Roux 58–9, thinks this stone, republished by Bousquet, *BCH* lxxxiii. 175 f., bore the statue of Castor.

(*b*) [Παῖ Διός, ὦ] Πολυδεῦ[κ]ες, "Ιων [καὶ τοῖσ]δ' ἐλεγείοι[ς]

    [λαϊνέαν] κρηπῖδ' ἐστεφάνωσ[ε τεά]ν

    [ἀρχὸς ἐπ]εὶ πρῶτος, πρότερο[ς δ' ἔ]τι τοῦδε ναυάρ[χου],

    [ἔστας ἀγ]εμόνων Ἑλλάδος εὐρ[υχ]όρου.

This stone (cf. Hiller, *H. Gr. Ep.* 59) has always been assigned to Arakos, the nominal Spartan *nauarch* to whom Lysander served as ἐπιστολεύς (Xen. *Hell.* ii. 1. 7), but his statue stood in the back row (see below). Roux shows that the stone is too deep for the back row and, with new readings, suggests Polydeukes, comparing Plut. *Lys.* 12. 1 for the part played by the Dioskouroi in the victory. Bousquet proves this conclusion by reading [Πολυ]-δεύκας on the top of the stone, and improves the readings and restorations; we print his text.

(*c*) Geffcken 97; Hiller, *H. Gr. Ep.* 58; Méautis, *Acropole* i (1926) 196 ff.; J. U. Powell, *Aegyptus*, xiv (1934) 468–72; Friedländer, *Stud. It. Fil.* N.S. xv (1938) 108–10; Pouilloux, *Choix*, 46.

The lettering is probably of the second half of the fourth century, but see Bousquet, *BCH* lxxx (1956) 580 f., who thinks it could be as early as 400.

εἰκόνα ἐὰν ἀνέθηκεν [ἐπ'] ἔργωι τῶιδε ὅτε νικῶν

ναυσὶ θοαῖς πέρσεν Κε[κ]ροπιδᾶν δύναμιν

Λύσανδρος, Λακεδαίμονα ἀπόρθητον στεφανώσα[ς]

Ἑλλάδος ἀκρόπολ[ιν, κ]αλλίχορομ πατρίδα.

5   ἐχσάμο ἀμφιρύτ[ου] τεῦξε ἐλεγεῖον : Ἴων.

For ἐχσάμο, cf. Nos. 77, ll. 18–19; 84, ll. 20, 34.

Back Row

(*d*)

[. . . . .ᵘ ος

[Λυσι]μαχίδαο

[Βοιω]τῶν ν[αύαρχος.]

What form the name took is uncertain; the current restoration [Ἀριάν]θιος is one letter too long. Pausanias (see below) gives the name as Ἐριάνθης; Plut. *Lys.* 15. 3, has Ἐρίανθος; the scholiast on Dem. xix. 65 Εὔανθος; the identification with the Theban Boeotarch of 424 (Thuc. iv. 91, Ἀριανθίδου τοῦ Λυσιμαχίδου) seems highly probable. See also Ziegler, *Rh. Mus.* lxxvi (1927) 33.

(*e*), (*f*) (adjoining blocks)

Κ[ιμμ]έριος	Αἰαντίδης	Θεόπομπος
Πελάσγο	Παρθενίου	Λαπόμπου
Ἐφέσιος.	Μιλήσιος.	Μάλιος.
		Ἄλυπος ἐποίει.

(on the top of block (*f*),

Αἰαντίδης

Παρθενίου

Μιλήσιος.

Τείσανδρος ἐποί[ησ]ε.)

The manuscripts of Pausanias give Μίδιον or Μύνδειον for Theopompos' ethnic.

(*g*), (*h*) (adjoining blocks)

Α[ὐτ]όνομος	Ἀπολλόδωρος
Σαμίου	Καλλιφῶνος
Ἐρετριεύς	Τροζάνιος.

(*i*)

[Κώμ]ων

[. . .]ωνδα

[Μεγα]ρεύς.

(*j*), (*k*) (adjoining blocks) (On the top of *j* Bousquet (*BCH* xc. 438) reads *Χα*]λκιδεύ[ς).

$$- - - - \qquad\qquad - - - -$$

$$\ldots\ldots\rho\epsilon - - \qquad - - - -$$

$$Κορίνθιος \qquad Z[- - -]$$

No Chalkidian appears in Pausanias' text; he names two Corinthians, Aristophantos and Pythodotos; La Coste-Messelière and Bousquet have argued that this is Pythodotos. The letter on block (*k*) has also been read as Σ and *T*. Pomtow suggests [Κλεομήδης | - - -] | Σ[άμιος] from Pausanias' list. This ignores the clue provided by a later inscription on the block (*FD* iii. 1. 68, corrected by Bousquet, *BCH* xc. 429 f.): κώμα Λακεδαιμονίων Τυρῖται βοῦς ἀνέθηκαν τῶι θεῶι Πυθίαν λάϊαν πεντήκοντα. La Coste-Messelière argues that these later inscriptions (see below) are always related to the original inscription, that the block must have carried a Spartan admiral with a village-name inside Sparta, e.g. ['Επικυδίδας | Λακεδαι-μόνιος ἐκ] | Z[άρακος]. Roux, accepting this argument and carrying it further, prefers to read the letter as *T* and restore *T*[υρίτης]; Daux and Bousquet (*BCH* xc. 285, 428) still maintain that the letter is Z.

(*l*) A block with the word κᾶρυξ on its top raises difficulties (particularly since Pausanias mentions no herald). The size of the block seems to assign it to the back row, but La Coste-Messelière has shown that the height of the statue must have corresponded to those of the front row.

(*m*) A block (*FD* iii. 4. 200) with a very mutilated epigram may also belong.

FD iii. 1. 69 does not belong to this monument (Pouilloux–Roux, op. cit. 47–50).

The Spartan triumph at Aigospotamoi in 405 was commemorated by the dedication of a large group of statues at Delphi, described by Pausanias (x. 9. 7–10; cf. Plut. *Lys.* 18). In the foreground stood the Dioskouroi, Zeus, Apollo, Artemis, and Poseidon crowning Lysander, beside whom were his seer and his pilot; behind them were twenty-eight portraits of ναύαρχοι who had engaged in the battle, with Arakos, the Spartan admiral at one end of the line and two Spartan squadron-commanders, Epikydidas and Eteonikos, at the other. The patina of the statues was later much admired (Plut. *de Pyth. Orac.* 2). The group was near the entrance of the Sacred Way, and Pausanias seems clearly to put it on the left of the path. However, two generations of scholars have, since the area was excavated, with very few exceptions, agreed on putting it on the right in a terraced enclosure and covered it with a variety of constructions (to the bibliography above add Daux, *Pausanias à Delphes*, 81–6). Roux (op. cit. 16–36, 53–5) has shown that this enclosure was Hellenistic, that Pausanias was right in putting the group on the left of the path, and that the statues were not covered.

The inscriptions illustrate the creation and after-life of a Delphic monument. Earliest in time come inscriptions which were not meant to be seen, but only to serve as a guide to those who set up the statues; (f), (g), (h), (j), and (l) have Μιλήσιος, Ἐρετρι[εύς], Τροζάνιος, [Χα]λκιδεύ[s], and κᾶρυξ by the appropriate feet-marks. The inscriptions proper appeared on the side of the stones, facing the spectator: (d), (e), (f), (g), (h), (i), (j), (k); for some reason one of the inscriptions on block (f) was duplicated at the same time as the main inscription, with the addition of the sculptor's signature. The important question is the date of the epigrams; (a) and (b) were probably cut later and (c) was certainly, we would think, cut a good deal later than the monument was set up. Most scholars have been content to assume that they did form part of the original monument, but that (c) at any rate had for some reason to be recut sixty or seventy years later (Pomtow, *Ath. Mitt.* xxxi (1906) 556, who thinks (e) is in the same hand). Roux argues, on the other hand, that the epigrams are epideictic additions to the monument, and that they were not cut till the fourth century because they were not composed till the fourth century; we confess to some sympathy with this view. With the third century a new phase opens, and those connected in some way with the persons commemorated here begin to use vacant places on the stone for recording documents of their own. This is possibly the case with the text on (k) discussed above; it is certainly the case with a proxeny-decree, Ἀλκιδάμαντι . . . ιου τοῦ Πελάσγου Ἐφεσίωι, inscribed on block (e) (*FD* iii. 1. 54), and another for Θεοπόμπωι Εὐφόρβου Μαλ[ίωι] inscribed on block (f) (*FD* iii. 1. 60). Cf. also *FD* iii. 1. 59.

ATHENIAN ARCHONS 500–403 B.C.

For earlier archons, see Cadoux, *JHS* lxviii (1948) and no. 6. For full references to support this list, see Cadoux, ibid., for archons of 500–480, and Hill, *Sources*², 397–401 for archons of 480–403. Only the year in which the archon entered office is given: thus the archonship of Σμῦρος extended from the summer of 500 to that of 499, and so on.

500 Σμῦρος	467 Λυσίστρατος	433 Ἀψεύδης
499 ?	466 Λυσανίας	432 Πυθόδωρος
498 ?	465 Λυσίθεος	431 Εὐθύδημος
497 Ἀρχίας (CR xii (1962) 201)	464 Ἀρχεδημίδης	430 Ἀπολλόδωρος
	463 Τληπόλεμος	429 Ἐπαμείνων
496 Ἵππαρχος	462 Κόνων	428 Διότιμος
495 Φίλιππος	461 Εὔθιππος	427 Εὐκλῆς
494 Πυθόκριτος	460 Φρασικλῆς	426 Εὔθυνος
493 Θεμιστοκλῆς	459 Φιλοκλῆς	425 Στρατοκλῆς
492 Διόγνητος	458 Ἀβρων	424 Ἴσαρχος
491 Ὑβριλίδης	457 Μνησιθείδης	423 Ἀμεινίας
490 Φαίνιππος	456 Καλλίας	422 Ἀλκαῖος
489 Ἀριστείδης	455 Σωσίστρατος	421 Ἀριστίων
488 Ἀγχίσης	454 Ἀρίστων	420 Ἀστύφιλος
487 Τελεσῖνος	453 Λυσικράτης	419 Ἀρχίας
486 ?	452 Χαιρεφάνης	418 Ἀντιφῶν
485 Φιλοκράτης	451 Ἀντίδοτος	417 Εὔφημος
484 Λεώστρατος	450 Εὔθυνος	416 Ἀρίμνηστος
483 Νικόδημος	449 Πεδιεύς	415 Χαρίας
482 ?	448 Φίλισκος	414 Τείσανδρος
481 Ὑψιχίδης	447 Τιμαρχίδης	413 Κλεόκριτος
480 Καλλιάδης	446 Καλλίμαχος	412 Καλλίας Σκαμβωνίδης
479 Ξάνθιππος	445 Λυσιμαχίδης	411 ⎰ Μνασίλοχος
478 Τιμοσθένης	444 Πραξιτέλης	(2 months)
477 Ἀδείμαντος	443 Λυσανίας	Θεόπομπος
476 Φαίδων	442 Δίφιλος	(10 months)
475 Δρομοκλείδης	441 Τιμοκλῆς	410 Γλαύκιππος
474 Ἀκεστορίδης	440 Μορυχίδης	409 Διοκλῆς
473 Μένων	439 Γλαυκῖνος	408 Εὐκτήμων
472 Χάρης	438 Θεόδωρος	407 Ἀντιγένης
471 Πραξίεργος	437 Εὐθυμένης	406 Καλλίας Ἀγγελῆθεν
470 Δημοτίων	436 Λυσίμαχος	405 Ἀλεξίας
469 Ἀψεφίων	435 Ἀντιοχίδης	404 ἀναρχία (Πυθόδωρος)
468 Θεαγενίδης	434 Κράτης	403 Εὐκλείδης

SUBJECTS

Numbers, except where otherwise stated, refer to Inscriptions.

INDEX III

WORDS AND PHRASES

This index contains a selection of words and phrases related to the political, religious, military, and economic life of the Greek states.

Numbers refer to pages.

μήνυσις, 119.
μισθός, 163; μισθοφορέω, 238; μισθόω, 26, 169 f.; μίσθωσις, 169, 244.
μνήμων, -μονεύω, 69–72.

νομοθέτης, ? 189 with 192.
νόμος, 37, 70, 264, 284; νόμιος, 36 f.

ξένια, 80, 102, 268, 276, 281.
ξένος, 36, 48 f., 112, 139; -νικός, 113, 210.
ξύλλεσθαι, 101, 103.
ξύν and compounds, see σύν.
ξυνόν, 63–65.

? οἰκήτορες, 122.
οἰκισία, 6.
οἰκισταί, 123 f.
οἰκιστῆρες, 6.
ὅμηρος, 139, 267; -ρεία, 268.
ὅπλα, 53 f.
ὁπλῖται, 268.
ὅρκος 5 f., 36 f., 70, 80, 113, 123, 138, 140, 152, 172, 175, 191, 284; ὀρκόω, 32, 70, 138, 189; ὀρκωταί, 138 f., 189, ? 281.

πανοπλία ? 118, ? 129, ? 192.
πάρεδρος, 230–3, 256.
πάτρα = φρατρία, 5, 7.
πέλτασται, 237.
πινάκιον, 118, 155, 218.
πλήθα, 37; πλῆθος, 22, 90, 99, 100.
πόλεις αὐταὶ φόρον ταξάμεναι, 86.
πόλεις ἃς οἱ ἰδιῶται ἐνέγραψαν φόρον φέρειν, 86.
πόλεις ὧν Ἀθηναῖοι ἄρχουσι, 92.
πόλεις ὧν Ἀθηναῖοι κρατοῦσι, 248.
αἵδε τῶν πόλεων αὐτὴν τὴν ἀπαρχὴν ἀπήγαγον, 179.
πολέμαρχος, 33, 66, 68, 189.
πόλις (= Acropolis), 67, 80, 185, 248.
πολιτεία (citizenship) 5 f.; (constitution), 267.
πρεσβεία, 80, 138 f., ? 202, 285; -βεις, 80, 172, 175, 177 f.; 189, 268, 285.
πρόδικος, 37.
πρόξενος, 4, 19, 268, 277, — καὶ εὐεργέτης, 202, 248, 251, 276, 278; προξενία, 268.
προστάτας, 37.
πρυτανεία, 130, 178, 185, 219; πρυτάνεις, 118, 155, 185, 186, 190, 193, 238, 261, 284, 287.

πρυτανεῖον, 80, 268, 273, 288.
πωληταί, 80, 108, 186, 190, 247, 264.

Ϙοινᾶνες, 36.

ῥήτρα, 14 f., 17; ϝράτρα, 31; ῥήτρη, 253.
ῥύτιον, 102, 104.

σάνις, 185.
σκῦλα, 154.
στάρτος, 94, 96.
στατήρ, -ρες, 11, 70, 95, 102, 105, 252 f.; Αἰγιναῖοι, 182; Κυζικηνοί, 162–4; Λαμψακηνοί, 162–4.
στρατηγός, appointment of trierarchs, 48; attendance in court, 186; board of generals (439–8), 152–4; in casualty-lists, 73, 126; co-operation with γραμματεὺς τῆς βουλῆς, 268, 285; grants for campaigns, 149 f., 167, 206, 208, 217, 230–3, 256 f.; number of generals for Sicilian expedition discussed, 237, 239; protection of Neapolis, 273, of πρόξενοι, 248, 276; settlement with Selymbria, 268, with Daphnus 270; supervision of oaths, ? 80, 138 f., of public sacrifices, 146, of envoys, 285; tribute responsibilities, ? 191. Samian generals, 284.
ξυγγραφαί, 129, 131, 169, 219 f.; ξυνγ-219.
ξυγγραφεύς, 218, 220; ξυνγράφω, 108, 191, 218 f.
σύλη, 30 f.
σύλλογος, 69.
ξύμβολα, 117.
ξυμβολαί, 66–8, 268 f.
ξυμμαχία, 79, 172–6; χσυνμ- 31, 80; συμμ- 79.
ξύμμαχος, 125, 172, 257; σύνμ- 18, 176; ξυμμαχικός, 114; ξυμμαχίς, 90.
σύμπαντες, 70.
συμπλέονες, 101.
συνανφότεροι, 101.
ξυνάρχοντες, 167, 205–8, 227 f., 230–3, 255; συν- 230, 250, 255–7.
συνέαν, 32.
ξυνθῆκαι, 268, 270; συν- 284.

? τάκται, 189, 198.
ταμίαι (of Athena): ταμίαι, 147, 205–7; ταμίαι ἐκ πόλεως, 149; οἱ τὰ τῆς Ἀθηναίας ταμιεύοντες, 156, 162, 165; ταμίαι ἱερῶν χρημάτων τῆς Ἀθηναίας,

OTHER INSCRIPTIONS REFERRED TO

Numbers refer to pages.

ADDENDA

1. Risch, *ZPE* lxx (1987) 1–9 (argues for ἐ[γόμ]ι in line 1).

5. Gawantka, *Isopolitie*, 101–11.

7. The expedition is dated 593/2 by Ray, *PCPhS* ccviii (1982) 85.

8. Ampolo, *PdP* xxxviii (1983) 401–16 (*SEG* xxxiii. 690) denies that Chios had more than one *boule* at the time of this text. O. Hansen, *Ant. Class.* liv (1985) 234–6 tries to improve the case for Erythrae.

10. Van Effenterre, *PdP* xxxv (1980) 161–75 (*SEG* xxxi. 357). See also Zancani Montuoro, *Schweizer Münzblätter* xxx (1980) 57–61. We may have dated this too early; if so, see Vickers, *Num. Chron.* (1985) 35–7.

11. Reconstructed drawing of the altar, *CAH*[2] IV p. 295.

12. Lochner-Hullenbach in Brandenstein-Mayrhofer. *Handbuch der Altpersischen* (1964) 91 ff.

13. *IG* IX[2]. 1. 3, 609.

18. Harrison, *GRBS* xii (1971) 5–24, arguing that the monument, with its first three lines commemorating an agonistic victory, was already in preparation before the battle. Amandry, *BCH* xcv (1971) 625–6 n.106, also prefers an agonistic victory and doubts whether the text refers to Kallimachos at all.

19. Bousquet *Rev. Arch.* (1970) 341, calls attention to Dinsmoor, *AJA* l (1946) 86–121, and La Coste-Messelière's reply, *BCH* lxxvii (1953) 179–82.

20. *IG* IX[2]. 1. 3, 718; Gauthier, *Symbola*, 351–6.

21. The finds from the Kerameikos referred to at the end are still only partly published. The most useful list is in R. Thomsen, *The Origin of Ostracism*, 93–4. For a general survey of the problems, see Lewis's 'Postscript 1984' to Burn, *Persia and the Greeks* at pp. 603–5. The date of the earliest among them has been controversial. Majority opinion puts a substantial proportion of them in 486/5, with later additions over a period, but Lewis, *ZPE* xiv (1974) 1–4, has argued for a fairly unified deposit from the late 470s. They involve one important new methodological point, in that many of them can be joined together; presumably these were used at the same ostracism. There is a valuable and well-illustrated discussion of those known before the Kerameikos finds by Vanderpool in *Lectures in Memory of L. T. Semple* II 215–70. The Xanthippos ostrakon (p. 42) is now *CEG* 439.

25. Bousquet, *Rev. Arch.* (1970) 341–2 points out that we ignored the physical traces of mounted objects on the stone; for a fuller refutation of our position see Amandry, *BCH* cii (1978) 582–6. Walsh, *AJA* xl (1986) 319–36, in a full discussion argues that the enemies were Greeks and that the stoa belongs to the 450s.

26. We are told of a new unpublished block apparently related to this text, which may totally change our ideas of this monument.

27. The base is discussed by Amandry, *BCH* cxi (1987) 102–15.

29. A third helmet has now been found; see *SEG* xxxiii. 328.

30. Herrmann, *Chiron* xi (1981) 1–30 (*SEG* xxxi. 985) publishes a very substantial parallel text, and offers changes in the old text; it now seems clear that the *aisumnetes* was referred to unfavourably in B4 and that the whole atmosphere is strongly democratic. It appears that Teos' 'colony' Abdera is very closely associated with Teos at this time, since similar imprecations are provided for them there. It is clear that we should have preferred ἐπὶ δυνάμει in line 31. Note also that the new text refers to a secretary (in the participial form) as φοινικογραφέων; cf. φοινικήια in our lines B 37–8. There is a parallel in a remarkable text from Crete published by Davies and Jeffery, *Kadmos* ix (1970) 118–54 (*SEG* xxvii. 631), in which a small community appoints a ποινικάστας to look after its records.

32. See S. Hornblower, *Mausolus* 85 ff. and elsewhere.

33. See Daux, *BCH* ic (1975) 150–4, Clairmont, *Patrios Nomos* 130–5, both with photographs (*SEG* xxxiii. 34). A very similar text from another tribe (Aegeis?) is published by Koumanoudes, *HOPOΣ* 2 (1984) 189–201, making our view that this is an exceptional record of a single tribe a good deal less likely. Our emphasis on the singular ἐν τῶι πολέμωι is unwarranted; cf. Arist. *Ἀθ. Πολ.* 58. 1.

34. Clairmont, *Patrios Nomos* 156. Dunst, *Ath. Mitt.* lxxxvii (1972) 153–5 (cf. Clairmont, ibid.) publishes a new Samian text, in which Inaros awards a prize to a Samian commander:

> Ἰνάρως Ψαμμητίχ[ο ὁ τῆς Αἰγύπτ]ο βασιλεύς
> Λεωκρίτωι Ἰφιά[δο Σαμίωι, τοῖς να]ύτηισιν
> τῶν συμμάχων ἐπ[..............ἀ]ριστήιον.

35. Bradeen, *The Athenian Agora* xvii 4; Clairmont, *Patrios Nomos* 136–8.

37. Meiggs, *The Athenian Empire*, 100–1, 599; Bradeen-McGregor, *Studies* 71–81. Mattingly's date of 418/7 has been widely supported; see e.g. Smart, *JHS* xcii (1972), 128–46; Wick, *JHS* xcv (1975) 186–90, *Class. Phil.* lxxvi (1981) 118–21. We acknowledge some force in the argument (Mattingly, *Historia* xxv (1976) 42–4) from the unusual formula in line 15, now attested in the 420s in *IG* I³ 165, but, although we now incline to accept the vertical in the archon's name, we think it is on the left of its space. The phi remains unconvincing on any photograph we have seen.

38. Ampolo, *PdP* xxxix (1984), 81–9; Musti, *Riv. Fil.* cxiii (1985) 134–57.

39, 50. Meiggs, *The Athenian Empire* (1972) has very full discussions of all problems. The latest texts of the quota-lists are *IG* I³ 259–90. New fragments of the first stele include one from the top of List 1 (Meritt, *Hesperia* xli (1972) 403–17), confirming the archon's name and adding considerable detail to Cols. II–III, and a very substantial fragment of List II, Cols. VII–VIII (Camp, *Hesperia* xliii (1974) 314–18, McGregor, *Hesperia* xlv (1976) 280–2, *SEG* xxvi. 28). For argument on the meaning of figures recorded as quotas, see Unz, *GRBS* xxvi (1985) 21–42.

40. Meiggs, *The Athenian Empire*, 112–15, 421–2; Engelmann and Merkel-

bach, *Die Inschriften von Erythrai und Klazomenai* I no. 4. We should have paid
more attention to a constitutional document from Erythrae itself (ibid.
no. 2); see Lewis, *Acts of the Eighth Epigraphic Congress* 59.

42. Piccirilli, *Gli arbitrati interstatali greci* I no. 1.

43. Piérart, *Ant. Class.* 38 (1969) 365–88. Problems in Milesian history have
been much discussed: see e.g. Gehrke, *Historia* xxix (1980) 17–31 (*SEG* xxx.
1337).

44. Meiggs, *The Athenian Empire*, 495–503. A good statement of the case for
dating the text to the 420s by Mattingly, *AJA* lxxxvi (1982) 381–5, but
Tracy, in *Studies Presented to Sterling Dow* (1984), 281–2, shows that the stone-
cutter is the same man who inscribed the accounts of Pheidias' statue of
Athena Promachos (*IG* I³ 435), which must belong to the 450s.

45. Thorough discussion of text and date by Erxleben, *Arch. f. Papyrus-
forschung*, xix (1969) 91–139, 212, xx (1970) 66–132, xxi (1971) 145–62.
Lewis, in ΦΟΡΟΣ ... Meritt (1974) 83–5, combines sections 7) and 8),
suggesting that a special fund concerned with Athena and Hephaistos is
being created, and that it is proposals for improper use of this fund, not use of
foreign money, which will incur the death penalty. For the latest discussions
of the epigraphic and numismatic evidence for the decree, see Carradice
(ed.) *Coinage and Administration in the Athenian and Persian Empires* (1987).

46. Mattingly (especially *BSA* lxv (1970) 129–33) has continued to argue
that this is later than nos. 68 and 69.

47. Bradeen-McGregor, *Studies* 94–9.

48. Clairmont, *Patrios Nomos* 165–9 (*SEG* xxxiii. 37).

49. Malkin, *Chiron* xiv (1984) 43–8 discusses the *temene*.

52. J. M. Balcer, *The Athenian Regulations for Chalkis* (*Historia* Einzelschr. 33,
1978).

55. Fornara, *JHS* ic (1979) 7–19 (*SEG* xxix.18) argues that all three
payments are for Samos and discusses the chronology of the revolt.

56. Bridges, *JHS* c (1980) 185–8 (*SEG* xxx. 6) has a better arrangement of
the relation between our fragments *b* and *d*, but we do not accept his further
conclusions (for which cf. Breslin, *The Ancient World* iii (1980) 104–6 (*SEG*
xxxi. 10)).

58. Bradeen, *GRBS* xii (1971) 469–83, discusses the lettering and maintains
our date.

59. On p. 164, insert after '4 T.' '1305 dr. is raised by the sale of surplus
ivory,'.

62. Coupry, *Inscriptions de Délos* 89, who simplifies the chronological problem.

63. The epitaph of Silenos (p. 175) is now *CEG* 12. Lewis, *ZPE* xxii (1976)
273–5, reaffirms, against Ruschenbusch, *ZPE* xix (1975) 225–32, that the
original texts of 63 and 64 were not contemporary and that both were
reaffirmed in 433/2.

65. Rhodes, *The Athenian Boule*, 75, on the decree-procedures. Hammond
and Griffith, *History of Macedonia* II 124 n. 7, date to late winter 429/8.

Piérart, *BCH* cviii (1984) 172, discusses lines 8 and 31, and has a good discussion of the tribute-lists of the Archidamian War (cf. Bradeen-Mc-Gregor, *Studies* 20–23).

67. The fourth-century dating is accepted by Jeffery, *BSA* lxxxiii (1988) 179–81. An unpublished fragment refers to Aeginetans and shows that the Chian friends of the Spartans were in exile.

67 bis. No collection of fifth-century inscriptions can now be without the first inscribed classical Spartan treaty, first published by Peek in 1976 (*SEG* xxvi. 461, xxviii. 408, xxxii. 398; Cozzoli, *Scritti Treves* 67–76); we print a composite text, without textual commentary and with much hesitation.

> [συνθῆκ]αι Αἰτολοῖς κ̣[αττάδε]
> [φιλία]ν καὶ hιράναν ἐ͂[μεν ποτ]
> [Αἰτο]λ̣ος καὶ συνμα[χίαν .. 3–4 ..]
> [.. 3–4]νμονος μαν[τ . 1–2 . hεπο]-
> 5 [μ]ένος hόπυι κα Λα[κεδαιμόνι]-
> [ο]ι hαγίονται καὶ κα[τὰ γᾶν]
> [κ]αὶ καθάλαθαν, τ[ὸν αὐτὸν]
> φίλον καὶ τὸνν αὐτ[ὸν ἐχθρὸν]
> ἔχοντες hόν περ [καὶ Λακε]-
> 10 δαιμόνιοι. μεδὲ κ̣[ατάλυhιν]
> ποιέθαι ἄνευ Λα[κεδαιμονίον]
> μεδενί, ἀνhιέμε̣[ν δὲ μαχομένος]
> ἐπὶ ταὐτὸν πόθ' ὁ̣ Λ[ακεδαι]-
> μονίος. φεύγον[τας μὲ δεκέθο]-
> 15 hαν κεκοινανεκ[ότας ἀδικε]-
> μάτον. αἰ δέ τίς κα [ἐπὶ τὰν τὸν]
> Ἐρξαδιέον χόραν [στρατεύει]
> ἐπὶ πολέμοι, ἐπικο[ρὲν Λακεδαιμο]-
> νίος παντὶ σθένε[ι κὰ τὸ δύνατον·]
> 20 αἰ δέ τίς κα ἐπὶ τὰ[ν Λακεδαιμο]-
> νίον χόραν στρ[ατεύει ἐπὶ πολέ]-
> μοι, ἐπικορὲν Ἐ[ρξαδιὲς παντὶ]
> [σθένει κὰ τὸ δύνατον ....]

Although Peek contemplated a rather earlier dating, we see no reason why the lettering should be earlier than the earliest known diplomatic contacts between Sparta and Aetolia in 426 (Thuc. iii. 100). The surest result seems to be the confirmation of the view (de Ste. Croix, *Origins of the Peloponnesian War*, 108–10) that the alliance formula of lines 4–10 was the primitive formula of Spartan alliances; it had previously only been known in cases where defeated enemies were brought into the Peloponnesian League (X. *Hell*. ii. 2. 20, v. 3. 26). Onto this formula is grafted the much more modern formula (cf. Thuc. i. 44. 1) of lines 16–23. But no satisfactory restoration of line 4 has yet been found, and the relationship of the hitherto unknown Erxadieis to the Aetolians remains uncertain.

69. Lines 30–1 are discussed by Lewis in ΦΟΡΟΣ ... Meritt, 85–6.

70. Walbank, *Proxenies* no. 70 with photograph. That this Herakleides came from Klazomenai is proved by a new fragment (*IG* II² 65) joined to the bottom by Walbank (*ZPE* li (1983) 183–4, cf. *ZPE* xlviii (1982) 261–3). The last lines now run (cf. *SEG* xxxii. 10, with later changes by Whitehead, *ZPE* lvii (1984) 145–6):

```
20                        [ἔναι ῾Ηρακλε]-
        [ίδηι] γῆς ἔγκτησιν κ[αὶ οἰκίας καὶ μετο]-
        [ικίο ἀ]τελειαν καθάπ[ερ τοῖς ἄλλοις πρ]-
        [οξένοι]ς καὶ ἐάμ πο βια[ίωι θανάτωι ἀπο]-
        [θάνηι, ἔναι] ϙερὶ αὐτô τ[ιμωρίαν καθάπε]-
25      [ρ ἐάν τις ᾽Α]θηναίων ἀϙ[οθάνηι καὶ τάδε τ]-
        [οῖς ἐγγόν]οις τοῖς ῾Η[ρακλείδο vacat    ]
                                        vacat
        [῾Ηρακλ]είδο Γ [..... c.8 .....]
        [προξέ]νο καὶ [ εὐεργέτο ]
        [Κλαζο]μενίο vacat
```

The timing of the earlier decree is still doubtful; cf. Lewis *Sparta and Persia* 69–72, 76–7, with qualifications by Stolper, *Arch. Mitt. Iran* xvi (1983) 223–36.

71. See under 44.

73. The date is discussed by Gomme-Andrewes-Dover, *HCT* iv. 270.

74. See Mitchel in ΦΟΡΟΣ ... Meritt, 107–9 for a false statement in our original lemma 2. For the parallel monument at Delphi cf. Bousquet, *BCH* lxxxv (1961), 69–71 (*SEG* xix.392), Jacquemin and Laroche, *BCH* cvi (1982) 191–204 (*SEG* xxxii. 550).

75. The text in *IG* I³ 287 includes a new fragment (Meritt, *Hesperia* xli (1972) 418–20) continuing col. II and expanding the list of Hellespontine names.

77. The text is frequently used and discussed by Gomme-Andrewes-Dover, *HCT* iv. The text referred to in the last sentence of the commentary (now *IG* I³ 291) is probably better dated to the Sicilian expedition of 427–4.

78. Gomme-Andrewes-Dover, *HCT* iv. 204–7.

79. There is a thorough study of those involved in the confiscations, with some textual observations, by Aurenche, *Les Groupes d'Alcibiade, de Léogoras et de Teucros*.

80. Gomme-Andrewes-Dover, *HCT* v. 196; Walbank, *Proxenies* no. 75 with photograph.

81. Gomme-Andrewes-Dover, *HCT* v. 181–2, 193–5. The letters are not purely Ionic: most of the lambdas are Attic.

84. Pritchett. *The Choiseul Marble*, 18–21, 104–16; W. E. Thompson, *Classica et Mediaevalia* xxviii (1967) 226–31. Spence, *ZPE* lxx (1987) 1–9, examines the certain and possible payments for the cavalry, and argues that its strength was down to 500 in this year. For the last paragraph of the commentary, see now *IG* I³ 376–82: there are many unsolved problems.

85. Osborne, *Naturalization in Athens*, D2; Bearzot, *Rend. Ist. Lomb.* cxv (1981) 289–303.

86. Gagarin, *Drakon and Early Athenian Homicide Law* (*SEG* xxxi. 17).

88. In *IG* I³ 119, Wilhelm's fragment is separated from this text, and published as *IG* I³ 120.

90. Walbank, *Proxenies* no. 87 with photograph.

91. Walbank, *Proxenies* no. 90 with photograph.

93. Two new substantial texts from Xanthos (Bousquet, *CRAI* 1975, 138–48; *SEG* xxviii. 1245) for the dynast Arbinas make it likely that this text is for his father Gergis. Line 4 should be [ἔρ]γων.

94. Osborne, *Naturalization in Athens*, D4.

95. Bousquet, *BCH* lxxxv (1961) 71–4 (*SEG* xix. 394) added a new fragment to *a*. In *Rev. Arch.* (1970) 342, he denies the existence of the last word on *d* and excludes *m* from the monument.

CONCORDANCE

	IG I³	*CEG*	Fornara	*SEG*
1		454		xxvi. 1144, xxvii. 679, xxix. 975
2			11	xxvii. 620
3				xxix. 777
4		143	14	
5			18	xxviii. 1565
6			23	xxviii. 19, xxxiii. 23
7			24	xxvi. 1812, xxx. 1669, xxxii. 1600
8			19	xxxiii. 690
9		362		
10			29	xxx. 424, xxxi. 357
11		305	37	xxxi. 31
12			35	
13			33	xxix. 468
14	1		44B	xxvi. 39, xxxi. 1
15		179	42	xxvi. 38, xxix. 20, xxxi. 28, xxxii. 20
16				xxx. 1080
17			25	
18		256	49	
19			50	
20			47	xxvi. 639
21			41D	xxvi. 59, xxviii. 28, xxx. 38, xxxi. 42–4, xxxii. 25, xxxiii. 28
22		367	38	xxviii. 429
23			55	xxvi. 444, xxviii. 400, xxix. 376, xxx. 384, xxxi. 332, xxxii. 388, xxxiii. 308
24		131	21	xxxi. 45, xxxiii. 31
25			43	xxviii. 494
26		2	51	xxviii. 29, xxix. 45, xxx. 33, xxxi. 32, xxxiii. 30
27			59	
28			54	
29			64	xxix. 411
30			63	xxxi. 984
31	10		68	xxviii. 1, xxix. 3

IG I³	*CEG*	Fornara	*SEG*
32		70	xxxiii. 682
33		78	xxix. 55, xxxi. 47, xxxiii. 34
34	421	77	
35	135		xxviii. 30
36	351	80	xxviii. 430, xxxii. 413
37	11	81	xxvi. 8, xxix. 5, xxxi. 4
38		91	xxvii. 659, xxxii. 933
39			xxx. 19–20, xxxi. 22–4, xxxiii. 19
40	14	71	xxvi. 3, xxxi. 5
41			xxix. 820, xxx. 1866, xxxi. 811, xxxii. 867, xxxiii. 731
42		89	xxvi. 424, xxx. 354
43		66	
44	35	93	xxxi. 9, xxxii. 2
45	1453	97	xxvi. 6, xxviii. 2, xxix. 7, xxxi. 7
46	34	98	xxvi. 7
47	37	99	
48	6		xxxiii. 37
49	46	100	
51	83	101	
52	40	103	xxvi. 10, xxvii. 1, xxviii. 4, xxix. 8
53	248	90B	
54A	459, 458	114	xxvi. 33
54B	460	114	
55	363	113	xxix. 18
56	48	115	xxvi. 11, xxviii. 5, xxix. 9, xxx. 6, xxxi. 10
57		112	
58	52	119	xxvi. 16, xxix. 12, xxxii. 6
59	449	120	xxxiii. 21
60	465	118B	
61	364	126	
62	402	121	
63	53	124	xxvi. 12
64	54	125	xxvi. 12, xxxii. 7
65	61	128	xxvi. 17, xxxi. 12, xxxii. 8
66		129	

IG I³	CEG	Fornara	SEG
67		132	
68	68	133	
69	71	136	xxxi. 13, xxxii. 9
70	227	138	xxx. 13, xxxii. 10, xxxiii. 12
71	36	139	xxxi. 9, xxxii. 2
72	369	134	xxvi. 31, xxviii. 18
73	78	140	xxviii. 8, xxxii. 11, xxxiii. 6
74		135	xxviii. 432, xxx. 428, xxxiii. 414
75	287	142	
76	329	143	
77	370	144	xxviii. 16
78	93	146	
79A	421.7–49	147D	xxvi. 32
79B	426.40–112	147D	
80	98	149	
81	373	150	
82		152	
83		153	
84	375	154	xxx. 22
85	102	155	xxviii. 9, xxxii. 13
86	104	15B	xxviii. 10, xxix. 15, xxx. 15, xxxi. 17, xxxii. 14, xxxiii. 15
87	118	162	xxviii. 12, xxix. 16, xxx. 17, xxxi. 19
88	119	163	
89	101	156	
90	110	160	
91	117	161	
92	123	165	xxvi. 26
93		177	xxxi. 1314, xxxiii. 1181
94	127	166	xxxiii. 18
95			xxxiii. 439